GIVE YOUR THOUGHTS LIFE

'… you have the Press, both open and free: use it. Give your thoughts life; let all good measures be brought forward, and well ventilated.'

William Colenso, *Hawkes Bay Herald* correspondence columns, 1859

Give Your Thoughts Life

WILLIAM COLENSO'S LETTERS TO THE EDITOR

Compiled by
Ian St George

OTAGO UNIVERSITY PRESS

Published by Otago University Press
PO Box 56, Dunedin, New Zealand
Level 1, 398 Cumberland Street, Dunedin
F 64 3 479 8385. E university.press@otago.ac.nz

First published 2011
Copyright © Ian St George 2011
ISBN 978 1 877578 14 4

Other compilations by Ian St George in this series:
Colenso's collections, 2008
Colenso's published papers 1 & 2, forthcoming
William Colenso: his life and journeys, a new edition
of this biography by A.G. Bagnall and G.C. Petersen
is also forthcoming

Publisher: Wendy Harrex
Designer: Fiona Moffat
Typeset by Book Design Ltd, Auckland

CONTENTS

爱

Chronology: William Colenso 1811–1846 *7*

Introduction *9*

Letters

1847–1859 *25*

1860–1869 *109*

1870–1879 *217*

1880–1889 *259*

1890–1898 *377*

The Final Chapter *479*

Index of Letters *492*

1811 *November 7* William Colenso born in Penzance, Cornwall.

1826 *September* begins six-year printing apprenticeship.

1831 Compiles third edition of *History of Mount's Bay* for his employer John Thomas.

1832 Begins work at St Ives.

1833 *October* leaves for London; meets Dandeson Coates of the Church Missionary Society: agrees to go to New Zealand.

1834 *April* returns to Penzance.

June leaves for Sydney aboard *Prince Regent,* arriving in **October**.

December leaves Sydney aboard *Alligator,* arrives at Paihia December 30; rowed ashore by Gilbert Mair.

1835 *February 17* prints first book published in New Zealand: *Ko nga Pukapuka o Paora te Apotoro ki te Hunga o Epeha o Piripai* / Epistles of St Paul to the Philippians and Ephesians.

December HMS *Beagle* in Bay of Islands; Colenso spends Christmas day with Darwin.

1837 *December Ko te Kawenata Hou o to tatou Ariki te Kai Wakaora a Ihu Karaiti* / The New Testament in Māori published.

1838 *January* in *Columbine* to Hicks Bay with William Williams, exploring East Coast–Poverty Bay region.

April Allan Cunningham arrives in Bay of Islands; epidemic of (probably) diphtheria kills many; Colenso very ill; first requests training for ordination.

1839 *January* to Hicks Bay.

March to Cape Reinga; first letter to Cunningham.

August hears of Cunningham's death; Busby dismissed as Resident.

1840 *January* Hobson arrives.

February Treaty of Waitangi; Colenso's first letter to W.J. Hooker; Wilkes (American Antarctic expedition) at Bay of Is.

April Dumont D'Urville's visit to NZ.

December Dieffenbach at Paihia; Auckland becomes capital.

1841 *May* Lady Jane Franklin visits.

August J.D. Hooker arrives on HMS *Erebus.*

October Andrew Sinclair arrives.

November (to *February 1842*) first Waikaremoana journey.

1842 First scientific paper published in *Tasmanian Journal of Natural Science*; proposes marriage to Elizabeth Fairburn.

June Bishop George Selwyn arrives in Bay of Is.

September sends over 600 specimens to W.J. Hooker.

1843 *April 27* marries.

June studying for holy orders at Te Waimate; Elizabeth teaching girls.

October to Gisborne; thence to

November Hawke's Bay where the Waitangi mission site is chosen; second Waikaremoana visit; paper on fossil bones published in *Tasmanian Journal*.

1844 Daughter Frances (Fanny) born.

September ordained a deacon.

December Colenso family leaves Bay of Islands finally for Hawke's Bay aboard *Nimrod*; 'Memoranda of an excursion' published in *Tasmanian Journal*; fossil bones paper republished in *Annals and Magazine of Natural History*.

1845 *February* first attempt to cross the Ruahines.

March first walk down coast to Wellington, returning via Palliser Bay and Wairarapa.

July to Wairoa; son Latimer born in August.

October to Wellington via Wairarapa.

1846 *February* to Wellington.

April to Tarawera.

August to Palliser Bay; fern paper published in *Tasmanian Journal*.

Further timelines for Colenso appear at the beginning of each decade of letters.

INTRODUCTION

If we attend to the course of conversation in mixed companies consisting not merely of scholars and subtle reasoners but also of business people or women, we notice that besides storytelling and jesting they have another entertainment, namely, arguing.

Immanuel Kant, Critique of practical reason, 1788

Does it not strike you as very remarkable ... that the good folks of Napier never meet to discuss public matters without quarreling about some trifle or other of the utmost insignificance ...?

'A collector of curiosities', Hawke's Bay Times correspondence columns, 1862

Colenso's correspondence

Printer, missionary, traveller, naturalist and eventually politician – the Rev. William Colenso became an avid correspondent in his later life, of which the last fifty years are well represented among his surviving private and public letters.[1] As he wrote to his friend J.D. Hooker in 1897:[2] 'I have been and am very busy, mostly in the writing way – letters, public & private; as I keep a tally of my scrawls – much like Crusoe in his days on the desolate island – I find, I have written from Augt.1, to Decr.31st, – 427 letters, some very long'; and to Lady Hyacinth Hooker in 1898: 'I am still very busy, daily at it, mostly writing letters, also naming parcels of plants sent in to me by strangers!'[3]

Altogether, he reckoned that he had written 1081 letters in 1898.[4] Even on the eve of his death, he was writing; his friend Coupland Harding told J.D. Hooker, 'The day before his departure he had been busy with many affairs – dictating answers to some of the letters that were accumulating, &c., and had methodically arranged his plans for the morrow.'[5]

Colenso's private letters to Allan Cunningham, W.J. Hooker and J.D. Hooker were published in the volume *Colenso's collections*, 2008. *Give Your Thoughts Life* presents a collection of his public letters, intended to complement the new edition of the biography by Bagnall and Petersen.

In his more than 200 letters to editors, Colenso wrote mostly for local Hawke's Bay readers. His few letters to papers outside Hawke's Bay were written during his national public life (1861–6), presumably because he had easier access to both national papers and those in other provinces, and usually when those papers carried items that called for his response. Nonetheless, he was a national celebrity for his opinions, as the small sample of clippings from papers outside Hawke's Bay scattered through this collection attest, and as, in the end, the widely published obituary notices witnessed. One Patea correspondent to the *Wanganui Herald* (28 January 1882), similarly sympathetic to the plight of Māori, tellingly signed himself, 'Colenso's ghost.'

'Print is a nice ego booster' and if you want your voice to continue to be heard long into the future, a letter to the editor will achieve this. Colenso, self-consciously aware that in many of his ideas he was in advance of his time, wrote in one letter, 'Of course, in all this, I know I am before the age; yet I have a joy. "I joy the age to come will think with me."'[6] However, his active involvement in local and national affairs gradually declined as he aged and his later frequent use of the correspondence columns may be seen as the participation of a socially isolated man.[7]

---

1 A truism: people keep letters written by famous people and most people achieve fame in the latter half of their lives.

2 Colenso to J.D. Hooker, 13 Aug 1897: see *Colenso's collections*.

3 Colenso to Lady Hyacinth Hooker, 19 Feb 1898: see *Colenso's collections*.

4 Colenso to Harding, 13 Jan 1899.

5 Harding to Hooker, 17 Apr 1899: see *Colenso's collections*.

6 14 February 1863.

7 '... do, for a moment, think of me. No wife, no bairns, no visitors—I, too, am living in a world "entirely alone" as to human society ....' (Colenso to Balfour, 29 Jun 1883).

Colenso's life in public service[8]

New Zealand's General Assembly passed the New Provinces Act in 1858 and Hawke's Bay was the first new province (separating from Wellington, one of the original six provinces established in 1852), in November 1858. It qualified because it had over 500,000 acres, a European population of at least 1000 and three fifths of its electors (men who owned land) petitioning for separation. Its first Provincial Council had ten members – three for Napier, two Napier Country, two Waipukurau, three single seats – and this was increased to fifteen in 1861 (Napier five).

Colenso was a Provincial Councillor for the Town of Napier from 16 February 1859 to 15 June 1869, 16 August 1859 to 3 February 1860, 13 February 1860 to 9 April 1861, 16 November 1861 to 28 June 1862, 19 July 1862 to 5 December 1862, 6 to 19 January 1863, 17 March 1863 to 4 July 1865; for Napier Town from 2 August 1865 to 28 April 1866, 11 May 1866 to 10 January 1867; and for the Town of Napier from 2 March 1871 to 19 September 1872, and 17 October 1872 to 10 March 1875. He was Provincial Speaker for a month in 1871. The intermittent nature of his tenure often resulted from his appointments to salaried positions (Provincial Treasurer, Schools Inspector), and the required resignations from elected office that followed.

The Provincial Superintendents during Colenso's time in public office were T.H. Fitzgerald (23 April 1861 to 25 March 1862), J.C.L. Carter (8 April 1861 to 5 December 1862), Donald McLean (26 February 1863 to 10 January 1867, and 9 May 1867 to 3 September 1869) and J.D. Ormond (24 September 1869 to 31 October 1876).

Colenso was a Member of the national House of Representatives from 1 July 1861 to 27 January 1866, during the Fox ministry (1861–2) and the Domett (1862–3), Whitaker–Fox (1863–4), Weld (1864–5) and Stafford (1865–9) ministries. Initially he was William Colenso, M.G.A. (Member of the General Assembly), and later M.H.R. (Member of the House of Representatives): Members were not designated M.P. until 1907. Until 1884, Members were paid £1 a day for expenses.

Searching for the public letters

The examples of Colenso's public letters in this book were initially identified by searching all those newspapers available in the National Library's 'Papers Past'.[9] Using the search word 'Colenso', I found the search engine depended on the word having been correctly interpreted by the optical character reading (OCR) software, which might 'read' Colenso as 'Oolenso' or 'Colenxo' or almost anything. In the end, I reverted to searching the correspondence columns of the available Hawke's Bay newspapers. No doubt some letters have been missed.

As mentioned, Colenso wrote mostly for local Napier papers, but he did write letters to national papers like Auckland's *Herald* and *New Zealander*, Wellington's *Independent* and *New Zealand Spectator and Cook's Strait Guardian*, as well as Dannevirke's *Bush Advocate* and

---

8   Most of the following is derived from Scholefield, G.H. 1950. *New Zealand Parliamentary record 1840–1949*. Wellington, Government Printer.

9   http://paperspast.natlib.govt.nz/

the *Waipawa Mail* during his visits to the Bush. In his private correspondence, he refers to many of these letters. Some of the national, Hawke's Bay and Bush newspapers of his time are unavailable in 'Papers Past'; some copies of these papers surviving elsewhere have been searched, but by no means have they all. Furthermore, there are many missing issues of the titles that are indexed in 'Papers Past' – importantly here, all issues of the *Hawke's Bay Herald* for 1886 and for 1871–6, and issues of the *Bush Advocate* during the period 1883–99: active years in Colenso's letter-writing life. The loss of the Napier papers is no doubt the legacy of the 1896 fire and 1931 earthquake and fire, which destroyed the premises of the Napier printers. But many issues of the national papers to which Colenso wrote could not be found either.

Among Colenso's letters to Harding are a few clippings of his public letters from papers that have not survived. Fortunately, he often mentioned his public letters in his private letters, and some were found by following those leads; even so, some potentially important letters could not be found.[10]

Thus the letters reproduced here are all that can be found at present. I also chose to include other newspaper cuttings (printed with a grey background) if they added information about the subjects of some of the more obscure letters – or simply if they interested me on browsing the newspapers. I have had to be selective – for a time there was scarcely an issue in which Colenso was not mentioned.

Napier newspapers

Colenso probably wrote more letters to the **Hawke's Bay Herald** than to any other paper. Its first editor, James Wood, was an Auckland reporter who came to Napier and in September 1857 started publishing the *Hawke's Bay Herald and Ahuriri Advocate* weekly for the population of 900.[11] Colenso, trained as a printer, just starting his business and political life after five years at Waitangi recovering from the loss of his family and career, rolled up his sleeves and lent a hand. Their relationship was thus cordial at the start.

---

10 21 Sep 77 to Luff: '… letter I wrote (on "Chinese Immigration")' (*Daily Telegraph*)

   13 Nov 77 to Luff: 'my short letter at Pub. Mg. re Ind(ian) F(amine) Fund' (*Herald*)

   31 Jan 78 to Andrew Luff (his last letter to Luff had been dated 4 Jan 78): 'You will note my letter in a D.T. re Hospital site—it attracted attention....'

   26 July 80 to John Drummond: 'I shall send with this a Paper "D.Telegraph" of Sat. evening … in it is a letter of mine about John Harding & the natives at Waipawa.'

   23 Aug 80 to John Drummond: 'I shall send you with great pleasure copies of my three letters … in defence of the Jews (the weaker side);—I got a few extra papers for my friends; as my letters were semi-historical, and something more, which (no doubt) you may detect. I can only write, as I think & believe, & feel, & speak,—for the truth.'

   28 Mar 81 to David Balfour: 'Weber's long letter appeared in the D.Telegraph against the Jews, and that so stirred me (as I have said above), I gave all yesterday in writing a reply, & in copying half for the D.T., which I hope may appear in this evenings paper.'

   5 June 95 to R.C. Harding: 'among other old mss., I found a copy (rough draft) of a letter to Ed. "Wkly. News", Auckland, written in 1870, walking-in to Gideon Smales!!'

   17 June 97 to R.C. Harding: 'in the Woodville "Examr." of yesterday was another short letter of mine.'

11 I am indebted for a good deal of what follows to Laraine Knight 2003. *First impressions: history of printing in Hawke's Bay*. Print Hawke's Bay, Hastings.

In his first editorial Wood wrote, 'The Ahuriri settlers have long been anxious for the means of making known their requirements, and of maintaining their legitimate political influence in the Colony ....' Colenso responded with alacrity, and had a letter in the 10 November issue. But Wood favoured the runholders (the 'squattocracy') and he and Colenso held opposing views on other important issues, so they became political competitors on the hustings (Wood was not above taking political advantage in his reporting) and their relationship deteriorated. Its lowest point was reached in the bitter exchanges of January 1863. In 1871, Wood appointed W.W. Carlile as editor of a daily half-sheet, then sold the business to his accountant P. Dinwiddie, in order to buy land; he died of yellow fever in Noumea in 1875. By 1878, the paper was run by Dinwiddie, Walker, and Company, but the jousting continued, with Colenso telling Balfour in 1881 that 'you ... will never again see a line of mine in the Herald— indeed, I have *not looked at one* for this year!!',[12] and the then editor Walker's satirical 1883–4 series, 'The Knife Grinders' Society'.[13] With time and Colenso's withdrawal from public life, however, there came a softening of the paper's treatment of him, until in his elderly years he was written of with great respect. In addition to his letters to the editor, Colenso wrote a paper on Captain Cook for the centennial of Cook's visit to Hawke's Bay (1869), and had booklets printed by the *Hawke's Bay Herald* on the condemned prisoner Kereopa (1871), collections of his public letters on the sabbath (1878) and on *Certain errors of the Church of Rome* (1898).

The *Herald* also published the **Hawke's Bay Weekly Courier** from 2 October 1879 to 1897, but that paper has not yet been included in 'Papers Past'. The National Library has an incomplete collection, and those examined simply reprint a selection of the preceding week's letters to the *Herald*.

Other Hawke's Bay papers came and went. The **Hawke's Bay Times** was published by the Yates brothers weekly from 4 July 1861 (later twice and three times weekly). Its aims were liberal but its correspondence columns were less vigorous and less often patronised than the *Herald's*. The paper reported at great length, often verbatim, the discussions at the Provincial Council and those relevant to Hawke's Bay at the General Assembly (in both of which Colenso was voluble and outspoken), so it is easy to understand why James Wood (in the heat of the January 1863 exchanges)[14] labelled the *Hawke's Bay Times* 'Colenso's organ'.[15] When the opportunity arose, Colenso responded with '... the *Hawke's Bay Times*, a paper with which I had no connection.' In 1864, Thomas Bennick Harding bought the business. His son Robert Coupland Harding purchased it in 1873, but the *Times* was discontinued in 1874. Many issues have been lost, and a search of those remaining reveals only a

---

12 Colenso to David Balfour, 28 Mar 1881.

13 *Hawke's Bay Herald* 10 Oct 1883 *et seq.* – see below. He wrote again (29 Mar 1882), 'I am pretty well sick—with seeing so much of trash in the "Herald" re those Irish folks; between them, the Everlasting "Races", & Cricket, I am often tempted to stop my papers'.

14 And apparently after losing the contract to report the General Assembly proceedings.

15 On 22 Jan 1863 the editor of the *Hawke's Bay Times* wrote, 'We are very gravely charged by the journal referred to (*Hawke's Bay Herald*), with being "Colenso's organ" and "the journal which enjoys his confidence."'

few Colenso letters. Coupland Harding continued publishing, however: he published Colenso's *Fifty years ago in New Zealand,* his *Presidential address* in 1888 and his *Ancient tide-lore* in 1889. The *Times* also published the *Hawke's Bay Weekly Times* from 1865–8: extant issues contain no Colenso letters.

The *Napier Daily Telegraph* was established in 1871 'for the purpose of providing an independent newspaper, untrammelled by party or sect .... The "Telegraph" is a well-written and outspoken paper, of democratic principles.'[16] Colenso referred to it in his private letters as the 'D.T.', and sent reports of the Hawke's Bay Philosophical Institute monthly meetings. The *Telegraph* printed Colenso's three literary papers (1883), *In memoriam* (1884) and his essay on the early Christian Church at Ahuriri (1889). Again, many issues are missing, and a search of the remainder shows few Colenso letters. The *Telegraph* also published the *Napier Weekly Mercury,* 1875–82.

The *Napier Evening Star* began publication in August 1879 and lasted only 6 weeks.

The *Napier Evening News* was published monthly from 4 January 1885 and wound up in 1896.

Hastings newspapers

The *Hastings Star* published twice weekly 1886–8, and the *Hastings Standard* began in 1896; neither attracted Colenso's correspondence.

Bush newspapers

During and after his years as School Inspector, Colenso made regular visits to the Seventy-Mile Bush, staying at hotels or guesthouses at Otane, Waipukurau, Takapau, Norsewood, Matamau, Dannevirke or Woodville.

The *Waipawa Mail* began in 1878 and continued twice weekly. Colenso wrote to Luff, 'I am *now* a subsr. to the 'Waipawa Mail': its principles are good, which is *not* the case w. our two Town ones. I have not looked at a "Herald" for this year! and I may not again: it is brought daily but only the servants get it. The "D.T." is just as bad'.[17] He wrote important letters to the *Waipawa Mail,* including a humane 1881 comment on the newspapers' treatment of the murderer Tuhiata, and a long historical account of the Taranaki incident involving HMS *Alligator.*

Colenso's name appeared often in the local news columns of the *Bush Advocate,* which began publishing in Dannevirke twice weekly from 8 May 1888. He wrote a few letters to the editor, notably in response to a correspondent ('Old Ratepayer', probably the draper named Hawkins) who irritated him.

The *Woodville Examiner* was published twice weekly from 1891; no Colenso letters were found in the issues searched, although he did write at least one letter to its editor.

Waipukurau had no newspaper until 1905.

---

16 *Cyclopedia of NZ* 1908.
17 Colenso to Luff 13 Jan 1881

Māori newspapers

James Wood published **Te Waka Māori o Ahuriri** weekly 1863–71; it was state-funded and pro-government, and after 1871 was published in Wellington. Colenso (Koreneho) wrote at least one letter in Māori, translated into English and republished from *Te Waka* in the *Herald* of 13 August 1867.

Te Wananga (1874–8) was published at Pakowhai Pa in opposition to *Te Waka*, using the printing press from the *Times*, which had wound up in 1874.

National newspapers

Colenso wrote his first letter to the **New Zealand Spectator and Cook's Strait Guardian** from his tent at Petone in 1847, near the end of his fifth biennial walk from Waitangi to Wellington to report to the Church Missionary Society. He wrote another on a similar issue in May 1848.

The **New Zealander** was published weekly in Auckland from 1845 to 1856. Colenso attended the General Assembly in Auckland until 1865. He contributed at least one letter, on Macaulay's 'New Zealander', probably to enhance the 'rather curious coincidence' (see republished letter *Hawke's Bay Times*, 13 May 1864).

The **Wellington Independent** (1845–74) covered Colenso's years in the House of Representatives in Wellington, and carried a few letters from him. It was replaced by the **NZ Times** in 1874.

What do letters to the editor say about their author?

Clearly, Colenso's letters to the editor are not ephemera. The idea that such letters should be read as noteworthy records or representations of a person's beliefs, from which we can draw proper conclusions when we read them, is supported by contemporary scholars.

Jürgen Habermas drew attention to the significance of social places, where members of the public discuss and negotiate the importance of things, in his book *The structural transformation of the public sphere: an inquiry into a category of bourgeois society*.[18] This book is regarded as the basis for modern public sphere theories, which propose that democratic decisions are reached through reasoned debate in public gathering places.

Perhaps the oratory of the Roman forum and the existential arguments of the Paris café have given way, in our mediated age, to a different kind of 'public sphere', the letter to the editor, the email chatroom, the radio talk-back show, the website, the blog, emails to radio programmes. Media sociologists think so and there is now a sizeable literature on the sociology of 'letters to the editor'. For instance, Perrin and Vaisey examined the 'mediated public sphere (of) the letters-to-the-editor column found in virtually all newspapers.' They concluded that:

> public debate in the letters to the editor column represents a pragmatic approach to solving a normative
> problem: the paucity of spaces in which citizens can enact the kind of public sphere demanded by their

18 Habermas, Jürgen (German 1962, English Translation 1989). *The structural transformation of the public sphere: an inquiry into a category of bourgeois society*. Cambridge Massachusetts: The MIT Press. p. 305. ISBN 0-262-58108-6.

understanding of democracy. It is, of course, by no means an ideal public sphere offering inclusion, deliberation, and extensive consideration of important issues. It is, however, a tool available for citizens to use in seeking to practise the democratic ideals they imagine to fulfill effective citizenship.[19]

Another researcher, Atkinson, wrote:

> *Traditional conceptualisations of the public sphere often view it as a physical place fixed in specific time and space, a site of literal geography such as a salon or a town square. But a more useful way to think of the public sphere might be to envision it taking shape in the two-dimensional world, such as in the column inches of a newspaper's letters to the editor, where time and space do not have to meet but can flow disconnected with communication being freer and more spontaneous than in a fixed three-dimensional location.*[20]

Finally, Reader and colleagues studied the published writers of letters to the editor: they tended to be white, middle-aged, well-educated upper-middle-class men who were avid readers, lived in the country and had strong political views (strong liberals and strong conservatives were more likely to write than were centrists).[21]

Although he was writing in New Zealand in the nineteenth century, Colenso matches the type. He wrote to Mrs. de Lisle (26 December 1898), 'Here alone and no town papers for 2 whole days, I know nothing of the gay and bustling world below (in town, I mean) & around me'. The correspondence columns of local newspapers were an important forum for that white, middle-aged, well-educated, upper-middle-class man who was an avid reader, lived in the country and had strongly liberal political views: had he lived today, Colenso would also no doubt have been a regular caller to talkback radio, operated a website and run his own blogs.

The provincial newspaper columns were the 'public spheres' of their time, places for geographically separated individuals to contribute opinions to the debates of an immature democracy. As Coupland Harding wrote, 'Newspapers then ... were live organs in every sense.'[22] But equally they were the vehicles for the passionately held views of bigots egged on by unscrupulous editors eager for exciting copy. Many of Colenso's public letters were answers to (or were met by) equally forthright editorials or published letters from contemporaries. During his time as a politician, many were composed in a sage, 'thus-spake-Zarathustra', senior-citizen, authoritative tone that would be read as condescending today. We can attribute this to his training as an evangelical preacher, although in mid nineteenth-century Hawke's Bay correspondence columns such a tone was commonplace. Colonial politics were argumentative, fervent, destructive and nasty – and the rants of opinionated, self-styled experts are thrilling in their vehemence. As William Dinwiddie wrote in 1921:

---

19 Perrin, Andrew and Vaisey, Stephen. Arguing in an anonymous public: writing and reading letters to the editor. Paper presented at the annual meeting of the American Sociological Association, Montreal Convention Center, Montreal, Quebec, Canada, 11 Aug, 2006.

20 Atkinson, Lucy. The public sphere in print: do letters to the editor serve as a forum for rationale-critical debate? Paper presented at the annual meeting of the Association for Education in Journalism and Mass Communication, The Renaissance, Washington, DC, 8 Aug 2007

21 Bill Reader, Guido H. Stempel III and Douglas K. Daniel. Age, wealth, education predict letters to the editor. *Newspaper Research Journal* 25, no. 4 (Fall 2004): 55–66.

22 Harding, R.C. William Colenso, some personal reminiscences. *The Press*, 27 Feb 1899.

The early colonial papers did not deal largely in local news. In the small settlements it may be supposed that everyone knew everything that was happening before the weekly newspaper announced it. The papers were largely political sheets issued in the interests of a party, and their chief contents are attacks, more or less venomous, on the leaders of the opposite party. It is wonderful how the party spirit manifested itself in the new settlements, and how vigorously it flourished. It may be remarked – that the resources of the English language were not sufficient to give expression to it, and political writers pelted each other with quotations from Latin satirists and Greek comic writers, and even from the Italian of Dante – for in all cases the original text was given. The fact surely indicates a somewhat higher level of education than is evident among the politicians of our own day.[23]

And Coupland Harding wrote, reflecting on Colenso's letter writing in 1899:

On a remote coastal sheep-station, visited every two weeks by the mail-man, the 'Herald' was read and re-read from title to imprint, and in the literary and political battles of the day,
'Always with a fearless heart,
Taking, giving, blow for blow,'
William Colenso was in the van. Quaint, eccentric, odd, sometimes to the last degree, were his 'Tracts for the Times', but always with the sub-stratum of solid argument and practical suggestion; tremendous were his battles with opponents such as George Worgan the aged, and Charles Pharazyn the youthful – both of whom preceded him (the latter very recently) to the Unseen Land. Readers of his voluminous newspaper correspondence could not fail to form some idea of his extensive stores of information, his methodical style, his British pugnacity, and indomitable energy. They would note certain curious mental 'kinks' and personal prejudices ostentatiously displayed, but only personal acquaintance could reveal the beauty and spirituality of the hidden life – the unfathomable kindliness of his nature.[24]

Colenso repeatedly insisted that he did not 'notice anonymous scribblers', viewing their anonymity as cowardly.[25] Although one can find a few anonymous letters on his favorite subjects written in his style, the only evidence that he ever did write anonymously comes from Coupland Harding, 'The only rhyme I know of his composition is a playful political squib, making no pretentions to poetry, published anonymously in the "Herald" early in 1860.'

Today many editors refuse to publish anonymous letters, 'arguing that they are upholding the principles of democracy, maintaining civil discourse, and preserving the traditions of journalism ethics.'[26] They suggest (as did Colenso), 'If you don't have the guts to sign your name, you don't deserve to have your say.'[27] Reader asserts, however, that a newspaper that refuses to publish anonymous letters cannot honestly describe its letters section as a true 'public forum' that is really 'open to all comers' and supports the 'traditions of democracy' because the elderly, women, racial minorities, and others who are socially and economically vulnerable prefer not to have

---

23 Dinwiddie, W. 1921. *Old Hawke's Bay.* Napier, Dinwiddie, Walker & Co. p. 3.

24 Harding, R.C. William Colenso, some personal reminiscences. *The Press*, 27 Feb 1899

25 His 1883 letter to the *Hawke's Bay Herald* 28 Feb ('A word about Te Kooti') expands his opinions on anonymous correspondents.

26 The editor of the *Hawke's Bay Herald* of 31 Jul 1858 noted below one anonymous letter, 'Reluctantly we give insertion to the above; for we consider that no man should be thus assailed by an anonymous writer.'

27 Reader, W. A case for printing 'name withheld' letters. *The Masthead.* Summer, 2002.

their names published. That was not always the case, of course, as Colenso's old foe J.D. Ormond admitted writing to the *Herald* as 'Fact'.

Colenso: a nineteenth-century liberal humanitarian?

By 'liberal' here, I mean the idea that liberty and equality are the most important goals: broad-mindedness, generosity of spirit, tolerance of change; not bound by authoritarianism, orthodoxy, or tradition. A liberal Christian in the nineteenth century was a Protestant who favoured free intellectual inquiry, stressed the ethical and humanitarian content of Christianity, and de-emphasised dogmatic theology. As Bagehot observed, 'Somebody has defined liberalism as the spirit of the world; it represents its genial enjoyment, its wise sense, its steady judgement ....'[28]

The Wikipedia definition of 'humanitarian' is one that I like: 'an ethic of kindness, benevolence and sympathy extended universally and impartially to all human beings. ... No distinction is to be made in the face of human suffering or abuse on grounds of tribal, caste, religious or national divisions.'

The idea of liberalism is said to have been founded in Adam Smith's economic theories, as developed in his book *The Wealth of Nations*,[29] and his earlier 1759 *Theory of Moral Sentiments*: '... he is certainly not a good citizen who does not wish to promote, by every means in his power, the welfare of the whole society of his fellow citizens.'[30]

The nineteenth-century expansion of the British Empire was motivated by a range of ideas and circumstances. Economically, Britain's industrial revolution made her a wealthy manufacturer of cheap goods that needed a ready market. It equipped her military forces, particularly her navy, to be the best in the world, and she sought strategic possessions to protect her future. The British perceived their civilisation to be the finest the world had known, their race to be the most noble, and their culture to be the most advanced; they felt a God-given duty to improve lesser peoples, or at least to teach them to aspire to their own greatness. The Victorians were a very religious generation, and their religion was Protestant, with the expectation that good came only from hard work. They were in harmony with the world, confident they were the chosen ones, and that God was on their side.

The British possessed a strong humanitarian impulse, spurred by their success in abolishing the slave trade in 1807, and freeing the slaves in 1833.[31] They knew it was their duty to help others less fortunate: as Prime Minister Palmerston said in 1839, 'Our duty – our vocation – is not to enslave, but to set free; and I may say without any vainglorious boast, or without great offence to anyone, that we stand at the head of moral, social and political civilisation. Our task is to lead the way and direct the march of other nations.'[32]

28 Bagehot, W. The first Edinburgh Reviewers. In Stevas, N. StJ (ed.) 1965. *The collected works of Walter Bagehot*, London, vol.1, p. 318.
29 Bellamy, R. 1990. *Victorian liberalism*. Routledge, New York, p. 20.
30 Smith, Adam. 1759. *The theory of moral sentiments*.
31 'If ever there was a time when the humanitarian impulse influenced government it was in the decade after 1831' (Hyam, R. 1976. *Britain's imperial century 1815–1914*. Batsford, London, p. 44.)
32 Lord Henry J.T. Palmerston, British Prime Minister 1855–65. In his letter to Hobson (13 Aug 1839), Palmerston

The principal missionary organisations were started at the end of the eighteenth century, the Church Missionary Society in 1799. The British and Foreign Aborigines Protection Society was formed in 1836, and in 1837 the Buxton Report 'asserted the imperial duty to safeguard native rights, and it proposed that a share of colonial revenues should be set aside for native education and religious instruction .... Britain's main concern should be "to carry civilisation and humanity, peace and good government, and above all the knowledge of the true God to the uttermost ends of the earth."'[33]

It was this evangelistic zeal to carry the word that so appealed to the young Colenso on his arrival in London from St Ives in Cornwall in 1833, and these ideas were to inform his beliefs, his actions and much of his writing over the next half century. The printer Colenso arrived in New Zealand in 1834, and he brought contemporary British humanitarian thought with him. That is nowhere more obvious than in his writing about Māori, beginning with his much-publicised rhetorical question to Hobson at the signing of the Treaty:

At this moment I, addressing myself to the Governor, said, –

'Will your Excellency allow me to make a remark or two before that chief signs the treaty?'

The Governor: 'Certainly, sir.'

Mr. Colenso: 'May I ask your Excellency whether it is your opinion that these Natives understand the articles of the treaty which they are now called upon to sign? I this morning'–

The Governor: 'If the Native chiefs do not know the contents of this treaty it is no fault of mine. I wish them fully to understand it. I have done all that I could do to make them understand the same, and I really don't know how I shall be enabled to get them to do so. They have heard the treaty read by Mr. Williams.'

Mr. Colenso: 'True, your Excellency; but the Natives are quite children in their ideas.[34] It is no easy matter, I well know, to get them to understand – fully to comprehend a document of this kind; still, I think they ought to know somewhat of it to constitute its legality. I speak under correction, your Excellency. I have spoken to some chiefs concerning it, who had no idea whatever as to the purport of the treaty.'

Later he came publicly to the defence of Māori accused of stealing, in his blunt 1847 letter to the editor of the *New Zealand Spectator and Cook's Strait Guardian*:

your paper too frequently sets matters in a very strong light against the natives, ...

Upon the whole, I think, Sir, you should be a little more cautious, in these times of extra excitement, as to what you receive and tell forth to the world as facts. Who can possibly tell the tremendous amount of physical evil (not to say moral guilt) which a continued course of inflammatory – though, it may be, infinitesmal – doses, will ere long cause to the whole system?

A year later he was similarly aggrieved,

---

was rather more prosaic: convicts escaping from New South Wales and whaling-ship deserters 'have formed (in New Zealand) a society which indispensably requires the check of some controlling authority'.

33 Hyam, 1976.

34 Colenso has been criticised for infantilising Maori in his reporting of the Treaty, but here he was simply trying to make a point to Hobson – deaf though the latter was to it.

Sir,—It was with no small amount of surprise and deep regret, that I read in your paper of the 26th ult. the statement, that the principal chief of Hawke's Bay, (and, in fact, of the whole district between that place and Turakirae,) Te Hapuku, had supplied the chief Te Rangihaeata with both arms and ammunition. I was surprised – although prepared from long experience to hear the natives evil-spoken of – because such a statement is altogether erroneous ....

Colenso's 1865 New Zealand Exhibition essay 'On the Māori races of New Zealand' is a masterpiece.[35] It is a scholarly work – although lacking the ethnological objectivity expected today, it was a tour de force of its time. Above all, however, it is a quintessentially humanitarian work; there is little hint of paternalism, but a tone of egalitarian and empathic admiration for the qualities of a people with whom he had travelled, preached, lived and made and received friendship, often as the first and only white man they had seen. He concluded his essay with.

The writer of this Essay has no hesitation in expressing his settled conviction; that ... taking all things into consideration, and viewing the matter from a philanthropic as well as a New Zealand point of view, – it would have been far better for the New Zealanders as a people if they had never seen an European.

His letter on the trial for murder of Tuhiata (1881) was, as the editor of the *Poverty Bay Herald* remarked, 'replete with sound common sense as well as generous sentiment'.[36] His letters on Kereopa Te Rau (1871), and Te Kooti (1883) might be seen as presaging today's liberation theology; they were written in a newspaper-mediated atmosphere of fear. Headlines such as 'Hauhauism and cannibalism', 'Discovery of mutilated bodies', 'Atrocity', 'Barbarous murder by Natives' were commonplace.[37] Colenso took a 'truth and reconciliation' stance, arguing that the Pai Marire movement that inspired these events was essentially Christian, and that in any case the events themselves should be forgiven as acts of war, and Kereopa treated with the dignity usually afforded to a prisoner of war. The authorities took no notice, and Kereopa was hanged as a common criminal.

Colenso's family spoke only Māori at home, his children learning to speak English only after leaving him for Auckland. He advocated a Māori department in the New Zealand University. In his superb 9 April 1869 letter (below) he suggested a pathway to peace after the wars, beginning with,

To this end let us all (Governor, Government, and people) be determined to do two things: 1. – To do justice; 2 – To acknowledge error.

1. To do justice – prompt and quick, even and fair, common-sense ....

2. To acknowledge error, frankly and fully, wherever and whenever such has unfortunately been done; even to the retracing of our steps if needful and possible. (Let us not think too highly of ourselves as the 'superior,' unerring race, adorned with a thousand highflown superlatives of our own inventing).

---

35 See *Colenso's published papers 1: 1842–1884,* forthcoming in this series.

36 The *Poverty Bay Herald and East Coast News Letter,* 7 Feb 1881.

37 Of the killing of the missionary Carl Volkner at Opotiki (when Kereopa swallowed Volkner's eyes) the editor of the *Hawke's Bay Times* had the alliterative indelicacy to write of 'The murder and mastication of a missionary' (12 Oct 1865).

There is a significant correspondence among the following letters on his moderate approach to alcoholic drinks. Teetotallers and prohibitionists, anxious about alcohol abuse and its affects on family life, were preaching and writing against the availability of drink, and for the closure of pubs. Colenso preached moderation in all things, interpreting 'temperance' as meaning just that – not prohibition.

He remained devoutly Christian throughout his life, but he preached a moderate approach to observing the Sabbath day. There is no extant correspondence between Colenso and his famous cousin, Bishop John William Colenso,[38] who wrote a lengthy critique of the Pentateuch declaring those first five books of the Old Testament to be Jewish history, not the 'word of God'; nonetheless William Colenso clearly held similar views, as his letters on the Bible in schools demonstrate. High churchman Selwyn appears to have forbidden the correspondence.[39] In his defrocked years, Colenso often criticised churches and organised religion – once offering money and land for a non-denominational and secular church building[40] – yet in his invited appearance (after 36 years) in the pulpit at Woodville, his first grateful sermon was on the return of the prodigal son.[41] Other sermons are mentioned in his letters to Hooker – they often traversed Darwinian concepts.[42] He wrote:[43]

The sublime truths anciently taught by the great Chinese Teacher Confucius to his countrymen, and also by the equally great Indian Teacher Buddha to his people, (though, at present, but little known, and even maligned, here among us in Napier, by narrow minded orthodox men of small calibre,) – will yet become the prized common property of the thinking world; together with those of the ancient Greek and Roman Philosophers – Socrates, Plato, Marcus Aurelius, Seneca, and others; – and, afterwards, those more plainly taught by the great Jew Teacher and Reformer Jesus,

38 There is, in the Otago Museum, a greenstone tiki presented by Prof. Charles Higham. It was owned by his grandfather, Rev. Higham, vicar of St John's, Wynberg, South Africa, who was on friendly terms with his Bishop, J.W. Colenso. Higham collected various items, including Zulu weaponry laid down by chief Cetshwayo's impis, and knowing of this interest, Colenso gave him the tiki, saying that it was collected by a 'Bishop' Colenso when travelling through the east coast of the North Island. The tiki is the only tangible evidence of contact between the two.

39 Colenso wrote to J.D. Hooker (30 Nov 1864), 'You may make (or have made) the acq. of my good (1st) cousin "Natal", at the meeting—not too great an heretic for you! Not a few of his views were mine: (we were very close correspondents until the Bp. of N.Z. divided us!—but enough).' He referred specifically to his cousin in his 20 Dec 1884 letter to the *Daily Telegraph*.

40 'something less denominational, and (consequently) more Christian' (Letter, 10 Nov 1857).

41 '… there would have been no service in Danevirke had it not been for Mr. Colenso, who willingly filled the gap when spoken to on the matter, and preached a very eloquent and edifying sermon on the prodigal son, which was of the most evangelical type, to a very crowded and attentive audience.' (*Bush Advocate*, 29 May 1888).

42 'I not infrequently allude to, & quote from, him (Darwin), in my sermons.' Colenso to Hooker, 13 Sep 1890 (see *Colenso's collections*.)

43 'Christianity versus Mahometanism', letter to *Hawke's Bay Herald*, 17 Jan 1888. He later preached '… in my first Sermon in the Cathedral on Xmas Day—(preached, not read,) taking for my text—"peace on earth, goodwill to man," (part of the "Angels' Song",) after dwelling on the fitness and benefits of these for man, & shewing how such had ever been inculcated by all ancient Teachers & Philosophers—Egyptian, Chinese, Greek, Jew, Rom., &c.,—Buddha, Brahma, Confucius, Antoninus, Cicero, Cato, Seneca, Socrates, Epictetus, Plutarch, Moses, Jesus, & Mahomet,—their truth & light, tho' many coloured and many sided, being identically one, as issuing from the one fountain.' (letter to J.D. Hooker, 4 Mar 1890 – see *Colenso's collections*).

– all will be (at last!) classed, as being Inspiration from the great Father of all – God (i.e., the meat not the bones): for 'Great is Truth and will prevail.'

Colenso would acquire no land from Māori when other missionaries, sanctioned by the Church Missionary Society, were doing so, and he famously opposed direct acquisition of land by runholders from Māori. Nonetheless, once McLean's systems of land purchase were in place, he began to buy land.[44] By 1891, he would be referred to as 'a gentleman of ample means' in one article in the *Bush Advocate*[45] and he had written (feelingly):

I consider it almost suicidal to both (Napier's) real progress and interests, to think of burthening her with heavy rates and taxes in her nonage under the high-sounding (though fallacious) phrase of improvements ....

... nothing ought possibly to be farther from Napier, and indeed from the whole Colony of N. Zealand than a thing so hateful as taxation—the curse of Britain! to escape which we have even consented to expatriate ourselves from the homes and hearths of our sires.[46]

Colenso habitually gave to good causes and sentimental appeals – his name often appeared as most generous donor in newspaper lists for bereaved families, church improvements, the victims of flood and fire. He wrote to the editor of the *Hawke's Bay Herald*, asking him to 'set forth speedily some useful plan by which to relieve the poor – the very poor – the starving, the outcast, the wanderer, the stranger, the homeless, – who are daily visiting Napier seeking work; and who do not know where to go, or what to do, to obtain a meal or a bed at night.'[47] He reiterated his plea to the Charitable Aid Board calling for support of swagmen – 'poor straggling wanderers – strangers, who almost daily visit this town and me, seeking work, food, necessary clothing, and a night's lodging.'[48] Similarly, he wrote to J.D. Hooker on 12 July 1884 'I have also during the last 3 weeks, been daily visiting a poor fellow in condemned cell *here* for murder (wife & 3 children!) he is to die on 15th – a sad case in every respect. –'[49] In Sydney on his way to New Zealand, he had been deeply affected ('It took years to lessen the startling reminiscences of that *day*') by the execution of a man he had supported.[50]

---

44 'I think I shall be quite ready to buy a few acres of land from the Govt—immediately after you have settled with the Chiefs'. Colenso to McLean, 1 Aug 1851. By 1855 he had bought a number of town sections.

45 25 Apr 1891.

46 *Hawke's Bay Herald*, 8 May 1858. (I don't think British taxes were his reason for emigration!)

47 10 Aug 1896.

48 14 Sep 1897.

49 The *Herald* reported (12 Feb 1884) on the murders of the wife and three children of Roland Edwards, who was plainly psychotic. Nonetheless he was tried and hanged, forty-one years after the introduction of the McNaughton Rules. The *Herald* reported after the execution, 'The so-called "patent scaffold," brought up from Wellington for the execution of Edwards, was a most disgraceful and ramshackle affair. There was no balustrade around the front of it, so that if the condemned man had swooned, or struggled, there was nothing to prevent him falling off. The step-ladder up which the wretched man had to climb to his death was only 24 inches wide, and was also unprotected by a balustrade on one side and on the other side a 6 x 1 board was nailed up in a temporary fashion. This ladder was also set up at an acute angle (about 60 degrees) so that only the firmness of the criminal at the last trying moment prevented a distressing scene. The idea, first, of constructing such an apparatus, and then carting it about the colony as occasion requires, reflects but little credit upon the authorities.'

50 See Colenso's 'Autobiography' in *William Colenso: Life and Journeys* (forthcoming).

Some recognised Colenso's philanthropy: Henry Hill wrote in his obituary, 'When the history of Early New Zealand comes to be written the name of William Colenso, F.R.S., F.L.S., printer, missionary, scientist, philologist, and, best of all, humanitarian, will be found among the list of the honorable roll of men who spent their talents in laying a strong foundation for the future of this land, and who when dying remembered the poor, the outcast, the unfortunate, and the young children in his will, without regard to age, creed, or nationality.'

Acknowledgements

I owe a huge debt to the National Library's 'Papers Past'. It is an extraordinarily valuable resource. Nothing immerses one's mind in the past more thoroughly than old newspapers, and to have them accessible from home is a great gift.

Also I thank the Alexander Turnbull Library, National Library of New Zealand, Te Puna Mātauranga o Aotearoa, which holds both microfilms and original newspapers, and the helpful and patient staff of the Newspapers section.

I thank Gail Pope at Napier Museum and Art Gallery for help and advice.

I take full responsibility for the inevitable transcription errors, although I hope these are few, after so much checking.

Conventions

Material other than Colenso's letters is presented with a grey background.

In his early writing Colenso used a form of American spelling, although later he not only reverted to English spelling in his private letters but wrote to Harding (13 Nov 91), 'I abominate those Americanisms—Labor! Color!' In his letters to the editors of the *Hawke's Bay Herald* and *Daily Telegraph*, some American spelling was retained throughout his life – presumably by the newspaper editors. Thus 'honor', 'labor', 'favorite' and similar spellings pepper the following letters.

The footnotes are presented in one sequence, with the author indicated in each case: W.C. = William Colenso, and I.S.G. = Ian St George.

LETTERS 1847–1859

WILLIAM COLENSO 1847–1859

1847 *February* via Tarawera to Taupo and thence to Mokai Patea, returning across the Ruahines. *April* to Wellington.
   October to Wellington again, returning for the first time via the Tararuas (Rimutaka Hill Rd). *December* crosses Ruahines for the second time.

1848 *April* to Wellington.
   November crosses via new route over southern Ruahines to Rangitikei.

1849 *March* to Wellington.
   November over Ruahines, returning via Tarawera.

1850 *March* to Masterton; affair with Ripeka begins; Donald McLean, Land Purchase Commissioner, comes to Hawke's Bay.

1851 *April/May* to Masterton.
   May Ripeka's child Wiremu (Willie) born.
   August writes to McLean, 'I think I shall be quite ready to buy a few acres of land from the Govt. – immediately after you have settled with the Chiefs'.
   October crosses Ruahines to Mokai Patea by new northern route.

1852 *January* Bishop Selwyn visits; John Fairburn takes Frances and Latimer to Auckland.
   September fight with Wi Tipuna.
   November suspended by Bishop.

1853 *January* Waitangi Mission house burns. Sends over 2000 specimens to WJ Hooker; fined for assaulting Wi Tipuna.
   March Waitangi flooded; refuses to leave Waitangi, living in his 'small and cramped weather-boarded store'.
   August Elizabeth leaves for Auckland with Willie.

1854 Acts as interpreter in Māori legal cases.
   August writes to J.D. Hooker.

1855 *April* buys land in Napier.

1857 Buys land in Meeanee river region; leases out his 200-acre farm at Tutaekuri; loses election for coroner to Dr. Hitchings; *Hawke's Bay Herald* begins publication, James Wood, editor, helped by Colenso.

1858 Hawke's Bay separates from Wellington and becomes a province; *Hawke's Bay Herald* appointed official provincial printer and newspaper.

1859 Elected Provincial Councillor; appointed Provincial Auditor and re-elected Councillor.

❖ 1847 TO THE EDITOR.
New Zealand Spectator and Cook's Strait Guardian 28 April.

In my tent, at Petoni,
Saturday evening, April 24, 1847.

SIR,—I was not a little surprised on reading in your paper of this day's date, of a "robbery committed by the natives at Ahuriri on the *Flying Fish!*" Had the paragraph, Sir, met my eye at any other place than Port Nicholson—or, had I not been well acquainted with the whole transaction—I should not have cared to notice it; but,—lest silence on my part should be construed by any one knowing me to be here into acquiescence—or, the New Zealanders be believed to be worse than they really are,—I feel myself constrained to say a word or two upon the matter. I must, however, necessarily be very brief.

The *Flying Fish*, Captain Mulholland, came into the Ahuriri harbour to refit rather than to obtain pigs, &c.; she being in such a state as not to be able to proceed on her voyage without it. Before she came in the captain and crew had fallen out; on her coming in they again fell out, and some of the crew subsequently left the vessel.

A heathen chief of first rank, K., visited the vessel, and, with the Captain's consent, "tapu'd" some "trade," which, shortly after, the Captain sold to another chief. On K.'s returning to the vessel he found his "tapu'd" articles gone, and made a noise about them. The Captain endeavoured (as too many, I am sorry to say, Sir, of my countrymen do) to ride the high horse—and failed. He got struck—which he told me, himself, was his own fault—and the chief took away some "trade," for which, however, a certain number of baskets of potatoes were to be paid.

In this state of things the Captain called at the Mission Station. I was from home in the Taupo country. Immediately, however, on my return, I visited him at Ahuriri, and had the relating from his own mouth. He had no complaint to make against the natives (so far from it, that I should not have known the particulars of K.'s conduct had I not been informed by some natives which led me to enquire of the Captain) but against his own countrymen, (not his crew,) who had robbed him, and who were pursued and taken and brought back by the Christian natives, and their plunder taken from them.

On my stating I should write to K., the heathen chief, to hasten his promised payment, as the *Flying Fish* would soon be ready for sea, Captain Mulholland said, he thought there was no need of my doing so, as the stipulated day of payment was not yet past. I, however, did so, and requested K. to give him a pig in addition for his having struck the Captain. To this K. assented, and made the payment within 4 days after, as the Captain (who afterwards called upon me) stated and as his note of thanks, written to me the night before he sailed, abundantly testifies.

The *Flying Fish* had to have every thing taken out of her in order to clean and caulk her without and within. The whole of her "stock-in-trade" and stores were piled upon the shingle bank at Ahuriri with no other protection than a sail; some hundreds of natives were about; and yet, Sir, her stores were not plundered by any but by Christian Englishmen! In fact, the Captain was obliged to set a native watch, to protect his property against his own countrymen.

I do not mean to say, Sir, but that the natives of Hawke's Bay are difficult to deal with; still, I venture to think that one step towards making them better is for more vessels than one to trade there, and to have those vessels manned (or, if not manned, commanded) by moral, if not Christian men, who will set them a good example. I scarce need add, that such vessels may depend upon what little aid and influence I may possess being exerted in their favor.

Apropos—statements similar to the alleged "robbery" have been formerly concocted in reference to other places in these seas, to secure the monopoly and scare away a new-comer.

"Facts," Mr. Editor, "are stubborn things,"—as you, yourself, have more than once said. And yet (though I believe I have said enough to satisfy any impartial person) I have not told the whole; some of the deeds of some of our countrymen in Hawke's Bay, I willingly for the present draw a veil over.

In conclusion, Sir, I may—as a well-wisher to the peace of the colony—be allowed to remark (though I don't pretend to know *how* it is, yet *true* it is)—that your paper too frequently sets matters in a very strong light against the natives. During the last 14 months in particular, I have been several times grieved at the relations therein contained concerning events which happened (I mean the bias—the *animus* which too plainly pervaded them), and which I knew were very widely different from what were therein related. I do not mean to say that *your aim* is to over colour or unnaturally to distort your statements; but I think, Sir, that when you have been led to publish forth to the world somewhat against the natives, and which, a few days after, has been found to be incorrect, you should, at least, make the *amende honorable*, and take the earliest opportunity of stating "the truth, the whole truth, and nothing but the truth."

Upon the whole, I think, Sir, you should be a little more cautious, in these times of extra excitement, as to what you receive and tell forth to the world as facts. Who can possibly tell the tremendous amount of physical evil (not to say moral guilt) which a continued course of inflammatory—though, it may be, infinitesimal—doses, will ere long cause to the whole system?

> *I am, Sir,*
> *Your obedient servant,*
> WILLIAM COLENSO,
> *Resident Missionary at Ahuriri.*

P.S.—I should also remark—in order to avoid ambiguity—that, the cause of Captain Mulholland's visit to the Mission Station was, to ascertain if he could obtain any assistance in a pecuniary way to enable him to engage and pay some white men to repair his vessel.—As the whole of his "trade" (tobacco) which he brought with him, did not amount to a fourth part of the quantity mentioned in your paper.

> *W.C.*

❖ 1848 TO THE EDITOR.
New Zealand Spectator and Cook's Strait Guardian 6 May.

Wellington, May 4, 1848.

SIR,—It was with no small amount of surprise and deep regret, that I read in your paper of the 26th ult. the statement, that the principal chief of Hawke's Bay, (and, in fact, of the whole district between that place and Turakirae,) Te Hapuku, had supplied the chief Te Rangihaeata with both arms and ammunition.

I was *surprised*—although prepared from long experience to hear the natives evil-spoken of—because such a statement is altogether erroneous, (as I hope presently to shew): I was (and must necessarily be) *grieved*, because such news (backed by your editorial remarks) is of a nature not only to alarm the quiet settler in the out-stations, but to make him view every little movement of the natives however inoffensive with distrust and anxiety—to cause both the Government and our friends in our mother-country to fear that war is again about to burst forth upon the colony—and to excite such powerful chiefs as Te Hapuku and his friends (seeing that they are continually misrepresented) into collision with the Government, or, at least, to cause those native chiefs to entertain a worse opinion of us than they have already.

I have stated my belief in the *falseness* of such information: and this I will now endeavour satisfactorily to shew.

On several occasions during the past two years, while conversing with Te Hapuku, I shewed him the folly of aiding Te Rangihaeata in any way—with men, arms, or ammunition; and I was glad to find, that he agreed in general in what I said. On my return journey from this place in November last, I heard that Te Rangihaeata intended if possible to effect an alliance with the Ngatikahungunu tribe, and to retreat upon the neighbourhood of Hawke's Bay, by way of the Manawatu river. I consulted with some of the more influential chiefs, and, having gained their consent, I, before I got home, sent him word, that he was upon no account to pass Te Apiti. Early in January, a messenger from Te Rangihaeata to Te Hapuku arrived at Wakatu, (the village of the latter chief, and near to my station) bringing with him two red and two white blankets as a present to Te Hapuku, and a request to assist Te Rangihaeata with arms and ammunition. A meeting of chiefs was held, and several professing Christian chiefs, headed by Leonard Te Kawepo my native teacher, spoke strongly against it. I was very ill at the time, but I sent to Te Hapuku to remind him of his promise and to encourage him to adhere to the same. And, a day or two after, Mr. W. Morris, master of the whaling station at Cape Kidnapper, calling upon me, I mentioned the circumstance to him, upon which he went to see Te Hapuku, and also advised him not to comply with the request of Te Rangihaeata. Te Rangihaeata's messenger obtained nothing whatever from Te Hapuku in return for his blankets, save some native mats. But, on his leaving Wakatu, and arriving at Raukawa at the end of his first day's journey, one of Te Hapuku's men, who had escorted him thus far, took upon himself to say to Te Waerenga, an old man (one of the distant relations of

Te Hapuku, formerly a Papist, but now a heathen) living in the village of Raukawa, that Te Hapuku had said, he was to give Te Rangihaeata's messenger a musket,—and thus he obtained *one* from him. The next Te Rangihaeata's messenger resumed his journey, and Te Hapuku's men returned to their village. On their reaching Wakatu and relating what had taken place, Te Hapuku became greatly enraged, and calling for one of his more courageous adherents (Hemi Kepa Te Uranga), ordered him directly to pursue Te Rangihaeata's messenger, and to follow him day and night until he should overtake him, when he was to take away and bring back the musket. H. Kepa overtook him at Te Waipukurau village, where, with the assistance of Paul Te Nera, and George Oneone (Christian chiefs), and Matthew Meke the native teacher, the musket was taken from him. He begged hard to be allowed to retain, at least, the cock, but this was refused; he then entreated to have the ramrod given back, and lastly the screw from the same, just to shew to his chief, but he pleaded in vain; Hemi Kepa brought back the musket to Te Hapuku.

I left my station, on my usual autumnal journey throughout my district, on the 23rd of March; up to which time no other persons had come to Heretaunga from Te Rangihaeata, I came by the way of the river Manawatu; and left Ngaawapurua (a village a little above Te Apiti, and the *only* route by which messengers from Te Rangihaeata could possibly travel towards Hawke's Bay,) on the 5th ult. and on the 7th ult. some natives of my Party who had remained at Ngaawapurua, left that place and came on after me to the village where I then was; up to which date no strangers had passed up the river. On the 10th ult. I finally left the Manawatu district, when my Christian friends, Paul Te Nera and Matthew Meke, and others, returned to Heretaunga by the same route by which we had come. And on my arrival here, I found a letter from home, from Mrs. Colenso, dated the 14th ult. (on which day too, I believe, the *Gypsy* sailed from Ahuriri,) which, while it gives me full information concerning the natives at my station and neighbourhood, contains not a syllable respecting the arrival there of "twenty-five of Rangihaeata's followers, and their subsequent returning laden with arms and ammunition!!"—An event which, if true, would have necessarily caused no little stir in the neighbourhood. But I may further add, such could not possibly have been the case, because there was not time for a party to pass from Te Apiti to Hawke's Bay (deducting the days in which the rain poured in torrents) during the short period which elapsed between my leaving Manawatu and the sailing of the *Gypsy* from Ahuriri. Further, Mr. Editor, allow me to say, that you are not quite correct in stating, "that a large quantity of arms and ammunition, obtained from the wreck of the American brig *Falco*, is known to be in the possession of Te Hapuku." For, none of the principal chiefs of Ahuriri nor their followers were at Table Cape at the time of the wreck of the *Falco*; and those natives who did reside there at that time, and who were concerned in that matter, and who subsequently migrated south to Heretaunga with their illgotten property, restored, last autumn, the whole of what they had left to me (some few, however, of them had, at my request, formerly returned what they had to Mr. Perry at Table Cape, prior to their leaving that place,) comprising, among many other things, muskets, powder, ball, and bayonets.

I pass by the mysterious shrouding (so to speak) of the affair—the departing from Heretaunga of the twenty-five armed men by night!—as being utterly unworthy of notice. It being well-known that the New Zealanders have a strong natural antipathy to night-travelling—and most particularly so where such is altogether needless.

You, also, (in your leading article in that number of your paper containing the information which is the subject of the present letter,) speak of "the natives as possessing the inclination to disturb the public peace, but as wanting the power to do so." I trust, Sir, that you may never have to chronicle the rising-in-arms of the Ngatikahungunu tribe;—an evil, compared with which all that has hitherto happened, both North and South, would appear as mere child's play. For, if once the sword of war is drawn in that quarter and against that powerful tribe, you may be assured of this, that the whole of the natives upon the Eastern coast, from the East Cape and inland to Taupo, inclusive, may be considered as united against the Government.

Knowing, as I do, the state of the native mind—the keen feeling of the first-rank native chiefs when falsely accused—and the absolute need of straining every nerve just now in order to preserve among us the blessings of peace—I could not conscientiously leave Palliser Bay (where I first saw your paper) for Wellington, and allow those natives who were then on their way towards Heretaunga with your news to depart without my writing a note to Te Hapuku upon the matter; a copy of which I subjoin, and which you are at perfect liberty to publish. I dare indulge a hope that I may possibly get an answer from him ere I leave this neighbourhood.

And further, and in conclusion, I would once more beg to be allowed to say—that, if ever peace is to be permanent among us—if ever this (hitherto unfortunate) colony is to flourish—it must surely be through a very different policy than that of laying hold of everything in the shape of *news* that will *"tell"* against the natives, and thus needlessly exasperating the native mind. If we and they are to dwell quietly together— if we really possess an intellect superior to theirs—and if *we* vaunt ourselves in being Englishmen—the descendants of a Christian nation the growth of nearly eighteen centuries—let us show our superiority, and evidence our desire to live peaceably with them, in our possessing a little of that pure and genuine philanthropy which thinketh no evil—beareth all things—and never faileth; otherwise our little children may yet become our teachers (or their children hand down their forefathers' deeds to the succeeding generation) when they admonishingly sing—

"None but a madman would fling about fire
And tell you—'tis all but in sport."

> *I am, Sir,*
> *Your most obedient servant,*
> *W. COLENSO*
> *Resident Missionary at Ahuriri.*

Copy of a note written to Te Hapuku, and sent by some natives going to Hawke's Bay, who were in possession of the report, stating,—that he had furnished Te Rangihaeata with arms, &c.

No te Kopi, Aperira 29, i tuhia atu ai.

E ta, e te Hapuku, Tena koe, e rahi ano toku aroha ki a koe, e noho mai na i to kainga. E ta, tena koe, tenei ano taku korero ki a koe; nui noa atu taku oho maori ki te korero i te Nuipepa, i taia mai nei ki Poneke; mohou ia te korero nei. Na te kaipuke mai tenei korero, na Tipihi. Na, ko te korero tenei, e, Erua tekau ma rima o nga hoa a te Rangihaeata kua tae ake ki a koe, me nga taonga ano, he paraikete, he aha, he aha; a, kua utua mai e koe ki nga pu ki nga paura; a, i hoki po mai ratou i a koe na.

Na, ko te korero tena; a, e mea ana ahau, he parau. Ae, apopo tae atu ai taku pukapuka wakakahore ki Poneke. E ta, me he teka ano te korero nei, kaua koe e aha ki a Hanara. Engari, me tuhi mai koe ki te Kawana, kia rongo tera kitei te tikanga. E ta, ma Mata (Mrs. Colenso) e korero to te Nuipepa ki a koe.

Tenei hoki ahau te haere nei ki runga ki te wakapae teka, heoi, kei te Atua te wakaaro mo tana pononga.

Naku,

Na to hoa aroha,

NA TE KORONEHO.

Ki a Te Hapuku.

§ 1852 SHIPPING INTELLIGENCE: ARRIVALS.[1]
The New Zealander 9 October.

Oct. 8—Thomama, 68 tons, H. Sturley, from Hawkes Bay, with 25 tons black oil, (66 casks) 350 bushels wheat, 650 do. maize, ½ ton whalebone, 4 casks pork. Passengers— Mr. Fairburn, and 2 children of Rev. Mr. Colenso.—J. Salmon & Co., agents.

§ 1857 OPEN COLUMN.
Hawke's Bay Times and Ahuriri Advocate 24 October.

SIR,—In the speech made by Mr. Colenso at the meeting last Tuesday, he made certain observations that were calculated to wound most acutely the feelings of Mr. Harris. Though the exordium for the introduction of these ungenerous remarks was devised with characteristic astuteness, yet the minds of those present were not imposed on as to their true character and the motive which dictated them: and Mr. Harris had the satisfaction of hearing expressed, in unequivocal terms, the indignation and disgust that were felt, and which such conduct, it is to be hoped, will always inspire.

Mr. Colenso chose also to imply that to Mr. Harris's own tone or manner of address might have been owing te Moana Nui's conduct towards him. This was

---

1 That is, arrivals in Auckland. Elizabeth Colenso's (née Fairburn) brother takes Fanny and Latimer to Auckland as the Colensos' marriage nears its end. I.S.G.

quite a gratuitous and unwarranted assumption on Mr. Colenso's part, and of a piece with the rest of his remarks about Mr. Harris. But Mr. Harris can well afford to treat with merited contempt this unworthy endeavour to detract from his official character. For Mr. Harris is well known to have filled for several years the onerous and responsible office of Clerk and Interpreter, and to have gained the unvarying approbation of his official superiors by the good sense, conduct and capacity with which he has performed and continues to perform his duties. His other good qualities and general demeanour have earned for him the good wishes and esteem of his fellow settlers, and he may rest assured that this estimation in which he is held will not be impaired in the minds of the Ahuriri settlers, by anything that Mr. Colenso may say or do of a nature with that which has provoked this letter.

Vispex.

§ 1857 THE NOMINATION.
Hawke's Bay Herald 7 November.

On Tuesday last, a Public Meeting of the electors of Ahuriri was held in front of the Court House, Napier, convened for the purpose of nominating two fit and proper persons to represent the District in the Provincial Council of Wellington....

At 12 o'clock precisely, J. Curling Esq., the Returning Officer... called upon those persons to come forward who were prepared to nominate candidates for the two vacant seats. The following gentlemen were then duly nominated and seconded:— Thomas Purvis Russell...; Robert Pharazyn...; Donald Gollan....; Thomas Henry FitzGerald....

Thomas Purvis Russell Esq. then mounted the hustings, or, rather, the dray that served the purpose of such, and said....

Robert Pharazyn Esq. then came forward and said....

T. H. FitzGerald Esq. then addressed the meeting....

The Rev. W. Colenso, in addressing those he saw around him as fellow settlers and fellow electors, said that he had not generally interfered in politics; but that, on the present occasion, when they were all assembled to exercise their birthright as Britons, he attended for the purpose of expressing his sentiments—the sentiments of the oldest settler in the District. He had one prefatory remark to make—if there was any place more than another where liberty of speech was allowed, it was the floor of the House of Commons or the public hustings. Like a famed reformer, he stood there to "speak the truth impugn it whoso listeth," and if any thin-skinned person chose to take offence, he could not help it. He would say to his fellow electors, vote for Gollan and FitzGerald; and he would establish his point, negatively as well as positively. The first in opposition to these candidates was Purvis Russell. What! vote for a man who had changed his colours! (*Laughter*) Mr. Russell had spoken largely here, and had done nothing in Wellington. (*Laughter*.) Then there was Mr. Duncan, of whom he knew but little, but who would no doubt vote for

Ahuriri so long as it went with Wellington, but no longer. Don't vote for him. He (Mr. Colenso) had been startled when he read of the insurrection in India, of the loss of the Dunbar, of the forebodings which some had entertained regarding the natives, and the desire to have martial law proclaimed throughout this District; but he was never so much astounded as when he learned that Robert Pharazyn sought to be returned member for Ahuriri. Ye Gods; only a few days ago he was a boy at school. They wanted the right men in the right place—not boys. Mr. Pharazyn, having been recently at school, should have learned the lesson *seniores priores*; and, in making his *debut* in public life, should have remembered the ancient saying, *dies togæ virilis*. Mr. Pharazyn came there a nominee. Dr. Pharazyn thinks so and so, and Mr. Pharazyn thinks the same. (No, understood to be from Mr. Pharazyn.) By whom was he supported? Why, by a little knot of office-bearers—men who dared not think or speak for themselves—men who trembled for their places and their salaries. They did not want inexperienced men; they had seen enough of them in the Council already. Nor did they want exclusive legislation for the runholder. Many of that class he respected, but there were others amongst them that he knew to be totally opposed to the progress of the country. For instance, a runholder once said in his (Mr. Colenso's) hearing that he never wished to see more then five Europeans in the country. Mr. Colenso then passed to the positive side of his argument, enumerating the merits of Messrs. Gollan and FitzGerald, although he did not agree with the latter in every thing. The organ of the Government had sneeringly said with reference to Mr. FitzGerald, send him to the Council, and, said the speaker, we will send him. (*Cheers.*)

The Returning Officer then called for a show of hands for the respective candidates.

The numbers were for Mr. Pharazyn 5; for Mr. Russell 6; for Messrs. Gollan and FitzGerald respectively, a very large show, probably from 30 to 40. A poll was thereupon demanded by Messrs Russell and Pharazyn; and the day of polling announced for Monday the 17th inst.

❖ **1857 TO THE EDITOR.**
Hawke's Bay Herald 10 November.

SIR,—In your Supplement of the 24th ult. (only this evening to hand), I note what you say concerning "an effort which is being made to establish a Wesleyan Chapel in Napier, &c."

Allow me to add, that, if such is, or should prove to be, the general wish of the inhabitants of Napier and its vicinity, I too shall be right glad in the same being both heartily and speedily carried out.

But, if, as I hope, something less denominational, and (consequently) more Christian, would both suit their wants and be quickly effected; I, for one, would willingly aid it.

I would, therefore, propose to my fellow settlers residing at Napier and, indeed, generally throughout the District, (who might, it is to be hoped, all be benefited thereby,) the speedy erection of a suitable Building for Divine Worship, upon the following simple and Catholic plan:—

1st., That it be wholly un-sectarian, and therefore free for any Christian Minister:—

2nd., That it be equally free to be used as a Lecture-Room for Useful Knowledge on Week-days, or Week-day Evenings:—

3rd., That Admission be free:—and,

4th., That the whole be under the super-vision of a Committee of—persons; to be chosen by ballot from among the Subscribers and regular Congregation every six months.

In furtherance of which I would be happy to give a building site at Napier, and also a subscription of £50, pledging myself to collect a second £50, should the expenses not exceed £250; and, should the Building Expenses amount to £400, I would then give both the site and £100 towards it.

I would also offer my own Personal Services, *gratuitously*, during the first year; *i.e.* to preach (d.v.) twice on the Sunday, and (if desired,) once a week on some weekday evening; or, assist any other Minister whom they might select:—and also, take upon me to give a Scientific Lecture once a month throughout the same year.

As the Clergyman Episcopally ordained to, and, therefore, (speaking Ecclesiastically,) as the Clergyman of the Ahuriri, (although I regret to say, now for 5 years suspended from duty, during which long time, however, I have continued to hope I should yet be saved any approach towards (*"Irregularity"*) I cannot but deem it my duty (however painful,)—under existing circumstances—thus to address, through your ready aid, my fellow-Christians and fellow-Settlers of Napier and the District.

> *I am,*
>
> *Sir,*
>
> *Very faithfully yours,*
>
> *WILLIAM COLENSO.*

Waitangi, Napier,

Nov. 2, 1857.

❖ 1858 OPEN COLUMN.
Hawke's Bay Herald 20 February.

SIR,—In your report of the Public meeting held on the 1st inst., (in your issue of this day,) you have, I think, reported me as saying what I certainly did not: *e.g*—"before severing a chain that could never be unsevered;"—rather, "before welding a chain that could never be unsevered":—that "more statistical information was needed":—rather; that "there was statistical information enough in that draft memorial to make several good ones":—again: that "it should be a document drawn up by an Englishman, to be presented by an Englishman, &c.":—rather (after I had alluded to Washington, and the *first* American declaration which had ended in their glorious

Independence, and that such a document was one which posterity had and would admire; I said,) that, "such a kind of document should also be drawn up by us as our children and grandchildren would not be ashamed of—one worthy of preservation in the future archives of Ahuriri—one drawn up by Englishmen, to be presented by Englishmen to an English Governor &c.".: again, instead of saying (in conclusion,)— "in ether case it was sham and a humbug": rather that "I had always opposed, and ever would oppose, all sham and humbug."—

Further: pardon me, Mr. Editor, when I say, that (believing you to be a countryman of Burns,) you ought to have known him better than so to "*murther*" the couplet which I quoted (thus corrected—from memory):

"Her prentice han' she tried on man,
And then she made the lasses O!"

> I am.
> *Yours very sincerely,*
> WILLIAM COLENSO.

❖ 1858 OPEN COLUMN.

Hawke's Bay Herald 8 May.

SIR,—Being desirous of making public a few additional remarks on the subject of Streets, Sewerage, and Drainage for our Town of Napier, I avail myself of your courtesy and "Open Column" to enable me to do so.

And, in order that I may be the better understood, I will endeavour to write plainly; —classifying under the following heads:—I. The Town of Napier, its advantages and disadvantages, its present wants and its present resources. II. The Wellington Streets, Sewerage, and Drainage Act, its peculiarities, and its unfitness for Napier. III. What is really needed, and how such may the better be obtained.

I. *The Town of Napier*, its advantages and disadvantages, its present wants and its present resources. (This I shall barely consider with sole reference to the subject of this Letter.) The site of the Town of Napier is, as we all well know, very peculiar. Perhaps no Town of modern times has been laid out on such broken, irregular, and varying ground. The length, N. and S., and breadth, E. and W., of the Township are about equal; throughout which and in every direction Streets have been plentifully marked out. And, while some of them lead up precipitous hills and over sandy beaches, and others through deep salt-water lagoons and fresh-water swamps, every Section, (amounting to about 600) good or bad, has quickly found a purchaser: not withstanding, the number of proprietors is but small when compared with the number of Sections. Now it is mainly owing to those two facts—its very peculiar configuration and state, and the present small number of proprietors,—that the great difficulty of its Streetmaking Sewerage and Drainage consists. For, had its site been naturally much like most other parts of the earth, which have from time to time been equally honored, the matter of putting it into shape and keeping it clean could be easily accomplished. Still, it has stone within itself for metalling and paving; and water also

for all Sewerage purposes. But here, at the very outset, a question obtrudes itself:—
Is any such Street-making Sewerage and Drainage Act as this Wellington one really
needed? Let me see:—I take my stand at the Royal Hotel, the S. terminus of Carlyle
Street, the principal thoroughfare; thence to the Land Office, at the N. end, is about a
mile; upon this Street I count, on the one side, 11, and on the other 5, houses; from the
Land Office I proceed over the second great thoroughfare, Shakespeare Gulley, on to
the Pilot's house at the extreme anchorage, a distance of upwards of another mile, and
here I find a much less number of houses: so that, as far as Sanitary measures (Sewerage
and Drainage) are included, there can not possibly be any need for them:—no, not
even if the climate of Napier was as pestilential as that of Fernando Po, or the banks of
the Tyber; how much less when the climate of New Zealand is so very well-known to
be everything but proverbial for its good quality, and ours, here at Ahuriri, among the
best of it! Still, it will be said, "Our roads and Streets must be made; Carlyle Street is
partly impassable in winter, and Shakespeare Gulley, during and after rains, is not much
better." True, must be the reply; but, with our limited resources, and very infantile state
of our young town, we must ever be content to do as our fathers did before us—crawl
before we run. "*Slow but sure*" must be our motto; and it will be well for us if we ever
bear it in mind; as by so doing we shall both keep out of the Bankrupt's List, and keep
from being laughed at for having undertaken what we could not perform. The modern
watch-word of "*Up boys and at them!*" (though spoken on the quarter-deck of a 120 gun
ship, amid much applause and world-wonder,) did not achieve so much as the wary
old British "*Steady boys, steady*":—so, steadily onwards, slow but sure, should ever be the
prosperous motto for Ahuriri. As an owner of land in the town of Napier, (and, perhaps,
soon to be a resident there,) I cannot but wish and seek her advancement; but I consider
it almost suicidal to both her real progress and interests, to think of burthening her
with heavy rates and taxes in her nonage under the high-sounding (though fallacious)
phrase of improvements. Nature makes no leaps; and that art, or state of society, is the
surest and best, because most like Nature, which imitates her. Some may here think
on Melbourne; but that gigantic youngling is altogether an exception. We have not
her gold foundation; notwithstanding ours may be equally as sure—perhaps more
stable (let a future generation decide), more after the growth of the old English *Oak*
than of that of the *Blue Gum*. But even the town of Melbourne, with all her gold and
her enormous population and intertropical climate and her Governor resident and her
influential Councils, allowed nearly 20 years to elapse before she thought it time to have
a Sewerage and Drainage Act: notwithstanding in less than a year after the first house
was erected she had more than double our present population. Passing indeed an act
for introducing water into the town, and entering into a contract with a company to pay
them £100,000 for doing the same, before she brought out the Sewerage Act.

II. *The Wellington Streets Sewerage and Drainage Act, its peculiarities, and its unfitness for
Napier.* Now this Act, Mr. Editor, I cannot but consider as peculiarly Wellingtonian; and
(not unlike several other of her Acts) one which has caused her Citizens (being
Englishmen) a good share of heart-burning and grumbling: for John Bull always

grumbles, even to bellowing, when he has to dip his hands into his pockets, especially for Rates, and that twice in one day! This Act, I have said, is peculiarly Wellingtonian:— 1st by its ostentation and specious objects (as if Wellington was a second Nineveh); as well as from its unhappy un-English feature of interference with the sacred rights of private property; which, in a small place like Wellington, ever-heaving with bitter political strife, is anything but a step towards a development of the better feelings of humanity, or a dwelling together in unity:—And, 2nd, from its being very much more suited to her as the N. Zealand Land-Company's town than to any other. For, be it known, that, when this Act was passed in 1855, (fifteen years after her birth,) the long straggling town of Wellington (salubriously enough situated for 2 miles and more on the edge of Port Nicholson harbour, well watered with several brawling streams, and plentifully ventilated with strong and healthy breezes,) possessed only 3208 souls, of whom upwards of 1500 were children! And yet, when the Act alone is duly considered, a stranger would naturally suppose, that the town or city for which it was framed was either dreadfully unhealthy, or overcrowded, or both. In the Act we find a whole host of officers, and offices and Works not merely legalised, but (as I take it,) made actually preparatory to any Streetmaking &c. being effected. (See particularly, clauses 35, 36, 37, 38, 49, 51.) A key however to this (and to much more of a similar nature and emanating from the same source,) is at hand; namely, that Wellington has had for a long time the modesty to consider herself as the town par excellence, of N. Zealand, and the only one of all already, or to be, born, fitted to become the capital of the Britain of the South! This unfelicitous gasconading characteristic has however already done her no little injury (scarcely yet, perhaps, clearly seen by her citizens); but, without enlarging just now on this point, what we have to guard against is, not to be so deceived as to follow with our eyes shut in her wake. Still, as I have said, the Act was in some measure *suited* to her as the *N. Zealand Land-Company's town*;—for in many of the proprietors of her town lands were not only absentees in the highest degree, but had also, as the saying is, got hold of those lands for "a song"; and it should not be forgotten, that one of that Company's binding engagements was, that "a tithe of all their purchases was to be reserved for the Natives"; through which they were thoughtlessly located in several spots in the Town of Wellington, to the subsequent grief however of the Citizens: hence, perhaps, might possibly be argued the correctness of such an "Algerine" manner of proceeding as that laid down in clauses 96, 97. Further, it should also be remembered, that Wellington (as I have already intimated,) is everywhere well supplied with fresh water; and has also close at hand, even on the immediate shores of her fine harbour, abundance of timber for fencing and other purposes; hence it may also be inferred, that, seeing she was entirely free from any cares respecting wood and water, and, consequently, never even once dreamily visited with the faintest penumbra of anything concerning a *water rate*, she could the better afford to be a little extra-expensive in the way of Street-making Sewerage and Drainage, not to mention *Fencing*.

Now from all those things—both good and bad—Napier is particularly exempt. She certainly does not wish to imitate the unlucky frog, and go on brooding over her immense qualifications till she bursts, saying,—"I am the most central; I have the greatest extent of natural grass pasturage, and of finest alluvial soil; and as to my sea-board, my Hawke's Bay waters are as productive as my plains, for they abound in whales, more so than all the other shore waters of N. Zealand; and, while vessels have been wrecked both N. and S. of me, in my open roadstead a fine first-class ship has lain 9 weeks without once lifting her anchor, &c., &c." No, no, Mr. Editor, Napier should never wish to shew the family likeness in this kind of way, and so vaunt herself like her elder sister Wellington. Again, among her town-land proprietors she has few or none really absentees; and no native reserves (to plague her) in the town; and therefore she needs not those stringently exceptional clauses. And, further, her population is very small, scarcely indeed amounting to the fractional number over the 3000 of Wellington; but then she is the youngest of the nine, and if not as beautiful or as aspiring as *Urania*, at all events is, and must be, the pet, because she is the nursling. Moreover, she is conscious that she has no timber yet handy (though plenty enough a little way off); and sometimes, after a sultry day or night, has certain fitful starts occasioned by an ugly visitant of a nightmare foretelling somewhat of a *water-rate*. Further, more than two-thirds of the area included in the township of Napier was not only both surveyed and sold by Government as "*Suburban Land*," but also in large sections of from 5 to 9 acres each, with excellent hints from the then Crown Land Commissioner, Mr. Domett, as to their being "beneficially occupied as paddocks and gardens." Now all this is utterly at variance with such Clauses as 70 and 80 of this Act, which, if received by us, would go well-nigh towards the totally prohibiting the keeping either a horse or a cow upon any of those suburban sections, and, consequently, against their beneficial occupation, seeing they are wholly *within* the town. And, in fact, our Bench of Magistrates (when considering the issuing and renewal of Publicans' Licences, on the same day in which the Sheriff held his Meeting for the election of Street and Sewerage Commissioners,) instead of making it imperative on each Publican to provide a 6-stalled stable, should rather have said, (acting up to both the spirit of the letter of the Wellington Act,)— "see that none of you allow a horse to be tethered upon your premises."

I have already (at the Meeting) remarked, on the great expense of the initiatory steps towards the carrying out of this Act, and therefore I need not to say anything more here under that head; other than merely again to call the attention of your readers to clauses 36, 37, 38, 39, 49 and 51.—I trust, that what I have both said and written will tend clearly to shew the utter incongruity of such an Act as this with the present wants and interests of the town of Napier.

I come now to my 3rd and principal consideration:—*What is really needed? and how such, may the better he obtained.* And here speaking of the present *real wants* of Napier, (with exclusive reference to the above mentioned Act,) we must also keep in mind our present resources. Now I humbly conceive, that, the putting the marshy part of Carlisle Street in a condition fit for the passing of wheel-carriages,—the metalling Shakespeare Gulley,— and the improving the Beach road on to the Pilot Station, are the Street improvements primarily needed. Those seem to be the points, in the way of Street-making, which more immediately call for energetic aid. As to Sewerage and Drainage, let all thought of such for the present, be scattered to the winds. It will, I think, be quite time enough to consider such when Napier like Wellington shall have passed through 15 years of being; or, at all events, when the proprietors of her salt-water lagoon sections shall have set the powerful and needful example of improving them. For, at present (referring for a moment to the said Wellington Act,) it is, as if an arithmetical problem was given:—— *e.g* If the exhalation arising from "1 ton of stable-dung" causes in "7 days" so much nuisance; how much is caused by that arising from 30 acres of putrid salt-water lagoons in the same time? But, whether present or future, it cannot for a moment be supposed, that a rate could ever be levied on the Town of Napier for the draining of those *Swamp* Sections, or even for making the Streets running through them. For it must not be forgotten that those swamp *Town* Sections were laid out of a larger size (some even being 2 acres,) and sold at a lower price by the Government simply because they were under water, and that whoever purchased them would have to make an outlay in order to make them of any service. Hence we had (for example) No. 291, ½ an acre, offered at £5, while its next neighbour, No. 276, containing 2 acres, was offered at £2. 10s. 0.

I think, Sir, that most of the land-owners and residents in Napier will fully agree with me as to the streets needing immediate aid; in fact, I might, truly enough say *all*, if some would but think less of their own isolated private, and more of the public interest. And now it remains to be considered how such needful aids may the better be obtained; or, in other words, the *Ways and means*.

1st *As to the Ways*:—let them be simple, suitable, and just. Simple, so as to be plain and easy; without stilts, or puffing, or mock display; and without needless expense in the matter of several paid officers or servants:—*Suitable*, so as to be always adequate to the wants of the rising town:—and *just*; so as every one residing, or holding property, in Napier, shall (*if really needed*) pay his fair quota towards improvements. Now, all this, I think, may be very properly and inexpensively performed by a Local Public Board; or, if they should need any extension of powers, such could very easily be obtained or, a plain Bill, framed on the broad basis of the foregoing conditions, might be duly considered and drawn, and be presented by our Members at the next Meeting of the Provincial Council.

2nd *As to the Means*:—not merely for the present (stated) occasion, but for the continual and growing wants of the town. And here, Mr. Editor, I would lay down the following suggestions for Public Consideration:—

1. That proper measures be taken in order to secure to the town of Napier, and for the sole benefit and improvement thereof, the unreclaimed and unsold lands of the harbour.

2. That, failing in the above, suitable aid be sought from Government towards the making the Streets and Roads of the said town—

3. That should Government refuse, or only partially assist, an easy Rate be duly levied on all Landed property in the town of Napier.—

4. That the rate be not uniform; with respect to the *situation* of land.—

5. That the rate be upon the broad principle of benefits derived, or derivable, from Street improvements; and, therefore, be somewhat as follows:—

6. (a) For all Land whether occupied or not.

(b) For all uninhabited houses, and for ground in profitable occupation.

(c) For or on account of all traffic, or income arising from the same.

(d) For all horses and carriages using such made and improved roads.—

7. That *Gough Island and Meanee Spit* be included.

8. That the Town be divided into suitable wards.

9. That one ward be not (generally) rateable for the improvements of another.—

10. That one local Board, and one sworn valuer be for the whole.—

11. That no unoccupied Land, or any belonging to any absentee, be distressable or saleable, for Rates.—

12. That appeal be allowed.

13. That the Board be annually chosen at a Public Meeting, and by ballot.

14. That all their accounts be annually and publicly audited.—Although I have gone so far as to propose a rate, it is wholly as a last resource; for nothing ought possibly to be farther from Napier, and indeed from the whole Colony of N. Zealand than a thing so hateful as taxation—the curse of Britain! to escape which we have even consented to expatriate ourselves from the homes and hearths of our sires.—

Now I sincerely hope, that the majority of your readers, being owners of land, or residents, in Napier, will give the foregoing suggestions attentive consideration; being prepared thereto by a strong determination to uphold that which is simple *suitable and just.*—and that too when the silver-loving side of the soul whispers, that to do so would be to act against one's own darling private interests.

> *I am, Sir,*
> *Yours very truly,*
> WM. COLENSO.

P.S. I have still a few words to say (in connection with the foregoing), and which I had quite intended to have said now; but as I have already exceeded all due bounds, I must leave the doing so till next week.

> *W.C.*

❖ 1858 OPEN COLUMN.
Hawke's Bay Herald 22 May.

SIR,—Your paper of the 8th inst. only reached me on the 15th—a circumstance I regret the more as (in a letter of mine contained therein) you have, by a small typographical error, made me to say the contrary of what I had written:—viz. "(b) For all *un*inhabited houses, &c.," should be, For all inhabited houses, &c.

In the P.S. of that same letter I had stated, that "I had still a few words more to say in connection &c.:" but, having subsequently had a public opportunity of addressing the inhabitants of Napier, when in a few strong words I said pretty much of what I had thought of dilating in writing, I will not trouble you any further on that matter.

In the same number of the Herald you give your readers a very full account of the Public Meeting held at Napier on the 30th ult. (and I sincerely hope, Sir; that they will at least, duly appreciate *your* most strenuous exertions, so very clearly shewn in the many closely printed columns in small type of that number.) In reading, however, the speech of Mr. Woodward therein reported, it occurred to me, that (while, on the whole, it is a tolerably faithful report,) there is some difference between it and the speech spoken—just such, if I may so express myself, as between a *sheep* and *mutton*. This opinion of mine, coupled with a few little wee things in the reported speech, has led me to infer, that, perhaps, Mr. Woodward had himself furnished you with it; or, at least, had the privilege of kindly aiding your notes. Now do not, Mr. Editor, for a moment suppose, that I am going to "pop the question" to you; so preserve, I pray, both your gravity and the *sella curulis*.[2] Neither will I venture on a critique; but, as I rose at the Meeting mainly to call attention to certain "fallacies and sophistries;" and as one of the greatest of them is all but quite ignored in the *reported* speech of Mr. Woodward (and yet my notice of it distinctly given); I deem it but an act of common justice to myself, as well as to your *distant* readers, to notice it;—leaving it to those who were present to decide as to the truthfulness of my remarks.

In Mr. Woodward's *reported* speech, he is stated to have said (speaking of the Constitution Act), that "it impowered the Provincial Councils to make laws for the peace, order, and good government" of their respective communities, terms that gave all the powers of sovereign legislatures, subject to the restrictions imposed by the Act." Now, according to my memory, and my notes (taken at the time), and my severe remarks (for I had felt my *loyalty* touched a bit,) on that particular portion of Mr. Woodward's speech, (most of which remarks, Sir, you have succinctly given,) and my (brief) conversation with Mr. Woodward *after* the Meeting, (when I again brought this one salient point before him,)—according to all these Mr. Woodward spoke differently. What I then clearly understood Mr. Woodward to say, had no reference to "Provincial *Councils*" nor to "their respective *communities*" nor to "sovereign *legislatures*" (nor to any *plural* numbers); but, to the simple and singular fact, which Mr. Woodward (as I took him, and I sat next to him,) emphatically stated, of *"the* SUPERINTENDENT *possessing sovereign power!"* And, indeed, Sir, there can be no manner of doubt about it; for,—after I had said (as truly reported by you,) that "I had heard it with the greatest astonishment, that the Superintendent possessed sovereign power":—I further said, that "I would then ask Mr. Woodward a question to his face" (which, turning to him, I did);—"Did Mr. Woodward believe that the Superintendent possessed sovereign power before he (Mr. Woodward) became a member of the Executive?" And to this question of mine, Mr. Woodward, half-rising from his chair, answered, "yes." Then, Mr. Editor, I proceeded, as you go on to relate.

I will not, Sir, make any more remarks; other than, in conclusion, to say, that instead of "precious Thistle and Bur Act," I said, "precious Thistle and Cur Acts."

---

2   The curule chair, official seat of consuls, praetors, and curule ædiles. I.S.G

I am, Sir,
Yours very faithfully,
WM. COLENSO.
Waitangi, May 17, 1858.

❖ 1858 TO THE EDITOR.
Hawke's Bay Herald 5 June.

SIR,—The season having again arrived for the planting of *Fruit-trees*, and being often asked for advice respecting the same, I willingly avail myself of your 'open column' and kindness to say a few words which may be of service to those of our fellow-settlers who are desirous of cultivating the trees of our Father-land, and thus conferring at least three noble benefits—1st. on themselves and their visitors, physically, in their fruits;—2nd. on the same morally, in the reminiscences of the *past*, which such trees and flowers and fruits must invariably convey;—and, 3rd. in transmitting the same—trees and ideas and kindly feelings—to the rising generation.

I wish to write particularly on the Sorts I believe to be the better adapted to our district; on the proper planting of the same; and on the *Soil and Situation* suitable for them; and that with especial reference to the King of British fruits, the Apple. A fruit, Sir, which I have long considered as one that will be still further improved by attentive and scientific cultivation in New Zealand, as well as one that will by-and-by become an increasing treasure both of wealth and utility to the inhabitants of this and the neighbouring colonies.—

In Westminister Abbey, in Poet's Corner, there is a monument bearing a bust in profile with this simple motto,—

Honos erit huic quoque pomo.—Virg.[3]

—Which monument was erected by Lord Harcourt (sometime Lord Chancellor of England) to the memory of a Mr. John Philips, one of Britain's genuine Poets, who, unfortunately, died at an early age, exactly 150 years ago. Although he is almost forgotten, he wrote among other poems a celebrated one in Miltonic verse on the Apple, which he entitled *"Cyder."* Thomson, in his "Seasons" (Autumn), thus truthfully notices him and the subject of his poem:—

"A various spirit, fresh, delicious, keen,
Dwells in their gelid pores; and active, points
The piercing Cyder for the thirsty tongue:
Thy native theme, and boon inspirer too,
Philips, Pomona's bard, the second thou
Who nobly durst in rhyme-unfettered verse,
With British freedom sing the British song:
How from Silurian vats, high-sparkling wines
Foam in transparent floods; some strong, to cheer
The wintry revels of the labouring hind;
And tasteful some, to cool the summer hours."

---

3   To honour this fruit too – Virgil, *Bucolics.* I.S.G.

And, inasmuch as *Philips* was a great smoker (in an age, too, when smoking was as nothing when compared with what it now is,) and commenced an ode of his with the praise of *Tobacco*, I may as well give it to please the many, and exercise a few of your pipe-loving readers (some one of whom, I hope, will favour us, through you, with a poetical translation):—

> *"O qui recisæ finibus Indicis*
> *Benignus herbæ, das mihi divitem*
> *Haurire succum, et suaveolentes*
> *Sæpe tubis iterare fumos."*—[4]

But to return from my digression:—my present letter shall be, *On the proper Planting of Fruit-trees*, to be followed by one, on *Sorts, Soil, and Situation*, in your next double number.

In one of our modern Cookery Books, there is a receipt for roasting a Hare, which is commenced with, "first, catch him": just so, Mr. Editor, would I speak to the purchaser of a Fruit-tree—first be sure that you get a *good* one;—not one (if an Apple) that is infected (although it may be invisibly) with that pest, the American Blight; nor one that has been grafted on a Hawthorn stock; nor one that has been grafted on an apple stock at one or two feet from the ground (which is too often done by gardeners, both to save labour in grafting, and to shew to advantage in size when removed from the nursery); nor one that has been raised in a very highly manured ground or nursery. Every obtainer of Apple-trees should be very suspicious of an infected locality. If he is so unfortunate as to have an infected tree, it should be dealt with precisely as an infected sheep,—if very bad, destroyed immediately; if a cure is to be hoped for, remove it quickly as far as possible from its fellows, and there try your remedies. Moreover, those grafted on Hawthorn, those grafted high on young Apple stocks, and those raised in highly manured ground, should never be chosen: the 1st is liable to deteriorate, as well as to be of very slow growth; the 2nd. has a quantity of useless wood which is very likely to put forth a host of finelooking shoots, which may perhaps be allowed to grow to the starving of the real branch (to say nothing of the extra risk in importing or carrying; while the 3rd. is almost sure to become *cankered*, if removed into a less stimulating soil, and if planted in a rich one to reward its planter with plenty of fishing-rods and whip-sticks instead of fruit.

Proceeding, however, to plant our tree, let the planter attend to the following simple rules; premising, that every *bona fide* Settler who has Fruit-trees to plant should be determined to do it himself, and not trust to servants.

1. Don't go about the job in a hurry; "good work requires time;" have a good *sharp* knife.

---

4   'Oh thou! from India's fruitful soil,
     That dost that sovereign herb prepare,
     In whose rich fumes I lose the toil
     Of life and every anxious care,
     While from the fragrant lighted bowl
     I suck new life into my soul.'
     – *The British Poets including Translations*, 1822. [Surely *Cannabis indica*, rather than tobacco?] I.S.G.

2. Choose dry (winter) weather for planting your trees; should they only reach you in wet weather, rather wait a week than hurriedly plant them in mire and half-broken clods.

3. See that none of the roots are crushed or torn in taking-up or carriage: if they are, cut off the wounded part, from above where it is sound, with a sharp knife.

4. Dig the pit very much larger than your tree apparently requires (at least, one spade deeper, all the better for going two spades); and fill up to the depth needed with surface earth, well broken, before you put in your tree.

5. Stretch out all the roots to their full extent (like the spokes of a cart wheel), giving them an inclination downwards.

6. Be sure *not* to plant the tree any deeper than it was before; rather (of the two) let it be shallower.

7. Fill the earth well in around its roots and under its main stem; break up the earth very small: use your hands.

8. Tread the earth well around the tree, and see that the earth is quite close to its stem at finishing; look at this afterwards at times throughout the year, as an open space around the stem is often caused by the wind shaking the tree, and which, if left, is very injurious to the plant.

9. If your tree is a little crooked, set the crooked side against the most windy quarter.

10. If your planting ground is very much exposed to any strong wind (say the W.), set your trees a little inclining that way.

11. If the situation of your garden or orchard is unfortunately very much exposed to high winds, a few screens (dead or living) kept up for a year or two, will amply repay all trouble. N.B. This should be borne in mind, in preparing or laying out Orchard ground, as *tutu*, and other native shrubs, or even fern, might be advantageously left for this purpose.

12. If your trees are very large, steady them in their places for the first year with a couple of braces, or stays, set opposite each other and tied to the tree; prevent them, however, from rubbing the bark of the tree; and be sure, in your tying, that you do not gird the tree tightly all round.

13. Having planted your tree, see that there are no broken branches, or bruised tips of branches; if there are any, better cut them off quite into the sound part with a *sharp* knife.

14. If your tree has a label attached by a wire, and you wish to keep it on, untwist the wire a little so as to be very loose; and *especially look at this during the year*, and untwist it as required.

15. If you plant late (say, after July), water your trees; especially if your situation is high and dry, or if there should be a dry spring season.

16. Should any *Suckers* arise (shoots which spring from the root), cut them off directly, and always as low down under ground as you can.

17. If your trees show any sign of unhealthiness, quietly endeavour to find out the cause. Beware, however, of *nostrums*: look to Nature.

18. Should a sheep, or, what is worse, a goat, get in and gnaw the branches of your trees, cut off as soon as possible the bitten part quite down to the sound bark. *Have good fences.*—

"Hail, Herefordian plant!————

————*Heaven's sweetest blessing, hail!*
Be thou the copious matter of my song,
And thy choice Nectar; on which always waits
Laughter, and sport, and care-beguiling wit,
And friendship, chief delight of human life.
What should we wish for more? or why, in quest
Of foreign vintage, insincere, and mixt,
Traverse th' extremest world ? Why tempt the rage
Of the rough ocean? When our native globe
Imparts, from bounteous womb, annual recruits
Of wine delectable, that far surmounts
Gallic or Latin grapes or those that see
The setting sun near Calpe's tow'ring height."—*Philips.*

> I am, Sir,
> Yours very truly,
> W. Colenso.

Waitangi,
June 1, 1858.

❖ 1858 OPEN COLUMN: TO D. GOLLAN AND T.H. FITZGERALD ESQUIRES, M.P.C. FOR AHURIRI, *(PER FAVOUR OF THE HAWKE'S BAY HERALD.)*

Hawke's Bay Herald 22 June.

My dear Sirs, I have this day received a printed circular from you, containing copies of your joint letter to Capt. Carter J.P., as Chairman of the Ahuriri Settlers' Association.

As one of your constituents—as one who publicly advocated your great fitness to represent us as our Members in the Provincial Council—as one who has watched with no small degree of interest your conduct in that Council, and who has, in common with many others, fully approved of the same, permit me to say a few words in reference to your letter to Capt. Carter.

That letter of yours, my dear Sirs, has both grieved and astonished me; *grieved,* at the bare idea of you our chosen men—thinking of resigning your seats (at this crisis) for anything less than a requisition to do so from a large majority of the electors: *astonished,* at you rating so highly Mr. Jos. Rhodes' letter, and at your opinion, that, failing to please the Association your only alternative would be to vacate your seats.

With you I lament, that Mr. Rhodes should have adopted "views so different" to what he once held and advocated and gloried in: with you *as a man,* I should also feel in reading his letter; but I question if Mr. Rhodes has so "suddenly" become a convert to his new views; and I greatly question the propriety of you, *as our Members* (whom the opposition would gladly see resign), allowing your just resentment, at your unfair ungenerous treatment, to predominate.

For, allowing the Ahuriri Settlers' Association all its due importance, (seeing that not a few of its members are both respectable and influential,) still, Mr. Rhodes did *not* write *as* the Secretary of the Association; and even if he had,—or, even if the Chairman himself[5] had written that Pandora's-box-like letter, I hesitate not to say, (and would, if required, prove,) that you ought not so greatly to over-rate it.

For you certainly were not elected only or mainly to represent the Ahuriri Settlers' Association—neither were you elected as nominees set forth by that Association: and I have yet to learn, that that Association, as a *body* either voted for your joint return, or energetically used their influence in your joint behalf. Therefore, with all due respect for many of the members individually of that Association, and for the Association itself as a body holding many just and proper principles, I cannot help thinking, that you have deferred vastly too much unto it.

Further; you know very well that you were not elected as some strangers have been (*e.g.* Mr. Ward, and Mr. V. Smith),—strangers alike to the constituency to the place and to the real wants of both place and people; had such been the case, then, perhaps, you would have had more reason to heed a letter coming from a respectable *bona fide* Settler of long standing, like Mr. Rhodes; but you know, that you were elected to your responsible and highly honorable (yet onerous) office, just because you were part and parcel of ourselves—chosen men of long-standing and experience and respectability, well-known to all your constituents, and well-knowing all the wants of the district.

Now, a part of my political belief is—that a man as a Representative of the people should always go unfettered to his work—that, being elected, he should no longer consider himself as quite at his own disposal, so as to resign whenever he should be opposed, or piqued, or when it might suit him that he should act conscientiously as well for the welfare of the minority who were against, as for that of the majority who had elected him—that once elected, he should be prepared both to see and hear many grievous things—or, rather, *not* to see and hear and feel so as to heed them—being determined to do his duty to his country: and, in thus conscientiously and straight-forwardly acting, not to care so very greatly as to his pleasing this or that person, or this or that party.

This is the night of your Public Meeting at Napier; I, unfortunately, cannot be with you. (Partly owing to my having been obliged to let loose my mare, to save her from the heavy flood of Tuesday night, and, although I walked several miles yesterday seeking, I have not yet caught her; and partly owing to an ugly visitant—Rheumatism). My not being with you I deeply regret. For, I wish, once more, publicly to give my full and sincere testimony to my belief in your able and praiseworthy joint service on our behalf and for the good of Ahuriri; and also to tell my fellow-electors, that I have every

---

5   May Capt. Carter pardon me for thus hypothetically speaking! W.C.

confidence in Mr. St. Hill, and this, too, after having known him well upwards of 13 years. And, I sincerely hope, that, if there be a single elector who, from not knowing him, has hitherto had a doubt as to his ability, this late manly circular of his just received (so very contrary to the unmanly and anonymous sneaking scribbling, with which our *one* Paper has been deformed of late,) will have completely dissipated it. In thus writing, however, I wish also to state that I have nothing personal against Dr. Featherston, whom I have had the honor of knowing for the same length of time; I bear in mind his former strenuous exertions in the cause of political liberty,—I regret the change of his mind,—and I respect his talents: but, his newly-adopted principle—

The enormous faith of many made for one;

That proud exception to all Nature's laws,

To invert the work, and counterwork its cause:—that of opposing the Representatives of the people,—which some, *anarchical*, I *monarchical*, call,—I differ from, *toto cælo*! For were he my own father, or were he the only man fit for the office of Superintendent in the whole Province (as some of his obsequious and obligated recipients would make some believe; little thinking, that, in swallowing such trash, they unman themselves!) I should, nevertheless, living as I am in the noon of political liberty of the 19th century, be under the necessity of voting against him; and this solely on account of that one hateful retrograding principle.

I had quite made up my mind, my dear Sirs, not to write a single political sentence until *after* the approaching 28th, as I had also determined to go to the poll and record my vote for Mr. St. Hill in solemn silence, (with no small amount of grief at the unreasonableness of a man of whom I had sanguinely hoped better,) and I also wished every elector to vote uninfluenced. Anonymous scribbling I never notice; and I only wish that some of us had observed the same rule. And even my neighbour's letter (notwithstanding his having manfully appended his name,) would not have moved me to seize a quill, had it not been for your joint one to Capt. Carter, of which I disapprove.

As I cannot be with you this night and at this hour, and as some may think such conduct rather strange, I have added the last two paragraphs of this letter.—

And am, My dear Sirs,

with the fullest confidence in you as our chosen Members,

Your very faithful constituent, WM. COLENSO.

Waitangi, Thursday night, June 17, 1858.

❖ **1858 OPEN COLUMN.**

Hawke's Bay Herald 3 July.

SIR,—No doubt there are many like myself, whose thoughts *this day* are on the events of yesterday. And while, on the one hand, the old adage, "*Nil sub sole novum,*" is true; on the other hand we have, "*many men many minds*" to match it: and therefore (if you may have room) I now trouble you with a tithe of my cogitations.

To tell you the truth, I feel somewhat ashamed of the Napier poll; and I wish you would publish the names of *all* who voted there *pro* and *con*; with those of Napier enrolled voters who, being present, held back. For, as Napier has been making some little stir in the cause of Reform during the last year in the New Zealand world, it is but an act of common justice to let those Reformers living at a distance know, how the poll at Napier came to be as it is. Besides, it will the better inform Dr. Featherston (and his party), so that he too may know, who and how many of the really free electors of Napier voted for him. As to those who chose not to vote, at such a critical period, it is but fair that their peculiarities should also be recorded, in order to be remembered.

I was the more impressed with painful feelings yesterday, when I saw *enrolled voters* refusing to exercise their privilege (although such voters were wholly opposed to the policy of the late government); while others, who valued their birthright, who had been more than a year residing among us, and who had come several miles to vote, found, to their surprise and disgust, that, as the new roll would not be scrutinised Magisterially before the morrow (*this day*), they were not allowed to do so!

And then I could not help thinking, that (unless some grave and weighty reasons could be assigned,—reasons sufficient to convince the majority of a jury of reasonable men,) such persons so refusing to serve their country, and that, too, at such a juncture, would not be altogether unfairly dealt with, if not allowed to vote in future—seeing they had abused a sacred trust.

And when I also saw well known *bona fide* and respectable settlers—men who had been some considerable time among us—proprietors of houses and lands and stock—(and that, too, to no small amount,) and also, yourself, Mr. Editor, the common Illuminator of us all—when, I say, I saw that you could not vote (owing to a "dodge," or a legal quibble,) and saw, moreover, persons voting for Dr. Featherston, whose old registered qualifications, either as to residence or property, were wholly *nil*, and knew, besides, that such (barring intoxication) could neither read or write—I could not help thinking on Dr. Featherston's own words—"that although heretofore all his predilections had run in favour of the people, as he must confess—still nevertheless he now wished to put the representation on *some other basis* than that of population."—

And when I further saw (and was much grieved in seeing) the unseemly activity at the doors of the Royal Hotel of some of the *Subs.* of the Land Office, (of whose conduct I shall say no more at present,) I could not help thinking, that, however un-English such a Bill may appear, something like the "Gag-Bill"[6] was absolutely necessary.

And when I saw a gentleman, (whose arrival among us last summer, as a settler, I was one of the first to welcome,) when I saw him acting the part of a "touter" for Dr. Featherston, and leading into the voting-room certain half-sober men who could neither read or write (and whose fitness and real qualification as electors were highly questionable), I could not help thinking, that he appeared much more advantageously and looked far more as a Briton when he trod the quarterdeck of his ship.—

6   In 1863 Senator Calhoun introduced a bill to the US Senate, commonly called the Gag Bill, prohibiting postmasters from receiving and forwarding any papers whatsoever containing anything relating to slavery; his aim was to preserve the status quo for the southern states. I.S.G.

And when I also saw my neighbour—the late *Secretary* of the Ahuriri Settlers' Association—now undignifiedly laboring as busy as a bee in getting votes for Dr. Featherston, in order to the undoing of all that he (my neighbour) had so long and ably been engaged in doing, I could not help thinking—*sic transit gloria hominis!*

And when I turned and saw the upper Tutaekuri *runholders*—and knew, too, what a long and rough and dangerous ride they had had, and considered their leaving their untended flocks;—and, also, saw enter the voting-room Mr. Alexander, another runholder and J.P., (and the oldest among us,) and knew, too, that he had left a sickroom to be present; and further, that these had all come to vote *for* the PUBLIC good—I thought on Nelson's last Battle signal, and thankfully felt, that Ahuriri yet had men who both valued their country and knew how and when to do their duty.—

And when I yet saw the Napier Schoolmaster enter and give his vote for Dr. Featherston; and considered, how he (the said Schoolmaster) had expressed himself relative to the Education Bill, and also concerning Dr. Featherston's answers to his repeated applications respecting the Napier School, (*endeavouring to view it as I believed he himself had viewed it,*) I could not help exclaiming mentally, "*Quid est homo!*"—

And when I, once more, looked round, and saw a vacancy—that *one* was *not* there, whom (if well and able) I could not but think ought to have been there, *viz.*, the Chairman of the Ahuriri Settlers' Association—I could not help thinking many things.—

And here, Mr. Editor, I must end; not but that I had *other* thoughts. No doubt, in my thus plainly revealing what passed through my mind, I shall vex some folks a little: I do not, however, wish to do so; I would very much rather they would by-and-bye quietly review their conduct as *Electors*, and its probable consequences. Be this as it may: you know what I once publicly stated—"that I had ever opposed, and would ever oppose, all sham and cant and humbug";—and I venture to think, that, while I am pretty well-known both faithfully and fearlessly to speak my mind, I am also known, *not* to say aught in malice.

I am, Sir, Yours very sincerely,
Wм. Colenso.

Waitangi,
June 29, 1858.

❖ 1858 OPEN COLUMN.
Hawke's Bay Herald 24 July.

Sir,—I had sharpened my pen to fulfil my promise, and so give you a 2nd letter on Fruit Trees; but your paper of the 17th inst. contains such an amusing extract from the Wellington "*Independent*," that my thoughts are turned another way. I cannot help thinking, that a man who dabbles in politics is likely to have both a hot berth and full hands; he may well enough be compared to a soldier on the field; or, better, perhaps, to a London fireman on a January night—roasting before, wet and freezing behind, with a momentary expectation of explosion by powder! Very comfortable, certainly;

but, *murus æneus conscientia sana.*[7] Although I have said, your extract is the ground of my present letter, I am well aware of the *sobriquet* by which the paper whence you had it is commonly known—"the lying Independent." I, however, would not so term it, but rather call it *unfortunate*. And this is, in great measure, owing to its clever editor (clever, mind; *not* talented; and there is a vast difference between the two, although, alas! too often the former is mistaken for the latter—the pinchbeck for the gold); for clever men dash at their work with the swiftness of swallows, and rarely care to refer to any authority—or, indeed, to what they may have already written on the same subject— hence they are continually making mistakes, and hence they have to bear the grosser term as a necessary consequence.—

We are oracularly told, Sir, that "FitzGerald and Gollan have fulfulled their mission, but not to the satisfaction of their constituents." Their constituents, however, know the contrary; and they also believe, that the term "jesuitical" (if at all proper here,) is far more in place applied to the conduct of the members of the late Provincial Executive Government—from the General Election 9 months ago down to their very recent sad discomfiture before Judge Gresson! No doubt the Pythian of Cook's Straits will find some way of evading its own sentence—or, rather, sentences, seeing that the above is followed by another equally truthful:—"From the hills of Castle Point to the plains of Ahuriri, not more than three or four votes will be polled for St. Hill." But what is the recorded fact? The fact, too, be it remembered, after all the long and active and "gallant" dragooning, both light and heavy; for we are triumphantly told, that, "Russell, Newman, Ormond and their gallant compeers sweep the whole district round"! Why the plain fact is, that those puissant champions of Dr. Featherston gained, *at their head-quarters*, only ONE solitary vote in excess of St. Hill! or, "from the hills of Castle Point to (the entrance of) the plains of Ahuriri," *two* votes *less* than St. Hill!! "So much for the inland country." And then the Oracle further says, "Joseph Rhodes... has raised Featherston's banner, and rallied round him a host of supporters for the red white and blue;.... and thanks to him, Charlton, and others, the St. Hillites will find themselves sorely discomfited." But, I again ask, what is the recorded fact? Why, first, that at Joseph Rhodes' own township and residence *St. Hill had a majority of five*! maugre the "energy and thorough English pluck," the "host of supporters," the glorious (but *sham*) republican "banner" of "red white and blue," and the dreadful "bomb" which that doughty Wellington-of-the-age sent into "the ranks of the enemy"! And, secondly, that, notwithstanding him, and Charlton, and others, (whose *labors* I have already noticed,) the Hawke's Bay, or Coast, majority in favour of Dr. Featherston was only *four*! While the gross total of votes recorded in his favour, throughout the whole of the Hawke's Bay District, only gives him TWO ahead of his opponent St. Hill!! 62 to 60.—May Dr. Featherston, like a wise general, *look and learn.*

Already it is known *how* some of those votes were obtained; and had I but a friendly Asmodeus at hand (like him in *le Diable Boileux,*) to shew the internal workings—what a revelation there would be! What an amount of influence of various kinds natures and

---

7   A sound conscience is a wall of brass. I.S.G.

degrees arrayed against St. Hill! All, or most of which, in a truly free state of genuine and virtuous Britons, ought not for a moment to exist. *Here,* (an Asmodeus would point out) some who were distantly related to Dr. Featherston—*there,* some who were related to his friends; *here,* would be seen some who had "snug berths" and who wished to keep them—*there,* some who, having Government Offices, had heard of Dr. Featherston's statement, of their not being half-paid, and therefore looked for an increase of wages; *here,* would be seen the owners of drays and holders of ferries, who, to please their masters the runholders, must "follow sort"—*there,* would be noticed those whose near relations are Government Servants or fortunate contractors at Wellington; *here,* would appear a queer animal, night *Meridarpax*[8]—*there,* would be seen another, *Hypsiboas*[9] named, who, when pretty nearly overwhelmed in the slough of care, instead of praying to Hercules (or Plutus), prayed to *Lithoptilon* the would-be-god of Cook's Straits, and was heard; *here,* would be seen some of the new genera of bipeds, (as recently classed by the profound naturalist Richmond,) *i.e.* "flat fish and flies"—*there,* would be discovered one who "dreamed all night and thought all day" about his getting the situation of Neptune's vice-gerent,[10] to look after those wicked *Sea Serpents,* and Mermaids (with Christian names), and other marine creatures as *Petrels,* &c., which lawlessly infest the Ahuriri waters, and to bring them to their bearings, for a good round annual sum out of the public purse:—but, Mr. Editor, I must stop. All those (with the exception, perhaps, of the newly classed and queer animals,) would have sided *against* Dr. Featherston, or rather, against his newly-adopted hideous *principle,* had it not been for those various influences above alluded to; and those of them who voted for him, or rather it, shut their eyes to the truth, that in doing so they voted against liberty and the rights of man! in defence of which some of their forefathers had bled—degenerate sons of able sires!—

Yes, Sir, and what is still more astonishing is the fact, that some of those very persons really believe that *they* are imbued with the true love of liberty and the rights of man, of candour and truth! Some of them are actually readers and admirers of the "*Westminster Review*"! hence they verily believe they are becoming mentally enlightened and enfranchised, and far wiser than their fathers; and yet they vote for one man to oppose the chosen representatives of the people! What a paradox!! But, Sir, I am still more moved and grieved when I see Scotia's sons so acting. Bards of ancient days, and History both mediæval and modern, all speak of Scotland as being pre-eminently the Land of Freedom.—

—"*The hills of the north,*
The land of blue mountains, the birth-place of worth;
Those mountains where Freedom has fixed her abode,
Those wide-spreading glens where no slave ever trod,
Where blooms the red heather and thistle so green."—

Scots! whose relatives and countrymen are even now engaged in erecting a monument

8 *Gr.* The name of one of Homer's mice – *a scrap-catcher.* I.S.G
9 One of Homer's frogs; – *a loud croaker.* I.S.G.
10 *Anglice.* Harbour Master. I.S.G.

to *Wallace*: Scots! whose *Knox* ne'er feared the face of man: Scots! whose *Burns* (though but a poor exciseman half-starving on his £70 per ann., was ever above a bribe,) — whose Burns had taught them—

"A king can make a belted knight,
A marquis, duke, and a' that;
An honest man's above his might,!
For a' that, and a' that:"—

And whose *Free* Church (in our day) hath shewn what *true* Scotchmen are composed of, and what they can do rather than sacrifice a truthful principle—leave their warm manse and their stipends and their homes, for the wild heather and the hill-side and the snow. Oh ye Scotchmen, who voted for Dr. Featherston, I am sorry for ye: sure I am that ye wonderfully differ from those revered worthies of your Father-land: sure I am, that none of ye should ever again attempt to sing, "*Scots wha hae*," or "*Auld lang syne.*" Ye should not ha' forgotten, that, in the honest pursuit of truth, ye can shut your eyes to no real facts or phenomena. I, an old settler, can not but lament the obliquity of your moral vision.

And then again the oracle declares, that "Gollan sits at Waipukurau like a pelican in the wilderness." It is true that he *sat*, while the others "swept the whole district," vote hunting. Gollan sat, and FitzGerald sat, and other influential friends to the cause of Reform sat, and I also sat; and we did this because it was the trial *principle*; not merely which of two men should be Superintendent. And now let any impartial person contrast the two parties—both as to their exertions *before* and *at* the election and the success of each. But "Gollan" is sneeringly said to "sit *like* a pelican in the wilderness." Good. Be it so. I accept it. The clever editor forgot all about the "pelican," and, owing to his overmuch cleverness, has spoken inconsequently (that I say not profanely), being tempted by the itching of a finger-ends sounding phraseology. He ought to have known how highly the ancients esteemed the pelican, and how modern naturalists speak of her. The ancients believed that she fed her young with her own blood, which she obtained by wounding her breast; hence they viewed her as the emblem of constancy affection and devotion. Hence, too, in later ages, the *pelican* became one of those honourable birds adopted in heraldry, and a pelican crest is a highly honourable one. Modern naturalists have discovered that the pelican has not only certain qualities in common with many other birds —*e.g.* the carrying an ample supply of food a very long distance to their young, their *social* habits, their peaceful demeanour towards other birds, and their longevity,— but, that in one good amiable and rare quality they are unique, *viz.* they will feed an injured bird of their species; hence the American Indians break the wing of a pelican and tie it up, in order to get a supply of fish. So that "Gollan" may very properly honorably and emblematically bear the arms his enemy has assigned him.

Further: the oracle says,—"All agree that for honesty honor and ability the name of Featherston ranks highest (*sic*) throughout New Zealand." And then he asks, "What appears against him?" What? I will answer; and that in one word:—*viz.* his audacious trampling on the very first principles of Responsible Government in continually daring to set at nought the Representatives of the people. Neither the Emperor of Austria nor Napoleon of France would dare to do as Dr. Featherston has done. Astonished at his conduct, I have in vain sought for a parallel in ancient or modern history. Such determined opposition to the people's representatives, such hindrance to the advancement of the Province, and to the public good, such ambitious views, are more worthy the consulship of Marius or the dictatorship of Sylla. It is true, Dr. Featherston is once more elected Superintendent; but he will assuredly find he has gained a Cadmean victory. Let not Dr. Featherston's interested adherents sing their *Io Pæans*, and plume themselves as if the matter was settled. Nothing, Sir, is settled, nothing *can* be settled, that is not in accordance with truth; hence the eternal heavings and throes of society. Nature is asserting, man is seeking his rights. Done with, for the time, it may be, and probably is; but settled, finished, it is not. Every oppression, every opposition to truth, or to the natural rights of man, is, for all the world, as a rule-of-three sum: as the greatness of the abuse is to the best interests of mankind, so, in proportion to the effectiveness of the statement, (or, of the power,) will be the length of time required for its abolition. And the common sense of mankind in general is the slate on which this problem is to be worked. For the time we (the Reformers) are in the minority; but what a minority! a minority embracing all those who are really free; a minority containing those who, obeying conscience, have volunteered to fight for a principle; a minority which, containing as it does a *living* principle, will be continually growing. This is our minority. Yes: "to brave unpopularity for conscience' sake, to fight in small minorities the uphill battle of principles not generally acknowledged, to embrace convictions with firmness and cling to them when the tempest howls,—this is what we understand by courage."

But as I have already, no doubt, exceeded the space you can afford me, I must bring my letter to a close ere my theme is half done. The Colonial Treasurer Richmond, in defining two genera, who unfortunately too often have to do with public matters, as "flat-fish and flies," forgot, I think, to add a third—or, it may be a sub-genus of the first, *viz.* the *Cuttle.* Such not only sees obliquely, but invariably squirts its own inky fluid when approached by either friend or foe;—as Cowper truly says:—

"*The man that dares traduce, because he can*
With safety to himself, is not a man."

And yet, Sir, after all, do what we can, do what we may, there are some persons, whose intellectual faculties are so dreadfully obtuse, that on them all facts all realities all reasoning seem to be thrown away. To such persons *post hoc* and *propter hoc* are alike. Ask them for a reason for their so voting, and they have none to give. It is so because it is so. As I did before, so do I now. Reminding me of a story which the learned Bentley, in his literary controversy with Boyle, tells of a certain priest who, for thirty years, had read *mumpsimus* in his breviary, instead of *sumpsimus*; and when a learned man told him of his blunder, replied, "I will not change my old *mumpsimus* for your new *sumpsimus*,"—a melancholy truth this! the more so, when such persons are (in common with the most conscientious and deep-thinking) the depositaries of sacred trusts, which should be used only for the public good.

I am, Sir, Yours very sincerely,

WM. COLENSO,

Waitangi,

July 19, 1858.

§ 1858 TO THE EDITOR.

Hawke's Bay Herald 31 July.

SIR,—The election is over; Featherston has in this district a small majority, and Mr. Colenso is "ashamed of the Napier Poll," which shame he expresses in a letter full of groans and parentheses. If we are to believe Mr. Colenso's own account, the state of that gentleman's mind on the polling day must have been truly deplorable; he was evidently full of weeping and wailing, and a little gnashing of teeth. No one can read the ex-reverend gentleman's letter without being struck by the elevation of sentiment which it displays; one would think it was written by a pitying angel, who, though himself raised far above the frailties and follies of our fallen nature, could yet grieve over the errors of mankind, and with compassionate gentleness urge them to return to that right track which they had forsaken.

Each person who voted for Dr. Featherston seems to have given Mr. Colenso an additional pang, and to have more and more convinced that reverend gentleman of the shocking depravity of human nature in general, and of Napier human nature in particular. Mr. Colenso mourned for the backsliding electors of Ahuriri, and would not be comforted, though fortunately he was able to mitigate the severity of his sufferings by remembering scraps of Latin; and, doubtless, had the electors been more numerous, he would have been forced to repeat the whole of the "Propria quæ maribus";[11] while had Featherston's majority been much greater, nothing could have saved the unhappy man but Greek in small doses.

But, seriously, is not this nauseating trash of Mr. Colenso somewhat insulting to the electors of Ahuriri. Such presumptuous dogmatising from any one would be most offensive, but from Mr. Colenso it is insufferable. Who is Mr. Colenso that he should give himself these airs of superiority and read the electors of Ahuriri a political lecture—coolly picking out the principal supporters of Dr. Featherston at Napier, and speaking of them as if in becoming such, they had committed a crime; whilst of those who have adopted the contrary course he writes in terms which only render the objects of his praise ridiculous.

Should Mr. Colenso dogmatise a little on matters with which he is known to be conversant, no one would be disposed to censure him very severely. Should he write an elaborate article on the plants of New Zealand from the "Monandria" to the "Polygamia," the style Mr. Colenso usually adopts might be suitable enough. Or

---

11 Literally 'Things appropriate to males', actually the name of a school Latin textbook. I.S.G.

were he to discuss biblical questions and give us a dissertation on the destruction of the cities of the plain, his opinions, simply as his opinions, would carry some weight, for with such subjects he may be presumed to be intimately acquainted. But when Mr. Colenso dogmatises in politics, his position is altogether different, for nothing we know respecting him would lead us to infer that he is more capable of forming an opinion on political subjects than any other educated man in this district.

But Mr. Colenso has not confined himself to political dogmatism. In his pedantic and miserably whining epistle, he affects to lament over the fall of those of whom he had hoped better things. By an unlimited use of italics and small caps, he endeavours to insinuate that those who voted for Dr. Featherston were actuated by interested motives to do what they knew to be wrong.

Mr. Rhodes' sensible, manly, and straightforward letter he formerly condemned, as it was natural such a man should; and, again, he groaneth in spirit, that "my neighbour" should have voted for Dr. Featherston.

The "Napier schoolmaster," who, by a life of unostentatious usefulness, has gained the respect of all who know him, and to whom the high praise of being the very antithesis of Mr. Colenso is justly given,—he condemns for having voted for Dr. Featherston, because Dr. Featherston's government supported the education bill, of which bill Mr. Marshall disapproves—as if every man who approves of the general conduct of a government is bound to defend their every act. If this were the case, government would be as impossible as education would be, were it necessary for a man to know everything before he knows anything. This remark of Mr. Colenso certainly shews no great capacity for dealing with political affairs. The paragraph referring to Capt. Charlton is merely silly; that relating to Captain Carter's absence on the polling day is both silly and impertinent. Surely that gentleman is as well qualified as Mr. Colenso to judge what was right and fitting for him to do in his own case; and I have yet to learn that Messrs. Gollan and FitzGerald are the exponents of the views of every member of the Settlers' Association.

The "dodging" talked of by the reverend writer, when he expresses his disgust at finding that the electors on the new roll were not permitted to vote, exists only in his own imagination; and is as unsupported by proof as his assertions usually are. He had better write to Governor Browne on the subject.

Mr. Colenso finishes his letter by assuring us that he is opposed to all cant and sham. This conclusion is singularly unfortunate. Why his whole letter is "cant."....
I have heard this question asked,—How is it that Mr. Colenso has become so violent a politician? Mr. Colenso will doubtless reply that his motives are pure and patriotic; that not for kingdoms, no, not for his own father, will he desert the cause of the people. In the vulgar tongue, this is "Bosh," clap-trap, and humbug. Can the Ethiopian change his skin or the leopard his spots? Can the man who for years did his best to keep Europeans out of this District suddenly become the unselfish patriot he wishes us to suppose him? No such thing: what he did formerly was for his own ends; what he does now is for his own ends. An uneasy, morbid

desire of popularity, together with the knowledge that he cannot obtain it among those whose good opinion is worth having, has made him aspire to the position of a demagogue; and a bitter dislike of all who differ from him, poorly disguised by an appearance of candour and Christian charity, has made him attack men in every way infinitely his superiors with a rancour which he may possibly mistake for virtuous indignation.

Of one thing Mr. Colenso may be quite certain, namely, that his opinions will be taken at their own worth; and what that is I have pointed out with sufficient clearness. Even that party to which he attaches himself, despise while they make use of him....

> *Yours, &c.*
>
> *Junius.*

[Reluctantly we give insertion to the above; for we consider that no man should be thus assailed by an anonymous writer. In this respect, 'Junius' might do worse than take a lesson from Mr. Colenso—Ed.][12]

❖ 1858 OPEN COLUMN.
Hawke's Bay Herald 14 August.

SIR,—In your last paper, of the 31st ult., I notice your stating, that "the news of the week, notwithstanding the number of arrivals, is not of much importance"; I, therefore, think the present lack of important matter to be a good time for me to fulfil a promise made to you some time back, and kindly published by you in your 37th number. I now essay to inform your many readers, as to the best sorts or varieties of *Apple Trees* suitable for cultivation among us.

And here, at the very beginning, I am, as it were, launching into both a broad and little known sea. For, not to mention the prodigious number of well-known and established varieties, my ignorance of what really good sorts are at present obtainable at Auckland and Wellington, Nelson and Canterbury, should almost deter me from writing on this head. Notwithstanding, I shall do my best, in telling what I know experimentally; and, also, in stating what has been said on this subject by others well qualified to do so.

Upwards of 20 years ago the Horticultural Society of London published a catalogue of Apples and Pears: which was, (and, perhaps, is) the only one to be depended on for accuracy; and is such a catalogue as none but a public body could bring to such perfection. In it they give, the *color, form, size, use, quality*, and *season* of each variety. Of APPLES, their catalogue contained 1396, and of PEARS, 677 named varieties, *exclusive* of synonyms. And when it is considered, how very much the science of horticulture has increased since that period, it is, perhaps, rather under than over, to state, that the varieties of apples and pears at present known exceed 3000!

---

12 Robert Pharazyn joined the fray against Colenso in the 21 August issue, and there followed a long period of bitterness between the two men – perhaps begun in 1848, when Colenso had refused to use his influence to get land for the Pharazyns (Bagnall & Petersen, p. 279). I.S.G.

As I am professedly writing for the information of those, who, in settling in a new country, have plenty to do, and, consequently, not much time to spare for the purpose of study; and as I wish that what I write should be of service to all; I shall, in writing of sorts, speak of them as *summer*, or, as *winter* fruit, and as suited for *kitchen*, *table*, or *cyder* purposes.

Of *summer* apples (*i.e.* fruit quite ripe and in perfection before March,) I have in my garden here, 5 old, 1 improved, and 2 new varieties. The 5 old ones are, *Devonshire* or *Red Quarrenden*, *March Aromatic*, *Nonesuch*, *Hawthornden*, and one (a yellow apple) name unknown; the improved variety is a *Nonesuch* scion grafted on another apple stock, by which the apple is greatly altered and improved; the two new varieties are, the one a small sweet very early apple and a great bearer, which I have named *New-Year*, and the other a very elegant and juicy apple having a peculiar transparent centre, which I have not yet named.[13] Of these 8 varieties, the *Hawthornden* and the *Nonesuch* have long been well known as excellent kitchen fruit; forming, in cooking, one uniform mass of rich pulp; while the *Quarrenden*, *March Aromatic*, improved *Nonesuch*, and new apple with transparent heart, are all very good as table fruit. Some also like the *Nonesuch* as a dessert apple, and some (particularly children) praise the sweet *New-Year*. Of those here mentioned, I can confidently recommend the *Hawthornden*, *March Aromatic*, *Nonesuch* and *Crystal-Heart*, as very suitable summer fruits for settlers; and where there are children (or a "sweet tooth," or a kind host,) a *New-Year* should not be forgotten; as it not only ripens earlier than any other, but it will be both acceptable and often visited in the Christmas holidays—if not remembered and talked of for some time after.

Of *winter* apples (*i.e.* fruit which ripen late, keep well and improve by keeping,) I have also in my garden 15 varieties:—viz. 8 old, 1 improved, and 6 new. The 8 old sorts comprise—*Ribstone Pippin*, *Royal* or *Autumn Pearmain*, *Court of Wick*, *Margil*, *Dutch Mignonne*, *Codlin*, *Yellow Pippin*, and a greenish yellow apple, name unknown: the improved sort is a scion from the *Court of Wick* grafted on another apple stock, by which the fruit is large and handsome: the new varieties are, *Waitangi*, *Napier*, *Settler*, *Bonum*, *Keepsake*, and *Phoenix*. Of the old and well-known sorts, I should particularly recommend to settlers the *Ribstone Pippin*, *Court of Wick*, *Margil*, *Dutch Mignonne*, *Codlin* and *Yellow Pippin*; and of the new kinds, the *Napier*, *Bonum*, and *Keepsake*, of which the *R. Pippin*, *Court of Wick*, *Margil*, *Y. Pippin*, *Napier*, and *Bonum* are table fruit. My *new* winter varieties are certainly not so estimable for the dessert as the old kinds, but they are handsome and of first-rate quality for the kitchen, and are better adapted for keeping, remaining sound and firm until October; the *Keepsake*, in particular, (one of the very best of all my new kinds,) a large and excellent kitchen fruit, I have kept sound, in the common way without packing, until the middle of November.

So much, Mr. Editor, for the kinds of apples that I both practically and experimentally know. I shall now give, from the catalogue of the London Horticultural Society, a selection of the best sorts, some of which may perhaps be obtained in New Zealand, or in the neighbouring colony of Tasmania. But here

---

13 This may be called *Crystal Heart*. W.C.

I would offer another cautionary remark—not to depend too much on the mere *name* of an apple. For I find, in referring to the aforesaid catalogue, that there are several apples of widely differing qualities bearing one name! For instance of the old kinds already mentioned, there were (20 years ago), 4 Quarrendens, 4 Hawthorndens, 8 Nonesuchs, 2 Court of Wicks, 2 Royal Pearmains, 17 Codlins, and 2 Ribstone Pippins; while of some other good sorts (whose fruit we have formerly eaten, and whose names we recollect with a sigh,) there were still greater numbers both good and bad of each kind, all bearing, through the carelessness, or ignorance or knavery of the cultivator, *one* name:—*e.g.* 28 kinds of Nonpareil, 18 of Golden Pippin, 7 of Newtown Pippin, 9 of Belle-fleur,[14] 11 of Queenings, 10 of Redstreaks, 8 Incomparables, 6 Gilliflowers, and of Russet and Pearmain of each a host! And when the amount and height of impudent adulterations of the last 20 years are considered (that our *imported* food and drink and clothing and medicine are not what they are called and labelled and would be sworn to be (if needed) in a Court of Justice—that our Mustard is not *Mustard*, nor our Port *Port*, nor our Woollens *Wool*—only think of this barefaced attempt ye wool-growers!) —a settler sending abroad for some good old sort of apple by name, and believing that it is sure to bear the like delicious fruits as those he knew once in his fatherland bearing the same name, may after all be disappointed.

SUMMER FRUITS. Carlisle Codlin, *k*. Irish Peach Apple, *t*. Sugar Loaf Pippin, *k*. Alexander, *k*. Siberian bitter-sweet, *c*. White Juneating, *t*. Large Yellow, *k*. *t*. Wetherell's White Sweeting, *c*. Leyden Pippin, *t*. Early Red Margaret, *t*. Summer Thorle, *t*. White Astrachan, *t*. Borovitsky, *t*. Oslin, *t*. Coussinette, *k*. Brebis, *c*.

WINTER FRUITS. Bedfordshire foundling, *k*. Alfriston, *k*. Bucks County, *c*. Devonshire Buckland, *k*. *t*. Beachamwell *t*. Cornish Aromatic, *t*. Dumelow's Seedling, *k*. Golden Harvey, *t*. *c*. Newtown Pippin, *t*. Golden Drop, *t*. Hick's Fancy, *t*. Belle fleur Brabansche, *k*. Downton Nonpareil, *t*. Adams' Pearmain, *t*. Coccagee, *c*. Herefordshire Pearmain, *k*. *t*. Keeping Redstreak, *k*. Stetting Jaune, *c*. Reinette du Canada, *k*. *t*. John Apple, *c*. Pitmaston Russet Nonpareil, *t*. Rostocker, *k.c*. Syke House Russet, *t*. Northern Greening, *k*. *c*. (Note. *k*. kitchen, *t*. table, *c*. cyder, &.c)

I further quote from the *Horticultural Magazine* (of a much later date,) the following:—"Select, from some respectable nursery, such of the following apples as may not already be in your collection; there are none of them of even a secondary quality; they are, for the purposes of a family, all that can be wished, and such as we would not be without. Franklin's Golden Pippin, *t*.; Fearn's Pippin, *t*. *k*.; Kerry Pippin, *t*.; Alexander, *k*.; Blenheim Orange, *k*. *t*.; Ribstone Pippin, *t*.; Nonpareil, *t*.; Hawthornden, *k*.; Royal Russet, *k*.; Scarlet Nonpareil, *t*.; Golden Harvey, *t c*.; Norfolk Baufin, *k*.; Juneating, *t*.; French Crab, *k*. *t*.; Court of Wick, *t*."

"Now turn thine eye, to view Alcinous' groves,
The pride of the Phæacian isle, from whence,
Sailing the spaces of the boundless deep,

---

14 Sometimes ignorantly called *"Newton Pippin"* and *"Belflod."* W.C.

To Ariconium precious fruits arriv'd:
The Pippin burnished over with gold,—
the fair Pearmain,
Temper'd like comeliest nymph with red and white.
O let me now, when the kind early dew
Unlocks th' embosom'd odours, walk among
The well-rang'd files of trees, whose full aged store
Diffuse Ambrosial streams,
Foft whisp'ring airs, and the larks matin song
Then woo to musing, and becalm the mind
Perplex'd with irksome thoughts."—Philips.

I am, &c.,

WM. COLENSO.

❖ **1858 OPEN COLUMN.**
Hawke's Bay Herald 28 August.
SIR,—

"Shut, shut the door, good John! fatigued, I said;
Tie up the knocker; say, I'm sick, I'm dead."—

Thus (if I recollect aright) our great English poet, Pope, commences one of his epistles: the occasion—his being tired with so many folks asking him to correct their verses. And surely I, wretched mortal! (and the generality of your readers) must be equally tired at seeing my name so often thrust tost fetched and jerked before the public, on account of my political sins. I had hoped I had quite done with politics, (quite time, some may say,) but, "goodness me!" what can a poor fellow do—how upon earth can he be quiet, when he is so pitched into (that I say not *pitchforked*) every week in your paper. And now, "Act IV., scene 4," lo! Mr. Robert Pharazyn, suddenly resuscitated, comes pop upon the stage! But, "Oh dear" (as Mr. Pepys in his diary might have written,) oh dear! the overweening vanity of some young men—who fancy themselves to be something when they are nothing. However, I should not complain; seeing, that, in the House of Representatives, one of the members said, that he feared it would require military force to make the colonial youth of Canterbury know their proper places—a colonial failing, Mr. Editor, a colonial failing. It is now 25 years since I left my father's house for this land, during which time I have in one sphere or another, been working hard for the good of my fellow-men (strange! if I should not have gathered a few fruits of experience in a quarter of a century!)—while here, in your, paper of the 21st inst., I have, unasked, an inexperienced colonial youth, who has scarcely numbered the same amount of years, thrusting himself publicly upon me as the corrector of my letter to you of the 19th ult., and as my very sage monitor! Surely there must be a deficiency with that party to whom he professedly belongs (and who endeavoured to foist him upon us as their nominee at the late election!)—or, the young man's "wish to see His name in print" (as Byron says,) must have been so strong that he could not be held in. Be it as it may, (astronomically speaking,) "a sad error, in computation this":—but, anon.—

Of course I shall pass unnoticed all my young mentor's grave charges of "bungling sophisms" and "sophistry" and "fallacy" and "false analogy" and of my being "less enlightened" and "less candid" than himself and party. I intend, however, in briefly noticing his own *"fallacies"* and *"false analogies"* to keep prominently before you, sir, his statement, that *"Mr. Colenso ought to know that a false analogy proves nothing, except dishonesty or incapacity in the person who uses it."*

First, then, Mr. R. Pharazyn says,—"the sophistry I refer to consists in comparing the elected head of a government to an hereditary head, and concluding that what would be tyrannical conduct in the one would be the same in the other." In reply, I say (remarking, by the way, that I made no such (foolish) comparison—the two tyrants of ancient Rome whom I had cited, Marius and Sylla, having been both *elected* by the people;)—in reply, then, I say, that, as to tyrannical conduct there is no difference; or, if any, the tyrannical conduct of an *elected* leader is every way worse than that of an *hereditary* one. I need not, sir, cite ancient or mediæval history; nor go back a few years of my own time to bring as a witness unhappy Poland.[15] Glance at the continent of Europe; see those two elected Heads, Louis Napoleon and the Pope of Rome; do their chains forsooth lie more lightly on their people because they were elected? rather, is not that very consideration the bitterest drop in the goblet which the patriots of France and Italy have to drink? Did not the young eagle the more keenly feel the arrow which brought him to the ground, when in rolling he saw that it was a feather from his own wing which had feathered the shaft?—Mr. R. Pharazyn, you, *"ought to know that a false analogy proves nothing, except dishonesty or incapacity in the person who uses it."*

Secondly: Mr. R. Pharazyn says—"There is just sufficient likeness between the Emperor of Austria and a Superintendent to make the analogy apparent; both are heads of governments; the assent of both is required to Acts before they become law." Here is another *"false* analogy"; being an echo of Mr. Woodward's king-making sentence—that a "superintendent has sovereign powers." But the truth is (or ought to be), that there is no likeness whatever between the Emperor of Austria and a Superintendent. Both are not heads of governments, in the same, or like, sense; for the Emperor of Austria has no man over him; but over a Superintendent there is, first, the Governor of New Zealand, and, secondly, there is the Queen (that I say not, also, a third, viz. the Provincial Council): neither is the assent of both in the same, or like sense, required to Acts before they become law; the Emperor of Austria says, "I will," and who shall say nay; the New Zealand Superintendent says, "I will," and lo! Governor Browne says "nay"; or the Governor assents to laws which the Superintendent wishes far enough off yet must obey; or a Judge of the Supreme Court with, a *"presto!"* brings him to order, makes him recant and eat humble pie.

---

15 "An *hereditary* monarchy is universally to be preferred to an *elective* monarchy. The confession of every writer on the subject of civil government, the experience of ages, the example of Poland, and of the Papal dominions, seem to place this among the few indisputable maxims which the science of politics admit of".—*Paley's Moral and Political Phil., b.6, c.6.* W.C.

Let it never be forgotten, that a New Zealand Superintendent in assenting to laws does so as the *locum tenens* of a deputy. And while the Emperor of Austria possesses all the mighty *influence* of appointing to places, a New Zealand Superintendent (speaking comparatively) has none,—he cannot appoint a common magistrate, or even a magistrate's clerk! Oh! oh! Mr. Robert Pharazyn you *"ought to know that a false analogy proves nothing except dishonesty or incapacity in the person who uses it."*

Thirdly: Mr. R. Pharazyn says,—"Twenty two members of the Council have passed certain Bills, and the Superintendent has vetoed all those that he considered to be injurious to the best interests of the province.... So that, Dr. Featherston having been elected by a large majority of the provincial electors, is clearly right in opposing the representatives of a section of the province." Here is another "fallacy" or "false analogy" of Mr. R. Pharazyn. For, the members and Superintendent are all alike men and freemen and elected servants of the public, and chosen for *one work*; (had the members been merely animals, or slaves,—or had the Superintendent appointed them as *his* servants, or had he been a god,—there would indeed have been a difference;) being then alike, as public men elected by the same body to *one work*, there is no difference; why then should the voice of *one* prevail against those of the twenty-two? only fancy the President of America vetoing *repeatedly* all Bills passed by ³/₄ths of the Senate! why the very sea would be "flaring" from Cape Cod to Tampico!! Suppose last year *Dr. Welch* had been elected Superintentendent, and, wishing to carry a point against the run-holders, had vetoed the Bills of the Provincial Council—if not exactly in their favour yet dealing fairly with them—"lauks!" what an uproar there would have been! an earthquake would have been as nothing to it. But we are further told, that "Dr. Featherston has been elected by a *large majority* of the provincial electors:"—wait a bit; we shall see. Dr. Featherston was, last year, elected by 834 electors; the 22 Representatives, about the same time last year, polled 4980 votes;[16] Where now is Dr. Featherston's "large majority?" But, further, still, Mr. R. Pharazyn states (meaning, I suppose, the election just concluded,) the number to be '890 electors';[17] but he knows very well that those Bills which were vetoed, were vetoed by the Superintendent who was elected by the 834 electors; or if he insists on the *present* election, he must also know that Dr. Featherston had a less *majority* by 120 over Mr. St. Hill than he had last year over Dr. Welch; and that he had been elected *not* by a "*majority*," but actually by a MINORITY of the electors; the whole number on the Electoral Roll being 2400! Surely Mr. Robert Pharazyn *"ought to know, that a false analogy proves nothing, except dishonesty or incapacity in the person who uses it."*

Now all these "fallacies" or "false analogies," on Mr. R. Pharazyn's part, arise (as I would charitably believe,) from his merely taking up at secondhand the opinions, and statements of other interested persons longer-headed than himself. Notwithstanding, since he has himself laid down the rule, that any such being used "*proves nothing, except*

---

16 See *Hawkes Bay Herald*, Nov. 21, 1857. W.C.

17 According to the Wellington papers, 886 is the real number for Dr. Featherston, and 576 for Mr. St. Hill; so that while Mr. R. Pharazyn runs Dr. F.'s number *on* to the next 10, he brings Mr. St. Hill's *back*, to the last; a little matter truly, but a straw thrown up tells which way the wind blows. W.C.

dishonesty or incapacity in the person who uses it";—I shall leave it to him to choose which of the two he will please to accept.

Further: I am forced, sir, to believe, that Mr. R. Pharazyn does not know the difference between political power rightly *possessed*, and political power rightly *exercised*. Now such power is *rightly exercised* only when it subserves the welfare of the whole community. For the avoidance of argument, it may be for the time conceded, that Dr. Featherston rightly *possesses* the power of Superintendent; but that he has rightly *exercised* it, is, I am very sure, lamentably far from truth, and plain enough to most, save to self-interested folks. Mr. Pharazyn, it is evident, thinks very highly of his own intellectual powers,[18]—which is by no means an uncommon qualification of young men; but, unfortunately for him, others do not think so; at any rate, there seems to be a sad confusion of mind in what little we have ever seen or heard. As a matter of course (such being generally the concomitant of vanity), he speaks very slightingly of what I have written and of my poor abilities—not even caring to consider, that, in all likelihood, I had passed through higher courses of studies than he had ever known; and that I had been engaged in public work from before he could have learned his A B C! Still, as I heartily wish him well, I would just remind him, that counter-assertion is not argument, and I would recommend him, to practice a little (if he can) the power of abstraction and detach accidental associations from truth itself. He speaks of my letter of the 19th ulto. as containing much "balderdash": that, however, is a question for the public. I have very lately gone again through that letter; and I feel thankful, sir, that I have been permitted and enabled to pen (and through you to publish) such sterling truths:—

"And joy a coming age will think with me."—

Very sure I am that the truths therein enunciated are wholly in accordance with the *"Westminster"*; and I would just hint to Mr. R. Pharazyn, that it would, perhaps, be not altogether unadvisable for him (seeing that he is an aspirant after political honours,) to lay up that letter in some safe place for a future reference, (it may be after the writer is no more,) when, I venture to predict, he will find the principles I have therein written to be among the received and prized truths of the day.—

Mr. Pharazyn also calls on me to "repent of having joined a party, not from a conviction that it was in the right, but because it was momentarily victorious." How wonderfully the former part of this sentence agrees with his address, 9 months ago, to the Electors of Ahuriri! Then he said,—"in one word, our opponents feel themselves great in opposition. Their genius lies in destruction. ... ... *To join a party, for whatever object, is to them the greatest of political crimes.*"[19] This needs no comment. As to

18 An article in the *Nelson Examiner* of July 31, speaking on this very subject, says:—"If we are to believe the *Independent* all the honest men opposed to them are fools, and all who have a grain of sense are unmitigated rogues; the electors who returned an adverse majority in the Provincial Council are a set of ignoramuses; and the members themselves a fair sample of those who sent them. They prove too much.... Then we have pleasant remarks on the "incoherent jargon" of one, the "virtuous indignation" of a second, "egotistical flourishes" of a third!" It is well, that what has been painfully noticed here, should have also been noticed in other provinces. W.C.
19 Address to Electors. *H.B. Herald,* November 7, 1857. W.C.

the latter part of his sentence, my having joined a party because it was "momentarily victorious": all I can say is, I do not understand him.

Before I conclude I would remind Mr. Pharazyn (and others who speak like him), that, situated as we are, political matters are looked at by us from widely different fields of view. It is my belief, Sir, that it is morally impossible for Mr. R. Pharazyn to consider our present political state impartially; if he can, he is more than a common man. For (setting aside his great inexperience,) he is not only deeply interested personally in carrying out his own ultra views, (which, fully followed up, must end in keeping away a numerous free and thriving population from the District), but his father (who is also Dr. Featherston's auditor), and relations are also alike interested in holding (as is well-known) the same principles; and I scarcely need add, that Mr. Robert Pharazyn has strenuously sought to be returned as our Member to the Provincial Council with the avowed determination of "going the whole hog" with Dr. Featherston's party. So that, in Mr. R. Pharazyn's case, there is not only self-interest (of first quality, and of colonial gage), but there is the equally strong bond of family ties; and the scarcely less one of vaulting yet disappointed ambition continually goading.

On the contrary I—the writer of "balderdash"—I have no peculiar self-interest to serve (I defy my opponents to point such out); I have no relations, nor even powerful or dear friends, egging me on by example and precept; and I have no political ambition whatever. Nothing indeed is farther from my wishes (if I know myself); very much rather would I be far away among the sequestered glens of the Ruahine range "culling of simples" (and enjoying myself among the grand and truthful solitudes of Nature), than here writing on political subjects.

And now, in conclusion, I would merely add, that I trust Mr. Robert Pharazyn will be benefitted by this letter, that he will have no just reason to complain of any discourtesy on my part, for if I have been more severe than usual, he should consider that he himself has evoked it. *Quis custodiet custodes.*[20]

> I am,
> *Yours very sincerely,*
> WM. COLENSO.

Waitangi,
Aug. 23, 1858.

§ 1858 TO CORRESPONDENTS.
Hawke's Bay Herald 18 September.
Mr. Pharazyn's letter was received at too late a period of the week for its insertion in this issue. It will appear on an early opportunity; although we have had several communications, both oral and in writing, expressive of opinion that the correspondence between Mr. Pharazyn and Mr. Colenso would be more fittingly conducted through the Post Office than the columns of a newspaper.

---

20 Who will guard the guards? I.S.G.

❖ 1858 OPEN COLUMN.
Hawke's Bay Herald 16 October.

SIR,—On reading another letter signed, "ROBERT PHARAZYN," in your paper of the 2nd inst., (only recently to hand), I was strongly reminded of what Dr. Johnson once said to a person who, having ventured into a dispute with the Doctor, had said, he did not understand him; when Dr. Johnson replied,—"I have found you arguments, Sir, I am not bound to find you understanding."

I must, however, beg to decline, Sir, saying anything more to your correspondent, Mr. Robert Pharazyn, ("Unhappy Robert!" as a gentleman termed him last week.) 1st—Because I have heard, from several quarters, that he is merely the tool (or scribe) of a small party, who club their united efforts in "getting-up" those epistles against me which have appeared in your columns: and, 2nd, (and principally), because I have been assured that he, (of course including his party), has stated himself to be the author of the mean and calumnious anonymous letter, which, under the pseudonym of "*Junius*" (!) appeared in your paper of July 31; and which you yourself, Sir, was obliged, (for the *first* time among us) to exercise your censorship over and suppress certain passages, as being wholly unfit for publication!

I can only regret that I did not earlier know of his having acknowledged himself to be the writer of that low and scurrilous letter; as, if I had known, I should not have stooped to notice any after writing bearing his name.

In conclusion, Sir, allow me to call your attention to a couple of quotations from living authors; (both of which must even by my antagonists be allowed to be unexceptionable;)—one being from the last number of the *Westminster Review*, (which opportunely enough was lent me only a few days ago,) and one from a letter of "*Rusticus Primus*," which appeared in your columns a few months back.

(For the information of your readers I will just add, that the reviewer is writing on one of his favourite and one of nature's men—the poet Shelley; who is "not only one of our first modern English poets, a man of genius, of extensive learning, and collegiate education, but who had also been twice married, having children by each wife, and who had travelled much on the continent of Europe; so that, as to any inferential comparison, 'tis "Hyperion to a satyr"; and yet he says:)—"The value of a young man's experience—and Shelley died at nine-and-twenty—is not worth much, and it is only by experience we can test anything in this practical world.... We perhaps can never rightly weigh the balance of any man's actions, because we never allow enough for the circumstances which should be placed in the other scale[21].... Before a man can write well he must have *felt*." *W. Review*, January 1858, pp. 19–21.

(I may also remark, that, in giving the following quotation, I am aware that I am quoting from an unknown author; yet, as he has repeatedly appeared in your columns as an acknowledged and staunch upholder of the opposition, I do so: and this

---

21 The wise saying of another of nature's men—Burns—will be thought of here:—
   "What's *done* we partly may compute,
   But never what *resisted*." W.C.

the more readily from the circumstance of his being commonly believed to be a near relative of your correspondent, Robert Pharazyn:)—He says:—"The dictum of New Zealand appears to be—not that great experience, deep reading, and much reflection should be the means of forming a wise councillor, but that the art of governing, like reading and writing, (as Dogberry sagely observes) comes by nature.—Brother electors, beware of self-seeking politicians." Letter of *R. Primus*, H.B. Herald, May 29, 1858.

> *I am, Sir,*
> *Yours very truly,*
> WM. COLENSO.

Waitangi,
Oct. 8,1858.

❖ 1858 OPEN COLUMN.
TRACTS FOR THE TIMES NO. 1.[22]
Hawke's Bay Herald 23 October.

"Dare lucem et dare servem."[23]

No. 1.—SHALL WE GO AHEAD?
Our petition for separation[24] signed by more than the requisite number of electors having been despatched to the governor, there can scarcely be a doubt that it will be immediately granted. The question—*"Shall we now go ahead?"* will therefore be put by many; and while a few may shake their heads and look "awfu' glum" by way of reply, a great number among us will no doubt take it for granted as a very sure thing, or as a matter of course. I, however, wish all *bona fide* settlers who really desire to get on, or go ahead, to consider the thing a bit—to give it a little attention; then they will soon see, that their cooperation is needed to ensure success.

---

22 Years later Colenso listed these letters and their meaning in a letter to R.C. Harding (I.S.G.):

Title	Date	Subject (if any)
Shall we go ahead	Oct. 23 1858	Petition for separation
Janus	Oct. 30	Two-faced persons in politics
Take time by the forelock	Nov. 13	The electoral roll
A square peg in a round hole	Nov. 20	Election of Spdt. for H. Bay
Who art thou	" 27	Truth in politics
Honey-dew tobacco	Dec. 4th	Adulterated products & politics
Darius and his groom	" 11	Election of Spdt.
"Cead mille failtha" (a hundred thousand welcomes)	" 18	Need of population in H. Bay
A mess of potage	Jan. 8 1859	Interference with franchise
All alive, all alive ho!	" 22	Allegorical natural history note on prov. Council elections
Shadows	Feb. 5	Candidates for Prov. Council
Substances	Apl. 30	Government in Hawke's Bay.
See-saw	May 7	Opposition in politics

23 To give light and (thus) to give help. I.S.G.
24 That is, separation of the Hawke's Bay from the Wellington province. I.S.G.

Nearly 2000 years ago, there was a mighty grumbling among a multitude in a large town; the cause—some having too little of the necessaries of life; when, in order to quell the disturbance, they were most reasonably advised, to look out men of honest report, who should attend to the matters complained of; this they did, and they soon prospered. Now our "great father" (as the Indians would call the governor,) has pretty nearly followed out this rule towards us: we have grumbled, and that to him; and he has sent us the "*New Provinces Act*" and told us, to select our men to attend to our business, that we too may get on, or go ahead.

Therefore, to every elector I would say, *Do you* WISH *to go ahead?* (For, if you wish fair prosperity for yourself you must also for your neighbour, and as certainly for the whole district). And as there can be no doubt that the reply will be, *yes*; I will rejoin, —then mind what you are after in the way of voting at the approaching elections: for on you, electors—individually—rests this great responsibility—whether your wives and little ones will prosper in this your now adopted country:—or, in other words, whether we shall go ahead. You know very well that no ship can perform a long voyage unless she is well found:—no good crop can be expected without good seed: no good articles can be made without good materials: even so, no real good can come to you—to us—to the whole district—without good men and true to carry out the practical business of the government of the district.

Therefore, brother-electors, allow one who has the real and permanent, and progressive welfare of the whole district at heart to give you a timely note. "Think for yourselves; act for yourselves." Mind what I once told you—"that the power is with the people"; that power is *now* in *your own* hands. Make a good use of it when the time comes; for, *after* you have voted, the power is for a season gone from you. You may use it for your own and your country's good; you may waste it; and worse still, you may use it to your own undoing. Depend upon it, that our going ahead rests at present solely with you; for if you do not find and choose *proper men* to man your ship, Scinde Island might as soon be expected to enter Wellington harbour, as that, we shall go ahead and you prosper.

Therefore, I once more say—*Mind what you are after*: pledge yourselves to no man. If ever a vote was a sacred trust it is so now;—now, when you have to use it for the first time, and that to set the thing agoing. Guard it, use it, as carefully as if it were a large sum of money of your own. Think for yourselves, act for yourselves; and in so thinking, so acting, do it with true British integrity of purpose;—and then we shall go ahead.

WM. COLENSO.

Waitangi,
Oct. 18, 1858.

❖ 1858 OPEN COLUMN. TRACTS FOR THE TIMES NO. 2.
Hawke's Bay Herald 30 October.

"Dare lucem et dare servem."

No. 2.—JANUS.

The ancient Romans worshipped many gods besides their full dozen of great celestial deities (*Dii majorum gentium*). In religious ceremonies the name of JANUS was always first invoked: not because he belonged to the superior class (for he was one of the second batch, or selected gods—*Dii selecti*), but because he presided over all gates and entrances, and it was through him only that prayers could reach the higher house. Moreover, Janus was represented with two faces looking two ways; and sometimes with the number 300 in one hand and with 65 in the other, to denote that he presided over the year—of which the first month (January) still bears his name. The native ornamented weapon (*taiaha*), with its double face and four mother-of-pearl eyes and its useful native proverb, has always served to remind me of the old Roman Janus.

Believe me, I am not going to invoke the aid of Janus, standing as we are on the threshold of a new (and it may be a mighty) era of good or ill for Ahuriri. It is, however, my desire to say a few words to my fellow-electors concerning some of the great-great-great-grandchildren of the old Roman Janus, who, in all probability, may shortly be expected to be scuttling about among us. For "the Derby day," though of very brief duration and held on an open downs, might just as reasonably be supposed to pass unheeded by the numerous flash gentry ever on the look-out for chances, as for the approaching maiden general election of Ahuriri to be uncontested by some of the numerous descendants of double-faced Janus. Unfortunately, however, our modern Januses (that I offend not classical ears I must also say, *Jani,*)—our modern Januses differ greatly from the old prototype in not carrying their distinguishing badge in their faces. Now-a-days the face is wholly one, (whether in conformity with the Lamarckian theory of development I shall not stop to examine;) while the heart is double. So that, in seven cases out of ten, the honest settler who has his bread to earn and his own and children's fortunes to better,—and who has no greater liking for entertaining evil thoughts of his fellow-men than he has for sowing Dock seed or Sorrel on his land, —such a one has really no time to spend in enquiry as to the truth of the statements of the modern Janus who is soliciting his vote. The elector hears him say, that his whole heart is bound up in the welfare of Ahuriri; and that through him (and his colleagues) the golden age will infallibly return. Looking only in his face and believing his words the elector gives him his vote: when soon Time (who, according to the Romans, was once Janus' guest,) shows him his folly, and that instead of the golden —the leaden age is come, and has to be endured with all its vexatious disappointments and burdens as it best may.

Let no elector ask, to have the different species of the genus *Janus* pointed out. He must take the definition of the *Genus*, and endeavour himself to find out the individual or species;—just as he would a cabbage an apple or a rose, of each of which there are very many kinds, and although new sorts are continually turning up yet there is no mistaking them,—no calling a rose a hollyhock, or an apple a cucumber. The genus *Janus*, then, inasmuch as it is *always developed late*, is best known by a good, hard and sharp look-out after its antecedents, or old qualities and qualifications; just such a common practical look-out, as a farmer exercises when seeking seed wheat, or it may be a good cow or a horse; or, as when a blacksmith is seeking among iron, for a bit of steel for some particular purpose; or a shoemaker a skin of calf among cordovan. No known creature requires such a good looking after as the genus *Janus*; owing to its duplex characters. In all its varieties it ever strives to make its dupes believe that it seeks their good and the welfare of the state; but, on the contrary, it seeks its own ends,—either in salaries or honours, in power or an easy billet, in carrying out the deep-laid schemes of selfish men, or pet projects of class policy; —and, like rust in steel, or blight in apple trees, once got in is scarcely ever eradicated.

I remember, a few years ago meeting with a good and able article in the "Times," in which the writer shewed, that while Nature in general intended every man for one thing in particular, for which she had also fitted him; the most of mankind strove to lay hold of two or more things, for which they were both unfitted and wholly unadapted, and hence a large measure of the misery in the world.

Brother electors, keep a good look-out after this genus Janus; endeavour to detect it, though unblown its flower, unknown its fruit. And, the better to do so, be yourselves somewhat like old Janus—looking two ways; the one way backward, at the past public acts and actions and present characteristics of every one who may wish your vote; and the other way forward, at what you may (knowing the past and the present) reasonably expect from such a one. Keep your eyes open. Water does not rise above its level. "Beware of self-seeking politicians."—

WM. COLENSO.

Waitangi,
Oct. 25, 1858.

❖ 1858 TRACTS FOR THE TIMES NO. 3.
Hawke's Bay Herald 13 November.

"Dare lucem et dare servem."

No. 3.—TAKE TIME BY THE FORELOCK.

Every well-wisher to good government amongst us should feel obliged to the Editor of the "Hawke's Bay Herald" for his gratuitous publishing of the Electoral Roll of the District, and thus giving extra publicity to a public document which can never be too well known. That Roll, however, is not what it should be—what it must be in order to be complete. As it now is it does not fully represent the county of Hawke in its entirety. For, 1st, there are not a few names inserted on wrong qualifications; and, 2nd, there are many settlers whose names are not on it. And as the beginnings of Responsible Government in its integrity spring from the correctness of the Roll, it behoves every elector to see that the Roll be made as perfect as possible. Of course it will be the positive duty of the Revising Officer (who will shortly be appointed by the Governor,) to look after all men of straw and all false qualifications; but every qualified settler, whose name is not already on the Roll, should consider it to be his duty (as well as privilege) to get his name speedily inserted.

As sundry important alterations have been recently made by the General Assembly in the Acts relating to electors and elections, some of which it is highly needful should be early known by all settlers whose names are not on the Roll; and as the time is short—when viewed in connection with the ever busy summer season of shearing and harvest and sperm-whaling, and our many scattered dwellings—not to mention our present imperfect postal communication, and that great colonial weed of putting off till to-morrow what ought to be done to-day,—all these considerations combined, urge me to call upon my fellow-settlers to take time by the forelock and see to it that their names are enrolled.

A few of the more important alterations in the above-mentioned Acts I will here briefly state:—

1. The *way* in which a claim to be enrolled as an elector is to be made; every such claim must now be accompanied by a declaration on the part of the person so claiming, to be signed by him before a Magistrate or the Registration Officer, to the truth of his claim, and any false declaration is liable to a fine of £20, to be recovered summarily:—

2. The time for making such claim is now limited to the month of March (instead of April, as formerly,) in each year:—

3. The manner of voting at elections is altogether altered; the system of voting papers containing the name of the candidate is wholly abolished, and now each elector is to name the candidate when his vote is recorded; and, further, the elector may also then be sworn, (if the Returning Officer thinks fit,) that he has not received any bribe or consideration for his vote, and the penalty for such false-swearing is that inflicted for perjury:—and,

4. The Revising Officer will have full power to strike off all false or insufficient claims from the Roll, even if not by any one objected to.

5. Now it is not unlikely that our general election may come off during the approaching autumn, so that there is time enough for every un-enrolled yet qualified settler to get his name enrolled, and thus be ready to serve his country in the very best way—by voting for *proper persons only* to carry on its government. I would once more remind all such settlers,—particularly those residing in the more northerly parts of the province (such as Wangawehi, Table Cape, Te Mahia, Waikokopu, Nuhaka, Te Wairoa, and other spots near,) as well as several others dwelling within 10 miles of Napier,—to look to this, and be very sure to send their claims in to the Registration Officer in time. And my chief reason for more particularly mentioning those parts is my certain knowledge of many settlers resident therein whose names are not on the roll; while I scarcely know of one in the more southern parts of the province whose name has been omitted. And, further, I would suggest to those electors whose names are already enrolled, as

well as to those, who shall straightway proceed to send in their claims,—to stir up all their neighbours to do their duty and to consider their privileges.

It was a good answer of the doctor to his patient who had sore eyes—"If you have more pleasure in wine than in your sight, wine is good." Just so, my fellow-settlers, if you have more pleasure in inattention and carelessness than in being active to secure your just privileges, (by which you may put the right men in the right place and so do your part towards prosperity and good government,)—why, then carelessness is good. But do not so act, (or, rather, *refuse* to act) as to cause yourselves any disagreeable reflections hereafter, *should* things turn out contrary to your desires. Remember the old saying,—

> *"For want of a nail the shoe was lost,*
> *For want of a shoe the horse was lost,*
> *For want of a horse the rider was lost,*
> *Being overtaken and slain by the enemy,*
> *And all for the want of a horse-shoe nail."*
>
> WM. COLENSO.

Waitangi,
Nov. 2, 1858.

❖ 1858 TRACTS FOR THE TIMES NO. 4.
Hawke's Bay Herald 20 November.

"Dare lucem et dare servem."

No. 4.—A SQUARE PEG IN A ROUND HOLE.

The time is close at hand when the electors of the new province of Hawke's Bay will be called on to build and launch their ship. Whether she is to be a steamer or a sailer, of iron or of oak, does not greatly matter; only, if of iron her rivets must suit; and if of wood her treenails must be round in order to fit their holes—otherwise she will very soon be in Davy Jones' locker.

Hawke's Bay is now a separate Province, and her settlers have now important duties to perform. Duties which cannot fairly be put off, nor thrown aside, nor shirked. Duties which, owing to the peculiar temper and circumstances of the times, can only be faithfully performed by a manly determination to do what is right. In order to do this every elector should think well and think deeply. For *our* commencement as a new province is very different from that of any of the older provinces of New Zealand. And in no one point more particularly so than in that of the *non-election of the Superintendent by the people.* (This is a fact which will appear more clearly by-and-by—seeing that John Bull, all over the world, always buys experience dearly.) Therefore, brother-electors, consider this well, ponder this deeply, before you give your vote to any one who may seek it in order to become a Member of Council. Many a man is fit for the office of Council Member who is *not fit* for that of Superintendent. Reflect then, that in voting for the one you are in all probability voting for the other. Look about you: talk a little more among yourselves as to fit men; prepare your stuff for your ship, of which you are the builders, but the men whom you may choose the navigators; so shall you avoid the disgrace and loss which is always sure sooner or later to arise from putting a square peg into a round hole.

For this very reason also, of the Members of Council choosing from among themselves a Superintendent, you will have persons seeking to become Council Members with no other view than that of gaining the superintendency—*the title and the salary*: just like old staunch wrestlers in a ring throwing young and inexperienced ones in their way to the *first* prize. And from this consequence arises, I fear, another equally certain, namely, that you are likely to have more unfit ill-adapted persons seeking to become Council Members, than any of the older provinces have yet had at any one general election. Now, do consider this. Be wide-awake. Recollect the thousand and one failures and sad errors which were said to have taken place during the late Crimean war, and which were mainly charged to the account of *red-tapism*—or, *the square peg in the round hole*. But those errors, many and grave though they were, were as nothing (*to us, here,*) when compared to the evils which will assuredly follow your doing the same thing. Therefore, I venture plainly and openly to advise you:—vote not for any man *because* he is rich,—or *because* he is a good scholar,—or *because* he may hold, or have held, any government or other office however high,—or *because* he is the thirty-third cousin of some lord, or *because* he is a clever chap, or *because* "he is a jolly good fellow,"—or *because* your wives are exceedingly intimate,—or *because* he belongs to and will uphold "through thick and thin" your particular class,—or *because* in voting for him you will have his custom or influence or favor,—or *because* he has "the gift of the gab,"—or *because* he is of the same family or town or country as yourself,—or, in short, because of any thing less than this—*that he is really and truly a fit and proper person to serve the public cause.* Believe me, brother-electors, a plain man of honest heart and practical ability is much more likely to serve your purpose and the welfare of the province, than any assuming upstart with no more brains than a hen be he who he may. As a late writer truly says:—"There is an immense amount of cool impudence nowadays, that puts on the garb of most innocent respectability, and that pushes incompetence into the post of genius, and prefers any quality to the one required if the possessor be well-connected. All see that this tampering with right is almost as fatal to the commonwealth as the most direct dishonesty. And then, when a great misfortune has happened, we have always the consolation of knowing that it is traceable only to the most unexceptionable of dunderheads and imposters; but, the blunder is there,—the evil is done."

Believing, as I do, that our welfare and going ahead as a province will mainly depend upon our having a *good* superintendent—an honest practical business-like man of comprehensive mind; one who has few or no private interests, nor "hobbies," but a man of integrity who holds equally dear the interests of all;—believing this, I, after long consideration, thus write to put you on your guard. And this I the more readily do, from my also believing with Adam Smith,—"The just man, the man who, in all private transactions would be the most beloved and the most esteemed, in those public transactions is too often regarded as a fool and an idiot, who does not understand his business."[25] Forewarned, forearmed: if you will use white pine instead of totara as piles for your building—if you will put incompetent persons into office—the square peg into a round hole—you must also be content to reap the consequences.

WM. COLENSO.

Waitangi,
Nov. 15, 1858.

❖ 1858 TRACTS FOR THE TIMES NO. 5.
Hawke's Bay Herald 27 November.

"Dare lucem et dare servem."

WHO ART THOU?

"I am TRUTH."

Whence cameth thou?—"I came forth from the throne of the Eternal."

Whither goest thou?—"I seek an entrance into the heart of every man."

Where wast thou during times past?—"Always on the earth, free as the winds which bore me; but always opposed, calumniated, ridiculed, kicked, expelled, throttled, put down, burnt, gagged, buried alive, tortured, thrown into wells, gibbetted and crucified."

By whom?—"By kings, by priests, by popes, by emperors, by lords, by bishops, by officials, by venal hirelings of the pen and the press, by powers."

Why?—"Because they hated me; because they loved tyranny, slavery, extreme wealth, absolute power, place and ease; because they themselves were unshackled by educational-twist, by custom and by precedent, by routine, by duncedom, and by hatred-of-change; because they listened to the loud cries of ignorance and darkness, and to the shriekings of bigotry, of superstition, of prejudice and of fear."

What is thy mission?—"To teach, to inform, to enlighten, to detect, to give knowledge, to strengthen, to cheer, to direct, to uphold, to settle firmly, to incite and lead enquiry, to cause reflection, to humanise, to make godlike, to free."

Dost thou think to succeed?—"Yes: I am but one but I am all-powerful and immortal, the gift of Him who sent me. The physical barriers of the universe are mighty—the moral ones are mightier far—and time seems long to the sons of men, but all are as nought to me. I never tire nor rest; I work every where; when crushed to earth in one place, I bide my time there, meanwhile I rise anew in another."

Hast thou at present any followers?—"I have many—scattered all over the globe; among all peoples, all tribes, all languages, all nationalities, all classes. But chiefly in Britain and her numerous colonies, and in America, are my more advanced followers

---

25 Theory of moral sentiments. W.C.

to be found. I have also very many rising ones in Italy in France in Germany and other places, which another short age will more fully develop."

Have not thy chief disciples, been always considered disturbers?—"Invariably so. We fare alike: the disciple is not greater than his master; in past ages they were always hunted to death; and even now

"The man who shows his heart,
Is hooted for his nudities and scorned!"

Why is this?—"Because my followers are always in advance of the age in which their lot is cast. This is proved, from the next generation raising monuments to the memory of those whom their fathers either murdered or suffered to die through cold neglect and want."

If then thy past chief ones have been so ill-used, and so very few among thy present followers escape ridicule coldness and persecution;—what reward hast thou to give them?—"The best the highest the most glorious: to use rightly their reason, the greatest gift to them of the Eternal. Hence they learn truly to know themselves; and, while they learn mentally to soar above all bounds and space, they become as humble as little children at their knowing so little; learn to despise pelf and honour and worldly glitter; and rejoice beyond expression at the new world of mind and freedom on which they have entered, and which ever remains with them ever comforting and strengthening them."

Since thou sayest, that thou teachest every where, perhaps thou doest so in every matter and thing?—"I do: such is my mission. I work alike in science and in art, in physics and in morals, in religion and in politics, in the minor events of the fleeting hour and in the hugest ones of the slow-revolving age, in the hamlet's path and in the path of comets, in the first prattling of an infant's mind and in the deepest conclusions of the wisest of sages. I taught both my New Zealand child how to make a flaxen fishing line and my British son how to form the electric band which now girdles the globe. I am naturally opposed to all secret conclaves, whether of the inquisition or the star-chamber, or vestries, or the 'closed doors' of petty colonial oligarchies. I abominate all humbug and moonshine and tinsel and ostentation and all vamped up externals. I dissect and shew the inner core and heart of things. I hate all insincerity, and have ever borne testimony against it; I did so 3000 years ago by the old Greek poet, saying,

'Who dares think one thing and another tell,
My soul detests him as the gates of hell.'[26]—

I inspired the British heart with love of freedom, liberty of the press, and of open trial by jury, and to stick to 'all fair above board': I am wholly against such teaching as 'all fair in love war and politics.' I counselled the sons of men in ancient days, by the wisest of their race, to 'buy the truth and sell it not'; and 2000 years ago my doctrine was openly and daily taught by the Founder of Christianity to the men women and children of Judea."

[*Exit* TRUTH.]

---

26 *Iliad,* ix. W.C.

O! mighty truth, thou must, thou shalt prevail! Go on: work, energise, operate, labour; thou hast much to do here in New Zealand—in Ahuriri; and thou wilt also find great opposition. Brother electors:—

"He is the freeman whom the truth makes free,
And all are slaves beside."—

WM. COLENSO.

Waitangi, Nov. 20, 1858.

❖ **1858 OPEN COLUMN. TRACTS FOR THE TIMES NO. 6.**
Hawke's Bay Herald 4 December.

"Dare lucem et dare servem."

No. 6.—HONEY-DEW TOBACCO.

—"He hath been a courtier, he swears.—If any man doubts that let him put me to my purgation. I have trod a measure; I have flattered a lady; I have been politic with my friend, smooth with mine enemy; I have undone three taylors; I have had four quarrels, and like to have fought one."—Just so, O thou inimitable Shakespeare! We live in an age of adulteration and paint, when impudent quacks and charlatans strive to carry their own private ends under the guise of serving the public. Strongly reminding one of the ugly vampire bat of S. America, which, by the aid of its wings flapping and fanning, gently sucks a man's blood until its huge belly is full. That "truth is stranger than fiction" is a truism; yet it is astonishing, that men who are sensitively alive to their own interests, and who even seek to follow the deductions of science, should in general consent to be hoodwinked in matters of Religion and Politics. Why should black be called white, or bitter sweet? Why, (for instance,) should spirituous liquors strongly adulterated which have killed and are yearly killing their thousands, be called "Cream of the Valley," and the "Water of Life"? or, why should a most horrible nauseous and highly poisonous vegetable substance be launched into the world under the *Christian* name of "Honey-dew"? For no other reason than this, that men, rational knowing 'cute white men, are content to be gulled by the knavish and designing, equally with the Fuegian and Australian savage, who is the dupe of mariners and chapmen through their gewgaws and trinketry. Even intelligent men too often forget, that there are men to be found now-a-days whose vocation seems to be how best to club their wits to deceive the unwary and confiding. "Men, who," as Sir W. Temple says, "under the disguise of public good, pursue their own designs of power, and such bastard honours as attend them."—Especially in matters of state (large or small,) and the getting-hold-of and retaining power in their own hands;—for this they will roar as gently as a sucking-dove;—use perfumed words dropping honey,—and hesitate not to speak all manner of ill (privately and anonymously, if they dare not openly,) concerning the man who sees through their stratagems—the honest man who is better than themselves.

May not a dog be choked with pudding? or a man with honey-comb? Can we conceive the Duke of Clarence to have had a sweeter death in his choosing to be drowned in a butt of malmsey in the Tower, than if he had been drowned in the Thames? or, would a silken halter effectually disguise the rough and unwelcome hands of Jack Ketch? These thoughts, and many similar, have passed rapidly through my mind during the past week; mainly owing to what I heard at Napier.

"Here comes an old trout; tickle him well and take him." At Napier an elector informed me that he had been called on by a certain person (A.) who endeavoured to induce him (B.) to pledge his vote at the coming election for a third (C.) and by no means to vote for another (D.) who had been spoken of as a Candidate. And thus A began:—"You know, B, what is good and proper, for you are an old settler; now you must vote for C, because he is a *religious* man; as to D, you must not think of him, for he you know is an *atheist* &c., &c."

[For the time I omit the names, as well as the blarney and soft sawder.]

Now I should like to know even believing (which *I do not*) the statement of A, that C is a "religious" man, and that D is an "atheist,"—I should like to know, I say, what such has to do with the matter of a FIT man as member-of-Council or Superintendent? Am I again to hear of such vagaries in the present year of grace, 1859, as that an ascetic or an imbecile or "a friend" or any man or what you please is fit to govern a free and rising people *because* he is "religious"? This would be to go back to the thirteenth century, to the times of Peter de Murrho (or Celestine V.); who was chosen Pope and Head of Christendom *because* of his being such a "religious" man; and who, after a short 3 months reign, abdicated, as unfit for the office of governing! Am I indeed to hear of a gifted man of comprehensive mind—a man to whom N. Zealand as a whole Colony is indebted—a man who, when even residing at a distance and using his talents in the service of a rival Province, was by *that* town and *that* province where he had *formerly* dwelt chosen solely on account of known merit as their representative in the great assembly of the Colony—a man to whom Napier and the Province of Hawke owes much, and to nothing more than to his conscientious uprightness and integrity:—am I to hear, I ask, and to be pained in hearing, such a man spoken of as being unfit to steer our craft because he is an "atheist"? At present I purposely abstain from asking, whether A is able to judge in such matters; or, whether A is not a little indebted to D for certain kind offices; or, whether A has not somewhat deviated from the golden rule of charity or apostolic religion in thus speaking ill, and that too of an absent one; or whether A really knows what constitutes an "atheist," or what a "religious" man.

The *time*, too, to the thinking mind, in which such an attempt was made, was singularly and strikingly unfelicitous. The day on which we received our long-looked-for July and August mails—which, informed us of the breaking-down of more of the barriers of superstition and bigotry at home, in the admission of a Jew into parliament—and of the sweeping away of those blots from the Prayer Book of the Church of England, as the religious services for Gunpowder plot, and Charles *the Martyr* (!) and the restoration of his precious son Charles II. Yes: this very time was that in which A made his nefarious attempt in the town of Napier!

Brother electors!—especially you of the town of Napier and neighbourhood —once more I say, *be on your guard*. Beware of honied words and fine promises and sanctified appearances. You have those among you who know how to play fast and loose, who know well how to run with the hare and walk with the hound. You have those among you actively *working*, who have openly avowed their holding to "all fair in love war and politics." Those men have hitherto opposed, and those men will ever oppose the true advancement of our province in its entirety. Believe not their honied words; believe not their planned their studied phrases; believe not their "sympathy with the working-man"; 'tis all syllabled moonshine used only to befog your brains. Take a hint from L'Estrange's thrush:—"Mother, says the thrush, never had any such a friend as I have of this swallow. No, says she, nor ever mother such a fool as I have of this same thrush."

Honest settlers of the province, you know me well. "I cannot cog, and say that thou art this or that, like many of those lisping hawthorn buds, that come like women in men's apparel, and smell like Bucklersbury in simpling time." As I said in *tract* No. 4, vote for no man merely because of this or that quality or qualification, if he is deficient in FITNESS FOR OFFICE AND HONESTY OF PURPOSE. A truly *"religious"* man, is indeed a great blessing, a treasure, an example, but such are very very rare; of such I need not speak. Jesus Christ was such; and all His *real* followers will ever be known by His one unerring badge of LOVE. But this one thing I will say, and I say it after long studying the subject and as a Christian man,—that I would rather be under an Atheist, or Jew, or Turkish Superintendent, *if he possessed the proper fitness for his office*, than under the greatest saint that ever wore a gown or cowl, without it.

WM. COLENSO.

Waitangi,
Nov. 26, 1858.

❖ 1858 OPEN COLUMN. TRACTS FOR THE TIMES NO. 7.
Hawke's Bay Herald 11 December.

"Dare lucem et dare servem."

No. 7.—DARIUS AND HIS GROOM.

"The thing that hath been it shall be." Verily it is both curious and painful to the reflecting mind to note how the world ever moves in cycles! The old father of history, Herodotus, informs us how it was in Persia some 2500 years ago. How that the great Persian King Cambyses being dead, a usurper, named Smerdis, possessed the throne until he was suddenly killed by a few Persian nobles, who then decided that they should again meet at sunrise on the morrow on horseback, and the one whose horse first neighed should be king. Darius (who was afterwards so celebrated) was one of them: and on his return to his house he told his clever groom, Œbares, of their determination, and caused him to set his wits a-working how to ensure to his master the wished-for honour. That night; Œbares took a mare to the place selected, and also Darius' horse. In the morning the six nobles were soon on the ground, and on coming to the spot where the horse had seen the mare the evening before, he instantly began to neigh, when the others dismounting and falling at Darius' feet hailed him king.

We are obliged sometimes to compare herrings with whales; we can't help it, though it may be impolite, the mind being master. Just so; late events have called-up the foregoing from old-buried depths of memory; and I am thinking how many 'would-be Darius' we have already among us, each working through his clever grooms and sagacious horses.

In the ancient case of the Persian, there was indeed a rare nugget to be gained: in the modern one of the Ahuririan, there is—what? anything but a pillow of roses to the best qualified, and a sure earthly purgatory to the incompetent.

Then, again, those Persian nobles did not profess to seek that high post—either, as being the best qualified for it, or for the public good. *They* were the magnates of the land. It seems the art or depth, of humbug was reserved for us moderns. Why is it that A, B, C, D, E, should think so very highly of their qualifications as state pilots, when those who know them best greatly doubt their possessing any such abilities? Is it, indeed, owing to their being the best qualified ones among us? This they dare not say. Is it owing to their being better born? They know better than to think this. Better educated? Highly doubtful. Is it owing to their reputation for general wisdom? Unfortunately the majority of them have this to seek; and their present acts shew their distance from it. Is it owing to their possessing a deeper purse? Very questionable; but if so, any lucky nugget-finder may arrive to-morrow from the gold fields and put them in the shade. But, if it be so, that they really possess *suitable fitness* and HONEST INTENTIONS TO SERVE THE COMMONWEAL, why do they not quietly seek to enter the good ship as able seamen to hand, reef and steer, and there to work with a will that she may duly perform her voyage? But no, not so—(as old John Dryden long ago sang):—

"Much rather woulds't thou choose a small renown,
To be the may'r of some poor paltry town,
Bigly to look, and barbarously to speak:
To pound false weights, and scanty measures break."

—Depend upon it, if those would-be Superintendents really possess the needful qualifications, such cannot long be hid. To me, our political prospect is anything but pleasant: and mainly (as yet) owing to the pride and vanity of a few noisy or puffed-up folk who wish to play first fiddle at Ahuriri! It is an ancient saying and a very true one, that "he who knows not how to obey knows not how to rule;" those persons plainly tell us—obey they will not, rule they will (that is, if they can)—how very modest! how unassuming!! Now all such aspirants should certainly be (at all events) believed by the many to possess suitable talents; but, alas! when one considers some of whom we have heard, it brings forcibly to mind the saying of the black slave—"I 'spect I'll wake up some morning and find myself playing on the pianny forty."

Men of Ahuriri! be wide awake to all would-be Superintendents; be ditto ditto to the whole generation tag-rag and bobtail of Œbares—whether grooms, duffies, toadies, touters, sycophants, lickspittles, or expectants. Remember, it is always when the game is played, that we discover the cause of the result. Darius, when he had gained the kingdom, erected an equestrian statue, with this inscription—"Darius obtained the sovereignty of Persia by the sagacity of his horse, and the ingenuity of his groom." Only fancy A, or B, or C, gaining our Superintendency, and then gratefully and openly acknowledging how he got it!! To be sure, such a proceeding would take away from the Electors a portion of the odium which will necessarily follow the success of an incapable. I, however, agree with Bright, "that, after all, our main hope and reliance is in the sturdy English, common sense of the working classes;" who generally are more free from that political cunning and knavery which has too often been the bane of Old England, and which must ever prove a curse to any people or nation.

With the sole exception of Domett, there is not one (among the whole batch of those whose names have been so unthinkingly thrust forward) who is any ways fitted for Superintendent. How on earth some of them were even once thought of for that office, is still a mystery—unless it was owing to the same principle as that of the old owl, who thought her young ones the handsomest creatures in Creation!

Many among you have repeatedly asked me for my opinion, and now you have it.

WM. COLENSO.

Waitangi,
Dec. 6, 1858.

❖ **1858 TRACTS FOR THE TIMES NO. 8.**
Hawke's Bay Herald 18 December.

"Dare lucem et dare servem."

No. 8.—"CEAD MILLE FAILTHA—(A HUNDRED THOUSAND WELCOMES).
Language is the vehicle of thought. Earthquakes happen; continents may become submerged; nations may be enslaved, or change their dormas, but not their national feelings: these are sure indications of a people's character. Lavater has laid down, that the character of a man may be detected not less clearly in the most trifling gestures —in the ordinary tone of his voice, in the way he takes a pinch of snuff or smokes his pipe, or mends a pen, than in great actions. Allow this and it follows, that such will ever be found the faithfullest signs of national character. What a chapter—interesting and instructive—might be written on the different forms of national greeting! A truly intellectual box of pemmican! Notice a few of the greetings of the East:—the ancient *'Shalum'* (Peace) of the patriarchal Hebrews; a pastoral people, always more or less at war; the *'If God will,'* of the modern fatalist Arab:—*'Thy visits are as rare as fine days,'* of the amatory and poetical Turk. *'How goes the perspiration?'* is that of Egypt, which stamps a feverish dry climate to the life. *'Have you eaten your rice? Is your stomach in good order?'* are the deliciously kind enquiries of the timid trepang, bird's nest, and chow-chow consumers of China. (Well might a clever modern writer ask—'Could such

have taken root in Aberdeen or Kentucky?') Then, step to the West; notice a few of the 'words that burn':—the *'Chaire'* (Rejoice! be glad!) of the ancient Greek, and the *'Ti-Kaneis'* (what dost thou?) of the modern degenerate cheating and chattering one; —note the contrast. The primitive Romans (with whom virtue signified manliness, and a man's whole value was in the measure of his valor,) said, *'Salve!'* Vale! (be healthy! be strong!)—how widely different from that of the modern priest-ridden Italian! The Spaniard says, *'May you live a thousand years!'*; the Frenchman *Comment vous portez-vous?* (how do you carry yourself?). Now a real Englishman would never be able to conquer his innate dread of humbug and flummery so far as to use the hyperbolical phrase of the Spaniard, or the superficial gingerbread and filigree sentence of the Frenchman. Even the kindly *'Hoo's a' wi' ye'* of the canny Scot, carries a spice of national *pawkiness* in it. And the Irish motto at the head of this tract, with their *'Long life to your honour—may you make your bed in glory!'* plainly shews the violent enthusiasm of the inborn Irish character, the very soul of a people endowed with peculiar lively feelings. (How I love a true Irishman! Give me an open honest Englishman, a sturdy liberal Scot, and a loving faithful Irishman, and I'd back my trio of worthies against all the world.) And then we must not forget those of the land we live in,—the hearty and open New Zealand *'Haere mai,'* and *'Nau mai'* and *'Ho mai koutou'*—meaning, come hither,—all thyself and thine welcome hither, and, bring yourselves hither and have no care as to board and lodging. All, however, both east and west, must give way to the real true honest blunt sound and hearty and no-mistake salutation of John Bull —*'How are you?'* and *'How do you do?'* Here is both theory and practice. To be! to do! Why, these are everything, the whole contexture of life. What a text to write on! —as a modern genius says, *'How are we?'* Happy if the advance of knowledge in the 29th or 30th century (to come) shall enable its Brougham or Whewell to answer, *'Pretty well, I thank you.'* But anon.

Now, I confess, I have been lured aside from that which I had purposed when I commenced this tract—namely, to write on what I conceive would strike a chord in the heart of all real settlers, and at the same time (if followed out,) confer a lasting benefit on both our adopted country, and our honoured Father-land. All real settlers heartily wish the province as a whole to go ahead; all such, possessing pluck are determined that it shall. What is really wanted in order thereto, is POPULATION. We do not want money or live stock, or a line of steamers or an electric telegraph. Already we have the elements of wealth in profusion around us; all we want is population. If the offer were now made me, of either a gift of £500,000 for the province, or 2000 good immigrants, I should immediately and joyfully choose the latter. Let this be the first aim of our new government when settled, to do their best towards securing immigration. Let, also, the real settlers do their part, so that the immigrant (on his arrival) may both read in our honest countenances as well as hear from our truthful lips—*'Cead mille failtha'*—a 100,000 welcomes! I want for my countrymen to have something better before them (on their landing), than to work on the roads, or to wait till sheep-shearing to get a job in shearing the sheep or packing the wool of the few fortunate first comers. This may very easily be managed by 'one and all'[27] uniting in the work.—1st. By the government—setting apart (as acquired from the native owners) more or less of the whole of the Ahuriri plains for agricultural purposes and real occupants;—by the government granting land to agriculturists (where needed) on deferred payments, and also rations (if required) for the first year, or even longer;—2nd. By the settler already *comfortably* settled knowing when he has enough, and so ceasing to buy up every morsel of land which the government may have or offer for sale. Or, if it be said, (as it has been said,) 'If I don't buy another will,' then let the rich (really or prospectively) among us put their heads together for the real benefit of the province and their poorer fellow-countrymen. For which purpose some such plan as this might be adopted: let a club, or society, be formed for the purpose of purchasing desirably situated agricultural land from the government: let a suitable sum be subscribed for this purpose, each giving according to his ability—according to that with which God hath blessed him—(not in driblets of £2 and £5, as have been done for the service of the God of their fathers (!) but in £50 and £100 and £200—and some of the more fortunate among us can very well afford this): let such land be sold to fit agricultural immigrants—to be *bona fide* occupiers—at cost price including charges: let, I say, these things (or something like them) be done by us in a kindly brotherly Christianly real-British, way; and let them be once made known in England through the press, and we shall soon have the pleasure of seeing the many elements of wealth in our province at present lying dormant and wasting, put to their proper and legitimate uses by a cheerful and happy and steadily increasing population. For it must not be forgotten, that while, on the one hand, there are thousands of our fellow-countrymen at home who are bent on emigrating; there are also, on the other, many colonies both old and new bent on inviting them to their respective shores. And, further, it should not be forgotten, that were we to have a large increase of able working-class immigrants to-morrow, such would scarcely remain; or, if remain, not happily and contentedly—seeing that such barriers existed between them and the first-comers. Let us all consider this—especially the rich among us—and acting rightly towards our poorer brother, invite him and receive him with open countenance and a hearty greeting of '*Haere maï*'—'*Cead mille failtha*'—a 100,000 welcomes!

> *"Alas! I have walked through life,*
> *Too heedless where I trod;*
> *Nay, helping to trample my fellow-worm,*
> *And fill the burial sod—*
> *Forgetting that even the sparrow falls*
> *Not unmark'd of God.*
>
> *"I drank the richest draughts,*
> *And ate whatever is good—*

---

27 "one and all" = *Durdatha whye!* the Cornish motto. I.S.G.

Fish and flesh, and fowl and fruit,
Supplied my hungry mood:
But I never remembered the wretched ones
That starve for want of food!

"The wounds I might have healed!
The human sorrow and smart!
And yet it never was in my soul
To play so ill a part:
But evil is wrought by want of thought,
As well as want of heart."

                    WM. COLENSO.
Waitangi,
Dec. 13, 1858.[28]

❖ **1859 TRACTS FOR THE TIMES NO. 9.**
Hawke's Bay Herald 8 January.

"Dare lucem et dare servem."

No. 9.—A MESS OF POTTAGE.
Christmas has come and gone! and so has my ugly and unwelcome visitor, rheumatism. The new year also has begun—the year of the spanking young heir attaining his majority—the year of liberty, of jubilee, to Napier and Hawke—the year to be hereafter gratefully remembered by generations yet unborn—the year in which the settlers of the province and the members of their choice will have great duties to perform. May all have that clearsightedness and disinterestedness which will enable them to perform those duties rightly!

I have called this tract 'a mess of pottage' (without however intending to intrude on the good old English fare of the season);—and we know well, that 'too many cooks spoil the broth.' Now in all good messes—whether English soup or Irish stew, Scotch haggis or Spanish olla podrida—the grand secret is, to have just such a blending of viands and condiments as that no one shall predominate. For all made dishes the French have ever borne the bell; and yet they use garlic commonly in their pottages, but just in that nice way that the nauseous bulb is not detected. Only fancy a French cook at a club putting into his soup two or three thumping heads of garlic instead of one! Goodness!! what a row!!! enough to disturb poor Soyer's repose. Fellow settlers! you will all acknowledge the truth of this—see then that you do not act the like part. 'Be wide-awake' (once

---

28 This piece brought a response from six Colenso supporters: '... we, the undersigned, believing at the same time that a section of the settlers of this district, whom your correspondent calls "respectable," are arrayed against him, – consider it our duty, as honest working men, to inform you that we are highly pleased with the articles that have appeared from the pen of Mr. Colenso, and, moreover, consider that the political information contained in them is far above any thing that has appeared from any other writer. It appears to us that Mr. Colenso exposes truth in colours too vivid to please those who are opposed to him; if there are parties who take insult and offence at the manner in which Mr. Colenso exposes "self-seeking politicians," it would appear that their own consciences condemn them ....' (*Hawke's Bay Herald*, 8 Jan 1859). I.S.G.

more I say,) as to whom you vote for—as to who shall be your Council members. Let no one peculiar kind of viand or condiment predominate, or you will soon find that you have indeed cooked a very pretty mess of pottage—a fine kettle of fish for yourselves! It is well known that among us are several class interests (I would there were none.) To the electors of Napier in particular I would say—Choose from among yourselves fit men to represent you and your town interests. If you should have any runholders among you (or any from the country districts) seeking your votes, be timely warned—or your mess will be odorous with mutton fat, and prove rather indigestible for your delicate town stomachs. Do not however misunderstand me: I neither wish to see a *fit* runholder excluded from our Provincial Council, nor the runholding interests depreciated. No doubt runholders will be returned from the country districts; but we shall find that it is infinitely more to us to have a good fair mess—or, in other words, to have the different great interests among us properly balanced,—than to hear by every mail the progress towards settling the eternal din and bother of the so-called 'balance of power' in Europe—which, by the way, never can be balanced.

'A mess of pottage!' Yes: the oldest book among us tells us what a pretty kind of thing a certain freeholder once made of it in the infancy of our race—how that he *sold his birthright* for a mess of pottage. And he repented of it afterwards but it was too late. Now, fellow-settlers, see that none of you do this. You may do it; but the poorest among you cannot do it as Esau did—through hunger. *No man can possibly want in New Zealand.* There may be some excuse for an elector at home (in the *old* country, with its over population hard times hard taxes and harder unfeeling Tory landlords,) for such an one voting against his conscience, against the public good:—such cannot exist here. Utterly impossible it is that you can ever find any excuse for remaining in flunkeydom. Notwithstanding I have heard strange tales. I have heard rumours of certain 'pains and penalties' to be visited on the refractory, on the disobedient, on the labouring man who shall dare to assert his own inalienable British birthright:—'If you do not vote for so-and-so, no more carting for you;—no more boating for you;—no more employ for you.' 'If you do not vote for so-and-so, money lent shall be called in;—certain favours shall no longer be granted';—and so on. But, gracious God! are we indeed Englishmen—sticklers for British rights and liberty and rule—and for (what's more) the common rights of man *as man*—and yet dare we perpetrate such things? Shall our honored fatherland expend millions in redeeming the West India slaves—and much yearly 'blood and treasure' in putting down the accursed slave traffic—and the very New Zealand chiefs throughout the three islands have abolished slavery, and yet we hold our fellow-men in thrall? Can 'Rule Britannia' ever again be sung here amongst us (at the expected visit of Governor Browne, or at the separation fete, or at a dinner to be given to the members,) without a certain constriction of throat—alias, conscientious choking—when we glance round the room at the singing of the chorus—

'*Britons never never never shall be slaves!*'

Fellow settlers! fellow-countrymen! you especially who are in the situation of masters, or possessed of influence,—do away at once and for ever with all such abomination. I was informed, by a person who took round our petition for separation to obtain signatures, that at three runholders' stations the men in their employ refused to sign, at the same time saying, that they wished to sign it, but that 'they had been bound down (or made to promise) by their employer not to sign, and that while they agreed with the petition and regretted their promise, they would stick to their word.' Here was honor on the part of the working-man! here was dishonor—grievous thick heavy leaden stygian mean unprincipled conduct—on the part of the employers! and yet these persons call themselves gentlemen! and Englishmen!! and 'sympathisers with the labouring classes'!!!

It is to be hoped that all such attempts have *passed*. Otherwise such 'gentlemen' will certainly hook it under the 'Corrupt Practices Prevention Act'—and there is 'a chief among us' who is on the look out, and who will glory in hooking some of those 'respectable' first class pikes. Listen:—'Every person who shall directly or indirectly, by himself or by any other person on his behalf.... impede prevent or otherwise interfere with the free exercise of the franchise of any elector, or shall thereby compel induce or prevail upon any elector either to give or to refrain from giving his vote at any election.... shall be guilty of a misdemeanour punishable by fine and imprisonment, and shall also be liable to forfeit the sum of £50 *to any person* who shall sue for the same, together with costs of suit.'[29] Further: those who shall be convicted of any of these offences lose their electoral rights for 3 years, and will have their names published in a kind of *Black* List. And both the person bribing and he who is bribed are alike liable to the common penalties of fine and imprisonment, with this difference that a further penalty of £100 may be inflicted by the Supreme Court on the person offering a bribe, and a penalty of £10 on the person accepting it. These stringent remedies have been provided against those sad interferences which have too often prevailed over freedom of election among us. So that now no Road Surveyor nor Contractor nor Paymaster nor Gauger nor influential Electioneering Agent, can turn the scale through the influence of his office or situation, and so swamp the independent electors who are above his schemes. But it will be of little service for the cook to have pepper and salt, or the doctor remedies, unless such are *used*.

Fellow Countrymen! especially you of the laboring class, be above being bought. See to it, that your British stomachs rise with honest pride against it. Why should you be made niggers?

WM. COLENSO.[30]

Waitangi,
Jany. 8, 1859.

---

29 S.4, of the above mentioned Act; the whole of which is well worthy of speedy publication in the *Herald*. W.C.

30 H.R. Russell replied, 'My attention has been directed to the following statement and remarks made by Mr. Colenso in his "Tracts for the Times" No. 9' – here he quoted extensively from Colenso's paper – 'Believing the whole affair to be a pure invention, brought forward to suit political purposes, I challenge Mr. Colenso either to prove his statement or to make the most ample retractation and apology. I am, Sir, Your obedient Servant, H.R. Russell. Napier, Feb. 10, 1859.' I.S.G.

LETTERS 1847–1859

❖ 1859 TRACTS FOR THE TIMES NO. 10.
Hawke's Bay Herald 22 January.

"Dare lucem et dare servem."

No. 10.—ALL ALIVE, ALL ALIVE HO!

Walk up ladies and gentlemen, walk up! The most wonderful collection of birdsisses and beastisses iver seen.—Here's the Chameleon wot changes his coat seven times a day; and here's the beardless Monkey wot measures 41 inches from the tip of his nose to the end of his tail, and only 39 inches from the end of his tail to the tip of his nose!—Walk up, walk up, *feeding time close at hand.*

—Who among us has not rejoiced in his boyish days on hearing of the vans of wild beasts coming to his native town? Who, when a boy, has not run wild with joy in beholding the docile Elephant the handsome Panther and the majestic Lion? Verily Natural History—whether in sixpenny or in 5-guinea volumes—whether in the assemblage of living creatures in the Zoological Gardens, or in the solitary white mouse, dancing bear, dressed-up monkey, or dumb tortoise of the Italian hurdy-gurdy grinder—Natural History, from the time of Father Adam down to our own day, has ever been a fascinating science; one which has never failed to draw out the hearty yearnings of the human soul both old and young.

Anciently 'twas said.—'Africa is the fertile home of monsters:' modern times have been astonished at the very peculiar animals of Australia and New Zealand. Of those of Australia I shall not now say anything: of some of these of N. Zealand, (of our adopted home,) I shall hazard a few remarks.

Class 1. MAMMALIA. (*Beasts.*)

This great division of the Animal Kingdom is but poorly represented in N. Zealand; we have but one or two terrestrial families belonging to the 3rd *order*, CARNARIA (*or Bats,*)—one of which (*Vespertilio tuberculatus*, Forster,) I shall briefly notice. The N. Zealand *Bats* are rather rare and only to be seen flying at twilight. For years there had been a long and warm controversy, as to the Bat being bird or beast; and without doubt it partakes of both. Hence it is a good natural type of a two-faced person, of a *changeling* in politics, of the turncoat or rat: one whom self-interest or the loaves and fishes have charmed. Such an one never works really well, not even with the party who bought him over; hence he (Bat-like) always hovers in the twilight, between the day and night, and having caught a few foolish flying Moths (as stray sops,) he hies away to his 'cave in the earth' to digest his meal at his leisure.

Of the 9th order, CETACEA (whales,) we have several genera; one of which is a species of the celebrated Dolphin (*Delpinus Zealandiæ*, Quoy.) Ancient writers have written largely on the love of this creature for man—of his coming to shore on being called to be fed—his delighting in music and odours—and his carrying men on his back, through the sea. We, moderns, however, have not noticed these qualities. It is probable enough that our N.Z. *Dolphin* (like many other beasts) would not object to be fed at the expense of others, and would not reject music and sweet scents; but as to his carrying men safely on his back through the seas—tell that to the Marines! Being also a voracious creature, he is a good natural type of a *place-hunter*,—one who wants an easy billet—one who promises roundly and fairly, smiling all over his countenance. But be timely warned; don't trust him: at all events, get not on his back, (*i.e.,* make him not a Provincial Councillor,) for assuredly you will find him a slippery customer, and in a stormy sea you are not likely to have the luck of old Arion.

Class 2.—AVES (*Birds*).

Of this world-admired class we have very interesting specimens; of the glossy-plumed *Alcedo* family we have a species of the well-known Kingfisher (*Halcyon vagans*), called by the Maories, *Kotaretare.* The ancients said, that there was invariably never any stormy weather during the time this bird was making its nest, laying or sitting: hence, that period (about the winter solstice) was called 'the halcyon days,'—when the seas were calm and navigable. Now *our* Kingfishers are very small and shy and dull plumaged; and though of late our times have been not a little stormy, so that halcyon days (or, in other words, *peaceful and prosperous* ones) would be highly acceptable, I fear we shall see but a small amount of them unless we get *that* real good tried and well-fledged Kingfisher from Nelson, of which we have heard so much, through whom and his experience in *nest-building* we might reasonably hope to see halcyon days.

Then there is the Wood-hen; (*Ocydromus Australis,* Strickland;) or, Weka of the Maories—a bird belonging to the Rail family. This bird is worthy of notice, if it were only on account of the New Zealand proverb respecting it—'*E hoki rua ranei te weka ki te mahanga?*' (Will the Woodhen return twice to the snare?) During the last two years this proverb has often been thought on by me, and it seems as if we were fast nearing the time when we should particularly remember it, and the effective moral it teaches; and so avoid choosing men as Provincial Councillors and Superintendent who would quickly take us back to a much worse snare than that from which we have but lately been delivered.

But of all our New Zealand birds the Kiwi (*Apteryx Australis,* Shaw,) is the most curious. This bird, as is well known, is without real wings, and its hairy feathers little resemble those of other birds. For a long time the existence of a wingless bird was doubted; it almost seemed a contradiction in terms. Nature, however, always balances her works: not so man. A bird, with *one* wing or *one* leg, or a beast with *one* eye or three legs, would indeed be unnatural,—but not a bird without wings, or an animal without eyes—such are now known to exist. Just so it has seemed to me (when considering a late decision made by a high legal authority—and its probable consequences—respecting a Superintendent spending the public money unapplied and uncontrolled by the Provincial Council,) that the mere stripping away the 'Peacock's feathers' from a Superintendent, leaving him to squander as he pleases the public cash, is equally as unnatural, under Responsible Government, as that of a bird with one wing or a beast with one eye. Either two wings or none: let us have no unnatural flutterings. Let the fact then of the *Kiwi,* coupled with the present state of a neighbouring province (not to mention the secret aspirations of a few among us), be to us a powerful natural example, warning us as to whom we choose for our Superintendent.

Class 4.—PISCES (*Fishes.*)

Just one real fish I give you in this collection,—and that is a species of the famed Remora (*Echeneis lineata*, Menzies). This very curious fish, though small, was believed by the Ancients to possess the power of staying the largest ship under sail, by merely sticking to it, which it does by an organ composed of transverse plates situate on the top of its head. Remarkable and well-known instances of its ability are fully related by Pliny in his Natural History. While, however, we know nothing of its power to stay a ship, it is still used to catch fish and turtle by the Indians on the coast of Mozambique. A live one is made fast by a ring to a cord, and is then let go into the sea, when he soon adheres to a fish or turtle, and both are hauled up together into the canoe. Now we should also learn a useful political lesson from the little *Remora*: let us just put an unfit man into the Superintendent's office, and we shall soon find that our ship won't sail— that we have got a Remora sticking to her keel, or (in other words,) we are in a *fix*!

Choose then, Electors, true and honest men for your Provincial Councillors; and so shew that you have not conned in vain a lesson of New Zealand Natural History. As far as I at present see, I know of no better plan by which to avoid many of the evils I have touched on in this Tract, than by our endeavouring to secure the well-known, tried and experienced Alfred Domett as our Superintendent.

WM. COLENSO.

Waitangi.

❖ **1859 TRACTS FOR THE TIMES NO. 11.**
Hawke's Bay Herald 5 February.

"Dare lucem et dare servem."

No. 11.—SHADOWS.

Do we really exist? Is there such a thing as matter? Is there an islet off Cape Kidnapper and a shingly beach at Ahuriri? Is there snow on the Ruahine Range and mud in Carlyle Street? Is all we see and taste and feel real? Are we to shut our eyes and believe all we hear? or open them, and be guided by our reason and our senses? There have been men—very wise men—who have both believed in and attempted to prove the non-existence of matter: there have been also others who have argued for the eternity of matter. One of the grand doctrines of the Hindoos is, that all we see is *brahm*, or illusion; and we have no need to go out of Ahuriri to find those who (when "a little elevated") have more than once believed a post to be a man. Some religionists make a virtue of disbelieving their own senses: and many in all ages have confused the unreal with the real, the shadow with the substance; hence has arisen the numerous (and apparently well-attested) stories of spectres ghosts goblins and fairies; hence too is derived a large proportion of the humbug and sham that is in the world. It is to be hoped, that the highly civilised part (at least) of the human race is getting better, through the rapidly advancing light of Science and the proper use of Reason, but, after all, when the many obstacles and the carelessness and wilfulness of man are duly considered, it must be confessed very slowly. Persons who will not use their reason—who will not discriminate between the shadow and the substance—are like those foolish skaters on the Serpentine, who, in spite of the "DANGER" boards of the Royal Humane Society, go carelessly on until they find the ice breaking around, and cold death embracing them. Then, again, there is another class, who may well be termed, *one-idea men* (some of whom have from time to time "bored" us in the "open column" of the *Herald*;) such see little or no difference in the glorious stars over their heads—or in Arrow-root and Potatoe starch—or in sunlight and moonshine; and, of course, to them an essay on shadows must be 'as clear as mud,' and therefore entitled to a most superlative sniff. To be sure, persons are not to be flouted for their want of intellect, but for their non-using it. And I verily believe that very much more is to be set down to carelessness and laziness on their part, than to niggardliness on the part of Dame Nature.

I, myself, am but a plain man of common observation; simple enough, however, to believe my senses. It is my opinion, that the real things are those very things I see and feel and know by my senses. Now that a thing should really be perceived by my senses and at the same time not exist, is to me a plain contradiction. And when I so speak I do not mean by *my* senses in particular but by those of *all* others who choose to use their reason and to examine into things. All knowledge is of service; and a very useful knowledge is to be derived from a proper study of *shadows*. I allude not to that artistic distribution of shade in paintings and mezzotints known as *chiaro-obscuro*; nor to that more severely rigid delineation of shadow so necessary to true perspective: neither do I mean those celebrated aerial shadows of world-wide fame, long known as the Spectre of the Brocken—the Fata Morgana in the straits of Messina—the Mihrage of the African deserts—and the Castles in the clouds of the Polar circle.—But to the *Shadows* which are to be met with in our every-day walk through life. As a general rule, it may be said, that, the more difficult to get at the substance or mass which throws the shadow the more available the shadow itself should be. The height of an inaccessible mountain, or of a steeple, may be known by its shadow; so also may the longitude of any place by the immersion of one of Jupiter's satellites in the shadow of that planet.

I shall not stop to consider whether the real pith of my subject is more of a physical or of a metaphysical nature,—of the mere animal, or of the more highly refined intellectual soul. For the present I have enough at hand in the sad aberrations around me. The principle is pretty nearly the same—whether seen in the Fantail-fly-catcher hopping from twig to twig and displaying his open tail, or in the swelling Turkey strutting in the sunbeams;—whether in the highly refined *belle*, with her balloon-like skirt of crinoline her rouge and ostrich feathers, or in her smirking savage Hottentot sister, with her cowrie and brass bracelets and the reeking entrails of a newly slaughtered bullock, wound round her person;—whether in the 4-year old urchin just breeched, or in the 40-year old one who chucklingly fancies himself 4½ inches higher from his having just obtained the addition to his name of ESQ., J.P., or A.S.S.—the principle, I say, is pretty much the same in every case; each creature fancying himself to be really bigger and of vastly more importance than he really is, so that all such greatness, being quite accidental unsubstantial and unreal, belongs only to dream-land and justly comes under the denomination of Shadows.

Just bring a man well into the very focus of public opinion (and there is nothing in all the world to be compared to that)—let his accidents (whether *Esq., J.P., L.C, Sh-ff,* or *ASS,* it matters not,) be puffed aside; his public antecedents retrocedents and precedents be fairly viewed—and lo! it is as if you had a mite or an animalcule under the microscope; he is turned inside out, he is altogether denuded of his cloak of shadows, and he either improves or not, as the case may be, under the piercing scrutiny of the Public eye.

But how few really improve! or, rather, how very few come up to what they were supposed to be! and why is this? Because men will insist on looking at the shadow instead of the substance—at the coat instead of the man. Just strip that would-be gentleman of his gold chain, and ring, and purse, and his swagger soon subsides, and it is soon patent to all that he never could have been a gentleman.—Just take from a man the spending of the Public Money, and the power and influence he had thereby is gone; let him lose all hopes of a good feed at the public expense, or of the post on which he has set his heart, and his patriotism rapidly evaporates.—Just let a man who has been carrying smartly on and apparently well to do in the world, but all on the credit of others, let such an one be stripped of his shadow and he will prove a man of straw.—Just try a great chatterer on any subject which demands deep insight and a well connected flow of thought, and 'tis like digging for water on Barrack Hill. But I might go on thus with common every-day examples until I had easily filled a whole sheet.

I have heard mention of a great number of persons as candidates for the honor of Provincial Councillors. Be it so; the arena of the Council Room will surely prove them —surely strip some of them of their plumes stilts and bustlers. It may be at the outset some will think themselves to be fully as large as their own early-morning shadows; but *there* (or I am much deceived,) they will be as if they were on the equator at noon.

I do not see why we have not a Board of Examiners appointed to try all political aspirants. This might be done before or after Election. In the present day, in addition to those of the highest professions, examinations are constantly being made of candidates for very many offices—even down to that of a country village Schoolmaster;—and is the body of the State of less consequence? Perhaps a generation to come will see the need of this.—

—Had some Board of this kind been established at Wellington (at the beginning of Responsible Government,) what an immense benefit it would have proved! What a means of prosperity to the place and Province! What a saving of time and money and reputation! What a preserver of every good and kind and manly feeling! What a touchstone and detector of shams and shadows! For, believing as I do, that man is as naturally a Creature of Order as he is of Society, and that being a Creature of Order he is also one of Law (*i.e.* of Law natural and suitable); it follows, that while all good laws are promptly and entirely submitted to, all bad ones are as naturally opposed, and are sure some time or other to be repealed. Now those bad or unsuitable laws—(*e.g* at home, the Game Laws, the Church Rates, and all those affecting liberty of conscience; here, the so-called 'Algerine' Act, the impossible Thistle, the unique Cur, and the unfair Fencing Acts,)—now all those laws are owing to selfishness, or to narrow-mindedness, or to incapacity on the part of the lawmakers. Our own Provincial *bad* and unsuitable laws have cost us (in sheer making) some hundreds of pounds; and 'tis not too much to say that they never would have disgraced our name and Statute book, had we had real men and not shams and shadows in the Wellington Provincial Council.—

Then again there are *Shadows* of another class—which, possibly, some of our would-be Councillors will find *by experience* disagreeably close to their heels;—Shadows, black blue brown and grey, broad long and tightly fitting, umbras and penumbras, a host! These are of the kind the dog saw in crossing the stream on a plank with a piece of meat in his mouth. Imagine a man leaving the healthy every-day bustle of his Sheep or his Farm or his Store, to put on a suit of black and sit quietly and orderly and without his cutty pipe for 6 or 8 hours daily, giving close and undivided attention to dry statistical matters;—such an one, if a *shadow*, will ere long be trying Holloway's Pills, to be shortly followed by a wish for a whittling knife and stick (after the American fashion,) and before half the first Session is over will have huge and ugly thoughts that he has thrown up the real for the unreal, the substance for the shade.—Imagine another, who, in addition to the foregoing, has left a snug home and wife and family; ere long such an one will do more than dream of *dulce dulce domum.*— Imagine a third, who, besides his uneasiness from inactivity, hears continually from his home, that his presence is necessary to his well-doing; such an one will assuredly be haunted by a horrible shadowy nightmare.—Imagine a fourth (if you can) who, in the height of dog-day elective zeal has thrown up his official situation (£200 a year it may be) to serve his country; ere long, if a shadow, he will begin to think he has paid too dear for his whistle!—Imagine yet a fifth, who, from having dreamed he saw some shadowy representation of a throne, became discontented with his honourable and useful situation, and thenceforth wriggled and strove and promised and smiled, and gained both a requisition and a seat in the Council;—

—*"Such a nature,*
Tickled with good success, disdains the shadow
Which he treads on at noon."—

—When lo! his eyes too are opened; he is now as a fish out of water, for he finds that he is out of his place, and that in stretching after the shadow he has lost the substance!! Now all this great grief and vexation of spirit comes upon the children of men through their contemplating their shadows instead of their realities, and so venturing to seek

—*"The bubble reputation*
Even in the cannon's mouth."

Let no one say I have shaded too darkly my sombre subject of shadows. Wait: time will shew. One of our most eminent English poets has sung much more gloomily of one of our chiefest and choicest human affections:—

"And what is friendship but a name,
A charm that lulls to sleep;
A shade which follows wealth and fame,
And leaves the wretch to weep.'—
And a greater than he, hath gone much further, saying,—
—'Life's but a walking shadow, a poor player,
That struts and frets his hour upon the stage,
And then is heard no more."

Wm. Colenso.

Waitangi,
Jan. 27, 1859.

❖ 1859 OPEN COLUMN.
Hawke's Bay Herald 5 March.

Sir,—Your last issue (Feb. 19) has a letter from Mr. H.R. Russell, containing a 'challenge' to me,—'either to prove a statement or to make a most ample retraction and apology!'

Nor is this all. Mr. H.R. Russell, in the same letter, says, that 'he believes' my statement 'to be a pure invention brought forward to suit political purposes':— that is (in vulgar language), a barefaced falsehood brought forward with dishonest intentions!!

Now how any well-bred man can so publicly write of any-one's words, and subsequently demand either proof or apology, I have yet to learn.—And I should also like to know, what right Mr. H.R. Russell has to challenge me concerning that statement?—seeing, too, that it was as large as the whole province of Hawke, and embraced all the runholders, amounting to a few scores.—

I ask, Sir, what peculiar right has Mr. H.R. Russell thus to challenge me? Have indeed the runholders held a meeting on the subject and unanimously deputed Mr. H.R. Russell to make the enquiry? or, is Mr. H.R. Russell their acknowledged head and leader? or the greatest man among them? that he should thus act as coryphæus and champion of all the Runholders of Hawke?—

If any of the above hypotheses is correct, then Mr. H.R. Russell would be entitled to either proof of my statement or retraction and apology,—provided he sought it courteously as a gentleman: if, however, none has been allowed, then every honorable man will grant, that an apology is due to me from Mr. H.R. Russell for his uncourteous and uncalled-for language towards me in particular on account of a most wide and general statement.

I am, Sir,
Yours very truly,
Wm. Colenso.

Waitangi,
Feb. 24, 1859.

§ 1859 NAPIER.
Nelson Examiner and New Zealand Chronicle 12 March.

The elections for members of the Provincial Council had commenced, and the following members had been returned:—for the town of Napier—Mr. T.H. Fitzgerald, Rev. W. Colenso, and Dr. Hitchings; for Napier Country District—Messrs. H. Tiffen and J.C. Carter; for Clive District—Mr. J. Rhodes. The elections for the Te Aute, Waipukurau, and Mohaka District were to take place in March. The Napier races, in consequence of the elections, had been postponed to the 15th instant.

❖ 1859 OPEN COLUMN.
Hawke's Bay Herald 26 March.

SIR,—Allow me to point out a slight error in your last number—in the speech of the native Renata, as spoken by him (and, I believe, translated by me) at the Separation Fete Dinner.—You state,—'It was the wish of himself and friends to continue loyal subjects of Queen Victoria: *and not to countenance the movement of a native king.*'

What Renata said, was;—'It was the wish of himself and friends to continue loyal subjects of Queen Victoria; and that, if the Native King his plans and his policy were identical with those of the Queen's Government he and his friends would countenance him; but if opposed they should not do so.'

Of course you will see, that my only object in writing is, that the Native Chiefs about us may not feel offended at having such unconditional sentiments put forth as theirs at this present peculiar crisis; as (it is well known) they are now daily expecting the arrival of the Native King and several hundred of visitors from stranger tribes.

> *I am Sir,*
> *Yours very truly,*
> *W. COLENSO.*

Waitangi,
March 22, 1859.

§ 1859 OPEN COLUMN TO THE EDITOR.
Hawke's Bay Herald 30 April.

SIR,—You and most of the electors are aware, that my being nominated as a candidate for the superintendency of this province, was not only not of my own seeking, but contrary to my wish. You may imagine my surprise then at Mr. Colenso's base and dastardly attack on me, on Saturday last, (he being a member of the council then sitting, and I only a spectator, and therefore not having the power of replying,)—especially after the matter had just been settled by electing a person of his own party to fill the office of superintendent, in order to prevent a deadlock, and to enable the business of the province to go on. I should not have deigned to notice this miserable calumniator, had it not been to tell him and the public generally that it was not only because I thought it better that the superintendent should not sit in the council, that I refused to stand for the Waipukurau, but that I would not disgrace myself by sitting in the council with Mr. Colenso. As to not representing a constituency, the fact of five of the members being my own supporters (and almost a sixth, for the member for Te Aute got in only by accident,)—and especially the two for the Waipukurau being elected to support me, gives the lie to that calumny. One word more and I have done with him. He says that I am unknown; better to be so than to have a name held in contempt and disgust by nearly all the people in the province, as Mr. Colenso's is. But I have a name that all his venom and malice can never tarnish. I am, Sir, Your obedient Servant, Alfred Newman.

❖ **1859 TRACTS FOR THE TIMES NO. 12.**
Hawke's Bay Herald 30 April.

"Dare lucem et dare servem."

No. 12.—SUBSTANCES.

My last was on shadows—unrealities: this shall be on substances—reality. Yes: men of the province of Hawke! on what I deem to be real; although its true utility and value will be more surely known to, and proved by, a generation yet to come.—

"I have not seen, I may not see,
My hopes for man take form in fact
But God will give the victory
In due time; in that faith I act.
And he who sees the future sure,
The baffling present may endure,
And bless, meanwhile, the unseen Hand that leads
The heart's desires beyond the healthy step of deeds."

Mistake me not: value not substances according to their gross densities; otherwise Garry's anvil will bear away the prize. There are various substances—from gold to gauze ribbon—from mutton fat to wool—from lead to magnesia—all of different specific weights and values; and there are still others—substances, that is, *realities,* (as opposed to shadows, or unrealities,) which are both more subtil and more potent—such as, the electric fluid—the different gases we swallow in every draught of water—and the intellectual thinking part of man.—Would that every Briton clearly understood and valued his birthright! Would that every settler in this new province of Hawke rightly viewed the greatest two of all his realities—his religious and legal privileges!

Of the former, that is of the religious, I shall not now speak (I hope to bye-and-bye); of the latter, that is, of his *legal* privileges as a British colonist, I shall now essay a few words.

It has been sneeringly asked by the opposite party; (who, by the way, have always opposed the dissemination of truth and light, and therefore have the least right of any to put such a question;) what right have I to write such *tracts* ? The answer I leave for my many approving readers to make.[31] I say now, once for all, *I write as nature's priest*. Do not, however, mistake me: Man, as lord of the creation, is by birthright nature's priest. But it is only to the patient, to the painstaking, to the humble, to the truthful seeker, that she reveals her store. Only such men unlock her treasures, and through them the world is enriched. To all others she is as hard as flint;—a perfect sphynx preserving an eternal silence. '*Know thyself*,' is her first lesson; and the man who cons this truly possesses the *sesame*, or talisman, which ever gives him entrance to the hearts of his fellow men. I write, I speak from my heart, what I believe and feel; hence it is that I strike a chord in the hearts of the many. This is the only true way of writing, of speaking; *from the heart to the heart*. Hence it is that the words in lovers' letters seem to jump out of the paper and are always understood;—that love's language is universal;—and that national proverbs and good ballads never fail to stir the inmost depths of man's being. There is a spirit in man—in every man, even in a child—which immediately detects what is merely said as compliment, or flattery, or humbug, or to gain one's own private ends;—and what is said in truthful simplicity from the depth of the soul. This latter always strikes home; it does not so much instruct or teach, as it finds a suitable spot in the soul, a seed already sown, a germ already waiting for the welcome ray or communication which is to evolve it. Such writing or speaking is living, is blood warm; it carries before it all barriers. It is man's soul speaking to his fellow's soul. "When I hear, or read, any such, I say, 'Ah! there's a living man; one who is like myself; one who has both laughed and wept, both experienced and felt.'" Yes: such an one lives for all, and all live in him.—

Men of the province of Hawke! I have now a few words to say to you on your electoral privileges. If you all really knew the value of them, you would prize them more than you do. To me—looking forward as I do to a happier period for all freemen—they are realities; precious substances pregnant with good! more to be prized than gold or pearls. For such, poor humanity has been struggling many thousand years—struggling through seas of blood. For such, a great part of Europe is still heaving and swelling like the billows of the ocean. For man in power has ever striven to keep down his fellow-man, whether in Church or in State.

Men of Napier! listen to one of your chosen members. Note the words of a man who has passed through much adversity—much contumely:—a man, composed of flesh and blood like yourselves:—a man, over whom both honours and wealth have now little power. Why? Because he has seen the hollowness of them, and has therefore been enabled to rise above them.—

Men of Hawke! You have in your own possession a great privilege—a valuable *substance*:—power. Prize it; use it rightfully for your own and your children's good. I have looked anxiously over the list, published in the Hawke's Bay Herald, of the persons who have newly qualified themselves as voters, and I confess I am disappointed;—there ought to have been three times the number. Oh! if you really knew the great

31 While inland last week in Te Waipukurau district, I again received the public thanks of some working-men for my Tracts; with a hope that I would continue them. W.C.

value of the boon you have thought so little of:—of the boon, to gain which your forefathers laid down their lives, you—every soul of you who has not sent in his qualification as a voter would have acted differently.

Men of Hawke! we have now Responsible Government—Representative Government of our own—and farther than this man cannot go towards perfection in the art of Government. But, bear in mind, that it is to *you*, to the electors, *to the basis* of the pyramid, that we have ever to look for the soundness and perfectibility of the superstructure. This I call, substance, *reality*: for, rightly used, your governing men cannot go greatly wrong. And, why so? Simply because the *power*, the reality, is with *you*—with the many, with the Electors; so that, if your governing men or elected representatives go far astray the fault will ever be your own. Your representatives are merely your own mouth-pieces, speaking for you; therefore they ought not, and, if you use your power rightly, they can not, they dare not, do, what you would not have done.—

This power, which you have legally and rightfully as men and as British colonists, you should prize highly; for by it alone when rightly used you both can and will have good Government.

But, like all other good things, it must be *used*; and to use it properly will require some little watchfulness on your part. If your chosen representatives dare to act irrespective of the welfare and wishes of those who chose them and sent them into the Provincial Council, call them immediately to account; spare them not. Pass not tamely over the first slip, or it may lead to greater and graver errors.

Both history and experience tells us that the worst of tyranny has ever proceeded from a small elected body; when such have once kicked away the ladder by which they mounted, they become an unprincipled oligarchy, vastly more costly and overbearing than any one despot could possibly be.—

I believe, and therefore publish, that no Representative of the people has any right to propose, or uphold, or vote for, any person or act or thing, which those who sent him into the Provincial Council would not approve of. And this I hold, because he is there only as their mouthpiece or organ, and therefore has no right to bring forward or advocate any peculiar or interested views of his own.

For a young and newly-born Province we have a very fair and goodly revenue. See then that your representatives use it rightly, as you would reasonably have it used. And do you help them here; you have the Press both open and free; *use it*. Give your thoughts life; let all good measures be brought forward, discussed, and well ventilated. Above all, see to it, that your available revenue is used for *the good of all*; and that no *Class*-interest is maintained and preserved at the expense of others.

This, I call, substance—reality or true Government; when, the power, being with the people, that power is by them delegated to certain chosen Representatives who act honestly and rightly for the good of all.

A strong cart horse in a stable eating oats, and outside drawing a heavy load, is in very different positions; so also is our little steamer the *Wonga Wonga*, when inactive in harbour, and when going against wind and tide: working for the good of the community, both are admired and both useful. Just so it is with your Representatives whom you have chosen and sent into the Provincial Council. It is you, Electors, who have called them into being; it is you who have given them power; it is you who have made them what they are: see to it, then, that they work for your good; otherwise call them to account. Let them see, that still with you is the *substance*; that you have the power; for, by so acting, you will be very sure to have in due time good government—a blessing, which, more than half of the States of Christian Europe, and nine-tenths of the whole world, is still sighing and hoping and fighting for!

At the same time be not captious: be not ever ready to find fault. Remember, that 'good work requires time:' and that your chosen men are, after all, only men (new chums it may be in political matters) and not angels.

Men of Napier! you have heard me say, 'I would not go fettered into the Provincial Council;' and this is right, as a freeman speaking to freemen. I have also understood, that in your voting for me and sending me thither, it is to sit there as *your* Representative—as *your* organ, to make known *your* wishes. If I cease to do so; or if I set aside yours for my own individual interests or designs, I then cease to be your Member, and you have a perfect and legal right to call upon me to resign; which call I must necessarily obey. Do you, also, Men of Hawke! act thus towards all your Representatives; and you will find, that you indeed possess a valuable substance—a reality—which thus used will be sure to bring you a valuable return.

It is related of George III that he once said, 'He wished every man in his dominions could both read and possess the Scriptures:' that was a good wish; it is a pity he did not do more towards effecting it. It is my wish, that every man in the Province shall be enrolled as a voter, and should know his privileges and duties as a voter; and towards this my aim shall ever be directed both in speaking and writing.

Men of the Province of Hawke who are generally called 'the working classes!' Englishmen, Britons, Americans,—Sawyers, Shepherds, Servants—Settlers all, see that you claim and obtain and use your rights as voters; in so doing you will possess a reality—a substance—in common (it may be) with your present masters or employers. It is only in your so doing that you are their equals; it is only here that you shew yourselves to be men like themselves. When I think how many of you are still unqualified as voters, and how much some of you monthly spend in grog (at the present high rate of wages,) I confess I am grieved, at your want of thought. Would that every one of you would become a 'teetotaller!' until at least he should have laid by £20, which, as things are, will enable him to buy 40 acres of land, make him a voter, and as such equal with his master, give him a valuable and substantial right, and enable him bravely as a man to aid in forming a liberal and free Government, through which your newly-adopted country is to rise, and your children and descendants will be benefited.

WM. COLENSO.

Waitangi,
April 25, 1859.

❖ 1859 OPEN COLUMN. TRACTS FOR THE TIMES NO. 13.
Hawke's Bay Herald 7 May.

"Dare lucem et dare servem."

No. 13.—SEE-SAW.

Who has not, when a child, enjoyed a good game at see-saw? Pleasant indeed is the sport! so is its recollection, even when dimly viewed through a long avenue of 50 years! Pleasant also is it to notice how deftly the crack young see-sawer manages when the plank slips a little out or in; or when his playfellow is heavier or lighter than himself. Who can say, that at such a game nothing is learnt of the power of correlative forces? of contraries? of opposition? Who shall say, that his see-sawing ended with the days of his childhood? rather, say, that man goes see-sawing to the grave. Alas! the world is full of it: not merely man with man; or company with company—ever opposed, opposite, and antagonistic, the heavier struggling hard to retain his filched piece of the plank, and enjoying but the fears and screams of his uptilted opposite —class-interest with class-interest, and state with state. Worse still! in no place is there a more determined see-saw game played than in the United States Congress, or in the British House of Commons!! Is not this sad? Yes: very, to the superficial observer; to the hoodwinked stiff-and-starched one-idea conventionalist; but not so to the truthful student of nature—to him who looks more than skin-deep into things.

It has more than once occurred to me, that a by no means unuseful essay might be written on Governmental see-sawing—opposites, or *opposition*. It is certainly a fact, that the more civilised or free any people or state has ever been, the more loftily and lengthily they dared to see-saw, or to oppose each other, and to "talk the matter over." Not but that both uncivilised and servile peoples have also talked; but such has ever been all form and ceremony, unmeaning palaver and twaddle, the mere animal following of the pack after their leader. Only a free people could produce such opposition—only a free people could hear such orations as those of Cicero and Demosthenes,—of Pitt and of Sheridan, of Burke, of Brougham, and of Bright. Yes: here is a good subject for a deep and lengthened study:—OPPOSITION; *its naturalness; its need; and its wholesome tendency.*

Opposition! this word, to some, sounds akin to ghost, or vampire, or some other horrible phantasy. Especially to the superficialist. Let him only hear of opposition, and anon he thinks of tartarus and the devil and his children! No doubt the word is both ambiguous and abused;—but so is the Polynesian word *tapu,* and the Latin word *sacer,* and our common English words, god, pound, knave, &c.; such equivocal words occur in all languages. But, undoubtedly, there is a sound proper good and beneficial opposition, as well as a factious and evil one. It strikes me, that (strange as it may sound,) opposition will be found to be one of the greatest physical conservators of nature;—her main-compensating power, or balance-wheel. And even morally, (to rise no higher,) no man possessing a sane mind and capable of deep reflection, will dare say, that he is not indebted to his failings for his being a wiser or a better man.

My axiom, then, is, that *opposition is natural*: as old Pindar also hath it (*Olymp. IX.*)
"All that is natural is best."

Look, "around, above, beneath;"—from the highest to the lowest, from the biggest to the smallest, all nature is full of *opposition*; and that, too, for the best purposes—Life, Harmony, Order. Consider the heavens, with their innumerable suns, planets and stars, all ever-whirling with astonishing rapidity, all performing their different motions,—

"Cycle in epicyle, orb in orb,"—

More correctly than the best chronometer, and (as far as we know) only doing so through *opposition*—*i.e.* their equal though vast centrifugal and centripetal (or giving-out and pulling-in) powers. Observe, also, another great (though still imperfectly known) natural agent, Electricity, (only recently pressed into the service of man,) consider, again, its own two great elements of *opposition*, in its negative and positive (or attracting and repelling) natures! Glance at the Animal kingdom; mark well the beautiful contrivances of diastole and systole, or the dilation and contraction of the heart; by which continual *opposition* life is preserved! View the Vegetable kingdom; notice the two currents of sap and their opposite circulation in the living plant, always ascending and descending! And then contemplate the wise *oppositian* through which the two great kingdoms of nature are maintained—the one (vegetables) giving-out oxygen and taking-in carbonic acid, the other (animals, whether living or dead) taking-in oxygen and giving-out carbonic acid. Hence the perfect adaptation of the two great kingdoms of living beings to each other;—each removing from the atmosphere what would be noxious to the other;—each yielding to the atmosphere what is essential to the continued existence of the other.

Thus we may see, throughout physical nature,—the naturalness, the need, and the wholesome tendency of *opposing* powers, or of *opposition*. Happy if, in so reviewing, we shall be led up through nature unto nature's Author:—

"Nature is but a name for an effect

Whose cause is God:"—

and with him of old, admiringly say,—"O Lord, how manifold are thy works, in wisdom thou hast made them all!"—

Nor is such less clearly seen by the philosophic mind in the moral world. No doubt, much of what we have of Truth, Justice, and Religion, is mainly owing to this great conservative power—*Opposition*: As I take it, it is through this eternal (and apparently discordant) clashing, that Truth now and then emerges from her well;—that Justice and Rights-of-Man are sometimes allowed successfully to plead;—that Religion, not excluding Revelation, is maintained pure simple and unsophisticated. How very much Christianity, in the midst of so many and so widely differing vagaries and follies and high-culminating worldly-wisdoms, is indebted to opposition; and that too among her best bodies of followers, He who is her Author alone knows!

And thus, even as we know opposition to be needful and wholesome in animate and inanimate nature, in the physical moral and religious worlds, even so is it in the Governing Economy, or Politics, of States and Provinces. But here we should learn to discriminate between that opposition which is really useful and good, and that which is factious and vile. For, as I said before, the word is ambiguous; and every good has its counterfeit. And, 1st., Men of Hawke! know, (and knowing, prize and store, and *use, when the time comes,*)—know that all *opposition* which is, or has been, or may be, made against the Governing body, (or Supreme governing man,) is not necessarily factious and evil. When the Governing body, or Supreme governing man, (as the case may be,) goes wrong—when that body, or man, ceases to act for the good of the people, then opposition is a virtue and a necessary end, and, at such a time, it is NOT the *opposition,* or opposing power, which is factious and disorderly, whether from many or few, but the false governing one in opposing the Public good. The time is for ever gone, when the doctrine of non-resistance, or "Kings (or governments) can do no wrong," can be any longer taught to Englishmen—whether in Old England or in the Colonies. How very much of the miseries under which poor humanity has long groaned may be fairly carried to the account of the belief in that dogma, I scarcely dare trust myself to think, much less to say.

And, 2nd., be assured that, the more highly civilised and free we are, the more needful and abounding opposition will be. For Human Nature fully developed is just as a chance pumpkin or corn plant, growing on a dunghill or highly manured lot of ground—the richer the soil the more of leaves and stem besides the fruit. The more clever and bold some intellects may be to devise well-concocted schemes of seeming good, the more certain some others equally gifted will arise, to enquire into and sift and scrutinise; and out of this see-sawing, or *opposition,* good must ever to freemen eventually come. The man of trained, or well-disciplined mind, will always be careful what he takes for granted, and in nothing more so than in political schemes of seeming good. That opposition, however, is ever good, come from what quarter it may, which is beneficial to the Province and people;—even if those laws and measures which are known to be theoretically good are set aside through it. For liberty consists not in being governed by the laws which are absolutely best, but by those which are deemed best by the people who have to obey them.—

And, 3rdly., Men of Hawke! from what has already been said, learn to discriminate and detect the really factious and evil opposition. Consider, capacities,—bias,— principles—motives—interests—tendencies. Shallow and prejudiced minds are like bad-sighted and fearful folks; such cannot see either a rock or a whale ahead, and will never venture out of their depth without their old corks or bladders; such will always be sure to raise an incessant cackle of factious opposition. Types of this class may be not seldom found in some thickset sturdy individual on juries committees and vestries. Selfish individual motives and principles are also mostly factious; so are class or party, or monopolising interests, where the many are called on to suffer to benefit the few; so is that opposition which is sometimes organised in order to delay, seeing it cannot hinder, the coming good, and which is too often elaborately and finely clothed with specious phraseology. And a pretty common mark, by which all such may be generally known, is that of a cat-like acting, or secrecy;—secret meetings, secret plans, secret and stealthy steps. Now all such is truly a factious and evil opposition; whether it proceeds from the ruler, ruling body, or ruled.

WM. COLENSO.

Waitangi,
May 2, 1859.

❖ 1859 OPEN COLUMN.
Hawke's Bay Herald 6 August.

SIR,—I believe you already know that I never notice anonymous letters. Exceptions, however, are found to all rules. And, inasmuch as *"Enquirer"* (in your last) made a very proper enquiry, and that too in decent language, I am happy in being ready and willing to supply an answer.

I am also the more desirous of doing so; lest "Enquirer" (or others) should unhappily draw the erroneous inference, that the Superintendent's writ and my own address to the Electors of Napier (both appearing at this time,) were elicited by or through his enquiry.

The facts, however, are simply these:—While the Provincial Council was sitting and near its close, a question was put (by, I believe the Superintendent himself, who had also previously obtained leave to bring in a Bill relative to this very matter,) as to the opinion of the Members concerning certain *special* Acts of the Provincial Council of Wellington—*viz.*:—such as "The Officers and Contractors Act;" whether such special Acts could be considered as legally applying to the Hawke's Bay Provincial Council? Some of the Members were of opinion that they would apply; while others did not think so. You know, Sir, and the Public also, that we were not desirous of commencing our Provincial career by enacting too many new laws; and so it was finally agreed, *nem. con.*, that the Superintendent should write to head-quarters and get the opinion of the Attorney-General on the subject.

He did so: but no answer had been received up to his leaving for Wellington in the "Wonga Wonga." During his absence, however, an answer did arrive, which was duly laid before Capt. Carter on Saturday the 23rd of July; but, as the steamer was then coming in with the Superintendent on board, Capt. Carter thought it better to defer acting.

On the following (that is to say, *last*) Monday, the Superintendent first saw the Government letters which had been received during his absence; and, of course, he lost no time in acting accordingly.

The opinion of the Attorney-General is, that all such Acts, although special, are in force until by the Council of Hawke's Bay repealed; and therefore all Members of Council accepting any official appointment (whether of emolument or to the Executive) will have to go again to their constituents.

I am, Sir, yours truly,
WILLIAM COLENSO.

Napier,
August 2, 1859.

❖ 1859 TO THE INDEPENDENT ELECTORS OF THE TOWN OF NAPIER.

Hawke's Bay Herald 6 August.

BROTHER SETTLERS!—A few months ago you chose me as one of your Representatives in our first Provincial Council. You did me that honor unsolicited. I entered the Council unfettered as "a Tribune of the People."—

I subsequently accepted the office of Provincial Auditor; and, in consequence thereof, I have (according to law) lost my seat in the Council. Notwithstanding I have every confidence in you; believing, that you will again choose me to be one of your Representatives.—

I believe this, lstly, because I accepted this very office I now hold of Provincial Auditor *the better to serve your interests*. The Province has great need of a tried man of courage and of independent mind and station to fill that important situation. Had such an office been created and properly filled at the very onset of our separation from Wellington, our Treasury would have been much richer. You know that the salary is small: and you should know that the duties (as laid down by our Superintendent) are important and responsible. They are not merely those of common Auditors, *viz.,*:—to cast up and correctly place accounts already paid, (duties which may be performed by common clerks,)—but, to scrutinize all demands on the public purse,—to control and check the expenditure of the public money,—and to see that none is spent beyond the amounts and for the purposes sanctioned by the people's Representatives in Council;— and all this has to be done before any of the public cash can be drawn or paid.

Secondly:—I believe that you will re-elect me, because you will agree with me that it is highly needful that the Provincial Auditor should have a seat in the Council.—

Thirdly:—I believe that you will again choose me, (notwithstanding any opposition—open or concealed—which my old opponents may raise,) because I fully approve, and have supported, and shall (if elected) cordially support, the highly suitable policy of our worthy Superintendent.—

Fourthly:—I believe, that you will again call me to the honourable post of your Representative; because, during the late sitting of the Council, I served you both faithfully and zealously.—

Fifthly:—I further believe, that I shall again become the man of your choice; because you know that I have ever heartily and fearlessly aided our Common Cause—with head and heart, with tongue and pen—and that our good cause, though strong and settled, is yet too young not to require the watchful and constant care of all its earliest friends.—

Believing thus, brother Settlers, and having confidence in you—I ask you for your votes: I calmly await the issue.

But, if, on the contrary, you can dispassionately think, that I have not faithfully and zealously served you; and you really know of a man altogether better adapted to serve you as your Representative—by all means choose him. Only (I would beg to be allowed to remind you) be quite sure, that he will fully uphold the policy of your present Superintendent; (particularly that part of the same which refers to the

Provincial Lands and to the Wellington Loan,) which policy I conscientiously believe to be the one best suited to the interests of our Town and Province.

In conclusion, allow me further to say,—that I shall, in this present election, pursue precisely the same course that I did in the last: *viz*:—I shall solicit no man's vote: I shall organize no Committee: I shall use neither influence nor friends: I shall not even ask any one either to nominate or to second me on the day of election. Of course I shall be there, to do my duty as the case may be.—

> *I am, Brother Settlers,*
> *Your true friend, and*
> *Very obedient Servant,*
> *WILLIAM COLENSO.*

Napier,
August 2, 1859.

§ 1859 THE AUDITORSHIP.
Hawke's Bay Herald 24 September.

SIR,—The duties of Auditor are thus defined in "An Act to provide for the Audit of the Public Accounts of the Colony of New Zealand," passed by the General Assembly last year.

"1. To examine the accounts of all persons entrusted with the collection, custody, receipt and issue of Public Money and stores of the General Government of the Colony."

"2. To call upon Accountants in the service of the General Government of the Colony, for all necessary or proper explanations respecting their receipts and expenditure, and respecting all matters necessary to enable the Auditor to discharge his duties under the above Act."

And it is provided in said Act that *the Treasurer shall at the end of every six months, send an account of the receipts and disbursements to the Auditor for examination, &c., &c.* The accounts are then, after being audited, laid before the House of Representatives, and finally examined and passed by an Audit Committee.

This is all very business-like and in accordance with the usual practice in every part of the world, I believe, whether the accounts are those of a State, province, county, corporation, or merely those of a public company or trust estate. And as our accounts are neither very intricate nor likely to include a very large expenditure, the duties of an Auditor for the small province of Hawke's Bay, ought to be a very simple matter, not requiring a week's work in the year; and therefore a very small salary should be sufficient. £50 per annum would be a handsome remuneration.

But it seems, if we are to believe the pure and single minded patriot who now holds that office in our province, that the provisional Superintendent has laid down duties attached to the Auditorship, of "an important and responsible nature;" and quite of a novel character. Let us see what the former individual says on the subject in his laughably pompous address to "The Independent Electors of the Town of Napier," when he announces himself as Colenso, the first of the resuscitated order of the tribunes.—By the way, the *Times*, in a recent article on the condition of the Roman people at the present day, speaks of "Rienzi the *last* of the tribunes" as "an atrocious humbug;" but of course, I make no comparisons.

Mr. Colenso says the duties of his auditorship "are not merely those of common Auditors, viz.,—to cast up and correctly place accounts already paid, (duties which may be performed by common clerks,) but to scrutinise all demands on the public purse—to control and check the expenditure of public money, and to see that none is spent beyond the amounts and for the purposes sanctioned by the people's representatives in Council—and all this has to be done before any of the public cash can be drawn or paid."

If our provisional Superintendent has really laid down any such duties, I beg leave to tell him that he is conducting the public business, perhaps in a new, but certainly in a very loose manner. It is the peculiar duty of a *Superintendent* to scrutinise all demands on the public purse, and to issue warrants through a Treasurer, or responsible clerk acting as such, for all items of expenditure. It is the business of an *Auditor to examine and report on the periodical accounts*. Where is the check if this usual practice be departed from? It will be seen at a glance by any practical man of business how very naturally an Auditor, entrusted with such powers as Mr. Colenso *says he is*, might; nay, probably will, imperceptibly and by degrees become master of the public "till"; and I am not aware that there is any bond of security required from an Auditor, for the faithful performance of his duties, whatever these may be.

How preciously verdant William Colenso Esq., must think his "Brother Settlers!"—the Independent Electors of the Town of Napier—the *twenty two* people of whom he stands so valiantly forth as the tribune—when he expects them to swallow his brazen faced assurance that he accepted this very office of Provincial Auditor "the better to serve their interests." And it is quite refreshing to hear him trying to gammon them about "the province having great need of a tried man of courage, and of independent mind and station (!!!) to fill that important situation,"—basely insinuating in the next paragraph that, previous to his appointment, the treasury had been extensively plundered. Having thus filled their minds with dark suspicions he gently leads them to what was, after all, uppermost in his thoughts—the salary. "You know," says he, "the salary is small." Is £150 a year so very small an object to a man in his *position or station*? Many 'common clerks,' (how contemptuously he looks down from his perch on these inferior beings)— both in public and private service in New Zealand, of as good abilities, of greater experience in lay business, and certainly quite as respectable in every way, work long hours, day by day, throughout the year, in situations of great trust, for such a salary or little more.

On reading that precious piece of balderdash and unblushing effrontery—
Mr. Colenso's late electioneering address—I was irresistibly and ludicrously
reminded of the pretty little story of Red Riding Hood and the wolf. When that
interesting innocent reached her poor, sick, grandmama's cottage in the wood,
with a basket of fruit for her regalement, a hungry wolf, which had made rather
a tough banquet of the old lady, and then taken her place in bed disguised in her
habiliments, gammoned our little favourite to put herself in his clutches in a manner
very similar to the proceedings of our friend the Auditor when trying to gain the
confidence of his constituents. "What great arms you've got grand-mama" says the
rather astonished Red Riding Hood.—"The better to hug you, my dear," replied
the horrid wolf, and immediately after transferred the confiding cherub into his
victualling office.

And so with the first of the tribunes. Some of his backers thought it rather
strange after all his professions that he should turn out to be only a greedy place-
hunter, and had been expressing their surprise accordingly; on which he coolly,
and with unparalleled assurance, only to be approached by his kinsman the
aforesaid wolf, informs his brother settlers—"I accepted this very office of Provincial
Auditor, *the better to serve your interests.*"

Beware, I say, of noisy patriots, who are only wolves in sheep's clothing; and as to
the Auditorship, the Council will, I trust, spoil that pretty little job when it meets.

I am, &c.,

ECONOMIST.

§ 1859 TO THE EDITOR.
Hawke's Bay Herald 15 October.

SIR,—You will greatly oblige by inserting the following questions, and answering
the same as the common illuminator of the people:—

1. Did William Colenso Esq., sign the warrants in the month of September,
   as Wm. Colenso, Auditor, acting for T.H. FitzGerald Esq.
2. If William Colenso Esq., did sign the warrants as acting for T.H. FitzGerald
   Esq., Superintendent, was the act legal without his having been gazetted as
   Deputy Superintendent.
3. Can his Honor at any time he thinks proper depute another man to use the
   powers vested in him by the Constitution Act, without notifying the same in
   the "Gazette."
4. When William Colenso Esq. signs warrants as acting for T.H. FitzGerald Esq.,
   is Wm. Colenso Esq., not then nominally Superintendent.
5. Can you inform the public how they ought to address the Provincial Auditor,
   as his offices seem multifarious. I think his title must be doubtful, and more
   particularly so as the Returning Officer addresses him simply as "William
   Colenso Esq.," and people take the Returning Officer as a high authority
   in such matters.

Yours truly,
ENQUIRER.

Napier,
Oct. 12, 1859.

❖ **1859 OPEN COLUMN.**
Hawke's Bay Herald 22 October.

SIR,—You have already more than once called the attention of your readers to the "Native King movement." There is a branch, or rather, perhaps, the very stem and support, of the same now actively working among us; which is highly antagonistic to the advance and prosperity of the Province and of its Settlers; and which every Settler should be made acquainted with, and should lend his aid to expose and bring to nought, of course I mean the *Runanga*—Native Parliament, "Wittenagemote," Council, or Inquisition. This Confederated Society or Association is now in "full-swing" among the Natives of this District; and, flushed with success, having succeeded so well among them, it is now seeking not only to oppose the Settlers' good; but also the Government both Provincial and General. I have very good reasons for believing this *runanga* to have vastly more powers here (over the Natives) than in Waikato whence it originated and emanated; and I am apprehensive (and sorry indeed to have to pen it) that it has lately received strength through the unwary acting of some Europeans. During Mr. McLean's late sojourn among us I had the opportunity of more than once conversing with that officer on the subject of the *runanga*, and our views of it (I am happy to say) agree: Lands, that Mr. McLean had purchased from the rightful owners and paid for, are now sought by the *runanga* to be restored—the purchase-money being brought back by the *runanga*, while the unpurchased Lands of the District are entrammelled by the written promises of many of the Proprietors to the Native King, to whom they have been made over, with the avowed determination never to sell a portion of them to Europeans. Roads, (both Te Aute and Middle,) on which some thousands of pounds have been spent, are sought to be immediately stopped. And Cattle to be restrained from grazing on wild open Native Lands. While the Natives themselves (especially the middling and lower classes) are most unmercifully dealt with; their own chiefs being powerless to help them—either through having consented to, or joined, the *runanga*, or their being afraid of it! Now the *runanga*, Sir, obtains this immense power, because, being of native origin and not unrelated to the *tapu* ('taboo'), it quite falls in with the native genius; and it is the more effectual from its working (*sub dio*) *i te aroaro o te tokomaha* (open and in the presence of all), quickly energetically powerfully and authoritatively for the public (Native) good!! and this under the guise of seeming good—yea, of religious good—the most detestable of all disguises. Inquisition-like it meddles with every thing: it will neither allow its decisions to be reconsidered nor delayed. And if the question is asked (by a white,) why such and such is done, he is curtly answered with "It is the will of the *runanga*;" ("*Le Roy le veult!*") or, "It is for good"!! However heavy their money fines may be, they are immediately paid, or rather taken by the officers of the *runanga* in the shape of Horses and other property. Two young Chiefs, Te Kuru and Wi, sold to Mr. McLean in July last some land at Porangahau (which they clearly inherited from their ancestors); Te Kuru was paid £130 and Wi £300. Very recently the *runanga* has been to Porangahau, and this money (though in great measure spent) was there collected and offered to Mr. McLean, who most properly and justly refused it. Now the *runanga* has brought it to Napier to the Provincial Government, and finding the Provincial Government will have nothing to do with it, will still (they say) seek to return it to the General Government at Auckland! The "Queen" (Hineipaketia) and the Chief Hori Niania also publicly sold some of their Land to Mr. McLean for £300.—this also is sought to be set aside by the *runanga*. I could give you, Sir, a great many cases, large and small, in which the *runanga* has promptly and mischievously acted, were such necessary, or had you room.

On Saturday last the Superintendent met the Chiefs Te Moananui, Paraone, and Karaitiana at Napier, (according to arrangement made with them by letter,) to talk over and agree about carrying the Middle Road over the open and wild Native land between Ngawhakatatara and Patangata; and so save the twice crossing the dangerous Tukituki river within the short distance of 3 miles, as well as the heavy travelling in its shingly bed.—A matter by which the Natives themselves living on or near the line of road would be equally benefitted with the whites. (His Honor, I should have premised, had, last week, endeavoured by letter, &c., to get them to meet him at Ngawhakatatara, but was hindered through the *runanga*. At that place, however, he saw the Chief Paratene, who resides there, and who readily acquiesced to the road passing over his portion of the Land.) Well: those chiefs, part proprietors of that tract of land, came attended by the *runanga*, and the Waikato Native Minister plenipotentiary of the Native King. The "talk" lasted from noon till sunset; during which the Chiefs were patiently heard, and all their many reasons and arguments adduced were met and answered—I think, I may safely say, fully; but, like as it is with us—

"*The man convinced against his will*

Is of the same opinion still"—

So with them: for as fast as they were driven from each and every position they always managed to fall back into the impregnable solid square of the *runanga*; against which neither the dash of cavalry, nor the modern sword-bayonet, nor even Sir W. Armstrong's steel gun would (I fear) have any effect! His Honor was pleased to ask me to help him on the occasion, as Interpreter, &c.,—and at last, on seeing to what a height of imprudent folly they had arrived, I could not refrain from quietly warning them (as an old friend, and as a Member of the Provincial Council,) that, inasmuch as they had sold their back lands to men like themselves and not to winged birds, and had kept the frontages over which roads to the interior must be had, that the time would both surely and quickly come when their consent to roads bridges and public improvements would neither be asked nor required.

One point however was gained, yet not without difficulty—the Wahaparata bridge was at length, but not till we were about to part, yielded. And yet their objection to that bridge (for the making of which the Public Contract has long been signed and the materials on the ground) we were wholly unprepared for.—

But what, Mr. Editor, grieves me—more, than even the unthinking and vexatious conduct of the Natives—is, the unwary conduct of certain whites, to which I have above alluded.—Now Mr. McLean fully agreed with me, that the better way to dispossess the Native mind and so to overcome the *runanga*, was by wholly and always ignoring it, and never in the slightest possible way to acknowledge it; and I am happy to find that that officer constantly did so while at Porangahau, though at no small inconvenience hinderance and expense. I have been credibly informed, that at a meeting of the *runanga* held a fortnight back at Te Waipukurau, to hear (among other matters) charges preferred against Matthew Meke an old Native Teacher there, (which however he denied, but which were said by the *runanga* to be proved, and the poor creature fined £100!) a Settler present strongly urged Matthew "to confess to the *runanga*." Of course the shrewd *runanga* sees its authority seemingly acknowledged by a European,—and perhaps, by a man who should have said (if he cared to say anything),—"Matthew, do not heed this unlawful tribunal; pay no attention to it." Further: Matthew having no money wherewith to pay, the *runanga* took his horses; and I have been also credibly informed, that another Settler (from Te Aute district,) said, "If Matthew confesses I will arrange with the *runanga* about the horses": here (supposing it to be true) is another most unwise strengthening of this mischief-making *runanga*. Again, I have been informed, that a Settler at Waipureku who had had a trifling article stolen, and who had found it in the possession of a native living near, had after making some stir about it received the article back (or a pecuniary recompense) through the *runanga*: this also (if true) is certainly a most inconsiderate mode of acting. And I greatly fear, Sir, that through some of our fellow-settlers thus continuing to act—in order to get debts paid, or stolen or missing articles found and returned, the *runanga* will point to its use to and support from Europeans, and vaunt of its working for *good*, and so become firmly established, only eventually the better to annoy the real good and prosperity of the Province.

Another statement, which, I am sure, both grieved and vexed the Superintendent on Saturday, was made by the Chief Karaitiana—viz. that one great reason why they were so much against the roads being formed was, that they had been repeatedly told by several whites, that the completion of such roads would be their own sure enthralment and ruin,—and much more to that effect. Now is it not almost beyond belief, that such insanely speaking whites should be found among us? Is any language strong enough to condemn, or any punishment too heavy to be inflicted for such atrocious conduct? Who can tell what the ultimate consequences of the unthinkingly casting about of such sparks may be? I well remember, Sir, the consequences of similar conduct in the very commencement of the Native war at Wellington in March 1846, and which took place while I was staying in that town: Sir G. Grey, with the kindest intentions, suddenly left Wellington one morning in the government steamer for Porirua, to see the Chief Te Rauparaha; had his Excellency then seen him, I have little doubt but that war might have been prevented. Be this as it may, while the steamer was going out of the harbour some low thoughtless whites told the Natives living at Kaiwharawhara—"Ah! Governor gone to make-a-tye, and hang-up Rauparaha!" In a twinkling sundry Natives were on horseback racing against time to Porirua, and reached there just before the steamer, and quite in time to get Rauparaha to run to the woods, and so utterly to frustrate all the Governor's good intentions.

I may further be allowed to state, that I have told the Natives, (in their highly figurative way,) that the *runanga* has no foundation—is a thing of yesterday—a mushroom without either ancestry or legs:—that there can not be but three sources of authority, to (or among) them—viz, 1. the Queen, and through Her Majesty all lawfully constituted secular authorities: 2. the Church in Ecclesiastical matters: 3. the principal Chief of each tribe in certain matters affecting his own tribe:—and as the *runanga* clearly comes from none of them, and is not supported by them, it cannot have any proper authority. Now the *runanga* wishes to establish itself on Church or Religious authority; in fact it asserts as much! And I cannot help thinking, that it is a cause of regret that those who possess official authority in the church, or churches, do not act more energetically and decidedly in this matter; as by their so doing they would effectually cut the very sinews of the *runanga*, and thus its hold on the minds of the many would be for ever weakened if not destroyed.

In conclusion I would add, (and I hope that I shall be believed to have a little insight into Native matters, as well as to have the welfare of the Province at heart,) that I would highly recommend to all a firm and temperate mode of acting with reference to the *runanga*: never allow of its authority in any degree or share: no, not even if by so doing a person might gain much thereby.—It may be some one may have lost his horse—or may need Native workmen—or cannot be paid money justly due without applying to the *runanga*: still, be patient; never look to it for aid; never allow of its proceedings. And, whenever it is spoken of, speak of it (if you notice it at all—for often *silence* will be found to be the best,) in quiet calm language, as a mere passing shadow—a wind—a whim of the day.

> *I am, Sir,*
> *Yours very truly,*
> *WM. COLENSO.*

Waitangi,
Oct. 17, 1859.

LETTERS 1860–1869

WILLIAM COLENSO 1860–1869

1860   Appointed acting Provincial Treasurer.

1861   *January* accepts nomination for Parliament, eventually elected; meets
Coupland Harding at a book auction.
July joins opposition benches in Auckland; moves from Waitangi to Napier.
Willie returns from relatives in Northland; 1861–4 Inspector of Schools.
Hawke's Bay Times begins publication.

1862   *June* found guilty of illegally occupying the mission land at Waitangi; his old
chapel at Te Awapuni burned by Hauhau; appointed School Inspector for
the Province.
September writes to J.D. Hooker, so recommencing regular correspondence
with Kew.

1863   Re-elected to Provincial Council, but resigns: writes *To the electors of the town
of Napier*; re-elected in March; dropped by McLean as Provincial Treasurer.

1864   Political skirmishes; exhibition essays ordered. T.B. Harding buys *Hawke's
Bay Times* from Yates brothers.

1865   Resigns seat on Provincial Council, re-elected 2 weeks later.
March defeated by McLean in election.
June Mantell writes asking Colenso to start a Māori-English dictionary;
Exhibition essays written; Colenso elected FLS; Wellington becomes capital.

1866   Militia battles Hauhaus near Napier; Colenso working on a Māori-English
dictionary.

1867   Infected forefinger impairs writing.

1868   Colenso working on a Māori-English dictionary; two New Zealand
Exhibition papers published in *Transactions of the New Zealand Institute* Vol. 1.
Willie leaves for England.

1869   Colenso working on a Māori-English dictionary.

❖ 1860 OPEN COLUMN.
Hawke's Bay Herald 4 February.

SIR,—One month of our new year has already gone and we have entered on the short second; and the next month (March) is the one in which by law all persons wishing to become Voters must send in their claims to the Registration Officer. If they do not they lose their right for another year. And this also extends to the amending or altering of qualifications; that is, all such must be done in the month of March. Now we very well know that there was no small outcry made last year by a large number of Voters, at their being unceremoniously struck off the Roll by the Revising Officer. But the wrong is not by any means to be wholly placed to his accounts. In many cases it was the fault of the claimant, through not properly describing his qualification; and in others, through not giving a proper legal qualification. It was partly too (as in my own case) the fault of the transcriber of the attested qualifications—who made a "mull" of his copying. While, no doubt, a pretty good share is to be laid to the Revising Officer for the haste in which he hurried through his business and closed his Court. But, Sir, be it as it may, the past is past. Now then, what should follow?

1. Do you yourself, like a veritable good Editor and guardian of the People's Public rights, begin sounding forth and weekly reminding them of their duty and privilege throughout this and the next month.

2. Do you, all of you, friends Countrymen and Settlers of this new and fast-growing Province of Hawke's Bay—all of you who have not yet been Registered—all of you who have been struck off and yet possess proper qualifications—all of you who have since got more and additional qualifications in other Electoral Districts of the Province—do you look to it, that you mind and register in time. Don't forget that you must register yourselves in March, or you lose all chance and right for another year. I speak particularly to the working classes and the newly arrived among us.

3. Do you, all good settlers and well-wishers to the prosperity of our Province of Hawke's Bay who are already registered and Voters,—do you all keep a good look-out in your various neighbourhoods, and see to it that you do your duty to your Country and to your unregistered neighbour, and remind him of what he has to do, and put him in the way how to do it.

4. Let us all unite in shewing to the N.Z. Provinces, and to the world at large, our *bona fide* number of freeholders and qualified electors. Depend upon it there is no better way of stopping the "chaffing" and taunts of Wellington, and of those others (if any there be) like her;—and of shewing forth the wisdom of Governor Browne and his Ministers in forming and carrying the New Provinces Act. Indeed: is it not a duty which we owe them? And will not our shewing forth our true British strength tell in the House of Representatives soon about to meet? And while we have (as true chips of the old block—John Bull,) grumbled heartily at the Revising Officer; now let it be seen, that we are determined to a man to use our utmost exertions in again, demanding

and securing our just and legal rights and privileges. Most particularly would I call upon all who last year were struck off the Roll to be very sure timely to reassert their proper and amended claims. If not, then the Revising Officer (who will be sure to be on the lookout,) may justly turn round in his turn, and say,—"great cry, little wool."

5. Sir, I should very much like to see two things done: the one, for a Public Meeting to be called, here in the town of Napier, to consider this matter; the other, for a Working Committee to be appointed, in order to enquire after all unregistered persons—to communicate with them,—to put them in the proper way of legally registering,—to point out the legal objection which may be made,—to scrutinise the published Roll of the Registration Officer,—to attend the Revising Officer's Court on behalf of registered electors residing at a distance,—and so do their utmost to secure to all their electoral rights.

I quite think it is highly needful fully to exert ourselves in this cause, for I well know the many enemies we have to deal with; on the one hand, the backwardness and the want of thought, the every-day moil and toil and the terrible colonial disease—procrastination or putting-off; on the other hand, the old Philistines, who hate nothing more than the idea of "the 40-acre wretches" becoming Voters, and so being equal with themselves. Such men (though few) will not be wanting to throw impediments in the way. But "forewarned, fore-armed."

In conclusion, Mr. Editor, allow me again to beg of you, as a good and trusty "*Herald,*" to sound your clarion truly and well, and to keep on sounding until the great tournament is ended, and for a guerdon you shall have much more than a fair lady's praise.

I am, Sir,
Your most obedient,
WILLIAM COLENSO.

❖ 1860 TO THE EDITOR.
Hawke's Bay Herald 11 February.

SIR,—In fulfillment of a promise made in my short address to the Electors of the Town of Napier in your last week's issue, I now write. I intend to confine myself strictly to facts; and so deliver "a plain unvarnished tale," without rhetorical flourish.

In June, 1859, after some preliminary arrangement, (of which I may just mention two parts, *viz.* that my engagement as Auditor was not to occupy more than half of my time,—and that my aid as Interpreter &c. was to be afforded when I should be in town attending to my duties as Auditor;)—well, in June I accepted (as I take it) the office or offices I have ever since held; as will clearly appear from the following Official letter notifying my appointment;—as well as from the open and well-known fact of my having been from that time so engaged.—

"Superintendent's Office,
Napier, June 15, 1859:

"SIR,—I have the honor to convey to you an official notification of your appointment to the office of Auditor for this Province, at a present salary of £150. per ann., which you will be entitled to draw from the 1st instant; and should you be willing to give me the assistance I may require in transacting with the Natives from time to time, I will recommend the payment to you at the next meeting of Council of a sum not less than £50. per ann. for services you may render me in the management of Native affairs."

> (signed) T.H. FITZGERALD,
> Superintendent.

As a necessary consequence it followed that I lost my seat in the Provincial Council. Therefore, in August last, the Electors of the town of Napier were called on to elect a Member, and they again did me that honor.

At the late meeting of our Provincial Council, (called together for a few days only to pass the necessary estimates,) my name appeared on the estimates (as laid in manuscript on the Council table) as *"Auditor and Interpreter,"* with a proposed increase to my salary of £50. per year (*as, indeed, promised by the Superintendent in his letter containing appointment*). This addition was at first opposed by the Members for Waipukurau, but ultimately carried by a large majority.

I, however, felt so much hurt at the opposition which had been made,—and which I considered most uncalled for, as my *constant* attendance on my duties was so notorious,—that I feelingly said, (as reported by you), that "I objected to any increase of salary, although, at the same time, I was not half paid for the work I did."

Very soon after I received another Official letter; of which I also give a correct copy.—

> Superintendent's Office,
> Napier, Dec. 1, 1859.

"SIR,—I have the honor to inform you, that your Salary has been voted by the Provincial Council at the rate of £200. per annum, from 1 January 1860."

> (signed) T.H. FITZGERALD,
> Superintendent."

After a few days consideration I replied to this letter as follows:—

> "Auditor's Office,
> Napier, Dec. 9, 1859.

SIR, I have the honor to acknowledge the receipt of your Honor's letter of the 1st instant, informing me that my "Salary has been voted by the Provincial Council at the rate of £200 per ann., from 1st January 1860.

"Before, however, that I proceed to give you, Sir, my thoughts and determination respecting the above,—I feel that I am, in all honourable duty, bound to thank your Honor for placing the proposed increase to my salary on the Estimates, (and so fulfilling your promise made in your letter to me conveying my appointment,) as well as for the kind truthful and firm statement respecting my services made by you in the Provincial Council.

"As we were both in our seats in the Council (as members for Napier) during the passing of and the discussion on the Estimates for the 1st quarter of 1860, I have no occasion to repeat here what was then said by some of the Country Members respecting the proposed addition to my salary; and which (eventually) led me to state, that "whilst I considered myself not half-paid for my services, I would not accept of the proposed increase.—

"This was my expression then: this is my determination now.—

"It is true, that, subsequently, the Members for Waipukurau both severally said (in this office), that they regretted what had been said; and had they but fully known how things really were, no opposition would or could have been made, &c., &c. Yet, as such statements were only made to me privately, I cannot allow them to have any weight towards altering my publicly expressed resolution.

"At the same time, Sir, I desire most heartily to fulfil the duties of my office as Provincial Auditor: and all the assistance I can possibly render you in all your public transactions with the Natives, either as Interpreter or Native Secretary, I hope also to be ever ready to give to the utmost of my ability while I may have the honor to hold my present office.—

(signed) "WILLIAM COLENSO."

Which answer of mine I have also acted upon,—having only drawn, on the 31st January last; my old and usual pay,—*viz.* £12. 10s.

And here I would submit two plain questions—1st.,—What *new duties* have I now to perform, which I had not from the date of his Honor's letter to me in June last? And, 2nd.,—What new office have I that I should again be called to resign the seat in the Council to which the electors of the town had elected me?

Sir, I have no doubt but that the many who read this will quite agree with me, and reply alike to each question,—NONE. "*Then why did you resign*" will of course follow; and to this very proper enquiry I have an answer ready.—

—Because I know that it would very soon be said, (by those who are waiting for opportunities,)—"Colenso shirks the question!" "Colenso is afraid to resign and go again to his constituents!" And so, rather than such shall be said of your Member,—rather than give them the merest semblance of a hold upon me—and through me, the Council or the Electors of the town,—I have taken the "short cut" and resigned, to cast myself again in all open confidence upon the good-will of the town of Napier.

I am, Sir,
Yours very truly,
WILLIAM COLENSO.

Napier,
Feb. 7, 1860.

❖ 1860 OPEN COLUMN.
Hawke's Bay Herald 14 April.

SIR,—I was not a little surprised to see in your last week's issue certain remarks stated by you to have been made by Mr. Alexander, (member for Napier country district,) and placed by you under the general head of *Provincial Council*; giving the unwary to suppose that such remarks were really made to or before the same. That Mr. Alexander did speak much as you have reported is no doubt correct enough; but, the council having previously adjourned, there was none then sitting. No notice could therefore possibly be taken of what he then said; to say nothing of the great irregularity of speaking on a subject of which no motion had been given, or for which leave has not been specially obtained; especially when (as in this case) the words or conduct of a member of council is strongly reproved. Had you, Sir, allowed those words of Mr. Alexander to remain in the obscurity to which they were unanimously consigned, I venture to think you would have acted more wisely. As it is, and as I take it, I have no alternative but to ask you to publish the following letter to Mr. Alexander—a gentleman whom I have long known, and for whom I have ever had the highest regard.

> *I am, Sir,*
> *Yours truly,*
> *WM. COLENSO,*

To A. ALEXANDER ESQ., M.P.C.

"Per favor of Editor of Hawke's Bay Herald"

DEAR SIR,—My attention has been called to a statement in the "Herald" of last week, in which the Editor reports you as publicly saying:—"The natives were grieved to hear that remarks to their prejudice had been made in the council by one who knew them well and intimately, and who should have regarded them with feelings of more deference and respect." Now there can be little doubt but that I am the individual referred to by you. And as such a remark is now published to the world as coming from a gentleman who has not only long and intimately known both the natives of Ahuriri and myself, but who, also, heard what I did say in my place in council at the time alluded to (when speaking on the motion concerning the resolution of sympathy and thanks to the Governor of New Zealand and to the Superintendent of Taranaki). Sir, I have taxed my memory; I have enquired of those who were present at the time, both in the council and in the gallery; and I have looked over what I am reported in the "Herald" as having said on that occasion, and I cannot tell what it is to which you, or the natives, or both so pointedly allude. What did I then say beyond the truth which is now by you so strongly objected to? which is so very grievous to be borne? If any such very prejudicial remarks were made by me in the council, why were they not *then* met and opposed? Why did not Tareha's friend do so? at a time, too, when my sayings were living and present and could be noticed. On the contrary, Did you not say, that you "generally agreed with what had fallen from both the members for Napier"? that you "entirely concurred in what had been said regarding the course pursued by the Governor; and quite agreed that it was proper and just for the council to express sympathy with the settlers of Taranaki who were quite victims to the aborigines of that part of the country"? [*vide* "Herald," March 31st.] Further, Did any other member offer a single adverse remark? Was not the council unanimous upon that resolution? Sir, I believe that I may very fairly question *your* right to make any such condemnatory remark, when I consider the very strong applauding language you (generally too so cautious) used respecting what the two town members had said who had preceded you in the debate. I, also, think, that I may properly enquire, (seeing that you yourself are commonly spoken of as having been their informant,) Who told the natives that any such prejudicial remarks concerning them had been made in the Council? And, why, in their making such a complaint to you, were they not by you at once set right? You could have told them what had really been said: you could also if you pleased, have translated for them word by word all I said (as reported in the "Herald") with the whole of the resolution of the council. If it be so that they object to what I really said, or to the resolution, I have nothing further to say—save, that I am prepared to stand by both alike. If, on the contrary, they object to some strange language they have been led to believe me to have said, or to some bugbear of their own, or to the surmisings of a guilty conscience, they must fall back upon the authors.

In conclusion, I will add, that, at the time of your (irregularly) making the statement referred to, I was recommended (for several reasons) not to notice it. So it dropped. And, as I have already said, I think it would have been much better if it had not been again resuscitated. As, however, it has, I find myself obliged to call your attention to it for some explanation; which, in the present excitable time, I cannot but think highly necessary.

> *I am, Dear Sir,*
> *Yours sincerely,*
> WM. COLENSO.

Napier, April 10, 1860.

§ 1860 LOCAL INTELLIGENCE—PUBLIC MEETING.
Hawke's Bay Herald 21 April.

On Monday, pursuant to invitation by public advertisement from William Colenso Esq., one of the town members, a large number of the electors met at Ferrers' hotel. T.D. Triphook Esq. having been called to the chair, opened the meeting in a few words. Mr. Colenso then proceeded to address the meeting—first apologising for not being so fully prepared to speak as he would have liked, owing to his attendance that day at a meeting at the pa whakaairo. He then stated that, with, reference to the last session of the Provincial Council, although the reports which appeared in the "Herald" were very fair and as full as could be expected, yet that much remained which could not be fully explained within the limits of a newspaper. He then referred at some length to the subjects—15 in number—which he had initiated during the session;—the resolution of sympathy with their fellow colonists at Taranaki and of approval of the Governor's policy; the memorial for an increase of representation; the publican's licensing bill, the object of which was that the indiscriminate sale all over the country of spirits in 2 gallons should be restricted by the issue of a license &c. Having adverted to these at some length he would ask the electors to say whether or not he had done his duty. On many of these subjects, particularly in the land regulations, he had stood alone, and had done anything but increased the number of his friends, for he had incensed the natives and many of the country settlers. To be in this position and then to find that his constituents were not prepared to back him up, was to be in a very unenviable one. He considered that his constituents should either be prepared to do so, or to accept his resignation. He was quite ready to continue in council and do his duty in it, but only on condition that the electors approve of his conduct. Of the 15 subjects he had mooted in the council, not one had reference to his own interest; on the contrary, he had, by making enemies, lost considerably. He had no wish to back out of the duties of their member—especially with troublous times in prospect—but the electors must do their duty and give him such support as they could.—

§ 1860
Hawke's Bay Herald 21 April.
TO SPADE LABORERS.
TENDERS will be received until the 23rd instant, by WILLIAM COLENSO, for the digging, levelling, and clearing about 3 acres of enclosed ground, adjoining his dwelling-house on the hill at Napier.

For particulars, &c., apply to JOHN WADE, On the Premises.

§ 1860 ELECTION FOR GENERAL ASSEMBLY.
Hawke's Bay Herald 28 April.
On Thursday, pursuant to announcement by the Returning Officer, a meeting of electors was held in front of the school room, Napier, for the purpose of nominating a fit and proper person to represent this district in the General Assembly....

Mr. Thomas Edwards proposed Wm. Colenso Esq., which was seconded by Mr. Wm. Smith....

Mr. Colenso came forward to address the meeting. If ever a man was taken on the hop, he was to-day; he was totally unprepared, for such a thing. He would ask to be allowed to withdraw.

In the first place, he did not wish to put the province to unnecessary expense; in the second, Mr. FitzGerald was much the fitter person to represent them. Between that gentleman and himself there was, except on one or two points, no great difference of opinion. The Returning Officer here pointed out to Mr. Colenso that under the Act of last session of the Assembly, he could not thus summarily withdraw. There was a certain form of doing so prescribed in the Act. Mr. Wm. Smith asked Mr. Colenso if, in so withdrawing, he also withdrew his opposition to the land regulations. He (Mr. Smith) seconded Mr. Colenso's nomination because of his strenuous opposition to the same, in distinction from Mr. FitzGerald's support of them. Mr. Colenso said that, seeing he could not withdraw in one way, he trusted those who were his friends would hold up their hands against him at the show of hands, and thus allow the honor to devolve upon Mr. FitzGerald. He did believe, apart from the land regulations, that Mr. FitzGerald was their man. With regard to these, he (Mr. Colenso) trusted that Mr. FitzGerald would see fit so to modify his opinions as more nearly to meet the views of his constituents. It was the part of a wise man to be always learning something; and he (Mr. F.) should not be an exception. But if there was a knotty question, that of the land regulations was the one; and the superintendent of a province had so many contending influences to reconcile, that it was one to him of peculiar difficulty. He hoped the electors would on the one hand hear an explanation of his policy from Mr. FitzGerald himself; and, on the other, both bear and forbear—give and take.

§ 1860 PUBLIC MEETING OF SUBSCRIBERS TO THE NAPIER SCHOOL HOUSE.
Hawke's Bay Herald 5 May.
In accordance with invitation to that effect issued by the recently appointed trustees or managers of the Napier school house, a meeting of subscribers, numerously attended, was held on the evening of Tuesday, the 1st inst.

On the motion of Mr. William Morris, seconded by Mr. James Grindell, the chair was taken by Mr. William Colenso.

The Chairman having read the advertisement by which the meeting was convened, expressed a hope that the trustees would be able to give a satisfactory explanation of their reasons for breaking off negotiations with the Superintendent in the matter of the school. It was a sad thing, with so many children about, to see so great a want of means of education. He had attended the meeting, not dreaming that he would be called upon to act as Chairman, but because he felt deeply interested in the cause of education, etc.

❖ 1860 OPEN COLUMN.
Hawke's Bay Herald 12 May.
SIR,—It was with no small amount of surprise, that I read (in your paper of last week) two statements said to have been made by myself at the Public Meeting of the subscribers to the Napier School.

You state, Sir, that, on my putting (as Chairman) the motion to the Meeting for the adoption of the Report, I said—"I *trusted* the Motion would be adopted." Allow me, Sir, to correct this; as it was morally impossible I could have said so. I might have said,—I "*supposed* the motion would be adopted"; or, "I *believed* it would" (from the many unmistakeable indications I had noticed of the temper of the Meeting). Again:—I am also reported to have said, that "*two-thirds of the contents* of the Irish National School-books were scripture lessons." Now, what I really said was, that, "I believed two-thirds of the Scriptures (such as should be read by the young, and alluding particularly to the New Testament,) were to be found in the Irish National School-books."

I also stated, (as a main reason why the objectionable term 'anti-religious' should be struck out from the Report,) that those Irish National School-books were assented to after long and deep consideration by the Clergy of Ireland;—including the Archbishops and

Bishops of the United Church of England and Ireland—the Archbishops and Bishops of the Roman Catholic Church in Ireland—and the Moderator and other influential Ministers of the Presbyterian Church there; and, that, therefore, an Education which comprised and encouraged those books could not be "anti-religious."—

Nearly £50 worth of those valuable books have already been received; some of which have been issued to schools: our Superintendent having lost no time (after the passing of the Education Act) in sending for and obtaining a good supply.

No doubt, Sir, that, in the considering of Schools for most Protestants *alone*, some such plan of Religious Education as that touched upon and approved of in the Report is theoretically good and pleasing. But, unfortunately, it is so in *theory* only. In *practice* such will assuredly be found to fail. And this not from any radical defect in itself, but from the sad defects and bias in our common human nature. Such a plan has been tried over and over, and always with failure. In fact, constituted as we are, the continued prosperity of any such a plan is chimerical and impracticable.—

As I equally dread any approach towards Religious controversy either among our small community or in the columns of a Newspaper, I studiously refrain from remarking on what I heard at that Meeting.—At the same time, as a Public man— as one who in that capacity assisted earnestly in framing and carrying the present Hawke's Bay Education Act,—I can not but consider it in some measure to be my duty to state my present opinion of that same Act; seeing, also, that, as Chairman, I was virtually hindered from declaring my sentiments at the Meeting.—

Sir,—as a man who has both studied and labored not a little for the welfare of my fellow-men,—as one deeply interested in the matter of Education—as one who has been many years engaged in the work of Instruction, and also as a Protestant Clergyman—I conscientiously avow my belief, that the Hawke's Bay Education Act is well-fitted for the general instruction of the Children of the Province, and one which all churches and denominations of Christians would do well to support.

Nevertheless, I do not for a moment suppose the said Act to be perfect; neither do I say that it is such an Act as I might like to see, provided we were all of one mind and way of thinking: but, when I duly consider our many varied and heterogeneous and (and perhaps) stubborn and inflammable minds;—the sad waste of time and talents which has for generations been made throughout Christendom, by each party struggling to have the upper hand in the matter of Teaching;—the still more rancorous spirit which all such party-striving inevitably engenders,—and the daily increasing wants of the many children around who are swiftly and for ever passing from the early and limited time and term of teaching:—I say, Sir, that when I duly consider all this, I am more than ever obliged to be of opinion, that the Hawke's Bay Education Act is both well-suited to the present time, and well-adapted to meet the wants of the Province of Hawke's Bay in matters of Education generally.

Oh! that men—Christian men—could but learn to view and consider things comprehensively, so as to speak and act for the general good! that they would but understand it to be their duty how and when to yield a little of party views, so as to obtain the hearty cooperation of the many! and so united, cordially labour together in love on the great and broad and open platform of improving the world!

> *I am, Sir,*
> *Yours truly,*
> WILLIAM COLENSO.

❖ 1860 OPEN COLUMN.
Hawke's Bay Herald 25 August.

SIR,—We have all heard of a "time to be silent and of a time to speak." For some time I have been considering whether the "time to speak" has not quite arrived; at least, for one who, from his position, knows a little more of public matters than many who have been both scribbling and talking about them and who (at the same time) is not a popularity hunter—does not intend to *rat*—and holds public offices without being glued to them.

In speaking then, or writing, Sir, on some of the common topics of the last few weeks, I shall essay to do so both calmly and reasonably; being vastly more inclined to sorrow than anger in consequence of what I have both heard and read, concerning our "Provincial bankruptcy"—"shameful squandering of public money"—"breach of faith to poor men"—"expensive government" and "fruits of separation." And here, Mr. Editor, you will please to allow me *en passant* to say that no small portion of my regret has arisen from the manner in which you yourself in your *Herald* have been pleased to speak of our present position. I cannot help believing, Sir, that it is ever the duty of every faithful officer or helper of the commonweal—from the lowest subaltern to the highest Field Marshal, or from the editor of the smallest sheet of news to the thunderer in the *Times*, to inspirit and cheer the people, instead of dispiriting and making them sad; especially in times of gloom, depression and anxiety. Huc, in his travels, tells us the Chinese have a saying,—"beware of making your hearts small" —and the Maories have a similar one; and we all know the value of a plucky chap, or a single encouraging expression, in a squall or gale of wind. If it be true that the arrival of a Merry-andrew or a first rate Punch and Judy, in a village does more to dispel the vapours than a doctor's shop; very sure I am that your lugubrious querulousness throughout your last four or five numbers has been a means of keeping the influenza among us—or, at least, of increasing its potency. Strike a higher chord man! to "There's a good time coming boys!" instead of your hurdygurdy griping ditties of "There is nae luck," and "Job's tears." Surely we have quite enough of the dismal in the melancholy tidings from Taranaki which every post and every *Herald* gives us?

But I must remember that I have promised to write calmly and reasonably. This I shall now try to do. And I hope that every *bona fide* settler in this Province, being a reader of your paper, will also calmly and reasonably consider what I say.

First, then, with reference to our "Provincial Bankruptcy" (as it is called). Sir, you very well know that the total amount of the Estimates for the year ending 1860, (as passed by the Provincial Council) was £45,444—of which sum about £24,000 was for roads and bridges and public works—and £6000 for harbour improvements.

Nearly the whole of this large sum of £45,400 (or at least £40,000) was looked for from the Land Revenue of the present year. As every building was immediately required,—and as the whole Province was in great want of roads and bridges, —(every cluster of settlers being clamorous to have a road to their homes made at once; and we well knew the wetness and short days of a New Zealand winter, and that roadmen and mechanics could not possibly live in such a season under their calico tents, (scarcely any party being anywhere snugly hutted,)—it was determined to make the most of the summer and to push on every road and work. And in order to this, the first meeting of the second session of the Provincial Council took place for a few days in November. Mark, then, a consequence:—the Province, instead of spending merely £22,722 in six months (just half of the sum voted for the 12 months), has spent in that time nearly £34,000; leaving but £10,000 to be raised and expended during the second half of the year. Where now is the "bankruptcy?" Rather let us admire and talk of the extraordinary fruitful yield of our newly-born Province of Hawke's Bay! which, in six months—with a frightful and threatening native war raging, and with the greater part of her own rightful Customs Revenue stopped, by-the-way by Wellington—could actually raise £7000 more, in half the year, than her estimated Revenue! That there should be a "tightness," or temporary want of money in the Provincial chest, under all the circumstances is not at all strange; it is no more than was to be expected, and should reasonably cause no alarm. I grant, if the Province had not been able to raise during the six months half of the money estimated for the year, then there would be some cause for alarm. Such, however, I have shewn, is not the case. Further: what has for the time increased the said "tightness" is the fact, that several heavy contracts amounting in all to a few thousand pounds, and for the completion of which no time was specified, have all been concluded nearly about the same time—making thereby an unusually heavy demand on the chest at once, and that too at the dead season of the year. Sir, if we calmly view the several great classes around us—sheep-farmers, agriculturists, merchants, and whalers, we shall find in every class a striking parallel. Would the owner of 5000 sheep be reasonably termed a "bankrupt," because he could not meet every pressing demand made on him in August or September? Or, would it be right to call the farmer who had 200 acres of grain crops a "bankrupt," if he could not promptly settle every account in November? And so with the merchant and whaler. Each great class has its own peculiar harvest or in-gathering time of wealth: just so with the Province; only with her it extends over the year. A 12 month's revenue must fairly be allowed to meet a twelve month's expenditure. While with her there is one far more sure and stable element than is to be found in any of the above mentioned great classes, namely *Land*. While Hawke's Bay has so many rich acres to dispose of she can never become " bankrupt."

Secondly: As regards our "shameful squandering of the public money." Sir, it is always difficult to deal with general charges, especially when made in a loose and vague way. Another of these usual weekly tirades has just appeared in your paper of this day, signed "An Honest Man" (*sic!*) If the writer is an Englishman, how is it that he has quite forgotten the wise and true adage of his forefathers, that "No honest man is afraid to tell his name?" It may be that public money may have been wasted; but can any one say that the Government has wilfully and designedly wasted it? It may be that the Government has not had in every case a shilling's worth for a shilling; but can any one prove such to be by its connivance or fault? Folks should bear in mind what exertions the Government has made in order to secure the best and the cheapest; and they should not (willingly) forget that very much of that which in other Provinces is cheap, is here necessarily dear. Our timber, whether *totara* or *kauri*, has to be imported; so that in this article alone, what would be 10s. or 12s. per hundred feet in Wellington Province is here 25s. Has any work been executed without first advertising for tenders, both in our local paper, and in those of other Provinces? And if the accepted tender (although in every case the lowest) has been high and the work greatly needed, is the Government to blame for accepting it? It may be that your Council may have sanctioned too great an expenditure (through not foreseeing the present native war); but if so, (and which remains to be proved) such expenditure was intended for the public good, and has been at all events spent right royally among us. And certainly so many thousands spent within the Province must have benefitted the settlers of the Province. Sir, very sure I am of two things: the one, that many persons who work for, or who supply the Government (including, as I know, not a few of these very railers themselves,) seek by every possible way to "stick it in" to the Government—or, in other words, to get as much money as they can from the public purse:—the other, that our much-abused Superintendent has ever striven hard (even to the introducing of "Requisitions" into every department) to lessen and control the daily expenditure. So that I myself (to give an example) cannot get a box of pens or a quire of paper without his sanction and signature. Would that every one in Government employ had but his energy and public spirit, and had heartily co-operated with him in this matter!—

Thirdly:—concerning our "breach of faith to poor men"—meaning thereby the workmen on the roads. A few plain words will suffice to shew the true state of this matter. In September, 1859, our Superintendent went to Auckland. At that time our laborers were very few, nothing like enough for a single line of road; and military labour (which we had had the advantage of on our town roads) was then nearly at an end, and soon after stopped. In order to get suitable laborers for the works, and to encourage immigration to the Province, his Honor offered a bonus (a week's wages) to every fit and able man who would come to Hawke's Bay to work on the roads; and, on his leaving Auckland, left the same terms with the government agents there. Several availed themselves of his offer, and came hither by different vessels. Early in January instructions were given to the agents, that no more were to be sent down. Notwithstanding, they continued to come. About that time positive orders were given to the captains of the 'White Swan,' 'Eliezer,' 'Zephyr,' and other vessels trading from Auckland, not to bring any more; still they brought them. And I have now by me (in the Audit office) the last accounts sent in by the captain of the 'Zephyr,' and others, in January last, for the bonus due to them as part passage money for several persons brought down by them; which accounts were refused to be paid by our "squandering" Superintendent, because those captains had been previously warned, and which money they consequently lost. Even after this many others arrived, both from Auckland and Wellington; in some cases having been written to by their acquaintances or chums, who had come on before them. Of course, those men who so came hither were received on the various roads and works, but without any bonus. In fact, the Government had no choice; the settlers either would not or could not employ them; and the men must either have been employed by the Government, or be in the daily reception of rations as Charitable aid from the same. They could not be allowed to starve. And it should be borne in mind and duly appreciated, that the roads were not stopped working until actually more money had been expended on them than had been voted. What then was the necessary consequence? Why, 1st that twice the number of men were employed than was originally intended: 2nd, that bad good and indifferent were all at work together; the bad, unfit, weak and old, spoiling the good, fit, strong, and young, or making them discontented: 3rd, the works which could have well supported half the number throughout the year, could only afford employ for all during the half of that time: and, 4th, instead of obtaining a selected industrious, thrifty, and useful lot of first-class immigrants (as was fondly hoped), who might by-and-by become independent and valuable settlers in our Province, it was found we had got some, of whom it may be safely said "their room was better than their company." Now, Sir, who is to blame for this? the Government? Not a bit of it. It was the men's own fault. Though, no doubt, a share of the blame (if blame there be) rests on the agents and captains, who, as a matter of course, chiefly thought of themselves. The men forgot the common saying "The more the merrier, the less the better fare."

Fourthly: I have to notice the (so-called) "expensive Government." Meaning, as I suppose, the expensiveness of that part of the Government which is, or has been, called into being through our having been made a Province. Really, Sir, I wonder some folks are not a little more modest; a little more careful. Would that people who will write, did but seek to make themselves fully acquainted with (at least) the subjects on which they choose to write. *Ne sutor ultra crepidam.*[1] Would that some folks did, or could think, ere they rush into your "Open Column." But what may not be looked for, when the old owl thought her young ones to be the handsomest birds in creation. Yesterday, by the "White Swan," I received some Wellington papers, and among them were two copies of the *New Zealand Spectator* of the 11th and 15th instant. In this of the 15th the sapient editor says (speaking of Ahuriri, and commenting on your information,)— "Complaints are general: of the insolvency of the Provincial Government; a fact which need not excite any surprise when the extravagant scale of its salaries is considered.... The Superintendent's salary is £600 a year, so that the inhabitants pay a tax of 5s. a head including children for the support of this one officer"!!! Admirable! He might just as truthfully have said that the officer commanding the 65th, costs his men £1 each!, or that the captain of the "White Swan" costs his crew £2 per

---

1   The shoemaker should not go beyond his last. I.S.G.

head! However, I have only to refer to the *Spectator* of the 11th instant (of only 4 days previous), to find words wherewith to oppose his precious statement. In this paper he gives us a full account of a public meeting held in Wellington for the relief of the sufferers at Taranaki; and at that meeting Mr. Moore, a well-known public gentleman and old settler, said—"He thought Wellington had done nothing for Taranaki, for the Government grant was nothing; *as there was not a man in Wellington who had paid a shilling towards it*." Now, Sir, either this speaker or that writer must be wrong in principle; for, while the two cases were decidedly parallel, their words are diametrically opposite! If the editor of the *Spectator* is correct, the £1000 voted by the Wellington Provincial Council from the public chest for Taranaki, is as much to be charged to every man, woman, and child of the Province of Wellington, as the £600 voted by Hawke's Bay Provincial Council for its Superintendent:—but he is not. Further: in your *Herald* of this day we have "An Honest Man" from Waipukurau saying,—"In this Province alone the last estimates passed amounted to £45,444. 16s. 7d., for a population—men, women, and children—of 2323, being a proportion of £20 to each individual." What a wonderful financier, political economist, and man of brains! (Oh! for Mr. Pepys and his diary!) Now, Sir, (throwing aside such stuff) every one who thinks knows that the fewer the people the more expensive (comparatively) must any form of Government be. Just so: the fewer the people the more expensive (if in like manner calculated) must the parson, or the schoolmaster, or the parish doctor, or the purveyor of a dinner, or the constable, necessarily be: there is no mistake about it: it cannot be helped. But now, Sir, what shall we say, when the premises whence the Editor of the *New Zealand Spectator* and "An Honest Man" of the Waipukurau drew their conclusions are alike vicious? Is this Government indeed supported by a "tax" that they have dared to make such a statement? It is, or ought to be, well known that this Government costs the settlers nothing. They would pay no more if the Government was much more expensive than it is; nor no less if there was no Government at all. I wonder what would be said if the Government had raised the price of all rural lands (as lately done at Otago) from 10s. to 20s. per acre? But, to return:—what is the real expense,—the real and whole sum total of salaries, as voted by and paid to this Provincial Government? Or, in other words, what in fact have we extra to pay in consequence of our separation from Wellington? I will give them:—

	£
Superintendent	600
Clerk	200
Provincial Council:—	
6 Members, £30 each	180
Speaker	100
Chairman of Committees	50

Messenger	100
Clerk	50
	480
Auditor, £200: Interpreter, £100	300
Registrar of Deeds	250
Director of Public Works	300
Total	2130

For (not to mention the officers of the General Government, such as the Resident Magistrate, his clerk, the Collector of Customs, &c.,) it will not, I think, be disputed that, if we had still continued part of the Province of Wellington, such officers as the Pilot and his boatmen, the Provincial Surgeon, the master of the Hospital and the Surveyors, would have been as a matter of course granted, and their expenses be much as they are now. And then the present Commissioner of Crown Lands and his two clerks, the Provincial Engineer, the Treasurer, and the Police, are all officers originally appointed by the Wellington Provincial Government, and, as a matter of course if we were still part of Wellington Province would be continued in office by her. Further: I may also remark—it is scarcely fair thus to grumble and that so early. As well might the sheep-owner in first investing in stock and run and homestead and drafting pens—or the merchant in laying in his stock of wares—or the whaler on his first outlay. Our investments of various kinds, particularly the steam-dredge, we have good reasons for hoping will return us amply for our outlay.

However if it be intended that our salaries ought to be I have little to say on this head. Such may, or may not be right. I hold, Sir, and I have always held that a man who receives the public money without rendering an equivalent is no other than a robber. And any Government which gives away the public money without obtaining an equivalent, or endeavoring to do so is fraudulent and base. It may be that some, or all, of our salaries are (through present and fortuitous circumstances) too high and will have to be lowered. It may be found convenient and expedient to unite some offices, so as to lessen the present expenditure; or it may be that the holders of some offices (seeing they cannot well be united to others) may so arrange as to have only to give half their time in their office for a half salary. Time is money with us all; and as I know somewhat of the value of time, I am a stickler for *quid pro quo*. Our next, or some future meeting of Council may settle all this; but I venture to think that Hawke's Bay has to keep a sharp look-out, lest through her incessant grumbling, she drive every able, faithful, fitting, and zealous officer from her service; and as we have not a great choice of men, the loss may be discovered too late.

Fifthly: I have heard that a few have gone so far as to "regret our separation from Wellington!" I have not, however, myself heard any one go to such a length as this; and I cannot help thinking that such a strange and farfetched notion could only have been uttered by some one of the notorious "minority of six." But, be this as it may, let us again come to facts. And when we speak of fact, we can only mean what we know or have experienced. And just as I know that fire burns, and that strychnine poisons, even so I know how it would now be with us had we never been separated from Wellington. Our revenue would have been carried thither for the advancement and embellishment of Wellington as the chief town of the Province; and this, owing to her known embarassment and want of funds, we may be quite sure would have been more especially the case. Not only should we not have had our steam-dredge in the harbour, and the buoy at Pania rock, and Government buildings, and roads and bridges; but we also should not have had the spending of all our money among us. For, be it known, and be it well pondered, that (rightly or wrongly spent) upwards of £25,000 has been spent here among us by our Government during the first six months of this year, and owing entirely to separation from Wellington! Yes, Sir, £25,000; of which sum it may safely be affirmed, reasoning from past dear-bought experience, and from what we know of the pressing monetary wants of Wellington;—a very small portion would have been spent here had we not been separated from her. Let any reasonable man knowing the past go through Napier, or stand upon any of the hills of Scinde Island overlooking the town, and let him ask himself (as I have done)—What would this town now be had we not obtained separation? Talk of "regretting separation!" as I take it, it is all the same as a rule of three sum; or, rather, as a sum in the Rule of Proportion: on the side of our still being part of Wellington we might at the utmost have, during the whole year (provided we proved strong at kicking and were not easily rebuffed) just £5000—instead of £45,000—or as 1 to 9. Whilst on the side of Hawke's Bay independent and separate we have the WHOLE—instead of the one-ninth, or perhaps, tenth! Now our extra expenses in the shape of salaries, through incurring which we secure all our Revenue, or £45,000, amounts to a trifle over £2000, as I have already shown. As much, then, as the whole of any desired good is better than a small part, so much are we easily proved to be the better for separation from Wellington:—*q.e.d.*

In conclusion, Sir, I trust you will forgive the length of my present communication. Its importance (if correct, as I deem it to be,) is great; and my public position—both as Provincial Auditor and as a member of the Provincial Council for the Town of Napier, prompts me to write fully and truly what I know, for the information and quieting of many of the scattered settlers of this Province, who, I fear, have been of late and in these exciting times unduly alarmed.

> *I am, Sir,*
> *Yours very truly,*
> WILLIAM COLENSO.

Waitangi,
August 18, 1860.

§ 1860 TO THE EDITOR.
Hawke's Bay Herald 8 September.

Sir,—I observe that the Reverend William Colenso, in a five column letter which he lately inflicted upon the readers of your valuable journal, begins it by accusing you of writing in a querulous and lugubrious style of the state of the Provincial Treasury. The rev. gentleman is surely the last who should bring such an accusation. Witness his dolorous whinings, during last session of the Council, over the hour taken for dinner by certain clerks in Government employ; and his dismal wailings over the supposed deficiencies of the Waipukurau Bench, or the unheard-of deliquencies of the publicans and sinners with which our Province is said to be infested. Yet the good man, all the while, not only takes his own dinner hour out of his official complement, but spends half his time at his rural residence of Waitangi, during which visits his office is shut up.

But to return to the charge against yourself. Your slight reference to the existing state of things did not strike me as being particularly gloomy; but how could you, in common honesty, put a bright polish upon the very rusty state of our Provincial Government affairs? As well might you labour to convince your readers that black is white, as satisfy them, if you tried, that things are not rotten in our little "State of Denmark." The true course is to "tell the truth, impugn it whoso listeth."

By the way, what does Mr. Colenso mean, with reference to the money that has been spent in the Province, by saying that it has been "right royally spent." Would he have us infer that it has been spent upon the reigning royal family of Hawke's Bay, of which he is a favored scion; or does he mean that the Province has right royally squandered its means, just as a drunken workman may be supposed to "knock down" his week's wages in the grog shop on Saturday night?

With reference to the letter generally, I think the Provincial Government has much reason to exclaim,—"Save me from my friends."

> *Yours, &c.,*
> SCRUTATOR.

❖ 1860 OPEN COLUMN.
Hawke's Bay Herald 8 September.

SIR,—Having noticed an assertion in your last week's Herald, that—"The proceedings of the (Native) Conference are actually over, and the members of it on the way to their respective homes, before the Governor's opening address is placed in the hands of the chiefs of this district!"—I have the honor to inform you, that "the Governor's opening address" was not only received here by our Superintendent before his late visit to Wellington (six weeks back), but that they were at that same time, in the hands of the chiefs of this district.

> *I am, Sir, Yours truly,*
> WM. COLENSO.

Napier, Sept. 4, 1860.

[Our information was received from a gentleman well known as an authority in native affairs, who had just returned from the interior, and who, in travelling, visited several pahs at which the Governor's speech had not been seen. And our own copy of the *Maori Messenger* containing the address in question had only just come to hand at the time we penned the paragraph to which our correspondent adverts. Ed. *H.B.H.*]

❖ 1860 OPEN COLUMN.
Hawke's Bay Herald 27 October.

SIR,—That some among us should be led in these stirring and excitable times to take strange and, sometimes, even perverse views of public matters, is not greatly to be wondered at. A considerate man, however, will always make every allowance for the peculiar standing of the observer, as well as the varied circumstances under which any object has been by him viewed. Granting this, it must also be yielded that a man is in common justice bound to ascertain the truth of a charge before he makes it. And if this simple and easy rule but be generally adhered to, how many erroneous charges arising from ignorance would annually fail to be made!

In your last week's paper I notice a letter from your correspondent F.C., who, writing on the rise, &c., of the Taranaki war, (and apparently on the popular and common sense side,) cannot omit aiming a blow at the Government. But as it has been with others so it is with F.C.; his charges mainly arise from ignorance, as I shall shew. He says:—"It was the duty of the Government of the Colony to lay a *clear, distinct, and strictly correct* account of the whole affair before Maori as well as the white population; and no better vehicle was required for this end than the "Karere Maori," provided the authorities took care that a sufficient number of copies were struck off and distributed, to allow one or more to every pah throughout the Colony. That the Government did not do this appears to me to be a serious error." Again, he says:—"But Rangitake's sitting quietly while Teira offered his land, and while the kaitaka mat lay at the feet of the Governor, appeared to shake their (F.C.'s Maori hearers) belief in the justice of Rangitake's cause, and led me to the opinion that a clear, distinct account from Mr. McLean, or some other influential official, printed and circulated among them, would at least have caused a difference of opinion among them, if it had not actually led them to admit the justness of the conduct of the Governor. That Mr. McLean has explained these matters to some of the Maori people whenever opportunity offered, I do not doubt, *in conversation*; but a printed account would have been of infinitely more importance, and would have been eagerly read and discussed by them all."

Sir, in the "Karere Maori" of July 31, (the very Government Maori serial mentioned above by F.C.,) this matter is given pretty fully. In that periodical (on this special occasion swelled from 4 or 6 to 62 pages) Mr. McLean himself again gives a clear and distinct account of the whole affair. Commencing at page 41, and ending at page 51, his recital occupies no less than 11 closely printed pages. Already, at page 48, has the statement been made, which is so earnestly desired by

F.C. to be yet made, viz:—that of "Rangitake sitting while Teira offered his land, and while the kaitaka (parawai?) mat lay at the feet of the Governor," &c., &c. And further, several copies of this periodical were very shortly after its publication in the hands of the principal natives of this Province. And if there had been but *one* copy among them—or *one* M.S. letter containing these facts,—F.C. must know well, that in less than a week after its having been received by any one chief of this Province it would have been known alike to all. F.C. has surely known enough of the natives, and also knows enough of their language to have known that their word or relation in important matters affecting themselves, (especially grave political ones,) should ever be cautiously entertained.

> *I am, Sir,*
>
> *Yours, &c.,*
>
> *WILLIAM COLENSO.*

Napier, Oct. 24, 1860.

❖ 1860 OPEN COLUMN.
Hawke's Bay Herald 3 November.

SIR,—Believe me, I unwillingly address you on this occasion. A sense of duty, however, prompts me to notice and refute the strange statements of your correspondent "Sincerity," which appeared in your last issue. Had Mr. Sincerity confined his remarks to myself,—or, had your paper a merely local circulation,—I certainly should not answer his letter. But, seeing that the Bench (of *three* magistrates), the Rev. Mr. St. Hill, Mr. Grindell, and myself, are all more or less attacked, to be altogether silent would be anything but proper.

I pass by the grammar of your correspondent (as he may be a foreigner, and therefore to be excused); also, his sneering and lowering remarks upon the magistrates (as he may have had a case unexpectedly decided against him in this very Court, and such might cause him to see things as if he wore green specs.); and shall proceed to notice what he says touching Mr. St. Hill and myself. Remarking, by the way, that Mr. Sincerity's statements are all of the *argumentum ad hominem*, or, rather, *ad populum* class; and therefore, at this peculiar time, calculated to do very much more harm than good.

Of Mr. St. Hill he says,—that "he took far too much interest in the case on behalf of the Maori race." And asks, "What right had Mr. St. Hill to converse with, or, perhaps, to prompt Capt. Lambert, one of the J.P.'s. who took the lead of the Bench on this occasion?".... "Have we not had enough of the interference of clergymen in public affairs? Have we to sit quietly by and see them exerting themselves on behalf of the Maories? Have we to come to the conclusion that they will always cross our path in favor of the so-called "ignorant," but, I say, cunning race? Whatever the intentions of these two gentlemen are, I will say they came into court for a specified purpose, and I maintain that they had no more right to interfere in the usual course of justice than any one else."

Alas! for the fussy vehement, and overtoppling indignation of Mr. Sincerity!! Now what are the facts of the case? the plain naked truth? Why, simply, that Mr. St. Hill sat as far from the Bench as the walls of the court allowed him,—that he never rose from his seat to speak to the Bench, but that Capt. Lambert (in an interval while the clerk was making his entries,) did rise and say a few words to him, of (as I believe, who sat next to him,) a purely common-place nature:—and that Mr. St. Hill, after quietly sitting for about 2 hours, silently left the Court.

How could it be supposed that any person—much less such a personification as *Sincerity*—could trump up such a story as this from such very slight grounds!

Concerning myself: I am (*in addition*) charged with—

1. "Interfering."
2. "Suggesting additions to evidence made on oath."
3. "Not only trying but succeeding in making alterations in the evidence given by a Maori in a Court of Justice."—
   (Shall I call this a wickedly clever climax—suggesting—trying—succeeding?)

But what are the facts,—the plain unadorned and simple truth?

1. That the defendant's attorney (Mr. Allen)[2], at the commencement of his cross-examination of the plaintiff Te Moana-nui, had more than once charged the Interpreter to the Court (Mr. Grindell) with holding a conversation with the plaintiff in the Maori language. (Forgetting that the defendant (John Blane) was standing between him and Te Moana-nui, and that he (Mr. Allen) had himself just said that "the defendant well-knew the Maori tongue.")
2. That the Bench decided, the defendant's attorney should propose his cross-examination questions to the Bench for their approval, prior to their being put to the plaintiff by the Interpreter of the Court.
3. That owing to Mr. Grindell the Interpreter being also Clerk to the Court he had a very heavy duty to perform, which I may truly call a 7-fold one, *viz:*—
   I. To attend to a question put by the defendant's attorney, often deep subtle, and peculiar, and very difficult to be rendered in the Maori language, and then to its modification by the Bench.
   II. To write such down.
   III. To put such in the Maori tongue.
   IV. To hear and obtain Te Moananui's answer.
   V. To translate orally and off-hand the same to the Bench.
   VI. To write the answers (translated) in the Court books.
   VII. To read it, *as written*, to the Court.
4. That I, being in the Court, and holding the office of Interpreter to the Provincial Government,) was asked by the Bench, whether the charge made by the defendant's attorney against the Court Interpreter was correct; and was also requested by the Bench to watch the case on behalf of all parties.

---

2   A gentleman who has only been a few months in the Colony, and who consequently knows very little of the Maoris and less of their language. W.C.

So much for the charge of "Interfering."

Further: touching my "suggesting additions." All the suggestions I recollect having made, were three; one to the defendant's attorney, one to the Interpreter, and one to the Bench. (1.) The defendant's attorney put,—"Have you ever had any transactions with the defendant?"—On this (and merely in order to save time and any further *strong* remarks from that gentleman to the Interpreter, and to make it plain to the Maori,) I suggested, that it would be requisite to define the "transactions," so as to be by the Maori understood. (2.) The Interpreter had used the words. *"rironga mai"* (good and pure Maori,) two or three times to Te Moana-nui, who, however, did not seem clearly to comprehend them; when I suggested (to the Interpreter,) *"hamaitanga"* (a word of similar meaning) to be used instead. (3.) On the word *"kite"* being used (as commonly) for to see, I remarked (to the Bench), that that word also meant *to know, to understand, to beware of,* &c.,—and, that the plaintiff, from his answers and remarks, had so understood it.

I scarcely need add, that I never once spoke to Te Moana-nui during the many hours the examination lasted.

So much for my "Suggesting additions."

As to the charge of my "not only trying but succeeding in making alterations in that evidence,"—this is soon disposed of.

I have already shewn how closely and heavily the Court Interpreter was engaged, and that, too, while he knew the Court was waiting for him!

On two occasions only (as far as I recollect), after he had read his *written* answers, did I remind him, that he had omitted writing a small portion; at one time, *one* word; at another, a short sentence of *four* words. *Which words he had himself less rendered in English to the Court when first giving his oral translation!*

So much for my "making alterations in Sworn Evidence"!!!

Let any one ask the defendant (John Blane), who heard all that I said, and who knew all the Maori language spoken in Court, whether I had dared to act as Mr. Sincerity had dared to say I did?

Had I not, Mr. Editor, already taken up so very much of your valuable paper, I should like to say a few concluding words to this Mr. Sincerity: but, as it is, I will merely call his attention to my letter in your last issue,—"that a man is in common justice bound to ascertain the truth of a charge before he makes it." And so I leave him to his own sincere and unenviable musings, and to the fair judgment of your many readers.

I am, Sir, yours &c.,

W. COLENSO.

Napier, October 29, 1860.

P.S.—In your next, and with your permission, I intend giving an illustration of Maori examination in a Court of Law.[3]

---

3   He didn't. I.S.G.

❖ **1860 OPEN COLUMN.**
Hawke's Bay Herald 17 November.

SIR,—Just, a word or two (with your permission) in reply to your correspondent F.C. in your last: I have not room for more. *This* letter of his has fully confirmed my suspicion with regard to the *animus* which incites him. Proved, by his unfair and garbled quotations from my letter, and by his building on such false premises; an excellent illustration of *suppressio veri* and *suggestio falsi*. F.C. says,—(as from me!) "The *ture whawhai* was dated January 25th, and issued at Taranaki Feb. 22nd; the 'Government account' of the matter was published July 31st, or more than 6 months after the proclamation of the war! Is not the charge of neglect on the part of the Government fully proved by Mr. Colenso's own showing?" To which I answer, NO. For, 1st, I had stated, that, "in the *Karere Maori* of July 31st Mr. McLean had himself AGAIN given a clear and distinct account of the whole affair; even to the occupying of 11 closely printed pages":—And, 2nd, F.C. ought to have known, that the Governor had given from the very outset of the Taranaki struggle a clear account of the whole sad affair; every *Karere Maori*, from the beginning of the outbreak downwards, being occupied with a perspicuous statement of the same. In the February number of that serial is given not only an account of the Governor's visit to Taranaki, &c., but also, that very valuable paper of His Excellency which contains such an able and lucid statement of his Native policy, and which I had myself the honor to bring before the notice of our Provincial Council in March last.

As I view it, any further words are but wasted on such a dishonest writer as your correspondent F.C. Therefore, in taking a final leave, I would direct him to a sentence in my former reply to his 1st letter—"That a man is in common justice bound to ascertain the truth of a charge before he makes it."

Yours &c.,
WILLIAM COLENSO.

Nov. 9, 1860.

❖ **1860 OPEN COLUMN.**
Hawke's Bay Herald 24 November.

SIR,—Through the Electoral Roll for the town of Napier, which appeared in your last Saturday's "Herald," I am again reminded of a duty which I have to fulfil. A self-imposed one it is true, and one that would have been long before this attended to had not my time been very fully occupied. I mean the present state of the *Electoral Roll*; or the number of voters of this Province. I believe, Sir, that you are aware I attended the Revising Officer's Court each day of his sitting, and heard him go through the whole of the Roll. And, in the first place, I feel bound to state, that that gentleman exerted his utmost powers *not* to strike out any claimant; a matter, I assure you, by no means so easy *legally* as (I dare say) three fourths of the electors think. He had heard of my having striven to arouse the public mind to a proper sense of their electoral rights; and, while he did not wonder at the apathy exhibited, (which, he said, was too common everywhere,) he remarked, that it would have been far better if an agent had been appointed to receive and inspect all claims before they were forwarded to the Registration Officer.

And now, through you, Mr. Editor, I wish to acquaint the electors of the Province of three things:—1. That many of their claims were made in a very loose and unsatisfactory manner,—some not signed by the claimant,—others not signed by a magistrate,—and many with a very faulty or incorrectly described title.—2. That had there been any opposition a large number would have been necessarily struck off. —3. That several are left on the roll *for this year only*; as, if not amended, they will be struck off at the next revisal; of which public notice was given by the Revising Officer.

If you can find room I will endeavour to give a pretty correct list of bad or untenable claims in law; all of which were sent in to the Registration Officer, and are merely allowed to remain on the roll for the present. You will see they are mostly bad through their vagueness or indistinctness: It is *bad* to say:—

Five acres west bank of Tukituki.

Part of Mr. Smith's purchase.

Purchase from John Smith.

Part of section No. 100. (*How much?*)

Moiety of section No. 100.

On the east bank of Tukituki.

40 acres, Mohaka. (*Number* of application not stated)

Application No. 200. (*Acreage* not stated.)

Town section No. . (Number left blank!)

Ditto. (When more than one claim.)

Household and leasehold.

Household and freehold.

Freehold, Ruataniwha.

Household, Napier.

Two men living together, the one puts in, A.B., Stores,——;—the other, C.D., Houses,——; both proprietors being one.

Any person already on the roll making a subsequent application, should state, whether such is additional,—

or, an alteration,—

or, an amendment,—

or, a substitution for his *former* claim; even when made for *another* district than *that* of the former claim.

All claims above one should be numbered,—1, 2, 3, 4, and so on.

Persons of the same name (as John Smith) should clearly specify themselves, by adding trade, or calling, or by Senior, Junior, tertius, &c.

Every claimant should bear in mind, that he has formally to sign his name twice to his application, (*besides* his statement made in full including his name in the body of the application,) and that one of his signatures must be made before a Magistrate.

So that his name must in every case be written three times on each application. J. Lamb of Porangahau was struck off because the declaration (part of the application) was not signed; and J. Heslop of Puketapu was struck off, because his application was neither signed nor declared! and so on with others. Claimants should also bear in mind, 1. that if their purchases or properties have only been recently acquired or occupied, (within six months,) their claim is invalid—2. that if they are foreigners, they must first become naturalised, or, their claim is not good.

And, lastly, I will state, (as my own private opinion,) that claimants who are on the Roll, and who may have disposed of their properties which formerly qualified them, in making a fresh application (and which may be in a new District) should state, that they were no longer entitled to their former claims. At all events such would look well and wear an honest face.

I should not omit to add that the Revising Officer stated he had sent to the Land and Survey Office for a map of the town to aid him in his investigations, but that such was refused. I believe, however, that the head of those departments was not there. Of course the Revising Officer could have issued a summons compelling both production and attendance. The public are not a little indebted to the clerk of the District Court (Mr. Grindell), who very kindly ran to and fro making several necessary enquiries, through which several names were allowed to remain.

In conclusion, Mr. Editor, allow me also to add that, having *again* come forward publicly in this electoral matter, I shall hope henceforth to take it more easily. I first wrote a "tract" about it; I next wrote a warning letter in your paper; I subsequently advertised (at my own expense) a public meeting, to organise a committee to look after such matters, and attended it with a few others, and failed; and last, I have spent several cold hours in the open Court with the Revising Officer, which has caused me to trouble you now with this long letter, as a kind of finish to an onerous public duty.

> *I am, Sir,*
> *Yours very truly,*
> *WILLIAM COLENSO.*

Napier, Nov. 20.

§ 1861 OPEN COLUMN.
Hawke's Bay Herald 19 January.
SIR,—The ancients held a superstition that the conjunction of certain bodies of supposed opposite tendencies and affinities, boded calamity and misfortune to the state. Such coalitions as we have witnessed of the three F's, with Hadfield, Stokes, & Co., are now almost eclipsed in this Province by the fraternising of Charlton, Colenso, & Co. This union looks ominous. Men of Hawke! be on your guard; give no promises, sign no requisition, nothing good can come of such conjunctions. What can it mean? Colenso, the disgraced churchman, the man who for many years opposed by every way in his power the location of Europeans in this district

—who almost monopolised, not only all profitable trade with the natives, but all good opinion too—who systematically maligned all new comers as evil persons thirsting to make a prey of the simple-minded Maories. This, a source of great gain to him, was all very nice while it lasted, but when the Maories, disgusted with his immoral intrigues, turned their backs to him, then, forsooth, he holds out the hand of fellowship to his countrymen. Then who so great a patriot as he? Now begins his land jobbing, now his cunningly devised and insidious measures for obtaining popularity. This, he in some degree achieved by wickedly traducing one class of the community, at the same time flattering and wheedling others; using his pen to beguile honest credulous people into the belief that he was seeking their advantage and enlightenment. Hence those nauseous "Tracts for the Times," and other egotistical rot that appeared from time to time in your journal. Next we trace him grasping place and pelf, supporting a Government condemned at all hands for its extravagance and waste of the public funds, and crowning his successful career of charlatanism by getting his creatures to present a requisition to him to stand for the General Assembly—which requisition (a wonder of wonders) is hawked about by Captain Charlton, the "sea lawyer," (as some have christened him,) the friend and champion of the calumniated runholders; one of the non-complying six; the exposer of the Superintendent's many delinquencies; the denouncer of Colenso, as the prince of humbugs; the (in short) pattern of an honest, clever, independent practical politician. Yes, Sir, Captain Charlton touts for Colenso on the one hand, and, on the other hand, abuses the Superintendent—all in the same breath. Truly the quart bottle trick is here altogether eclipsed; thimble rigging and mummery could no further go. I ask through you, Sir, will the people of Hawke's Bay be content to be so mis-represented in the New Zealand Parliament? will they prefer the scheming, greedy, money loving, suspended churchman, to a *bona fide* settler, who has expended his means in the employment of labour, the encouragement of trade, and in the cultivation, and improvement of the country; one with whom gentlemen need not shrink to associate. I have too good an opinion of the manly feeling and common sense of the constituency of this province to believe such a thing possible. Surely the admonitions of a friend should be esteemed beyond the flatteries of a self-seeking sophist.

> I remain, Sir,
> Faithfully yours,
> GEORGE WORGAN.

P.S. One most striking inconsistency is apparent at this time; to wit, persons who loudly condemn the waste and mismanagement of the Superintendent, yet lend their support to Mr. Colenso, "the Superintendent's *chief trumpeter.*" Electors look to this. I would beg respectfully to suggest that it might materially tend to the establishment of a mutual confidence between the constituency and the would-be-representatives if a meeting could be convened when all questionable points would be cleared up by means of question and answer.

❖ 1861 TO THE ELECTORS OF THE DISTRICT OF NAPIER.
Hawke's Bay Herald 5 January.

To His Honor T.H. FitzGerald, Esq., J.P., Capt. J.C.L. Carter, J.P., M.P.C., Capt. R.H. MacGregor, 65th, J.P., Alex. Alexander Esq., J.P., M.P.C., John Chambers, T. Lowry and W. Boorman, Esqs., Capts. G. Charlton, J. Henton, and Alexander Blair, Messrs. John Stevens, James Hallet, R. Brenigan, M. Sullivan, W.W. Yates, F. Sutton, J. le Quesne, W. Villers, J. McKain, Jos. Torr, Peter Searles, and the other electors, who have signed the Requisition.

BROTHER-SETTLERS AND FELLOW-ELECTORS.—I cannot any longer refrain from replying to your public call,—contained in the Requisition so very numerously and respectably signed, which you have this day placed in my hands,—that I would consent to be put in nomination as your representative in the New Zealand Parliament.

Although more than two months have elapsed since I first knew of the wish and intention of my fellow-settlers to put me in nomination for this high honour and very important duty, I have hitherto abstained from taking any step in the matter. I have been induced to be so far inactive, partly from possessing no private desire to go any further into the strife and turmoil of political life than I have already ventured, lest I should get beyond my depth; and partly from a hope that some more fit person might be found to go for us;—the names of such I recognise among those attached to the Requisition;—would that their time was less fully occupied!

I believe that I may truly say, that you pretty well know my mind upon many (if not all) chief political matters, whether Provincial or Colonial: as proof of which I may with honest pride refer to your plain and straightforward Requisition, signed as it is so universally—by members of our Provincial Council and by magistrates, by officers in the army and by professional gentlemen, by freeholders and by runholders, by merchants and by master mariners, by tradesmen and by the working classes.

Notwithstanding, I will here briefly state my opinion upon several of the more important political topics of the day. For there may be some one among our many voters still desirous of knowing my present sentiments; and it is always good to go into action with one's colours flying.

1st. It would be my aim to support the Governor and his present able Ministry: they deserve such from all true-hearted settlers, and from those of the Province of Hawke's Bay in particular.

2nd. I wish for peace, but not a dishonourable and hollow one; rather let us have a 7 years' war than that. I should, therefore, be conscientiously obliged to vote for a powerful, energetic, and steady carrying-on of the war until the requisite basis for a sound and lasting peace is obtained. And this I should do, not merely from what has taken place at Taranaki, but from what I believe to be more or less the sad state of things generally in this Northern Island (south of Auckland), the rank and diseased growth of several years; and from what I conceive to be now absolutely requisite for the future peace and welfare of the Colony. As I take it, the spirit of headstrong resistance to the lawful authorities must be now once and for ever quelled;—the supremacy of British rule must he universally and freely acknowledged, no more to be opposed;—Law, the fountain of all order, must be fully respected;—the rights of individual natives (being now British subjects) to sell or otherwise use their own several lands, must be supported and confirmed;—and compensation, if not for the expenses of the whole war, at least for the losses sustained by our unfortunate countrymen in Taranaki, must be made.

3rd. I should support the New Provinces Act, and this not merely as regards ourselves, but to seek to have its benefits thrown open as widely as possible. And, in so speaking, I do not only mean with reference to the future *new* Provinces, but also with hopes of bringing back the first six of the N.Z. Provinces to be more like what was originally intended they should be in the Constitution Act;—enlarged Municipalities with ample powers, instead of Lilliputian Kingdoms. For I have an utter abhorrence of ultra-provincialism; as being a costly, arrogant, and selfish form of Government; one leading to envy and disunion, and wholly unfitted both to us as Englishmen, as well as to the rapid growth, and full development of our adopted country. At the same time I think, the New Provinces Act may by careful and judicious amendment in a few of its clauses be further improved, and made more commonly serviceable.

4th. With reference to Land, I am still of the same opinion as when I spoke so fully on this subject in our Provincial Council in March last. I should generally uphold Sir George Grey's Regulations; unless such may yet be altered for the good of *all*. I should earnestly seek to obtain both for and from the natives the recognition of their common and individual rights to landed property even as ourselves: and should strive hard to get an immediate alteration of the Native Land-Purchase Department—at least in this Province.

5th. Touching the (so-called) Wellington debt,—I repudiate it *in toto* as I have ever done; and will never willingly consent to pay any portion of it. I should cheerfully agree to a fair debtor and creditor account being rendered; on the one side, of what we have had carried away (by her),—and, on the other, of what we have had expended (as from her), adding thereto whatever penalty shall be deemed to be fair for our unfortunate and half-ruinous connexion; and then let her pay back to us what in all equity shall be shewn to be our rightful and honest due.

6th. I should use my endeavours to obtain the great advantages of Steam Communication being granted to us, in common with all the Provinces, at the expense of the General Government. And should ever heartily seek to advance the united prosperity of our Province and Colony.

Again thanking you for the honour you have done me;—believing that you will quite uphold my opinions herein expressed;—and looking forward to meeting you shortly at the hustings.

I am, brother Settlers,
Your very faithful servant,
WILLIAM COLENSO.

❖ 1861 OPEN COLUMN.
Hawke's Bay Herald 19 January (1).[4]

SIR,—Reading, on Saturday last, the letter signed "George Worgan," in your paper of that date, I had nearly made up my mind to answer it fully in your next issue; but, having been led to *think* on him this day while using these words,—"That it may please Thee to forgive our enemies, persecutors, and slanderers, and to turn their hearts," —I feel it now to be a duty not to notice the sad letter of the poor, unhappy old man.

> *I am, Sir,*
> *Yours truly,*
> WILLIAM COLENSO.

Waitangi,
Sunday night, Jan. 13, 1861.

❖ 1861 OPEN COLUMN.
Hawke's Bay Herald 19 January (2).

SIR,—It is my humble opinion, that no one will ever charge you with having "puffed" the Province of Hawke's Bay. Perhaps, however, you uphold the good old rule, of cuffing scolding and flogging being every whit as needful for the young one as bread and milk?—That such treatment is the very best to bring him early to know himself, and to develop his young powers, and to assert his liberty, and to think and act independently? Perhaps so: at all events such will undoubtedly cause him to squall when so ill-hearted. Hence this cry of mine.—

In your leading article of last Saturday's *Herald*, you say,—"We look anxiously forward to the future Government of the Province. It will commence 1861—so we are informed—some £6000 in debt"—and so on. But what are the *facts?* Here they are:
—On 1st November, 1860, Province was indebted to the Union Bank, £6307 11s.

On 1st December, 1860, Province was indebted to the same, £4458 10s 10d.

And, on 1st January, 1861, the debt was £4021 14s. 6d.

Besides which, on the 31st December, 1860, the whole of the interest then due, amounting to £240 18s. 10d. was paid; otherwise the debt on 1st January would have been less than £3800.

And at this present time there are recorded applications in the hands of the C. L. Commissioner, made within the last three months, for upwards of 30,000 acres of land, the sale of which will come off early in March.

> *Yours, &c.,*
> WILLIAM COLENSO.

Napier, January 16, 1861.

---

4   This in reply to an earlier Worgan letter in which he clearly identified Colenso with a correspondent who used the *nom-de-plume* "Rua Taniwha": he wrote, "I would first observe my conviction that the signature (Rua Taniwha) is a mere blind; the reptile whose venomous spawn has been allowed to defile your pages lives not on the fair plains of Rua Taniwha; No, no: nothing but a compound of the festering drainage of commingled salt and fresh water could have produced anything half so loathsome. Let the crawler beware my heel!" I.S.G.

❖ 1861 OPEN COLUMN.
Hawke's Bay Herald 23 February.

SIR,—Permit me, in a few words, to supply an omission in your report of Provincial Council proceedings in the last "Hawke's Bay Herald." Especially as without it your report has a very different aspect. Under the head of "Schools," (*Estimates*, February 13,) you state that, (in opposing the application for a grant of public money towards the support of a school for Maories in the Pa Whakaairo,) I said,—"Bishop Selwyn had obtained a grant of 5000 acres in this district for the education of the natives, and he (Mr. Colenso) saw in a blue book before him that the Rev. Samuel Williams had received £1300 of public money within three years for the same purpose."

What I really said was—First, I called the attention of the Council to a motion made by the Superintendent in our last session,[5] and passed unanimously, with reference to this very item of expenditure—Schools: viz., that to ease the increasingly heavy expenditure under this head we should apply for full powers to deal with our town "Educational Reserves;" and, that as we had then determined such to be fair with regard to them, such a rule would be equally fair as to the larger ones. That ample provision had long ago been made by Sir George Grey for the education of the young natives of this district, in a grant of upwards of 5000 acres of land at Te Aute; in addition to which was the annual grant by the General Assembly of £7000—a portion of which also fell to this district, as appeared from a blue book then on the table, which shewed in the three years, '54, '55, and '56, (no later being in our possession,) the sum of £990[6] to have been granted to the Rev. S. Williams solely for Te Aute school. That the ministers of the different Christian denominations ever wished to have the teaching of the children of their respective churches: that the Maories of the Pa Whakaairo were professedly of the Church of England, and that the parents of many of the children were also communicants in that church: and that a chief aim of the Bishop of New Zealand had ever been, the better to educate the Maori children, to remove them from the daily horrors of a Maori pah. That, while I wished to see all Maori children taught English, &c.,—in this Council granting the aid sought, would be giving the public money to a purpose already amply provided for; and also doing that which would go a great way towards defeating one of the principal objects which the promoters of Maori education had ever in view —namely, the removal of the children from the pahs; and that, further, in granting the application, we might quite expect similar ones to be made from every pah in the Province, &c., &c.

> *I am, yours &c.,*
> WM. COLENSO.

Napier, Feb. 20, 1860.

---

5   *Vide* "Hawke's Bay Herald," March 10, 1860. W.C.
6   £1,030 was mentioned by me—looking at the sum total, including balance. W.C.

§ 1861 PAGE 4 ADVERTISEMENTS.
Hawke's Bay Herald 13 April.

LIST OF THOSE PERSONS who during the month of March, 1861, sent in their Claims to the Registration Officer of the District of Napier, and Clive, for the purpose of having their names placed on the Electoral Rolls for the year 1861–62....

Colenso William, Napier, freehold, 1, Porangahau, sub. secs. Nos. 41, 53, 71 and 72, acres 97.

Colenso William, Napier, freehold, 2, Blackhead, township, sections No. 39, 41, 55 and 57.

Colenso William, Napier, freehold, 3, Havelock township, sec. No.—and sub. Nos. 15 to 19.

Colenso William, Napier, freehold, 4, Abbotsford township, secs. 8 to 10 and 81, 83, 84, 85, being 3½ acres of Nos. 16 and 46 Government map of Waipawa.

Colenso William, Napier, freehold, 5, west bank of river Tukituki, and opposite Te Tamumu, 180 acres, application 146.

Colenso William, Napier, freehold, 6, Tarawera 686 acres, applications Nos. 27 and 49.

Colenso William, Napier, freehold, 7, Mangatarata, 100 acres, application No. 50.

Colenso William, Napier, freehold, 8, Clive, sub. secs. Nos. 216 to 236.

Colenso William, Napier, freehold, 1, Napier, suburban sections 39 to 44 inclusive.

Colenso William, Napier, freehold, 2, Meanee river, sub. sections Nos. 7, 9 and 23.

Colenso William, Napier, freehold, 3, Whareponga, western side of harbour, sub. secs. Nos. 58 and 59.

....

❖ 1861 TO MR. H.B. SEALEY, OF NAPIER.
Hawke's Bay Herald 20 July.

Per favor of the Editor of the Hawke's Bay Herald.

DEAR SIR,—I have read in the Hawke's Bay Times of yesterday your long letter concerning me; and am thinking your own "second thoughts" will scarcely approve of it. Homer makes Æneas say to Achilles—

"Reproach is cheap: with ease we might discharge
Gibes at each other, till a ship that asks
An hundred oars should sink beneath the load."

Had you been returned instead of me, I would not strive to weaken you on your entering the field; on the contrary, I would gladly have aided you against our Provincial foes. I leave to-morrow for Auckland per Zephyr. *Vive valetque.*

> *Yours truly,*
> *W. COLENSO.*

Napier, Friday, July 19, 1861.

§ 1861 TOWN OF NAPIER.
Hawke's Bay Herald 16 November.

The nomination for this district took place on Thursday the 14th inst., in front of the Government Buildings. As usual on such occasions, the attendance was large....

Mr. William Colenso was proposed by Mr. John Steven, seconded by Mr. William Reardon....

Mr. Colenso was the next speaker. He came before them, he said, a tried man.

Mr. Allen.—Yes: *Mene, mene, tekel upharsin.*

Mr. Colenso.—Speak in English, that the people may all understand you.

Mr. Allen.—They all understand it; it is in the Bible.

Mr. Colenso.—I have heard of a certain personage quoting Scripture for his own purposes.

Mr. Allen.—I have heard you quote it many a time.

Mr. Colenso (in continuation) would not make a set speech, but still had a few words to say. [We commenced to take notes of his "few words," but when we found that they were likely to occupy about three quarters of an hour in the utterance (which they did), had to give the task up in despair. Nearly half-an-hour, to begin with, was taken up in describing his own sensations under a double attack from the press of the Province—the *Times* having urged that no paid officers of the Government should be allowed to enter the Council; and the *Herald* that makers of set speeches, and orators otherwise longwinded should be carefully eschewed. He subsequently touched upon various subjects, and answered question upon question from the body of the meeting.]....

A show of hands was then demanded for the respective candidates. A good number appeared for Messrs. Triphook, Colenso, and Begg; a few for Mr. Wilkinson; and one or two for Mr. Skeet and Mr. Edwards respectively. The show was declared to be in favour of Messrs Colenso and Begg; and a poll was demanded on behalf of the other candidates. The poll takes place this day.

§ 1861 ADVERTISEMENT.
Hawke's Bay Herald 24 December.

£30 REWARD.

WHEREAS some evil-disposed person or persons have very recently forcibly broken into the weather-boarded building in the field at Waitangi (near the Ferry, Waipureku); and, besides stealing therefrom several articles, have wickedly and maliciously done a very large amount of damage in destroying Glass, Books, Writings, Natural History specimens, Medicines, &c., &c. The above reward of £30 will be paid by William Colenso, the owner of the aforesaid property so wantonly destroyed, to any one giving such information to the Inspector of Police as shall lead to the apprehension and conviction of the offender or offenders. £10 to be paid on the giving of such information, and £20 to be also, paid on their conviction.

E ta ma, e nga Maori, titiro mai, ETORU TE KAU enei Pauna Moni hei utu mo te tangata e hopu ranei e whaka-atu ranei i te whanako nana i pakaru kino te toa a Te koreneho ki Waitangi.

Waitangi,

Dec. 23, 1861.

§ 1862 PROVINCIAL COUNCIL.
Hawke's Bay Herald 8 February.

Mr. Colenso wished to know what question was before the Council. The Speaker said there was none....

Mr. Colenso pointed out that a fatal objection existed to the proposed sanctioning of three months' expenditure by resolution....

Mr. Colenso said that the demands made by the natives for a crossing place for ferries had always been resisted upon principle....

A motion... was negatived through the opposition of that highly economical gentleman (where his own salary is not concerned,—Printer's Devil) Mr. William Colenso....

Mr. Colenso... could not agree with what Mr. FitzGerald had said, that the Act was a sham....

Mr. FitzGerald seconded the motion. Mr. Colenso opposed it on the ground of economy....

Mr. Colenso trusted Mr. Tiffen would re-consider this decision, as the request of the council was one that would have to be complied with....

Mr. Triphook seconded the motion. Mr. Colenso opposed it....

Mr. Colenso opposed the suspension of the rule. This should only be done in cases of urgent and pressing necessity....

Mr. Colenso questioned whether they would be doing their duty to their constituents by passing such a resolution....

§ 1862 PROVINCIAL COUNCIL.
Hawke's Bay Times 13 March.

The SPEAKER observed that the question before the Council was that it be adjourned for a week.

Mr. COLENSO maintained that he was speaking to the question, and if he chose to speak until 6 o'clock in the morning he (the Speaker) was bound to sit and hear him.

❖ 1862 OPEN COLUMN.
Hawke's Bay Times 20 March.

To Mr. James Parker, *Chairman of the Public Meeting held on the Green, Napier, Saturday, March 15th, 1861.*

Sir,—When I attended the public meeting called by Messrs. Searles and Mullaney on Saturday evening last, I did so because (1) all the town members were by public advertisement requested to be present, and (2) myself in particular had been invited by Mr. Mullaney; consequently, I supposed I had some right to be there.

When, upon putting the second resolution (calling upon the Superintendent immediately to expend the £637 *balance* at the end of the year from the sum voted for harbour improvements), I stepped forward to say a few words in order to set right what was a grave error, and which I KNEW to be such from my office as Provincial Treasurer;—common courtesy should have sufficed to have obtained for me leave to speak, so as to give the explanation I had to give in the fullest manner. And, having so given it, common sense should have told you to pause ere you put such a resolution to the meeting and common sense should also have prompted the meeting not to carry it.

For, it cannot be denied, that a man in my public position does not often go forth voluntarily to utter untruths to a public meeting. If you believed that I spoke the truth, you should have shewn it by amending your second resolution.

And so, when Mr. Peter Searles charged the Superintendent (amongst other things,) with having given extra monies to a government officer—monies which had not been voted; and when he further stated that I *(William Colenso)* had received the same for myself under the head of "contingencies" common decency and love of fair play should have urged you to demand for me a hearing, and you should not have listened to Mr. Peter Searles' repeated statements, that "the town members were not there to speak," and that "there was to be no debate on the matter."

For, it cannot be denied, if facts—if the truth was what was wanted by the meeting such undoubtedly would have been the case.

However, sir, I will now repeat the statements I made at the meeting:—1st. That there is no *(real)* balance of £637 standing over from the sum voted for harbour improvements. For, in addition to the sum of £5812 16s. 11d. (paid by me as Provincial Treasurer up to the 31st of Dec. last,), there is also the sum of £792 14s. 9d, paid by me in January for *work &c., on the Harbour Improvements during the three last months of* 1861. Of course you did not know this; but you ought to have known (from the December quarterly abstract lately published) that the Director of the Public Works had then £390 in hand, unaccounted for; and which it was to be presumed was also spent. And you knew (or ought to have known) that of this extra sum of £742 14s. 9d., Mr. M. Mullaney (who appeared not to relish my attempted explanation) himself received £352 0s. 6d.

2nd. That the Superintendent did not give to me any such sum as £30 16s. over what had been voted (or, in fact, any sum at all). The sum total of £379 16s. (Treasury Department Expenditure) is made up as follows, viz.:—

To James Smith, for a press (had in 1860)	£27	0	0
To ditto, for shelves, &c.	4	10	0
To W. Miller, for a table (had in 1860)	4	2	0
To F. Sutton for stamps and postages	1	5	8
To J. Wood, W. & H. Yates, & others, stationery	2	18	4
To W. Ray, for copying documents for General Government	3	0	0
To G. Griffiths, for fire-proof iron safe	49	0	0
To P. Searles, for placing same	0	10	0
	£92	6	0
To Mr. E. Lyndon, for acting in my absence at Auckland	60	14	4
To W. Colenso, as treasurer, from 1st Jan. to 31st Dec	226	15	8
	£379	16	0

So that, instead of my having received £30 16s. over and above what was voted, and in a smuggling, clandestine, (thievish) way, I have not only *not* received what was voted but have fallen far short of the £300 salary, about which so much noise has been made. This, however, you would not now have known, had it not been as it were wrung from me through ungenerous treatment and unjust statements made at the Public Meeting on Saturday evening last.

I have the honour to be, Sir,
Your very obedient Servant,
WILLIAM COLENSO, M.P.C.

❖ **1862 OPEN COLUMN.**
Hawke's Bay Herald 28 June.
SIR,—When, in the Civil Commissioner's Court on Monday last, I asked for the warrant authorising the police to lay informations under the Native Land Purchase Ordinance,—I supposed, that the warrant, though not to be produced, was at all events in existence, and perfectly legal (in fact, the Crown Prosecutor stated, that such was in the possession of the Superintendent.) I now, however, find, that *there is no such instrument*—that it was, from the very first, informal and therefore returned to the General Government for correction, and that, owing to its informality, all the informations laid by the police under it in 1860, were obliged to be withdrawn by the counsel for the prosecution (*Vide* leading article, *H.B. Herald*, Dec. 15, 1860.)

And, further, I find, on referring to a subsequent number of your valuable paper (*Vide H.B. Herald*, Feb. 2, 1861), an important letter from the Colonial Secretary to the Superintendent of the Province, dated Dec. 29, 1860, and requesting him "to direct that no new action for the present be taken under the Native Lands Purchase Ordinance."

And which determination no doubt, so operated with the General Government as to cause them to withhold the issuing of a fresh warrant authorising the police to act.

> *I am, &c.,*
> *W. COLENSO.*

Napier, June 25, 1862.

§ 1862 NAPIER.
Otago Witness 19 July.

There have been some proceedings lately at Napier which are exciting attention, relative to an action of ejectment brought by direction of the Government against the *soi-disant* Rev. W. Colenso, before the Civil Commissioner. The land it appears was made over by the natives to the Church Missionary Society some years ago, and Mr. Colenso and his friends urge that it is not native land, even though the Church Missionary Society repudiate the possession. Mr. Colenso is a member of the Assembly, and no doubt we shall learn the merits of the case shortly from the proceedings in the House of Representatives.

§ 1862 THE NEW POLICY.
Daily Southern Cross 16 July.

The new policy—as it is developing itself at Hawke's Bay—is that of the Bishop of New Zealand, who holds that in the government of the colony the real interests of the settlers should be held secondary and subordinate to the imaginary interests of the Maories. Owing to the arrival of the northern mail since our last publication, we find we have not room, as we then promised, to give an extended report of the case tried before the new Civil Commissioner at Napier on the 23rd ultimo, in which the ministry was plaintiff and Mr. Colenso defendant. The facts of the case may be thus stated—Mr. Colenso was charged, at the instigation of Mr. Crosbie Ward, with a breach of the Native Land Purchase Ordinance, in occupying ten acres of land not comprised within a grant from the Crown. It appeared from the evidence that the land in question had, in the year 1843, been granted by the natives—with the sanction of the Crown—to the Church Missionary Society, for a mission station, and that Mr. Colenso then came to reside upon it, laying out a considerable amount on buildings, fencing, gardens, and other improvements. Ten years after this—*i.e.* in 1853—the Bishop of New Zealand wished the defendant to leave the place, which he refused to do without compensation. In March last, the trustees of the Church Missionary Society stated, in a memorandum to the government that they had no intention of applying for a Crown grant for the said land and that they saw no reason why it should not again revert to the natives. Soon after, the land commissioner at Napier received the following letter:—

"Crown Lands Office,
Auckland, May 1st, 1862.

"Sir,—I have the honor to request that you will proceed without delay to cause an information to be laid under 'The Native Land Purchase Ordinance' against the person named in the margin (William Colenso) for illegal occupation of the old Church Missionary reserve, situate on the road between Napier and Clive, and known by the name of Awapuni.

"By warrant under the hand of his excellency the late Governor, every member of the police force within the Province of Napier is authorised to lay such information, and his honor the Superintendent has been requested to give directions to the police to afford you all the assistance necessary in dealing with this case.

"It may be found most convenient that the information should be laid before the Honorable Colonel Russell.

"I forward to you an original letter from the Right Rev. Bishop Williams and others, trustees of the Church Missionary Society, from which you will perceive that the title to the land in question still vests in the Native owners. You will be good enough to return the paper when done with.

I have, &c.,

(Signed) "CROSBIE WARD."

"The hint," says the *Herald*, "thus conveyed that the ordinary courts of justice should be ignored, and the case be heard by the Civil Commissioner—who is simply a political agent of the Government, seems to have been faithfully acted upon, without reference to the legality or illegality, propriety or impropriety, of such a course. On the morning of Saturday, the 21st inst., a summons, signed by Captain Culling, the Resident Magistrate for Napier district, was served on the defendant, requiring him to appear on Monday, the 23rd inst., at the Resident Magistrate's Court. Monday, be it observed, was just four days before the projected departure of the steamer 'White Swan' with the members of the General Assembly. The defendant appeared on the day referred to, and found that the case, sure enough, was to be heard by the Honorable Colonel Russell in *propria persona*. The result was a judgment against the defendant, given in utter disregard, nay, in utter opposition to the evidence. The judgment, too, was pronounced the instant the defendant resumed his seat, and in such a manner as to impress the spectators with the conviction that it was a foregone conclusion. The whole proceeding, from first to last, was characterised by an indecent determination to convict at every hazard, and bore on the face of it the unmistakeable impress of persecution.

"The Court during the hearing of this case, was crowded with spectators, and the announcement of the decision arrived at, was received with a storm of hisses; while, out of doors, the proceedings were universally referred to in words of unmeasured indignation. The public felt but little interest in the intrinsic merits of the outstanding question upon which these proceedings were based—saving this, that they regarded the intention to reconvey the land to the natives as another of the humiliating and ruinous concessions to the aboriginal race which so eminently distinguish the policy of the present Government, and the end of which no mortal can fore-see.

But they saw, in the whole affair, an unscrupulous and unblushing violation of the first principles of justice, for the purpose of serving a political end. Mr. Colenso, we should mention for the information of the English reader, is a member of the House of Representatives—the representative of Napier. He is well known to be an opponent of the present Government, and being a fearless speaker, his opposition, if not weakened by some means or other, might prove very inconvenient to a tottering Ministry. The Native Land Purchase Ordinance has long been a dead letter, and Ministers have more than once expressed their intention to move its repeal in the approaching session of the Assembly. Hence, its violation has been of daily occurrence—scarcely a settler in the country (the Civil Commissioner himself not excepted) being innocent of occupying native land. In fact, leasing runs from the native chiefs has become a matter of open and ordinary business transaction. But by some process or other, the troublesome member for Napier must be silenced, or at least his influence weakened, and this obsolete ordinance afforded a ready means: while a pretext was not wanting, inasmuch as the natives had characteristically demanded, at the hands of the Government, his expulsion from the property."
—*New Zealand Advertiser*, July 5.

§ 1862 CONDUCT OF THE "MAORI MESSENGER".
Taranaki Herald 6 September.

Mr. Colenso, in moving, "That in the opinion of this House it is highly desirable that the Government serial called the *Maori Messenger*, printed for and circulated among the Maoris, should be placed under proper supervision and made as effective as possible; *vide* articles III. and IV. of May, and article III. p.6, of July, 1862," referred to the absolute want of proper supervision of this periodical, every number being full of errors of selection, of translation, and gross typographical errors, of which he produced examples from recent numbers, among the former of which were dry disquisitions on law, &c., and things which though all right in one part of the island, were dreadful curses to the natives of another part. If it were to be of any use it must be placed under proper supervision at once.

§ 1862 SUPREME COURT—CRIMINAL JURISDICTION— TUESDAY, SEPTEMBER 30.
Hawke's Bay Herald 7 October.

(Before His Honor Mr. Justice Johnston.) NETANE TE HUIKI, an aboriginal native, was placed at the bar, indicted for that, not having the fear of God before his eyes, and being moved and instigated by the devil, on the 26th day of May last he did feloniously and with malice aforethought, kill one Hiraina (his wife) against &c.

His Honor intimated that he would like to see as many natives as took an interest in the proceedings accommodated in the court; and said that he would be much obliged to any gentlemen not otherwise engaged who would explain the proceedings to them as the case went on. Mr. Colenso undertook to do so....

William Colenso, sworn, deposed:—I have been in the colony nearly 29 years. I have been nearly the whole of that time shut up among the natives, and have observed their habits and customs. Suicide was very common among them at one time. There was no superstition against suicide, but one in favor of it—a great deal respecting which will be found in Sir George Grey's collection of native songs. Suicide is of more rare occurrence now. It was at the time of which I have spoken more common among the females than the males; seldom have I known a male committing suicide.

§ 1863 THE ELECTION FOR NAPIER.
Hawke's Bay Herald 10 January.

The Nomination. The nomination for this district took place on Monday the 5th inst....

Mr. WILLIAM COLENSO was proposed by Mr. H. Groom, seconded by Mr. Brooke Taylor....

Mr. COLENSO had not intended to come forward; nor did he now intend to do so, but finding that he had been nominated, why there he was. He had sometime since seen an article, in the *Times*, stating that there were plenty of working men in town who were well fitted to represent its interests, and he had hoped to see some of that class nominated. The batch that had been nominated (himself included) was not such as to meet his approbation. Allusion had been made to the town and country districts being antagonistic; but this was a feeling which should be completely set aside. The runholding interest was not what it once was; 19 out of 20 of the runholders had converted their runs into freehold estates, or at least purchased portions in such a manner as to exclude all other buyers. That interest was no longer in opposition to the general prosperity of the province. As he took it, the great antagonistic interest of the day was the squatting system. It was those men who, in defiance of law, were leasing lands from the natives and paying them an exorbitant rent for the same, who had brought about the present state of things. That class was busy weaving a warp which might never be unravelled. Don't let the two classes of settlers be jumbled together, or considered as one. He trusted that the persons they might elect would stand together in a determination to resist by all means the present concessional policy; and that they would watch narrowly to see that the town of Napier had a fair proportion of the revenue allotted to it.

In reply to a question from Mr. JOHN BEGG, (which we did not catch) Mr. COLENSO said that but for the fact of his having stood in the gap, the Fox ministry would have succeeded, in the House of Representatives, in introducing a clause into the Native Circuit Courts Bill, under which squatters on native lands would be liable to two years' imprisonment.

Mr. JOHN BEGG.—Well, I think you would have done better to let it be introduced.

Mr. COLENSO.—So I would had the clause been intended to take retrospective effect, but as it was intended only to take effect from the time of its being passed, I opposed it as unjust. I said,—Either go back to the beginning or let it alone, altogether.

Mr. MILLER asked Mr. COLENSO whether he would support Mr. McLean as Superintendent.

Mr. COLENSO would rather the question had not been put, but, as it had, he would answer it. If Capt. Carter came forward again, he (Mr. C.) would support him for the office. With regard to Mr. McLean, he did not consider him, as some one had said, the fittest man to deal with native affairs at this time. He (Mr. C.) must first know Mr. McLean's policy before he could promise to vote for him. He thus spoke of him in the view of his being Superintendent. He believed that the Chief Magistrate of the Province had by virtue of his office a certain weight in native affairs; and that if Mr. McLean would hold, instead, a seat in the Executive, a double influence would then be brought to bear upon the native mind. There would be two good heads instead of one....

The Returning Officer then called for a show of hands, which proved to be in favor of Messrs. Smith, Kennedy, Edwards, Hitchings, and Colenso. A poll was thereupon demanded by Mr. Wood....

The polling took place on Tuesday the 6th—continuing from 9 a.m. till 4 p.m. There was no great excitement at any time, although rather more stir was apparent than on previous occasions....

The state of the poll was declared at 4 o'clock the same day by the Returning Officer, as follows:—

Smith 62
Kennedy 61
Wood 59
Hitchings 57
Colenso 45
Edwards 45
Wilkinson....... 32

The Returning Officer said that Messrs. Colenso and Edwards being equal, it devolved upon him, under the Regulation of Elections Act, to decide by a casting vote, which he would give in favor of William Colenso. He accordingly declared Messrs. Smith, Kennedy, Wood, Hitchings, and Colenso, to be duly elected as members for the Town of Napier.

After the lapse of a few seconds,—

Mr. Colenso said that he had waited two or three minutes for some one who was higher on the poll than himself to come forward, but no one appearing, he would say a few words. There was no Thatcher to-night to occupy their attention, and he hoped he might claim a hearing for a quarter of an hour or twenty minutes. He was the more anxious to avail himself of this opportunity because he did not write in the newspapers—not now at least. In one of the two papers he confessed he had very little faith. Well he would rather not, but would if pressed. And, first, although he would much rather have gone into the Council without the casting vote of the Returning Officer, he would thank those of the electors who had recorded their votes in his favour. Those votes, he was proud to say, had been given without any solicitation on his part or by anyone on his behalf. He was low on the poll, but the fact was, he was neither an Oddfellow nor a Freemason, and, above all, he did not belong to the miserable Scotch clique of Napier. He was an Englishman; he thanked God he was an Englishman; but had he not been born an Englishman, he would wish to have been born an Irishman, a free, open hearted, generous Irishman—anything rather than a mean, crawling, sly, close Scotchman. Mr. Colenso having indulged in this strain for some time, proceeded, as he said, to examine the pretensions of that magnificent lion M'Lean to the Superintendency of this Province. And, first, he could tell the townspeople that they were arrogating to themselves the appointment of this officer—forgetting altogether that the country had the larger voice in the Council, as it had often before shown. He would premise that Mr. M'Lean was an old acquaintance of his—their friendship having begun 13 or 14 years ago, and lasted till the present time. He had no ill feeling towards Mr. M'Lean —quite the contrary, but he considered him unfitted for the Superintendency of this province for several reasons. First, he was a General Government officer, and liable to be influenced and instructed by Sir George Grey. But they wanted their Chief Magistrate to be a thoroughly independent man—a man who, like Cæsar's wife, was above suspicion—a man who would work on his own hook—a man who could not be tampered with. Second, he was a Land Purchase Commissioner, and his duties might call him to Auckland at any time. The Native Land Bill would, he believed, be shortly in operation, and who, he would ask, was to acquire land under it?— Why Mr. M'Lean. And how could he perform the duties of both—Superintendent and Commissioner? Yet because M'Lean happened to be a Scotchman, his own countrymen chose to shut their eyes to these facts, and were determined, forsooth, to thrust him down everybody else's throat. Third, it had been said that Mr. M'Lean had great influence over the native mind. They might speak of the influence Mr. M'Lean had, but that was in times past; it was a thing of old—at a time when he had an unlimited purse at his disposal and dispensed it with a free hand. But should Mr. M'Lean become Superintendent, and, in that capacity, feel compelled to resist the demands of the natives—to refuse them money for a road or for shingle, then mark the re-action. He would also say beware of M'Lean and the concessional policy of which he was representative. He would conclude by referring to the discourteous, underhanded way in which this contemptible clique had treated Captain Carter, their esteemed Superintendent, than whom a more judicious, attentive, and honest man, never held the chief magistracy of any province. Capt. Carter, whose desire to resign was owing to circumstances which no longer existed, and who, he believed, was now willing to resume the office, had been removed from the field by the sly underhanded intrigues of a pack of beggarly Scotchmen who were fattening upon the wealth of the Englishmen of the district. [The *reverend* gentleman, having exhausted himself with sound and fury, here precipitately retired.]

Mr. KENNEDY, notwithstanding the tirade they had just listened to, was not ashamed of being a Scotchman. He thanked the electors for the honour they had done him, and would do his best to deserve the confidence they had shown in him.

Mr. WOOD just alluded to the foul-mouthed abuse which had been heaped upon his fellow countrymen, and remarked upon the exceedingly bad taste displayed by Mr. Colenso in the attempt they had just heard to create national distinctions in so small a community—to pit one country against another.

Mr. COLENSO.—Who did it first—why, your own paper. Mr. WOOD denied it emphatically. [And now challenges Mr. Colenso to prove it.]

Mr. WOOD (in continuation) said that Mr. Colenso had thrown a brand of discord into their little community which might not be fully extinguished for years. In reply to Mr. Colenso's remarks upon Mr. M'Lean, he (Mr. Wood) would only say that Mr. M'Lean, as a settler, was paramount to Mr. M'Lean as a Government officer; that he was a man who could not be tampered with—not even by Sir George Grey; that a two years' leave of absence would afford him the leisure to pay attention to provincial duties; and that his influence over the natives arose in a great measure from the honesty of his intercourse with them. And it was a perversion of the truth to say that Mr. M'Lean was the advocate of a concessional policy. As to the underhand supplanting of Capt. Carter, that gentleman (of whom he had the highest opinion) had repeatedly stated, long before Mr. M'Lean was thought of as Superintendent, that he had no intention of again accepting office, and had afterwards called at the *Herald* office for the purpose of having it made public that he would not oppose Mr. McLean.

Mr. COLENSO.—Why? You know why. Was it not on account of Mrs. Carter's illness, which was thought to last for 6 or 7 months. But that illness having since terminated fatally, he believed he could say that Capt. Carter, but for the promise that had been wheedled out of him, would be prepared again to accept office.

Dr. HITCHINGS thought that remarks were framed in a very bad spirit which brought up any differences about country or religion. He was sorry at much he had heard that day. With regard to the Superintendency, Capt. Carter had stated repeatedly to him that he had no intention of standing for that office; and, more recently, had said that Mr. M'Lean was the fittest man for it at the present time. They wanted no heartburnings of that kind, but to work together and get good roads, some of which were in a desperate condition.

Mr. EDWARDS thanked those of the electors who had polled for him. He found himself in a minority, but this was accounted for by the votes of the government officers. He could easily imagine that these men would be antagonistic to an independent member, for certain departments were full of gross abuses, which would not stand the test of too strict a scrutiny. It gave him pleasure to think, at all events, that he was side by side with Mr. Colenso.

Mr. COLENSO.—Did you vote for yourself? Mr. EDWARDS.—Yes.

Mr. COLENSO.—I did not, so of the two you are virtually the lower on the poll.

Mr. WILKINSON thanked the electors for the measure of support they had given him. He was rather glad than otherwise at the result, as he had some thoughts of going away for a time about the period the Council was likely to re-assemble. He had always understood that Capt. Carter had wholly withdrawn as a candidate for the superintendency; otherwise he would have felt a delicacy in moving in the matter of his successor. He thought, however, that in this matter, Mr. Colenso had travelled out of his way in making the statements he had done.

Mr. COLENSO entered into further (and, we may add, revolting) explanations relative to Capt. Carter's changed views and the cause which had led to such change. He concluded by declaiming against the conduct of one or two false friends who, under the guise of sympathy, had gone to Capt. Carter and wheedled him out of a promise to support Mr. M'Lean. They had acted, in a way that no Englishman would have condescended to do.

The meeting separated shortly after this—not, however, without a wordy warfare between Colenso and John Begg.

§ 1863 EDITORIAL.
Hawke's Bay Herald 13 January.
Many of our readers are aware that the validity of the return of Mr. William Colenso as a member for the Town of Napier, at the late election, has been questioned by the candidate who was beaten by the casting vote of the Returning Officer. Two objections have been raised to this return—the first, that the name of Mr. Holder (who recorded a vote for Mr. Colenso) is on the roll for Napier as Richard Holder, instead of Henry Richard; the second, that the name of Mr. Anderson (who did likewise) appears on the roll after that gentleman had been objected to by the Registration Officer as having parted with the property upon which he qualified, and the objection been sustained by Mr. Hart in the Revision Court.... It will be a species of retributive justice should Colenso lose his seat through an informality in the vote of one of those very men upon whose devoted heads he heaped so much, virulent abuse.

§ 1863 FROM OUR OWN CORRESPONDENT, WELLINGTON.
Hawke's Bay Herald 20 January.
One of your M.P.C.s for Napier, Mr. William Colenso, has rather astonished the Scotch folks here by that extraordinary election speech of his, which I fear has not done much to elevate either his dignity or reputation, such as it is. Had the honorable gentleman been dining that he made such a display, or was it simply an ebullition of political spleen?

§ 1863 MR. COLENSO ON THE SCOTCH,[7] FROM THE *WELLINGTON INDEPENDENT*, JAN. 15.

Hawke's Bay Herald 24 January.

"Sir," said an old Waterloo officer, "I hate prejudice and I hate the French." It appears that a sentiment similar in character pervades the mind of Mr. William Colenso, a legislator of the colony, and now by a special providence, and by the casting vote of the Returning Officer, one of the Provincial Council for the Province of Hawke's Bay. Mr. Colenso has no ill feeling towards Mr. M'Lean, in fact he rather likes him despite his nationality—but he thanks God he is an Englishman, and hates the Scotch. Such, in substance, if not in words, is the speech delivered by that gentleman, at the recent Napier election, where seven candidates sought the sweet voices of the electors, of whom five, with Mr. Colenso forming the tail, were chosen. There appears to have been a happy unanimity of sentiment existing among the successful candidates, on the main question on which the election turned, viz.: the choice of the future Superintendent. They all save Mr. Colenso thought Mr. Donald McLean was the man best fitted to succeed Captain Carter, who, from the pressure of a great domestic calamity, did not intend to accept office again. Mr. Colenso, however, would not have 'the M'Lean,' or be dominated over by the nominee of a beggarly clique of Scotchmen; so when his own return was secured, he favoured the electors with the following exposition of his opinions on things in general and Scotchmen in particular. He is reported to have said—[His precious speech having already appeared in these columns, need not be repeated.]

§ 1863 EDITORIAL.

Hawke's Bay Herald Wednesday, 28 January.

Mr.—we beg his pardon, the *Reverend*, William Colenso, has usually, in referring to the *Herald*, "laid it on very thick." In writing for its columns (which, by the way, he has done probably to the extent of quires) he has generally opened with such expressions as,—"Mr. Editor, your valuable journal"—"My dear Sir, your excellent paper"—"My good Sir, your admirable summary." In the Council he has repeatedly alluded, in terms of exaggerated commendation, to the accuracy of its reports; and, on the hustings, in the presence of a large number of electors, he expatiated on one occasion upon the frantic eagerness with which the members of the Mechanics' Institute in Auckland were wont to wait for its arrival and to devour its interesting contents. (Upon hearing which, by the way, we mentally ejaculated "Walker"!) His admiration for the *Herald*—especially when, at some trouble and expense, we exposed the arbitrary and illegal character of the proceedings taken against him in the Civil Commissioner's Court—was altogether unbounded; and *why*? Simply because in the cranium of the reverend gentleman the bump of self-esteem is inordinately developed, and because, all unconsciously, we ministered to his ruling passion.

---

7   A pun? The 'Wellington correspondent' (above) asked rhetorically, 'Had the honorable gentleman been dining that he made such a display?' I.S.G.

From sickening adulation he has now turned to bitter invective—wherefore the change it is difficult to conceive; unless on the supposition that he believes himself to be the only man in the province competent to deal with the native population or fitted for the office of Superintendent, and that, in supporting Mr. M'Lean for the latter, we sadly derogated from the dignity of the *reverend* gentleman. We were wholly unconscious of offence towards him when, upon the termination of the polling, he poured upon our devoted heads his vials of wrath. We do not, however, complain —far from it; the censure of such a man being to us infinitely more grateful than the most complimentary expressions. Nor should we now notice his *reverence* were it not for the very serious character of the charges he has made against this journal, and for the possibility of their being read where the degree of weight to be attached to ought emanating from such a source might be overestimated.

First, then, he has publicly stated that the course pursued by him on the husting —that of stirring up dormant feelings of nationality and seeking by that means to pit one portion of our small community against another—was originally followed in the columns of the *Herald*; that this journal was the first to lend itself to so iniquitous an attempt. To that charge we reiterate the unqualified denial that has already been given it. The course ascribed to us is one against which we have ever carefully guarded, and the assertion to the contrary is no better than a downright untruth. In the spirit of fair play, we again call upon Mr. Colenso to sustain his assertion by proof, for which purpose we are willing to furnish him with a file of the *Herald* from its first issue, and to afford any extent of space that he may require. Should he act upon this suggestion and succeed in the effort, we shall not lose a moment in publicly retracting the offensive expression we have just used; but, should he fail, his "feelings as an Englishman" will doubtless prompt him to withdraw, with equal celerity and publicity, his injurious accusation.

The second charge is contained in a long-winded letter which appeared last Monday in the *Times*, and which, for the information, of our readers, we re-print in another column. It will be seen by those who have patience to read it through that he brings against this journal the very grave charge of misreporting, for purposes of its own, the speech he delivered at the close of the poll. He represents us as having "vilely misrepresented" him ; and, further on, he uses the expression "falsely reporting" as applied to the account of the election proceedings that appeared in the *Herald*. Now false reporting, with the view of gaining an end, is, in our estimation, a much graver offence on the part of a newspaper proprietor than the publication of a false and malicious, if outspoken libel; inasmuch as for the one, redress can always be obtained; whereas for the other it cannot, except by the uncertain process of bringing public opinion to bear upon the publisher. A journalist who would misreport to gratify personal or political feeling is unworthy of public confidence; and hence it is that we devote more space to this part of the reverend gentleman's epistle, than to many of our readers may seem necessary or called for.

Mr. Colenso, though dealing very extensively in generalities, is very cautious in descending to particulars. He names but two respects in which he alleges his words to have been misreported, which he does in the following terms,—"As an instance, I may just call attention to what he has reported I said against Sir G. Grey!! and of my 'revolting explanations' concerning my dearest friend in Hawke's Bay, Captain Carter." Now his allusion to Sir George, as reported, is as follows,—"He (referring to Mr. McLean) was a General Government officer, and liable to be influenced and instructed by Sir George Grey." Granting for a moment that His Excellency's name has been substituted for that of the ministry of the day, which is the utmost that can be averred, where is the vileness? The one assertion indeed would be even more offensive towards Mr. McLean (could he take offence from such a quarter) than the other. But that the sentence as given in the *Herald* is a faithful report of what was really said we have the evidence of our note book, of our own senses, and of some twenty or thirty onlookers—many of them Colenso's own supporters, who have already borne testimony to the fact.

The next charge, as particularised, is that of having characterised the reverend gentleman's explanations of Capt. Carter's position in the matter of the superintendency as *revolting*. This remark, we may observe, was within brackets and was no part of the report, properly so called; but for its use we are equally responsible. We have attended many election meetings—probably a hundred —and have heard much that was coarse and indelicate; but certainly nothing to equal the indelicacy of a candidate bringing forward on the hustings, for political purposes, the name of a lady—much less the name of one whose remains had just been committed to the silent tomb. We then deemed it revolting, and would now characterise such conduct by a still stronger epithet, did one occur to us at the moment.

The report in question, to speak of it now in general terms, was certainly a misreport in two particulars. First, it left out several strong expressions applied by Mr. Colenso to the objects of his special aversion, of which we distinctly remember "sneaking" as one; and, generally, it toned down rather than exaggerated the reverend gentleman's observations. Second, it made no attempt to portray the demoniac expression of countenance he assumed during their delivery—the impression of such upon the spectators being as if long pent rancour and hate had suddenly burst the bounds which prudential considerations had hitherto interposed to their outbreak, and had gushed forth with violence irresistible.

The general accuracy of the report has received the testimony of every person present to whom we have named the subject; and there can be no doubt that, if any can complain of misreporting, it is that class against whom his reverence's malignity was directed. We challenge him to prove the contrary, or to substantiate a single instance of misreporting to his prejudice.

Our space will not permit us, at this time, to say more than one word upon his letter as a whole. It is, we may premise, but a second edition of the "Tracts for the

Times"—a series of papers with which, some years ago, our readers were nauseated, and which, in point of humbug and hypocrisy, were worthy of the pen of the immortal Pecksniff. We but ask our readers to give this letter a careful perusal, as nothing that we could say would more effectually shew the character of this self-styled "Tribune of the People" than the miserable clap-trap of which it is so bright a specimen.

❖ **1863 TO THE ELECTORS OF THE TOWN OF NAPIER.**
Hawke's Bay Times, Napier. 3 p. Hawke's Bay Herald, 28 January.

"Veritas visu et mora, falsa festinatione et incertis valescunt."[8]—TACIT.

"Diligimus omnia vera, id est fidelia, simplicia, Constantia; vana, falsa, fallentia, odimus"[9]
—CIC.

"I speak unto wise men; judge ye what I say."—PAUL.

GENTLEMEN,[10]—Permit me to call your close and unprejudiced attention to this letter, containing the reasons which (combined) have led me to resign the seat in the Provincial Council of Hawke's Bay, to which some of your number lately elected me.

I. *Because of the unreasonable attempt at forcing a pledge upon me at the nomination.* I call this conduct "unreasonable," because, (1.) you well know that I (who have stood on the Napier hustings 6 or 8 times) have ever resisted and refused to pledge myself to anything, even when I knew my refusal might be the very means of my losing the election. And, further, I have uniformly said—"Never fetter any man of your choice with pledges," (mostly demanded in an hour of popular excitement); always, however, excepting the *one* pledge which I have ever voluntarily given (and which you should always obtain), viz., to resign whenever requested to do so by two-thirds of those who had voted. This pledge should be sufficient for both parties; for I am very sure it will not be found politically or morally safe to go farther. (2.) Because, while you wished me to pledge myself to vote for Mr. McLean as our future Superintendent, not one of you could tell me Mr. McLean's POLICY; not one of you knew anything about it; therefore, I was most "unreasonably" called upon to pledge myself for a man, of whom (politically speaking as Superintendent of our Province) I knew nothing, as against a man (our present Superintendent) of whose policy I knew something;—to pledge myself, in short, merely for a man,—*not* for a principle, nor for any known line of sound policy. (3.) Because, many among you well knew that the most cordial good feeling (and, I may say, agreement in Maori matters generally) had ever existed between Mr. McLean and myself; and, as you all well knew, that it has been charged against me as a political crime my ever standing by and supporting the Superintendent of

---

8 'The truth is established by investigation and delay: falsehood by haste and uncertainty.' Tacitus: *Annales* II: 39. I.S.G.

9 'We delight in things that are true, that is, that are faithful, simple, permanent; such as are vain, false, deceitful we abhor.' Cicero. I.S.G.

10 The 1893 electoral bill first allowed women to vote. I.S.G.

the Province, you might easily have coupled these facts together and reasonably have inferred—that, on Mr. McLean becoming our Superintendent and producing a suitable policy, I should most willingly and heartily have supported him also. Such, indeed, (as I have been informed,) was clear enough to several electors;—such, indeed, was the only logical deduction.

II. *Because of unfair treatment.* Not a few of you, gentlemen, have heard me say, (for I well remember saying it on two public occasions,)—that in healthy constituencies there must ever exist between the electors and elected a mutual confidential understanding of warm, close, ready, and constant support; and this most reasonably, because the elected person is but their own mouthpiece. Now many of you who recently voted against me have repeatedly and publicly acknowledged, that I have hitherto politically served you faithfully and to the best of my ability. If so, were you not fairly bound to continue to support me at this last election? And was I not fairly entitled to look forward to, and to rely on, your ready support? Some of you, who recently voted against me, (and whose continued support I had reasonably calculated on,) told me on the hustings that I had hitherto served them well; and that, excepting the present election, they had always voted for me. Could you not then have confidence in me for the future? Ought you not to have both had and shewn such confidence after 4 years' experience of me? As I view it, your own words fairly considered are proof of the unfair treatment I have received at your hands. Such a mode of acting entirely unsettles all confidence in electors;—enfeebles the man of your choice when in Council;—restrains truly honorable men from coming forward to serve you;—and, sooner or later must prove injurious to the Commonweal. I might also fairly enough complain of the *manner* of acting adopted by some few among you at the late election—as against an opponent (myself) who never canvasses, nor condescends to use any threat, or promise, or art, or cajolery; but, as I know very well there are some among us who believe in the hacknied phrase,—"All's fair in love, war and politics,"—(at least, those persons have shewn their firm belief in the *political* part of the adage by acting (shall I say *dirtily* acting?) up to it,) I shall be silent, notwithstanding I greatly doubt if such conduct will bear their own close calm investigation, or give them any satisfaction when reviewing it hereafter. Pirates firing broken glass, or the Chinese stinkpots, have never been copied or supported in reasonable and civilised warfare; and Lord Dundonald's secret of wholesale destruction, (with many others of a similar kind) was rightly disapproved of by the Government at home.

III. *Because I wished you to believe what I told you on the hustings on the day of nomination, —that I was not desirous of a seat in the next Provincial Council.* Some of you that day doubted the truthfulness of that statement of mine; they viewed it as a mere catch-word. Such statement, however, was perfectly correct. My mind had been made up for some time, and mainly from the following grounds:—1. The experience I have had of how very little can be really effected in Provincial Councils or General Assemblies by one person, however zealous, or single his aim.—2. The very great dislike I have to what is known as political "log-rolling."—3. The waste of time, and unprofitableness of such a situation to a man constituted like myself—*i.e.*, of one who only goes there to aid and benefit his town or province, and who never absents himself from his duty.—4. The belief that I had, that many of those old settlers—working men—with whom I had been consociated from the beginning of our Provincial Government, would not again come forward for re-election (I included Messrs. Carter and Rhodes, subsequently elected).—5. The extra amount of labour which might fall upon me if re-elected (as an old working hand, always in his place,) among so many new hands.—6. My increasing desire for quiet, and for more time for scientific studies.—7. The possibility of my ere long leaving the Province.

IV. *Because of the misconception, or delusion, which still existed among many of the electors.* I had hoped, on and after the day of the declaration of the poll at the late election, that what I had boldly said on that occasion (regardless of consequences), would have wholly disabused the minds of several of the electors, as I addressed myself particularly to the *thinking* men among them. Such, however, (as far as I know), I am sorry to say, has not been the case. *Why*, it is not for me now to say. One thing I know, that few men now in New Zealand, holding the post of town member in your Provincial Council, would have served you and the town interests (as against the country) so zealously and fearlessly as I have done; and you must know, that, in my so doing, I have made myself many enemies among the country gentlemen and runholders. As an instance, however, of the delusion which still exists among the electors, I may state, that, since the polling-day, in talking with one of them who had voted against me, (a respectable elector and a Scotsman), he said,—"But, Mr. Colenso, you pitched into the people of Burns, of whom I have myself heard you say you were an ardent admirer." I replied, "My good sir, I am (and ever must be) a great and steady admirer of Burns; but it is just because Burns would never have joined in any sly, underhand measures that I admire him. Think you, were *he* here among us at this recent election, he would have joined his Countrymen in any such measures? NO. Burns himself *suffered* from similar causes, and devoted his noblest efforts in exposing all such; whether under the mask of religion, morality, or politics." Burns is with *me*, Scotch electors of Napier; not with you, if you own to any sinister underhanded influence, albeit you are Scotchmen.

V. *Because of the unjust and absurd attempts made to unseat me.*—My knowledge of human nature tells me, that such conduct would generally result in the very opposite to that of a resignation; and perhaps, under other circumstances, I would not have resigned. But when I saw that among my opponents, *(even after the election was over)* were those who seemed utterly devoid of any generous sentiment; who stopped at nothing; who clutched eagerly, as drowning men, at straws—first, doubting the Returning Officer's *right* to vote—second, disputing the *legality* of Mr. Holder's vote—third, denying altogether that of Mr. Anderson's (although *on the revised Roll!)*—and, fourthly, endeavoring by low and unworthy means to foment and increase the excitement (already too high) between myself and some of the Scotch settlers, (which excitement I had, indeed, in some measure, caused,—though not as vilely represented in the *Herald* paper) —when, I say, I saw all this, I thought it better to resign. Never before, however, have

I had such practical proofs of the wisdom of the saying,—that "no man should judge his own case:"—for I have herein seen the utter incompetency of a man to do so, although possessing a pretty clear head and some amount of legal knowledge,—aye, running to the most absurd conclusions, even against law, respecting his own case;— and another, selfishly cunning one, completely losing his hitherto cautiously measured step, overtoppling and even falsely reporting[11] through his dreadful excitation! anti all—(under the guise of virtuous indignation at lowered nationality!!)—to bolster up HIMSELF! *O tempora! O mores!*—

—*"Absentem qui rodit amicum,*
Qui non defendit alio culpante; solutos
Qui captat risus hominum, famamque dicacis;
Fingere qui non visa potest, commissa tacere
Qui nequit, hic niger est, hunc tu, Romane, caveto.[12]
—HOR.

Before, however, that I conclude, (although my letter is already too long,) I must not omit saying is few *more* words to those Electors who are from the far North—or Scotland. I say "a few more," because I particularly invite their close attention to what I have already written. Especially as the Scots are a people who rank very high as metaphysicians, close reasoners, and lovers of truth. All that I may have said, or that I am believed to have said, against you AS A PEOPLE (on the hustings, at the declaration of the Poll on the 6th. inst.,) I pray you to forgive, and, if possible, forget. I sincerely regret so offending any of you, and now publicly apologise. Favorably consider, I pray, the place, the circumstances, and the excitement, and the well-known fact, that only the *wearer* of the shoe knows how it pinches. Bear in mind that my oldest and best Provincial friends are Scotchmen (Alexander, McLean, Gollan, Lyon, and others, not one of whom I should willingly offend, much less wish to lose). At the same time— having said this—having thus publicly apologised to you Scotchmen, *as a people,* I cannot allow myself to withdraw what I *really* said on that occasion against that clique, or party among you here in Napier, who so ably (?) and indefatigably worked against me on the occasion of the recent election. Strange *facts,* that have since been made known to me; together with the great indelible one on the Poll-book—of only ONE Scotchman having then voted for me—all these prove, how some then wrought, and... *something* besides.

And now, gentlemen electors of Napier, permit me to take my political leave of you. Those of you who have supported me I thank again, most sincerely, for all past favors and in more than I one sense regret that we should thus have parted. Perhaps it ought not to have been so; perhaps we ought not to have parted at this peculiar time—THIS COMING CRISIS: but so it is. While I live I cannot but have the interests of Hawke's Bay

---

11   As an instance, I may just call attention to what he has reported I said against Sir G. Grey!! and of my 'revolting explanations' concerning my dearest friend in Hawke's Bay, Captain Carter.—W.C.

12   'He who backbites an absent friend, who does not defend him when another censures him, who affects to raise loud laughs in company and the reputation of a funny fellow, who can feign things he never saw, who cannot keep secrets, he is a dangerous man; against him, Roman, be on your guard.' Horace. W.C.

deeply at heart. And seeing that I have a large stake in the prosperity of the Province; —that I am well acquainted with the whole of it, its resources and its requirements; —that I am among the very oldest of its settlers;—and that you have but few public men; —I should perhaps, after all, do wrong, if I were not to hold myself ready to respond to your call, should that call again come *while I may continue to reside in Napier.* But before such response could ever again be honestly and cheerfully made by me, a very much better understanding must be arrived at among us. You, my constant supporters, and the electors of Napier generally, must awake from political lethargy; you must be ready and willing to do your share of the great work. There must be nothing more of a "touch-and-go" kind; it must be fair play and mutual help. It has been, that confidence after recrimination has been stronger and freer than it was before; and surgeons say that a united bone is all the stronger for having been broken.

Lastly, allow your old servant (who has your best interests at heart,) at parting politically to offer a word of advice:—Seek to strengthen your incoming Superintendent: reflect a bit,—*choose a good useful man to fill the present vacancy.* Consider those already elected as members of the Provincial Council; are there more than two (or three at most) of the whole number who from their position, and knowledge &c. of the Province, are fit to be entrusted with Executive duties? And would those three persons accept that office? I am pretty sure two of them would not. And yet three will be required, which (as the law now is) must be chosen from the Provincial Council. See, then, you make a wise and discreet choice in selecting another member for the Town. It is just your only chance left of doing anything for yourselves, and, at the same time, strengthening your future Superintendent. And may you, and your next Superintendent and Provincial Council, act more harmoniously and usefully than you have all hitherto done.

I have the honor to be, Gentlemen Electors,
Your most obdt. Servt. and well-wisher,
WILLIAM COLENSO.
Napier, Jan. 22, 1863.

❖ 1863 CORRESPONDENCE.
Hawke's Bay Times 6 February.
SIR,—I have just seen, in a copy of the *Herald* dated "Saturday, February 4," a query by "Enquirer." If Enquirer is an elector, and has the manliness to give his real address, he shall have his enquiry fully answered by
WM. COLENSO.
Wednesday.

§ 1863 TO CORRESPONDENTS.
Hawke's Bay Times 30 January.

OUR correspondent "Jim Crow" has reminded us of a fact which had, owing to the pressure of other matters, for the moment escaped our notice. There can be no doubt whatever but that under the Contractors Act Mr. James Wood, being a large contractor under the Provincial Government, must vacate his seat, and come before his admiring constituency a second time. We confess to being very glad that this opportunity is offered to the electors of Napier to correct the error which they have made in returning Mr. Wood. That individual does not appear to us to possess any characteristic which in the slightest degree entitles him to the distinction of an M.P.C. for Napier. And furthermore, it seems to us that for a man like Mr. Colenso, according to our view of the case the *only*—(mark, the *only*)—man connected with the Provincial Government of this Province who is possessed of any ability whatever, to go begging, while the electors return such a sorry humanity as Mr. Wood, is a flat contradiction of the electoral privilege.

§ 1863 HAWKE'S BAY.
Wellington Independent 12 February.

Mr. William Colenso has resigned the seat in the Provincial Council. He publishes a long letter detailing his reasons for taking that step; which the *Herald* of the 24th January thus comments on:—His letter is a curiosity in its way. He complains of having been *vilely* misrepresented in the report of the election proceedings which appeared in this journal; yet makes an apology to the Scotch, as a people abjectly asking forgiveness—although, of course excepting the dirty Napier clique. He bids his constituents a political farewell in one part of his letter, and, further on, nibbles for another invitation to come forward. It is necessary to add that the whole is interlarded with scraps of Latin.

§ 1863 TO THE EDITOR.
Hawke's Bay Times 13 February.

SIR,—Just back from the country, I have been looking into the late Napier news, to see if Mr. Colenso had noticed any of his antagonist's bitter attacks. At the same time I scarcely thought he could, after having been openly called a liar on the hustings by him. And here I might say it is worth noticing, and marks the man, to see how Mr. Wood turns that off in his news, he there with some pomposity says, —(if I remember the precise words: I know we had a good laugh over them) —"Mr. Wood denied it emphatically"! Well, let that pass. I am not going to take up the sticks in defence of Mr. Colenso. I know well he does not want help from me,—but I never have believed the Devil to be so black as he is painted. I saw on my way back that copy of Wood's newspaper in which he speaks of Mr. Colenso's demoniac countenance, and of the gushing forth of his great rancour and hate towards the Scotch, which had long been bottled up, &c., &c., &c. I was struck with this statement of Wood's, and, thinking as I rode, I considered it to be very malignant, marking the man again. In short, it is worse than bare malignancy, it is both false and ungrateful on the part of Wood, and this I think I can show. As no other person has come out, and as actions speak louder than words, I will just give you, Mr. Editor, two matters which came to my own certain knowledge, and there may be many more like matters unknown to me though known to older residents. About 18 or 20 months back, I heard Mr. Wood himself say, that the Scotch could not have got up their church in this town, had it not been for Mr. Colenso's noble and disinterested conduct concerning the land on the hill, which was as good to them as a gift of £500. Mr. Wood also remarked that it was the more generous on the part of Mr. Colenso, as he did not attend their worship. And Mr. Tom FitzGerald told me about 3 or 4 years back, that Mr. Wood would have got on but badly when he set up—he not knowing much of printing—had not Mr. Colenso helped him, and that he, Mr. F., had known Mr. Colenso to ride in from his old residence, purposely to help him, and had seen him throw off his coat, and with his own hands wash Wood's dirty printing dabbers. This last fact I give as I heard it from Mr. F., and though I believe it to be true I don't vouch for its truth, and I think Mr. S. Begg was present at the same time and heard Mr. F. say so. So that Mr. Wood is somewhat indebted to Mr. Colenso, both individually and nationally, and should have been a little more careful in giving vent to his spleen. I just give you two matters of fact, which have been brought fresh to my remembrance through reading Wood's statements, and you may print them if you please. I am, &c., &c.,

JUSTUS.

P.S.—I have said £500. I think that was the sum Mr. Wood mentioned, but he might have said £400 or £500.

§ 1863 EDITORIAL.

The Independent 14 February.[13]

The career of Mr. William Colenso as a Provincial politician has come to an abrupt close. By his own act, he has quitted the hot arena of the Provincial Council Chamber of Hawke's Bay, and now seeks, in the cold cell of private life, that repose and leisure for his scientific classical studies, which his previous position did not afford. Perhaps it is well that this should be so; who knows, but that like the first Greek prose writer he may still devote his elegant leisure to the service of his adopted country: Cadmus of Miletus chronicled the foundation of his native city, and wrote the history of the colonisation of Ionia—and Colenso, in imitation of his illustrious prototype, may yet make Napier similarly famous and have his memory cherished by future generations as the historian of Hawke's Bay. Degenerate Scotch materialists think of this!!
The man "who is far before his age" lives unhonored amongst you. "The modern Cadmus" feels the chills of neglect, but posterity will yet atone for your injustice.

---

13 This editorial in the *Wellington Independent* was copied in the *Hawke's Bay Times*, 20 February 1863 and the *Hawke's Bay Herald* the next day. I.S.G.

Philosophers are however but mortal after all, and Mr. Colenso forms no exception to the rule. Putting aside for the moment, the almost mountebank display recently made on the hustings at Napier; we regret that he should have thought it necessary on the occasion of his resigning to favour the colonists with another ridiculous exhibition. Not content with issuing a terribly verbose, and inscrutable valedictory address to the electors of Napier, he has favored this journal with a letter, which will be found elsewhere, containing an attempted explanation, and justification of his recent doings. While committing political suicide, he can't even do it quietly—but contrives to expire amidst a gorgeous Coruscation of words. The gist of the letter simply amounts to this, that our previous comments on himself—"our Editorial castigation" as he terms it, was merited, "if he had been the fool that the selfishly cunning writer of the so-called report had made him." This not very clear sentence taken in conjunction with the rest of the letter, amounts to the charge that Mr. James Wood the Editor of the *Hawke's Bay Herald* has of *malice prepense*, published a false report of the speech in question. This is certainly a very grave accusation against a gentleman occupying the twofold position of a journalist and a member of the Provincial Council, and should at least be supported by reasonable evidence. We have again gone very carefully over the files of the Hawke's Bay journals, the *Times* as well as the *Herald*, and on comparing their reports with Mr. Colenso's letter; cannot find anything which in the least degree justifies the charge.

Mr. Colenso from lengthened political experience should be perfectly aware that the words of a speaker cannot always be reported verbatim and that an alteration of phrase when the meaning is strictly preserved, does not constitute a misreport. At the very most this is all he can complain of. He admits having made an attack on the Scotch, and only denies the use of certain words; but if we may take *his own version* of what he did say, it would be hard to judge whether that, or the reported speech was most insulting. Besides, Mr. Colenso should remember that we have only his own testimony on one side, and he cannot, from position be considered a perfectly unprejudiced witness; while on the other hand, we have a gentleman whose reputation as a journalist, and character as a local politician depended on the honesty and accuracy with which he recorded public proceedings. It is surely very petty for Mr. Colenso to ascribe a host of underhand motives to Mr. Wood, in the columns of another journal. The issue ought to have been settled elsewhere, and we observe with regret that his accusations in the present letter are infinitely stronger against Mr. Wood than those contained in his address to the electors. The former is only published here, while the latter first saw the light in Hawke's Bay, and admitted of almost immediate refutation. So far as this journal is concerned, we simply acted as we have always hitherto done, in taking the report of the speech from a journal of acknowledged respectability; and if it were incorrect, the error should rather have been exposed in the columns of the *Hawke's Bay Herald* than in those of the *Wellington Independent*. As a matter of opinion, we may however say that we believe the report was substantially correct, and that conviction is borne out by the circumstance that its re-publication in both the *Southern Cross* and *New Zealander*, has evoked no contradiction.

We do not profess to be quite so well acquainted with colonial "Dodges" as Mr. Colenso, nor can we emulate his dexterity in supplying copious talk with only the appearance of reason. In this, he almost rivals Hudibras, of whom it is said,

"On either side he could dispute,
Confute, change hands, and still confute."

We scarcely appreciate this kind of trifling, and therefore think it unnecessary to do more than just allude to his gratuitous assumptions as to the motives which dictated our previous comments. His ingenuity in suggesting explanations really evinces an immense amount of perverted talent. Perhaps it was because the writer "was a Scotchman and an Odd Fellow," or perhaps "a leading member of the late Ministry was having a blow at an old political opponent." The former of those insinuations only provokes a smile, the latter we indignantly repudiate. As a public man, with no inconsiderable notoriety, his recent displays have been made the subject of legitimate comment. In one breath he now craves pardon for the past, and heaps fresh insults on his opponents. His valedictory address to the electors had better never been made, his letter better never been penned. Both only make matters worse than before, and simply serve to show how far political bickerings may for the time cause a polished gentleman, and a Legislator of the Colony to forget the dignity of his position.

❖ **1863 TO THE EDITOR.**
Wellington Independent 14 February;
republished Hawke's Bay Herald 21 February.

SIR,—An acquaintance has just shewn me your paper of the 15th instant, in which you have been pleased to devote a whole editorial to myself and to my late (?) doings! I confess I feel some doubts as to the proper course open to me—whether to write to you or not. Had your old established paper a mere colonial circulation, I should certainly not care publicly to notice your elaborate article. I should just act in this, as I have under many other equally strange charges and statements made concerning me—quietly live it down. For, I am very sure, that as far as the Province of Hawke's Bay is concerned, ditto a large part of that of Auckland, and no small portion (I think I may safely say) of that of Wellington, it would be a mere waste of time and words, if not highly ridiculous, for me to think of answering what such a man as James Wood, the printer of the *Hawke's Bay Herald*, pleases to write concerning me on any matter in which himself or his pocket is concerned.

Sir, I wholly grant the correctness of your editorial castigation, *if* I had been the fool that the "selfishly cunning" writer of that so-called report, had made me. But it does seem strange, very strange—to me at least, that you, sir, the editor of an old-established journal,—you, who have long known me (may I not say personally,) pretty well,

—you, sir, who so often have warned us here in another Province against believing the canards of the *Spectator* and of the *Advertiser;*—you, who know that even the reporting of the General Assembly debates by disinterested and able reporters, possessing every convenience, was but very lately protested against for its erroneousness; that you knowing all this, should so suddenly jump to the conclusion, that *all* that interested James Wood said, in his "vile report" of our late election proceedings, was true! Mark me, Mr. Editor, I say, all that Wood had said; for, if you had any reasonable doubt on your mind, (as an editor of several years standing and a judicious man), as to any portion of that "vile report" of his, then you should have reasonably suspected the whole, and then you ought to have withheld your editorial pen until you had made further enquiry. And (may I not ask,) had you no doubts, no misgivings, as to some portion of that precious report? Sir, I know you are a man like myself, and moreover an experienced man, and I therefore know you must have had such doubts. Why, then, did you not act justly towards me? Have I to conclude, that, seeing you are a Scotchman and an officer in the Odd Fellows,—or, rather, shall I say, an old Wellington settler and an out-and-out supporter of the "Fox-Featherston party,"—such a golden opportunity should not be lost of hitting "the old enemy of Wellington;" more especially when such could be done by using the very words of a quondam acquaintance. Or, am I to adopt the opinion of some here—that, seeing sometimes an able man of the late ministry (as it is reported) writes articles for your journal, that that gentleman has once more tried his hand against an old political opponent? Sir, I cannot bring myself to adopt the latter.

Mr. James Wood, as it is well known, is generally *his own reporter;* in this case most unfortunately for him and for his little paper. For, had any one else, not immediately concerned, been reporting, all, I have no doubt, would have passed off well enough. (As, for instance, in the *Hawke's Bay Times*, a paper with which I had no connection), whatever was *really* said by me however grating, would have been properly placed (as it has already been by thinking minds), to the excitement, the place, and the very great provocation I had received. My real remarks as to my not being either a Freemason or an Odd Fellow *rightly construed,* only shewed that through my non-social *status* with them I had not their votes. The words "mean, crawling Scotchmen," were *never* used by me; at the same time, I did plainly enough denounce "the underhanded secret, mole-like working" which a certain party had carried on against me. And as to the words,—"had he not been born an Englishman, he would wish to have been born an Irishman, &c;" (which words are lumped in by excited Wood into *one* sentence with the former!) I did not use those words as so set down; although I did say—in my *second* address, after all the other candidates had spoken, I (being obliged to speak again, through James Wood having given me the lie direct in plain English, and after having been often interrupted by some of his own Scotch supporters and friends who were in the fore-front of the hustings with no very seemly remarks)—that "I did not believe in the ancient doctrine of metempsychosis; but if I did, or if there were truth in such, and I could not be again born an Englishman, and I could choose, I would elect to be born an Irishman, rather &c."

And surely, sir, there can be no great need for me to lengthen this in order to point out the *reasons* why James Wood was so fearfully excited; unless it be that you, living at a distance, were ignorant of them! The *present* main cause, sir, was my having dared to touch upon his own paper,—saying, (in answer to some one from the crowd,) "I had no confidence in it." (Much indeed as there is in that part is reported by him—*before* he "overtoppled.") But there were *other* latent and congenuous causes smouldering in his bosom, (of which I need mention but two). First, his again losing the Government printing for 1863, which he had felt cock-sure of getting. And second, the advertisement which appeared about three weeks ago for tenders for advertising, (which you yourself *not knowing* the real state of the case, had also unwarily animadverted on,) both of which mortal sins against the *Herald*, are mainly laid by James Wood at my door, as one of the Hawke's Bay Executive. Now, sir, having stated this plainly, may I not appeal to you—as an old printer and an experienced Editor, pretty well acquainted with colonial politics and dodges of would-be Provincial politicians—whether such a man in such a place, under such influences, united, could possibly report faithfully? Talk of prejudices—of party-feelings—of green-glasses—of nationality!

"Hyperion to a satyr."

And then you also speak of my "false and malicious attempt to arouse ancient national jealousies!" Is this the old Editor of the long established *Wellington Independent* thus speaking?—and thus speaking of *me*? Do you not know—nay more, have you not in some of your old numbers, noticed approvingly my long known absolute and real hatred of all such national distinctions, and would that they had all been left behind us? Yes, whether civil, political, or ecclesiastical. Did I not, several years ago, write and speak against your St. Andrews and St. Patrick's and St. George's days being held there among you at Wellington?—Calling on you to do away with such mummery and barriers to the advancement of our common humanity, and unite in one colonial day of hilarity and welcome and brotherhood. And have you ever heard of my altering? Of course, in all this, I know I am before the age; yet I have a joy.

"I joy the age to come will think with me." Sir, I believe this of you, that on calm reflection you will allow all this. Further, for James Wood of the *Herald*, under all the circumstances, there is a certain allowance to be made for his "vile report;" but, really I see but very few extenuating ones for the remarks of McKenzie & Muir of the *Wellington Independent*.

You, also, remark on my "forming a tail,"—*i.e.* being the lowest on the poll of those returned (46 to 62). I scarcely know whether you mean this as a reproof to me, or to the Napier electors; for, although *at present* politically differing, (you and I,) I believe that you, as an old colonist and a watcher of political events, will readily own that I have endeavoured to serve Napier and her interests. However, as you are well acquainted with Provincial elections, it will suffice for me to inform you, that every one of the 46 who voted for me, did so *unsolicited*; nay, more, several of them nobly withstood strong solicitations to the contrary.—

You may yet know more of our late Napier election, *of what took place before it,* and during its continuance, if such be worth your knowing—bye-and-bye. Time is the great revealer of all things. Sir, I have resigned my seat in the Hawke's Bay Provincial Council, and I shall enclose a copy of my letter to the electors of Napier, on my so doing for your perusal.

> *I am, Sir, Yours very truly,*
> WILLIAM COLENSO.

P.S.—(28th.) Since writing the above I find James Wood has returned to the charge of railing; hoping thereby to bolster up himself—which he much needs. Let me call your attention, in closing, to his acknowledging his misuse of the Governor's name in his "vile report," but in so doing, poor creature, he goes from the pan to the fire! saying, "it was the Domett Ministry whom I spoke against from the hustings"!!! What will you at Wellington think of that? I, William Colenso, speaking publicly against the Domett Ministry!—*Jam satis—ohe.*

> W.C.

❖ 1863 OPEN COLUMN.
Hawke's Bay Herald 29 August.

SIR,—I am desirous of calling your attention to a portion of the leading article in the *"New Zealander"* of the 21st inst., containing a very grave and unpleasant misconstruction arising from an apparently slight error in your 'Herald,' of the 15th inst.

The Editor of the *"New Zealander"* says:—"When Archdeacon Brown, and the settlers around him, were warned to escape for their lives from Tauranga, and when Wm. Thompson issued his mandate to slay and spare not, we gave it as our conviction that he had a great ultimate object to attain in clearing the Bay of Plenty of its "FLEAS." That object, we said, was to receive shipments of supplies, and send off gunpowder and warlike munitions and stores, unwatched and unnoticed, from Tauranga to the Thames. Our then convictions have been more than confirmed, they have been all but realised by intelligence received from Napier yesterday, by the Wonga Wonga.—On the 12th instant, the schooner Janet, 23 tons, Paul, sailed from Napier for Tauranga, with 160 bags flour, and 100 native passengers. Of this *significant shipment,* the "Hawke's Bay Herald" of the 15th writes thus:—

"The flour per Janet, shipped in large quantity by the natives here, and in handy 50-lb bags, has given rise to much speculation as to its ultimate destination—some going so far as to say that each bag contained a canister of gunpowder. Who doubts the perfect correctness of these 'speculations'? and who but feels surprise that the Auckland was not rather instructed to cruise off the Mayor Island,[14] than at the mouth of the Wairoa?" And so on.

Now all this is owing to an error in the Herald of the 15th inst., (most unintentional on your part I have not the slightest doubt). There you state (as quoted),—the Janet sailed hence for *Tauranga* instead of *Turanga.* The former place, in the Bay of Plenty,

---

14 Off Tauranga, Bay of Plenty. W.C.

being Wm. Thompson's nearest seaport; the latter, the (now) common Maori name for Poverty Bay.

It is very easy to understand how such an announcement of flour ("powder") and a hundred native passengers hence to Tauranga (Bay of Plenty), must have increased the suspicions and fears of Auckland. And I venture to think, such fears and suspicions would have been greatly lessened had you also stated, (what I, at the time, understood, to be the case,)—that the 100 natives had mainly come down in the Janet from Turanga to the mill-feast here—had brought down a large lot of seed potatoes to the Natives of Ahuriri, and were now taking back flour in return. Of course, of the powder, I know nothing.

> *I am, Sir,*
> *Yours truly,*
> WM. COLENSO.

P.S. I notice also the same error of Tauranga for Turanga, to be in the "*Waka Maori*," published by you.—W.C.

❖ 1863 M. FITZGERALD v. COLENSO.

Hawke's Bay Times 4 September.

SIR,—Having been often asked the particulars of the above-mentioned action, (owing to, I regret to say, its not having been clearly reported either in the *Times* or the *Herald*,) and having (as I hope) yesterday paid the *last* bill of costs on account of the same, I wish, with your permission, and for the information of the public, to state plainly the case itself, the working of the "Minor Jury Sittings" (Supreme Court) here in Napier, and, in conclusion, say a word to the gentlemen who may form the Napier Juries.

I. *The case itself.* This (as I take it) is exceedingly simple. Notwithstanding, to make it the more plain, I shall be obliged to give a little necessary introductory matter.— Messrs. Triphook & Wright were my Land Agents, up to their leaving for Canterbury. On the 6th February last I received back from Mr. Triphook my various maps and plans. Shortly after Mr. M. Fitzgerald called on me, as agent for Mr. Tuke, to know my terms for some land near Puketapu: I told him. He called two or three times, in as many days, and eventually made me an offer in writing for the same. His offer being a complicated one, I took two days to consider it, (taking also professional advice,) on the third day I told Mr. F. that I would accept his terms; he said, he would immediately inform his employer, Mr. Tuke. After this nearly a fortnight passed, during which I saw no more of Mr. F. On the day, however, of the election of our Superintendent, (February 26th), I accidentally met Mr. Tuke in Shakespeare-road, when he informed me, (in a few words spoken as he hastily passed by,) that he should not purchase the land. I thought his conduct very strange, but as I had had no communication with him about it, I said nothing to him; the next day (the 27th,) I called Mr. F. into the Treasury office, and told him what Mr. T. had said. Mr. F. acknowledged that he had known of such being Mr. T.'s intention; and, moreover, that he (Mr. F.) was so displeased at it, that he had told Mr. T. he would not communicate it to me adding, that if I brought the matter into court he would appear as a witness in my behalf, &c., &c. Mr. F. then seeming to be so straightforward and honorable, and I at that time so very busy in the office and also with public matters (our Council being about to meet), I asked him to become my land agent, handing him over the maps, &c., as I had recently received them back from Mr. Triphook, and *arranging with Mr. F to give him a Schedule of prices with full letter of instructions, at the close of the sitting of the Provincial Council.*

A day or two afterwards Mr. Maney called on me, respecting a piece of land near the Meanee bridge. I sent him to Mr. F., and soon after Mr. F. saw me, ard arranged with me as to terms.

About the same time Mr. P. Dolbel came to me to renew his enquiries after the land near Puketapu, which Mr. F., as Mr. Tuke's agent, had made me an offer for. *As Mr. Dolbel had commenced his enquiries last year about that land, and knew both the acreage and price, I did not send him to Mr. F.*

On the 7th of March, (the day after Napier races,) Mr. F. called again at the Treasury office, and said that while on the race course Mr. Ormond had been speaking to him about the land near Puketapu, but that he (Mr. O.) could not speak decisively about it for a month or so; and that he, (Mr. F.) supposed, from what Mr. Ormond had said, the land would be too large for him. I told Mr. F. that I had recently again seen Mr. Dolbell, who had renewed his old application for that land, and that I had also given him a week to consider my terms; and unless Mr. Dolbell should refuse them I could not attend to any offer from another person.

I may also mention, that, during that week I got a tracing, &c., of the land near Puketapu made for Mr. Dolbel, from the maps at the Land Office by another Surveyor, notwithstanding my having a colored map of the same land, on a large scale among the maps, &c., in Mr. F.'s possession, but I was careful not to trouble him in the least about it, although I was in the habit of daily seeing him; Mr. F's residence and office being the next house to my office.

At the end of the stipulated time Mr. Dolbel accepted my terms.

Mr. F. never saw Mr. Dolbel about the land.

Before the close of the Session of the Provincial Council I had resigned the Office of Provincial Treasurer, consequently, (being now free from public duties, and having little else to do,) I informed Mr. F. I should act for myself, and hence Mr. F. did not receive from me the promised schedule of prices.

Soon after Mr. F. sent in his bill, in which, while he charged as Commission for the transaction with Mr. Maney, the very moderate sum of £3, he charged as "Commission" on the whole amount of the land sold by me to Mr. Dolbel, £34 15s. 0d, although he knew that three fourths of the purchase money were to remain in mortgage on the land, (for 7 years if required) at 8 per cent.

The day following I called on Mr. F., and told him, how very greatly I was surprised at his bill of charges and that, in concluding to take back my maps, &c., from him, and for the future to act for myself, I had already determined to give him £15, (say, £5 for Mr. Maney's matter, and £10 on so suddenly and unexpectedly resuming my papers, &c.,—as I had thought he might be not a little disappointed at my so doing,) and which sum of £15 I then offered him; but which he would not accept, claiming "the Commission to the last shilling upon the whole amount of the purchase money." On leaving him that day he agreed to my proposal, to bring the matter immediately before Captain Curling, R.M., and to abide by his award.

About ten days after this I met Mr. F. in the street, when to my surprise he informed me, that he had altered his mind, and that he should bring me into the Supreme Court. He had engaged Mr. Wilson, our then only disengaged Solicitor, (Mr. Brooke Taylor, being Registrar of the Supreme Court, was not able to act for me,) and on the arrival of the steamer with the Judge, Mr. F. left Mr. Wilson and engaged Mr. Allen who had also come to Napier by the steamer.

Before the trial, the £3 charged by Mr. F. as commission on the land sold to Mr. Maney was paid by me into Court.

The Judge, in summing up, informed the Jury clearly, that what I had told Mr. F. on the 7th of March relative to Mr. Dolbel, had quite taken that piece of land out of Mr. F.'s hands, and that Mr. F. *"had no claim for commission"*; but that, if they were of opinion, *"anything was due to him for work done,"* they were to find for him such an amount as was fair and reasonable.

After a short consultation the jury returned a verdict of *"£20 for the plaintiff,* Mr. F., he paying his own costs." The Judge, however, told them he could not receive their verdict so given; and that they should only find for the amount (if any) for work done. On this they again briefly consulted, and returned a verdict of *"£17 for Mr. F.,* being half his charge for commission."

II. Of *"Minor Jury Sittings."*—This case of Fitzgerald v. Colenso is the first case tried here under this new Act and I dare say what the Judge said in favor of this new mode of action will be remembered by those who were that day in Court. At present, sir, it will be quite sufficient for me to call the attention of the public to one remark only which fell from His Honour the Judge, viz., the desirability of removing cases from the District Court into the Minor Jury Sittings (Supreme Court), partly on account of its *inexpensiveness,*—the costs being but very little more than they would be in the District Court. What the *costs* in the District Court might have been in this case I do not exactly know; I am informed such would have been *under £10.* I do know, however, the amount of costs I have paid, amounting to £22 10s., of which sum £15 15s. was to the plaintiff's lawyer, who (I should also in justice state,) struck off a few pounds from his bill, owing to its being (as he called it) "a hard case." Therefore, sir, unless the costs in the "Minor Jury Sittings" (Supreme Court) are to be very materially lessened, I cannot see the great desirability of removing cases thither from the District Court; mine, too, being *per se,* a very simple inexpensive case, and one to be quickly disposed of.

III. *A word to Napier Juries.*—And here, before I say anything, I would state, that I feel assured the Jury on this occasion thought they had acted rightly,—and in erring (*if they have erred*) did so unintentionally. But, from certain candid admissions made to me by some of them since the trial,—taken together with the law as laid down by the Judge on the occasion, and, also, their first verdict,—I cannot but conclude that I have had heavy uncalled for expense, little law,[15] and less justice. And, therefore, I hope that a due consideration of the case in all its bearings will be a means of causing a future Napier Jury to act equitably,[16] and save many a poor defendant from unintentional wrong and unlooked for expence.—For, firstly, the Judge laid down as *law* that Mr. F. could not claim any "commission," while he could "for work done" if there was any. Yet Mr. F.'s bill was *only* for "*Commission*,"[17] and the Jury eventually found for him "*half his charge for commission;*" not for any work done, (during the 8 days—*i.e.* from the 27th Feb. to the 7th March,—the time the said land was in his hands,)—which indeed could not be shown,—for Mr. F. admitted, on his cross-examination by Mr. Carlyon, that he had *not* even entered the Land in his Registry Book. Hence it is plain, the *second* finding was against Law as laid down by the Judge. Mr. F. throughout took his stand for commission on the whole amount of sale of the Land; he never pleaded any work done; and, I think, the Jury should have either found for him entirely;—or, following the Judge's ruling (both in law and equity,) for me. Secondly, on comparing the first and second verdicts of the Jury, it is clear, that they only allowed me £3 to pay Mr. F.'s law costs,—whereas I have paid (a reduced bill of) £15 15s to his own Solicitor. Thirdly, some of the Jury have since admitted to me, that in returning their verdicts, they had lost sight altogether of my having paid into Court previous to the trial the sum of £3, (being the amount of Mr. F.'s charge as Commission on the land sold to Mr. Maney, and an item of Mr. F.'s bill produced in Court,)—their verdicts *included* that sum also. And here I may also in passing note, that, while the Judge was addressing the Jury and near the close Mr. Allen (Mr. F.'s counsel) leaning across the table said to me—"Forty shillings! that will be their verdict."

Further: in England, and also in the Australian Colonies, it is the rule, that when a plaintiff drags a defendant into a superior Court, where an inferior and less expensive Court exists, and the plaintiff gains the action, that he is justly made by the Judge to bear the *extra* expenses caused through his electing the superior Court. Now Mr. F. not only did not adhere to our arrangement to bring the matter before Capt. Curling in a plain and simple way, he also recklessly increased the law expenses,—for instance, one of the heavy items in his lawyer's bill was for "SEVEN witnesses." I hope, ere long, such a salutary rule as the one referred to will also obtain here.

Of the conduct throughout of Mr. Fitzgerald, the plaintiff, in this action, I do not wish to speak. Silence is often the most expressive.

In conclusion, I will just add that I have had dealings with more than one firm in Napier as Land Agents acting for me, and I have never before heard of such a strange charge. My first agent was Mr. J.A. Smith, and, during the time he so acted, I sold three parcels of those lands which he had to sell for me, (and of which *he had the list of prices,* and also gave information concerning the same to each of the parties before

---

15 Legal protection against wrong. W.C.

16 Equity—fair play. W.C.

17 Mr. F. was paid *separately* £1 11s. 6d., for putting a plan of the estate on the margin of the deed; also £2 2s. for riding thither and setting out the lower E. boundary. W.C.

they came to me,) viz.,—one to Mr. Perry in Waghorn-street,—one to Mr. Bousfield on Scinde Island,—and one to Capt. Carter (for Mr. Leadam) on the W. side of the harbor. And not only did Mr. Smith not dream of charging Commission (as indeed he honorably witnessed in Court, being one of Mr. F.'s witnesses,) but, in his account-current for that year, having inadvertently charged Commission on the section I had sold to Mr. Perry, (Mr. Smith having also sold him one,) he credited me with the same sum, as having been "charged in error;"—which old account-current of his was also produced in court, and elicited praise from Mr. Allen.—Afterwards Mr. Triphook, and, subsequently, Messrs. Triphook & Wright became my agents; and during the time my lands were in their hands I also sold two parcels—one, to Mr. Wright, on Scinde Island, (before he entered into partnership with Mr. Triphook) and only last October, one to Mr. J. Begg, at Whareponga, (this latter too, under very peculiar and well-known circumstances): I scarcely need add, that those gentlemen never dreamed of such a thing as charging me commission on lands sold by myself.

Trusting that you will both forgive the length of this letter, and believe with me, that I am performing a public duty and indeed a benefit in making this case in its various bearings generally known.

I am, &c.,

WILLIAM COLENSO.

Napier, August 29, 1863.

❖ 1863 OPEN COLUMN.

Hawke's Bay Herald 30 September.

SIR,—I read with some considerable interest the notice, "Native Dispute," (under your heading of "Local Intelligence") which appeared in your issue of the 16th inst. And I have since closely examined your two subsequent numbers, fully expecting that you would follow up the matter. I scarcely need add, that I have been disappointed. I fear, however, it would be of little use my referring you to many places in the life of the *Herald* (in past years), where, with perhaps less to call for it, and at a far less critical period in our brief history, you have acted very differently. For what is the seed or the root of this "dispute," which you inform us seriously threatens to disturb the peace of this district? Who is the cause? perhaps some greedy run-holder not satisfied with what he has already; at all events it is some "inland settler" (name, perhaps, known to you), acting *illegally*. For all such contracts or leases are now by law illegal; and so they must be hereafter if this Province is ever to go-ahead. Of course, in so speaking, I wholly leave out of sight both Hapuku and Karaitiana: with the real Maori owner I have nothing to do.

May I ask a question, Sir—How would you like (as one of the Volunteer corps) to go to the front to quell any disturbance which might easily and rapidly grow (in these times) from this "dispute" or from any such illegal, and it may be greedy, proceedings on the part of a runholder? I know it is not for me, Sir, to suggest to you what may be best, (though time was when we thought alike on such matters) but, as I take it, you should lend all the weight and influence arising from your share of "the Fourth

Estate," (1.) to keep the public peace, by denouncing all disturbers of it; (2.) to prevent the best and choicest of the plains in the possession of the Maories (of which number Raukawa is one) from falling into the hands of the mere runholder, and to seek to preserve them for the agriculturalist (3.) to inform the public (when you happen to know) the name &c. of such offender to the Commonweal.

I only hope that this "inland settler" and *illegal* fomentor of Maori discord, is neither a J.P. nor a General Government official, nor a holder of any kind of commission from the Governor; for if so, and any disturbance follow, I know pretty well what my duty (as a M.H.R. from our Province) should be at the General Assembly.

> *I am, Sir,*
> *Very faithfully yours,*
> WILLIAM COLENSO.

Napier,
September 24, 1863.

❖ **1863 CORRESPONDENCE.**
Hawke's Bay Times 2 October.
SIR,—I beg to draw your attention to an able common-sense article which appeared in the *Otago Daily Times* of August 26, (reprinted in the *Otago Witness* of August 28,) on the unauthorised expenditure of that Province, as one not a little suitable to us at this time and well worthy of republication in your paper, if you have room.

It appears that the Superintendent of Otago had expended no less a sum than just a *quarter of a million* (£224,000) without authority! And that the compliant and kind Provincial Council had even negatived a resolution seeking to know how this enormous sum had been spent!!

The following sentence should be carefully studied and treasured up in memory —both in Hawke's Bay as well as in Otago—"Of one thing it [such conduct] is likely to convince the General Government—*the impolicy of granting the control of large loans to men who show themselves little acquainted with the form of constitutional government.*"

There is also, in the same paper, (*Otago Witness*), a series of letters between the Superintendent of Otago and the Manager of the Union Bank of Australia; which is very useful and highly suggestive to every one interested in Provincial Government matters but, I fear, too long for republication in your columns. From them, however, we learn that while that Bank had contracted to allow the Otago Provincial Government to overdraw to the amount of £30,000, it had really *overdrawn* to the extent of £150,000!

The last letter from the Superintendent of Otago to the Manager of the Union Bank of Australia, withdrawing the Government account from the Bank, being a short one, you may perhaps find room for.

> *I am, Sir, Yours, &c.,*
> W. COLENSO.

Napier, Sept. 24, 1863.

❖ 1863 CORRESPONDENCE.

Hawke's Bay Times 9 October.

SIR,—I was surprised to see in the *Herald* of Saturday last the startling statement that Wiremu Tamihana (William Thompson), the celebrated Ngatihaua chief of Waikato had recently been in our immediate neighborhood. I confess, I did not believe it (my knowledge of N.Z. etiquette assured me he could not thus have been here and returned). However, on Monday I made diligent enquiry, and found it to be an absolute myth! Judge, then, how very greatly I am surprised to find in the *Herald* of this day (being, too, a "summary for England") not only the same untrue statement repeated, but with fresh additions as a comment upon the "fact" of W.T. having been here, and the probable consequent disastrous results to us all!! Now, this is really too bad. The *Herald* is known to be at least semi-official, and should give the public the earliest and most truthful information respecting the Maories. Such a *reiterated* statement (though known here to be false) may be productive of much injury both among settlers and Maories in the outlying districts of this and the two neighboring Provinces. From the enquiries I have made, I may positively state, that W.T. has never been in this neighborhood nor (for what we know) a step on this side of Waikato.

I sincerely hope your paper of Friday next will be issued in time for the English mail steamer due here tomorrow, so that, at least, the antidote may be commensurate with the bane.

> *I am, yours, &c.,*
> WILLIAM COLENSO.

Napier,
October 7, 1863.

❖ 1864 CORRESPONDENCE.

Hawke's Bay Times 15 April.

SIR,—I noticed, in your last week's issue, the official advertisement from the Registration Officer, reminding the Electors that the present month is the only one in which objections are legally to be made against any name on the Electoral Roll. As the making any such objection by any private person, especially in a small community like ours, (however good the intention of the objector, or however beneficial the ultimate result,) is sure to be, by some, considered invidious or unnecessary,—I wish to make it known to all qualified persons, that I shall be happy in obtaining a few to join me in forming a Committee of Scrutiny, for scrutinising the Electoral Rolls of the Province; in order to object in due form against ALL persons erroneously placed thereon. I do this wholly apart from any political bias; and should be glad if Electors opposed to myself (politically) would join me,—as my only wish is to see the Electoral Roll purified. A note addressed to me (by post, or left to your care,) from any qualified person shall be immediately responded to.

I find, that at Canterbury such a Committee has been formed, having Mr. Fitzgerald, M.G.A., at its head, and is now working.

I am,

Yours truly

W. COLENSO.

Napier, 9ᵗʰ April, 1864.

❖ 1864 TO THE SECRETARY, WELLINGTON CHAMBER OF COMMERCE.
Wellington Independent 21 April.

Napier, March, 12, 1864.

SIR,—Having been requested by the Commissioners of the Royal Exhibition at Dunedin to contribute the Essay "on the Botany, Geographic, and Economics of the North Island of New Zealand," and having undertaken the task, I naturally seek for every aid which will the better enable me to fulfil the same. And being well aware that the Wellington Chamber of Commerce possesses much valuable information relative to the indigenous vegetable resources of its Province; and believing that it would willingly aid in making such known, especially on such an occasion as this; I venture, sir, to solicit the assistance of your Chamber in preparing the said Essay, and would be greatly obliged in receiving from you, at your earliest convenience, any information respecting the useful indigenous vegetable resources of your Province—whether timbers, barks, gums, drugs, fruits, vegetable fibres, &c.—as well as the quantities annually used within the same.

I am, dear sir, yours very truly,

WM. COLENSO.

❖ 1864 MACAULAY'S NEW ZEALANDER ON LONDON BRIDGE.
Hawke's Bay Times 13 May.

[Having also republished, in our issue for ( ) the quotation alluded to below by Mr. Colenso, we now copy his letter from the *New Zealander* of March 26th. —*Ed. H. B. T.*]

To the Editor of the *New Zealander.*

SIR,—In your issue of the 18th ultimo, you have the following quotation from a London paper:—"A DROP OF COMFORT.—There is just one consolation arising out of this now old New Zealand war. If we abolish the New Zealanders, we shall abolish that eternal fellow of Lord Macaulay's creation, who, on the average, finishes three hundred and sixty-five leading articles every year. If there *is* no New Zealander, he can't well come and sit on the broken arch of London bridge, and sketch the ruined Cathedral."

Of course, we have all heard over and over the quotation from Lord Macaulay, but I very much question its "creation" by him. Lord Macaulay was certainly not the author—the originator of that idea. I confess I have often marvelled at no one of the many critics and scholars connected with the press in England having long ago pointed out the source whence, in all probability, Macaulay derived it. That Macaulay was a very extensive reader, and possessed a very retentive memory, his works everywhere show. And while it is scarcely fair to charge such a man with being a plagiarist (at all events, certainly not a wilful one), one cannot forget how in his celebrated Essays he has severely lashed some of those authors whom he was reviewing for the crime of plagiarism. I doubt, however, whether Macaulay himself intended the short sentence now under consideration in any other light as a referential one. His own words, "when *some traveller* from New Zealand," would almost lead to such a conclusion. However, sir, I will just give you the quotation at length, which I believe to have been the origin of the idea with Macaulay, and which will be found in pp. 6 and 7 of the translator's preface to La Billardiere's celebrated voyage in search of La Perouse, (Stockdale's quarto edition, London, A.D. 1800)—a work which it is almost certain Lord Macaulay must not only have read, but have read with great pleasure:—

> *"Having mentioned providence, a word not very common in some of our modern voyages, we are tempted to add a consideration which has often occurred to our minds, in contemplating the probable issue of the zeal for discovering and corresponding with distant regions, which has long animated the maritime powers of Europe. Without obtruding our own sentiments on the reader, we may be permitted to ask whether appearances do not justify a conjecture that the Great Arbiter of the destinies of nations may render that zeal subservient to the moral and intellectual not to say the religious, improvement, and the consequent happiness of our whole species? Or, whether, as has hitherto generally happened, the advantages of civilisation may not, in the progress of events, be transferred from the Europeans, who have too little prized them to those remote countries which they have been so diligently exploring? If so, the period may arrive when New Zealand may produce her Lockes, her Newtons, and Montesquieus; and when great nations in the immense region of New Holland, may send their navigators, philosophers, and antiquaries to contemplate the ruins of ancient[18] London and Paris, and to trace the languid remains of the arts and sciences in this quarter of the globe."*

If my conjecture be correct, and if such have not been already publicly noticed, it is rather a curious coincidence that it should be first publicly pointed out in New Zealand, and that, too, in the columns of the "NEW ZEALANDER" newspaper.

In conclusion, sir, it may not be altogether amiss to give also the quotation from Macaulay (so often referred to) in his own words.

Speaking rhetorically of the Roman Catholic Church, Macaulay says:—

> *"And she may still exist in undiminished vigour when some traveller from New Zealand shall, in the midst of a vast solitude, take his stand on a broken arch of London bridge, to sketch the ruins of St. Paul's." (Essay on "Ranke's History of the Popes," vol. 2.)*

> I am, sir,
> Yours very truly,
> W. COLENSO.

Napier, March 5, 1864.

---

18 This word is italicised in the preface. W.C.

§ *The* Hawke's Bay Times *of 11 July 1864 carried a good (i.e., long) example of a Colenso speech at the Hawke's Bay Provincial Council.*

§ 1864 SKETCHES IN THE PROVINCIAL COUNCIL.
Hawke's Bay Times 26 August.

.... Last, but not least, amongst, the Apostles is Mr. Colenso. We have reserved our notice of this gentleman to the last, because he appears to us the most noteworthy amongst the lot. He has a remarkably intelligent face, a fine forehead, and in fact looks like a clever man, which he is. There is, however, a lurking look of chronic dissatisfaction in his eye, which indicates that he is a man whom it would be difficult to please, and who, in consequence, shines more as an oppositionist than anything else. Mr. Colenso is an industrious speaker, but there is much in his speeches which is worthy of commendation, and much which might have been dispensed with. He evidently studies his part carefully, and looks upon the duties of representative of the people as by no means a light matter to be treated with indifference. He appears, moreover, to seek to infuse into that Council a more earnest and business-like tone, which, indeed it greatly needs. Mr. Colenso, it is hardly necessary to say, is, *par excellence*, the opposition, from which it would seem, if we are to take that circumstance as a fair indication, that the present Government is popular. We respect the courage with which Mr. C. supports his cause against such long odds and the plucky manner in which he resents the frequent insults hurled at him. It has been objected that he is rather irate and loses temper: we should like to see the holder of that opinion in Mr. C.'s shoes, undergoing the outpourings of abuse from the mouths of some ten or a dozen first-class blockheads. There are some people who under such conditions, would bow and immediately join the conquering hosts, and bray, as long and as loud as the rest; there are others again, who would most likely resent a great many things which Mr. C. stomachs, by the adoption of a species of argument which is more forcibly expressed by action than in words. Mr. Colenso manfully bears his burden in spite of all. He studies carefully the subjects under discussion, such as they are, and is armed at all points with facts and figures, a kind of armour which, when attacked by his careless and ignorant compeers, is found to be irresistible before their absurd clamors. Mr. Colenso is a very good example of a hard-working member and it would be well indeed for the Province if the other members took as much pains and devoted as much time and trouble to their duties as he does. The reason why the members of this Council side with the Government is because they are incapable of thinking for themselves; for as the Government supports the runholding interests in which they are all but Mr. Colenso bound to, it answers just as well as the best.

§ 1864 THE NEW ZEALAND EXHIBITION.
Hawke's Bay Herald 15 November.

We are gratified to learn that an interesting collection of exhibits is already supplied by a few of the settlers of this province—sufficient, at all events, to ensure our not being ignored altogether (as seemed at one time probable) at the New Zealand Exhibition. We subjoin a list of contributions up to the present time....

MR. WILLIAM COLENSO:—

Cook's Voyages, great Government edition (*editio princeps*), 8 vols., royal quarto, and Atlas (elephant folio), maps and plates

Flora Antarctica, 6 vols., Royal quarto (colored plates)

Raoul's folio Botanical work on plants of Middle Island, plates

Forster's (classic) *Generum Plantarum*

Owen's Monograph on the Moa

      "   "   " *Apteryx*

Mr. Murray on Flax Plant, N.Z., (printed on paper made from it) 1838

Paper made from N.Z. Flax, 1838

New Testament, N.Z., printed at Bay of Islands, 1837

Common Prayer (complete), N.Z., printed at Bay of Islands, 1839

First book printed in N.Z. (Feb., 1835)

First English book do. do., (1836)

Specimens of earliest Printing (public papers) in N.Z., in 10 sheets (A.D., 1835–40), including Treaty of Waitangi, &c., &c.

First book printed for New Zealanders, 1833

Sundries—1st Sermon, 1st Almanacks, 1st Gazette, &c.

1 copy of a journey of a Naturalist in N.Z., printed in Van Diemen's Land, 1844

1 copy of *Filices Novae*, N.Z., printed in Van Diemen's Land

1 round Box, containing Chrystallised Volcanic Sulphur specimens from Islands in the Bay of Plenty

1 best Native Bordered Mat

1   "   Black String ditto

1 Axe of Slate, from Island of Mangaia

1 Native Carved Tinder-box

6 "Moa" Bones (a set)

    2 Tarsi

    2 Tibiæ

    2 Femora

1 Saw, made of Sharks' teeth, from Byron's Island

1 Carved N.Z. Tablespoon

    6 Native Stone Axes (1 large one being of "green-stone" or "Jade")

    1 Antique Bell, with inscription in Javanese characters—obtained in interior of North Island in 1837

1 round Box, containing—

    1 pair N.Z. Helices ⎱ 8 land

    3 pairs N.Z. *Bulimi* ⎰ shells

    Specimen of Tin Ore, Thames

1 Gold Seal, with a N.Z. engraved stone—A.D. 1836
2 ancient Fish-hooks—human bone
Specimen of Cord, N.Z. manufacture (A.D. 1836) on reel
1 Fancy Maori Basket
3 Geological specimens of furthest Southernmost land (valuable)
1 ditto of Auckland Island
20 specimens of Red and White Carnelian, from Thames and West Coast Bitumen, East Coast (2 pounds)
2 Whales' Teeth (H. Bay)
1 large specimen Calcite, Caves, H. Bay
1 large Paper Mulberry Cloth, from Pacific Islands
1 large Mat (best quality but old) N.Z. manufacture
1 Tea chest, containing—
    1 *Deinacrida gigantea*, in. sp.   ⎫
    1 large Guana-lizard, *Hatteria punctata*, do. ⎬ in glass
    1 glass bottle Ambergris (H. Bay)
    1   "   Maori Rouge, before burning, or Red Oxide of Iron
1 specimen Contorted Carnelian from West Coast
40 Cones of *Pinus Pinaster*, grown at Waitangi, Hawke's Bay
90 Geological, Mineralogical & Fossil specimens from North Island
12 Volcanic ditto ditto
14 specimens Copper Ores, Cornwall, Great Britain
26 ditto Tin, Lead, Iron, Antimony, Mundic, Manganese, Uranite, Blende and Serpentine, from Cornwall, Great Britain

❖ **1865 CORRESPONDENCE.**
Hawke's Bay Times 15 May.
SIR,—In your issue of the 6th instant you have a long extract from the *Southern Cross* on the "Occupation of Waimate," in which the story of "Jack Guard and his captive wife" is given, and said to be *truthfully* related.[19]

Such, however, is not the case; very far indeed from it. And therefore, as you have an "open column," and as I hope you care more for truth than part, I trouble you now with the truth of a small portion of that story.

I was well acquainted with Captain Guard, as also with some of the officers who were in that expedition (particularly with Dr. Marshall, surgeon of H.M.S. *Alligator*), from whom I received the whole story as it happened.

But it is from Dr. Marshall's interesting published narrative (1836) that I rather choose to select the few following sentences, merely adding, for the information

19 In 1890 Colenso wrote a much more detailed account from Dr. Marshall's diary (The first Euro-pean fighting at Taranaki. In A.A. Sherrin *The Early history of New Zealand*, part 1 of *Brett's Historical Series: Early New Zealand*. Auckland, pp. 435–58.). I.S.G.

of many of your readers, that Dr. Marshall was not only an eye-witness of all he relates, but a truly amiable, good, truth-loving man, whose memory his friends still love to cherish!

Southern Cross and H. B. Times

"At Te Namu, a pa between Cape Egmont and Waimate, Mrs. Guard was recovered with her infant child.

"She had been forced to live with a native chief, and had often been ill-treated and even wounded by the natives. In the conflict in which she was taken she had received some wounds in the head; and after this the head of her brother (heads seem to have been at a premium then as now), who had been killed and his body eaten, was constantly exhibited to her, after offering her part of the flesh."

Dr. Marshall's narrative

"The tribe on the beach... deposited their female prisoner and her infant in a canoe, launched it from the shore, and brought them off alongside the Alligator's gig. In a few minutes they were on board the ship, and under the protection of His Majesty's pennant. She was dressed in native costume, being completely enveloped from head to foot in two superb mats, the largest and finest of the kind I had ever seen. They were the parting present of the tribe among whom she had been sojourning. She was, however, barefooted, and awakened, very naturally, universal sympathy by her appearance. From her own lips I gathered the following particulars of what had befallen her."

(Premising that, the day before:—"In Te Namu pa, the lodging allotted to her was discovered at once by the size of the door—the addition of a small window, on the ledge of which was the soap she had that day used—and inside, her child's frocks and her own stays.) The door had been enlarged for her accommodation; the window had been made in compliance with her request; and a singular proof of considerate kindness and deference to her supposed delicacy of feeling, was furnished in the owner having caused the entrance and window both to be secluded by a close paling set up in front of the house, which effectually screened her from observation from without.... Of the treatment she had all along experienced at their hands her report was extremely favorable."—pp. 188, 190.

Speaking of "Jack Guard," you also say:—"A true type of those daring spirits of the olden times, who used to manage the New Zealander by, what shall I call it?—well, by *honest* John Bull pluck."

Dr. Marshall relates a conversation he had with Mr. Guard:—"Mr. Guard scouted the idea of New Zealanders becoming christians. I asked him how he would propose to effect their civilisation in the absence of christianity? The reply, made in serious earnestness, and in a tone of energy and determination, at once unmasked the man, and made one's heart sick at the thought that, upon the uncorroborated testimony of such a man, an expedition was fitted out against New Zealand, likely to be fraught with disastrous consequences. "How would I civilise them? Shoot them to be sure! A musket ball for every New Zealander is the only way of civilising their country!" (p.162) The writer of this has also more than once heard J. Guard say the same.

As Dr. Marshall's book is well-known in England, and of course Jack Guard and his *peculiar views*, it is considered to be somewhat unhappy for the colony that the *Southern Cross* and the *Hawke's Bay Times* should now be found apparently enforcing such opinions, particularly as the colonists have been often wrongly and calumniously charged at home for holding them.

> *I am, &c.,*
>
> *WILLIAM COLENSO.*

Napier, May 9, 1865.

§ 1865 THE NEW ZEALAND EXHIBITION.
North Otago Times 18 May.

In the Hawke's Bay collection is a singular bell, which, from the characters of an inscription upon it, is deemed to be of Javanese manufacture. This was obtained by the exhibitor, Mr. Colenso, in the interior of the North Island, so long ago as 1837, before which time it had been in the hands of the Maoris for several generations. Of course a long Maori legend is attached to it, but where it came from is not explained thereby to the satisfaction of the critical European mind. No doubt some prao or junk has been wrecked on the coast, driven thither by adverse weather; or the voyage may have been made by some adventurous spirits, who, like the navigators to whom we owe all our geographical discovery, were bent on knowing what the world is made of. From land to land, the voyage from the Eastern Archipelago to New Zealand is not so difficult an affair. The inscription on the bell has, I believe, been lately copied, and the copy sent to London, where no doubt some learned Orientalist will decipher and determine whose handiwork it is.

§ 1865 TO THE ELECTORS OF NAPIER.
Hawke's Bay Times 31 July.

GENTLEMEN,—No doubt most of you have seen in last Tuesday's issue of the Government organ, a letter signed "Fact," and many of you will also readily identify its tone and expression as that of a most malignant opponent of our late worthy Town member, both in the Provincial Council and the House of Representatives. Now what is the aim of the writer? Simply to prevent if possible, the re-election of Mr. Colenso, so that, he, the writer, may be able to dodge and shove his little schemes through more easily, and quietly, and snap his fingers at the people of Napier. His letter has an ulterior motive too, that of ousting Mr. C. from his seat in the House of Representatives. But I would say to him—John, shrewd as thou mayest think thyself, entertain no such ideas as these, for thou art known unto the people, who will refuse to be blinded by thy cunning, for they have proved him by his deeds and are satisfied, they have therefore determined that he shall still be their champion and he will fight and vanquish thee, O John the Shrewd, because of thy opposition to our will. Therefore hold thou thy peace and kick not against the pricks.

THREE CHEERS for COLENSO!! and Down with the Squatocracy!—Yours, &c.,

AN ELECTOR.

Napier, 25th. July, 1865.

❖ **1865 TO THE EDITOR.**
Hawke's Bay Herald 29 July.

SIR,—Being still here—through the non-arrival of the Egmont—I have opportunely seen the letter signed "Fact" in your issue of this morning.

Of course, "Fact" (writing as he did on the 20th inst., and knowing my passage was taken to leave Napier on the 21st), little thought that I should be here to see, read, and reply to his accusations.

Before, however, I proceed to do so, I would just tell "Fact" two things—first, that he is well known to me even in his *present* disguise; and, second, that I am right glad I am *here* to meet his charges, to which I may add my belief, that he will not find many in Hawke's Bay to go with him in his doubly dark attempt at assassination of character,—to wit, under the assumed garb and name of "Fact," and behind my back in my necessary absence; when I could not possibly be here to speak for myself, nor even heard in my own defence! before what he wished should be accomplished. "Fact," who has sometimes quoted scraps from Shakespeare, should not wholly have forgotten what Shakespeare says as to such dastardly conduct:—

"Who steals my purse steals trash;[20] *'tis something, nothing;*
'Twas mine, 'tis his, and has been slave to thousands;
But he that filches from me my good name,
Robs me of that which not enriches him,
And makes me poor indeed."

—Now then for "Fact's" figures, statements, and conclusions.

1.   That "I sold myself and the people in (Mr.) Fitzgerald's Superintendency for a *sinecure* office and a salary of £250."

---

20   *Othello*, Act 3, Scene 3, 155–181. I.S.G.

My answer is,—My salary under Mr. Fitzgerald was £150 (not £250), and as to the office being a *sinecure* (that is, having nothing to do), I leave that to those who knew me when in office, and how I worked therein for the good of the Province. Best proved, I think, by the true *fact*, that the people of Napier have always repeatedly returned me as their member.

2. That "the Society paid me for improvements I had made at Waitangi;—that I got out of them two lump sums of £70 and £92, besides other sums, &c., &c."
    My answer is,—That I never received a single penny from the Society for any of those "improvements" at Waitangi. What the Society did pay, in part, for, was towards the outlay on the *large* Mission-house which stood at Waitangi, which contained 15 rooms on the ground floor, and was burnt down with out-buildings in 1853, which house "Fact" never saw.

3. That "a second time I received the enormous sum of £350 of public money for those so-called improvements."
    My answer is,—That I did receive £300 (not £350) on my being obliged to leave the place, according to the award of the arbitrators, backed (I may say) by the common-sense feeling of the people generally of Napier, as shewn at their public meeting, and by *their* petition to the General Assembly in my favor, as recorded in the *Hawke's Bay Herald* of the day.[21] And, further, I may inform "Fact" that I was so far from wishing to receive the said £300, that I actually offered to pay £400 to be allowed to remain and enjoy my "improvements"; this *latter* I wished, and strove hard to accomplish it.

4. (Last, greatest, jolliest, and best!) That "I have actually bagged during the past year £500 of public money;—that I got this wholesale plunder, through advocating in the House, in my place as representative of the people, that a lexicon of the Maori language should be prepared, and that £500 should be paid to me for preparing it. Anyhow, I carried the motion and got the job for myself. Perhaps, "Fact" goes on to say) "I may have written the book;" but, while "he does not know about that," he again asserts, "I have nobbled the *five hundred pounds*."
    My answer to all this is the plain truth, as it stands recorded in the journals of the House of Representatives, from which I now copy *verbatim*:—
    "*Resolved,*—That it is highly desirable, as soon as the finances of the Colony will permit, that a sum of Money be devoted for the purpose of commencing a standard Library Dictionary or Lexicon of the *Maori* language." (7th August, 1861, p.126.)
    And this is ALL, to the present!! No Maori Lexion has been (as far as I know) ordered by the Government;—no sum stipulated (or even mentioned) for doing it;—no monies paid.
    And now, Sir, if "Fact" has any spark of British manliness left in him, let him shew it by being as ready openly to acknowledge his error, as he has been ready to charge me with it.

---

21 2 August 1862. W.C.

Once more to use his words—"Hoping that the sketch of the Napier 'patriot' (by "Fact") will not be thrown away upon the Napier public,"

I am, &c.,

WM. COLENSO.

July 25, 1865.

§ 1865 TO THE ELECTORS OF HAWKE'S BAY!
Hawke's Bay Times 7 September.
In the absence of Mr. COLENSO a move is being made to get you to pledge yourselves to return M'Lean as Member of the House of Representatives at the forthcoming General Election. Be not deceived! Rivet not the fetters round your own necks by signing any such document. The illegal squatter who refused to put in execution the powers entrusted to him for the prosecution of that class; the man who evidently seeks the position for the purpose of getting £2,000 bonus for nothing; the Superintendent who winks at the sacrifice of Public Revenue for the benefit of his own adherents;—

IS NOT THE MAN FOR YOU!!

Be up and doing, and by a long pull, a strong pull altogether, drag to the ground INABILITY AND CORRUPTION!

☞ REMEMBER THAT YOU HAVE BUT ONE VOTE

❖ 1865 TO THE EDITOR.
Wellington Independent 26 October.
SIR,—In your issue of this day you have stated that—

"Mr. Cracroft Wilson, C.B., moved that the statement of Joseph Jeans, now on the table of the House be printed; and in doing so called the attention of the Speaker to the fact, that Mr. Colenso had put two marks of interrogation against a certain word in this document, and his initials in the margin."

"The Speaker said his attention having been drawn to this defacing of public documents, he must request that the like might never occur again."

As it is but right that the public should fully know what this "defacing of public documents," really amounts to, I beg to trouble you with the following:—

On the 1st of August copies of several papers relative to the murder of Mr. Volkner were laid on the table of the House; among them was a letter from Mr. J. Mackay, Civil Commissioner, to the Government, covering a "statement of Joseph Jennings, a Portuguese resident at Opotiki," (relating what he knew, or had heard, of the murder of Mr. Volkner,) in which letter Mr. Mackay said, "I beg to call your attention to these documents, as they contain, what appears to me, to be the most distinct and straightforward account which has yet been given of that unfortunate affair."

I, Sir, who had read with much interest the various (and far more full) statements which had been made by Captain Levy, by his brother, by Mr. Hooper, and also by Mr. Grace, (and which had all appeared in print), I on reading the said papers early in August, drew a line, in pencil, *under* the word "straightforward," and put (as a query) two ?? in the margin. At the same time honestly writing my name in full in the margin, and so openly avowing it, little dreaming of doing any wrong.

This, however, some eight or nine weeks after those papers had been read by all the members, who of course, had noticed my very simple remark, has been suddenly made a grave charge against me by Mr. Cracroft Wilson, C.B., and has been termed a "defacing of public documents" by Mr. Carleton, the Acting Speaker.

I am, Sir, Yours, &c., WM. COLENSO.

Wellington, October 21, 1865.

§ 1865 PARLIAMENTARY PHOTOGRAPHS.
Wellington Independent 21 October.

Under this heading a writer in the New Zealander gives a pen and ink sketch of the members of the House of Representatives. He thus naughtily caricatures the member for Napier:—

"... Mr. William Colenso, of Napier, who makes it a standing rule to speak upon every question, and upon every amendment to every question, and if amendments to amendments were allowed, would speak upon them too, but they not being allowed he takes it out in committee, and does not let a single clause of any bill pass by him unnoticed. But he is greatest of all in Maori translations, and not a single one has come before the House yet, from that unfortunate Treaty of Waitangi downwards, that he has not found fault with. It must positively be shameful the set of ignoramuses who put themselves up for Maori scholars in this country, if we are to trust Mr. Colenso's judgment on their works; for when you hear a thin harsh voice proceeding from near the fire-place, on the Speaker's right, you may be sure that the member for Napier is 'pitching in' to some unlucky translator."

§ 1865 A STORY OF A BELL. FROM THE *COLOMBO OBSERVER*, JULY 27.
Bruce Herald 2 November.[22]

Schiller we think it was who wrote a sublime poetic description of 'The Founding of the Bell.' Edgar Poe's ballad of 'The Bells' is only second in descriptive power to his 'Raven.' Shirley Brook's exquisite bit of fun is less known. A scientific papa describes to his little daughter, in all the hard words of acoustic science, the mode in which the tintinabulations of a bell are produced, and is rewarded for his pains by a slap on the cheek, and the exclamation—

"You bad old man! to go and tell
Such gibberygosh about a bell."

But from New Zealand—land of mysterious Moa as well as of truculent Maori— we have a tale of a bell to which all others must yield. Last mail brought to

---

22 And widely published in other papers, including the *Hawke's Bay Times* of 16 November 1865. I.S.G.

Ceylon copies of a photographic representation and lithographic sections of
what is described as 'the upper portion of an antique bell, from the New Zealand
Exhibition of 1865; the property of W. Colenso, Esq., M.H.R., (Member House
of Representatives), Napier.' It is added that 'this interesting relic was obtained
in the interior of the North Island of New Zealand by the exhibitor in 1837.
The inscription, which has been sent to England for translation, is believed to
be Javanese. It had been in the hands of the Maoris for several generations. Its
history, which Mr. Colenso has written, is long and interesting.' A facsimile of
the inscription is engraved on the paper, and a gentleman, formerly in Ceylon,
recognising the characters as Tamil, asked a friend in Colombo to obtain a
translation. This latter gentleman brought the paper and the translation to our
office, and our readers may imagine the hilarity which ensued over the words—
"The Bell belonging to the Moheiden Box"—Moheiden Box or Bux is one of the
most common names of the small class of native brigs which ply between the grain
ports of Southern India and Ceylon. A vessel of the name, plying probably in the
Eastern Archipelago, may have been either taken by pirates, or driven out of her
course and wrecked on the shores of New Zealand. It is easy to see, therefore,
how the bell may have fallen into the hands of the Maoris. Its history may be long
and interesting, but certainly since the time when Edie Ochiltree dissipated all the
finespun theories of Mr. Jonathan Oldbuck about Aikin Drum's lang ladle; since
the Pickwickians puzzled themselves over the inscription which turned out to be,
'Bill Stumps, his mark;' or, to come nearer home, since the worthy Dutchwoman,
Anne Plock, claimed as her grandmother's the ring supposed to have been dropped
at Manaar by Aunius Plocanus, the Roman knight, there has been no such prosaic
resolution of a mysterious inscription.

§ *The **Hawke's Bay Times** of* **23 November 1865** *carried a report of a public
meeting called to assess Colenso's performance:* VOTE OF CONFIDENCE IN MR. COLENSO
UNANIMOUSLY PASSED! *A lengthy report ended with,* "The motion was unanimously
carried amidst loud acclamation."

❖ 1865 CORRESPONDENCE.
Hawke's Bay Times 4 December.
SIR,—I am of opinion that you deserve thanks for departing a little from the usual
routine of a Newspaper Editor, and republishing, in your issue of the 16th inst., the
letter from "Old Lanka" to the Editor of the Wellington Independent, concerning the
ancient bell found in the Northern Island of New Zealand.

Such a strange attempt at drollery, and at accounting for an ancient relic found in a
far-off land, as that made by some would-be Ceylon *savant* in the Colombo Observer,
in the article "A Story of a Bell," (also reprinted by you,) was never before heard of!
He has, however, the felicity of being "alone in his thoughts" (not glory).

While at Wellington I received a copy of the letter written from Ceylon to Otago about the bell; in which it was stated that the inscription was in Tamil, and that it had been translated as follows:—

"THE BELL BELONGING/BELONGS TO THE SHIP MOHIDIN BUX"

—The word belonging, or belongs, being written *twice* in the inscription; and that its age had not been ascertained.

Now such information is far from being either final or satisfactory.

Among other things it is still enquired:—

1. What is the meaning of *Mohidin Bux?*

2. When was the name of *Mohidin Bux* first given to ships of Southern India?

3. Was any peculiar kind or class of vessel meant by the *Tamil* term translated ship? and if so, are such vessels now being built? and if not, when did they cease to be built?

4. When did the ancient *Tamil* character used in the inscription on the bell go out of use?[23]

5. Have such peculiarly made and inscribed bells been cast since European commerce with Southern India? and if not, when did such cease to be cast?

6. What is the nature of the mixed metal of which the bell is composed? and has such composition been used in modern times?

7. How did it come into New Zealand? and when?

It is believed that this ancient relic may yet prove to be an important witness. Many skilled sons of science and Oriental linguists are even now at work in different parts of the globe, respecting this bell. Its tale has yet to be told.

> *I am, &c.,*
> *W. COLENSO.*

❖ 1865 THE COLENSO BELL.

Hawke's Bay Times 4 December.

SIR,—May I be allowed further to ask you to republish a short letter from Mr. Thompson, of Dunedin, (just to hand), respecting the ancient bell found in New Zealand? I do so that the opinions of the eminent Oriental scholar, Mr. Crawford, contained therein, may be known; although I do not quite agree with him as to how "the North Island (of New Zealand) was originally peopled by the Maori."—I am, &c.,

> *WM. COLENSO.*

THE COLENSO BELL.

TO THE EDITOR OF THE DAILY TIMES

SIR,—I have read the remarks of the Editor of the Colombo Observer regarding "the Colenso Bell," found in the North Island, New Zealand, and must take exception to his facile and facetious explanations.

---

23 The characters in the inscription are much more ancient than the *Tamil* and cognate characters used by the Serampore Mission in their translations, and also by the British and Foreign Bible Society from the beginning of their publications. W.C.

The inscription on the bell is undoubtedly Tamil: but the date of the style, idiom, and orthography, is not proved. This has, however, so been proved—that it is not modern.

In a letter that I have received on the subject from John Crawford, Esq., F.R.S., that Oriental authority makes the following remarks:—"It is a sacrificial Hindoo bell, such as was in use when the Hindoo religion was prevalent in Java; and this is known to have been the case down to A.D. 1478."

—Mr. Crawford adds that the bell must have been received by the Maori through the remote Islands of the Archipelago.

As to the remarks of the Editor of the Colombo Observer, he truly states that "Moheiden Bux," (the name on the bell) is a most common name,—I would suggest—so are Abraham and Moses. The name being common does not detract from the supposition of its being antique.

He further states that it is easy to see how the bell fell into the hands of the Maoris viz,—by being on board of a vessel taken by pirates, or driven out of her course and wrecked on the shores of New Zealand.

I confess I see great difficulties in either hypothesis. The most remote countries visited by the most enterprising traders of the Malayan Archipelago, viz., the Bugis, were the north and eastern portions of New Guinea and the Northern Peninsula of Australia. Now, to carry the "Colenso Bell" from either of these parts by pirates, or shipwreck, 2,400 geographical miles would have to be traversed, and this against the prevailing winds and ocean currents—a feat yet unheard of. Authentic instances of the Polynesian Islanders being drifted great distances are to be quoted; but in no case such as this against wind and current.

To seek a solution of the problem of "a Hindoo sacrificial bell" finding its way to New Zealand we must revert to the suggestion of Mr. Crawford (than whom as an authority none can be higher), that it found its way by Polynesia, or in other words, by the route through which the North Island was originally peopled by the Maori.

As the "Colenso Bell" has warmly interested several ethnographists of known learning, we must await the result of their investigations before concluding that the little symbol has no bearing or import on the history of the Aborigines of New Zealand—I am, &c.,

J. T. Thomson.

Dunedin 30th October, 1865.

❖ **1865 MR. COLENSO AND SEPARATION.**
Hawke's Bay Times 7 December. ***Hawke's Bay Herald*** 9 December.

SIR—With permission, and through your columns, I should like to say a few plain words to the electors of the Electoral District of Napier on the subject of Separation;[24]—or, rather, of my having voted for it through believing in it, and of my future conduct respecting it.

---

24 In this case, separation of the Middle (South) island from the North. W.C.

And this I the more readily do, because some of my supporters have told me,—"they regret my having voted for it"; others have asked me "if I could not modify my views"?—while others (I hear) speak of all Separation in a raw-head-and-bloody-bones kind of way,—as containing every thing that is evil! but (it may be) hobgoblin-like, unreal, and undefinable.

No doubt Separation is a word big with meaning;—and, moreover, there are many kinds of Separation, some of which would be at any time positively injurious; but I do not intend to enter into a consideration of any of them in this letter.

Two or three points will, I believe, be granted me by all:—1. That I formerly opposed Separation;—2. That I voted for it reluctantly, while the Weld FitzGerald Ministry was in power;—3. That I still consider it as an evil;—4. That if good government for the Colony as a whole can be had without it, so much the better; in which case I should (as before) oppose it;—and 5. That it is not impossible that I may (from having seen, heard, and read so much about Separation, and of many existing evils sought to be corrected by it), that I may know a little more of it, and of what it really means, and what good it might affect if properly brought about (*as I understand*), than some of those who now most loudly oppose it.

Be this as it may, I think I see a reasonable way to get over the difficulty, and to reassure several of my supporters, from whom I am sorry to differ. Always bearing in mind,—that it is on the matter of Separation *alone*, that (as far as I know) any difference exists between us. If I knew of any other I would not now write.

This, then, I am prepared to pledge myself to, (that is, if such should be the wish of two-thirds of the electors) namely, *not to vote for Separation, neither to support it, while two-thirds of my constituents continue to be against it.*

I am the more inclined to offer this pledge from the information I continue to receive, that a large number of the electors of Hawke's Bay are against Separation. For while, on the one hand, I could not consent to go to the General Assembly as a mere delegate from the electorate—on the other hand, I must, as their representative, ever have a due regard for their wishes.

Further, it must not be forgotten that we have now another Ministry in power, from whom much in the way of reform may be reasonably expected. So far, then, times have altered since I gave my reluctant vote.

Again, if Separation be a truth in Nature,—one that must come to pass,—the fact of the Napier constituency and representative not helping her on will not very materially retard her progress. And should Separation ever be carried in the General Assembly of New Zealand, such will not be done through the addition of the single vote of a member for Napier. Separation,—to be agreed to by the Imperial Parliament of Great Britain, and so to become law,—will only be affirmed when such has been carried in the General Assembly by a large majority. No New Zealand majority of "one," nor "low fluke" (as in the removal of the Seat of Government) will ever effect such an important question.

Commending these few sentences to the fair consideration of the electors, (and purposing to write to you again next week on another branch of this subject,)

I am, yours, &c.,

WILLIAM COLENSO.

Napier, December 2, 1865.

❖ 1865 CORRESPONDENCE.

Hawke's Bay Times 11 December.

> *"They could not have a perfect constitution of Government which enabled ONE CLASS to legislate for its own benefit.... There ought to be no class feelings. The Legislature should be a fair, just and impartial umpire or arbitrator."*
>
> —*Speech of J.S. Mill, M.P., to the Electors of Westminster.*

SIR,—I wish to call the electors of the Electoral District of Napier fairly and fully to consider the few important words of Mr. J. Stuart Mill, which, at the head of this letter, are again brought to their notice. I feel the more strongly inclined to do this, —1. From my firmly believing, that by unfair or one-class legislation New Zealand as a Colony and Napier in particular will be materially damaged and kept back from going ahead:—2. That the strong bias towards such *one-class* legislation is already too great in the General Assembly; as seen also in the Provincial Council and Government of this Province. Therefore words of timely warning may not be in vain.

Of course I know the vast difference between the welfare of the people at large, and that of the few. A good government seeks the welfare of the many; of men before animals,—people instead of sheep.

We have long known how it is here among us in our Provincial Council; where, out of fifteen members eleven are runholders: just so, or worse, is it in the Executive of the Province. How injuriously such a state of things has acted, to the detriment of the Province, is notorious.

From the Province of Hawke's Bay, small and young as she is, no less than five of her settlers are selected to be members of the General Assembly; three of whom are chosen by the Government, and two by the people. Of these five, four are of the *one class* of runholders,—

Lieut. Col. Russell,

Major Whitmore,

Mr. Henry Russell, and

Mr. J.D. Ormond.

The first three, be it also observed, are *members for life*.

Now if the electors of Napier can so far forget themselves,—their duties, their liberties, and their welfare, and also the future advancement of the *whole* of the people of the Province—as deliberately to choose another from the same *one-class* runholders,—and so to have the whole five of their members in the General Assembly selected from that *one class*,—then they must be prepared to reap the fruits of that *one-class legislation* which will assuredly follow; which Mr. J. Stuart Mill denounces and which it has long been the strenuous aim of all British politicians and statesmen and of all lovers of their country to put down. Experience in all ages have told us that those fruits are bitter.

At this moment this new and richly-stored Colony is groaning under a heavy weight of taxation, such as is not even known in older countries. On the one hand, our commonest necessaries—boots and shoes, shirts and trousers, tea and sugar, shovels and pick-axes, saws and scythes,—the clothing, the food, and the tools of the many—are all taxed; while on the other hand,—iron hurdles, wire and iron posts and straining machines for putting them up, woolpacks and wool lashings, sulphur, arsenic, and tobacco for sheep-wash, and even leather collars for sheep dogs, are all free from any tax. It is well-known that a reform of the present obnoxious tariff is loudly and generally called for; and such will without doubt be made at the next session of Parliament. Several schemes were devised before and during the last session, by men and parties in and out of the House. Prominent among them was the proposal from the Canterbury Chamber of Commerce; they had evidently given no small attention to the subject, and had printed their new scheme of taxation in a small book, which they circulated among the members of the Assembly. In it, while they take good care to keep most of the runholder's imports (as before) free of tax, they also propose,—that silver and gold plate, jewellery and precious stones, carriages, pianos, chinaware and engravings, and also the new luxury of ice, shall be *free* of duty. Characteristically adding,—that, while "leather collars for dogs," and (drugs) "specified for scab in sheep," shall both be *free* of duty; "paper collars" for men and boys, and "drugs" for (scab, or itch in) the poor of mankind, shall both *pay duty*! And, while the rich man's "gold and silver plate" shall be *free* of duty, the "plated ware" of the poor man shall *pay duty!!!* And, as a further sample of their fair impartial reasoning, they also state, that "on the item *wool-packs,* which forms a considerable part of the imports of the South Island, as compared with those of the Northern, a *duty on them would be unfair to the South Island.*" (Surely such an argument was never heard before!—as if a great English brewer, or exporter, were to say, Because I require and use (through my great trade and profit) five hundred times the quantity of casks bottles and cases used by another, therefore I must have them free!)

At the next session, about twenty persons from Canterbury Province alone will have seats in the General Assembly, nearly all of whom will be run-holders. To which will have to be added about as many more from the other Southern Provinces. Four runholders, as has already been shewn, will in all probability be there from Hawke's Bay. Will the electors of Napier still add to their number? if so,—if this pernicious *one-class* legislation is to be so unnaturally so unwisely fostered, then this Colony and this Province will be greatly retarded in its progress, and ourselves and our children will have to bear many heavy and grievious burdens. Politically speaking there is nothing so likely to hasten the evil of Separation, as this evil of *one-class legislation*. As we sow, so shall we reap.

Let no one distort my words and meaning; and say, I am writing against the runholders. I am not now writing against them as a class of settlers among us;—but *against the electors choosing them only to legislate for the welfare of the people.*

I am, yours &c.,

WILLIAM COLENSO.

Napier, December 5, 1865.

❖ **1865 TO THE EDITOR.**

Hawke's Bay Herald 19 December.

SIR,—I notice, with regret, in the leading article of your paper of this day, that you charge me with "perpetual railing at the runholder." This, I think, is saying a little too much; particularly as in the letter on which you are animadverting, I took care wholly to disown any such intention. You freely and unasked republished my 1st letter (on separation) to the electors of Napier; (for which I thank you and feel obliged;) could you not also republish in your next issue my 2nd letter to them? (the one which you have this day censured;) that your numerous readers among the runholders and their friends may see and judge for themselves of my "very bad taste," and "perpetual railing against them."

I am, yours &c.,

WILLIAM COLENSO.

Napier, Dec. 16, 1865.

[Mr. Colenso's second letter is an appeal to the electors for support—such as is usually considered an advertisement. Nevertheless, we should have published it before now, had its length, about a column, and late demands upon our space, not prevented our doing so. The remark with regard to Mr. Colenso's "perpetual railing against the runholder" had less reference, however, to his letter to the *Times* than to his speeches, session after session, in the Provincial Council.—Ed. *H.B.H.*]

§ **1865 EDUCATIONAL.**

Hawke's Bay Herald 23 December.

The examination of the boys attending Mr. Marshall's school took place on Monday last, in the presence of the parents and friends of the children....

Mr. Marshall then proceeded to award the prizes.... The pencil drawings of Joseph Rhodes, and William Colenso (which with others helped to ornament the walls of the school-room), were much admired.

§ **1866 CORONER'S COURT.**

Hawke's Bay Times 22 January.

Mr. W. Colenso here stated that he believed he could throw some light on the matter. He was accordingly sworn, and deposed:—I reside at Napier. I was yesterday standing by the Masonic Hotel, waiting for a trap, when I heard the

report of a rifle, followed almost immediately by the cry that a man was shot.
I hurried to the spot, and saw the man being carried into his house by four men.
I called to them to keep his head raised, and followed them into the house. I saw
his face, and death was written upon it. Water was procured, and I bathed his head
with it. I asked if a doctor had been sent for and was answered in the affirmative.
I told the man to trust in GOD for his case was hopeless. He assented. He was
sinking rapidly. As I saw how rapidly he was sinking I thought he might be unable
to make any declaration when the justices arrived, and concluding he was *in extremis*,
I asked him several questions. I first asked him who had shot him, and he replied
"Dick Farrell." I asked him if it was done accidentally, and he said "yes." I asked
him if he had had any words with him, and he replied "no." I asked him if he
had had any previous quarrel, and he replied "no." He again said that it was done
accidentally, in the presence of his partner, Mr. Williams. He knew he was dying, for
his first words to his partner were, "Harry, I'm a dead man." As I was supporting his
head I could distinctly hear every word he said. Mr. Lee drew up a short will for him
at his own dictation. Afterwards the doctor arrived, and, finding him in great agony,
and sinking fast gave opium to alleviate the pain, and brandy as a stimulant. Some
time after this the justices arrived. He had sunk very much then and was suffering
much pain, though he would have suffered more had it not been for the opium.
The words in which his deposition is written all passed through me. When he was
asked if it was done wilfully or accidentally, he replied "Wilfully." I asked him how
it was there was that discrepancy in his statement. He replied, "O don't ask me any
more questions, I'm in too much pain to answer them."

❖ **1866 CORRESPONDENCE.**
Hawke's Bay Times 26 February.
TO HIS HONOR DONALD M'LEAN, ESQ.,
SUPERINTENDENT OF HAWKE'S BAY.

SIR,—Nearly 20 years ago, I asked a prinicipal Maori chief of these parts, (a man well
known to you though now dead,)—"What he considered to be the duty of a chief
towards his tribe?" Of course, our views differed greatly: he believed that a chief
was bound to get all he could for *himself*; while I thought, he should seek the greatest
amount of good for *his people*.

Pardon me, Sir, when I say, that, of late, this old question has again popped up;—
not, however, now with reference to a New Zealand Maori chief, but with especial
reference to yourself, as our chief Magistrate and present Superintendent of this
Province,—and I am again obliged to fall back upon my old supposition, viz., that
A CHIEF (whether hereditary or elected) SHOULD EVER SEEK THE GREATEST AMOUNT OF
GOOD FOR HIS PEOPLE: I trust you will fully agree with me in this.

We are now in the midst of a general election for the House of Representatives.
You know, Sir, that I have served the Town and Electoral District of Napier as its

member during the past five years. I recollect well certain conversations you and I have had at various times within that period, concerning some of the business done in the General Assembly and my close attendance there, in which you (as a Hawke's Bay landholder) highly approved of my conduct. This fact, coupled with my belief of your Honor's duty to the Province (as intimated above),—not to mention our long acquaintance,—would have quite led me to expect *your* coming forward on the approaching nomination day (as an elector) to nominate ME for re-election,—had it not been for a "Requisition"[25] which has appeared in the 'Herald.'

And here I may remark, Sir, (while I honestly avow my conviction, that the least now said about that unhappy "Requisition" the better for all parties who were therein *actively* concerned,)—that if, on the prorogation of the General Assembly or on its subsequent dissolution, a Requisition, fairly and openly got up and plainly speaking its true meaning, had been presented to you signed by *only half of the number* whose names appear on the present one, I should hesitate long ere I could bring myself to consent to contest the present election with you, notwithstanding my prior and reasonable claim.

But as we well know that such has *not* been the case, and as I wish you, Sir, to do the utmost amount of good for the people of this Province, of which you are officially the present head, I therefore ask you to consider this letter, and (under all the circumstances) to withdraw from the contest, and to come forward on the day of nomination—like a good chief and just and honest Superintendent—and propose me, the old and tried servant of the people and of the Province, for re-election, and so both avoid an unseemly and unnecessary contest, and strengthen the hands of the *one* member for Napier in the General Assembly.

Do not, however, misunderstand me, as if I herein asserted or insinuated my better ability; such is not the case. I ground my claim (as against you, Sir,) upon three things,—1. My long and faithful service,—2. My acquired knowledge of the work, and—3. By having plenty of spare time (to which I might also fairly add, my having assisted in putting-in the present Stafford Ministry.)

I confess, too, to a feeling which I have, that (though I wish myself to be returned, believing I should again, as heretofore, faithfully and usefully serve our Province,) I should not like to see you (*as our Superintendent*) beaten:—some, however, may call this a *weakness* on my part. I well know that you cannot depend on the names to the printed "Requisition" as *against myself*; obtained too, as very many of them were, through misrepresentations, and *at a time too when a far different Ministry was in place*; and I know by experience the great difference that there is in the weight of any member of the House when he is merely a member and not a member by law, but not a Representative willingly elected by the united votes of a free people.

No doubt had I carried in the General Assembly what I strove hard to do,—to have *another member* granted to us for Hawke's Bay, (making our number of members

---

25 I have been unable to find copies of the *Hawke's Bay Herald* for 1866, so cannot explain this reference. I.S.G.

equal to that of Taranaki; a smaller Province,) then, Sir, we might have stood together
before the electors at the approaching election.

Commending this to your earnest consideration,

I am, Sir,

Yours very faithfully,

WILLIAM COLENSO.

Napier, 21st February, 1866

§ 1866 AN OPINION ON MR. COLENSO'S LETTER TO MR. M'LEAN.
Hawke's Bay Times 1 March.

SIR,—The letter which appeared in your columns yesterday (Monday), addressed
by Mr. Colenso to Mr. M'Lean, is a piece of the most unmitigated twaddle that it
has ever been my misfortune to read in a public journal. Many persons who would
have supported Mr. Colenso in his re-election as member for Napier in the General
Assembly are now getting quite disgusted with him, and if he fails of success I am
bound to say it will be entirely his own fault—Yours truly,

AN INDEPENDENT ELECTOR.

§ 1866 NAPIER.
Daily Southern Cross 20 March.

We have Napier news to the 18th, but nothing of importance. The first portion
of the Maori prisoners have been despatched to Chatham Islands. The nomination
took place on the 16th. Mr. Donald McLean (Superintendent) and Mr. William
Colenso were nominated, the show of hands being in favour of the former.

§ 1866 EDITORIAL.
Daily Southern Cross 29 March.

The election for Napier terminated in the return of Mr. D. McLean, the
Superintendent, against Mr. William Colenso, the late member, by 146 votes
against 32. Not one-half of the electors voted. Mr. Colenso did not canvass,
and had no committee: Mr. McLean's friends did all that money, influence, and
intimidation could do,—at least Mr. Colenso charged them with it, and we have
reason to believe truthfully so, on the hustings. Amongst the placards posted by
Mr. McLean's committee was this:—"Vote for Colenso, who sold himself to the
Auckland clique!" In short, Mr. Colenso has been sacrificed for being independent
in his principles, fearless in his speech, and honest in his action during the last
session of the Assembly. Mr. McLean expects to be made Native Minister, and
when in office proposes to carry out the scheme of annexing Poverty Bay and East
Cape to Hawke's Bay.

§ 1867 THE APPROACHING ELECTIONS.

Hawke's Bay Times 18 March.

.... I may state here, sir, that although I have stated that I entertain no hope of seeing either Colenso or Edwards again in our Council, I intend to vote for the former gentleman should he come forward; and, certainly, as a writer in the New Zealand Herald said, about two years ago, "Without him (Mr. Colenso) the Provincial Council of Hawke's Bay would be a sham and a humbug"—I am, &c., HOTSPUR.

❖ 1867 THE BLIGHT BIRD.

Hawke's Bay Herald 13 August.

The following letter, translated from the *Waka Maori*, was written in reply to a letter from Hapi Kinihi, published in that paper (a translation of which was published in a former issue of the *Herald*), asking for information relative to the Blight Bird. The translation has been kindly furnished us by the writer, who has added the postscript which will be found appended:—

(To the Editor of the *Waka Maori*.)

FRIEND,—If you are agreeable, permit my letter to be printed in the *Waka Maori*, as a reply to the enquiry of Hapi Kinihi; because his question was a proper one, and so indeed was all his letter. It would be well if the generality of Maories were like him in that respect— to observe and search and enquire, that their knowledge might increase concerning the many works of the great Creator who made all things both small and great.

Now that small bird, about which Hapi Kinihi enquired, is a real New Zealand bird; but originally came (to us) from the Middle Island, which is its native home. The southern Maories call it *kanohi mowhiti* (ring-eye); by others it is called *tauhou* (stranger); while another of its maori names is *poporohe*. In the Summer season this bird remains in the hill forests to lay its eggs and rear its young; in the winter it comes down to the seaside to seek its food in the warmer parts. It was first seen here at Ahuriri in 1862; in my journey to Te Wairoa I saw it at Aropauanui, with its nest and young; there were four young ones in the nest which were nearly fledged, the Maories of that place took them from a thick shrub on the banks of the river. They told me that it was a new bird to them, they having first observed it there in the preceding year, 1861.

The settlers at Wellington say, that this bird was first noticed there in the year 1856, when it flew across the Straits from the Middle Island. It suddenly appeared at Wellington, and not long after it just as suddenly disappeared. For three years it was absent altogether, after which it was seen again at Wellington, since when it has constantly resided both there and here, increasing rapidly in numbers. Its principal food is the scale insect (*Coccus* sp.) which so disgustingly and injuriously sticks to the peach trees, also to the *ngaio* and other Maori trees. Hapi Kinihi describes correctly its gregarious habits, flying and consorting in flocks. I suppose there are a hundred, or even more, gathered together at this present time here in the trees in my garden. When they commence seeking their food, one of them remains as a sentinel on the topmost branch of a high tree, and if he sees a hawk or a sparrow-hawk flying, he utters a peculiar note, when all the little busy eaters immediately fly away without noise into the thick *koromiko* shrubs to conceal themselves, where they remain as quiet as mice; and when the enemy is gone off the watchful little sentinel utters a different note, on which they all fly out of their concealment and recommence eating. Sometimes, though more rarely, they are also on the ground among the grass under the trees seeking insects, when the sentinel keeps a good look out, and warns them also of the approach of man! They have very good reason to dread their enemies—the sparrow-hawk in particular,—as one of these bold birds, (which has been too frequent of late in my garden) has been seen to catch and carry off no less than three of them; domestic cats also kill them too easily.

It is also amusing to observe how dexterously this little bird strips off the scale insect from the branches, turning itself over and over, back downwards like an English tom-tit, peering under every twig and leaf and into every crack, so that nothing shall possibly escape him; sometimes 4, 6, or 8 of them will get on the top of a slender rose or chrysanthemum bush in the sun; and enjoy themselves in swaying it to and fro, or in pulling out the chaff of the dead chrysanthemum flowers,—just as fast as an English goldfinch does the thistle down. When they retire to roost they sleep in pairs, cuddling quite close together like love-parrots; and before they fold their heads under their wings they bill and preen each other's head and neck most lovingly, uttering at the same time a gentle twittering note.

There are also some other species of this bird (*zosterops* genus,) varying slightly from this one, found in the small Islands of this ocean lying to the N.W. of New Zealand, viz., in Norfolk Island, and in Lord Howe's Island.

I am, &c.,

W. COLENSO.

Napier, July 7, 1867.

[It may here be stated, that the writer of the foregoing would long ago have written in English for publication in the newspapers what he knew of this little bird (Ring-eye), had he not from time to time noticed in several colonial papers the most strange assertions concerning it. In one paper it was said to be "the English linnet!" in another, the Acclimatisation Societies (of the moon or elsewhere,—not however stated,) were roundly thanked for introducing it!! in another it was said to have migrated "hither from Australia,—and so on. None enquired (like the Maori Hapi Kinihi), all asserted,—more or less of error!]

§ 1867 EDITORIAL.
The Daily Southern Cross 8 November.
"Students of the Maori tongue," says the *Otago Daily Times*, "will be pleased to learn that the first part of the Maori-English and English–Maori Library Lexicon, now in course of preparation by Mr. William Colenso, of Napier, under the auspices of the Government, will probably be published next year, although the remaining part

of the work will not be completed until 1872." The *New Zealand Times* states that it appears, from correspondence between the Government and Mr. Colenso, laid on the table of the House of Representatives, that the work will be very elaborate, and will contain every known word in the Maori language, with clear unquestionable examples of Maori usage.

§ 1867 SUPREME COURT.
Hawke's Bay Herald 30 November.

William Colenso, sworn, deposed: I reside in Napier. I am conversant with the Maori language, and am now preparing a Maori lexicon for the Government (Mr. Colenso here read Ihaka's lease in the original Maori. With reference to a verb which occurred in the lease, which had been previously translated "parting with," Mr. Colenso stated that when the Commissioners came from Sydney in 1842, he had translated the same word "transfer," which he considered the proper word.) I believe the word *reti* to be a corruption of "let." It is not a pure Maori word. *Kainga* I understand to mean decidedly something more than the house or the ground on which it stands.

His Honor: May it not mean dwelling place?

Witness: If dwelling-place only had been intended, *nohoanga* would have been repeated. *Whare* is a house; *whare-nohoanga* a dwelling-place. *Kainga* has several significations. It may mean a place where canoes come to, a place to gather shell-fish, or a place under cultivation.

His Honor: Is it not derived from *kai*?

Witness: *kai* has many other meanings besides food. Much would depend upon who drew up the document, whether a Maori or a white man; I understand it was drawn by Mr. Locke. I am decidedly of opinion from the construction of the document that something beyond dwelling-place is intended.

§ 1868 SHIPPING CLEARED OUTWARDS, JANUARY 25.
Hawke's Bay Herald 28 January.

John Bunyan, barque, 520 tons, Allan, for London, with 832 bales wool, Watt Brothers; 400 bales wool, Newton, Irvine and Co; 203 bales wool, Kinross and Co; 113 bales, 36 bags wool, Stuart and Co; 5 bales wool, Routledge, Kennedy and Co; 10 bales and 10 bundles sheepskins, 406 ox hides, 16 calfskins, 17 qr-casks and 4 hhds (70 cwt) tallow, Watt Brothers. Passengers, Mrs. Allan and child, J.W. Atkinson, Masters William Colenso[26] and Alfred Carter.—Watt Brothers, agents.

§ 1868 PORT OF NAPIER.
Hawke's Bay Herald 18 July.

From a telegram received by William Colenso Esq., on Thursday afternoon, and kindly placed at our disposal, we learn that the John Bunyan from Napier, arrived on the 11th May. She sailed on the 28th January, and, consequently, made the

---

26 Willie leaves for England. I.S.G.

passage home in 103 days. There were three passengers on board—Mr. Atkinson, Masters Carter and Colenso.

❖ 1868 THE GUERNSEY LILY.
Hawke's Bay Herald 8 August.

(To the Editor of the "Daily Southern Cross.")

SIR,—Some three months ago I noticed what you had then stated in your paper respecting the blooming of a Guernsey lily for the first time in Auckland, and was so struck with the relation that, at first, I thought of writing to you about it. No doubt I was the more induced to do so from the fact of having cut flowers of the said plant standing in a flower-vase on my table at the time of my reading those remarks; and those flowers, as I looked at them, seemed ready to join me in a hearty laugh. However, on reading a second time what you had stated—viz., 1. That it was a "Jersey" lily; 2. That it was the first time of its blooming in New Zealand; and 3. That it was notably the first which had bloomed beyond the confines of the island (of "Jersey" of course)—it altogether seemed so strange that I abandoned all thoughts of writing.

Now, however, that I have just seen (in your paper of the 4th of July) an account of its having also bloomed two or three years ago at Canterbury, I am inclined to trouble you with a few words about the plant, being also urged thereto by some acquaintances who have often seen it in bloom here in our gardens, and who had also read what you had stated about it in your paper.

The Guernsey lily (*Amaryllis sarniensis*) was introduced into Hawke's Bay about 10 years ago, by the late Superintendent of the province, Captain Carter. It has done very well here, in the open border. I have now more than 20 individual plants in my garden, where some flower every year; some stalks bearing more flowers (12–14) than they generally do in other places; five plants bloomed together in my garden in 1865. It never was found in Jersey; nor, indeed, is it truly indigenous to Guernsey, although now common there. Its native country is Japan, whence it was early introduced into Europe (through the Dutch,) and first flowered at Paris in 1634, and in England, at Wimbledon, in 1659; and has long been common throughout Europe in gardens and greenhouses.

This Amaryllis is by no means a difficult plant to cultivate in our south latitudes, nor is it rare in flowering,—especially when compared with some of its congeners. I may instance a Crinum, which I received from New South Wales in 1837, and which first flowered in 1860, after 23 years' cultivation and patient waiting;—and the Agave (or great American aloe), which you have common in Auckland, is another well-known instance.

If our Southern neighbours should wish to cultivate the "Guernsey lily," I would venture to suggest (in order to ensure its regularly blooming) that they should take care its leaves are not injured by the frosts of winter. It is certainly a very handsome plant, and shows particularly well by candlelight.—I am, &c.,

W. COLENSO.

Napier, July 24, 1868.

❖ 1868 THE EDUCATIONAL RATE.
Hawke's Bay Herald 8 September.

SIR,—In the HERALD of this morning you inform your readers, that "steps are being taken for the appointment of a Collector of the Educational Rates." I am sorry to hear this. I had hoped that the mess the Government of a neighbouring Province has just got into, in endeavoring to enforce a similar unjust rate, would have proved a warning.—I beg to offer a few remarks on the subject.

It seems strange that neither you nor your contemporary have said a word to the people of Hawke's Bay as to the iniquity of this so-called Education Rate, when both of you have told us so very much about the obnoxiousness of the Auckland Poll-tax one. As I view it, the *obnoxious principle* is exactly the same in the one as in the other. Is it not at Auckland, because every man, great or small, rich or poor, is made to pay a *like* sum? and is it not so here, when every house, little or big, is rated alike? Indeed, here it is worse: the principle of our new Educational Rate Act is actually worse (in degree) than that of the Auckland Poll-tax one. There, a man in business, earning his daily bread by the sweat of his brow, having a detached shop (as some of our townsmen on the White Road and elsewhere), would only have to pay a single rate; while here, such hard-working men with a detached shop, however small, will have to pay a double rate! while yourself Sir, and your neighbour Mr. Tiffen, Bishop Williams, and His Honor the Superintendent,—with all your large establishments around you—will only have to pay a single rate!

Again, under the Auckland Act, if a man is so poor as not to be able to pay it, he can legally be relieved therefrom, by the written testimony of two others; but in the Hawke's Bay Act there is no merciful provision whatever of this kind. And so the Hawke's Bay Government advertisement of this day, in pointing out the duties of the Collector, wisely forecasts that a principal one will be—"to attend at Magistrates' Courts whenever required to give evidence."

Further, the Auckland Act is only for *one* year; this (if Hawke's Bay people don't look out) will be perennial.

Sir, hitherto, wherever and whenever Rates have been made for whatsoever purpose, they have been *levied fairly*; this, indeed, is essential to a Rate; without it, a sum demanded is not a rate, but a tax. This great principle you yourself (in some measure) upheld at the Meeting about the Conservation of the River held at Meanee last week. The principle of this Educational Rate Act is not so, and is therefore plainly unjust.

Nor is it unjust only; it is also excessive; far, very far, beyond what is actually required. This I will also show.

But first let me briefly state my belief as to Education.—1. I hold that the State should educate the child: that is (*as we now are*) those children whose parents cannot do so, and who will allow them to be taught.—2. That State Education must be wholly secular, and confined for the present (as far as this Province is concerned,) to Reading, Writing, and Arithmetic. (If there should happen to be any gifted lads among the lot so taught at the expense of the State, such lads will not remain content with such teaching, and will easily find their way to higher.)—3. No general Rate should ever be levied in this Colony to sustain sectarian teaching.

Now what is the real state of the case? Here, in Napier, we have a known number of boys and girls between the ages of five and fourteen. 1st, take from them all those whose parents can afford to pay for their schooling (as such would certainly not like to have their children educated as paupers; and, I should suppose, would just as much resent anyone's offering them a few shillings towards their Education, as they would their offering them a pair of shoes or a loaf of bread for their children):—2ndly, take also those, who, for various well-known reasons, will not be allowed by their parents to go to any school; 3rdly, further take all those unfortunates, who, from narrow priestly or ministerial influence, would not be permitted to attend a Government secular school:—then, 4thly, *the residue are all we have to provide for*, a small number indeed, just sufficient to employ one fit schoolmaster and one schoolmistress. And is it for these few that this heavy Educational tax is now to be imposed upon us?

I shall, perhaps, be told, that the Hawke's Bay Government has determined (for the time at least) to keep up sectarian school teaching. Such may be; but I feel assured they will never collect a tax sufficient to do it. The time is for ever gone by—even in the Old Country—for taxing the public to maintain teachers purposely to teach harsh dogmas and sectarian catechisms. Here in Hawke's Bay, *just now*, it is indeed an evil hour for the Government to attempt such a thing The signs of the colonial times, in the matter of taxation, are portentous. *We have no money to throw away*. Not that a proper Rate fairly levied for proper Education can ever be thrown away; but proper Education and true Religion has nothing whatever to do with the difference of sectarianism of any kind or name.

Sir, you tell us, truly enough I believe, (in your leading article of this day,) that "unfortunately the (Colonial) Government does not see its way to any reduction in taxation;" and, "that *direct taxation* must be the means whereby the Provinces will obtain their future revenues. So that the colonists of New Zealand have before them the pleasant prospect of paying high Customs duties, stamps, &c., and of also being called upon to contribute directly in aid of the treasury of the particular locality in which they happen to reside. This too, in addition to tolls and road rates already, in some cases, falling heavily upon struggling settlers." Such being the case, is this (I would once more ask) the time for the Hawke's Bay Government to endeavour to collect such an unjust and heavy Education tax?

Sir, I have not yet quite made up my mind as to whether I shall pay it or not; for quietness sake, and to save time, I *may* do so; but, as a great principle is involved and as further Provincial taxation is not far off, I do not think I shall, save by compulsion; and to this conclusion I am obliged to through the unjustness and excessiveness of the said tax and it being imposed to uphold sectarian teaching. I sincerely hope the people of Napier will timely arouse themselves and imitate the people of Auckand.—

> *I am, Sir, yours, &c.,*
> *WILLIAM COLENSO.*

Saturday night,
Sept. 5, 1868.

§ 1868 THE WELLINGTON PUNCH.
Marlborough Express 26 September.
News from the Front.—The Hauhau chief has sent to Napier, demanding Colonel Whitmore's head and the right thighbone of Mr. Colenso for a Waddy. He threatened to burn the town.—The Government telegraphed that they have consulted Mr. G——e G—h—m,[27] who recommends moderation, i.e., sending the head first, with a complimentary letter, and a dozen cases of brandy.

❖ 1868 TO THE EDITOR.
Hawke's Bay Herald 17 November.
SIR,—For some time past I have regretted to notice your almost continual attacks on Mr. Stafford[28] (a man to whom, to say the least, Hawke's Bay, as a province, is greatly indebted), and which, I think, culminated in your issue of Saturday last, wherein you state (conspicuously, and directly after your article) that "Mr. Stafford is said to have received on Wednesday evening intelligence of the Poverty Bay massacre,[29] and, next morning, to have left Wellington for the Wanganui racecourse!"

Now this may be quite as truthful as the statement of your contemporary in his paper of the 5th, in which he gives a detailed account of *his* having observed the transit of Mercury over the sun on the evening of the 4th—exactly twenty-four hours before that event happened!!

But, be that as it may, the taste, or the political animus, which caused it is certainly most objectionable; and therefore it is that I, as one of your old subscribers, protest against it. To me there is just as much real connection between Mr. Stafford and the sad doings of the Hauhaus here on the East Coast, as between Tenterden steeple and Goodwin Sands.

Surely, Sir, just now events are serious and sad enough to be truthfully dealt with as realities. Allow me, as an old settler, and as being deeply interested in the welfare of the province, to beg of you not to mix up politics or expediences with momentous passing events of life and death, of weal or woe to Hawke's Bay. And to ask of you (now a settler of some years' standing) to stand up for truthful reports, and to expose all shams.—To wit: where on earth is the need of a night patrol of militia in this little isolated and all but impregnable town of Napier? (of Tanners "Cavalry," too!!) Where

27 George Graham came with Hobson and was present at the signing of the Treaty. He became a member of the House of Representatives, and was known for his sympathetic approach to Māori issues: he opposed the wars, land confiscation, and land sharking.. I.S.G.

28 Stafford, Edward William, 1819–1901, Runholder, provincial superintendent, premier, sportsman. In 1867 the four Maori electorates were established to incorporate pro-government Māori into the political system. Stafford asked Governor G.F. Bowen to pardon some former 'rebel' chiefs. Te Kooti's attack on Poverty Bay in November 1868 heightened the sense of crisis and almost obscured the fact that Titokowaru (Taranaki and Wanganui) was the greater danger. The ministry did, however, concentrate its forces on the west coast of the North Island, so bringing on itself the fatal enmity of McLean, superintendent of Hawke's Bay. McLean was sacked by Stafford from the government agency in Hawke's Bay in March 1869. (*Dictionary of New Zealand Biography*). I.S.G.

29 Te Kooti's Hauhau had burned farmhouses and killed people. I.S.G.

is the enemy to come from? By balloon into the midst of Napier? Is not the fact of such nonsensical shams being done (allowed or ordered) a strong and valid reason for alarming all the outsettlers?—I am, yours, &c.,

WM. COLENSO.

Napier, Nov. 16, 1868.

P.S.—If there is real danger to the town, why not call a public meeting?

[We insert this letter, but we confess to some amazement as to its tone and tenor. So far as we ourselves are concerned, we have said nothing regarding Mr. Stafford that we do not believe to be true.—Ed.]

§ 1868 TO THE EDITOR.

Hawke's Bay Herald 21 November.

SIR,—Amidst the appalling intelligence that we have received and are daily receiving from the scene at Poverty Bay, there is one amongst us—your correspondent the Rev. William Colenso—who has had the offensiveness to hurl at the survivors and relatives of that sad catastrophe, wanton insult and injury, by upholding Mr. Stafford's criminal conduct, and telling us that he is our friend and benefactor. Anything more insulting to the community at the present juncture cannot be conceived. Away with him, to his friends the Hauhaus!

—*I am, Sir, PUCK.*

Napier, Nov. 19, 1868.

❖ 1869 THE EDUCATION RATE.

Hawke's Bay Herald 23 February.

SIR,—In the HERALD of the 20th, in speaking of the Education Rate, you say that you "republish (from the *Times*) what is probably a *revised* report" of what was said at the meeting on Monday evening; and as the editor of the *Times*, in his paper of this morning, has not thought proper to take any notice of your statement, and as his silence might be reasonably taken as meaning assent, I write now to say that I know of no revision of the report, having not only never seen it before it was published, but also had no communication whatever with either reporter or printer. Had I seen it I should have corrected a few words—such as "Te Aute school estate being worth £5000;" what I said was—containing 5000 acres.—Yours, &c.,

W. COLENSO.

Napier, Feb. 22, 1869.

❖ 1869 TO THE EDITOR.
Hawke's Bay Herald 26 March.

"More in sorrow than in anger."—SHAKS.

SIR,—In your article of this morning you have the following:—"The crowning act of folly on the part of Mr. Stafford and his colleagues, has been consummated in the withdrawal from Mr. M'Lean of the General Government agency. Ministers, by this act, have deliberately insulted a public man of long experience and high standing, —they have raised on the part of 95 (?) per cent of the European community the strongest feeling of indignation,—and they have lost the only hold they could be said to have upon the friendly tribes, more especially those of the East Coast. We are glad to find that Mr. Stafford's insolent treatment of the chief magistrate of this Province is not likely to be overlooked, either in Hawke's Bay or other parts of New Zealand."

I deeply regret that you should have thus written; and, though I have neither time to waste nor inclination to enter on the unseemly political squabbles of the day, I feel that it would be wholly unbecoming in me to sit silent and allow such statements to go forth to the colony, without at least offering some passing notice.

Why don't you put the matter truly before your readers? You know very well, that Mr. Stafford has not "insulted" nor offered any "insolent (*sic*) treatment to the chief magistrate of this province." The fact of the late Government agent, Mr. M'Lean, being at the same time our Superintendent, was a purely accidental one; unless, indeed, you believe that Mr. M'Lean held that office because he was the Superintendent. Supposing that either of our former Superintendents held office now, and Mr. M'Lean residing here,—do you think that either of them would have been appointed General Government agent in preference to Mr. M'Lean, merely because one of them happened to be Superintendent? Or, supposing (if you can) that the Government agent in the Auckland province, Dr. Pollen, could go so far as to flatly disobey the Government of the colony, and they were consequently to dismiss him, would any of the Auckland papers (however politically opposed) speak of it in such a silly way, as "insolent treatment" of a medical gentleman of long standing, or, of the medical profession?

Mr. M'Lean was the General Government agent here, and most persons (including myself) approved of the appointment, but all in reality for very various reasons. (Some of which you well know.) The moment however that Mr. M'Lean, as the agent, the subordinate officer of the Colonial Government, refused to carry out the instructions of his superiors, and not only so but opposed them, and (don't forget) gratuitously interfered with their arrangements, and that too at a highly critical period, what course remained? As I view it, there really was no other alternative left, if the Government of the colony wished to keep up even the semblance of self respect for themselves as British gentlemen and as a Government. And, mark well, the present Ministry (like Mr. M'Lean) are all old colonists, persons too who have not only held office for many years but who are absolutely intimately acquainted with all our East Coast localities and people.

But even were it otherwise; were Mr. M'Lean everything that we could wish, or you suppose him to be, and the Colonial Government a set of greenhorns and ignoramuses, I cannot for the life of me see how it were possible for them to have acted differently. Whether in civil, naval, or military service, such conduct on the part of a Government (even when right in itself) must ever be so followed up. History tells us of officers having been shot for much less. And have you (or, even, Mr. M'Lean,) duly reflected as to how such conduct, if passed over, would operate on our numerous colonial officers and Maori chiefs in the field?—none of whom (it appears) are overburdened with that first requisite of a soldier—prompt obedience. Put the case for a moment, Mr. Editor, to yourself. Supposing you chose to enjoy a little more of your *dulce domum* in the country, and you employed an agent—a sub-editor—in town to conduct your paper, how would you act if such an one chose to interfere with your arrangements and to disobey your orders,—your political or semi-political instructions? Would his classical attainments—his being deeply read in Vattel and D'Tocqueville—or his great acquaintance with Maori matters save him? Heaven and Earth! how the *Jupiter tonans* of the Herald office would come down! Nasmyth's steam sledge-hammer, or Mr. Punch's genteel kick, would be as nothing to it.

No doubt several who respect Mr. M'Lean are sorry that he is no longer the General Government agent,—but, as before, for various reasons. At the same time many of his friends are more sorry that, in the matter of flatly disobeying, he acted as he did. Some say, "he was led away to do so, in the heat of the moment, by his *Fidus Achates* or Mephistopheles" (whoever that may be); but while of that I know nothing, I do know this, that many of his friends have not so far lost all their old British belief of what is due to the higher powers as not to agree with me as above—namely, that things having gone so far the Colonial Government really had no other alternative.

You further call our attention to the astounding fact, that "the *Gazette* notice annulling the appointment of Mr. M'Lean as General Government agent was inserted without that gentleman having received any intimation whatever of what was intended." But here, too, I cannot see anything uncommon or irregular. I presume Mr. M'Lean heard from the Government in the usual way by the first mail, which no doubt also brought the *Gazette* to which you refer. I do not see how it could possibly be otherwise with a *Gazette* published at Wellington and Mr. M'Lean living here at a distance; unless you are prepared to show, that the said *Gazette* was got out purposely to give that one notification; or, that Mr. M'Lean was not officially informed of it by the *first* mail. And when (in continuation) you go on to say, "It was only, indeed, from the telegram that appeared in the HERALD that he became acquainted with what had been done,"—you surely forget, that you had already told us in the preceding HERALD (of 20th), that "such was not altogether unexpected by you." And if not by you, an outsider, do you think it was less so by Mr. M'Lean himself?

You also inform us of the indignation meetings which are forthwith to be held—at which, cataracts and avalanches (Oh! terrible), are to be produced. "Well: you and

I know a wrinkle about such meetings. Will it be a roaring for Bacchus, or for his train? The "cakes and ale," and pickings, and all that.

But—and pray don't be offended with me—just consider for a moment how Mr. M'Lean has ever himself acted towards those who, as Provincial Government officers, were his inferiors and subordinates. (Don't forget, please, that I emphatically say they were such for the time, through their being Provincial Government Officers.) Has he not mercilessly got rid of several of the best officers of the Provincial Government of Hawke's Bay—merely because they were politically opposed to him, or would not be his toadies? Don't wince, man. I'll give you their names. First, myself, William Colenso, whilom Provincial Treasurer and Inspector of Schools; did not Mr. M'Lean, in 1863, drive me from my offices, because, as member of the Provincial Council for the town of Napier, I opposed some of his schemes, though only fairly and openly, and in my place in the Council? Was any fault ever found, ever hinted, with the manner of my performing my official duties? And was I not summarily dismissed, although I had but lately come in to Napier from the country at great expense to reside in consequence of my office? Second, the late Crown Lands Commissioner (but he, good man, has so much of blessed charity, or of spaniel-like love, in his disposition, that his case can only be passingly referred to, albeit true). Third, our oldest and best chief clerk, Mr. H.E. Webb. Fourth, and more recently, our talented draughtsman, Mr. August Koch,—all, alike with myself, old officers of the Provincial Government from its very beginning, and all removed by Mr. M'Lean because we would not toady. And to this sad list, perhaps (as I now learn from your paper of this day) may also be added the name of Capt. Buchanan!

Now, such being the case, is it fair for Mr. M'Lean to wince, or to foster indignation; or for his friends (*sic*) to simulate such a hubbub? Fair, why, man, he is just served as he himself has served others.

In conclusion, it may, perhaps, be advantageous by-and-bye, for the province and for the colony, to have Mr. M'Lean again reinstated as General Government Agent. I should have no objections to that, provided that a responsible Purser be also appointed, and that all supplies of every kind for the future be obtained through public tender and contract, in the common way. *Verbum sat sap.*—I am, &c.,

WILLIAM COLENSO.

Napier, March 23, 1869.[30]

❖ **1869 TO THE EDITOR.**
Hawke's Bay Herald 30 March.
SIR,—In your issue of the 26th instant you say, "Mr. Colenso made a long and wordy statement, in which he maintained that either the rate could not be collected till the end of the year, or that the Act was repugnant to the Constitution Act." There was, however, another proposition, and perhaps the most important one (which I fully

30 Several articulately offensive letters were sent to the *Hawke's Bay Herald* 6 Apr and 30 Mar 1869 in response. I.S.G.

stated to the Court, and which, also, the rate-collector admitted on oath), viz., that I had tendered to him in coin 6s. 8d.—four months' rate—being the whole arrears of rate to that time, and that I should also pay the residue as it became due.

May I ask you to insert this in your next issue?—I am, &c.,

WILLIAM COLENSO.

Napier, March 27, 1869.

❖ 1869 TO THE EDITOR.
Hawke's Bay Herald 9 April.

"A word in season."—"A time to speak."
"Can ye not discover the signs of the times?"

SIR,—In the HERALD of this day your article concludes with these words: "All that is wanted is CONFIDENCE, the want of which shuts out capital and labour, and impairs the energies of all." These are true words, and to them I heartily assent. But how is this confidence to be brought about? First, we must have *peace*; a true, substantial, firm, and lasting peace; from this will naturally spring confidence, and mark, *from this only*. To this end let us all (Governor, Government, and people) be determined to do two things: 1.—To do justice; 2—To acknowledge error.

1. To do justice—prompt and quick, even and fair, common-sense, not tedious legal justice. "Do ye to others as ye would they should do to you" if you were in their place.

2. To acknowledge error, frankly and fully, wherever and whenever such has unfortunately been done; even to the retracing of our steps if needful and possible. (Let us not think too highly of ourselves as the "superior," unerring race, adorned with a thousand highflown superlatives of our own inventing). Let us remember the fable of the man sitting astride on a lion, and the lion's truthful remark. Let us endeavour to consider our political conduct in the light of God's truth,—to which scrutinising light it will have to be submitted.)

In order to this:—

I. Let the war be immediately and everywhere stopped.

II. Let a truce be proclaimed.

III. Let an accredited messenger be sent from the Governor to the Maori King Tawhiao (not as king, but as the acknowledged head of many great tribes) to ask his aid towards making peace; and from him to the various Hauhau leaders; and a similar messenger to the chiefs of the principal friendly Maori tribes. The basis of such peace to be:—1. A general amnesty. 2. The return of all (nominally) confiscated lands, subject to certain conditions; such as, on the one side, all useful surveys and substantial improvements to be repaid; on the other, certain spots which it is necessary should be retained to be paid for. 3. Common freedom to all religions however absurd.

IV. Let Peace Commissioners be appointed from both sides, and a place be mutually arranged for their meeting.

V. Let powers be given to them to settle equitably our difficulties, and all great vexed questions.

If this is done, and the British Commissioners be fit and high-minded men—men of comprehensive views, and able to grasp the whole subject,—and if all the terms then and there agreed to be hereafter honestly and promptly carried out,—then, I venture to prophesy a firm and lasting peace to the Colony of New Zealand; otherwise you will not, cannot have it—at least for a long generation, a long and weary time of bloodshed and misery to both races: and, note well, that such a peace so obtained by conquering or destroying isolated tribes, whenever that may be, *will not be lasting.*

I have long entertained those views; I now openly avow them. I know, in doing so, I shall be assailed by the unthinking, with—

1. What of the murders, atrocities, massacres, and cannibalism?
2. What of the present numerous semi-military bands?
3. What of the expense and loss?
4. What of our British name and reputation?

I reply, to the first question—Who began the war with the "Hauhaus?" Who unjustly treated them—men, women, and children—by illegal wholesale banishment without trial? Who, on those Chatham Island "prisoners" returning to their own lands, in a most creditable, and gallant, and peaceful manner, foolishly and insanely, and without authority, attempted to capture and destroy them! instead of bringing them bread and water, and giving them the right hand and welcoming them back? Who carried on the war against them *in Maori fashion?* Quietly mark this, and note—they have *(for the first time with us)* also carried on the war against us and our Maori allies in Maori fashion, which we call murder, massacre, and atrocities (and so deceive ourselves, as if such were really different from our own "civilised" mode of warfare)! but hitherto we have only begun to know what it is; and note well, I beg, that to the present time hunted "Hauhaus" have not retaliated upon a single European living quietly on lands fairly purchased or leased. We have already killed something like seven or eight to one; besides inflicting irretrievable loss and evil. Moreover, fanatical outbreaks and rebellious *emeutes*, everywhere occurring in this world's sad history, are never rigorously revenged.

To the second question, I reply—The sooner they are disbanded the better for the colony.

To the third—Bear it; it can be borne to restore peace and confidence; it is by far the better, the easier, and the cheaper load.

To the fourth—It will gain additional lustre, which ten years' war and eventual success will never bring it. Our Maori foe cannot, will not reflect tauntingly upon it, as we have driven them from all their strongholds, and killed seven or eight to one.

Having said a word to the unthinking, I would also say a word to the really thoughtful among us, including the God-fearing man, and in particular to those of all the churches who believe in God's particular providence and in His stern retribution.

1. Note how successfully this handful of men ("Hauhaus" and "rebels" we call them) have sped; note how they have been hunted; the enormous powers of all kinds brought to bear against them—armies, seven or eight to one—the most improved ordnance and big guns, as well as superior rifles and ammunition; heaps of prayers and invocations, public and private; all the power and strategy of the "superior" race, both "spiritual and carnal,"—and note the result. The different Hauhau leaders, on whose devoted heads in particular high prices have been set, who have bravely stood to the death in every fight amid showers of balls, are all still safe, as if they were invulnerable, while not a few of our best and good men are gone! With death in every form, including starvation, and want and misery, and with little of human aid, they have been long familiar.

2. Note also, I pray—The strange, the utter reversal of what is promised to the God-fearing man, of what has hitherto been his lot—freedom from fear and dread. How comes it that so great a panic everywhere prevails? That instead of a few of the "superior" race overawing a whole band of Maoris ("one putting a thousand to flight," as was formerly the case), now two Maoris even at a distance, or even a fire on some distant hill, are enough to arouse ugly misgivings, and to cause a whole settlement of stalwart whites to flee as affrighted hares! Everywhere the majority of the settlers are suffering from this foolish affection, even where they are dwelling together in large numbers, and where there has been, and is no cause whatever for any such fear. How comes all this? Think over these questions quietly, and dare to follow them out. Is ours altogether a righteous cause? Have we the god of battles with us, or have we not?

Now it is just because I believe all this, that I am not sorry that Mr. M'Lean is no longer Government Agent; for while he held that situation and stuck to his old schemes (policy I cannot call them), no real confidence could ever arise, as a firm and lasting peace could not possibly under such schemes ever be restored,—for, at the most, as soon as a so-called peace had been at an enormous expense patched up in one place it would break through in another: it would only be the old, miserable union of "iron and miry clay." I know very well that some few (if they dare speak their thoughts) would say, "Exterminate." To this I reply, you can't do it; and if you could, it would take you years to accomplish. Be warned in time: your (present) "friendlies" (mercenaries, on whom some of you depend so very much) would not allow of it.

Sir, I did hope that the arrival of a son of Her Majesty the Queen among us, the first arrival too of a Prince of the blood royal on those shores, would be advantageously made use of in the way I have above indicated. From my knowledge of the national feelings of the New Zealander, I cannot help stating as my firm belief, that such might have been beneficially done,—and even now it may not be too late.—I am, etc.,

WILLIAM COLENSO.

Napier, April 6, 1869.

❖ 1869 NATIVE AFFAIRS.
Wellington Independent 3 August.

SIR,—I trust you will kindly allow room in the columns of your paper for this letter, although it is long. You may not wholly agree with it; nevertheless, though various our endeavors, our object is one—*Peace*. Yesterday morning our Hawke's Bay Herald informed us what a state many of the good folk in your city of Wellington were in, owing to the news reaching you of Te Kooti having joined the Maori King at Tokanga-mutu. To me it was really good news (if true) and I will tell you why. (1) Because, as I viewed it, properly followed up, it might lead to peace. (2.) Because it would be very likely to restrain Te Kooti and his marauding band from again swooping down on our more exposed out-settlers.

1. I have said—"Properly followed up it might lead to peace." My own opinions on the only sure and proper way to a firm and lasting peace have been some time before the public (see below) and all that has happened since has only confirmed me in those views. I think highly of Mr. Rolleston's motion for a commission of enquiry (with one alteration), provided it is rightly managed, and believe that real good would result to both races from it. I demur altogether to Mr. Attorney General's statement—"The Maoris now in arms have put forward no grievance for which they seek redress. Their object, so far as it can be collected from their acts, is murder, cannibalism, and rapine. They form themselves into bands, and roam the country seeking a prey." (Opinion, &c., 30th June, 1869, Parliamentary Paper, p.3.) They have grievances, which they have patiently borne, and they have long endeavored to express them. (See, for instance, the petitions from the Poverty Bay and East Coast tribes to His Excellency Sir G. Bowen, Parliamentary Paper, A. No.16, Session 1868.) And it is because they cannot get their grievances promptly attended to that they have been driven to desperation, and that they are now in arms, and (*worse*) in such a state of mind—deadly enmity—towards us, which is sadly increasing, and will, I fear, in time be found to have infected the present "friendlies." Now from my long and intimate knowledge of the Maori—past and present—I feel convinced, that if they are met by us frankly, honestly, and liberally, they will meet us in the same spirit, and it must be *bona fide* on our part. If such is the case, then Mr. Rolleston's motion is a step in the right direction; but to render it effectual this amendment must be made, viz., to omit all Judges of the Native Lands Court (a well as all other Government Officials, both General and Provincial), and in the selection of Commissioners to be very sure to have no one who has ever obtained any of their lands or runs, for himself or his relatives, or who is, or who may be, interested in the acquiring of any such. The Maoris are naturally very suspicious, and see through all such miserable manœuvres. If no fit persons are to be found in our North Island better then let the Commissioners be chosen from among Middle Island gentlemen, albeit strangers to the Maori manners and customs. Further, if Commissioners should be appointed, let the fourth estate (the Press of

N.Z.), and the colonists generally, patriotically refrain for a while from injudicious comment upon the Maori people—their sayings and doings.

2. "It would restrain Te Kooti and his marauding band, &c." Yes: thus. Te Kooti would be under the immediate rule of the Maori King and his Executive (shrewd and able men), so that he could no longer act as he pleased, the more so from the fact of his not being *by birth* an A1. chief (*i.e.*, the acknowledged head of any tribe), and having joined the King party he would have to obey Tawhiao. At the same time, however, we must be careful in rashly concluding that Te Kooti, being an inferior chief, can be therefore easily overcome; we must not forget the Hauhau element,—he is now a name, an authority, a notoriety, among the great and increasing body of Hauhau fanatic, which makes him of far greater importance than if he were the head chief of a tribe, however large that tribe might be.

Before I conclude I would also state my belief, that it is far from prudent to be guided by the opinions of any Maori chiefs, however influential or friendly, who may have been with us in arms against the Hauhaus, or whose relatives or people may have in former years suffered from the Waikato tribes, as such cannot but give the old innate Maori opinion, arising either from their never dying hate and love of revenge, or from fear that they themselves may at some future day be retaliated upon by a spared foe.

I trust I shall not be deemed to have trespassed in thus once more putting my views on such an important subject before the Colony. It is because I believe them to be correct, that I do so; and because I see no other easy way out of our difficulties.— I am, &c.,

WILLIAM COLENSO.

Napier, July 24, 1869.

[Mr. Colenso has sent us another letter which has already appeared in the "Hawke's Bay Herald." We have not space for it—*Ed. W.I.*]

§ 1869 EDITORIAL.

Star (Christchurch) 22 September.

… looking beyond our own province to the proceedings of the New Zealand Institute, we have every reason to be proud of the contributions which have been made to the literature and scientific knowledge of the country. The essays on the botany, ornithology, and geology of New Zealand, and especially Mr. Colenso's essay on the Maori races, contained in the published transactions of the Institute, are far more than literary efforts for the present, possessing as they do an interest for all time.

❖ 1869 LIEUT. SAXBY'S PREDICTION.

Hawke's Bay Herald 24 September.

"Hubert. My Lord, they say, five moons were seen to-night.

King John. Five moons?

Hubert. Old men and beldams, in the streets,

Do prophesy upon it dangerously.

——I saw a smith stand with his hammer, thus,

The whilst his iron did on his anvil cool,

With open mouth, swallowing a tailor's news."

SHAKESPEARE—*King John.*

SIR,—Allow me to say a few words on the "predicted tidal wave," which, some say, is to play the very "Dragon of Wantley" with us, and to swallow up poor Napier.

I should have earlier essayed a few words to some of your more credulous readers, with a view to allaying their foolish fears, as I have had not a few enquiries made, both personally and by letter, concerning this said sea invasion; provided that any appeal to reason can do so much in a time of uneasy excitement and apprehension; only you, in your article of the 17th, said, "We have taken steps to get a scientific opinion on the matter, which, when received, we shall at once place before our readers."

First, then, I would call their serious attention to this fact, that we have in England a noble and united band of hard-working public men of first rate scientific attainments, whose whole life has been more or less spent in the study of astronomy and meteorology; now these say nothing whatever about any such alarming occurrences, not even in the British Nautical Almanac for 1869, wherein every little deviation or apparent aberration of nature from her old established rules and laws is accurately noted.

Secondly, the same may be said of the numerous skilled astronomers of all other civilised kingdoms, particularly of those of Germany, France, the United States, &c., by none of whom either officially or independently has anything of the kind been published.

Now such being the case, are we in the face of all this, to adopt the single utterances of such men as Saxby or "Zadkiel," or any others of the cunning followers of "Francis Moore, physician?"

The Chinese have a proverb, that "no lie is so bad as that which has truth in it," (which is a pretty good exponent of the depth of experience of that ancient people,) and so in this case of the "tidal wave," (bosh!) there is just this amount of truth in it,—that very likely at that date, from the situation of the planetary bodies, the sun the moon and the earth, there may be a somewhat higher tide than usual; but certainly no higher than some of us old settlers have already more than once seen at Port Ahuriri.

Indeed, if any credit is to be given to any portion of Saxby's statements, past, present, or future, (which, I confess, I am not inclined to do,) then, I would call attention to that portion in which he says—"this year the two hemispheres will be affected alike;" if so, then, by his own showing, the equilibrium will be preserved.

You state in the article referred to, that "Saxby had alluded to the accuracy of a former prediction;" (oh!) and you speak, undesignedly no doubt, as if you endorsed it. Any "accurate prediction," however, on his part, according to the usual and common meaning of the words, I deny. It was just such a prediction as any one might make in saying the sun will rise at 6 o'clock on Saturday morning next,—or, the westerly winds will blow strongly several times during the month of October, or, that thrice during the month of November the shopkeepers in Shakespeare road will have to close their doors on account of the great dust, and that * * * and * * * will be then seen wearing blue specs. It is a wonderfully easy matter to "predict" after this fashion:—I could make 26 such every year, that high tides would arise on my 26 predicted periods and do great damage in some parts of the world; and sure enough such would afterwards be found to have taken place somewhere!

It would seem as if we still needed not a little of reasonable enlightenment on even natural matters. A few dozen of cheap edition copies of Lecky's noble work on "The Rise and Influence of Rationalism," circulated among us, might prove a step in the right direction towards removing many such preposterous and credulous beliefs.

Some may remark, "Ah! it is all very well for you, W.C., there on the hill at Scinde Island to talk like this." Well: I believe I should talk and act the same if I still lived at my old residence at Waitangi, low and close to the sea; and even now I am quite willing (if my doing so would tend to make any of Saxby's too credulous followers more easy,) to spend the said fated day and night locked in in any decent room on the lowest flat about Napier.

I quite agree with you when you say, "We should not be surprised if the 5th October passed without any unusual occurrence." I would, however, that you had not given publication to that foolish anonymous letter from Wellington. Surely the writer, if in earnest, which I doubt, must forget that such a general high tide as would "wholly sweep away" our western town, would also shew little mercy on the shops and stores on Wellington beach! But he, too, travels far to vent his cheap pity.

Writing of Wellington reminds me of another false prophet, named Schmidt, a character not wholly unknown to the old settlers here: I knew him a little too well. In January, 1855, he went overland hence to Wellington; he was there at the time of the severe earthquake, which happened on the 23rd of that month. Very shortly afterwards he gave a kind of lecture on volcanos and earthquakes, and "predicted" that a far severer shock would take place in the night of a day which he named; consequently, it being a time of great fear and excitement, and small shocks being also common, many left their homes and passed the dreaded night on the hills in the open air. But that night passed off quietly, and the prophet Schmidt quickly skedaddled to the Middle Island.

For my own part I would that all such vagabond and vainglorious false prophets or alarmists, who live by their wits, whether theological or natural, as Schmidt, Saxby, Cumming, or Baxter, were just fairly though rudely dealt with, as Peter of Pomfret is said to have been by King John,—laid hold of and put into ward until the predicted time had passed, and then, if correct, rewarded; if not, immediately strung up *à-la-lanterne*.

Such fellows, in my estimation, are far worse than "Hauhaus."

In conclusion, I will just give an extract from a letter written yesterday by a Maori, and received this evening by the inland mail; he says, (after mentioning the deaths which had recently occurred among his people,)—"Here is yet another new talk among us, it is currently reported and by some believed, that the ocean is soon to come in rolling over the land even over the Ruahine mountains, and then the moon and the stars are also to fall!"

Credulous, easy men of Napier, don't laugh at the Maori.—I am, &c.,

WILLIAM COLENSO.

Napier, Sept. 22, 1869.[31]

§ 1869 TO THE EDITOR.
Hawke's Bay Herald 1 October.

SIR,—In your publication of the 24th instant, there appears a letter from Mr. Colenso, containing, a great deal of frothy matter, the object of which appears to be to throw ridicule upon the prediction of Mr. Saxby for the 5th of October, and to exhibit himself, (Mr. W.C.) in the light of a much more scientific and learned man than Mr. Saxby. The most charitable construction to be put upon the last ebullition of Mr. C.'s forward imagination, is, that the great labour and research necessary to the compilation of the Maori Lexicon upon which he is supposed to be engaged, have driven him mad.

Does Mr. C. know anything at all about Mr. Saxby or his prediction? I trow not; or he would know that, instead of "a tidal wave," that gentleman has stated, that, on the 5th of October, from some peculiar situation of the planetary bodies, an unusually high tide may be expected. I have generally understood, though I cannot profess to any scientific knowledge of such matters, that a tidal wave is the result of an earthquake.

What egotism Mr. C. shows, when he says he "would be quite willing to spend the fated day and night locked in in any decent room on the lowest flat about Napier." Poor dear man! what a vast amount of physical and moral courage he must be possessed of. Of course he totally ignores the fact that most houses in Napier are provided with windows, which occasionally are made to open.

Mr. C. seems fond of bringing up to our recollection old times, with his high tides and his Schmidt; old settlers remember many curious and remarkable facts in the early history of Hawke's Bay, as well as Mr. William Colenso.

The last time your correspondent gave vent to his over-boiling feelings in your columns, was, I believe, in that memorable letter of his, wherein he characterised

31 Saxby wrote to the *Standard* (his letter reprinted in the *Daily Southern Cross* of 30 Sep 1869) denying all knowledge of any claim to predict tides, and expressing dismay that such a hoax could have been perpetrated in his name. His relative George Saxby of Te Kopanga wrote in his defence and in high dudgeon to the *Hawke's Bay Times* of 1 Oct 1869, the day Semper Eadem's letter (above) was also published. I.S.G.

the murderers of our friends, and in some cases our relations and their wives and families, as a noble band of patriots, and now he speaks of such men as Mr. Saxby, Dr. Cumming, and old Baxter, as worse than them, and places some foreign adventurer (Schmidt) of whom we know nothing, on an equality with these clever men.

Does Mr. William Colenso know anything of Mr. Saxby when he ventures to assert that he lives by his wits? Is such an expression, to say the least of it, gentlemanly or Christianlike? I am given to understand that Mr. Saxby holds a responsible situation under the English Government, and spends much of his time and money in studying this particular branch of science he has adopted, and in making public the result of his labours; such a man would surely be one of the last of whom the ugly expression could be used, "he lives by his wits."

Amongst other predictions, I think I may venture upon one, and that is—that if Mr. Colenso is not a little more guarded in his expressions, he will either be sent to Karori[32] or become one of the first inmates of the lunatic asylum in Hawke's Bay when it is built; With which prophetic remark,—I am, &c.,   SEMPER EADEM.

❖ **1869 COOK'S CENTENARY.**
Hawke's Bay Herald 1 October.
SIR,—In your last issue you say "Wednesday next, the 6th October, will, we believe, be the centenary of Capt. Cook's first landing in New Zealand."

There is a little error here, as Captain Cook landed on the 8th. Five years ago I wrote thus:—"On the north-west shore of Poverty Bay, in the evening of Sunday the 8th. October, 1769, being early summer, Capt. Cook, Sir Joseph Banks, and Dr. Solander, had the pleasure and privilege of first landing in New Zealand. This present year of grace, 1864, has been lately signalised by Great Britain and the civilised world as that of the ter-centenary commemoration of the immortal British Poet, 'of all nations and of all time'; and, surely, five years hence the colonists of New Zealand will suitably commemorate the Centenary landing of the adventurous and celebrated British Navigator COOK—*the great Navigator of and for all nations*—on these shores with his illustrious band of devoted disciples of Natural Science!"[33]

At the time of writing the above (March, 1864), I hoped that Poverty Bay would continue to increase in prosperity, and that steamers from north and south would, in October, 1869, take many a colonist there to celebrate on the spot the centenary of our great countryman's discovery and landing.

Captain Cook entered Hawke's Bay on Thursday, October 12th; anchored that night not far from Long Point; continued to coast within it until Sunday, the 15th October, on which day the second fatal affray with the natives took place off our south cape, which he then named Cape Kidnappers.

---

32 Karori Lunatic Asylum had 12 beds and 23 inmates in 1871. W.C.
33 Essay on the Botany of New Zealand (North Island), page 1; in *Transactions and Proceedings of the New Zealand Institute*, 1868, vol. I. W.C.

Most heartily do I wish that Friday, the 8th October, will be suitably celebrated by the Colony; particularly by us here in Hawke's Bay, and this for several reasons. I may mention the following:—1. Ours is the only Province in New Zealand bearing a name of his giving: 2. Our town of Napier is the only New Zealand town built on a site of his seeing: and, 3, he has said many interesting things, about our Bay (which he sounded all round) and its neighbourhood.

True, the time is now short; but could not something be done among us towards commemorating his landing—something in which all could unite? Say, a general holiday proclaimed by the Government,—cricket and rural games in Clive square, or on the hill, a tea or evening party, *soirée*, or *conversazione*, in the Oddfellows' Hall, with music, songs, &c., &c. Something in which all settlers could unite.

As your next Friday's paper (bearing, too, a name of Cook's giving) will be published on the 8th—the very day of his landing, I will, with your permission, prepare for its columns an epitome of what COOK saw and did here during his first week in New Zealand.—&c.

WILLIAM COLENSO.

Napier, Sept. 30, 1869.

[We have to thank Mr. Colenso for his kind offer, of which we shall gladly avail ourselves.—ED.][34]

---

34 Colenso's paper 'In Memory of Capt. J. Cook, R.N.' was published in the *Hawke's Bay Herald*, Napier: 8 Oct 1869, p. 3. It is reprinted in *Colenso's published papers 1: 1842–1884*, forthcomig in this series. I.S.G.

LETTERS 1870–1879

WILLIAM COLENSO 1870–1879

1870 Colenso working on a Māori-English dictionary.
1871 Third edition of Williams's Māori dictionary published; Colenso re-elected to Provincial Council; *Hawke's Bay Times* winds up. James Wood sells *Hawke's Bay Herald*;
December 'Fiat Justitia' published by *Hawke's Bay Herald*.
1872 *July* appointed Inspector of Schools, 1872–8; still working on a Māori-English dictionary.
1873 Willie working as a sailor.
1874 Hawke's Bay Philosophical Institute founded, Colenso secretary.
1875 Writes to Cheeseman expressing renewed interest in botany.
1876 McLean dies; Colenso contests his seat and is soundly defeated; Willie settled in England.
1877 Reads his first paper to the HBPI: 'On the day ... Captain Cook ....'; four papers in *Transactions of the New Zealand Institute* 10.
1878 *Tracts for the times No. 1: on the Sabbath* published by *Hawke's Bay Herald*; resigns as School Inspector; Henry Hill appointed in his place; retires; James Morgan and wife servants; his dogs maliciously killed; William Williams dies; *Waipawa Mail* begins publication; five papers in *Transactions of the New Zealand Institute* 11.
1879 Advertises 'Tracts for the times No. 2' (never published); five papers in *Transactions of the New Zealand Institute* 12.

❖ **1870 TO THE EDITOR.**
Hawke's Bay Herald 16 December.

SIR,—It is not from want of inclination that I have not intruded on your "open column" of late. I have, more than once, wished to notice (or "shew up") some of the strange, erroneous, and even mischievous "notions" which from time to time have appeared therein, more particularly the long aberrant letter of "Cosmopolite," which appeared in your issue of the 9th instant, and also the disparaging little one of "Tradesman," which you published in the HERALD of yesterday.[1]

You have yourself noticed Cosmopolite's effusion; though, as I take it, much too mildly and cursorily—yet that will do for the time. It may lead him to reflect a wee bit, and perchance to cease scribbling post-prandial epistles.

For the sake, however, of keeping up the respectability of our province (not to mention that of your paper), as well as to keep you clear from the meshes of any legal net, I should like to notice the little £. s. d. letter of "Tradesman;" not by any means merely to shew his (apparent) hardness of feeling and moral obliquity of vision, but to draw his and your attention to its mischievous tendency (possibly not perceived by "Tradesman,") as well as to the danger he is exposing himself to of prosecution in the Supreme Court for libel.

I neither know "Tradesman " nor Chaundy, nor is it at all needful. It has been suggested to me that "Tradesman" is really a publican; such may be, but I rather incline to think him to be what he calls himself; not one however of our more respectable Napier tradesmen,—such he cannot be (seeing he comes out so strongly for so small a debt as £3 13s.), but of that select class known here as "nippers."

But, to his letter:

First, then, "Tradesman" finds great fault with our Resident Magistrate, for having given the unhappy Chaundy "four and seven months in which to pay an undisputed debt of £3 13s. 0d.;" but which, in reality, (with costs, as "Tradesman" knew, and as reported by you) is £4 12s. 3d. He also overlooks (as all such folk do) what you further, briefly yet strongly, reported, *viz.*—"the debt was admitted by Mr. Lee; he merely asked that time might be given to pay, on the ground of defendant's poverty." And Chaundy on oath stated,—"I am a labourer, I have a wife. I have earned very little money for four months past. I had to pay away all I did earn in the settlement of other debts. I owe still about £20. I have the contract for carrying the mail to Kereru." [Perhaps about £40 per annum.] Surely, for the honour of our Napier tradesmen, great and small, not another could be found who, knowing the case, would join this "Tradesman" in his disparaging reflections on the R.M. for his considerate judgment in this matter!

But there is another and far different feature arising from this case, which, if "Tradesman" had noticed and publicly commented on (seeing he knew of it also), I should have agreed with him, and saved myself the trouble of writing this; but such would not have suited his purpose of having a fling at the new R.M. On the very same day on which this case was heard, the 6th inst., an official declaration

---

1 'Tradesman's' short letter criticised the Resident Magistrate. I.S.G.

of bankruptcy was made by this same William Chaundy, and which appears in the *Hawke's Bay Times* of that date. Here, then, two or three questions naturally arise, of far greater importance to the trading community, and indeed to all, than such a trivial one as that which has so aroused the virtuous indignation of "Tradesman":—

1. Did Chaundy depose truthfully in Court, when he said he only owed "about £20"?
2. What sum is requisite for law expenses, &c., to bring a man through the Bankruptcy Court?
3. Would any lawyer in Napier undertake to do so for a less sum than £20—*Cash*?
4. Seeing the Magistrate's judgment was so very merciful, (all that Chaundy could have ever expected,)—how came it, that, within two or three hours afterwards, he filed his declaration of bankruptcy? Did be intend to do so before he went into Court? and did his counsel know of it? or did he fall into the hands of some bad adviser? Less than the *cash* law expenses as a bankrupt might have cleared him with his creditors, and shewed him to be an honest man.

Moreover, there is still something to be said about this Chaundy. Did he not appear in the Resident Magistrate's Court here some eight or nine months ago, as defendant in a similar case of debt, when Mr. Lee, as counsel, also appeared for him, and obtained from the late Resident Magistrate the time of six and twelve months in which to pay it in? Has this debt been paid—in part? I believe not, though, perhaps, included in the deposed amount of £20. Of course, "Tradesman" knew all this, but, as it were such a merciful precedent judgment on the part of the *late* Resident Magistrate, towards the *same* man too, and in a very similar case, he overlooked this also!

Under all the circumstances of this case it will be for the Post-office authorities, acting for the good of the public, to determine, whether William Chaundy is a fit person to continue to hold the contract of carrying Her Majesty's mail over a wild and open country.

Secondly: the whole tone of Tradesman's letter, short as it is, is bad mischievous and evil (not to say untruthful and unjust) against our new R.M.; and, as I think, libellous and criminal in law, and one which might justly obtain from a special honest educated jury heavy damages. "Tradesman" says, "It is pretty plainly shewn that the Resident Magistrate's Court is *not* the place to recover debts": that he "has heard of very peculiar" (meaning, unjust,) "decisions given by the same gentleman" (the Resident Magistrate): that "the Government has made a bad bargain" (in placing him here):—and that "great satisfaction would be felt" (by the public) "if the Government would restore the Department to the same state of efficiency as it was before the new Resident Magistrate arrived." I purposely pass by, as unworthy of notice, Tradesman's low sneering at the good and proper old English style or prefix, of worship, or worthy, correctly given to our R.M. by your contemporary; as well as his insinuation (quite in keeping and savoring of the counter,) about our R.M. "receiving a much higher salary than his predecessor"; merely remarking, by the way, on this last that "Tradesman" knew well that our present R.M. performs more and higher duties than his predecessor did, being also District Judge; and that, in the two offices being combined and held by one person, there is really a considerable monetary saving to the Government and public.

I scarcely know of anything more prejudicial to our moral getting-on, more subversive of our doing well, whether as a people, province, or colony, than such foolish low and wicked animadversions on the Dispensers of Justice, as those I have remarked upon. The British are evidently a law-loving, law-supporting people; and the good British Magistrate must necessarily be a hardworking, pains-taking, patient, plodding man;—perhaps doubly-so in a place like this, newly settled by various races. Now just let the public mind be once brought to believe, that justice is *"not"* to be had in our Law Courts, owing to inability, or any other lack, on the part of the judge! and what an amount of bitter fruit will surely follow! Again: what can be more painful to any ingenuous mind, than to have one's honest exertions to do one's duty, to do impartial justice *tempered with equity*, (for which our R.M. courts were originally established,) continually disparaged and sneered at by those who are unwilling or incapable of understanding them?

As a true John-Bullian, I know very well our right to grumble and growl at any adverse decision, but, the growl over, there is an end of it. Not so, however, low *published* general disparaging remarks, which insidiously sap the public faith in our best institutions, and so tend to make settlers suspicious and uneasy.

Although this letter is already too long for your columns, I would, for "Tradesman's" information, just call his attention to what Mr. Justice Blackstone tersely says on libel, particularly of libelling a Magistrate:—"Libels, in this sense, are malicious defamations of any person, and especially a magistrate, made public by either printing, writing, &c., in order to provoke him to wrath, or expose him to public hatred, contempt, or ridicule. The direct tendency of these libels is the breach of the public peace.... It is immaterial with respect to the essence of a libel, whether the matter of it be true or false, since the provocation, and not the falsity, is the thing to be punished criminally; though, doubtless, the falsehood of it may aggravate its guilt, and enhance its punishment." And Lord Coke has said, "That the greater appearance of truth there is in any malicious invective, so much the more provoking it is." And I think I may venture to add, that we all pretty well know how His Honor Mr. Justice Johnston would view a person prosecuted before him for ridiculing and defaming a Magistrate and Judge in the honorable and painful performance of his duty.

I think I ought also to say, that I have felt the more impelled to write thus,—not merely from my long acquaintance with our late R.M., who has been more than once hinted at by "Tradesman" in his letter (at whose removal from office, I, with many others, felt grieved), whose generous mind would be the first to object to being alluded to and invidiously compared in such a way; but also from my having carefully read all the decisions of our present and new R.M. which have appeared in print, and that I have been struck with their clearness cogency justice and equity,—and, if I may hazard as much,—their legal knowledge and ability; the product only of careful and painstaking investigation and thought. I have not the honor of being intimately acquainted with our new R.M., but, I, with many others, am thankful that we have such a Magistrate. And believing as I do, that "Righteousness exalteth a Nation,"[2] I would there were more like him in our Province, and less of those of his vilifiers.

Hoping you may find room in your next paper for this, and that both you and Napier *Tradesmen*, duly considering the probable consequences of such a letter as "Tradesman," if allowed to pass unnoticed and unrebuked, will agree with me in condemning it. I am, &c.,

WILLIAM COLENSO.

Napier, Dec. 14, 1870.

§ 1871 EDITORIAL.
West Coast Times 5 May.
Several specimens of the New Zealand thrush have lately made their appearance in Napier and the suburbs. These unwonted visitors have probably been driven down from the Ruahine Mountains. One specimen is now in possession of Mr. Colenso, who intends having it stuffed.

§ 1871 EDITORIAL.
Nelson Evening Mail 9 June.
Provincial Councillors often entertain very exalted ideas of their own importance and of the legislative powers of the body to which they belong. An amusing instance of this has recently occurred in Napier, where Mr. Colenso actually asked the Council to assent to a series of resolutions regarding the necessity for the enactment of a Usury Law. The resolutions are really refreshingly cool. They recite that monies were commonly and largely borrowed on the first settlement of the Province at very high rates of interest by many of the early settlers, for the purpose of taking, occupying, and stocking of sheep runs, and that such monies were in general thus largely borrowed at a time when both sheep and wool were worth in the market from four to six times their present value, and when highway and other rates and tolls were unknown; and in entire good faith and belief that those early prices for the staple commodities of sheep and wool would continue and that as notwithstanding the utmost care, attention, and prudent economy on the part of those parties that have so borrowed, it is now found to be impossible any longer to pay such high rates of interest; it therefore seems fair and just that under these greatly altered circumstances the loss should be equitably borne by both lender and borrower. Mr. Colenso accordingly proceeds to recommend the unanimous application to the Assembly to pass an Act compelling the lenders in the cases referred to, to accept 6 per cent interest, but having some doubt as to whether the Assembly would consent to fix the rate so low, and in the event of that body

---

2 This is the motto for the seal of the Kingdom of Hawaii (Sandwich Islands). W.C.

not consenting to make the maximum legal sum to be henceforth due and paid as interest upon the said old loans less than 8 per cent, that the sum of 2 per cent, per annum shall be at every payment thereof deducted therefrom, the same to be paid over to the Provincial Treasurer of Hawke's Bay on account of the said Province, and to be by the Provincial Council dealt with as its ordinary revenue. It is almost needless to add that Mr. Colenso's no doubt well-meant, but at the same time utterly absurd proposals found little favor in the eyes of the Council, and were, after a good deal of time had been wasted in debating them, rejected.

❖ **1871 Fiat Justitia; being a few thoughts respecting the Maori prisoner Kereopa now in Napier gaol, awaiting his trial for murder. Respectfully Addressed to the considerate and justice-loving Christian Settlers of Hawke's Bay, and also to our Rulers, in a Letter to the Editor of the *"Hawke's Bay Herald."*[3]**

§ 1871 HAWKE'S BAY.
Otago Witness 16 December.
Napier, December 8th.—Mr. Colenso has written a long letter to the Herald against the execution of Kereopa. Every exertion is being made to procure proper evidence for production at the trial. Mr. Commissioner Clarke and nine witnesses are expected to arrive from Tauranga tonight. At the examination yesterday, Kereopa expressed a desire to be taken to the place where Mr. Volkner was crucified, and to be crucified there himself. The Eperaima bridge, 130 feet long, was blown down the night before last, and entirely destroyed.

At a cattle sale yesterday store steers were sold at from 75s to 90s ; yearlings, 80s to 50s. Sheep same as last quotations.

❖ 1872 SHOULD KEREOPA BE HUNG?
Nelson Examiner and New Zealand Chronicle 3 January.
Mr. Colenso has addressed a long letter to the Hawke's Bay Herald, protesting against the sentence passed upon Kereopa being executed. The letter, which is a clever piece of special pleading, is too long to republish, but we give Mr. Colenso's own *resumé* of it:—

1. That at the time (1865) when Mr. Volkner met with his sad fate, we had been at war with the natives for several years, during which they had suffered greatly.

2. That it is well known that the natives had been repeatedly told, both by word of mouth and by letter, by several Europeans high in office (both spiritual and civil)

---

3 Reprinted by Dinwiddie, Morrison & Co., Napier, as a leaflet. Re-published in *Colenso's published papers 1: 1842–1884*, forthcoming. I.S.G.

and their friends—some of whom, as the present Premier the Hon. Mr. Fox, and Dr. Featherston, and Mr. Fitzherbert, the present Superintendent of Wellington, are still connected with the Government of the colony—that the said war was "an unjust and unholy war" on the part of the Government, and that it was shamefully forced upon the natives.

3. That our own repeated killing of their women aud children (no doubt unintentionally), and other barbarities always more or less incidental on long and heavy war, aroused the worst feelings of the natives against us, and set them on barbarous reprisals; which, though in their own old mode of warfare was quite common to them, they in all their former wars with us had never initiated.

4. That Opotiki, where Mr. Volkner resided, was, for many sad reasons, in a very excitable state at the time of the Hauhau party reaching it, and of his being killed.

5. That the fanatical Hauhau party under Patara, sent forth from Taranaki, where the war began by Te Ua, the Hauhau prophet, visited Opotiki and the East Coast in order to induce the tribes to join the West Coast natives in the war.

6. That on the arrival of the Hauhau party at Opotiki and their being joined by the inhabitants of that place, their acts and deeds were, under all the exciting circumstances, those of a politico-fanatical *emeute*, or mad fanatical tumultous mob.

7. That all history tells us of such sad times and scenes often and everywhere occurring.

8. That at such times everything is for the time beyond all reasonable control—even in the oldest and most Christian countries and cities.

9. That maddening acts of zeal committed at such times, are seldom severely revenged; or, if revenged, done immediately on the spot; never after a period of years.

10. That Mr. Volkner, much as we deplore his death, was killed at that time by the frantic mob, as a spy or "betrayer:"—much as in the American war General Washington hung the British officer, Major André. (Perhaps, of the two cases, all things calmly considered, General Washington's act was the worst).

11. That many other European settlers, men, women, and children, at least as equally innocent of wrong as Mr. Volkner, were also from time to time killed by the natives.

12. That the murderers of these were by proclamation specially excepted from pardon.

13. That these murderers were subsequently pardoned without trial, although coroners' juries had returned verdicts of wilful murder against many of them.

14. That the chief Te Pehi, who by proclamation had been also specially excepted from pardon, for his gross perjury and for treacherously attacking the troops of the Queen, was also pardoned without trial.

15. That three natives, names known and given, who had in the same year murdered the Governor's messenger, and for whose apprehension £1,000 had been offered—have not been prosecuted, and are allowed to go at large.

16. That the Hauhau prophet Te Ua, and Patara, the leader of the Hauhau party who killed in conjunction with the Opotiki natives Mr. Volkner, and who were the originators and directors of all the subsequent mischief, were also pardoned.

17. That the "loyal native" chiefs, including the members of Parliament, say, (1.) that inasmuch as the Government have pardoned the great Hauhau leaders in wrongdoing, the Government cannot now refuse to pardon the subordinate ones; and (2.) that the Government have already exacted a dreadful revenge at Opotiki for the killing of Mr. Volkner, killing, in all, more than fifty Maoris; and that it is unjust to shed more blood on account of Mr. Volkner's death, after, too, such a lapse of years.

18. That it is believed that the doing so would be certainly secretly charged against the Church or against a section thereof.

19. That the "loyal natives" are, in many parts of the island (more or less, rightly or wrongly) dissatisfied with the Government.

20. That it should be the steady aim of the Government to endeavour to lessen that spirit of dissatisfaction now so prevalent among the "loyal natives"—and that not by promise, or flattery, or money, but by prompt and cheerful acts of justice.

21. That care should be taken not to increase the spirit of dissatisfaction by doing that towards one of their nation which in their opinion is unjust.

22. That Christian justice (which we have endeavoured to teach the natives) is ever tempered with mercy.

23. That the Imperial Government dislikes our repeated shedding of Maori blood, especially for long past political offences; and that our Government has been informed, that "it has given the Imperial Government great pleasure to hear, that" (out of thirty Maori prisoners in one batch condemned to death), "there were no executions."

24. That the sad death of Mr. Volkner by the hands of the infuriated politico-religious Hauhau natives in the *emeute* at Opotiki in March, 1865 (nearly 7 years ago), *has been fully avenged, and that* IN THE WAY THE GOVERNOR HIMSELF CHOSE.

25. That our laws do not admit of double punishment for one crime.

[It is intended, we believe, that Kereopa shall be hung to-morrow.]

§ 1872 EDITORIAL.
Wellington Independent 5 January.

(Kereopa's crime) was unprovoked and cruel even in Maori eyes, and he does not appear to have had the sympathy of any one of his own race. If he has found apologists, it is amongst those mawky sentimentalists we occasionally meet with amongst Europeans. Such men as Mr. Colenso, whose influence, luckily for the colony, is now extinct.

§ 1872 POLITICAL.
Wellington Independent 20 January.

(Kereopa) has been since hanged, and so far from his punishment having in any way been resented by the natives it appears to have received unanimous acquiescence in its justice. We regret, however, to say that Kereopa found an apologist in Mr. Colenso of Napier who with the accustomed sickly sentimentalism of the Philo-Maorists, has sought—if not to justify Kereopa's crime—to palliate it. It is needless to say that very few persons can be found to sympathise with this attempt to prove that "killing is no murder."

§ 1872 EDITORIAL.
Evening Post (Wellington) 21 August.
The learned Dr. Buller is not the only aspiring literary genius who is acquiring the rudiments of his profession at the expense of the taxpayers of New Zealand. It is very gratifying to find a paternal Government fostering our local literary talent, but we should be still more gratified if we were shown some tangible result therefrom. For many years past, Mr. William Colenso, of Napier, has been supposed to be engaged upon the compilation of a Maori lexicon, and whatever progress Mr. Colenso has made, it is quite certain that he has dipped pretty deeply into the public purse "on account." What sums have been lavished upon Mr. Colenso, and what *quid pro quo* he has returned, it is impossible to say. The non-completion of work has been apologised for by the dilatory lexicographer year after year upon the plea of ill-health. Yet we find that he has accepted the post of Inspector of Schools in Hawke's Bay, the duties of which will entail long and wearisome rides to outlying districts. As one of the local papers observes:— "When a gentleman is too infirm to sit at home and compile a dictionary, it can hardly be expected of him to undergo physical exertions absolutely necessary before he can perform the duties of a school inspector." Either Mr. Colenso is in good health or he is not. In the one case he ought to finish his famous dictionary,—in the other he ought to resign his inspectorship.

§ 1872 NAPIER, FROM A CORRESPONDENT.
Wellington Independent 22 October.
We had a Provincial Council election here recently, but the affair was very tame, little or no excitement being manifested by either side. The candidates were Mr. William Colenso (who had resigned the seat in consequence of having accepted the appointment of Inspector of Schools), and Mr. T.R. Newton. At the close of the poll, the numbers were announced as follows:—

Colenso 83 Newton 82. If it had not been for the ignorance of the *modus operandi* of the ballot by two of Mr. Newton's supporters, the result of the election would have been exactly the reverse of what it was. It appeared that instead of obliterating the name of the candidate they proposed to reject, they wrote the name of the favorite, leaving both names remaining on the printed form. Their votes were of course declared null, and this turned the election in favor of Mr. Colenso.

§ 1873 THE ALLEGED MISSIONARY LAND SHARKING.
Daily Southern Cross 11 October.

The subject of the early missionaries of the Church of England in New Zealand having engaged so extensively in land purchases from the natives, has engaged a good deal of attention lately. The following extracts from "The Story of New Zealand: Past and Present—Savage and Civilised," by Arthur S. Thomson, M.D., surgeon-major 58th Regiment, and published in London in 1859, will be read with interest. At page 154 and following pages, vol. 2, Dr. Thomson says:—"At an early date, it will be remembered, several of the English Church Missionaries purchased land from the New Zealanders, and the statement of the quantity claimed and the awards given, will be found in the subjoined table, where also will be seen the honoured names of Messrs. Maunsell, Ashwell, Chapman, Morgan, Colenso, and the early missionaries who resisted this world's temptations:—

Rev. Alfred N. Brown, missionary, entered the mission in 1829, and Mr. J.R. Wilson, catechist, entered the mission in 1833; they jointly claimed 3,840 acres of land, and were awarded by the land commissioners, 2,987 acres.

Rev.—Maunsell, missionary, entered the mission in 1835, claimed no land.

Rev. R. Taylor, missionary, entered the mission in 1835, claimed 50,000 acres; awarded 1,704 acres.

Rev. Henry Williams, missionary, entered the mission in 1823, claimed 22,000 acres; awarded 9,000.

Rev. Wm. Williams, missionary entered the mission in 1826, claimed 890 acres; awarded 890 acres.

Mr. Benjamin Ashwell, catechist, entered the mission in 1835, claimed 20 acres; awarded 20 acres.

Mr. Charles Baker, catechist, entered the mission in 1828, claimed 6,242 acres; awarded 2,560 acres.

Mr. John Bedford, wheelwright, entered the mission in 1836, claimed 250 acres; awarded 60 acres.

Mr. Thomas Chapman, catechist, entered the mission in 1830, claimed no land.

Mr. George Clarke, catechist, entered the mission in 1824, claimed 19,000 acres; awarded 5,500 acres.

Mr. William Colenso, printer, entered the mission in 1834, claimed no land.

Mr. Richard Davis, catechist, entered the mission in 1824, claimed 6,000 acres; awarded 3,500 acres.

Mr. James Davis, store-keeper, entered the mission in 1824, claimed 1,015 acres; awarded 335 acres.

Serena Davis, teacher, entered the mission in 1824, claimed no land.

Mr. John Edmonds, stonemason, entered the mission in 1834, claimed no land.

Mr. W.T. Fairburn, catechist, entered the mission in 1819, claimed 20,000 acres; awarded 2,560 acres.

Mr. S.H. Ford, surgeon, entered the mission in 1837, claimed 8,400 acres; awarded 1,757 acres.

Mr. James Hamlin, catechist, entered the mission in 1826, claimed 6,774 acres; awarded 3,937 acres.

Mr. James Kemp, catechist, entered the mission in 1819, claimed 18,552 acres; awarded 5,276 acres.

Mr. John King, catechist, entered the mission in 1814, claimed 10,300 acres; awarded 5,150 acres.

Mr. P.H. King, catechist, entered the mission in 1834, claimed 2,305 acres; awarded 2,305 acres.

Mr. W. King, assistant, home in New Zealand, claimed no land.

Mr. Octavius Hadfield, catechist, entered the mission in 1838, claimed no land.

Mr. S.M. Knight, catechist, entered the mission in 1835, claimed no land.

Mr. Joseph Matthews, catechist, entered the mission in 1832, claimed 2,200 acres; awarded 2,200 acres.

Mr. Richard Matthews, catechist, entered the mission in 1837, claimed 3,000 acres; awarded 4,792 acres.

Mr. John Morgan, catechist, entered the mission in 1833, claimed no land.

Mr. Henry W. Pilley, catechist, entered the mission in 1534, claimed no land.

Mr. James Preece, catechist, entered the mission in 1830, claimed 1,450 acres; awarded 1,450 acres.

Mr. W.G. Puckey, catechist, entered the mission in 1821, claimed 4,800 acres; awarded 2,300 acres.

Mr. James Shepherd, catechist, entered the mission in 1820, claimed 11,860 acres; awarded 5,330 acres.

Mr. James Stack, catechist, entered the mission in 1834, claimed no land.

Mr. W.R. Wade, superintendent of the press, claimed no land.

Marian Williams, teacher, went out with her father, claimed no land.

Church Missionary Society, claimed 11,665 acres: awarded none.

Families of Church Missionaries, claimed 6,200 acres; awarded 3,100 acres.

Total area of land claimed, 216,763 acres; awarded 66,713 acres.

"Two Wesleyan missionaries bought land from the natives, but the great majority of the clergy belonging to that Church kept themselves aloof from land-sharking. The Roman Catholic missionaries arrived too late to take advantage of the trade; not that they would have done so, for the missionaries of that Church in other Countries have generally obeyed the spirit of the holy injunction to the first Christian missionaries in the world: 'Take nothing for your journey, neither staves, nor scrip, neither bread, neither money, neither have two coats apiece.' The Church of England missionaries claimed 216,000 acres of land, and the Commissioners awarded 66,000. The foregoing statement shows the exact quantities claimed and awarded. The Bishop of Australia had in 1847 some misgivings about these lands; and in 1846, Governor Grey, thinking some of the awards illegal and unjust towards the natives, asked the missionaries to relinquish certain portions without reference to the Courts of law,

and Bishop Selwyn used his influence to accomplish this object. The missionaries were told that their conduct was injuring the Society they belonged to, and affecting their own character: Punch suggested that Father Taylor should have his picture hung up in the Church Missionary Society's hall with the words 'fifty thousand acres' under it; the judicial board of the Privy Council declared against them; but all these modes of attack were in vain. Archdeacon Henry Williams and others refused to relinquish a rood unless the Governor withdrew some verbal accusations hurled against them.... The Council of the Church Missionary Society... informed Archdeacon Henry Williams and some others, that they must either give up their exclusive grants of land or leave the service of the Mission. The Archdeacon chose the latter course: one missionary was superannuated; the resignation of another, accepted; and the others offered to relinquish their lands. When Archdeacon Williams had suffered suspension for five years he was restored. The treatment the venerable missionary received—the man who had borne the burthen and heat of the day, 'the father of missionaries,'—for a society he had served with zeal for more than a quarter of a century, was severely stigmatised by several in New Zealand: but other parts of the world and other times will doubtless affirm that the Archdeacon's suspension and restoration were alike creditable to the Church Missionary Society.[4]

§ 1874 EDITORIAL.
Wanganui Chronicle 26 March.

At length tidings have been heard of the great "Maori Lexicon," upon the compilation of which Mr. W. Colenso, of Napier, has been employed since 1866, his labours being now and then refreshed by grants of considerable sums of public money! These tidings are conveyed in a report from Mr. Colenso to the Native Minister, dated 30th August, 1873, but which has only just seen the light. They are not, unfortunately, what might have been wished. Mr. Colenso frankly says to the Minister, "I allow that the work is in a most unsatisfactory state, not only to the House, but to the public, and to the Government, but most especially to myself," but then proceeds to repudiate the inference to be drawn from this assertion, by adding, "I cannot allow that I am, or have been, to blame in the matter." The present condition of the magnum opus is described thus:—A large quantity of matter has been accumulated, which has been put into place, in a kind of rough order, in the M.S., but not a single page of it is ready for the press; it is, moreover, merely roughly and quickly written with abreviations, intended for Mr. Colenso's own copying, and the whole has to be thoroughly and closely considered and re-written. Practically, therefore, it is only intelligible to the writer. This distressing state of affairs is aggravated by the deplorable condition of Mr. Colenso's health. He declares he is getting more and more infirm with advancing years, that he is suffering from chronic rheumatism, while a contraction of the thumb and forefinger of his right hand prevents his writing

---

4 Dandeson Coates, the powerful secretary of the C.M.S., had written to Lord Glenelg in 1837, 'It is too high wrought, too Utopian, to believe that a miscellaneous body of men will expatriate themselves, to a savage land at the antipodes, merely out of a benevolent regard to the civilisation and moral improvement of the Natives .... it is not without difficulty that the Missionaries have been able, on some occasions, to obtain a sufficiency of land for their objects ....' The above quotation from Thomson is an edited version – he had a lot more to say about the Anglican missionaries' 'land-sharking'. I.S.G.

long continuously. Then, his time is pretty well occupied with the duties of Inspector of Schools for Hawke's Bay, and the only "feasible" proposal which he can make in regard to the work is this: That he should proceed at once to do all that he can to get a portion of the lexicon, though uncompleted, ready for the press, say, from A onward; the first parcel to be forwarded to the Government in January, 1874, (it would be interesting to know whether it was so forwarded) to be followed by other portions throughout the summer. By these Cyclopean efforts, a "small 'portion'" of the work will be ready for members by the next session of the General Assembly, and will doubtless be eagerly enquired for. After the prerogation of the Assembly, Mr. Colenso proposes that the printing shall begin. Then will come the tug of war.

❖ **1874 EARLY DAYS OF THE NEW ZEALAND PRESS.**
Otago Witness 26 December.
SIR,—In the interesting account of the adjourned meeting of the Press Club, which you have published in your issue of the 2nd inst.,[5] a few things are stated, in the speech of His Honour Judge Chapman, which are not altogether in accordance with fact; and as it is in my power to correct them, I venture to do so, relying on your courtesy to give what I now write due publicity in the columns of your paper. I feel the more inclined to address you—1. Because what I have to state is closely connected (historically, so I may say) with the introduction of the Press into New Zealand, a matter in which both yourself and the Press Club cannot but be deeply interested; and, 2nd, because what has been publicly uttered by a gentleman of so long standing in our Colony, and holding such a high position as Mr. Justice Chapman (on such an occasion, too!), is sure to be received with great attention, and, most probably, be repeatedly published in all parts of the English-speaking world. While, however, I proceed to show some of the errors made by Judge Chapman in his speech, I would be understood as merely doing that which His Honour himself would undoubtedly have done had he been fully aware of it; although some may be ready to detect a vein of the *ad captandum* genus running throughout this portion of the learned Judge's remarks.

Judge Chapman says:—"He would now come to what would be of interest to his hearers, the early history of the Press of this Colony, particularly the newspaper press.... The first number of the paper (the New Zealand Gazette) was issued on the 18th of April 1841.... Although this was the first newspaper in the Colony, he did not mean to say that the Press which printed the New Zealand Gazette was the first printing press. The Missionaries had a small printing press at Pahia, (*sic* Paihia), many years before, which they used to print little books for the instruction of the Maoris— printing prayers and so forth, extracts from the Scripture printed in Maori, and a little Grammar and Accidence for teaching the Maoris English. He had some of the printing work done by the missionaries, and he thought that the printers of the present

---

5 Actually in the 7 Nov 1874 issue. This is the same Henry Samuel Chapman who wrote with 'biting malevolent sarcasm' about Colenso in 1847 (see Bagnall & Petersen, p. 266). I.S.G.

day would turn up their intellectual noses at it.—(Laughter.) It was not very good press work, but it was useful in its time." Then the Judge goes on to say:—"There was also another little press in the Colony; Colonel Wakefield brought with him a little toy-press.... It was the second printing press introduced into the Colony of New Zealand."

Now, then, for the facts.

The printing press of the Church Missionary Society, which arrived with me in New Zealand in 1834, was not a "small" one, it being a Stanhope press, royal size; and this was soon followed by a Columbian press of the same size. These were constantly used, not only to print "little books—Prayers and so forth, and extracts from the Scriptures, and a little Grammar"—but to print tolerably large books, viz.:—In 1835, the Epistles to the Ephesians and Philippians, and the Gospel of St. Luke, in 12mo, containing 79 pages; in 1837, the whole of the New Testament, in small pica, 8vo, containing 356 pages, of which edition 5000 copies were printed in 1839, the Psalms, in 12mo, containing 128 pages, of which 20,000 copies were printed; in 1840, the complete Prayer Book of the Church of England, in long primer, 12mo, with its Epistles, Gospels, Psalms, Occasional Services, Articles, and Rubric, and also 42 additional Hymns, forming a book of 372 pages; besides which there were large quantities of smaller books printed, such as Catechisms, Yearly Almanacks, Daily Prayer Books, School Lessons, Primers, parts of the Old Testament, as of Genesis, Exodus, Deuteronomy, Isaiah, Daniel, Jonah, &c., &c., each containing from twelve to fifty-two pages in 8vo, and in 12mo. The first English book, being "The Report of the New Zealand Temperance Society," was printed in 1836, and the first Gazette in English was printed for the Government in 1840.

As all these were composited wholly by myself without assistance, and, in part, also printed—and that under great difficulties,[6] of which neither missionary nor printer of the present day can possibly form any correct idea. I will not say anything as to the quality of the work; yet, in again looking at the printing of those works (copies now lying on my writing table), I feel pretty sure that no "printers of the present day would turn up their intellectual noses at it". Moreover, should the members of the Press Club at Dunedin wish it, and also pay the expenses, I will, with much pleasure, send them, per registered mail, copies of the works for their inspection and opinion—but to be returned to me.

I may further mention that those books were also bound by myself: the art of book-binding, with many other useful arts, I was obliged to learn at that early and eventful period of our history.

---

6   Curiously enough, only a few days ago, in looking over the library of my lately deceased friend, Mr. Edward Catchpool (who for long time was the Collector of Customs at this port, and who was also one of the first printers in Wellington, who, in its earliest days, printed a newspaper there—which seems to have been wholly overlooked by Judge Chapman), I found an interesting book, entitled, "The British Colonisation of New Zealand," and published for the New Zealand Association in 1837—which I had never before seen. At page 206 of that work is an extract from a letter of mine, written from New Zealand in March, 1835, in which I say—"I have been engaged in printing 2000 copies of a book of 16 pages, containing St. Paul's Epistles to the Ephesians and Philippians. A printer in London cannot form a correct idea of the disadvantages under which I laboured in getting this up and sending it out. In consequence of not having a single lead," which, with printing paper and several other absolutely necessary things, had been left behind, "I was obliged to substitute paper and spaces," placed flat, "for blank lines, &c., &c." W.C.

In conclusion, I may be permitted to add that I believe I shall—at least by all the members of the Press Club—be readily pardoned for saying that the first printing-press in New Zealand under my superintendency has much to be fairly proud of, in having printed the first and only edition of the complete New Testament in the Southern Hemisphere, and the first English book and English newspaper in New Zealand, —I am, &c.,

WILLIAM COLENSO.

Napier, Nov. 28, 1874.

§ 1875 THE SUPPLEMENTARY ESTIMATES.
Evening Post 19 October.
Mr. William Colenso never having completed his Maori Lexicon, although pretty well paid for it, is to get £100 for writing an elementary English and Maori school book.

§ 1876 EDITORIAL.
Daily Southern Cross 2 September.
UNLIKE his calculating cousin of Port Natal, MR. WILLIAM COLENSO, the Inspector of Schools for the Province of Hawke's Bay, is not content with measurements and calculation based on rigid rule and the strictest arithmetic, but in his educational report revels in what may be classed as "miracles," and Arabian Nights fictions. When discussing or narrating educational statistics, and the progress of schools and scholars, the fitness of teachers, and the hygienic condition of school-houses, it is to be expected that high-flown rhetoric and fanciful comparisons would be carefully avoided, and the strictest matter-of-fact accuracy of narrative and illustration would guide the mind and pen of the writer of an official report of this description. Mr. COLENSO, however, sublimely soars above all such sublunary restrictions, and his report, which has just been published in the Hawke's Bay *Provincial Gazette*, is unique in its way, both as to felicitously imaginative descriptions, and a true disregard for the customary rules that are supposed to regulate English composition. There is a fulness—a kind of gushing overflow—of sentiment which distinguishes much of Mr. COLENSO's report, which, we are glad to observe, notifies an increase in the number of scholars. Last year the total number of scholars on the books was—boys, 820; girls, 582; total, 1,408. The total average daily attendance was 1,137, or 321 in excess of the average of the previous year. The attendance is given at 26 schools, conducted by 26 principal teachers, who are aided in some of the larger schools by male and female assistants. The schools, it appears, "are now much too small for the number of scholars;" and this defect is frequently, and with original emphasis, referred to throughout the report. In one of the detailed reports of the schools, Mr. COLENSO, speaking on this subject, says, "Very much more room, however, is needed, as the children are *packed together like herrings in a barrel.*" We italicise the last six words. What can teachers, what can parents of children

conceive of the value of accuracy of description when, in a document such as an official report on schools, the public are gravely informed that the children are packed together like herrings in a barrel? The statement reminds us of an old story which, because of its appositeness, will bear repetition, regarding a woman who was a witness before a well-known English Judge, who was engaged in trying a prisoner for burglary. In the course of her evidence, in which she was rather voluble (and it is your too-willing and voluble witness who comes to grief), she remarked "I was so frightened I could have crept into a nut-shell." The Judge, in a mild voice, asked her to repeat what she had just said, as if he had failed to catch the statement. Glibly the creeping into the nut-shell process was repeated, whereupon the Judge sternly said, "Woman, on your oath *could* you have crept into a nut-shell?" So, similarly, Mr. COLENSO, on your veracity, *were* the children packed "like herrings in a barrel," and, if not, what possible good purpose can be served by the use of such extravagant and ridiculous hyperbole in a document professing gravely and circumstantially to describe the condition of a public department which is of such great importance as is that of education?

After mentioning that "no less" (meaning no fewer) "than twelve boys had gained special prizes for essay writing" in one school, Mr. COLENSO again refers to the necessity for more room, and observes, in somewhat nursery-maidish English,—"*However* the scholars manage to do so well as they do, seeing that they are so crammed, is a marvel." But for the context and the previous reference to the subject, it would be difficult to comprehend whether Mr. COLENSO meant that the scholars were crammed physically or mentally, inside or out. If he means "crammed together," as he no doubt does, then the fault of the herring-packing is repeated; and it is not surprising that he should look on the whole thing as something approaching to a miraculous arrangement. Altogether, this is a style of loose writing which is least tolerable among men who profess such high scholastic attainments as are supposed to enable them to judge and criticise the results of the performances of those who are teachers of the new generation.

On the somewhat vexed question of school prizes we observe that Mr. COLENSO thinks prizes produce advantageous effects, and he affirms that "no small amount of diligence and improvement on the part of scholars is to be fairly ascribed" to such prizes.[7] It is pleasing to find that in nearly all the Hawke's Bay schools there is "much greater activity and diligence exhibited among the scholars in applying themselves to learning than there was formerly." He points out, too, that when this is not the case the fault is mainly that of "the parents or teachers, or both." There can be no doubt that if a pupil is permitted at school to escape while only half doing his work, or succeeds in just escaping censure, when, by a little diligence, he could from

---

7   Colenso set the following problem for students at Waipawa School during his 1873 visit: 'A B C D went into partnership. A put into the business £674/13/6 for 4 yrs, 5 mths, 19 days. B put in £2463/14/8 for 2 yrs, 3 mths, 24 days. C put in £896/17/9 for 6 yrs, 8 mths, 17 days. D put in £346/18/7 for 3 yrs 4 mths. Their gross gain was £2487/13/2 and expenses in working the business was £596/15/9. I wish to know the nett gain and what was each partner's share.' The problem was answered correctly by James Woodhouse Bibby (1862-1959) an 11-year-old Form I boy. Inspector Colenso presented him with a book as a prize. I.S.G.

his capacity gain much praise, the teacher is to blame; and if parents fail to back up the earnest efforts of an earnest teacher in enforcing study, duty, obedience, and respect, then the parents fall very far short of their duty at once to the teacher and to their own children. And we fear there are too many cases where this, perhaps, unthinking, inattention is to be found. It cannot too soon be remedied.

The Inspector concludes his report by the two following paragraphs.—

"For my own part, now that the Provincial system of Government is abolished, I heartily wish that the Colonial Government will shortly establish a suitable, liberal, and comprehensive plan of general education. One, by which education shall be for all alike,—both guaranteed and civil, or, in other words, compulsory and secular; such a system once well begun,—in good and ample school-houses and with first-class trained teachers,—would soon become established, grow more and more necessary and national and be heartily welcomed, and yield in due season an abundant crop of fruit.

"No doubt the time will arrive when every public school in this colony will not only have its *trained* teachers, but when all the teachers will act upon one improved system of teaching. But, while I say this, I must be clearly understood to mean, that a *trained* teacher, as such, is only the more valuable to his school and to the public, when he has also the especial *natural* qualifications of a teacher in him,—which no *mere training* can possibly impart; otherwise the untrained though educated man, *possessing the aptness, the mind and the heart*, which enables him to *love* his work in its entirety, and which peculiarly fits him for the office of teaching, will prove the better qualified and most useful man; such an one will be sure to gain the hearts of his pupils, and the corresponding advantages will be great and solid, and though not so showy will be seen."

He is a trifle metaphysical in the last sentence, and, while the pulsation and regular pumping work of the heart is necessary for the physical and mental health of the human subject, we must say that, as in the ordinary business of every day life, we should (to use a common and, at least, as sensible a metaphor), as a rule, prefer a trained teacher with the "stomach" for his work, to an educated untrained man, however much of pure love and affection he may cherish for the world at large.

§ 1877 THE NAPIER ELECTION.
Hawke's Bay Herald 9 February.

The nomination of candidates for the vacant seat for the Napier electoral district took place yesterday in the Courthouse....

Mr. W. Thomas proposed Mr. William Colenso. Mr. T. Moore seconded the nomination, remarking that he was sure that Mr. Colenso would prove a faithful servant....

The Returning Officer then took a show of hands, and declared that Mr. Sutton had the majority, the numbers being as follows:—

Sutton.................. 24
Buchanan 23
Tiffen.................. 16
Rhodes.................. 5
Colenso.................. 3

Mr. Tiffen having demanded a poll, the Returning Officer announced that it would be held on Thursday next the 15th instant.... If any of the candidates wished to address the meeting they could do so now; he would merely suggest, in the mildest possible manner, that lunch time was at 1 o'clock. (Laughter.)....

Mr. Colenso, on rising, was received with very great applause; and his first remark, that he was an old hand at elections, elicited quite a universal roar of laughter, mingled with demonstrations of applause. He reminded the meeting of the injunction of the good Spartan mother to her son to come back from the battle either with his shield or on his shield. Well, Mr. Colenso said, that was what he was going to do; he would either be at the head of the poll or dead on his shield. (Great laughter.) He was going to fight the battle fairly, and they might judge of his mode of fighting by what he had already done. He had advertised his address only three times. (Laughter.) He was not like those who let their addresses hang in the newspapers for weeks together. He did not exercise any of those manoeuvres, such as bowing and scraping, crying and promising. (Laughter.) No, he would stand much as he had always done, and he would win either honestly or not at all. (Applause.) He could not but confess that he did not understand the newspapers at all. There was one of them, the editor of which, certainly, was young, for his beard had scarcely grown—(laughter)—and that paper had said of him (Mr. Colenso), "The absurdity of his expectations now is due to his past history. Some ten or fifteen years ago, he was the representative of Her Majesty's Opposition in Hawke's Bay. He voted in all matters dead against his colleague, the present Minister of Public Works. Recently, however, he has gained the determined enmity of most of his old party by going over to the Government side and accepting the post of Inspector of Schools." What namby-pamby stuff! (Laughter.) However, after that the paper went on to say that he (Mr. Colenso) "filled the post with remarkable ability." Well, it was the old story, "Save me from my friends." At all events, it could not be denied that he had been more usefully employed than any of the other candidates who were seeking the votes of the constituency. He now would say a few words about each of those candidates. (Great laughter.) Yes, he meant to polish off the whole four, and having removed the *impedimenta*, he would have room for himself to reach the head of the poll. He would begin with Mr. Tiffen. (Laughter.) If Mr. Tiffen had gained knowledge by going round the world, it was well for him, but he had little grown by the travel. (Laughter.) What had Mr. Tiffen ever done? Had they not seen Sealy undo whatever Mr. Tiffen did? (Laughter.) What was Mr. Tiffen going to do in the House? What had he to do with the laws that were to govern the country? Would he not be better among his ferns and his flowers, his grapes and so on? (Laughter.) Mr. Tiffen would be altogether out of place in the House of Representatives. There was one thing, certainly, that Mr. Tiffen would do; as soon as 10 o'clock arrived he would put on his hat and go. (Laughter.) Mr. Tiffen would never pipe all day and all night too; and when the Speaker's bell rang, Mr. Tiffen would not be there. (Laughter.) He (Mr. Colenso) could not help thinking of the scene in "Hamlet," where, after seeing the players, Hamlet and Polonius being together, Hamlet shows Polonius a cloud, and asks if it is not almost in shape like a camel? Polonius answers, "By the mass, and it's like a camel indeed." "Methinks it is like a weasel," says Hamlet. "It's backed like a weasel," replies Polonius. "Or like a whale," again says Hamlet. "Very like a whale," returns Polonius. (Roars of laughter.) And that was Mr. Tiffen, continued Mr. Colenso. (Renewed laughter.) They must not find fault with him (Mr. Colenso) and think him too severe; they must remember this was their Saturnalia. Now for Mr. Sutton. (Laughter.) Mr. Sutton's seconder had given one good reason for Mr. Sutton's return—that working men were wanted in the House. He (Mr. Colenso) agreed with that, but unfortunately for the reasoning of Mr. Sutton's seconder, it was necessary that the working man should be a clever man, able to grapple with matters of large importance, not with such matters as were dealt with in County Councils, road boards, or municipal councils, but matters affecting the policy of New Zealand; and Mr. Sutton was not the man for that! He (Mr. Colenso) recollected when a small measure was brought into the Provincial Council for licensing wholesale dealers in spirits. There was £10 to pay, and Mr. Sutton scouted the measure out. (Great laughter.) After some further remarks about Mr. Sutton, Mr. Colenso dealt with Mr. Buchanan, remarking that his proposer, Mr. Villers, had been brought over from Petane with a hook in his jaw, the bait being the Ahuriri bridge. One objection against Mr. Buchanan was that he was a runholder, though Mr. Buchanan said he was not. Then, Mr. Buchanan was not a resident in the town or in the district. Mr. Buchanan got in the Provincial Council twice, but only by flukes; he was beaten lately in a little riding—even his own people wouldn't have him—and he was beaten for the Provincial Council eighteen months ago. Had they come to such an emaciated condition that they must take Mr. Buchanan, and so backed as he was? He (Mr. Colenso) had that faith in the people of Napier as to believe that they would not do any such thing. In speaking of Mr. Rhodes, Mr. Colenso said that the objection against him was that Mr. Rhodes was still of the class termed runholders. He (Mr. Colenso) had no down against runholders, but that class was already amply represented both in the House and in the Council, and the electors should beware of increasing the strength of that class in the legislature. Mr. Rhodes was also like Mr. Tiffen, and as soon as 10 o'clock struck he would be off from the House. The question had been asked in the newspapers what right had he (Mr. Colenso) to come forward as a candidate? It had also been said in a newspaper that he was only poking fun, and did not mean it. If they wanted to know why he came forward, there was his justification (holding up a blue book of the votes and proceedings of the House). It was said in the Home Letter of the newspaper he had referred to that his

(Mr. Colenso's) coming forward was an absurdity, and that on occasions he had voted against Mr. Ormond, the Minister of Public Works. Well, the book he held in his hand showed that he (Mr. Colenso) had voted in 84 divisions, and Mr. Ormond—he was not Minister of Public Works then—had voted about nine times, and on two or three occasions they were against each other. But was he right or Mr. Ormond? Mr. Colenso then mentioned the various measures that he had opposed, and gave reasons to show that he had been right in his opposition in each case. He then went on to say that one reason why he could more usefully serve the constituency was that he had served a five years' apprenticeship in the House, and, he asked, inasmuch as he had served the constituency faithfully had he not a better claim than an outsider? (Applause.) Mr. Colenso then defended the course he had taken in regard to separation. He had fought to keep out of the House the Superintendents. He saw that they would bring in their Provincial Secretaries and their clerks, and that each cock would fight for his own dunghill; he had fought for the purification of the House, and he had gone in for separation, believing it would be better to have two provinces than one. Now that the provinces were abolished the case was different. There were men of wisdom, though, who still believed that separation would be good. He did not think so. He believed in New Zealand, one and undivided. Mr. Colenso then referred to the Good Templars and to the Catholics, claiming their votes—the Good Templars', because he had been a temperance man all his life; and the Catholics', because all the candidates being Protestants, there was not one of them so liberal as himself. (Long continued applause.)

❖ 1877 MR. COLENSO AND TEMPERANCE.
Hawke's Bay Herald 14 February.

SIR,—As a rule I never reply to anonymous letters; but you have one in your paper of this day (Tuesday) which, for 3 reasons, I would notice.—1. Because the slanderer has dared falsely to assume an honorable name (I.O.G.T.[8]) which does *not* belong to him, —neither are those letters—(or any of them) the initials of his own well-known name: —2. Because of his malevolent intention,—although some allowance is generally granted to *such* low principled persons at election times:—and, 3. Because no lie is so base, or so deep, as that which contains half of the truth. I know that the writer will attempt to wriggle out of this,—by his placing the fault to his "*bad memory!*" (which he has already mentioned,) as an easy way of escape: but such an evasion won't do for *him*. (I could give him a useful recipe for "lying and a bad memory," if he will take it to Bowerman, or Ellis, and then swallow it after it is mixed.) He knows, very well, that the letter which I last year wrote, (and which he has "the audacity" to refer to,) was *not* against Constable Madigan for *doing his duty*, (which I, for one, should ever be foremost to uphold him in,)—but, *for his overstepping his duty*, and interfering with the *gift* of a jug of beer to a working-man for his Sunday's dinner.

---

8   International Organisation of Good Templars. I.S.G.

And so with what followed in my letter on that occasion;—namely, my possibly going to Havelock on a Sunday and giving away beer.

All that was written to prove the principle of our common British liberty; or, in other words, to test, whether a poor man, or a hard-working man, at home for the Sunday, should be allowed to accept his beer as a gift, if any one offered or gave it to him.

And such a true and honest principle as this all honest Englishmen should uphold; or they may find, when too late, that their giving-in on this tack will surely lead to greater loss of common liberty, or rights. I am, &c.,

WILLIAM COLENSO.

Napier,

Feb. 13, 1877.

❖ 1878 THE EDUCATION ACT.

Hawke's Bay Herald 19 January.

SIR,—A *second* letter from Mr. W.L. Williams having appeared this morning in the HERALD,—in which he again lays it on thick, hot, and heavy, on the Hawke's Bay Education Board, (and, as it appears to me, without just cause,)—induces me to trouble you with a few lines in the hope of placing some of the matters so complained of by Mr. Williams in a little clearer light. I should not, however, care to do so were the members of our maligned Education Board here on the spot; but, of the five gentlemen who constitute the same, Mr. Rhodes and Mr. Lee are at Wellington, and Mr. Ormond and Mr. Chambers are at their country homes, and only one, Mr. Newton, resides in town, and he, I presume, has too much of real business to attend to, to notice the mole-hills of Mr. Williams. It is true that Mr. Williams prefaces his first letter, of Monday, the 14th inst., with an apology for his rushing into the fight, by saying:—"As I have not yet thoroughly mastered he Education Act, 1877, it is with some diffidence that I call attention to some mistakes, &c." And (as Mr. Williams only returned to Napier by the steamer *Taupo*, on Sunday Evening the 13th) such was allowable; but, then he follows up his attack—after 1 week's interval, with no one caring officially to notice his first assault,—he should, I think, have been better prepared; for, as it is, a certain *animus* is plain enough;—which, from a Christian minister, and in such a cause, would surely have been better avoided.

1. In his first letter, Mr. Williams says, "It devolves upon the Auckland Education Board, and not upon the old Hawke's Bay Board, to take the first steps under the Act for the school districts of Gisborne, Ormond, and Te Kapu."

Curiously enough, the Auckland Education Board does not think so; as is clearly shewn by what took place at their late sitting, held on the 11th instant. In the Auckland *Weekly News* of last Saturday, 12th, it is stated:—

GISBORNE.—This was an application for money to fence the school building. The Chairman (Mr. H.H. Lusk) said this application was placed in an awkward position, by the fact, that the whole of Cook County was omitted from the schedule of the new

Education Act, as being within the Provincial District of Auckland, and was placed within that of Hawke's Bay.... The tenders had been called for and accepted. The inspector said he thought it would be a pity if the whole thing must be broken up.—The chairman.—The question is how can we, the Board for the Provincial District of Auckland, enter into a contract for work to be done in the Provincial District of Hawke's Bay? The Secretary said, there might be a refund of liabilities.—The Chairman: Still that does not affect the question as to the right of the Auckland Board to enter into contracts for work to be done in the district of Hawke's Bay."

—So that the Auckland Education Board is here, in their views, at one with the Hawke's Bay Education Board. I know very well that two blacks will not make one white,—and both Boards may be wrong. Still, there is the fact against Mr. Williams.

2.   Mr. Williams finds repeatedly great fault with the New School districts, as for the *first* time cast by the Hawke's Bay Education Board, saying:—

—"It certainly looks as if the old Provincial District of Hawke's Bay had been mapped out into school districts, and, in enumerating them, the Mohaka district had, somehow, been forgotten."

But could not Mr. Williams have charitably considered it in another light? which is, also, the true one, viz.—that the Gazetted Road Board Districts of the Hawke's Bay Provincial District were adopted *pro tem* by the Hawke's Bay Education Board, and their boundaries taken at the beginning of the putting of the new Education Act into active operation, as affording something suitable and ready to hand for starting from to form those boundaries of the new School Districts; bearing, also, in mind (1.) that it was imperative to form them at once: (2.) that no time was to be lost: (3.) that all such bounds could easily be rectified: and (4.) that the new Board could very much better do all that. And this would serve to explain the apparently anomalous position of Mohaka,—of which Mr. Williams also complains.

In thus writing, however, I do not mean to defend all those School Districts, as now carved out and plotted on the map; very far from it; the Education Board itself would not do so; but that is a matter which time alone,—or time with experience,— can rectify.

3.   Lastly,—in the concluding words of his letter of this morning, comes Mr. Williams' Parthian dart! It is so exquisitely and keenly double-barbed, that I venture to copy it wholly. He says,

—"It is not very creditable to the existing Board that they should have been ignorant of the fact, that the school at Te Kapu has been under the control of the Auckland Education Board ever since its first establishment, and that it never had any connection whatever with the Hawke's Bay Education Board."

Did Mr. Williams really believe in the necessity for writing one iota of this *telling* sentence when he penned it? Did Mr. Williams not know—aye, and very well know, too,—that the members of the Hawke's Bay Education Board were all old settlers, —gentlemen who had always taken an active part in the Government of the Hawke's Bay Province from its formation?—that four out of the five members who constitute it, had been for many sessions members of its Provincial Council, and that its chairman had also repeatedly filled the office of Superintendent throughout many years? Did not Mr. Williams also know, that whenever I have gone to Te Wairoa to inspect the school there, that I have always steadily refused to visit officially the school at Te Kapu, though close by; and that even when solicited to do so by the people of the place, and at the same time willing myself to visit it,—saying, That such was in the Province of Auckland, and so beyond my Instructions from the Superintendent of Hawke's Bay?—

I will answer this: Yes, Mr. Williams well knew all *this*. Then, why did he pen that sentence? Ah! that is out of my depth; let him answer *that*.

In conclusion, and as an old man knowing something of the matters in hand, —I would quietly venture to suggest for Mr. Williams' consideration,—whether when he writes again he could not concoct a much more wholesome dish,—by omitting a little of the *fortiter* (mustard and pepper) and adding more of the *suaviter* (oil and yolk of egg)?—At all events such would be more palatable and useful; as generally, I think, here, in our temperate S. latitude, the public taste runs less on cayenne and chillies. —I am &c.,

WM. COLENSO.

Napier, January 18, 1878.

§ TEN POUNDS REWARD

WHEREAS some trespasser on my premises did last night about 11 o'clock brutally kill my brown retriever Dog Carlo, here close to my house: the above reward is therefore now offered to be paid by me to any one who will give such information to the Inspector of Police as will lead to the conviction of the offender. Public Warning is also hereby (once more) given, that all persons caught trespassing on my grounds, whether by day or night, will be prosecuted.

TWO GUINEAS REWARD will be paid by me to any policeman on conviction of any person whom he may apprehend trespassing on my grounds after dark.

WILLIAM COLENSO.

Napier, February 14, 1878.

❖ 1878 THE LATE BISHOP WILLIAMS.
New Zealand Herald 9 March.

SIR,—I was not a little surprised—pained, perhaps, I might better say—to see in the WEEKLY NEWS of February 16th, a letter from Mr. Gideon Smales dated the 12th inst., correcting (as he says) an error of yours respecting Bishop Williams and his "New Zealand Grammar and Dictionary." Mr. Smales professes to have had "deep feelings of sympathy and veneration" for the late Bishop, when reading your short sketch of his life, but those feelings were soon overcome by Mr. Smales's greater love of truth; hence he proceeds instanter to correct your serious error. I fear, however, with Mr. Smales it has been *dictum de dicto*, and therefore what he has written will not stand the test of sober scrutiny. And, as no one in New Zealand (not excepting our late Bishop's own family) knows more about the matter in question than myself, I cannot but consider that in some measure it devolves on me to say a word or two on behalf of the truth and of my dear and lamented deceased friend. You had, in your short sketch, briefly and simply stated, "The first grammar and dictionary were compiled by him [Bishop Williams.] Much has been done since, but in point of time the Bishop led the way." And no doubt, in your saying so, you were generally correct. I have carefully said "generally correct;" I would prefer saying quite correct; but I do this in order to allow Mr. Smales the full benefit of the few true items he has adduced. At the same time I cannot help thinking that even supposing all he has mentioned were quite correct, they would altogether be but of small amount, and surely not imperatively required to be brought forward in the columns of a newspaper in unseemly opposition just at that sad moment when the mortal remains of the late Bishop were not yet conveyed to the grave? Mr. Smales says:—"The facts are, Captain Cook published the first vocabulary of the language, as may be seen in his works." (yes; at vol. iii, p. 474, we have that vocabulary, containing 32 common words, nearly all nouns, and the first 10 figures, making a grand total of 42 words.) Then Mr. Smales says:—"Several other vocabularies were published from that time (1773) to the time (1820) when Professor Lee published his grammar and vocabulary at Cambridge." (Has Mr. Smales ever seen them? those "several other vocabularies," which, he states, were published during those 50 years, before Professor Lee's? And would Mr. Smales prefer Professor Lee's orthography, based on an alphabet of 20 letters?) Then, Mr. Smales proceeds:—"Various publications were printed by the different missionary societies and others up to 1842, when Dr. Maunsell published the first Maori grammar. In 1841, Bishop Williams's dictionary with a short grammar was published." (I have partly compressed both your own and. Mr. Smales's remarks.) Now, "the facts are" (to use Mr. Smales's words):—1. That the first sheets of Bishop Williams's Maori Grammar were composited and printed by me early in 1838 (soon after the printing and binding of the first Maori New Testament were completed). 2. That the Grammar would have been printed early in 1833, only for the pressing want of school books and of the New Testament. 3. That it was again set aside (in 1838) in order to print, &c., the whole Prayer Book of the Church of England (nearly 400 pages), which, with much other pressing work for schools, was only finished in November 1841, when the printing of the Bishop's Grammar and Dictionary was resumed: and, as it always gave way to the printing of works for the Church Mission (and for the newly arrived Government), it was again delayed, and so not commonly published until 1844. The Bishop, however, in his preface to the first edition, says "That the whole of the work was prepared for the press six years ago." Further, I may remark, that Bishop Williams's MS. Dictionary was always at the service of every one who cared to avail themselves of it; and several gentlemen (outside of the Mission) did so—among whom were Mr. Busby, Dr. Marshall, Baron Hügel, Dr. Ford, Mr. John

Busby, Captain Clendon, Mr. Allan Cunningham, Dr. Dieffenbach, &c., besides those Church Missionaries who came after—as Dr. Maunsell, Rev. R. Taylor, and others. To me, Bishop Williams's MS. Dictionary was an invaluable help, especially in 1835, when I was acquiring the language. In conclusion, I will just copy from the old printing office account books of the Church Mission which I have now before me (records, I may call them!) a few entries of my having (as Superintendent of the Church Mission Society's Press) issued copies of the first sheet of Bishop Williams's Grammar (and also of the Maori New Testament complete) in 1838–9, to Mr. Busby, Rev. N. Turner, Dr. Day, Mr. Ford, Commodore du Petit Thouars, Rev. Dr. Lang, Bishop Broughton, of Australia, Capt. O.P. King, R.N., Rev. Maunsell (now Archdeacon), Rev. R. Taylor, &c., &c. Some, no doubt, of your early Auckland and Bay of Islands settlers will remember many of those persons, most of whom, with our lamented Bishop, have preceded us a short way in our journey—I am, &c.,

WILLIAM COLENSO.

Napier, February, 1878.

❖ 1878 THE INSPECTORSHIP OF SCHOOLS.
Hawke's Bay Herald 9 April.

SIR,—As you have "trotted me out pretty freely" in your columns during the last fortnight, perhaps you will now allow me to have my say respecting the whole matter in question; although I may, possibly, (and in order to clear it), take up a little more of your "Correspondence" space than is usually allowed. But, I am not the aggressor; you have provoked it. All I ask, is a "fair field and no favor."—

I should, perhaps, have written before, only I had no spare time,—having been for a fortnight absent in the Country visiting schools, and since my return engaged in writing for the Education Board; and (speaking for myself,) I am a little too thick-skinned, after so many years of Public Service, greatly to heed the tilts of Lilliputian reeds and lances! And even now I don't think I should care to write on this matter, were it not for your own sub-article in your paper of the 1st April. For all my doings, as the Inspector of Schools,[9] have always been open and before the whole public,—especially Teachers, Scholars, Parents, and, more recently, the Board of Education. And happy am I,—aye, far beyond many other public officers,—in being able both to believe and to say, that *I have them all with me!* At the same time, I think, it will be allowed, that no one has a more arduous duty to perform than an Inspector,—whether he be one of Roads, Gaols, Asylums, Railways, Public Works, Steamers, Sheep, or Schools; the duty, if performed truly, is a heavy one entailing a great responsibility:—on the one hand all look to him; on the other, if he, in the least, touches, or approaches, vested interests, rights, or properties, fancied or real, the many interested "have a down" on him! So that thrice happy is that individual who can well and truly perform his duty without giving great offence.

---

9   Colenso's resignation from his post as Inspector of Schools was reported in the *Hawke's Bay Herald* of 18 Mar 1878, and a number of letters were published in the following issues. I.S.G.

In your paper of last Monday (April 1st) you say—"With reference to the subject of Mr. Colenso's resignation, the undesirableness of allowing an Inspector to have any voice whatever in the appointment of Schoolmasters, is, to our mind, quite palpable." (With much more to the same effect.) And your friend "Alpha," whose letter you published the next day, (but which letter you had had some time by you, as I find from your paper of March 30,) writes very much in the same strain, only more flippantly and thoughtlessly, or (I might truly enough say,) wildly.—For instance,—where "Alpha," lashing himself up to a white heat like an angry tom-cat, asks—"Who invested our late Inspector with superior authority in educational matters? Or, on what grounds does he arrogate to himself the right of being consulted respecting the appointment of teachers? If the reason assigned for Mr. Colenso's resignation be correct, they imply an amount of assumption and presumption seldom equalled far less surpassed." And, again,—"Mr. Colenso had no right to arrogate to himself functions which nowhere pertain to his office," &c., &c. (!!) High-flown language and heavy words these on the part of "Alpha;" but, unfortunately for him, and for *you*, too, they have no foundation whatever! as I will show.—

Here, however, I halt, to enquire, whether you were led astray by "Alpha," or "Alpha" by you?—

His letter was in your possession and read by you on or before the 30th March, but your remarks were first published. And (to this I would call particular attention,) had you in your lengthy Report of the meeting of the Education Board held on the 18th March, (fair and good as far as it goes, but, unfortunately, with a most important *suppressio veri*,) had you then published *the grounds* of my Resignation it would have saved you, as Editor, from subsequently committing yourself in your sub-article,—and, possibly your friend "Alpha" also from his rash writing! In that Report of yours you rightly mention "my official letter to the Board of February 9, 1878," and the "direct opposition" thereto on the part of "the Board," as being the chief grounds of my Resignation; but you do not inform the Public as to the contents of my letter or its meaning! Probably you never cared to know anything about it,—though professedly the caterer for the public in all important public matters! and so, through your supineness, both yourself and your friend "Alpha" are where you are,—between the horns!—

And now I will give the Public a copy of that Official letter.—

"Napier, February 9th, 1878.
SIR,—I have the honour to call the attentive consideration of the Board to the following, *viz.:*—

1. That, unless in case of very great emergency,—"No person shall be eligible for appointment as Teacher to any school who does not produce a Certificate of competency from the Minister of Education, *and* such other Certificates of fitness as shall be required"—(in conformity with clause 45 of the Education Act). I trust this clause will be borne in mind by the Board,—even in cases in

which Committees should ask for the Board's appointment of any one specially recommended by them (the Committees) as Teacher. For it is to this being upheld and carried out in its integrity by the Board,—and also to Section 3 of the same clause 45,—that I look forward to much real good rising to some of our Schools.

2. That, as a general rule, no Teacher shall be removed from one Government school, where he is the Teacher, to another, merely on his bare letter to the Board asking for such removal; or, on the mere letter of the Committee, of that School, asking for his removal from the School where he is the Teacher to their School: to effect any such removal some very sound reasons should be adduced.

3. That the several local School Committees be early informed by the Board of their adoption of the above for their (the Committees') guidance.

For, unless these rules are generally rigidly adhered to by the Board, and also made known by them, many slightly-considered applications will be sent in to the Board, and much undesigned mischief may arise to several of our rising Schools; for Schools do not generally profit by change of Teachers, and never by the loss of good ones; for when Teacher and School well know each other they always work more cordially and advance more rapidly.

(Signed) W. COLENSO, I.S."

The Chairman,
Hawke's Bay Board of Education, Napier.

I think that all will plainly see what I sought in that letter. Certainly no wish on my part; to *appoint* Teachers anywhere; neither "assumption" nor "presumption," neither "arrogancy" nor "the asserting of superior authority," (as your friend "Alpha" says,)— but only the upholding the rights of our Teachers and the good of our children; and so not to leave them altogether to the tender mercies of a hastily-chosen and ill-assorted local "Bush" Committee.

But *you*, Mr. Editor,—from your long knowledge of me and from the published annual Reports of the Schools,—you should have both known me better and also my official doings during the 7 years I have held the office of Inspector of Schools (I say nothing of the earlier time, when I was also Inspector of Schools, 1861–4). Did you ever know me once to make an appointment of a teacher or, even to seek to do so? Were not all the several Teachers of Schools who have been appointed during (say) the last 7 years, so appointed by the local Trustees of the various Schools? In the past 7 years I made *one* recommendation to the then Superintendent of the Province, (and that because there were no local Trustees there,) viz. to Norsewood Scandinavian School; and, recently, I recommended to the Board, at a time of serious exigency, (as you well know,) Mr. Gush, and Mr. Wright: these are all my (so called) "appointments;" and I believe the Public concerned will generally support me in them.

"Alpha" has one sentence in which I cordially agree;—"Doubtless Boards will always attach considerable importance to the opinions of Inspectors and rightly so."

Now that is all I have asked, and should ask, for. My official letters to the Board shew this. I find, moreover, that the Educational Boards of Wellington and of Auckland pay very great consideration to their Inspectors, with respect to the appointment of Teachers. In the Auckland *Weekly News* of March 9th, to hand *since* the date of my letter of Resignation, (I quote from memory, not having that paper now by me,)—in their Report, occupying two columns, of the proceedings of the then last weekly meeting of the Auckland Education Board, it is stated,—that, out of between 30 and 40 matters concerning their Country Schools, all separately named,—there were 9 respecting Teachers: of these nine, five were appointed (*mark!*) on the recommendation of the Inspector, while four, being new, were deferred for the Inspector's report thereon. The Auckland Board has, also, the further advantage of an *Examining Committee.*

Of course, this speaks volumes! and wholly upsets both your and your friend "Alpha's" views on this subject. At the same time, the concluding sentence of "Alpha's" first letter I wholly agree with; he says,—"However capable Inspectors may be of giving advice, Boards must exercise their own discretion as to the right course to be pursued in filling up vacancies, and be specially careful to throw no obstacle in the way of the promotion of *really deserving teachers.* And no less necessary will it be to see that the Act is fairly and impartially carried out, and that no influences, denominational, political, or otherwise, are allowed to prevent this from being done."

And, I think, it will be surely found, that, whoever may hold the high office of Inspector of Schools,—if he be a fit and proper person, and if he also does his duty,— that his official opinion generally in the matter of Teachers, cannot, ought not, must not be set lightly aside; for he is the permanent and skilled officer; he knows the Teachers all, well; he knows moreover, the *peculiar* requirements of each and every School and School District which a Board, changing as it does and must every year, cannot possibly personally and really know. And as to the Inspector being "biased," and "having favourites of his own appointment," &c., &c., and all that kind of trashy gallimantry brought forward so prominently by "Alpha"!—surely all that may safely be left to the Teachers themselves and the Public,—to the *Daily Telegraph*, and the HERALD. Let *our Experience* of the past speak! May I not, in going out of office as Samuel of old, ask, aye proudly ask,—"Witness against me: Whom have I defrauded? Whom have I oppressed?" in this matter of Teachers.—

One word respecting "Alpha," and I have done with him. In his *first* letter he begins by saying,—"On reading "P.F's." letter, one is reminded, that however satisfactory a man's reasons for his course of conduct may appear to himself, he is wise to keep them to himself." And, again, in his *second* letter, (so quickly written, too, after the former one, as if "to order"!) he begins with saying,—"It is astonishing how absurd people can be when blinded by their own selfish interests. None are so blind as those who do not wish to see." Aye, "Alpha," just so, I would reply; only adding two other classes; the one, who ignorantly rushes into a war of words, not knowing or understanding the causes; to which class "Alpha" certainly belongs:—the other, that of those venal hacks, or scribblers, who, possessing a little smattering of apparent knowledge and a spice of cleverness, (resembling the quick smart dashing of the swallow glancing in the sunbeam,) take up matters for pay or profit. Let "Alpha" look to this—And let him also remember—that assumption and abuse of an adversary is not argument. One is always strongly reminded, when a writer jumps out, or bolts,—in that kind of way, like "Alpha,"—of the old saying,—"No case, abuse the counsel." Very sure I am, that "P.F.," (whoever he may be) understood the matter he was writing of far, far, beyond the poor comprehension of "Alpha"—(who, however, I must allow, was in part cheated, or led astray by *you*). "P.F.'s" letter shews the writer to be a man of trained mind, of calm clear thought,—one capable of taking up a subject and pursuing it closely to its logical conclusion;—in every respect so very different from "Alpha." And that "L.K." has also written truthfully and plainly, and feelingly, and that without any apparent low designed or insidious sneering, which so cleaves to "Alpha," and of which, strive as he may, he cannot wholly divest himself.

Long as this letter already is, I must be allowed to make a further remark on a letter from the Teacher of Kaikoura School (Mr. Crawford), which also appeared against me in your paper. Two things, if I recollect aright, (for I first saw the said letter in the "Forty-mile Bush,") Mr. Crawford charged me with: first. *Lying:*—in his denying the truthfulness of what I had said (in a few words) in my Official letter to the Board respecting his removing to the Woodville School. On this direct denial of this I say nothing; only that, notwithstanding the same, some may continue to believe me, and some may choose to believe him. But if it were so that his heart was always so set on the Woodville School, how came it to pass, hat he had secretly made every arrangement last October with the Trustees of the United Methodist School here in Napier, to have their School? and from which he was only, and that at the last moment when he came to Napier to sign the agreement, dissuaded by me from carrying into effect.—Where was Mr. Crawford's thought of Woodville School then? 2nd. *Stealing:* which Mr. Crawford (in his sad "murthering" of Shakespeare) also charges me with —"Filching from him his good name" (!) Bless the man! How? when? where? and in what way? I would ask. It is true, I openly and officially, in doing my duty, told the Board,—that I did not consider Mr. Crawford a fit person to be removed from Kaikoura School to Woodville School, to have the charge of the School there. And why? (1.) Because the people of Woodville had informed me, that they had 50–60 (in one letter, 70–80) children ready for school. Hence (2.) I was seeking to get a good A.1, trained Teacher, with, if possible, a trained female Teacher as wife, for that large and growing School. (3.) For Mr. Crawford is not a trained Teacher (though a good writer and accountant, at home in a quiet office,) neither has he the physical strength to stand the daily wear and tear of a heavy school,—to say nothing of want of quickness and of tact in getting through those daily duties;—then Mr. Crawford has a large family mostly of small children, and his wife, poor lady, an invalid. Indeed, Mr. Crawford had also told me, when he was so desirous a short time ago of returning to Napier to take charge of the U. Methodist School, that "one of his reasons was, to be near to a medical man on account of Mrs. Crawford." (Perhaps Mr. Crawford may find it convenient to forget, or even to *deny* this, also?) However, I, for my part, am quite willing to "bide-a-wee," and let Time (the great revealer) show, who was right in the matter of a *proper* Teacher for the rising generation at Woodville School. It may be that the old, old, story, of trying to serve two masters, will be found to have had much to do with it. Be all that as it may, Mr. Crawford must very well know, that in my late Yearly Reports, and in my visiting his School at Kaikoura, and in all my connection with him, I have ever sought publicly and privately to do him ample justice; just the very opposite (I should think,) of "Filching his good name"!! But, because Mr. Crawford under all his disadvantages could manage a small school of little children in a settled quiet village like Kaikoura,—it surely does not follow that he could get along so well with the bigger school of rough lads in the new Bush Settlement of Woodville—

I purposely abstain from making any comment on the sly Pecksniffian under handed mode of proceeding in that affair; this, too, will be better understood by-and-by.—I am, &c.,

WILLIAM COLENSO.

Napier, April 6, 1875.

❖ 1878 TO THE CHAIRMAN BOARD OF EDUCATION, NAPIER. *Hawke's Bay Herald* 4 May.

Waipukurau, May 1, 1878.

SIR,—I have the honour to call your attention to the following.

I should not, however, write did I not know from HERALD of this morning, that the Education Board meets again to-morrow, and that my name in connection with my late office had been prominently before the Board yesterday.

I note what you are reported to have said in your opening address, viz., "that in considering the applications received, they should consider whether the late Inspector should not be induced to accept office;" also the question put by Captain Russell, —"whether there was any probability of Mr. Colenso continuing to hold the office:" and, further, your reply thereto.

It is wholly owing to the foregoing that I now write.

For I had supposed (wrongly perhaps),—that having resigned my late office on 31st March, (but contingently on 8th April,) and the late Board having subsequently officially asked me to continue in office until 30th April, to which I had immediately assented,—that the way was open for the new Board, meeting on that same day the 30th (*if they chose*), to ask me further and at once to remain in office; or to ask me to withdraw my resignation; to either of which I should have assented.

For, although repeatedly requested (by many, too, whom I have long known and highly respected,) to withdraw my resignation; I failed to see how I could possibly do so, that resignation having been by the late Board officially accepted.

However, (having made this explanation,) I write now to say, that,—owing to the very numerous strong and pressing requests made to me (both personally and by letter) by all the old experienced Teachers of our schools, and by several of the newer ones, together with the still stronger solicitations and persuasions of many of our oldest and principal settlers and also those of their children,—I am willing to continue to hold the office of Inspector of Schools, if such is the wish of the Board.

And as I am now here at this place, and am anxious to visit the Porangahau School before that I return to Napier, (having already inspected all the other southern ones,) I should much like to have the reply of the Board at once and by telegram; for, if the Board accept my proposal, I leave hence immediately (weather permitting) for Porangahau, as I can not well come back again to go thither in the winter; and if on the contrary the Board should decline it, then I return to-morrow to Napier. I have, &c.,

(Signed) W. COLENSO.

❖ 1878 PHILOSOPHICAL SOCIETY.
Hawke's Bay Herald 17 July.
SIR,—I thank you for your (painful) notice this morning of the failure of the meeting of the Philosophical Institute last night. So far, you are right, but you have omitted a portion, which, I think, ought also, in all fairness to be told—at least for the information of the members of the said society. *Another* member, a lady, Mrs. May, also attended, kindly bringing with her four other ladies; those five ladies came at the proper hour, 7.30,—and, I assure you, I was very glad to be there to receive them, —they sat until 8.20, patiently awaiting the arrival of some Members, but no one came save Mr. Smith! You, sir, and a few others, may guess my enviable situation as the Honorary Secretary to the said *Philosophical Society!*

To Mrs. May as one of our members, (always ready and willing to support every thing tending towards the advancement of Science, Literature, and Art,) and, also, to the other ladies, who, as visitors, so amiably accompanied her, I beg again to tender my deepest thanks and humble apologies,—as the Honorary Secretary to the said Society; who, in the performance of the duty imposed upon him, had unfortunately to announce the said meeting, and so to have caused them so much trouble and disappointment. —I am, &c.,

W. COLENSO,

Hon. Secy. H.B.P.S.

Napier, July 16, 1878.

§ 1878 *Hawke's Bay Herald* 18 July.
SIR,—I see by a letter in your paper that Mrs. May, accompanied by four or five... young ladies, went to the Philosophical Institute to hear Mr. Colenso read an essay on birds and fishes, and in consequence of the smallness of the attendance were disappointed. Now, I would respectfully suggest that Mrs. May bring those young ladies to the Mutual Improvement Society, where they would learn more philosophy than by going to the Institute. I am sure the members of the literary

club would be glad to receive all ladies who might feel disposed to attend, and as visitors are allowed in, their presence would give an impetus to the society and make it, what I have no doubt it will soon become, the most important association in Napier. When I was in Dunedin last year, several of the ladies there attended, and the societies were all nourishing. In most of the principal towns in the colony there are a number of literary girls, and they avail themselves of every opportunity of improving their minds. Besides, any gentleman or lady would feel a pleasure in taking their daughters to such places, and it would be looked forward to with interest by the young ladies, who often find time hangs wearily on their hands.—I am, &, *Mater Familias*.

Napier, July 17, 1878.

❖ **1878 SUNDAY-SCHOOL PICNICS.**
Hawke's Bay Herald 6 September.

SIR,—Now that our Parliament have ceased for a while, perhaps you may find room for a few lines from me.

Yesterday I read, in a late number of the London *Times* (just to hand by mail), of a very influential deputation of Irish gentlemen, who had recently called on the Rt. Hon. Mr. Lowther, M.P., Chief Secretary for Ireland, "to present a memorial; signed by a very large number of Irishmen, asking to be enrolled as volunteers, 'in support of the honour of the Empire' under regulations similar to those governing the Volunteer forces in England, Scotland, and the Colonies." Lord Monck, who was the first speaker, said, (among many other very good remarks,) that he, and those with him, thought,—that a judicious enrolment of a loyal Volunteer force would prove of vast advantage to Ireland; would be a sure and ready engine in the hands of the Government for putting down those sectarian outbursts; for the Government could refuse the parts where those disturbances occurred the power to form a corps. The Government could say,—"As soon as you show a clean bill of health and *do away with your 12th of July and St. Patrick's Day disturbances*, we will grant you your wish, but so long as that sort of thing goes on we cannot permit you to have Volunteer corps."

I have always believed in that:—"Do away with (the cause of) disturbances" and heart-burnings. Thirty-five years ago I both spoke and wrote against the first public celebration of "St. Andrew's Day" (as it is called),—saying,—"Banish all such from this young Colony, (S.S. Andrew, Patrick, George, David, and the Orange Days,) and let us here go in for a United Colonists Day." To me,—it seems not altogether unlikely, that, a few years hence, some such question as this may form a legitimate one for our Debating Clubs,—which is the greatest cause of mischief to New Zealand, the introduction and keeping up of those fearful Sectarian blemishes, or the introduction of house sparrows and rabbits?"

For my own part I felt convinced, that it should be the aim of every good Colonist, —of every well-wisher to the human family,—to do all in his power firmly and consistently to put down narrow Sectarianism.

Yesterday two little girls called on me, (one at a time,) each with a begging card for donations to their respective Sunday School picnic. (The same thing happened last year.) And I was obliged to refuse to contribute—in that way—towards the upholding of narrow Sectarianism. At the same time I felt it was both an ungracious and unpleasant thing to do, to such nice young children whom I know and respect; for though I briefly told them my reasons, I fear they could not comprehend them.

I told them (just as I said last year),—that I would willingly give liberally, if their Teachers and Ministers would unite and have one really good holiday together, —taking the children (say) by train to the country; by which they would be able to see (perhaps with many of them for the first time!) the beauties of Nature, the growth of our district,—and the wonderful works of God.

I hear, that all the Protestant sects are moving just now; each to have their own little S. School pic-nic. Good: but why not *unite*? and do it *well*, nobly and *charitably*! with all the several little S. Schools in our country townships also joining—like so many streamlets—and swelling the stream! that would be something like a holiday! a day of gladness and joy not likely to be forgotten.

I trust that no one who knows me will for a moment suppose,—that I propose such a plan in order to save money! In subscribing, as it is, suppose I were to give (say) five shillings to each, (as some do, "and have done with it"!) that would not amount to much,—say, £1 5s, or so. But, to enable the teachers and ministers to carry out the large-hearted and nobler scheme, I am willing to give £5, and to do the same every year as long as I may live.

A month ago you told us, in your paper, of the opening of the new Presbyterian Church at Waipukurau,—and that on that festal occasion there were ministers of various Protestant sects—Church-of-England, Presbyterian, and United Methodist,—all taking part in the proceedings,—like "brethren dwelling together in unity" and helping one another—"shoulder to shoulder." Therefore, I ask again, Why not join in having a grand united S. School pic-nic for the benefit of the little ones?

And here I may, perhaps, in conclusion, set down, what a very intelligent person who was present at that meeting said to me in relating it, (though, possibly, our plain speaking and my plain writing may offend some one,)—he spoke of it approvingly, as "a great success" and as "a goodly show to see and to hear them,"—adding, "but was it a reality or a sham?" I replied,—"God knows, and they know, and time will show."— *Verb. sap.*—I am, &c.,

WILLIAM COLENSO.

Napier, Sept. 4, 1878

❖ **1878 A few thoughts and facts concerning the "Sabbath" and its due observance.** *Hawke's Bay Herald* **24, 27, 28 September; 1, 5, 22, 31 October; 14, 15, 21, 29 November; 4, 12 December.**[10]

---

10 These letters were collected and published as a booklet: 'Tracts for the times No. 1: On the Sabbath and its due observance' republished in *Colenso's published papers 1: 1842–1884*, forthcoming. I.S.G.

❖ 1879 THE COMMUNION.
Hawke's Bay Herald 5 March.

SIR,—I was a little surprised to read in your issue of this day the following—"An innovation in the form of receiving the Communion has been adopted by the Rev. C.J. Byng, at St. Matthew's Church, Dunedin." (Those words I take to be your own, or supplied). Then you go on to quote from the *Daily Times*,—"Contrary to all recognised procedure, the Communion was celebrated yesterday, after the Evening Service."

There is, however, allow me to, say, no "innovation" here; neither is it "contrary to all recognised procedure,"—very far from it. The same being the practice in very many churches belonging to the Church of England, both in London and in country towns and parishes in England. Neither is it new there, for I well remember it being so when a boy.

As to Mr. Byng's additional saying (as quoted by you), that "Our Lord always communicated in the evening," I make no remark on such a very strange statement. But I do on another queer bit of news of yours, contained in your issue of February 21st, which, when I first saw it inland, last week (on my return from the Forty-mile Bush) rather startled me; therein you say—

"A Confirmation Service will be held in St. John's Church, by the Right Rev. Bishop Stuart, on Palm Sunday, the 6th of April next."

Now I knew that Bishop Stuart was at that time absent, and therefore such could not possibly have come from him.

Permit me, further, to say, that the Church of England knows no such a day as "Palm Sunday," such is not to be found in her Church Calendar; it is therein merely and plainly called "the Sixth Sunday in Lent." The Church of Rome, however, has it; and the wretched Ritualistic clique[11] (who have done the Church of England so much injury) use the term, prankingly of course; it is this clique also who are dead set against Evening Communion, the better to carry out their own Romanistic views.

And as this is not the first time of late that I have detected in your columns the appearance of "the cloven foot" of Ritualism (although but slightly shewn), yet, as a straw thrown up is sufficient to indicate the path of the coming storm, and as "coming events often cast their shadows before,"—I, as an old member and Minister of the Church of England, give timely warning to the members of the Church of England here to be on their guard.—I am, &c.,

WILLIAM COLENSO.
Napier, March 4, 1879.

❖ 1879 FAIR PLAY.
Hawke's Bay Herald 4 April.

SIR,—Your paper of this morning contains a letter signed "Fair Play" in defence of three boys who were brought before the Magistrate yesterday for stealing rails. Had "Fair Play" not wilfully belied his assumed name, perhaps I should not now

---

11   That is, the Oxford movement. I.S.G.

be writing; for, if "Fair Play" is a parent, or near relation of one of those poor boys I could not have noticed his letter—under the circumstances—feeling as he must for his child; but, if "Fair Play" is nothing of the kind, then, as I have said, he has belied that name,—in assuming it and acting to the contrary,—in abusing our well-known and long-tried Inspector of Police, and also the R.M. (both, too, fathers of families), well knowing that from their official position they could not reply to his charges; and, also, in his more than gross insinuation against our old and valued medical friend Dr. Hitchings,—as to his having any claim to the dividing fence of his own freehold! Bah!

I pity those three unfortunate Boys, particularly the two younger ones (although I do not know them); but I do not pity nor feel in any way for their unhappy parents; indeed, I would that the law could have been put in force against *them*, and so let the boys go free on their own simple confession; for the receiver and encourager of theft is generally worse than the thief,—always so in the case of parents.

For my part I knew nothing of this affair until it was all over; but I heartily thank Dr. Hitchings for taking it up, and Mr. Inspector Scully for his part in it. With him I hope something will shortly be done in the matter of a proper reformatory—and I trust the Magistrates and Grand Jury will at the next meeting of the Supreme Court in Napier make a very strong presentment to the Judge respecting the urgent necessity of such an institution.

Curiously enough yesterday, at the very hour of trial (ignorant of what was going on), I was engaged at the Survey Office with Mr. Baker, the Chief Government Surveyor, respecting the necessity of early replacing a trig. station block which some boys had dug up and stolen from my paddock just in front of my house; it was of little worth to them (or to their parents) save as a lump of firewood.

For some time past I have suffered considerably through some persons (believed to be "boys") breaking down and stealing the rails of my fences—particularly, I may say, of the long dividing fence between my land and that of Dr. Hitchings. My late man, James Morgan, was completely tired with so much extra labor consequent on such often-repeated wholesale robbery in fitting and replacing rails. At last I consented to his nailing them into the post-holes, and then they were hacked out and taken away! Those rails were mostly V.D.L. timber, and altogether, including labour, cost me a considerable sum.

Further, I may mention that I had this land of mine surveyed, roads through it laid off, and cut up into quarter-acre sections, each section being fully pegged with extra large totara pegs, with their numbers burnt in, and well driven into the ground; in a short time all were drawn up out of the ground, and carried off by "boys" for firing, the Government trig block, the biggest of the whole lot, and nearest to my dwelling-house, being left for the last. Perhaps "Fair Play," (with his wee quantum of legal knowledge, or quibble) may further suppose that the parents of these "boys" did not see, or, seeing, did not know, the burnt and stamped figures and marks on those prepared totara surveyor's pegs? I venture to state that £50 would not cover the loss to me of those surveyor's pegs and consequent professional labour, as now that work must be done over again.

At present I say nothing of the almost continual stealing of garden produce—as fruit, vegetables, and roots, and, also, ducks. For these matters I have complained to the police, and have all but come to the conclusion to give up all attempt at having fruit or vegetables, and so escape the continual annoyance of having them stolen— generally, too, just before they are fit to use!

In conclusion, sir, allow me to say, that I feel these things the more when committed by our own European "boys" (and men and women!); from the fact that I have lived more than twenty years among Maoris, and never had anything stolen; and yet the Maoris are looked down upon and talked of, by those European thieves and swindlers, as the inferior race!!—I am sir, &c.,

W. COLENSO.

Napier, April 3, 1879.

§ TWO SERVANTS WANTED

WANTED (by this day month), a handy man and his wife without children; man as Gardener and General Servant,—woman as Cook and Housekeeper. Testimonials to character required. To save trouble on both sides, none but steady folks need make application. Apply by letter only to W. COLENSO.

Napier, May 13, 1879.

❖ 1879 THE INNOCENT PUNISHED.
Hawke's Bay Herald 19 May.

MR. W. COLENSO writes us a letter, too long for publication in extenso, upon the the case of the convict Habron, concerning whom a paragraph cut from a Home paper appeared in our issue of last Thursday. Habron, it will be remembered, was about two years ago sentenced to death for the murder of a policeman at Manchester, but was reprieved on account of his youth. The infamous Peace, who was recently hung, admitted when in gaol that he killed the policeman. Mr. Colenso sends us an extract from the London Daily Telegraph, showing that the authorities, after a close investigation, found indisputable proofs of Habron's innocence. He has been accordingly liberated, and will receive a sum of money as compensation for the degradation and punishment he has gone through, the money to be invested for his benefit under the supervision of trustees. The same paper has an admirable article upon the danger of finding prisoners guilty on purely circumstantial evidence. No circumstantial evidence could be stronger than was that against Habron, yet he has been proved to be innocent. By the mere accident of youth he escaped hanging. The Telegraph says:—"The main warning for Justice to derive from this memorable case is to be ever on her guard against circumstantial evidence combined with police prepossession. The ordinary official mind is too much like a bull which, after lowering its horns for a charge, closes its eyes. In this instance, we fear not only that facts were strained against the prisoner, but that evidence was set aside which ought to have told in his favor.... So blindly tenacious of a prepossession are officials, that when even the respite was granted they still stuck to the belief that, if Habron had not actually fired the pistol, he was accessory to the fact, and the re-examination of the case was commenced, it is said, with prejudice still strong against him. Altogether a more suggestive rebuke was never given to human justice. It has inflicted on this honest boy the long bitterness of impending and shameful death; it has wasted 2 years and 8 months of his early manhood in useless and degrading toil; it has killed his father with a broken heart, and stamped the ignoring of crime upon his family; and finally it owes its own deliverance from the perpetration of all these measureless wrongs to a murderer's volunteered confession. William Habron, therefore, must not be merely provided for and forgotten. His name and story must remain ever present to the mind of the Queen's Judges and Secretaries of State as long as the law inflicts sentences, which, once executed, can never be reversed."

Mr. Colenso upon this remarks:—"No evidence is superior to circumstantial evidence when it is perfect, fully clear and complete; but (if) even only *one link* of the whole chain is wanting, then it is to be held in doubt and not to he trusted."

❖ **1879 MR. COLENSO AND ST. JOHN'S CHURCH.**
Hawke's Bay Herald 11 July.
SIR,—I have been rather pointedly asked to-day, by more than one,—Why I, as a member and minister of the Church of England, and as a pewholder, &c., of St. John's—why I did not attend the Church of England meeting held last night? And on thinking over what was said, I have concluded it to be a part of my duty to write a letter to you upon your report of that said meeting in your paper of this morning.

First, then, I would say, for the information of the many (newly-arrived) attendants at St. John's, that my reason for not attending at that meeting (at which I greatly desired to be present) was this—that I am both a member and minister of the Established Church of England, and that being such (from long before St. John's, or even Napier, was built,) I have ever consistently refused to lower myself by *again* subscribing to any *new* Synodical rules and regulations framed here in N.Z., and so professing to belong to a mere colonial clique or ecclesiastical sect. I openly refused to do so, in that church of St. John's when such illegal subscription was first required, in the time of the late Mr. Wilkinson's churchwardenship; commenting, on that occasion, on the impertinence (or, in colonial colloquial language, the "cheekiness") of the thing,—to ask *me* to do so! And, therefore, noticing the words of the advertisement in your paper calling the said meeting, (including even the obsolete A.D:, brought in at the end like a curly little pig's tail!)—by which words mere boys of yesterday and of no experience, not to mention others newly arrived here (who had never helped in building the church!) would be put over my (aged) head if I attended the meeting: I restrained myself (as I have often done) and so stayed away for peace' sake;—allowing them (to use an expressive Scotch phrase) "to gang their gait."

Second, in reading your long Report of this morning, I was—what? shall I say, surprised,—or concerned,—or distressed,—or pleased? to use any one of those words would not convey my real meaning, because there was just a little of each! Neither would my meaning be clearly conveyed in my saying,—"I was struck all of a heap!" Indeed, I have no one word handy which would quite supply my meaning, unless, perhaps, I may use the term "bitter-sweet." *Financially*, no doubt, your published Report seems to be a great success,—especially in these dull times; but even here, I regret to find, that *all* the accounts were not before the meeting, not having been audited! and, therefore, the action of the meeting, in strict law, (as far as law may be applied to such sectarian meetings,)—the action of the meeting was illegal in passing such accounts.—Then, as to the 160 additional *Communicants* within the past year; if of these the number of boys and girls lately "confirmed," &c., and of the easily-led (or "silly") women were also given,—then more might be known as to its true basis. For I have lived long enough to remember the old abominable *Test and Corporation* (Sacramental) *Act*, and its workings; and, also, to know a little of the designing and insidious outward requisitions of the pretentious High Church and Ritualist parties in our dear old Mother-Church-of-England, to put reliance on any such figures,—or, indeed, such persons. We have had energetic "Communicants"—aye, and Church-wardens, too,—here amongst us in Napier, whose room before long was found preferable to their company. But I must drop this, for the present, and turn,—

Thirdly, to what seems the most surprising of all,—the Chairman making a long, piteous (*ad misericordiam*) and leading speech, in the midst of the proceedings, and interrupting others (instead of quietly hearing what the Church members had to say on the matter before them), and so finally determining the votes of those present,— or, at all events, of all the younger and tamely-led members. Of course, from the fact of Mr. Hovell being a very young man and consequently inexperienced, much may charitably be set down to that. Still, this, as I view it, Mr. Editor, (as a mere pewholder, mind, my *lowest* right,) was fourfold wrong;—1. Because, as Chairman (and such an one, too,—*interested* I mean,) he had no right whatsoever to do so.—2. Because it is a great hardship (as Mr. Price and others justly said,) that pew-holders (*alias* ticket takers of seats for the season) with their families could not possibly all get to their pews in time; and such must ever be the case, I fear, here in our long and straggling town of Napier, with its great disparity of all official clocks and times: while, no doubt, it is as easy as winking, for Mr. Hovell, living next door to the church to slip out bareheaded (even in rain) from his snug and cosy parlour.—3. Because it (*viz.*, the throwing open the seats or pews to all hands *before* the morning (or evening) prayer begins,) is against all good old established Ecclesiastical rule in England, (even where pews were *not* paid for,)—there the pews or seats were thrown open,—in some, after the reading of the Psalms,—in others after the First Lesson; and such should be the rules here, being fair and suiting all parties. 4.—Because the Chairman, Mr. Hovell, seems to have forgotten or mistaken his real position in the Church; *viz.*, the Minister, or Servant, or Mouthpiece of the Church or Congregation when assembled. He plainly assumes (I would hope in ignorance,) that which the late Mr. Townsend took on himself to say, when nearing the close of his stay among us, *viz.*, that he, forsooth, was the Master, the Shepherd, and we the (silly) sheep! I happened to hear that precious Sermon of his, and I did not lose much time in calling on him and telling him of it: I did not *hear* him repeat any such priestly stuff afterwards: I do not, however, say he did not do so.

Further, and in conclusion, I note, that Mr. Hovell signs himself "Incumbent," and this not for the first time,—and you, too, Mr. Editor, in your Report also use the term. Allow me to tell you (both) that such is wrong,—is, in fact, illegal: there are no *Incumbents* in the whole District. It is a downright assumption; of course, done in ignorance of Ecclesiastical law. I may here add a story (known, I think, to some of your readers.) I remember, when connected with the General Assembly, that a petition to the higher powers was drawn up, and one young minister in orders, among others, wrote his name to it, adding (just as Mr. Hovell does) Incumbent: but, on due consideration, that addition had to be carefully erased from the parchment (causing no little trouble) before the petition could be presented,—or it would not have been received.—I am, &c.,

WILLIAM COLENSO.

Napier, July 10, 1879.

❖ **1879 MR. COLENSO ON THE DRAINAGE POLL.**

Hawke's Bay Herald 4 October.

SIR,—From our Napier papers I gather, that the opinion of the ratepayers of the borough is to be taken by vote, in order to decide the knotty yet important question of high, low, or middle level. I regret this. I do so, because I cannot bring myself to see that this is the fittest way of arriving at what is really the best for the benefit of the borough. I am no believer in the wisdom of deciding any question by general voting, unless the same is pretty well understood, in all its bearings, by the voters; which, I fear, would not be—indeed, cannot be reasonably expected—in this matter.

It seems to me that it would have been far better if a number of our townsmen (say, a dozen), were chosen at a public meeting of ratepayers—to examine closely into the business; to consider all plans, &c.; and with power to call for evidence affecting the same, and having done so, to decide among themselves as to which plan should be adopted, and to report thereon to the Municipal Council.

Of course, the selected dozen should include our professional men (surveyors and engineers), and those others among us whose judgment in such matters can well be depended on, and who are themselves interested in the future welfare of the borough. For my own part, I could willingly agree in the decision of such a skilled jury, or committee, so acting; but I cannot say as much for the mere number of votes of the ratepayers; many of whom know nothing about the subject, and not a few of them care less. Indeed, I would just as soon submit the matter to the decision of a cast of dice, as to this determination by general voting.—I am, &c.,

WILLIAM COLENSO.

Napier, October 3, 1879.

LETTERS 1880–1889

WILLIAM COLENSO 1880–1889

1880 Willie marries his cousin Sarah Colenso in Cornwall; six papers in *Transactions of the New Zealand Institute* 13.

1881 Seven papers in *Transactions of the New Zealand Institute* 14.

1882 Gives Kahungunu a block of greenstone; three papers in *Transactions of the New Zealand Institute* 15.

1883 *Three literary papers* published by *Daily Telegraph;* writes 'Autobiography' for his sons; one paper in *Transactions of the New Zealand Institute* 16.

1884 '*In memoriam*' published by *Daily Telegraph*; paper published in Penzance *Transactions*; argues with G.M. Thomson about ferns, and with Cheeseman about orchids; four papers in *Transactions of the New Zealand Institute* 17.

1885 Restarts Māori lexicon; five papers in *Transactions of the New Zealand Institute* 18.

1886 Offered Honorary Life Membership of the Hawke's Bay Philosophical Institute; elected FRS; seven papers in *Transactions of the New Zealand Institute* 19.

1887 Five papers in *Transactions of the New Zealand Institute* 20.

1888 *Fifty years ago in New Zealand* published by R.C. Harding; Presidential address published by Harding; *Bush Advocate* begins publication; eight papers in *Trans.* 21.

1889 *Ancient tide-lore* published by R.C. Harding; *A few brief historical notes* published by *Daily Telegraph*; three papers in *Trans.* 22.

❖ 1880 THE NEW BUILDING REGULATION.
Hawke's Bay Herald 30 March.

SIR,—In your issue of this morning you have published, in full, the important by-law No. 19, respecting the future building, &c., in our borough; which by-law in the main is a very good one as far as it goes; but I think the time is fully come when something should also be done by our Corporation to prevent the reckless cutting into the hill-side properties, which has for some time been carrying on here in our midst; and, by their so doing, present such thoughtless or careless cuttings with expensive lawsuits,—very likely save human life, and be a means of increasing their own rates; not to mention the strict preservation of legal boundaries, and the symmetry of some of the principal outlines of our rising town.

I, myself, have long been a great loser through such careless unprincipled mode of acting; and this, I regret to say, through both public and private parties. The damage that I have suffered (and am still increasingly suffering); along my E. boundary running parallel with Carlyle-street, is plain to all, and many have been the remarks and the enquiries made to me about it,—some, too, by strangers and visitors, who have been astonished at such a state of things being allowed in a civilised community,—super-abounding as we are in law and police!

And there is a double if not a fourfold hardship in this case; which I may as well (with your permission) bring before the public. 1. I put up the substantial boundary fence between me and my neighbours of *puriri* posts and V.D.L. rails; my neighbors, however, one and all (with two solitary exceptions of owners of ¼-acre sections) put off paying their half, or share: and never to this day have paid anything: 2. When I found, through the reckless cutting and undermining of *public* men, my fence was in danger, and was being carried down into Carlyle-street, I made an attempt to stop the mischief; at first, I was told that the work was under the Provincial Engineer, Mr. Weber,—on writing to him I was informed, that he had handed it over to the Corporation; I then wrote to the Town Clerk, and was informed that was out of his line, but he would send my letter to the Municipal Engineer, Mr. Peppercorne: on this I relied. (I may here observe that I was busy at this time and absent from Napier, going my country rounds as Inspector of Schools.) On my return I found the work of destruction and positive injury to my property, still going on! and more fencing carried down!! I now sought Mr. Peppercorne, and was told that he had nothing to do with it, having handed it over to Mr. Dunbar, whose party were there at work for the new Railway Station. I sought Mr. Dunbar, he was absent; and at last I was told that the contractor (a man from Wellington named Skelly) was the person to whom I must look! He, too was away; at last I saw him, but got little from him save that he was sorry, &c.;—but the mischief was now done! and I have had to stand to the loss of posts and rails, to the repeated loss of land falling away, and to the continued shifting back of the fence from the boundary line, which in some places has now been done 4 times! 3. In due time the Government passed an Act to compensate owners of properties for the portions taken for Railway purposes; when I, finding that an officer had been appointed here to hear of claims and to make awards, and that among others, Mr. Johnston of Wellington, had been awarded by him £400 for a strip of useless watery swamp adjoining Munroe Street, *which swamp land had been filled in for the Railway with earth and stone taken from my land* (as above);—I applied for some compensation, and got laughed at! 4. And now I find, that carters here among us will still secretly undermine and carry away from the lowermost layer of sand laid bare there, (though, in some instances, kindly warned by the Inspector of Nuisances,)—and that as every heavy rain naturally brings down more and more of the soft earth and soil, to the sections below, owing to their cliffy cuttings, the owners of those sections are unprincipled enough, for the sake of a few pence, to sell the said earth (my land!) to contractors and carters; little thinking of the awkward consequences to themselves! Further, and recently during the late rains, several panels of my fences have been carried down into Milton Road, and into section No. 103, Tennyson Street, Clive Square, (occupied by a man named Davie) with, of course, much of my land. Now in both these instances I had timely warned the parties concerned (Mr. Peppercorne for Milton Road, and Mills and Tait, contractors, on part of selves and Davie,) of the dire consequences which must follow; but got little for my pains! And so it has also been in the case of the Napier school hill-side cutting, of which I had timely warned the Education Board, but the Napier School Committee however are now doing their best to mend this matter; and so will, no doubt, the Corporation,— but, money might have been saved, for "Prevention is always better than cure." But what possible redress can I have from men of straw like Davie? Just another Skelly affair over again; only a blacker one as this injury is from an old Napier man and a neighbor!

Now if there were a by-law respecting this matter of injury to boundary and loss and damage, (seeing there is provision made in the by-law No. 19, you have published this day, concerning dangerous walls and fences, §42,—and, also, another good by-law already passed, providing against privies and cess-pits being made within 3 feet of the boundary fence,) then I could easily have put it in force,—bring the unthinking fellow up, and get him fined right-off, and there would be an end to it with him; while others would take warning.

I see, by late Auckland papers, that the Native owners of a hotel at Rotorua (vexed at the decision of the Magistrate), said, they would burn down their house and so end it! but the Inspector of there quickly told them, that if they did so, he would take them into custody. There, in a half-wild place, they *could not do with their own* as they liked; while, here, in the very centre of a town, a man *may injure his neighbour's property* and go on quietly day after day doing so, and the police looking-on with folded hands!

I hope, therefore, our Corporation will see the necessity of speedily passing such a by-law affecting this matter as will be equitable and give relief. I have long quietly borne with the present unfair state of things. Of one thing, however, the public may rest assured,—that, sooner or later, some lives will be lost, through this reckless cutting into soft earth and making and leaving such dangerous cliffs, overhanging inhabited back-premises; innocent women and children will surely be sacrificed, and that without warning! Indeed, as it now is, the danger is so great in some places, through their careless cuttings, that I should not like to reside in the front dwelling-houses; —some night, perhaps, a thrilling cry may be heard!

My letter is already too long, but I also wished to remark on a sentence in your sub-leader in your paper of this morning upon this said by-law; where you speak of the past severity of volcanic action at Wellington, &c., and of the shocks having been sufficient to level brick buildings. True; but I would tell you, (as I had told the folks at Wellington, in the very days of their great calamity, when I was present), that much of that (their brickwork being thrown down), was owing to the wretchedly bad mortar they had used. As a proof I mentioned my own 3 chimneys at Waitangi, which were large and high and only built by myself, but with good mortar, made of lime which I had also burned, and no stint; those stood all earthquakes; while the few brick chimneys there were at that time at Wairoa and at Poverty Bay were all thrown down. With you, therefore, I agree that we have nothing to fear from brick or concrete walls falling through earthquakes, if good materials are used.—I am, &c.,

WILLIAM COLENSO.

Napier, March 29, 1880.

❖ 1880 MR. COLENSO AND THE MUNICIPAL COUNCIL.
Hawke's Bay Herald 9 April.

SIR,—In your paper of this morning, in your report of M.C. proceedings, you represent Cr. Ashton as saying "that my letter to them respecting town section 316 was as long as the *Australasian* newspaper;" and, therefore, it was taken as read, and so passed by.

I write now merely to inform you and your readers (especially Town Ratepayers), that my letter referred to is *not* a long one,—and would probably occupy about one column of your paper.

Of course there was no need to read my two letters a second time before the M.C. assembled as such, they having already, under their other name (Committee of Public Works), both read and considered them, and also decided how to act with them; but it was highly requisite that Cr. Ashton should keep within the bounds of truth respecting them,—especially when the one he so facetiously refers to affects me seriously (and, as I take it, unjustly, yet, perhaps, in ignorance,) to the amount of £300.

No doubt it was by far the easier way of dealing with my letters for the M.C. to refer them both to their solicitor. The *first* one mentioned probably required this; the *second* one did not; it only required a little close attention, and knowledge, of figures sufficient to work a simple sum in cubic measure, (which, at all events, Cr. Large should know something of), and a heart to justice to a complaining ratepayer. Very likely my letter was a highly distasteful one; but I can assure our M.C. that if they do not pay closer attention to matters involving figures and payments of money they will receive many more such letters from the Borough, and that before long.

It is not proper to impute motives to a body of public men elected by ourselves but one is almost tempted to think, that the manner of performance last night and the performers, was a matter snugly arranged beforehand in the "Green Room!"—at all events *before* the 2nd act commenced. And I should be the more inclined to believe this, if the Chairman, as Manager, Mr. Swan (to say nothing of Mr. Ashton) knew anything of the "casting of parts."—I am, &c.,

WILLIAM COLENSO.

April 8, 1880.

❖ **1880 A MOUNTAIN OF A MOLEHILL—*ALIAS* ROASTING A MAORI.**

***Hawke's Bay Herald* 28** May.

SIR,—In your paper of this mornmg you have a strange story—of a Native having been yesterday actually brought up (on "remand" too!) before the Court in Napier, for putting another Native, who was ill, on a rude kind of earth oven or vapour bath! (Heigho! when are such pragmatic intermeddlings to end?) I write to inform you, that such means of obtaining relief in illness and pain, were formerly commonly practised by the New Zealanders. A notable instance of it was first seen by Captain Cook, who amusingly relates it in true sailor fashion in his *large* work. I have also known it to be done and to afford great relief when properly performed (as I have mentioned in my "Essay on the Maoris," section 21, vol. I., "Transactions N.Z. Institute," 1866).— Sometimes, however, there would be a "burn" (or scald) left in spots, arising either from the hot steam, or from a *porte-moxa*-like application of a hot edged, or pointed, stone; but such "burns" were never by the old Maoris considered worthy of the least notice, being indeed far less painful than what they suffered from their tattooing,—and scarcely ever worse than the destruction of skin often caused by a severe blistering with blister plaster! Of course, this latter made and applied by a duly authorised Medical man *secundum artem!*

Having alluded to a *porte-moxa*, I may as well add, that this mode of burning the skin with fire in spots (which has for some time been in use among European Surgeons), has long been used by the Chinese, and by other Oriental nations, to relieve pain, &c. So that some poor John Chinaman may ere long be hauled up, or "run-in," by some ignorant and fussy Constable,—for such wicked "burns!"

To me—the whole affair is most laughable! Constable Livingstone might just as reasonably ferret out and apprehend any poor white (some old woman, perhaps, away in the Country!) for using a rude Turkish vapour bath, or a series of cold water ones; or for Homœopathic treatment,—or for causing a credulous patient to swallow at one time 36 of Holloway's pills (according to Holloway's own prescriptions!)

You, also, have heightened this story by your sensational heading! And I quite expect to see the same reproduced by telegrams both N. and S., (especially by the Napier correspondent of the *Auckland Weekly News,*—so notorious for all such matters,)—as a dreadful act of horrible cannibalism by the Maoris of Hawke's Bay.—I am, &c.,

WILLIAM COLENSO.

May 27, 1880.

❖ 1880 THE BIBLE IN SCHOOLS.
Hawke's Bay Herald 7 June.

SIR,—In your paper of this morning you give us a copy of the petition for Bible reading in the public schools, to be brought forward for adoption and signature at the meeting convened for Monday next. You also have in the same paper, a letter signed by "A Lover of the Bible," evidently written in support of the same scheme. I regret to see them both. Allow me to give a few reasons, out of many, for my so saying. Were the meeting an *open* one, I would attend, and there "say my say."

I take up the text of the petition first. What Bible is it that is here called (in rather dark and stiltified language) "the authoritative Exponent of the National faith?" which Bible is sought to have read daily in schools "without note or comment?" It cannot be the old and larger Bible of the Roman Catholics, because they never have and would not allow of it; therefore it is the Protestant or smaller Bible. Here, then, at the outset, is the grand difference; this great division between the *two* "authorised" Books, or Bibles, of the Christian Churches; which this petition (supposing it to become effectual!) would serve to keep up, and that too by the great injustice of excluding all the Roman Catholic youth from the public schools! still serving as fuel for the fire, the making of old religious (or Church) feuds the stronger, more bitter and lasting. Of course I shall be reminded by Bigots, Shallow-pate, & Co.,—there is the "Conscience clause!" true; I know it, I will come to that by-and-by.

Now this grand distinction between those two Bibles, both containing, alike "the elements of the nation's faith" (whatever that may mean), is an obstacle that cannot be got over:—So much then for the book—the Bible.

But supposing it could,—or (what is sought in the said petition,) that the Protestant Bible should be so daily read "without note or comment." Anything more bald more wretched in the way of training the young I can scarcely conceive. (And, please, bear in mind, that I write from long practice and experience in the matter.) For, there in the schools, on the one hand, the children would have the scientific elementary works of the day, written in clear modern language, teaching them, as far as is known, the truth about all natural things; which truths, be it ever remembered, are as surely from God as the best of the Bible is. Truths, whether in Astronomy, Geology, Natural History, or the sciences generally; on which subjects, of course, any amount of questions might be put, and encouraged too, and answered by the competent teacher,—to a willing pliant class, whose whole minds would be absorbed in their pleasing work, drinking in such daily instruction as the grass does the nightly dew, and growing too thereby. While, on the other hand, in reading the Bible; no questions must be asked! Lesson over; shut books! Why? (1.) Because many awkward questions might arise, which, if answered after the old one-groove and stereotype fashion, would disagree with the other and truthful teachings of the school; and therefore soon found out, even by children, not to be the truth! or, (2.) Because of the incompetency of the teacher to answer them completely? or (3.) Because of his sectarianism, which prevents him from answering them truly? or (4.) Because the Bible is the Word of God?—

I leave it to the supporters of the said scheme to decide, which of those 4 reasons they prefer.

Very likely they (or most of them) may prefer the last one; still saying (as of old but with far less reason,) that the Bible—all within its covers from Genesis to Revelation— is the Word of God.

And, first, I will apply myself to this. If so, is it right and proper—on the part of the children—to have God's word merely read in that hurried hireling kind of way? Is that the way to have proper reverence paid to God and to the holy Scriptures?

Is that the way to inculcate the holy truths therein taught on the youthful mind? To be read merely as an additional reading exercise,—in many cases, too, a hard one, often an irksome one; especially when the noisy glee of their frolicsome and happy schoolmates comes rolling in through the open windows, calling away their attention and distracting their minds,—embittering them, I might have said, (guided, perhaps, by the Devil!) Here, if anywhere, would be seen the truth of the old saying,—Where the treasure is, there is the heart; and the heart would assuredly be with the players outside. And the sure consequences would follow; the bitter crop to be reaped from that seed,—that the Bible, its reading and its study, would get to be so disliked by them as they grew up.

If the Bible be the Word of God,—then, I say, it should be carefully and reverentially approached and read; not hurriedly or as a forced and distasteful task; with all the needful explanation possible, given in the most winning way, and that only by competent teachers.

It has long, very long, seemed to me, that the proper Christian way to work the so-called "Conscience clause" (here, among us, and under present circumstances,) is for the several Ministers of Religion to work *more* than they do, and work heartily too. If the Bible be the Word of God, let them, as His paid servants, teach it, open it, explain it, to the lambs of their respective flocks. There is the whole of the Saturday (to say nothing of the Sunday-schools,—when, however, they are generally otherwise employed); let them on the Saturday assemble their children belonging to their respective sects or denominations; all of them have time enough to do this; and if they enter on this duty with a good heart, willingly and zealously, I have no doubt of their being useful to the children; far more so than any, or all of our school teachers could possibly be in merely hearing the children read the Bible daily "without note or comment!" But then, again, that real usefulness will depend whether those Ministers are sticklers for dogmas and forms, and old-fashioned obsolete untruthful Catechisms!—more desirous of keeping the youth of both sexes in a kind of sectarian thrall or bondage, than in teaching them the pure enlightening unfettered Truth.

"*Holding back all noble feeling,*
Choking down each manly view;
Caring more for forms and symbols
Than to know the Good and True."

With your permission I will send you the remainder of my letter for your next issue; when I will notice the letter of "A Lover of the Bible."

   Yours, &c.,

   WILLIAM COLENSO.

Napier, June 4, 1880.

§ 1880 THE BIBLE IN SCHOOLS.

Hawke's Bay Herald 7 June.

The Rev. De Berdt Hovell at St. John's Church, and the Rev. J. Spear at Meanee and Taradale, yesterday preached on the subject of the Bible in State schools. Mr. Hovell adduced statements to prove that neither Jews nor Roman Catholics objected to the Bible being introduced into the public schools, and urged that only atheists and heathen really opposed it. We are requested to state that a number of members of Mr. Hovell's church intend to take steps to show that they totally dissent from his views, and that "atheists" and "heathen" are not the only objectors to State religious teaching.

❖ 1880 THE BIBLE IN SCHOOLS II.

Hawke's Bay Herald 8 June.

"A Daniel, still say I; a second Daniel!

I thank thee, Jew, for teaching me that word."

SIR,—Did you ever perceive a certain indefinable something in the face of a cow, horse, or dog, which instantaneously reminded you of some person you had formerly seen, or of an absent friend?—one, it may be, whom you had not seen or heard from for many years: if not, I have and that more than once. Yet, if you were to ask me to define it I could not—save by the word, expression or cast. Well, on reading the letter of "A Lover of the Bible" in yours of Friday last (already alluded to by me in my letter of the 4th), in which he brings forward so largely Mr. M. Arnold, as supporting the reading of the Bible in our public schools,—the words of Shakespeare in his inimitable *Merchant of Venice* (which I have given above as a motto) rushed into my mind! and I have, ever since been in a measure haunted by them. I do indeed thank "A Lover" for bringing forward Matthew Arnold[1] in this matter; but whether "A Lover" has read Matthew Arnold's works on the Bible? (such as, *"Paul and Protestantism," "Literature and Dogma," "God and the Bible,"*) is quite another matter; also, whether "A Lover" would agree with him in what he has written therein I trow not! However, since "A Lover" has brought this witness forward, in support of his views, he cannot reasonably object to my cross-examination of Mr. Matthew Arnold, on what he has said concerning the Bible.

  From my being well-acquainted with Matthew Arnold's works, and in the main highly approving of them, nothing is more certain than this, that he would never

---

1 Arnold was, like Colenso, Inspector of Schools. I.S.G.

approve of *such a kind* of Bible reading as this hurried and distasteful one now sought "without note or comment." And "A Lover" should have known this, at least; for, as it is, his quoting Matthew Arnold seems like sailing under false colours,—or, in other words, making a man's words to mean the contrary of what he intended. To this remark I would also just add one other word, viz. that I believe "A Lover" and "Biblos" (in your paper) and "Codex" (in your contemporary) to be one and the same person,— or, at all events, all written at one instigation.

There are two particularly prominent points in the letter of "A Lover" on which I would first say a few words, before I proceed to examine Mr. M. Arnold.

1.   The wonderful "kindling of trains of thought and remembrance through Bible names—as, Zion, Tabor, Hermon, and Sharon,—operating on the imagination of the young readers of that Book!" This, to me, is strange; yet not so, either, when I bear in mind the glamour or false glare that for years (or ages) has surrounded them. How? Through ignorance; and through the clergy, generally, keeping it up and delighting to have it so! For too many of them still firmly believe that "Ignorance is the mother of Devotion."

I will give an instance or two of that false glamour I have mentioned, which will explain my meaning. About 18 months ago I wrote a series of Papers, which appeared in the HERALD, on the Reasonable and True Keeping of the Sunday; and in doing so I had occasion to mention the puny and insignificant sizes of the petty kingdoms of Israel and of Judah, which, together, formed what has been termed "the Holy Land." I therein said,—"Those two kingdoms together, were not so large as the small tract of country extending from Napier to Cape Palliser in length, and from the Ruahine mountain ranges to the sea in breadth. While that of Judah alone could be comprised between Napier and Takapau." And some of the tribal portions, said to have been cut up and allotted by Joshua to the 12 tribes, were not so large as some of our sheep-runs here in Hawke's Bay held by one man! I had also quoted from the Bible, the number stated to have been slain on *one side only* in a single battle between the two kings of those two small states, namely, "500,000 chosen men"! While, as a set-off, the total loss of the Allied army in the great and memorable battle of Waterloo, including British, Germans, Hanoverians, Brunswickers, Prussians, and Belgians, was 4,172 men." I, also, showed up therein, several other things taken from the Bible, in plain and convincing unmistakable language. And often, since the publication of the above, have I received letters and notes and verbal thanks, from old and middle-aged, and from young persons too (who dare to think for themselves), for opening their eyes a bit to those plain natural things, which they had never before heard of, or once thought of, in that way, and so removing the glamour from their eyes concerning some of the Bible statements. And such remarks of theirs do not, can not, stop there: I am also asked Why do not the present working paid Ministers do this? Why do they not explain the Bible truthfully? Is it owing to their ignorance, or to their carelessness, or to their dislike to let in light on all such matters,—fearing the result?—These questions *they* must answer: I can assure them they are asked.

2. "The Bible being the only contact the scholar had with philosophy and poetry."
    —I don't know what is the state of things in the English schools, but such is not
    (or, rather, *was not*) the case here; much of choice and beautiful and feeling poetry,
    taken from the works of our best British poets, was commonly read and explained,
    and committed, too, to memory, in our Provincial schools,—and, I should suppose,
    is still. But, apart from that, if the Bible were only dryly read in our Public Schools
    as a daily task "without note or comment;" where would be the poetry of such
    a performance? One might just as well speak of the sweet sugariness of vinegar!
    It is another thing and all very well (as we shall see,) for Mr. Matthew Arnold
    (he, too, being the Professor of Poetry in the University of Oxford,) thus to write
    of showing and educe the grand old Hebrew poetry of the Bible in *his mode* of
    reading it and teaching from it with enlarged culture in schools; but here,—in the
    wretched way proposed! precious little would, or could, ever be seen or known or
    mentally felt of the poetry of the Bible.

Mr. Matthew Arnold, examined, says:—"An inevitable revolution, of which we all
recognise the beginnings and signs, but which has already spread, further than most of
us think, is befalling the religion in which we have been brought up. In no country will
it be more felt than in England.... There is a time to speak and a time to keep silent. If
the present time is a time to speak, there must be a reason why it is so. And there *is* a
reason and it is this. Clergymen and ministers of religion are full of lamentations over
what they call the spread of scepticism, and because of the little hold which religion
now has on the masses of the people; many of whom are now found rejecting the
Bible altogether. Let me quote from the letter of a working-man,—a man, himself,
of no common intelligence and temper,—a passage that sets this forth very clearly;
'Despite the efforts of the churches,' he says, 'the speculations of the day are working
their way down among the people, many of whom are asking for the *reason* and *authority*
for the things they have been taught to believe. Owing to questions of this kind, and
to their lack of culture, a discovery of imperfection and fallibility in the Bible leads to
its contemptuous rejection as a great priestly imposture.'... We regret the rejection as
much as the clergy and ministers of religion do. With Catholics as well as Protestants
this is so. What the religion of the Bible is, how it is to be got at, they may not agree;
but that it is the religion of the Bible, for which they contend, they all declare. 'The
Bible,' says Dr. Newman, 'is the record of the whole revealed faith; so far all parties
agree.... And yet, with all this agreement both in words and in things, when we behold
the clergy and ministers of religion lament the neglect of religion and aspire to restore
it, how must one feel that to restore religion as they understand it, to re-enthrone the
Bible, as explained by our current theology, whether learned or popular, is *absolutely and
forever impossible!*—as impossible as to restore the predominance of the feudal system, or
of the belief in witches! Let us admit that the Bible cannot possibly die; but then the
churches cannot even conceive the Bible without the *gloss* they at present put upon it,
and this gloss, as certainly, cannot possibly live. And it is not a gloss which one church
or sect puts upon the Bible and another does not; it is the gloss they all put upon it,

and call the foundation of belief common to all Christian churches. It is this so-called fundamental basis which must go, and it supports all the rest.... Those who 'ask for the *reason* and *authority* for the things they have been taught to believe,' as the people are now doing, will begin at the beginning. They will never consent to admit, as a self-evident truth, the preliminary assumption with which the several churches start. If they are to receive the Bible, we must find for the Bible some other basis than that which the churches assign to it, a truthful basis and not an assumption; and this, again, will govern everything which comes after. This new religion of the Bible the people may receive; the common and repeated statement now current among the churches of the religion of the Bible the people never will receive.... Meanwhile there is now an end to all fear of doing harm by gainsaying the received theology of the churches and sects. For this theology of theirs is itself now a hindrance to the Bible rather than a help; nay, to abandon it, to put some other construction on the Bible than this theology finds, is indispensable, if we would have the Bible reach the people.... The correspondent we have above quoted notices how the lack of *culture* disposes the people to conclude at once, from any imperfection or fallibility in the Bible, that it is a priestly imposture. To a large extent, this is the fault not of the people's want of culture, but of the priests and theologians, who for centuries have kept on assuring the people that perfect and infallible the Bible is.... Our mechanical and materialising theology, with its insane licence of affirmation about God, its insane licence of affirmation about a future state, is really the result of the poverty and weakness of our minds.... To understand that the language of the Bible is fluid, passing, and literary, not rigid, fixed, and scientific, is the first step towards a right understanding of the Bible. But to take this very first step, some experience of how men have thought and expressed themselves, and some flexibility of spirit, are necessary; and this is culture.... Without culture we cannot have this experience; although it is true that even culture itself, without good fortune and tact, will not fully give it. Still our best and only chance of it is through means of culture.... But it is for the Bible itself that this discerning experience, so necessary in all our theological studies, is most needed. And to our popular religion it is especially difficult; because we have been trained to regard the Bible, not as a Book whose parts have varying degrees of value, but as the Jews came at last to regard their Scriptures, as a sort of talisman or charm given down to us out of Heaven, with all its parts of equal value! And yet there was a time when the Jews knew well the vast difference there is between their books, of the Old Testament; there was also a time when Christians knew well the vast difference between the books of the New Testament. This, indeed, is what makes the religious watch-word of the British and Foreign School Society: *The Bible, the whole Bible*, and nothing but the Bible! So ingeniously absurd; it is treating the Bible as Mahometans treat the Koran, as if it were a talisman all of one piece, and with all its sentences of equal power.... We have said, and it is important to maintain it, that popular Christianity at present is so wide of the truth, is such a disfigurement of the truth, that it fairly deserves, if it presumes to charge others with atheism, to have that charge retorted upon itself; and future ages will perhaps not scruple to condemn it almost as mercilessly as Polycarp condemned the religion of heathen antiquity. For us, the God of popular religion—of the churches and sects of the day, is a legend, a fairy tale; learned theology has simply taken this fairy-tale and dressed it up!—Clearly it is impossible for us to treat this fairy tale with solemnity, as a real and great object, in the manner which might be most acceptable to its believers. He does well, who, steadily using his own eyes in this manner, and escaping from the barren routine whether of the assailants on the Bible or of its apologists, acquires the serene and imperturbable conviction,—indispensable for all fruitful use of the Bible in future, that in travelling through its reports of miracles he moves in a world, not of solid history, but of illusion, rumor and fairytale. Only, when he has acquired this, let him say to himself that he has by so doing achieved nothing, except to get rid of an insecure reliance which inevitably some day or other would have cost him dear,—of a staff in religion which must sooner or later have pierced his hand."

Here "A Lover of the Bible" (who had long been sitting very fidgety) meekly said, that he should prefer a Nonsuit.

That will do: You may stand down Mr. Matthew Arnold.—I am, &c.,

WILLIAM COLENSO.

Napier, Sunday, June 6, 1880.

§ 1880 PARLIAMENTARY ITEMS.
Bay of Plenty Times 17 June.

Colenso who received £1100, instead of £700 as agreed upon, for a Maori lexicon, and completed only a small portion of the work, has the impudence to demand further payment or the return of the manuscript. The specimen page laid on the table of the House shows that at the rate he worked two or three generations would be required to complete it.

❖ 1880 MR. COLENSO ON A SMALL INLAND TAX.
Hawke's Bay Herald 28 June.

SIR,—I was not a little pleased with your article in your issue this morning,—that is, with very much of it; and was quite inclined to shout "Bravo!" and to throw my wig into a corner, when I read your words,—"For once we find ourselves in almost perfect accord with the member for Clive." In my opinion you should have stopped there; having spoken, and said a really good thing,—subside into dignified silence, and wait for the applause.

But, no! You then go on to say: "The one point in this where we differ from the member for Clive is, that we think a small land tax should also accompany an income tax." Now this I did not, I could not, expect from you,—seeing you have hitherto strenuously opposed this flagrant property tax, (which I have always thanked you for doing,) and which is, in fact at least, only another name for a land tax.

But I would ask you, Are you not aware that "a small land tax" (or, as it is with some, a tolerably big one) is being paid already, and that, too, for several years? Had you lands any where in town or in the country you would have known it,—have *felt* the pinching tight shoe on your toes, and squalled loudly enough. Just show me, if you can, a single acre of land in all Hawke's Bay that does not pay "a small land tax"—or, rather, *two*, or more, taxes, or rates, which is just the same thing. Know you not, that all the country lands, including those of the poorest settlers, are already doubly taxed, or rated,—by Road Boards and by Counties? As to land taxed, or land rated within the Borough, I need say nothing of that,—for *it is felt too keenly*. And then, in addition thereto, both in town and country, there is no prospect of such rates lessening,—though even now heavy and detrimental to settlement; and, worse still, there is but small prospect (judging from the past) of those rates or taxes, so laid on and so collected, being laid out fairly and economically for the benefit of the many!—

To talk of an income tax *and* a land tax together,—is just as sensible as to speak of making all printers pay for a licence to print, and then further, to tax their printing, especially their advertisements! I don't say, however, judging from what I am obliged daily to see, but that a tax on advertisements would not be beneficial both to the State and to subjects. "Anon, Sir."—I am. &c.,

WILLIAM COLENSO.

Napier, June 20, 1880.

❖ 1880 EARLY PRINTED BOOKS.

Hawke's Bay Herald 24 July.

SIR,—In your paper of yesterday, under the heading of "Napier Municipal Council," you state, that at the meeting of the Council on last Wednesday night, a letter from the Sydney Exhibition Commissioners was read, containing a list of awards to Exhibitors in this district; and that among them you have—

"W. Colenso, Early Printed Books and *Gazette*; fourth degree of merit."

As this sentence "Early Printed Books"—does not inform your reader as to what those Books were, (and as some, by their enquiries, have already supposed them to mean ancient European ones,) I send you the list of them, hereto annexed, taken from the "Official Catalogue," by which you will know they were all our own home work, being the first printed in New Zealand. Perhaps you may kindly find room for the said little list, together with this letter, in a corner of your paper.

If I had more time to spare and you space, I should be tempted to say a little on the relative awards of "merit," as published by you; if only to point out the great value in the eyes of those Sydney Jurors of "a picture of sea-weed" over No. 1 of my little lot! Our Colonial Jurors, however, at the N.Z. Exhibition in 1866, did not think so.—I am, &c.,

WM. COLENSO.

Napier, July 23, 1880.

New Testament, printed in Maori in New Zealand, 1837. First copy of New Testament printed in Southern Hemisphere (edition 5000 copies).

Prayer (Church of England), with Psalms, Rubrics, and 39 Articles, printed in Maori in New Zealand, 1839.

Early public papers, viz., (1) First Government *Gazette*, 1810; (2) first English placard, 1836; (3) first English circular, 1835; (4) first English prospectus, 1839; (5) first English proclamation, 1840; (6) second English proclamation, 1840; (7) third English proclamation, 1840; (8) fourth English proclamation, 1840; (9) treaty of Waitangi in Maori; (10) statement of confederate chiefs, 1835.

First book printed in New Zealand (Epistle to Ephesians and Philippians), February, 1835.

First English book printed in New Zealand, 1836.

First English sermon printed in New Zealand (Bishop Selwyn), 1842.

Two Maori almanacs, 1840 and 1843.

Letter from the Right Hon. Viscount Goderich to the chiefs of New Zealand.

Address from James Busby, Esq., British Resident, to the native chiefs (both printed in Sydney, 1833).

Account of *Phormium tenax*, by J. Murray, F.S.A., F.L.S., printed on paper made from its fibre, 1838.

All of these books printed in New Zealand were composited by the exhibitor, and some were written, bound and translated by him.

§ 1880 MARRIAGE.
Hawke's Bay Herald 30 November.
COLENSO—COLENSO.—On September 8th, by licence, at St. Mary's Church, Penzance, England, by the Rev. Prebenday Hedgeland, Mr. William Colenso, jun., of Napier, New Zealand, to Miss. Sarah Veal Thomas Colenso, daughter of Mr. Richard Colenso, decorator, of Penzance.[2]

❖ 1880 THE ATHENÆUM'S LAST COMMITTEE MEETING.
Hawke's Bay Herald 6 December.
SIR,—In your issue of this morning, you state (in referring to a meeting of the Committee of the Athenæum held on Friday night)—"A lengthy communication was read from Mr. W. Colenso, taking exception to smoking being allowed in the conversation room." And, as there is at least one material error contained in that short sentence, allow me to correct it.

My letter was not against all or any smoking being allowed in the conversation room—very far from it. Had I so written, I should myself have done the very (selfish) thing I had so prominently found fault with in my letter. What I had asked for

---

2 Willie married his cousin. I.S.G.

(in that letter), viz., that the morning hours should be allotted for the ladies and the non-smoking members—the committee has reasonably granted.

You call my letter "a lengthy communication." What grounds have you for so saying? "Lengthy," as compared with what? I know it was written on a single small sheet of note-paper, and my hand-writing is not particularly small. I do not know if you had any reporter present, (from the tenor of your item of information I should infer you had not). Two lines on a postal card might prove to be a "lengthy communication" with even a Lilliputian Senate!

I should not care to notice your error at all, had I not written on behalf of the public, and for the benefit of the members, and also of the Athenæum.—I am, &c.,

WM. COLENSO.

Napier, December 4.

❖ **1881 MORE SERIOUS ERRORS!**
Waipawa Mail 1 January.

"Those French fellows even call a horse a shovel (cheval) and a hat a chopper (chapeau)!"
—ENGLISH JACK TAR.

SIR,—I have been greatly pained in seeing a most glaring political error in the H.B. Herald of this morning. I would write to the Editor about it (living so near him), but I know too well from past experience it is no use to do so! I, therefore, address you, looking at the matter as being of great public interest, and not merely so, but of importance, too, towards the keeping of the future peace of the colony (as between its two chief races). The error itself, in its brief telegraphic original, is but small, comparatively; not so, however, the expansion and perversion of it by the editor of the Herald, who has used it as a text for a long unpleasant and disloyal sub-article, which I deeply regret to see.

It appears that Captain Knollys, the Governor's aide-de-camp, had just visited the chief Te Whiti officially, bearing a peaceful message from His Excellency offering to meet him, Te Whiti; to which Te Whiti replied, "Tu a maoa te tawa."

His answer, the Herald says, means, "The potatoes were cooked;" [Oh! thou gross quintessence of stupidity!] and thereupon falls to, tooth and nail, and comes out startlingly—worthy of a credulous disciple of Mother Shipton!

Now, if Te Whiti's brief and oracular reply to Captain Knollys is reported correctly (as to Maori orthography)—and I suppose it is, seeing that it is good grammatical Maori, a complete sentence in itself, and pregnant with deep and suitable meaning —then its grammatical, and proper rendering would be, "The hard tawa fruit (like a plum) is fast ripening;" while the true figurative meaning (as I take it) would be "Our difficulties are quietly growing towards (or nearly advanced to) a settlement." We have a similar English saying—"When the pear is ripe," &c.

The tawa tree is one of the large N.Z. forest trees; its stone-fruit (one of the few big indigenous fruits) is a long time slowly growing and ripening; and it is often used in their old proverbs. (See Ext. in one of my last papers on the ancient Maoris, in "Transactions N.Z. Institute," vol. XII., p.138.)

I can only earnestly hope that there are far better Maori interpreters and truer commentators to be found at Wellington than those of the H.B. Herald; and I would not now care to trouble you, to expose the blunder in translation, were it not for the editor's ill-timed comment or perversion thereof.—I am, &c.,

WILLIAM COLENSO.

Napier, December 30, 1880.

❖ **1881 CORRESPONDENCE.**

Waipawa Mail 5 January.

SIR,—Permit me to add a few lines by way of postscript to my letter in your paper of this day; and, in my doing so, I would first apologise to your readers for having omitted them, which omission entirely happened through my writing hurriedly to you to be in time for the mail to your town, and for your paper, and also to my being very busily occupied in writing for the outgoing English mail.

I wish to add that Te Whiti's pithy sentence, "*Tu a maoa te tawa*," may also mean that the hard stones or kernels of the tawa fruit are at length getting soft through their long preparatory steaming, though not yet quite fit for eating, and, if so, then their figurative meaning is much the same; possessing, however, (particularly to the native mind,) much more of highly suitable metaphor, arising from the extra trouble, time, labour, and patient waiting, to bring this to pass.

I may also observe that, curiously enough, this very subject—the mode of preparing the tawa kernels for food, as practised by the ancient Maoris—was part of my paper read here before our H.B. Philosophical Institute last; and as such may interest your readers just now (as serving to elucidate Te Whiti's words), I may further say that the large ripe berries of the tawa were formerly gathered up from the ground under the trees in bushels, in their season, and when denuded of their fleshy pulp (easily done by the aid of water), the kernels were laid in quantities in a very large earth-oven, previously prepared and heated (*umu-tao-roa*—slow baking oven), and therein slowly steamed for two or three days, until they became soft and were easily masticated;—and to this, in all probability, Te Whiti's apposite sentence may be attributed.

These stones or kernels somewhat resembled in shape those of the large date fruit of the shops, and were excessively hard.—I am, &c.,

WILLIAM COLENSO.

Napier, January 1, 1881

❖ **1881 MR. COLENSO ON AN INCIDENT OF OLD NEW ZEALAND HISTORY.**

Wanganui Herald 8 January.

I have this evening been reading in the Weekly News of December 4 (just to hand), a few of Jacky Marmon's sayings; also Mr. Dickson's letter commenting on some of them, and, while I almost marvel at you caring to publish Marmon's Baron-Munchausen-like tales (and in extenso, too)! allow me to point out a few errors—both in Marmon's relation respecting the loss of the barque *Harriet*, and in Mr. Dickson's letter.

I may first state that I happen to know a good deal about this affair, viz,—the loss of the *Harriet* at Te Waimate (south of Cape Egmont), and the bitter revenge which so quickly followed. For I had at Sydney made the acquaintance of Dr. Marshall, the surgeon on board H.M.S. *Alligator*, on her return thither from that expedition, and had received from him the whole sad account while fresh; besides, I have it now as fully written (journal fashion) by Dr. Marshall, who was a truly Christian gentleman. I have also Guard's statement—official document—made before the Executive Council at Sydney; and, lastly, on my subsequently coming to New Zealand, Guard himself was a fellow-passenger, and a most unpleasant one! during a long voyage in our wretched little and badly-found craft.

J. Marmon says:—"The *Harriet* was wrecked in 1829. That Guard was not the captain. That two of his children, with their mother, were rescued from the Maoris, to whom a few trifling presents were given."

Mr. Dickson says: "There was but one child saved with the mother;" he also finds fault with Marmon's statement that Guard's wife and child were safe and sound, Mr. Dickson saying: "This is hardly to be reconciled with the well known fact (sic) that though the child was uninjured, the mother had been left for dead when the natives precipitately evacuated the pa in terror at the shells thrown into it by the *Alligator*."

Now then for the plain truth. The barque *Harriet* was wrecked near Cape Egmont early in 1834 (not 1829). Guard was her master. Mrs. Guard and her two children, together with eight of the crew of the *Harriet*, were rescued, having been delivered up by the Maoris to the *Alligator* on separate days, more than a week apart, Mrs. Guard and her infant before the heavy firing by the marines and sailors took place. The delay seems to have arisen from, at least, two sources; (1) Guard's boy being in the possession of the chief of another tribe who was not then present; and (2) the Alligator leaving in the meanwhile for Port Hardy, South Island, where some nautical surveying was executed. The heavy fatal firing (after the delivery of all the prisoners) seems to have been begun wantonly, and without orders, and that too while the British flag of truce was still flying! Of course, several of the Maoris were killed, and their pa, provisions, canoes, &c., burnt and destroyed, even the dead were mutilated and outraged! Such were the few and trifling presents from H.M.S. *Alligator*.

But, as I see that Mr. Dickson is rather positive, I had better copy Dr. Marshall's own words respecting Mrs. Guard, as they are very interesting; doubly so, I may say, just now, when this recent harrowing tragedy has just been perpetrated there. "When the ship's boat came within hearing of the Maoris on the beach, they all set up a shout of gratulation, and several waded through the surf, up to their mouths in water, hoping to get near to the boat; but, failing to do so, deposited their female prisoner and her infant in a canoe, launched it from the shore, and brought them off alongside the *Alligator's* gig. In a few minutes more, they were safe on board that ship, and under the protection of His Majesty's pennant. She was dressed in native costume, being completely enveloped from head to foot in two superb mats, the largest and finest of the kind I have ever seen. They were the parting present of the tribe among whom she had been sojourning. She was, however bare-footed, and awakened very naturally, universal sympathy by her appearance.... From her own lips, I gathered all particulars.... and of the treatment she had all along experienced at their hands, her report was extremely favourable," during her five months' captivity among them.

Dr. Marshall further says:—"In the Namu pa (after it was taken by the troops) the lodgings allotted to her were discovered at once by the size of the door—the addition of a small window, on the ledge of which "was the soap she had that day used; and inside her children's frocks and her own stays. The door had been enlarged for her accommodation, the window had been made in compliance with her request, and a singular proof of considerate kindness and deference to her supposed delicacy of feeling was furnished, in the owner having caused the entrance and window both to be secluded by a close paling set up in front of the house, which effectually screened her from observation from without."

The whole of Dr. Marshall's long and particular narration is a highly interesting one and well suited to your columns (far better, allow me to say, than Marmon's sayings!); but bearing in mind what you had told me in this last winter re my letter and Parliamentary paper sent to you being "too long for insertion;" and also the saying "Once bit, twice shy" I hesitate to copy it.

Nevertheless I would also remark that I think Mr. Dickson is wrong in supporting that Marmon, in speaking of another murder—that of Puare, in which he had a hand— that he really meant Bishop Broughton (the first Bishop of Sydney), although Marmon's sentence (as given by you)—"a native missionary named Broughton, afterwards Bishop of Sydney"—seems, at first sight, to mean as much. It is true that Bishop Broughton visited the Bay of Islands at Christmas, 1838, in H.M.S. Pelorus, on official business, but his stay there was short, and, certainly, he was never in New Zealand before; indeed he told me so. How, then, could Bishop Broughton have been there at Hokianga? If there is any truth in Marmon's rambling statement, re that murder of Puare, I should say there may be a double confusion arising from the similarity and wrong use of names (1) Broughton, or Paratene, being a rather common name North, which Marmon (with many others) may have supposed to have been derived from Bishop Broughton, which, however, was not the case, but from a Mr. Nicholas Broughton, a good Christian, and a constant friend of both the old Church Missionary Society and their early missionaries; and (2) from the common practice among those low whites of the early days, of calling a baptised or Christian Maori "a missionary" i.e. one of the missionaries' followers. However, be that as it may, by merely altering one word in Marmon's sentence, viz., for "afterwards" read "named after the,"—the said sentence is intelligible enough, to me at least; and, so altered, it may be correct—viewing the said transaction from J. Marmon's standpoint.

In conclusion, I may observe, that I should not care to notice any saying of Marmon's but for Mr. Dickson's letter—I am, &c.,

WILLIAM COLENSO.

❖ 1881 A FEW THOUGHTS ON THE LATE SAD MURDER AT OPUNAKE.
Waipawa Mail 15 January.[3]

"The rope followeth the bucket."—Ancient Eastern proverb.

Sir,—The last dread sentence of the law having been fully carried out on the Maori criminal Tuhiata, I have been expecting to see in one or more of our papers some suitable remarks upon this sad strange case; none, however caught my eye. I have, therefore, determined that I would submit a few which have occurred to me for the consideration of your readers, hoping that I may thereby be the means of provoking or stirring up thought.

And here I would anticipate and meet a question, which some one may be inclined to put,—Why do I undertake this peculiar duty? and my answer will be,—1. Because of my having dwelt so long in N.Z. and among the Maoris (now nearly half a century), and because of the strangeness of such a crime among them:—2. Because of my having had to attend criminals under sentence of death, both in the condemned cell and on the scaffold:—3. Because I am so well acquainted with the circumstances attending the capture by the Maoris, at that very spot where this murder was committed, of the first white woman who was ever in those parts of N.Z. many years before N.Z. became colonised. (This story, which is highly interesting, I hope to write an account of for your next week's paper.)[4] I trust these reasons may suffice.

Æsop's Fables, which we read with delight when young (whether in their original Greek or modern English dress), always carried a moral with them; and surely a fitting moral, or reflection, or something of that kind,—something useful, something beneficial, to ourselves, and the rising generation,—may be fairly drawn from this recent shocking affair which, barely a month ago, stirred all N.Z. from the North Cape to Stewart's Island.

At that time, however, and for some time after (down to, I may say, the period of Tuhiata's execution), there was no lack of extravagant and exaggerated, and even indecent language, respecting both the unhappy Maori and his deed; mostly, I believe, the productions of those mischievous and misleading "Special Correspondents," who both take, and are allowed, far too much liberty; one sentence only as a sample I have need to quote to bear me out, and that shall be from your own paper of December 8th,—where your "correspondent," writing from Auckland, says,—"The murder of Miss. Dobie, a deed that has no parallel in the history of all that is diabolical and infernal," &c., &c.

This I altogether deny; far worse murders, I am sorry to say, (if their horrid attendant circumstances can make them so,) take place continually at home in Great Britain,—to say nothing of Ireland! Every monthly mail to us teems with such. In the very last English paper I received, (dated November 2,) were accounts of two, or even three,

---

3   This letter was reported almost in full by the *Poverty Bay Herald*, whose Editor wrote, 'Mr. Colenso's communication … is replete with sound common sense as well as generous sentiment.' I.S.G.
4   He did so – see below. I.S.G.

dreadful murders, which had then just taken place; one, in Kent,—a double murder of an aged couple named Ellis, who were singly decoyed by night from their quiet home by an ex-policeman named Waller, (formerly of the Metropolitan Police force), and brutally murdered on the highway! they, too, being on friendly terms with him.

To deal plainly reasonably and truthfully with such a case as this—the late N.Z. murder, is something like the undertaking of a *post mortem* examination,—unpleasant, aye revolting; yet both necessary and beneficial. Therefore, in speaking truthfully of the sad deed itself, I cannot but briefly say, that it might have been very much worse; that is, attended by more dreadful and harrowing circumstances this must be allowed: let this suffice.

Of course, all your readers are pretty well acquainted with all that has been stated in the several Courts of Law respecting this murder. Very little indeed has there been brought forward of a clear kind, save the open admission by Tuhiata in a half-a-dozen words at the close of the first examination of his having done the deed,—his own subsequent statement before some of the Constabulary party respecting it, and, also his short letter to the Governor the day before his death. I (and no doubt many others) have regretted that the prisoner was not allowed to say what he greatly wished to say at the Coroner's inquest, and also to speak on the scaffold at the time of his execution, when he again wished to do so,—but was so ungraciously prevented by Archdeacon Stock! I have never before heard of any poor fellow (in modern times) being denied,—roughly and rudely denied, too! as on this occasion,—that poor, that last consolation. Such, indeed, was lately granted to the unhappy Chinaman who was executed at Dunedin,—who was even asked to speak! I could say a good deal on this head, but, for the present, I refrain.

The Wellington correspondent of the "Hawke's Bay Herald," (not a "Special,") who, it appears, was present at the trial, thus writes of the prisoner:—"The demeanour of Tuhiata throughout the long trial has been a standing source of wonder to all beholders. He is a fine strapping young Maori, and for a native may be considered good-looking. Certainly there is nothing about his face that would stamp him as such a ferocious criminal as his actions have proved him to be, his countenance having a pleasing and good-tempered aspect about it." He also says, that Tuhiata received his sentence composedly; and in a smiling manner, (though heavily-ironed) left the Court. And just so, it seems, he showed himself on the fatal scaffold,—allowing for the Reporter's colouring, (I quote from the "N.Z. Mail" of January 1, 1881,)—"The governor of the gaol entered the condemned cell and brought out Tuhiata with his arms pinioned at the elbows with a strap. The Governor of the gaol led the way; Tuhiata walked steadily along the passage with an easy lounging stride, and stolid unconcerned face: mounted the steps, and, directed by the hangman, placed himself on the very centre of the drop." Of course, in addition to all this, (which, from the accompanying tenor of those communications, with others, seems to have been unwillingly conceded,) there are the repeated charges of "callousness," of "obduracy," of "recklessness," of "unconcern," of "the habit of shedding blood,"—with other like statements which, I venture to think, *may* not be true here.

Why? because that this poor fellow had already done all that lay in his power towards atoning for his foul offence. He had early acknowledged his having done the deed;—that it was also a great crime—that he was willing to die for it;—and that he, there and then, offered himself to be put to death immediately, in any way the justly offended Europeans assembled should choose. And all this, mind, without attempting to say one word in extenuation! Now this, as I take it, was the grand secret of Tuhiata's subsequent, quiet pleasing peaceful appearance, behaviour and attitude, throughout the whole of his remaining days, which were (I regret to know) unnecessarily days of torture. What more could any poor erring sinful man possibly do?

Tuhiata did, as I have often known Maoris to do in the olden time, (before their too common acquaintance with the "superior race" and "the blessings? of civilisation"!)—he acted immediately on the truthful promptings of his own conscience; he told the truth, the whole truth, and nothing but the truth, regardless of the consequences; and having done so he received that internal support which always surely follows such a confession, and which never forsook him. He realised (it may be in *another* way—far out of our thoughts) what we all profess to believe, that "if we confess our sins God is faithful and just to forgive us our sins," and this confession and forgiveness are described, by one who had experienced both, as being simultaneous and always united, (*Psalm* 32.5) one cannot be without the other. He took the great Father of all on His internal teaching at His word; he lived thus his few remaining days without once faltering,—without once complaining of his many discomforts, bearing up manfully under them all; and he died properly and manly as a poor sinner should die,—having openly confessed his great sin, and acknowledged the justice of his sentence. What more could he do? What more could the very best among us do, if, unfortunately under similar sad circumstances, placed in his situation?

No doubt there are some among us who would have very much preferred his (apparently) pious listening to the exhortations (whatever they were) of those Ministers who visited him,—his making large "Christian" professions,—and his having been Baptized, &c., &c. I, however, for one, rejoice and feel thankful that he did not relinquish the one firm hold of the right which he had taken, and understood and proved. No doubt there are also others, who would have been greatly pleased had he lived and died in continual dread and terror,—even to the behaving unseemly in his last moments, and dying struggling and howling like a dog! There *are such*, I know; to them I have nothing to say; I leave such creatures to the enjoyment of their own charitable thoughts now,—and to the boat and comforts of "the ferryman Vain-hope," including his modern crew of 8-bells-celebrants, hereafter !—as honest John Bunyan hath it.

And here I would fain ask a question, or two. How would any of our countrymen —of the "superior" civilised race—generally have acted, if so overtaken with such a heavy crime; would they—could they—have acted as manly a part as Tuhiata did? and have so consistently kept it up from the beginning to the close?—I fear not: as a rule, I scarcely remember an instance. Further: I would ask, what shall we think of that white man who sold Tuhiata the bottle of brandy on the morning of that sad deed?—and which, no doubt, was the great incentive to this robbery,—or, rather, to his attempt at extorting money from his unoffending victim, which led on to the murder? He may stand clear from human laws and convictions; but can he possibly stand clear in the sight of his own conscience?

If so, then, I pity him and would rather (of the two) the self-accusing conscience of the Maori, Tuhiata. I firmly believe, that this great and fearful crime of murder,—so wholly unprecedented and contrary to all of our long and ample experience here among the Maoris of N.Z.,—would never have been committed but for their having first become so wretchedly demoralised by the boasting Christian Europeans!

I should much like to pursue this subject farther, but I have already trespassed too largely on the columns of your paper.

I would, however, also, say a few words with reference to the unfortunate Miss. Dobie. And this I do, because you, Sir, reside among our Maori people, and your paper is read by scores of European settlers, who are living either near to, or among them; and I write this portion of my letter particularly for the benefit of the young women, daughters and sisters of our settlers, and their young female visitors. 1. Don't go strolling *alone* into lonely unfrequented spots, to gather Ferns, or to take Sketches of forest-trees or old pas or picturesque scenes; better by far repress all such curiosity, than go to such places without companions. 2. Should you, unfortunately, happen at any time when alone, to have your money, watch, &c., &c., rudely demanded from you by a Maori, (or, more likely, by a travelling "loafing" European,) and you have to give it; hand it over quietly, without any threat or remark. Rely upon it, our police will soon do you justice. 3. Should you, unfortunately, at any time when travelling, or when alone in "the Bush" or the country, be ill-used by any fellow, and hurt, and left for dead; just quietly endeavour to continue still, repressing your feelings, &c., (as you would if assaulted by a wild cow, or a bear,) until the wretch shall have gone clear off. By bearing in mind and attending to such little simple prudent rules as these, (just like as when a fire breaks out in a house,) life may be preserved, and great crime prevented.—I am, &c.,

WILLIAM COLENSO.

Napier, January 11, 1881.

[We hope Mr. Colenso will favor us at an early date with the contribution promised above.—Ed. W.M.]

❖ **1881 The first European fighting and killing at Taranaki: A striking incident in the old (modern) history of New Zealand.[5]** *Waipawa Mail* 22, 26, 29 January; 2, 5, 9, 12, 16, 19, 23, 26 February; 2, 5 March.

---

5   These letters contain an account of incidents involving the wreck of the *Harriet* and the subsequent actions by HMS *Alligator* (briefly mentioned in the 8 Jan letter to the *Wanganui Herald* above); it is very similar to that published as 'The first European fighting at Taranaki.' In Sherrin, R.A.A. 1890 *The Early History of New Zealand*, part 1 of Brett's Historical Series: Early New Zealand. Auckland, pp. 435–458.—reproduced in *Colenso's published papers*, forthcoming in this series. I.S.G.

❖ 1881 TURNING TO THE EAST.
Napier Daily Telegraph 13 July.

SIR,—Permit me to correct an error which appears in a letter in your contemporary this morning, signed "Moderation." (It is from no wish to enter into this present undignified church squabble that I now write in this matter.) Referring to the practice of turning to the east to recite the Creed, "Moderation" says,—"the Late Metropolitan of New Zealand Bishop Selwyn did so"—this, however, I deny. I never knew of his doing so in a single instance; and I have been present in church with him hundreds of times,—both in his own college church, as well as in those which were mine,—and I never knew him once to break the rubric (or law), for he always took the proper assigned position, at the north end of the table.

At the same time, his erratic good-natured chaplain, the Rev. W. Cotton, did so; and there was the striking peculiarity, if not the puerility, of practice plainly shown, (*then* an innovation for the first time, and great novelty in New Zealand!)—of two (or more) ministers being present, and only one (Mr. Cotton) whisking round to his position! No doubt he believed he was doing right; and, possibly, supposed that he was rightly teaching others in his so acting! But Mr. Cotton had not the far-seeing mind nor depth of judgment of Bishop Selwyn, who did not deem it worth while to disturb the peace of a mixed congregation over such little things.

I may also say, that having read attentively "Moderation's" letter, I cannot but conclude, that he is not a Moderate, in the true sense of the word, and he knows it. For, would it not have been far better, far more to the point, for him (if a Moderate) to have adduced the practice of the Bishop of the Diocese in this matter? of both the late respected Bishop of Waiapu (who was so known to have been a "Moderate," and also blessed with many years of experience and judgment in Church matters,) and of the present Bishop,—if the practice of a Bishop in the Church was to be adduced at all. And not to voyage far away to distant lands and islets?

But then the late dear Bishop of Waiapu had boldly and truthfully preached in St. John *warning* the congregation against that deluding, and dangerous book, "Hymns Ancient and Modern;" notwithstanding which,—certain recalcitrant curates of his Diocese persisted in retaining its use!!—I am, &c.,

WILLIAM COLENSO.

Napier, July 21, 1881.

[A meeting of the church members having been called for Wednesday next, for the discussion of the subject of the above letter, we must decline to publish any further correspondence on the questions in dispute.—Ed. D.T.]

❖ 1881 MR. COLENSO IN DENIAL.
Hawke's Bay Herald 23 September.

SIR, In your paper of this morning you have been pleased to bring me very prominently before the public. You commence your notice of me by saying,—

"Mr. W. Colenso was yesterday busily engaged in soliciting support from the electors."—

As this is utterly untrue, I seem to have no alternative left me but to *deny it wholly and publicly* through your paper, which I now do; and, at the same time, to ask you for your authority. I will give you a cheque for £20, payable to you (for the Hospital, or for any charitable purpose you may select) if you can truly give the name of one single elector whose "support I solicited" or asked.—

Such a thing I have never done at any time,—not even in the heat and excitement of our elections of the olden days,—all such being totally opposed to my principles; as is well-known to the old resident electors of Napier, both friends and foes (political). So, again, I ask you to give us the name of only one elector, out of the many you say I "solicited;"—and so gain £20, and convict me of lying.—I am, &c.,

WILLIAM COLENSO.

Napier, Sept. 22, 1881.

❖ **1881 NEWSPAPER ERRORS.**
Daily Telegraph 27 September.

SIR,—I have sometimes asked myself the question, Why is it that both you and your contemporary of the Herald make so many errors in your foreign telegraphic information?—generally, as to the dates and figures. In this morning's paper we were gravely told, that our July mail was delivered in London on Sept. 23! Knowing this, at first sight, to be an error and a serious one, (for you had both informed us, about a month back, of the safe arrival at home of the July mail,)—I quite expected to see it rectified in your paper of this evening; and lo! you have made it still worse, in saying, that it was our May mail hence!!—but it was the August one. Such errors make little difference to me, and probably to most of us here in town,—but I know that they are of greater importance in the country; especially just now, after the late Post Office enquiry.—

I am, &c., W. COLENSO.

Napier, Sept. 26, 1881. [The "error," if there be one, with which we are charged, is not ours, but Reuter's, through whose agency we receive our cablegrams. Mr. Colenso would have just cause to complain if we deliberately altered our messages to make the news fit into what we or anybody else might think was the correct groove.—Ed. D.T.).

❖ **1882 THE FEVER SCARE.**
Hawke's Bay Herald 11 April.

SIR,—I deem it a duty to thank you for your brief yet tardy remarks *re* the "fever scare," in your issue of this morning. Such, however, or something stronger, should have appeared long ago in both of our papers; still I thank you—"better late than never." I note that you, also, have used a very apposite proverb in your remarks about "a dirty bird, &c."; and, therefore, I copy for you what I found in the *N.Z. Mail* of Saturday last, as you may not have seen it, (a portion of a letter from Wairoa concerning Napier and its fever!)—as it is scarcely just to charge *all* the evil to "the Press Association's Napier agent for the evening papers."—

—"Now seeing that Napier town is simply one huge fever bed, that the business portion of the 'city' is built upon a sickening mass of putrid swamp and shingle soaked to repletion with the drainage from cess-pits, would it not be as well to admit that Napier town, as well as a harbor, is a failure, and to make a fresh start at the Kidnappers? Of what use is all this tinkering up of drains that lead nowhere, and patching up of harbor work that will never constitute a harbor if Napier is to become, some very hot autumn, one vast charnel-house."—

Of course I (that I say not, *we*) too well know the flippant careless scribbler, who writes too often for all papers roundabout in a similar thoughtless witless strain; and I have long thought (with others), that respectable papers should have quietly relegated him to the paper of his own village,—where, however, he is too well known!

I could say a very great deal on this autumnal fever visitation, having known more of it practically (I may say,) than any resident here in Hawke's Bay, and that, too, from a time when there were no other European residents than myself (and no "cesspits," &c., &c.)—then it was much more common than it has been since; but, at present, I forbear.—I am, &c.,

W. COLENSO.

Napier, April 10, 1882.

P.S.—In the same paper, I note the following telegram from *Nelson*:—"April 4. The scarlet fever does not appear to be spreading to any extent. One new case yesterday. Mr. Naylor, however, lost his 4th child from this disease this afternoon, the four children having died within a week. There have been five deaths in all, and other cases are said to be recovering." (And this is pre-eminently healthy Nelson; had one household *here* lost four in a week, what would such creatures as the Wairoa bird have screamed and scrawled!!)

❖ 1882 THE FEVER SCARE.
Hawke's Bay Herald 13 April.

"For none but a madman would fling about fire,
And tell you,—'Tis only in sport!"

SIR,—My letter to you of yesterday has been the means of my receiving several communications concerning the anonymous and wilful calumniators of our town. I had little thought they had been so numerous, or had gone so far in the way of mischievous lying. And I do think that something effectual should be done by our municipal authorities to bring those vicious adult larrikins to their proper senses. I am of opinion, that our Mayor should at once take the matter in hand, and first enquire of the Municipal Solicitor whether our public traducers could not be criminally prosecuted for malicious libel; (I believe they can;) and then call a public meeting of the Burgesses to obtain their consent to the prosecution. And, if money is needed, I am ready to join in a subscription, and to subscribe at once £10 for that purpose, and to double it if required.—And I have no doubt of the Merchants and Burgesses generally of Napier coming forward readily to fill up such a subscription list,—to any amount required for the just punishment of such evil-doers. Our Shakespeare has very truly said,

"A little fire is quickly trodden out,
Which, being suffered, rivers cannot quench."

With permission, I will give another brief extract, from another Wellington paper, the *Evening Post* of April 1st, just sent to me (which your readers will also see has been taken from another paper;—the *Wairarapa Daily*;)—

"A recent visitor to Napier writes as follows to the *Wairarapa Daily*:—'The stink as we passed through the streets was simply sickening. It appears there is a good deal of sickness about, over 400 cases of typhoid fever, and the whole town struck one as plague-stricken; half the shops had a shutter or blind drawn; flags half-mast high; and every token of disease. Carbolic acid choked you in the streets, and chloride of lime was sprinkled thick over every floor of both shops and hotels, making a delightful odour. I was only too pleased to get out again the next morning.'"

It is, and ever has been, justly considered to be bad enough to "filch" secretly the "good name" of any private person of the community; but when such depraved minds are further developed into the publishing of open bare-faced brazen lying!— to the far greater injury of the many, of the Commonweal,—the injury done is immense, and cannot be compensated by the infliction of any money fine, however heavy. In all such cases the "purse" would truly be as "trash." Indeed, my own opinion is, that all such fellows deserve the lash—equally with the garrotter and the wife-beater.

I shall hope to hear of this matter of a criminal prosecution being taken up and carried out.—I am, &c.,

WM. COLENSO.

Napier, April 12, 1882.

[We received Mr. Colenso's letter early yesterday morning, many hours before the republication in an evening paper of the extract from the *Post.*—Ed. *H.B.H.*]

§ 1882 INTERPROVINCIAL NEWS, NAPIER.
Hawera and Normanby Star 17 April.

Great indignation is expressed here at the accounts published in the Northern and Southern papers of alleged wide-spread and dangerous sickness here a short time since. There were a few cases of low fever, but the official returns show the deaths to have been fewer than usual. The vital statistics prove Napier to be the healthiest town in New Zealand. Mr. W. Colenso offers £20 to start a fund to prosecute the authors of the account published, if it is possible to find them.

❖ 1882 THE TREATMENT OF NATIVE PRISONERS OF WAR.

Timaru Herald 21 April.

SIR,—Without apology or introduction I write to tell you that I have been very much pleased in reading a long extract from one of your papers (*Timaru Herald*, 20th March, 1882) given us in our local—*Hawke's Bay Herald*—on Wednesday last. I could only wish I had a few copies of your paper containing it (in its entirety), to send to my friends in England by this outgoing mail. It is a long time since I have seen anything so real and so truthful, affecting the poor misguided and hunted Maoris who were in arms against us.

I send you herewith a copy of a pamphlet I published at that time (ten or eleven years ago), in which you will find not a little wholly in agreement with what you have now published in your paper. I hope you may find time to read it through. My writing it nearly cost me a prosecution![6] It is a great gratification to find another mind, both independent and at a distance, agreeing with one.

I think, however, your opinion of Te Kooti too severe; hitherto you have only known him through his bitter implacable foes! Perhaps what I have also published at the end of the said pamphlet, may serve to give you a more favorable opinion of him. Once more thanking you for your able article,

I am, &c., WM. COLENSO.

Napier, April 15, 1882.

[We have to thank Mr. Colenso for forwarding us a copy of his pamphlet on Kereopa.—Ed. T.H.]

❖ 1882 THE NEW ZEALAND OLIVE.

Daily Telegraph, 11 May.

SIR,—I note what you have said in your issue of yesterday (Tuesday) concerning the Olive tree and the *tawa* tree being one: viz.—"We cannot put our hand upon our authority, but we have a distinct recollection of reading somewhere a letter from England, in reply to a question relating to the introduction of the Olive tree, that the best and speediest way of naturalising the Italian Olive would be to graft upon the native *tawa* tree, which was stated to be a true Olive."

I know nothing of "the letter from England," mentioned by you, nor of its writer; but I suppose that (if your "distinct recollection" is correct) it must have been a *modern* one,—written, very likely, in consequence of so much having been said and published of late years about the introduction of the European Olive into New Zealand, as the basis of a future lucrative article of use and of commerce; and if so written, then assuredly it was not written by any authority, whether Botanical or practical Horticulturist, as it contains the great error of the *tawa* tree being an Olive, and of the grafting successfully of the Olive upon it! For, as I have already casually shown in your columns of yesterday, there is no Natural or Systematical connexion whatever

---

6   The issues of the *Hawke's Bay Herald* for 1871–6 are missing from Papers Past, so I am unable to find any information on Colenso's putative prosecution. I.S.G.

between the two trees, or their Natural Orders; indeed they are farther apart in the Natural System of Botany, than a cabbage is from a cucumber.

I had early discovered 3 species of *Olea* (or true olive) in New Zealand; one at the Bay of Islands, one at Wairarapa, and one at Patea in the mountainous interior, (this last in 1847,) and had severally sent specimens of them to Sir W. Hooker, the Director of the Royal Gardens at Kew. And I believe that I, myself, was the originator, or the first writer, of the *"grafting"* part of that statement mentioned by you; which I will now endeavour to show.

Nearly 20 years ago, (in 1864,) Sir G. Grey, then Governor of New Zealand, acting with the Imperial Commissioners appointed to carry out the New Zealand Exhibition, held at Dunedin in 1865, officially assigned to me the Public Essay "on the Botany of the N. Island of New Zealand," (and, also, the Essay "on the Maori Race,")—and, in Part III of that Botanical Essay, in considering the Economic Botany of New Zealand, I brought forward several N.Z. plants, which, probably, would be found useful in the Arts, (a few I had, myself, proved,) with observations on them, and also on the various soils, and Climates of N.Z., &c., &c., suited to plants of commercial value worthy of being introduced into the Colony; and, among other remarks, I said, that "the European Olive might be advantageously grafted upon the several indigenous olives of the Island." (Essay, ¶ 32.) This essay was also republished in its entirety (but without the *Notes*) in 1869, in the *first* volume of the "Transactions of the New Zealand Institute."

At the time of my writing of that Essay, I scarcely can suppose there were a dozen persons in the Colony who knew of our possessing an indigenous and true Olive in our woods; or, if they had happened to have heard of it, (from Sir W. Hooker's early publications of my Botanical discoveries in the "London Journal of Botany," 1841– 1849, and in other works of his,) they did not really know the trees themselves in our forests. Subsequently, however, through the publication of Dr. Sir Joseph Hooker's "Hand-Book of the New Zealand Flora," in 1866, and its extensive circulation here in the Colony, our possessing species of the Olive in our woods became known; and yet, (strange to say!) among all the immense amount of *talk*, aye, and of writing, too, about the introduction of the European Olive into the Colony (both inside Parliament and outside), I have never once noticed any one even hinting or alluding to the far easier and ancient and more speedily profitable mode of its early and successful propagation in the Colony,—viz. by its being *grafted* on the plentiful wild olive-stocks which are so very common here. One would have thought, (even supposing our Representative men to be generally ignorant of Natural Science,) that some of them must, at least, have often heard of Paul's striking natural imagery, in his Epistle to the Romans, (XI. 17.) about *the grafting of the olive*; and that the bare recollection of this would have sufficed to give them an idea, or working notion of the thing! But then, as I said before, probably they did not even know of the existence of the wild olive tree amongst us.

And here, Sir, you, or some others, may justly enough say,—"Why did I not write to some of the papers of the day, and so inform them?" Were I to keep doing this, respecting the many useful, new, profitable, and other things, I have formerly written and published, on religious and other matters, I might do nothing else. I continually see, in Newspapers, Books, Sermons, and Colonial Almanacs, the same old, often exposed, and obsolete errors constantly being hashed, and vamped and served-up anew! arising from ignorance or carelessness, or forgetfulness; and I am sometimes driven to reflect—

"Since ignorance is bliss,
'Tis folly to be wise."

In conclusion, I may briefly mention that my collecting, early last week while in the forests, berries of the olive and of the tawa trees, and bringing them with me to Napier, (with many other fruits and plants) to show at the meeting of the Hawke's Bay Philosophical Institute on Monday night was wholly irrespective of what you had said in the leading article in your paper of that same evening. Indeed, I had got all my specimens put in order and packed up for taking down to the Athenæum, during the morning of that day; it was a highly curious and undesigned concurrence, or coincidence, and that was all. I am, &c.,

WILLIAM COLENSO.

Napier, May 10, 1882.

[Our thanks are due to Mr. Colenso for the valuable information contained in the above letter. As most bush settlers are acquainted with the native names of trees, he would be adding to the obligation we are under to him if he would kindly furnish the names by which the New Zealand olive trees, most common in Hawke's Bay forests, are known to the Maoris. Is the *maire* an olive?—Ed. D.T.]

§ 1882 NAPIER MUNICIPAL COUNCIL.
Hawke's Bay Herald 18 May.

From Mr. Wm. Colenso, acknowledging recipt of three notices to abate nuisances, and stating that in his opinion no nuisances existed, that the water lying on two of the sections was caused by the action of the Corporation, and that he considered he had an equitable claim against the Corporation to fill up the sections.—Cr. de Lisle enquired where the land was situated of which the nuisances existed?—His Worship explained the positions of the sections, and stated that he had signed the warrants in the usual way, calling upon Mr. Colenso, amongst others, to fill up low-lying sections, and Mr. Colenso replied in this letter that there were no nuisances.—Cr. M'Dougall said that the matter resolved itself into the question whether the Council should act upon the report of the inspector of nuisances or give way to Mr. Colenso's repudiation. He would move that Mr. Colenso's letter be acknowledged, and that in relation to the nuisances complained of, the usual course be followed, namely, that the sections be filled in by the Council, and that Mr. Colenso be debited with the expense.—The motion was agreed to.

❖ 1882 THE NEW ZEALAND OLIVE.

Daily Telegraph 12 June.

SIR,—I set aside my writing to-night to respond at once to your wish expressed in your paper of this evening, (in your postscript to my letter,)—to give the Southern Maori names of the N.Z. Olive. Indeed I should have done so in my letter, but for the fact, that the name usually given by the Maoris here to one species of the Olive, is by the Maoris at the North given to a widely different tree, of quite another genus. A name it bears here is what you have this evening rightly given or enquired, viz., *Maire*, but there are other trees also bearing this Maori name in part which do not belong to the Olive family; that is, their names begin with *Maire*, and in common colloquial language among themselves, that portion alone of the name is all that is expressed, which abbreviation of a common name is also quite in keeping with their mode of speaking respecting persons and things generally; as, for instance, in MacLean—*Makarini* (in Maori), but oftener only the first syllable, *Ma* was used. And this was another reason for my not having written the Maori name in my letter,—to prevent confusion. At the same time I should observe, that in their so speaking there was no confusion anciently among themselves, as to the particular kind of tree meant; no more than with us, when we commonly speak of grain, corn, grass, dogs, apples, &c., &c., without distinguishing the precise kind.

Three names are (or were) used here among the Maoris for the species of Olive,— *Maire, Maireraunui, Mairekotae.* Other trees are called, *Mairetawhake, Mairehau, Mairetaiki, Mairerororo,* &c. And at the North the true *Maire* tree, is a very different tree altogether, being a species of *Santalum*, belonging to the same genus as the famed Sandalwood of commerce. I have only once seen it growing in these parts at the South, and that was near the head of the Ruamahanga river, in the upper part of the Wairarapa valley, where, strange to say, 3 trees grew together, and they were beautifully in flower; so that, *that tree* is also to be found in these southern forests,—hence 2 *Maires* here. Its flower and fruit, however, are both widely different from that of the Olive-*Maire*, whose flowers are very small and insignificant, and its fruit resembling in shape a very small Olive, and therefore cannot be mistaken.

In my letter I have mentioned "3 species of olive in New Zealand"; that is, 3 species described and published by Dr. Sir J. Hooker. I believe, however, that there are (at least) 2 more; one there, in the interior, and one confined to the country N. of the Thames,—making, perhaps, 5 species in all; but these last 2 have yet to be accurately determined.

Which species of all of them may prove to be the best adapted for grafting-stocks, has yet to be ascertained by experience.

No doubt the reason why the ancient Maoris gave the same name of *Maire* to 7 (at least) widely different trees, arose from their both being alike hard-wooded, and both used for the same purposes,—for making weapons of war, and for wedges used in splitting timber; one tree, also, being very common at the N., and one at the S. Such was their great hardness that their names were often used figuratively in their proverbs and songs, as indicating a valiant hero in fight, the chief of a tribe, &c.

The wood of both the N. and S. *Maires* ranks among the hardest of all the famed N.Z. hard woods.—I am, &c.,

WILLIAM COLENSO.

Napier, May 11, 1882.

❖ **1882 STILLING THE WAVES.**
Daily Telegraph 26 June.

"Hold thou the good: define it well:
For fear divine Philosophy
Should push beyond her mark, and be
Procuress to the Lords of Hell."—TENNYSON.

SIR,—The highly curious beginning of the long article in your Contemporary (H.B. Herald) of this morning has set me a thinking; and as I do not like to see anything erroneous piled up upon sandy foundation, neither anything publicly asserted to be "Biblical" or from the "New Testament" which is *not* so,—and as you in your paper of this evening have not referred to it, I will just do so.

Your contemporary begins by saying,—"'Pouring oil upon the troubled waters,' is a Biblical phrase, used oftener than any other by both clerical and lay writers.... It is to them only a simile—nothing more. Yet even those who deny the inspiration of the New Testament admit that the Apostles used similes thoroughly understood by their hearers, and in those days this knowledge could be developed only by personal and practical acquaintance with the operation referred to. It may therefore, well be inferred, that to 'pour oil on the troubled waters' was a common practice among the Galilean fishermen, and that its efficacy in calming the waves was undoubted."(!!!)

I fancy that not a few of the Herald's readers,—some of whom, in the country, may read this article tomorrow (Sunday),—will consider all the beginning as very fine, and very "Biblical."—

But, unfortunately, I (may I not say, We?)—I don't know of any such "Biblical phrase" or saying: Will the Herald kindly point out where it is to be found?

But the little error of its being called "Biblical," and it is not, would not alone cause me to write about it, were it not for what follows,—what is built upon it,—of the "common practice of the Galilean fishermen" (the Apostles, to wit,) "pouring oil upon the troubled waters of their lake" in time of severe storms, &c.—

Now, as I view it, there is a large amount of error here, (not, perhaps, intended)—for (1.) What was the size of that lake? About 13 miles long by 5 miles broad; or (say) as long as from Napier to Hastings, and as wide as from Napier to the fifth mile post on the beach beyond Awatoto!—(2.) What necessity could there have possibly been, on such a narrow sheet of water, to use oil for such a purpose? even supposing those freshwater fishermen knew anything of the "calming efficacy of oil when poured on the troubled waters."—(3.) Those "Galilean fishermen," with their small craft of lake-boats, were but men of very poor means, and could never have afforded to purchase Olive oil for such a purpose;—the Jews not using common animal oils of any kind.—

There is plenty (alas! far too much!) of errors of this kind (so-called "Biblical phrases" and pictures) abounding in books, and in fanciful cuts and plates for the young,—aye, and for the elders too!—which are greedily and wonderingly swallowed as true! Such as are in Raffaelle's Cartoons of "the Resurrection," and of the "miraculous draught of fishes" in this same lake, where little boats contain skates and thornbacks and other big *salt-water* fishes! and the monstrous birds in the fore-ground are as big as *Moas!*—(which picture, possibly, the Editor of the Herald might have been looking at the night before,—or have had "in his mind's eye" at the time of his writing that article.)

I cannot but consider it right to strip all plain and simple truths (especially asserted "Biblical" ones), of all fabulous excess, gewgaw, and fanciful imagery. Only a few years back, on a similar occasion, I had to remind your readers of the real size of the little kingdom of Judea—or "the Holy Land," (about which such a fuss was being made,)—that the whole of it could be comprised between Napier and Takapau—I am &c.,

WILLIAM COLENSO.

Napier, June 24, 1882.

❖ 1882 PROPOSED NEW BYE-LAWS.

Daily Telegraph 18 September.

SIR,—In your paper of Wednesday (13th), you gave the public official notice of certain proposed bye-laws to be considered by the Municipal Council on Wednesday next the 20th inst. I have been waiting patiently to see if any of my fellow-burgesses would remark in your columns on any one of them; and, as no one has yet done so, I will, with your permission, just call the attention of "the Mayor Councillors and Burgesses of the Borough of Napier," to at least one of those proposed Bye-laws; namely, that one—"as to lighting fires in the open air"; here it is.—

"Every person who wilfully sets fire to any inflammable material whatever in the open air, or who wilfully lights a fire for any purpose whatsoever in the open air, unless within a properly constructed fireplace or without the written permission of the Council to do so, shall be guilty of an offence." This subject is far too serious a one to afford fun or a joke, otherwise I might be inclined "to go" for this precious sentence—its logical meaning and its grammatical construction,—and so mercilessly dissect this one-sentence-bye-law! but, while I waive that, I cannot help offering a few observations, just to put my fellow-townsmen and visitors on their guard.

1. —"Every person who wilfully sets fire to any inflammable material whatsoever in the open air":—that is, who lights a match for his pipe,—or who lights a cigar, being composed of inflammable material,—or, who, in the non-moonlight nights, owing to the wretched glim of the public far-apart gas-lamps, strikes a match against a post to find out his whereabouts in his journeying homewards!—

2.   —"Or who wilfully lights a fire for any purpose whatsoever in the open air unless within a properly constructed fireplace"—that is, who lights his pipe in the streets, (unless our lawyers would be prepared *to prove* not merely to *contend*—for they would contend in Court for anything, on being sure of costs!) to prove, I say, the pipe to be "a properly constructed fire-place." [I should like to hear this well and learnedly handled and argued in Court, between the Municipal Solicitor and two of our legal gentlemen whom I could name.]

But I proceed and read on,— 3.—"Or without the written permission of the Council to do so." Ah! ah ! what have we here? Does this really mean,—especially when taken in connection with the foregoing clauses,—that the Corporation getting impecunious (or, in common terms, hard up for cash!) intends to issue street-smoking Licenses? I am not a smoker myself, and therefore have no foolish fears; but look out, all you street-smokers in this wooden town of narrow streets, with dry weather and high westerly spring winds at hand! look-out a-head, a bit!

However, it was not to warn our public street smokers of this new law about to be "ordained," (yes, that's the proper term, see Daily Telegraph,) that I took up my pen. For, possibly, whether I am right or wrong in my suspicions, something of this kind may yet become law—through the rapid advance of high civilization—and that before very long; so that street-smoking on narrow curbs shall be classed with perambulators, hurdy-gurdys, bicycles, wheelbarrows, big sun-shades, sweeping dust-raising raggletail dresses, and all other like street nuisances; which, though bad enough already, are sure to increase here among us, and so find work for the "bobbies."

My sole intention was, and is, to call attention to the unsuitableness of such a Bye-law for the *whole* of the Borough of Napier.

No doubt that, or something similar, is required for the town *proper* (so to speak) on the flat land below; where the houses actually adjoin each other, and where the dangers from fire are consequently very great. But such a Bye-law is most unsuitable for the hills (Scinde Island proper), it would there become a very great hardship in many places, and cannot be enforced and carried out. Of course, I more particularly mean those parts of the hills which are fenced in and used as grazing paddocks,—where the few scattered houses are many chains apart,—where 5 or even 10 acre fields intervene—and where large vegetable and other gardens and shrubberies exist. For much of the extensive refuse in those fields and gardens (arising from the Blue Gum and other like trees), can only be got rid of by burning, as it will not readily rot, which burning also serves to destroy thousands of our insect pests, in their various stages of growth and development.

Therefore I trust the Municipal Council will give this subject full and fair consideration in all its hearings; for here in this, as in many other instances (both past and present,) it will be found, that what may be, and is, a highly suitable Bye-law for the rich and densely-packed town below, is not at all advantageous nor fitting for the thinly-occupied hills above.

Indeed, it would be well for the Municipal Council always to bear this in mind; and so make the fair and equitable distinctions required between the small and thickly-peopled town and the large and all but empty suburban allotments; that is, until such time as the latter become gradually cut up and built on, and so really made one with the town or borough. For it is of little use for our Council merely to look over or to read the Bye-laws which have been made by older Boroughs in New Zealand; or to placidly resolve, that Mr. Town-Clerk do write to such a Borough to enquire as to any particular Bye-law and its working there; and that for this simple fact,—that there is no Borough, City, or Township in all this Colony so situated as we are here in Napier,—with our rough broken hilly *suburban* lands, without proper roads or means of access, *all in the very midst of the Borough!* Suburban lands being, in all the others, truly suburban and *outside* of the town or borough.

Our Municipal Council is yet young, and is also mostly composed of young men,—men of no very great experience in law-making, or, of what is of far more superior importance, the serious consideration of the bearing of laws; and it may permit an old man (who is not altogether ignorant of laws and their requirements, and who has had a little to do in past years for Napier both in legal Councils and Assemblies,) to make this remark,—one gathered from his elders and proved by his own experience,—that, the *less* all laws, whether general or bye, interfere with the liberty and common-sense of the people the better.

In conclusion, I would further observe, (in order to anticipate any adverse remark, such as, Why did I not write officially to the Town-Clerk on this subject, that my letter might be brought before the Council?)—that the amount of snubbing and contumely my late letters to the Municipal Council received, have led me to conclude, not to apply again to that quarter; not, at all events, until it has shown evident signs of amendment.—I am, &c.,

WILLIAM COLENSO.

Napier, September 16, 1882.

❖ **1882 TO THE BENEVOLENT: A CASE FOR CHARITY.**
Daily Telegraph 23 November.

SIR,—As both the D.T. and its contemporary the H. have ever been ready to advocate the cause of real Charity in their columns, I beg permission to say a few words in behalf of a very poor widow with a large family of small children; whose sad case should, I think, have been duly made public long ago through our Napier papers, and that, too, by some one well acquainted with their situation. For I feel assured that had such been done not a few in Napier and the Hawke's Bay District would have willingly responded to the call. This poor woman is now the widow of T. Scheffler, (who died in the Napier Hospital a few weeks back,) and she has been left with six small children, (the eldest being only about 8 years old!) with the probability of soon adding another to her little circle. It is well-known that T. Scheffler had long been laboring under an incurable disease, which also disabled him from constant work for some time previous to his death, consequently his little savings had all been consumed before his decease. The Waipawa County Council kindly allows her ten shillings a week, and this, perhaps, just keeps the widow and family from absolute starvation. But they are in want,—in great personal want,—and their miserable old house (or shed !) is neither wind nor water tight, and with only the cold and damp earth floor; and, unfortunately for them, their neighbors are mostly poor also, and therefore can do but little. Some small help however she has received, in the way of old clothing, &c., &c., which is gratefully acknowledged. And as she bears the sterling good character of a home-loving hard-working motherly and thrifty woman, all those little aids she has economised to the furthest:—More, I think, on this head I need not now write; I would much rather preach a sermon on it to a large audience.

I write this to you from Norsewood, where I have been residing more than a fortnight. I had privately heard of this poor widow's case last month in Napier,—and I looked forward, almost daily I may say, to some one from this neighborhood (Norsewood) writing to the D.T., or to the H., in behalf of this poor friendless destitute and uncomplaining soul and her big family of six wee bairnies! but as such was not done, and as I was coming hither, I purposely deferred my writing until I should have made full enquiry on the spot; this I have now done, and I therefore appeal to the truly benevolent (and especially to the Christian Mothers) of Napier and of Hawke's Bay to render some little and seasonable help.

This poor widow is a German, as her late husband also was; and this may be a reason for no public appeal having been made by her German friends or neighbors. But (as I take it) true charity looks neither to Nationalities nor to Creeds,—it is of too high, too holy a nature for that.

Any monies sent to me shall be faithfully applied, and a public account rendered of my stewardship; or such may (I suppose) be sent to the Rev. Mr. Sass, the German Lutheran Minister at Norsewood, to be used for her benefit: I mention this, although I have not spoken to him on the subject. Please add:—Rev. W. Colenso (1st Donation) paid, £2; ditto (2nd Donation, £1).—

I am, &c., WILLIAM COLENSO.

Norsewood, November 21, 1882.

P.S. I trust, the Editor of the Herald will kindly also take up this matter; and possibly re-publish my letter.—W.C.

❖ 1882 THE CASE OF CHARITY: THE POOR WIDOW AND HER 6 LITTLE ONES.
Daily Telegraph 28 November.
SIR,—I have to thank you for so kindly and so promptly publishing my letter to you from Norsewood, on behalf of the poor widow and her family; also, for publishing the list of subscriptions so kindly collected by Madame Politz,—which I was right glad to see, and to know that some kind and humane person had already been beforehand actively engaged in this matter: and I heartily thank them all—all round. I wish also to add, that, on my way back to town, I received (spontaneously and unasked for) the following subscriptions at Waipukurau:— £ s. d. Mr. Peter Gow 10 0 Mr. J. Grindell

10 0 Mr. W. C. Smith, M.H.R. (a 2nd Donation) 10 0 Mr. J. Grubb, (per Mr. Smith M.H.R.) 10 0 A Friend 10 0 —
I am, &c., WILLIAM COLENSO.
Napier, November 27, 1882.

❖ 1883 SHORTSIGHTEDNESS.
Daily Telegraph 2 January.
SIR,—Our town papers have recently informed us, that the Napier School Committee are about to convert the small town section No. 105, adjoining the present School-house, into a playground for the children of the School. I am surprised at this, and that for various reasons which I will give.

1. *It is far too small,* (without any probability of its ever being enlarged,) the whole available area being less than ¼ of an acre: and the number of scholars on the books being (as you lately informed us) over 600, and, of course, continually increasing; in fact I have been credibly informed, that the School-house itself, large though it is, is much too confined and must soon be enlarged; the bit of ground is too small and confined for even a gaol-yard.

2. *It is altogether unfitted,* from its situation, having the big School-house on the N.E. effectually blocking out the cooling sea-breezes of summer, and a very high hill at the back (N.W.) so that the sun at noon does not shine on it in midwinter! hence the confined spot will necessarily be exceedingly hot and close in the summer season, and cold and wet in the winter.

3. *It will consequently, be very unhealthy;* this unhealthiness will be largely increased through the prevailing summer winds, (almost invariably daily from the N.E.) carrying in a constant stream the stench from the dozen privies and urinals at the foot of the hill behind the school-house.

That a spacious healthy playground with its many requirements and belongings is greatly needed for the scholars of the Napier School is absolutely certain, and *must be had*: good open ground for cricket and football; room for a gymnasium house to be used in wet weather; proper alcove or shelter for their eating their little dinners, or luncheons, in, (seeing that many come from a distance,) instead of (as at the present) in the streets;—or on the low dirty steps under the porticos of the adjoining theatre with its filthy ribald scrawls and sentences, for them to con and decypher and imitate while eating;—or on the verandah of Ashton's Hotel;—for my part, I marvel at the many parents of those children so putting-up quietly with this great want for so long a time.

How, then, would I propose to remedy, it?

Answer. By removing the School-house to a far more roomy and suitable site.

Hold on! Do not mention the expense and trouble,—it will have to be done sooner or later; *it must be done,* and the sooner it is done the bettor for all. Our children are worth far more than our Cash!—our Flocks and Herds and Crops!!—although I fear, with some, they are a kind of *Stock* that are overlooked or too lightly valued.

We see what the United Methodist Free Church have just done, removed their big chapel, (although, according to the old saying, "Three removes are as bad as a fire")—and we also find it seriously proposed to widen Emerson Street,—of course by removing all the buildings further back, and some of them are very large,—a much heavier and more costly job than the removing of the School-house.

Such a roomy and every-way suitable site is at hand:—(1) On a portion of the level and open 7 acre allotment called the "Town Hall-Reserve;" or (2) on part of the reclaimed land,—both being public property.

And I scarcely need observe, that the present occupied School sites in Clive Square would let well and so return a good rental.

And here I should state, that during the last 6 months of my holding the office of Inspector of Schools, I was officially requested by the first (or Interim) Education Board, to point out a suitable site in the Town of Napier for the public Schoolhouse, then shortly to be erected under the new Education Act. I did so; I performed that duty; and after going carefully over the whole town, and considering its map and the future wants of the rising town and generation, I pointed out in my official reply, a portion of the said large 7 acre "Town-hall Reserve" (no longer wanted for that purpose) as being the best, if not the only, place every way fitted for the new School and its required roomy and healthy play-grounds.

I may also further remark, that nothing that has ever been done in this town with public money has so greatly astonished me as the placing the School-house where it now stands—(including the prodigal waste of money thereby incurred in buying-out the occupiers !)—on a small confined corner spot in a central thoroughfare every way unfitted for the proper carrying-on of a big School in a large and busy and growing town with its very narrow streets. This serious evil however will be much more clearly seen and felt in years to come,—if it is allowed to continue.

And here I will both anticipate and answer a question, which will be sure to arise among many of our newly-settled townsmen,—namely, why did I not move in the matter before the schoolhouse was built under the direction of the second (or present) Education Board?—

1. Because such a decision was quickly moved and determined by the Education Board, (just as in many other things since) without due consideration.
2. Because had I written to that new Board any amount of letters on the subject they would not have been attended to, however correct and fitting my letter might be; and that because I (the late, and for many years the only Inspector of Schools) had written them; the well-known adverse personal influence being far too great.
3. Because they possessed my official letter on the subject, written only a few months before.
4. I could also give other reasons.

I believe I may truly say, that there is no other School in this whole extensive district that is so badly situated in this respect of site and of the want of a proper playground as this, the largest school of all and in the head town of Napier.

I see, however, the same short-sighted folly (as to site) acted on in other townships;— at Woodville, for example; where the school-house is actually built on a corner section opposite to the Post-Office, in what I suppose will become the busy and crowded part of the township! instead of in a more retired and suitable spot.

Having now brought this highly important matter plainly before the Public, (and in so doing have both faithfully informed them, and delivered my own conscience,) I do hope that both the Education Board and the Napier School Committee will heartily unite in reconsidering the same, for, from the very small size of the bit of ground and its utter unsuitableness,—notwithstanding a sure outlay of heavy expense at tinkering and patching,—it can only at best become a wretched make-shift, unworthy of the name of a play-ground to the large town school, and can never he satisfactory. Though late, it is not yet the eleventh hour, and the thing is both urgently wanted and *can be done.*

I have entitled my letter "Short-sightedness"; very likely some one hereafter, writing with a much more trenchant pen on the *fruits* of this evil tree (should it be allowed to remain), may give his communication some more strong more startling name: for—

"Evil is wrought by want of thought,
As well as want of heart."

> *I am, &c.,*
> WILLIAM COLENSO.

Napier, December 30, 1882.

❖ 1883 A WORD ABOUT TE KOOTI.
Hawke's Bay Herald 28 February.

"The de'il's no sae black as he's ca'd."

SIR,—I have been not a little grieved during the past fortnight, in seeing so many bitter remarks and wild statements made in both of our local papers concerning Te Kooti; written, too, by their respective Editors as well as by anonymous writers. I venture, therefore, once more into the arena (in the cause of Truth), hoping to be able to say—or, rather, to repeat—a few words upon this subject, which are highly needful to be borne in mind when considering or writing on the same, and which, I regret to say, seem to have been wholly forgotten.

Before, however, that I do so, I would make one remark, namely, that I should have come out earlier had the writers of those anonymous and malevolent letters, which have appeared in our Napier papers, possessed the common fairness, the manliness, of putting their names to their letters (if, indeed, more than one have really been engaged in writing them); for I have a great and a growing dislike to all cloaked anonymous writing, which too often is closely allied to the skulking cowardly shooting of a man from behind a bush with a crape mask over the face! and, as a rule, I never answer, never notice any such effusions when directed towards myself. Such seem to me to be un-English,—that is, against the good old rule of our forefathers, of "all fair and above board."

Possibly, however, at Election times (such being a kind of Saturnalia, Carnival, or Free-licence time,) anonymous letters may be permitted,—"for the fun of the thing," as the boys say; but, sir, there is a vast difference between Comedy and Tragedy; between writing for "fun" and laughter, and writing traducing "the powers that be" and howling for human blood!

And yet, though I have said, that had I certainly known the writers I should have come out earlier to meet them; still, I should not have done so if I found that they belonged to one or more of those 4 classes, viz.—

1. A venal hireling scribbler.
2. One who had largely suffered through loss of relatives, &c., in those sad times of war (long past).
3. One known to be full of hatred to the Maori people.
4. A new and ignorant hand, who really knew nothing about it.

For I have no time to waste on such persons.

To return: Some 12–14 years ago I wrote pretty fully on this subject, in several successive letters in the columns of your paper, (and for your kindness at that time in publishing them I would again publicly thank you). Fortunately, may I not say, it was a subject with which I was well acquainted from beginning to end; possibly more so than anyone at present here among us. My situation at that time and for some years previous (official and private,) was highly favorable to my obtaining the most correct information, and I was also in a position to consider and weigh events calmly, *ab initio*,—a highly needful qualification.

I purpose, therefore, on the present occasion, reproducing a portion of what then appeared in the columns of the HERALD; and I am the more inclined to do so from the very large number of settlers and townsmen who have since those years (1869–1871) joined us: Moreover, adding, (1) that what I then publicly wrote could not be gainsaid; and (2) what I then ventured to point out as the proper steps to be taken by the Government, I rejoice to have lived to see accomplished—though late Governments, as well as individuals, too often only learn through long (and it may be bitter) experience.

On the 9th April, 1869, I wrote thus.—[7]

A LETTER TO THE EDITOR OF THE "HAWKE'S BAY HERALD," ON THE KIND OF POLICY NECESSARY TO BE SHEWN TOWARDS THE MAORIS.

"A word in season."—*"A time to speak."*

"Can ye not discover the signs of the times?"

SIR,—In the HERALD of this day your article concludes with these words: "All that is wanted is CONFIDENCE, the want of which shuts out capital and labour, and impairs the energies of all." These are true words, and to them I heartily assent. But how is this confidence to be brought about? First, we must have *peace*; a true, substantial, firm, and lasting peace; from this will naturally spring confidence, and mark, *from this*

---

7   This letter is reproduced above. I.S.G.

only. To this end let us all (Governor, Government, and people) be determined to do two things: 1.—To do justice; 2.—To acknowledge error.

1. To do justice—prompt and quick, even and fair, common-sense, not tedious legal justice. "Do ye to others as ye would they should do to you" if you were in their place.

2. To acknowledge error, frankly and fully, wherever and whenever such has unfortunately been done; even to the retracing of our steps if needful and possible. (Let us not think too highly of ourselves as the "superior," unerring race, adorned with a thousand highflown superlatives of our own inventing! Let us remember the fable of the man sitting astride on a lion, and the lion's truthful remark. Let us endeavour to consider our political conduct in the light of God's truth,—to which scrutinising light it will have to be submitted.)

In order to do this:—

I. Let the war be immediately and everywhere stopped.

II. Let a truce be proclaimed.

III. Let an accredited messenger be sent from the Governor to the Maori King Tawhiao (not as king, but as the acknowledged head of many great tribes) to ask his aid towards making peace; and from him to the various Hauhau leaders; and a similar messenger to the chiefs of the principal friendly Maori tribes. The basis of such peace to be:—1. A general amnesty. 2. The return of all (nominally) confiscated lands, subject to certain conditions; such as, on the one side, all useful surveys and substantial improvements to be repaid; on the other, certain spots which it is necessary should be retained to be paid for. 3. Common freedom to all religions however absurd.

IV. Let Peace Commissioners be appointed from both sides, and a place be mutually arranged for their meeting.

V. Let powers be given to them to settle equitably our difficulties, and all great vexed questions.

If this is done, and the British Commissioners be fit and high-minded men—men of comprehensive views, and able to grasp the whole subject,—and if all the terms then and there agreed to be hereafter honestly and promptly carried out,—then, I venture to prophesy a firm and lasting peace to the Colony of New Zealand; otherwise you will not, cannot have it—at least for a long generation, a long and weary time of bloodshed and misery to both races: and, note well, that such a peace so obtained by conquering or destroying isolated tribes, whenever that may be, *will not be lasting.*

I have long entertained those views; I now openly avow them. I know, in doing so, I shall be assailed by the unthinking, with—

1. What of the murders, atrocities, massacres, and cannibalism?

2. What of the present numerous semi-military bands?

3. What of the expense and loss?

4. What of our British name and reputation?

I reply, to the first question—Who began the war with the "Hauhaus?" Who unjustly treated them—men, women, and children—by illegal wholesale banishment without trial? Who, on those Chatham Island "prisoners" returning to their own lands, in a most creditable, and gallant, and peaceful manner, foolishly and insanely, and without authority, attempted to capture and destroy them! instead of bringing them bread and water, and giving them the right hand and welcoming them back? Who carried on the war against them *in Maori fashion?* Quietly mark this, and note—they have (*for the first time with us*) also carried on the war against us and our Maori allies in Maori fashion, which we call murder, massacre, and atrocities (and so deceive ourselves, as if such were really different from our own "civilised" mode of warfare)! but hitherto we have only begun to know what it is; and note well, I beg, that to the present time hunted "Hauhaus" have not retaliated upon a single European living quietly on lands fairly purchased or leased. We have already killed something like seven or eight to one; besides inflicting irretrievable loss and evil. Moreover, fanatical outbreaks and rebellious *emeutes*, everywhere occurring in this world's sad history, are never rigorously revenged.

To the second question, I reply—The sooner they are disbanded the better for the colony.

To the third—Bear it; it can be borne to restore peace and confidence; it is by far the better, the easier, and the cheaper load.

To the fourth—It will gain additional lustre, which ten years war and eventual success will never bring it. Our Maori foe cannot, will not reflect tauntingly upon it, as we have driven them from all their strongholds, and killed seven or eight to one.

Now just consider, how much of that I then ventured to point out (and for which I was then so inconsiderately laughed at by not a few,) how much of that has only recently been accomplished!

Again, in 1871, (on the occasion of the execution here of Kereopa,) I wrote:[8]

Perhaps in no one thing has our Government lost influence with the Maoris more during the last few years than in this—their perpetual hunting and slaying of the helpless ones in the interior under the miserable subterfuge of pursuing Te Kooti! We, the early missionaries to this people, had the utmost difficulty in bringing the native tribes to leave off their seeking recompense for offences in this kind of way—by armed murdering prowling bands. Eventually, however, Christianity triumphed, and it was put down everywhere. Now, however, the Government has revived it, and they, I fear, will bye-and-bye find out their very serious error. But their doing so has caused the natives to think and talk and brood over their wrongs more than ever. Look, for a moment, at that last sad case (one of many similar ones,) reported in your paper a few weeks ago: of the murderous band of mercenary bloodhounds surrounding a small village by night, and shooting down suddenly and unexpectedly 6 unoffending natives (3 men

---

8   These passages are taken from Colenso's 'Fiat justitia' published in the *Hawke's Bay Herald* and republished in 1871 as a booklet. See *Colenso's published papers 1*, forthcoming. I.S.G.

and 3 women) and wounding others! Were these British subjects? No one *here* lamented them; no Christian female settler even said, How shocking! But, had such a deed been done by the Prussians when overrunning France, all England would have rung with the atrocity, and our Napier papers would have copied it—but these, alas! were Hauhaus!

Our Premier, the Hon. Mr. Fox, on the 7th ult., in the House of Representatives, moved an address to the Queen respecting the melancholy death of Bishop Patteson, which address concludes in these words:—"And we pray that your Majesty may long live as the protector of the weak and defenceless in every part of the world."—To which good words I respond heartily, Amen. But, "Charity begins at home;" and our Premier might have thought of those wretched "weak and defenceless" Maories in the mountains of New Zealand, so long harassed and hunted and killed by the mercenaries of the Government. There was a time when he could speak eloquently in their defence, as "men of like passions with ourselves." As it is, such can only remind one of what Dickens so forcibly tells us of Mrs. Jellyby and her telescopic philanthropy for educating the African children of Borrioboola-Gha, while her own family around her were utterly without it!

Why it is, that the ministers of our various Christian churches have not long ago stood up unitedly in the defence of the oppressed, I cannot divine. In rude ancient times, the bishops, abbots, priors, priests, and presbyters, were always found in the van, loudly denouncing all such ill-usage, even when made by their own nobles and kings. But then the clergy led and tended and taught their flocks, being independent of them; now, alas! they follow in the ruck, and preach to please their sleepy fat sheep (as we have seen in the clergy of the American slave-holding States,) being wholly dependent on them.

On July 27th the late Dr. Selwyn, then Bishop of Lichfield, spoke thus on the same subject, in his place in the House of Lords. (This was also republished by you in the HERALD.)

In the House of Lords on July 27, the affairs of New Zealand were brought under discussion:—

Earl GRANVILLE trusted that the difficulties of the Colony, and the irritation in it, would only be temporary, and that *the Colonial Government* would learn the real nature of the responsibility which it had assumed and *adopt those measures of conciliation towards the natives which would put an end to the state of brigandage* rather than war which prevailed in it.

The Bishop of LICHFIELD thought he should be wanting in his duty towards the colonists of New Zealand, as well as towards the natives of that country, if he were not to address a few words to their lordships on the present occasion.... Every New Zealander desired to be a faithful subject of Her Majesty until that unfortunate idea of the Queen's right to the pre-emption of land took the precedence over every other idea, and the whole notion of government was lost in the simple question of in what manner and by what quickest possible means the property of the soil in New Zealand should be transferred from the natives to the Crown. Their great mistake in New Zealand had been their asserting from the beginning a sovereignty over a country which they could not govern. They had repeated all the errors committed in Ireland centuries ago, and had punished crime by the confiscation of land. Large tracts had been taken from the natives, and so-called military settlers were placed in them to defend the district. On one occasion he knew that a dealer came to these settlements and bought up the land of those supposed defenders of the country, who went away leaving the place undefended, and then a number of peaceful settlers came instead of those military men and scattered themselves over the district, and although they were exposed to every kind of danger, they were never injured because they were living in the King's country. In other parts, indeed, where peculiarly exasperating circumstances had occurred the case had been different. The men who had done all the mischief on the east coast and at Poverty Bay were men who had been carried off as prisoners to the Chatham Islands [and that without any trial, or investigation whatsoever, W.C.] where they were told that if they conducted themselves well at the end of two years they would be set at liberty. There they behaved in the most exemplary manner, but at the expiration of the two years they were informed that they were not to be set at liberty, whereupon a look of despair came over them, as if every hope they had of life were cut off. They had been placed on lonely and remote islands, they had looked forward to the day of their emancipation, and with that view they had behaved exceedingly well. But when they saw no hope left to them, was it surprising that they took matters into their own hands and escaped? Those men went back into their own country, where they were followed up by a military force, driven into the woods, their places stormed, and their houses burnt. The most unwise thing of all was that, in spite of warning, the military officers who had followed up those escaped prisoners went and settled down on the land which had just been taken from them. The New Zealanders would not be like the Scotch, the Irish, or the Welsh, if under such circumstances they had not resisted these excursions…. There were a few persons among the settlers, as there were also a few among the New Zealanders, who would at times rush into violence but the great majority of the colonists lived in peace and harmony with their native fellow-subjects, and their good will was in a great degree reciprocated by the natives."

And this is the ground on which I again take my stand; not that kindly brought forward yesterday in your paper by "Imprimatur," of acting Christianly towards Te Kooti,—high and correct and praiseworthy though that be; but one that is still much higher, older, and universal, viz. that of JUSTICE; strict Justice (even as I had chosen for a title to my pamphlet—"*Fiat Justitia*,"—let Justice be done). Let us learn, though late, to act justly in this matter; bear in mind Bishop Selwyn's noble and truthful words; "bury the hatchet" and, as loyal peace-loving people, support the Government. I, for one, (and there are many with me,) heartily thank the newly-arrived Governor and the Native Minister Mr. Bryce for what they have done in the matter of the General Amnesty—*excluding no one*. And I deem this last political act of Mr. Bryce, of so publicly so freely so genuinely pardoning the unfortunate the wronged Te Kooti, as the very best of all his public political acts known to me.

"There's a heart that leaps, with a burning glow,
The wronged and the weak to defend,
And strikes 'as soon for a trampled foe,'
As it does for a soul-bound friend.—
—'Tis a rich rough gem, deny it who can;
And this is the heart of an Englishman."

I am, &c.,

WILLIAM COLENSO.

P.S.—The whole of the foregoing extracts, with a great deal more of authentic official high and interesting matter bearing on this subject, was also published by me at that time in a closely-printed pamphlet (alluded to above) of 23 pages; and as there seems to be a large amount of ignorance abroad, respecting the doings of those unhappy days,—and as there may be many among us who would like to know more of what really took place,—I shall send 3 copies of the said pamphlet to the Reading-room in the Athenæum, and 3 copies to the Working-men's Club—it will well repay perusal.

—*W.C.*

Napier, February 26, 1883.

❖ **1883 "MUCH ADO ABOUT NOTHING!"**
Hawke's Bay Herald 14 March.

SIR,—I have twice read the short letter of "F.R.H.S." in your paper of this morning; and the above well-known old and plain motto is just my conclusion upon it: although, I confess, I had nearly gone a step further, and adopted instead, that of the mountain in labor and the *ridiculous mouse!*—as being still more suitable.

But who is it, in particular, that "F.B.H.S." labors to "show up," or to "let down?" Is it you, Mr. Editor, for your blundering want of botanical knowledge? (such being, as he says, "above or below your comprehension!"). Or is it the kind-hearted and liberal Mr. Tiffen? or his obliging hard-working gardener?—or the judges at the late Horticultural Exhibition? or the committee of the young ("newly-fledged") society? Not knowing the anonymous writer, it is hard for me to say who it is that he seems to have such a "down upon!" Possibly it is the whole lot of you mentioned above. Be this as it may, two things seem pretty clear:—1. that he is no true "Botanist,"—no lover of flowers for their own sake; and—2., no real well-wisher to our young Horticultural Society, and to the many exhibitors and zealous coworkers at the late show.

So much for the *animus* (or feelings and aim) of "F.R.H.S." Now, then, for his big-little show of botanical learning!

1. As to the correct generic name of the lovely prize plant shown, *Fittonia*—he says, that this is not its proper name, but that it is *Gymnostachyum*—I will, however, venture to tell him that I think he is wrong in so saying; for I have Veitch's catalogue before me, in which, while *both* the names of *Gymnostachyium* and *Fittonia* are entered in it as belonging to *one* plant (the former name merely given as indicating an error,) we are informed, that for *Gymnostachyium* we must look to *Fittonia*.

2. As to his correction of a mere common error of the press—and that, too, a single letter! and one which by its omission, makes no difference whatever in the reading—either of grammar or meaning. [Sometimes, however, both these occur, through the want, or addition, of a single letter, and then it is awkward.] "F.R.H.S." corrects your "*gracilium*" to "*gracilimum*," and takes you to task for so blunderingly and ignorantly leaving out the first *m;*—but he himself has, in his attempt at correcting you, done the same, or worse, himself, for he has omitted an *l.*—the word should be *gracillimum*. Now were I inclined to follow "F.R.H.S.'s" example, and to carp at a wrong letter and to charge it home to him, I might notice his (or your) having here in this very sentence—intend*i*d for intended.

3. Again he pitches into you for another mere typographical error; one, also, that (as before) causes no difference in either the grammar or meaning,—that is, it cannot though altered be taken for another word. "F.R.H.S." corrects your ("*rubonervia*" to "*rubronerva*;" but should it not have correctly been *rubrinervis?*—("This to thy right eye, Philip!")

And now Mr. "F.H.R.S.," I take my leave of you; ta, ta! Don't jib, and be sulky. And please remember, that if you should be tempted by Mephistopheles (or something nearer) to come out again after this fashion of yours against our "newly-fledged" Horticultural Society, (for it is not fair to ill-use a wee toddling bairnie,) remember that this Old Man is here on the watch;—and so you had better think twice, and perhaps give him a wide berth.—I am, &c.,

WILLIAM COLENSO.

Napier, March 12, 1883.

P.S.—*Tuesday Morning*, 13th.—I had written my letter late last night; and now I find in your paper of this morning that Mr. Tiffen had very properly written a letter in reply to "F.H.S." Of course, had I known of his going to do so I should not have troubled you, but as there are a few extra points in mine not touched on by Mr. Tiffen, I shall still send it to you.—*W.C.*

❖ 1883 DR. COLENSO, THE LATE BISHOP OF NATAL.
Hawke's Bay Herald 23 June.

"*If Ongar can hide the sun from us with a blanket, or put the moon in his pocket, we will pay him tribute for light.*" —Shaksp. *Cymbeline.*

SIR,—As the nearest living collateral relative of Dr. Colenso, whose recent death has been announced by you in your paper this morning, (which, I may be allowed to observe, has taken me by surprise, not having heard from my family of his having been ailing,—and his also being so remarkably hale and healthy,)—perhaps you will permit me to add a few lines to what you kindly gave us this morning from *Men of the Time*, concerning the late Bishop's works, labors, and persecutions.

The compiler of that brief biographical memoir, while stating, that,—"During the Bishop's stay in England (in 1874) he was prohibited from preaching in their respective dioceses by the Bishops of Oxford, Lincoln, and London;" has omitted to remark, that, notwithstanding those "prohibitions," Dr. Colenso did preach in all those dioceses, as well as in others.

He preached in London, at Westminster Abbey; in Oxford, at the Church of Balliol College; and, notably, at Claybrook in Leicestershire (adjoining to Wickliffe's famed Rectory of Luttorworth,) where—having been invited by the vicar to preach in his church, and subsequently indecently (though ecclesiastically) personally opposed on the Sunday morning in that Church by the Bishop of Peterborough,—Dr. Colenso preached standing on a table on the village green, the school-room whence they had adjourned not being large enough, to a large and most attentive audience; in this respect following the noble example of John Wesley, a century before, in the neighboring county of Yorkshire.

"And now, for this man, too, life's toil is over;
His words are all said out, his deeds are done;
For this man, too, there comes a rest, however
Unquiet passed his time beneath the sun.

  *   *   *   *   *

"Think you, that God loves our tame levelled acres
More than the proud head of some Heaven-kissed hill?
Man's straight-dug ditch more than His own free river,
That wanders, He regarding, where it will?

Enough! High words abate no jot or tittle
Of what, while man still lasts, shall still be true;
Heaven's great ones must be slandered by Earth's little,
And God makes no ado."

           —*Yours, &c.,*
           W. COLENSO.

Napier, June 22, 1883.

❖ 1883 MR. COLENSO AND THE AUCKLAND WEEKLY NEWS.
Daily Telegraph 13 July.

SIR,—Will you kindly find room in your columns for the accompanying letter (written by me 3 weeks back to the Editor of the Auckland Weekly News; but which, it seems, he will not do me the scant justice of publishing in his paper,—or noticing in any kind of way.

I should not greatly care to trouble you in this matter, were it not, (1) that the Auckland Weekly News has several subscribers here in this District, (indeed, one of them has kindly brought the discourteous sentence complained of to my notice,) and, (2) that this is not the first unjust remark of the kind that has appeared in that news paper respecting my papers published in the annual volumes of the "Transactions, N.Z. Institute"; neither is this my first letter of complaint to the Editor of that paper of such matters,—but all, apparently, alike written by me in vain. As an old original subscriber to the Auckland Weekly News,—one who, when in 1863 as a member of the

House, gladly assisted in launching the craft,—the treatment I have received from its Editor is, to say the least of it, both unbusinesslike and ungenerous.—

I am, &c., WILLIAM COLENSO.

Napier, July 13, 1883.

[To the Editor of the "Auckland Weekly News," Auckland.]

SIR,—In a review of the *Transactions N.Z. Institute*, vol. XV., given in your paper of June 16th., you have the following sentence respecting my 3 Botanical papers published in that work:—

"W. Colenso contributes lengthy descriptions of supposed new ferns and flowering plants, some of which have been described by other authors."

Of course, it is not to be expected that the Editor of a paper, or the Reviewer of such a scientific work as this should be fully acquainted with the technicalities it contains; but this statement of yours is far too sweeping to be quietly passed over. Having, perhaps, the largest Botanical library of any private person in the colony,—time at my command,—good health,—love and zeal in the pursuit of my favourite science,— and, possibly, some knowledge of our Botany; I will thank you to point out *those plants*, (discovered and lately described by me in the said volume of "Transactions,") *which*, you say, *"have been described by other authors."* For their sake, as well as my own, I make this request, that I may be enabled to make them full reparation.—Yours truly,

WILLIAM COLENSO.

Napier, June 22, 1883.

§ 1883 EDITORIAL.
Waikato Times and Thames Valley Gazette 15 September.

We are glad to see, *Nature* says, that there is at last some prospect of the immediate publication of Mr. W. Colenso's Maori-English Lexicon, which was submitted to the New Zealand Government nearly eight years ago. A specimen sheet of twenty folio pages has recently been printed and presented to both Houses of the General Assembly by command of the executive authorities. From this specimen it is evident that the work is of an encyclopaedic character, embodying a vast amount of information collected from original sources on the languages, ethnology, traditions, religions, habits, and customs of the Polynesian races. The plan is at once simple and comprehensive. The various meanings of each word are first given in large type, and each meaning is then illustrated by one or more passage in small type from the native poems, myths, legends, proverbs and colloquial usage. Thus nearly four pages are devoted to the different significations and grammatical applications of the single word *a*, which plays such an important part in all the Polynesian dialects. To the particle *atu* as many as thirty distinct meanings are assigned, and these meanings are illustrated by no less than seventy-two quotations from the various sources above indicated. In some cases the quotations are Englished, and it would certainly be satisfactory if this could be done uniformly. In the English-Maori part the same plan is adhered to, only here quotations illustrating the different senses of the English words are omitted as unnecessary. Should the work be carried out on these lines it will enable the student to wait somewhat more patiently for the appearance of Mr. Whitnee's long-promised Comparative Dictionary of the Polynesian Languages.

§ 1883 THE KNIFE GRINDERS' SOCIETY.
Hawke's Bay Herald 10 October.

[Reported by the indefatigable secretary.]

I have noticed that of late you have not had any Report of the Proceedings of this Society,—a fact that I am quite sure your Readers, one and all, must have much deplored. I have also noticed,—(and have done so with much pain,)—that such reports as you have had have not been so faithful as if I had written them. I have, therefore, determined to do violence to my modesty and furnish the reports myself. I will not, however, stoop to the subterfuge (for so I call it,) of writing of myself in the third person;—that is, saying, "The Secretary read this," or "The Secretary did that." No, that may do for ordinary scribblers; but such a man as I am can well afford to boldly use the personal pronoun "I;"—*my* Efforts in preparing the renowned *Moresco Lexicon* would alone justify such a course. Then, again, the attitude I have always taken in regard to the interesting Race, the Morescoes,—not alone in reference to their language; but, also, their traditions, their character, and their many lovable qualities—has raised me so much above the common herd as to entitle me to ignore those puerile considerations which restrain people from asserting themselves in Public print, and I can say plainly *Ego hoc feci*.—(By the bye, it has always seemed to me that the Capital letter *I* does not sufficiently represent its important signification. Only one letter of the Alphabet to represent the Individual speaking? Surely that is not enough! In Latin they have three. And how much better it sounds!)

But to proceed.—The Knifegrinders held their Ordinary Meeting on Monday night. There was not, I regret to say, the usual crowd of Members present, and still more to my regret the Chief Knifegrinder was absent, and consequently the Chair was occupied by the Vice-Chief. It is of course, under any circumstances, a gratification to me to read, or speak, or lecture to an audience however small, but the gratification is much enhanced when there is a goodly Assemblage, and to observe, as I pause and look smilingly around me, the admiring faces of my auditors,—particularly the ladies, who, I assure you, veritably simmer with delight at the words of wisdom which fall from my lips. In consequence of my pleasure in this respect having been limited on Monday night, it was decided to have another Meeting in November;—it being understood by all the Members that the *principal*, if not the *only* object of the establishment of the Society is that of ministering to the admiration of my undoubted Talents and Great Acquirements, more especially in the Art of Knifegrinding.

The Lecture with which I favored the Meeting on Monday night was certainly long, but, as usual, it was *highly interesting*, and it was listened to from beginning to end with *breathless attention*! It related, chiefly, to the changes which take place in the Material out of which Knives are composed; and to the differences between the various blades in use in the progressive ages of the Globe.

The better to illustrate the Lecture I set the Knifegrinding wheel going, and turned out some beautiful *Specimens* for the delectation of the Meeting.

A vote of thanks, in which I joined heartily myself, was unanimously accorded to me at the conclusion of my Lecture.

Then came the most delightful part of the proceedings, and which I had purposely kept in store till the last, so that I might go home brimful with pleasure at having Myself admired. It had happened that only a few days before I had borrowed from the Vice-Chief Knifegrinder a copy of the *Toledo Blade*, published in Germany, and in it I found an article speaking in highly commendatory terms of the *Moresco Lexicon*, written by me (the Indefatigable Secretary), of which so much was heard formerly—specimens of the same having reached London and Germany. "This," I said, "is what this great serial says about ME!!" I then laid on the table two copies of my great Work, for the enrichment of the Society's Library. There was a general buzz of admiration, which sounded oh! so sweetly in my Ears that in the exuberance of my feelings I sat down in the Vice-Chief's lap, and only found out my mistake when he gently allowed me to slide down on the floor.

§ 1883 COMPENSATION COURT.
Hawke's Bay Herald 30 November.
Thursday, November 29. (Before his Honor the Chief Justice, and Messrs E. Lyndon and T.R. Hackett, Assessors.) W. COLENSO V. MINISTER FOR PUBLIC WORKS. This was a case brought under the provisions of the Public Works Acts to recover compensation for alleged damages accruing to plaintiff through the closing of certain roads required for railway purpose. The amount sought to be recovered was £396. Mr. M'Lean appeared for plaintiff, and Mr. Cotterill for respondent....

The assessors retired to consider the question of damages, and after an absence of over an hour returned with an assessment of £225 should his Honor rule that no benefit had accrued to plaintiff by the construction of the railway, and £125 should the ruling be that benefit had accrued....

❖ 1884 SCINDE ISLAND.
Hawke's Bay Herald 25 January.
SIR,—In your leader this morning you state, in writing of Scinde Island (Napier),—"It is said that Captain Cook sailed round the Island,"—and then, as usual, you proceed to draw certain deductions therefrom. May I ask of you,—By whom has this been said? I never before heard it. Were it not that you were writing on a very serious

subject, I would not trouble you with this question; looking on the statement as the veriest moonshine! But as, of late, so much nonsense has appeared in both of our Papers,—concerning our Bay and waters, rivers and travelling shingle, Cape and harbour and breakwater,—and all, more or less, draperied in the costume of truth and facts,—I have deemed it proper to write you this short letter lest that statement of yours uncontradicted should also be added to the multifarious heap I have alluded to, and in time to come be brought forward to do mischief.—I am, &c.,

   W. COLENSO.

Napier, January 24, 1884.

[It is a common belief that Captain Cook sailed round the island, and we are surprised that Mr. Colenso has not before heard it. We can give no authority except report for the statement, and therefore we used the qualifying expression, "It is said."—Ed. *H.B.H.*]

§ 1884 A KNIFEGRINDER'S LAMENT.

Hawke's Bay Herald 6 February.

SIR,—You will doubtless be grieved,—as I know all the People in Hawke's Bay will,—to learn that I have resigned the secretaryship of the Hawke's Bay Branch of the Knifegrinders' Society. I know that it will be a serious blow to the Society;—but it was the only means I had of showing my indignation at the treatment I had received from the Man who works the Wheel of the Head Society at Wellington—for the last ten years I have been the Life and Soul of the Society; and but for Me it is very doubtful whether the Hawke's Bay Branch would have contributed its quota, to the Parent Society, of scientific investigations into the art and mysteries of Knifegrinding. The difficulty of finding a worthy successor to Me was thoroughly recognised at the Annual Meeting yesterday, when I gave in my resignation,—and the Members went down on their knees, imploring me to retain the Office. But I was inexorable! I told them they could not do without me;—but I stuck to my resolve. And could I do otherwise? The Man at the Wheel at Wellington had had from Me no less than eighteen letters;—and beautiful, long letters they were, too,—fully ornamented with Capitals, colons, and semicolons, notes of exclamation and interrogation, dashes and parentheses;—And yet these eighteen epistles only evoked two official communications!! Could it be believed?—Then, as if that were not enough, three of my best ground Knives were rejected, (though no one living could have produced such models of Knife-grindery).—It was, in fact, presumption to reject those knives. However, I will not dilate on the subject;—it is too humiliating. I have my revenge, though;—I know there is no one in Hawke's Bay possessing My qualifications, and my retirement leaves the Society poor indeed!—I am, &c.,

   THE INDEFATIGABLE.

February 5, 1884.

❖ 1884 STAMFORD-STREET FILES.

Hawke's Bay Herald 23 February.

Sir,—In your paper of to-day you have a sub-leader on Stamford Street, and you begin it thus:—

"There seems to be some confusion in the public mind relative to the request made to the Borough Council to sell part of Stamford Street to Mr. Colenso and to Mr. Robjohns, who have properties abutting on that part of Stamford Street they wish to purchase"—winding it up by saying, our action in this matter "is a little disingenuous."

Now, why not have told the whole plain and simple truth? and so have cleared the "confusion" (if such there be) "from the public mind." You might have done so in a few words. As, however, you have not done so, but rather done all that you can to increase that confusion; I will now say a little thereon, and as briefly as possible.

1. "Stamford Street," as it now is, is merely a short blind alley between 2 town sections, only 2½ chains long, and leading nowhere.

2. Mr. Robjohns and myself are the sole owners of those 2 sections, and of course the only persons interested in that *cul-de-sac*, or bit of street.

3. I am informed, that, by law, we are the persons who have the right of purchasing it under all the circumstances from the Corporation.

4. If this bit, or end, of what was once Stamford Street, could be used by us (or by anyone) as a way into the adjoining railway station, we would not think of buying it: it would be madness to do so.

5. For, as the law now is, to go through this bit of street on to the Railway Station, for any purpose, subjects the trespasser to £10 fine.

6. And seeing there are so many Railway lines laid down there close together, and also the fixed determination of the Government not to alter them, (and I, though a loser hereby, think they are right on behalf of the public,) I believe that, in writing my letter to the Borough Council, I chose that which was best for the public good: viz., to put a few hundred pounds into the public chest, rather than to draw therefrom for private advantage.

So much for the bare facts.

Now supposing (on the other hand,) I had sent in a letter to the Borough Council, respecting this end remaining of Stamford Street, asking for it to be formed and made, would you not be one of the first to charge me (or, Mr. Robjohns and myself,) with seeking to improve the way into our own private properties at public expense? I think you would, in your usual happy manner! on anything respecting Mr. Colenso.

Councillor M'Dougall's remark in the Council on this occasion (as reported) was correct, being the plain common-sense view (apart from the *interested* twistings of Councillor Neal, who has land there on t'other side.—where, he says, the railway goods shed and stores should have been, and he still hopes shall be!) Cr. M'Dougall said,—"Either sell them the land, or make the street." Of course, if the Council should not now grant the prayer of my second letter, I shall be driven to apply for the making of Stamford Street.

You, also, kindly insinuate (in your usual happy manner), that the petition to Mr. Maxwell asking him not to open the end of Stamford Street, was "got up by Mr. Colenso" (in part, at least). May I tell you, that I knew nothing of it, never even once heard of it. On the contrary, I stated in Court on oath, that I would rather than £500 that Stamford Street had been kept open: and this I still say.

Before I close I would further observe, that I have thought I had lost quite enough in the deterioration of my properties on Wellesley Road and Stamford Street (myself and tenants), through the *laches* or supineness of our Borough Council— or, of some one ("some one has erred"), as shown from official documents in the late Compensation Court held here in connection with this very matter. Moreover, (having mentioned the Compensation Court), I may inform the public, that the very compensation for loss on this same property lately awarded me in equity by the Chief Justice, and published by you in your paper, is now *refused* me by the Government! who call on me to further prove my legal right to be paid it before the Court of Appeal at Wellington!! Perhaps this new move *you* may also think right. —I am, &c.,

WILLIAM COLENSO.

February 22, 1884.

❖ **1884 A LAST WORD ON STAMFORD-STREET.**
Hawke's Bay Herald 10 March.

SIR,—With your permission I would yet say a little more on Stamford-street. I ought to have inserted it in my former letter, to make that complete, for I had it in mind at the time, but I feared to make my letter too long for your space. And, as I view it, it affects the public as much as myself, if not more so; and therefore I wish to make it known for timely and due consideration.

In my letter (of February 22), I said,—quoting Cr. M'Dougall's words,—that "the Borough Council should either sell us the bit of street end, or form it, and make it;" and it is to this latter proposal (supposing it should be urged,) that I wish to offer a few remarks.

I dare say, that many of my countrymen among your readers will recollect similar holes or blind lanes and alleys at Home in the towns where they formerly resided, especially if those towns were old ones; and also what a nuisance many of them were made. And I have been from time to time informed (by papers and letters from Home), that since the adoption of stringent sanitary measures, all such places have been as far as possible shut up. Besides, there is yet another nuisance connected with them, which the police at Home know something about, namely,—that such dark blind holes in streets are commonly the lurking places of thieves and vagrants, and other disorderlies. I think this will be allowed to be a fair picture, not over-drawn or coloured, of many such spots at Home.

But here in Napier such blind alleys may become much worse! especially in such a place as our Southern Suburb—Wellesley Road, with houses only on its Northern side,—and that for several plain reasons;—from the fact of our Napier houses and fences being almost wholly constructed of wood;—from the growing larrikin and vagrant elements;—and from the exposed situation of that end of Stamford Street opening into Wellesley Road, and lying wholly open to the whole force of the southerly gales blowing over the inner sea,—there being no building sites, nor even a fence, on the opposite side of the said Road washed by the sea! or likely to be for some generations.

Hence I am driven to conclude, that if that short end of Stamford Street should be retained open and formed and made—leading as it does nowhere! then it will become a kind of catch pool for all manner of filth (which I need not describe); and what is worse (please mark this!) a place for all light stray waifs from the sea and long beach below,—as straw, and shavings, and grasses and rushes, raupo from the neighboring swamp to accumulate; blown thither by the strong winds sweeping along the strait close fences of Wellesley Road, and then into the open *depôt*—or public receptacle for rubbish! Which hole, convenient corner, or Noman's-land,—if not actually made a place of resort for vagrants and other disorderlies,—is sure to become one for match kindling and pipe lighting in windy weather, by day and by night, and probably for the beginning of a serious fire. For should a fire ever happen there at a time when the strong southerly wind is blowing, with those large wooden buildings, and inflammable stores, and so much loose timber in the yard around, it would be a great one, and possibly ruinous to the adjoining railway station. So much for the public good.

As for myself, I think I may be permitted to say, (as all Napier knows the loss I have already incurred—in the "corner" section at least—by the taking away and the stopping of Stamford Street,) that if the Borough Council should decide on keeping that bit, or end, of Stamford Street open, it will be another means of lowering the value of that unfortunate corner section of mine (331), for the reasons I have above adduced. On the other hand, one even and continuous line of close fence, and without any unsightly public gaps or breaks, on the N. side of Wellesley Road, would not only be a means of increasing the value of property there, and of making that road much more respectable in appearance, but would also prove to be of great security and protection from fire, &c., &c.,—as well, perhaps, as a reasonable means towards the prevention of any increase of insurance rates in that quarter of the Borough.—I am, &c.,

WILLIAM COLENSO.

Napier, March 8, 1884.

§ 1884 EDITORIAL.
Feilding Star 15 March.

It will be necessary, during the examination into the working of the Civil Service which is now taking place for the Commission to make a thorough inquisition into the working of the Wellington Museum. It is notorious that all correspondence addressed to the Curator and other officers of that Institution is shamefully treated.

Important communications demanding immediate reply are treated with contempt or subjected to utter neglect. We notice, that Mr. Colenso has discontinued his connection therewith on account of his being unable to elicit replies to his letters.

❖ 1884 STAMFORD-STREET.
Hawke's Bay Herald 11 April.

SIR,—In a sub-article in your paper of this morning you again repeat, aud that more strongly and offensively than before, your old charge against me about Stamford-street. You say—"This is the petition got up by Mr. Colenso, in aid of his private scheme for securing part of Stamford-street for himself."

Now I had fully replied in your paper of Feb. 23 to your first statement of this kind, wholly denying that I had anything to do with that petition; affirming "that I knew nothing of it, never even once heard of it," and so I say now. And at that same time Mr. Robjohns did the same, in a letter in your columns, and that without seeing me. Why then do you again bring forward this charge against me? Adding thereto what is just as false, namely,—that I have a "private scheme for securing part of Stamford street for myself," So far as I know I have no "private scheme." The little that I have done or said, I have done openly and publicly, both in your paper (with your permission), and in my two short letters to the Municipal Council.

Why then, I ask, do you reiterate this falsity? which I have so plainly and fully denied. If you (alone) will not believe what I have said, act the manly part and show your proofs, your authority, in support of your repeated assertions; or, failing to do so, acknowledge your error, and cease foolishly throwing editorial mud—that is unworthy of your paper.—I am, &c.,

WM. COLENSO.

Napier, April 18, 1884.

❖ 1884 MR. COLENSO AND NEBUCHADNEZZAR.
Daily Telegraph 8 May.

SIR,—Your paper of Saturday last has just reached me here, and I notice in the "Supplement" a text taken from the book of "Daniel" by Rev. J. J. Lewis respecting the great Assyrian monarch Nebuchadnezzar, and his supposed worship of "the King of heaven" as the one true God. Curiously enough, it was only yesterday that I was reading in a late number of the London Times, (having brought my file with me for quiet reading,) a most interesting account of the discovery of two inscriptions of King Nebuchadnezzar at Mount Lebanon; communicated to that journal by the learned Assyriologist M. Ch. Clermont-Ganneau. He says:—

"Those two large unknown inscriptions of Nebuchadnezzar, were found on Lebanon by M. Pognon, Assistant-Consul of the French Republic at Beyrout. . . These texts are engraved on the rock, in the Wady-Brissa, one of the wildest valleys on the eastern slope of Lebanon, near the Orontes. They measure about 5 metres

50 in breadth by 2 metres 80 in height. They are written, the one in archaic and the other in cursive cuneiform characters, forming a whole of 19 columns ... The two inscriptions each contain a different text. They commence by the titles of Nebuchadnezzar:—"Nebuchadnezzar, King of Babylon, the illustrious Pastor, the servant of Merodak the great Lord, his Creator, and of Nebo his illustrious son, whom his Royalty loves."

"M. Pognon" (an accomplished Oriental Scholar) "is of opinion, that these texts mark the site of a timberyard, whore trees were cut to be sent to Babylon. The name of Lebanon is repeated several times in mutilated sentences, where it is a question as to the wood employed in Nebuchadnezzar's buildings. ... The supposition of M. Pognon on the general purport of these two texts becomes very probable if one compares it with certain facts more or less known. We are aware, from the other inscriptions of Nebuchadnezzar which have reached us, that the great King of Babylon employed a considerable quantity of wood for his sumptuous building of temples and palaces. In one of these inscriptions, preserved in the British Museum, he even says expressly "that he has employed for the woodwork of the Chamber of Oracles the largest of the trees which he has had conveyed from Mount Lebanon."—

The whole of the description is very interesting, and is long. I have thought that the above extract from this communication of an historical fact respecting Nebuchadnezzar, (mere outline though it be,) worthy of sending to you for your readers just now. I note that Mr. Lewis takes for a real historical truth (!) the text he has quoted, together with all its strange apparel and circumstances; on this assumption, however, (with its diffuse superstructure,) I, at present, make no remark.—I am, &c.,

WILLIAM COLENSO.

Matamau, "70-mile-Bush,"
May 6, 1884.

❖ 1884 MR. COLENSO ON BUSH LICENSES.
Hawke's Bay Herald 10 June.

SIR—I am much pleased in reading your reasonable and fitting article on "Bush Licenses" in this morning's Paper; and hope what you have therein said may prove to be of timely service. Having myself had no small experience during the last 3–4 years, through boarding and lodging at various times at some of those very Licensed Houses that are now proposed to be closed, (and an ounce of fact being worth more than a pound of theory,) I cannot fairly refrain from saying a few words on the subject.

It is well-known that I occasionally visit the distant woods (70-mile-Bush), and spend some considerable time there. My sole objects in doing so, are—good health, to please myself, and (perhaps I may be allowed to say) to aid Science,—in seeking after new plants and animals, and in obtaining specimens of them and of others for the Royal Botanical Gardens and Museum, Kew, London. Now this pleasure and duty I should not be able to have were it not for those Licensed Houses.—

And here I would particularly mention the Central Hotel at Matamau,—in the very midst of 70-mile-Bush. At this Hotel I have often staid,—On some occasions a month at a time (owing to wet weather), on others a fortnight, or a week; and that, too, under both Landlords,—the first one Mr. Towers, and the present one Mr. Baddeley; I am a temperance man myself (not a sham one—under the Blue Ribbon or any other such like flag!) and a great disliker of drunkenness and of drunken habits; I have dwelt there as quietly and respectably as I could have done in my own house at Napier, (insomuch that I hope to go thither again,) and I have never seen anything to find fault with; on the contrary I have had ample proof, and that repeatedly,—that such houses, well-conducted, are real blessings, and that to all classes of the travelling community.

Indeed, it would be very unreasonable,—aye, an unjust and injurious, thing, to think of closing the new Hotel at Matamau, or of refusing a renewal of its license; seeing it was erected for the convenience of travellers and to meet a crying want, and that nothing has ever been alleged against it; and, on the other hand, its proved great and real service to the many passing travellers,—whether by coach or on horseback, with loaded drays or on foot. Such a high-handed proceeding as that of a refusal to renew the License to this Hotel, would have to be met or counteracted somehow, and that immediately, by the Government, otherwise business and travelling that way would suffer materially.

To give an instance: the through Mail train leaves Napier at a very early hour, and I, in travelling, have known of several cases where passengers have been obliged to leave Napier without breakfast; on arriving at Makatoku (11.30), the popular Driver of the Mail Coach, Jones, is ready, waiting for Mails and passengers to start, and off they go! Now were it not for those two Licensed Houses on the way,—the one near the Railway Station, and the one at Matamau, where a glass of good beer and a biscuit can be always had (as well as other good drinks),—who can say what evil might not too often follow, if those half-famished passengers were obliged to travel as far as Tahoraite, where the Coach halts to change horses and to dine—say, 2.30, or 3 p.m.,—and then swallowing their breakfast-dinners hastily, being goaded on by excess of hunger and "Coach-ready-Sir"? And then, mark, what might reasonably be expected to follow—dyspepsia, illness, *death*,—as in the recent case, 2 months ago, of the unfortunate Engine-cleaner at Makatoku;—through men going too long without refreshment, then eating quickly (and it may be ravenously and too much) for the weakened state of the stomach, which unhealthy state is further increased by the jolting that follows.

Thinking over this, reminds me strongly of the old Arabian proverb,—"For want of a nail the shoe was lost," &c.; and, as it is said, the Railway line is soon to be open as far as Matamau,—and the Coach to run through to Wellington thence daily on the arrival of the train from Napier,—and then the Matamau Hotel would be the *only* place of refreshment on the road for early call; it seems to me both unjust and injurious to the public to think of closing the Matamau Hotel.

What is really required everywhere is the following:—

1.   Good Licensed Houses with proper accommodation;
2.   Good Masters and Mistresses;
3.   Good unadulterated liquors.

All this I have often endeavoured to impress on several Good Templars and Teetotallers, with whom I have from time to time conversed. And these obtained, *true* Temperance would be advanced; and other good and reasonable things would surely follow.

I could say a good deal more on this subject, but my letter being already long I forbear.—I am, &c.,

WILLIAM COLENSO.

Napier, June 9, 1884.

❖ **1884 MR. COLENSO ON "STRONGBOW".**
Hawke's Bay Herald 16 June.

SIR,—In your issue of this morning you have a long letter from a certain being yclepd "Strongbow;" which is intended as a reply to, and (in his opinion) a crusher of, my letter to you of the 9th inst. You will please to permit me to make a few remarks on "Strongbow's" letter although in my doing so I depart from my old-established rule of not noticing anonymous scribblers. It is true, that in this instance, you have courteously informed both me and the public, that I can have the real name of "Strongbow" from you on application; and this, you further tell us is from him; (but whether voluntarily on his part, or required by you, you do not say.) But why should I trouble myself about his Name? seeing he is ashamed, or not manly and honest enough, to give it? Was he afraid of openly owning his written thoughts? or, (seeing he had used gross "personalities" concerning me in his public letter, which you, sir, were obliged to cut out and lay aside,) was he afraid of what might possibly follow,—a prosecution for libel, a challenge, or a public horsewhipping? Perhaps, if I were only a few years younger, I might be induced to call on you for his Name, and then "Strongbow" would have to look out,—albeit a head and shoulders (it may be) taller than myself: I might be foolish enough to take the law (for once) into my own hands,—remitting the ultimate consequences to a jury of my countrymen.

But, to me, there is no need to see his name in big Roman letters. I know it well enough. Certain portions of his letter bring to mind the old fable of the Ass in the Lion's skin, and his awkward attempts at concealment. "Strongbow" has given me in his letter the two angles, and I can easily find the third. So, whether he chooses the name of "Strongbow" or "*Long*bow,"—or, even the ancient kingly name of *Longshanks*, or (if I am right in my geometrical calculation,) that by which he is said to be commonly known in the country,—"Big Sulky," it is all one to me. The Riddle, or Enigma, is found out.

And in order to enable others to find the required answers, I will just call their attention to the following three things (as I take it), that "Strongbow" has let out of himself:—

1. He says, positively: "I am not a Good Templar, Blue Ribbonite, nor fanatical temperance man of any kind."
2. He says again positively:—"I have travelled over the Seventy-Mile Bush road hundreds of times."
3. He says, relatively:—"I would like to see Mr. Colenso and his batch of badly-treated travellers going out mustering on one of the back country sheep runs, when they would have to carry lunch on their saddles or go without."

—And here mark, that while "Strongbow" speaks of their "lunch on their saddles" (after having had a good breakfast at the Station), he omits to mention the flask of whisky in the breast pocket from the home store! forgetting, that "what is sauce for the Goose is sauce for the Gander."

Now consider the above 3 marks, and you may easily find out "Strongbow."

Having done with the writer, I will now turn to his writing. And, first, he cannot fairly quote my letter, which he criticises! He says,—"Mr. Colenso is very pathetic in recounting the hardships of the traveller who had to go without his lunch till 2 o'clock." Where have I said this? I never wrote about "*lunch,*" (with me, always, an unnecessary meal,)—nor "2 o'clock;" but about the probable long fast in wet and cold and wind, and confined to a sitting posture, it may be no breakfast, no dinner till 2.30, or 3.00, or even later, such I have myself seen, and then the probable and reasonable consequences. Again: our truly respectable large new clean well-furnished and orderly hotels, (of which we should be justly proud,) and also contumeliously styled by "Strongbow,"—"grog shops,"—"grog shanties,"—"grog mills," &c. Again: that such (hotels) are not required by the "few solitary travellers" on that main and only road between Napier and Wellington.

"Strongbow" says,—"I have travelled over the 70-mile Bush-road hundreds of times, and my experience impels me to negative Mr. Colenso's conclusions." Allowing that "Strongbow" has so "travelled," (mind, always on horseback, or by coach) and so, passing those hotels,—or, say, the one at Matamau,—without stopping; what does that show again of my experience of repeated and long sojourning there, —in winter and in summer, in wet and dry,—and my frequent travelling on foot for many miles both N. and S. on the main road, and often meeting with many poor fellows toiling along with their swags on their backs, seeking employ, and anxiously enquiring the hour (in the Bush), and—if new hands—the distance to the hotel, that there they might rest awhile, have their glass of good Beer (or whisky) with their bread and mutton, or cheese, which tired Nature required, and then go on their way strengthened—and thankful.

No doubt, "Strongbow" has (like myself) seen those poor sons of toil on the road; —but has he ever been known to give one of them a "sixpence,"—or a "bawbee," —wherewith to pay for a glass of beer, or a pipe of tobacco? Methinks I hear (or have heard) "Strongbow" reply, with becoming hauteur,—in the language of George Canning to the needy knife-grinder,[9]—

---

9 Colenso the knife-grinder: see satiric letters on the 'Knife-grinders' Society' (the HBPI) 1883–4 above (pp. 307, 309), and references to them in Colenso's private letters. I.S.G.

"I give thee 6d! I will see thee d——d first!"

But to shorten this part: there are many now who daily (I may say, continually) travel by that road, both going and coming, and their number will increase; and it is to the travelling public in general that I look to decide, who is right,—"Strongbow" or myself; as to the advantages and benefits, or the disadvantages and evils, arising to the whole community from those scattered Bush hotels.

But I have not quite done yet with "Strongbow." I must now gently note his knowledge of History; particularly as he has taken on himself to teach me (or you, Sir, or all of us) something of History both Ancient and Modern.—

Of Ancient History, "Strongbow" says:—"Mr. Colenso says, an ounce of fact is worth a pound of theory. So it may be occasionally, and here is another *fact* for Mr. Colenso.... Theory told Galileo that the world was round; facts afterwards proved him to be correct."—

Oh! dear! Shade of Galileo!! Stars and Stripes!!! Boys of the 4th Standard in our Common Schools!—listen to that!! "Theory told Galileo that the world was round; facts afterwards proved him to be correct." Why the rotundity (or, roundness, "Strongbow,") of the the world was known and proved 500 years before the Christian era! It was the revolution (or, turning "Strongbow,") of the world (or earth) on its own axis that Galileo confirmed, (on his discovery of the telescope,) and for that he was persecuted; and this also was known long before, and was the foundation of the present received Copernican theory.

Of Modern History,—Strongbow descants largely (in his way) on the dreadful evils arising to our children away in the Bush, from those few hotels; he says:—"Does Mr. Colenso think, that the interests of the settlers shall be overridden for the sake of a few solitary travellers—that the growing youth of the 70-Mile Bush shall be contaminated by the continual sight of drunkenness, and debauchery, and the continued temptation to become tipplers, &c." Ahem! (nearly as bad, as to recklessness of speech, as that of the Blue-Ribbon *Sub*. John Harding!) Now let us see; "Strongbow" has allowed, that my saying, "An ounce of fact is worth a pound of theory," and so I will give him a bit of our own real and well-known Modern History, to repel the whole of his "high-flown statement."—

I will just take 4 of our oldest villages, or "townships" now; which have each had for more than 25 years a hotel in it; two of them being also still very isolated out-of-the-way places: Havelock, Waipukurau, Hampden, and Porangahau. Those places, I may also remark, have witnessed scenes of drunkenness &c., in past and early times of disorder, that will never be seen again in Hawke's Bay. In all those long-settled places, children were born, taught in the Schools, brought up, entered on active life, settled, and married; and I (as the old Inspector of Schools for many years,) have known them all. I challenge "Strongbow" to point out the "contamination" among them! the drunkard, the loafer, the dissolute, the idler! Our Country Youth, as a whole, are far more sober and hardworking, than those of similar townships at Home. Indeed, I have more than once thought, in past years, when engaged in visiting officially among them, that those sights were after all more beneficial than otherwise to the children;—according to the mode of the ancient Greeks, the dealings of the Spartans with their Helots (slaves, "Strongbow,")—making them publicly drunk, &c., that their Grecian Youth in beholding it might learn and love to keep sober. And, further, too: some of our early settlers' children, were, alas! the children of those who, unfortunately, drank too much; but I don't find that in this respect they turn after their parents; neither is their general health, so depraved as "Strongbow" would make it appear to be; on the contrary, I think, (in not a few instances known to me,) they are healthier and more able than those of some weak teetotallers. Besides it must not be forgotten, that our British gentry generally, of whom we are rightly proud, are descendants of Heavy drinkers: Well do I remember the drinking days of the time of George IV.—In conclusion, I hope, "the grand and glorious physical and mental greatness of the coming New Zealanders," will be a *leetel* superior to that of "Strongbow," or they will be nowhere in the race! So, Ta! ta! "Strongbow," and Goodnight.—I am, &c.,

WILLIAM COLENSO.

Napier, June 13, 1884.

❖ 1884 CORRESPONDENCE.
Daily Telegraph 18 June.

> *"How now? Who's there?—*
> *—'Tis poor mad Tom.*
> *Glos. 'Tis the times plague when madness lead the blind."*
> *—King Lear. Shakespeare.*

SIR,—Of late the people of the Colony have been exercised not a little over insanity. Not that it has ever been wanting among us, in some one of its many and varied forms, as we ourselves know here, and as your notes of proceedings in the R.M. Court too frequently inform us. Its numerous Protean phases are often so subtle and so strange, and so very very small in their origin, as to elude the lengthened examination of the most skilful. Some medical men of experience and high standing in their profession have put it on record, that almost every man is mad at some time or other of his life; and from what I have read and observed during a number of years I am inclined to believe it. Indeed, I am even now obliged, in charity to some of my old Colonial acquaintances, to hold strongly to this conclusion; otherwise I can not account for some of their unreasonable sayings and doings,—their crazy, cracked, and reasonless views and utterances—more especially those who labour under some unattainable "fad" as Teetotallism and Blue-Ribbonism on the brain—

"They rant, recite, and madden round the land!"

Shakespeare, our great British delineator of human character under many and strange guises, frequently brings madness prominently forward, and that in a great number of forms,—from the mild and playful to the raging type, including also the simulated form; as when *Hamlet* says,—"I am but mad north-north-west; when the wind is southerly, I know a hawk from a hand-saw;" or "the mad-brained bridegroom" Petruchio, with his,—"Be mad and merry,—or go hang yourselves." From Shakespeare's frequent and varied uses and modes of madness, we may reasonably infer, that the malady was then, just as it is now, common enough in his time.

The unhappy man Donoghue, who was executed last Wednesday morning at Hokitika for the murder of Gifford, was (when placed on his trial some months ago) supposed to be insane. The Judge directed a Jury to hear and decide. Dr. Hector, and Dr. King the surgeon of the hospital there, examined the prisoner, and immediately and in the strongest manner pronounced him insane; the Jury however wanted further evidence; and four other medical men examined the prisoner, who all refused to say he was insane! consequently the trial proceeded, resulting in a verdict of guilty. It seems, that the population of the West Coast was greatly excited over those proceedings; first the murder of Gifford,—second the steps taken to prove the murderer insane,—and third the long delay. It seems, too, that the Government was in doubt, for, at length Dr. Graham was sent by them to examine the convict. However, Donoghue was at last hung; and the several medical men, no doubt, still hold to their opposite opinions respecting him.

I have very recently been reading, in the London Standard newspaper, a remarkable case of a most serious charge of insanity brought against a talented lady, Mrs. Weldon, by her own husband, who had employed that eminent and noted physician, (especially in such cases,) Dr. Forbes Winslow. Dr. Winslow had certified her to be mad, in the usual way, and she was about to be consigned to the Doctor's own (or to his mother-in-law's) Asylum, at the nice little figure of £10 10s a week, when she fortunately made her escape! (At that time her allowance from her husband was £1000 a year: she having, also, property of her own.) And now Mrs. Weldon brings an action against Dr. Forbes Winslow, for libel, and assault and false imprisonment, and £10,000 damages. The trial is a celebrated one, and that for many reasons; one prominent reason being this, that Mrs. Weldon nobly and cleverly conducted her own case in the Court of Queen's Bench, without any assistance from Counsel, before Mr. Baron Huddleston and a special Jury. The trial lasted 6 days and was most interesting throughout: the Court being densely packed each day.

The lady examines and cross-examines a large number of witnesses on both sides, including Dr. Winslow and his own medical associates of high standing, and her own husband. Dr. Winslow cut but a sorry figure in her hands, although his Counsel (2) took his part; now and then he appealed to the Judge, who told him, he must answer the question. I suppose he never experienced such an examination before, extending through two days. The Judge, however, was obliged legally to nonsuit her; although in his summing up he spoke largely in her favour, and most strongly against the present horrible practice of entrapping supposed or charged lunatics, that is carried out by Doctors under the law of England. It is worthy of observation, that, owing to this very trial, it has already been moved in the House of Lords, to amend the lunacy law.

A part of Mrs. Weldon's examination of Dr. James Edmunds, M.D., F.R.C.P., and of his answers, is so peculiar, so new in a Court of Justice, that it is well worthy a place in your columns,—as causing food for thought. She also put similar questions to Dr. Winslow, who gave similar answers.

Dr. Edmunds,—"I am a doctor of medicine, and member of the Royal College of Physicians. I have had a full experience in cases of insanity.... I examined Mrs. Weldon for 3 hours,—and upon the whole I came to the conclusion, my lord, that she was right, and as sane as she appears to be to-day."

Re-examined by Mrs. Weldon, "I take it you are not a Spiritualist?—Certainly not. You know that there is a great difference between mediums?—I have heard so.

And, that there 46 million Spiritualists?—I never heard it put so high as that. There are a great many men who are Spiritualists.

John Wesley was a medium and heard voices; should you say he was crazy?—No.

St. Paul, when he went down to persecute the Christians, heard a voice saying, "Why persecutest thou Me." Now, should you consider that St. Paul was a crazy person? (loud laughter,)—I am afraid I should have to say that he was in a little crazy condition.

Do you think Balaam was out of his mind when he heard his ass speak?—I think he must have been a little crazy (laughter).

Then there was Joan of Arc. Was she crazy? A little, I think.

Have you heard the story of Stokes, who gave evidence in the case of Harriet Lane, murdered by the Wainwrights, saying that he heard a voice saying, "Follow that cab?"—I should say that that was not craziness. It was an instantaneous act, and a kind of unaccountable impression.

Because I said, when I heard in Paris that my husband was selling my furniture, a voice told me to go back, should you say I was mad?—No; I should say it was a kind of automatic cerebration. Persons in a state of mental excitement may see something of stars before their eyes. It is common in slight cases of fever.

Mrs. Weldon.—I am a Spiritualist, and do not believe in mad doctors; but I do believe in spirits, which are much less harmless." (Laughter).

Dr. Edmunds having also, in reply to Dr. Winslow's Counsel, spoken of both crazy and insane persons;—

"Mr. Baron Huddleston.—What is the distinction?

Witness. A person might be crazy, but not of sufficiently unsound mind to be locked up in a lunatic asylum.—Sir Isaac Newton fancied he was a teapot."

Great applause in Court followed Mrs. Weldon's last address, which the Judge put a stop to.—

In his summing up, his Lordship said:—"I must express my astonishment that such a state of things can exist, that an order can be made by anybody on the statement of anybody, and that two gentlemen if they have only obtained a diploma,—through them any person can be committed to a lunatic asylum. It is startling,—it is positively shocking, that if a pauper, or as Mrs. Weldon put it, a crossing sweeper, should sign an order and another crossing sweeper should make a statement, and that then two medical men, who had never had a day's practice in their lives, should for a small sum of money grant their certificates, a person may be lodged in a private lunatic asylum. . . . I am bound to say, that having seen Mrs. Weldon's demeanour throughout this case I, speaking as a layman and not as a doctor, consider she is in the full possession of her senses, and has conducted her case with judgment, intelligence and talent," &c., &c.

In conclusion, I would remark, that Gloster's deep saying at the head of this paper is well worthy of consideration at the present time. For craziness is rampant just now. The poet Dryden has also a suitable observation in one of his plays, highly applicable here;

— *"There is a pleasure*
In being mad which none but madmen know";

and this, I think, belongs to senior wranglers and medallist Teetotallers.[10]—I am, &c.,
WILLIAM COLENSO.
Napier, June 16, 1884.

❖ **1884 FATHER DES CHESNAIS' LECTURE.**[11]
Hawke's Bay Herald 1 July.

No pleasure is comparable to the standing upon the vantage-ground of Truth.—Bacon.

SIR,—In your paper of this morning you have given your readers an interesting account of the Convent School Entertainment in the theatre last night,—of the music and singing, and of two Lectures by the Rev. Father Des Chesnais, on Public Opinion, Rationalism, &c.,—and no doubt the audience was well pleased.—

But I am not pleased with several of the Rev. Father's scientific and historical statements, which I cannot but consider erroneous; and therefore I trouble you with this letter. I do not mean to take them all up, (you could not afford me the requisite room,) only a few of the more prominent ones; and these I will briefly notice in a few plain words,—as I only seek the truth.

1. Of the Copernican system of astronomy, Father Chesnais says,—"As a proof that the Catholic Church had always believed in the rotundity of the Earth, he quoted the instance of the frescos in the Vatican, executed by Raphael *over a hundred years before the inception of the Copernican system* of astronomy;" Well: Copernicus was born in 1472, and Raphael in 1482, 10 years *after* Copernicus.

---

10 Colenso, the senior wrangler, confesses his pleasure in being as mad as his teetotal opponents! A correspondent ("Madman") missed the point in an unpleasantly sarcastic response in the *Telegraph* of 19 June. I.S.G.

11 He wrote to J.D. Hooker (12 Jul 1884), 'I have been also hard at it! fighting in our 2 Locals,—(1) against the wretched fanatical Teetotallers w. their "Local option", —who have just closed 4 Hotels in the woods on the Royal Mail Coach Lines (where I have often stayed many weeks) and now there are none for 40–50 miles! And also, (2) against a Romish priest (I enclose a copy of this letter in the packet of seeds, as it may interest you a bit; it has again procured me the black looks, and uncourteous "passings by" of the priests & Levites all round!)—this, of course!!' I.S.G.

At the early age of 23 Copernicus proceeded to Rome, where he was kindly received by the celebrated astronomer Regiomontanus, and appointed to a chair of mathematics, and there pursued his astronomical studies, being also a churchman.

2. Of the Mosaic Cosmogony, Father Chesnais says,—"That the Bible nowhere taught that the Earth was created in six days, and urged, that the days were periods of immense duration." This is a modern invention reluctantly advanced by those theological critics who, driven to extremity by the numerous increasing and overwhelming Geological proofs, are obliged to adopt it; but it is against what the Bible plainly affirms and teaches. In its plain, purely historical, and calm narrative, such a metaphorical use of the word "day" is rendered impossible by the repeated phrase—"And evening was and morning was," both forming one natural day. Nor can the circumstance, that on the fourth day only the sun was created to divide the day from the night, prove that the word "day" denotes, in the preceding verses, at least, an unlimited time; if it means day in one verse, it has the same signification throughout the whole narrative, or we should be obliged to take the day of Sabbath likewise as a "period of immense duration" of rest. How could the plants of the third "period of immense duration", have grown and prospered, if the sun obtained his power on the earth in the fourth "period" only? Whatever efforts have been made to prove that the days here represent "periods of immense duration", the advocates of this opinion have not been able to bring forward one single plausible argument; unless it be considered in harmony with the Biblical notions of Divine omnipotence, that God created the light, or the heaven, or the dry land, in a "period" of 50,000, or 100,000 years; of that omnipotence which "commands and it exists." The term "evening and morning" describes indisputably the lapse of one complete day, or of four-and-twenty hours, and this cycle of hours elapses, even if there were no sun to mark it. Sun and moon do not make the day; they only govern it. And as there were days and nights before the creation of the sun and the moon, so there will be, at the end of time, light without the luminaries which diffuse it; as is distinctly stated, both in the Old and the New Testament.

Father Chesnais "accounted for Moses using the terms 'day and night' by supposing that Moses saw six visions, each vision representing to him what took place during each of the long periods referred to." Now wherever the Scriptures intend to describe visions, they are careful to introduce them in a manner that they are clearly distinguishable as such, and can never be confounded with plain history. The prophecies of Ezekiel offer so numerous instances of such visions, that it suffices simply to refer to that part of the Old Testament. The Biblical records are written in the ordinary style of human composition, for they were intended for the perusal and study of man. This ancient and orthodox principle must remain our supreme rule and guide. The first chapter of Genesis is, therefore not a "creative picture," but a creative history; it presents not a series of prophetic "visions" or tableaux, but of acts and events; it is merely a simple prose narrative.

3. Father Chesnais said,—"that all the miracles alleged to have been performed by Moses, were confirmed by the discoveries of modern Egyptologists, and that in particular, the miraculous passage of the Red Sea, as recorded in Exodus, was proved by Egyptian remains now in the British Museum."—I simply deny this; mere oratorical display!

4. Father Chesnais said, "that in the ancient times no man dared to speak against the established religion under pain of death. As a proof of his assertion he instanced Socrates, condemned to death by hemlock for speaking slightingly of the gods." —I reply: (1) That Socrates was not so condemned, but for his being (as his accusers termed it) "a corruptor of Youth":—that is, he taught them to think for themselves. It is true, the other charge was also brought against him, but Socrates triumphantly refuted it, silencing his accuser Meletus in the Court. As Xenophon says,—"As to the charge, that Socrates did not respect the gods whom the city respects;—what proof did they bring? For he was seen frequently sacrificing at home, and frequently on the public altars of the city.—Concerning celestial matters in general, he dissuaded every man from becoming a speculator how the Divine Power contrives to manage them; for he did not believe that those acted dutifully towards the gods, who inquired into things which they did not wish to make known.—But if any one desired to attain to what was beyond human wisdom, he advised him to study divination; for he said, that he who knew by what signs the gods give indications to men respecting human affairs, would never fail of obtaining counsel from the gods." (*Memorabilia*, lib., I, IV.) And much more to the same effect in Plato. (*Apology, Crito*, and *Phædo*.)
(2) That those "times alluded to in which no man dared to speak against the established religion under pain of death,"—were pre-eminently those of the dark middle-ages, when the thrice-accursed Inquisition, established and fostered by the Church of Rome, had full sway, and tortured and slaughtered her thousands and hundreds of thousands with cruel mockings and rejoicings!

5. Father Chesnais said,—"He combated the idea, that there was any conflict between Religion and Science, as exemplified by modern research on the one hand, and the Mosaic cosmogony on the other."—To this I reply: (1) Between *true* Religion and Science there is no conflict, as both proceed from the one source of truth—GOD: but (2) Between the religion and creeds of the Churches and Science there is great conflict, and *must ever be, until the several Churches alter their human Creeds.*

6. On two points I heartily agree with Father Chesnais: (1) "that public opinion depended upon the books and newspapers people read":—*ergo*, people will increasingly read, aye and *think*; science, light, and truth will advance, and emancipate the nations.—(2) "That a higher state of civilisation than that now in existence was in existence before the flood."—Yes: but say, *the time* of the flood.

As such an event as the Noachian (or general) deluge, has long been shown and scientifically *proved*, never to have occurred.—I am, &c.,

WILLIAM COLENSO.

Napier, June 27, 1884.

§ 1884 INSPECTOR OF NUISANCES' REPORT.

Hawke's Bay Herald 7 August.

The Inspector of Nuisances (Mr. Black) presented the following report:—….
The owners of swamp sections in Hyderabad-road, near Onepoto, have with but one exception—Mr. Watson—failed to comply with the notice from the local Board of Health. The names are—George Hart, Thomas Coldham Williams, Samuel Joseph Kustin, and William Colenso. Summer is now close at hand, so that the reclamation of these swamps should be attended to at once. I would beg to suggest that legal proceedings be taken at once.

❖ 1884 MR. COLENSO AND THE AUCKLAND FREEMAN'S JOURNAL.

Hawke's Bay Herald 18 August.

We reprint at Mr. Colenso's request the following letter from him to the editor of the Auckland Freeman's Journal, which was published in its issue of the 8th instant:—

SIR,—Yesterday I received from some unknown friend at Auckland a copy of your paper of July 18th, in which I find some animadversions of yours on what I had brought forward respecting the two astronomers, Regiomontanus and Copernicus, in a late public correspondence here between the Rev. Father Chesnais and myself. Permit me to say a few words thereon.

1. I *now find* that what I had said about the time of Regiomontanus is incorrect, and that what you have told us is right, and I have pleasure in doing so. At the same time I shall give you the respectable authority for my error in quotation.

2. I would, however, observe (*in limine*) that this error is but a trivial one; at most, my mention of Regiomontanus was immaterial, not at all affecting the main subject in dispute, in clause 1 of my letter, viz., the *time of the birth, &c.*, of Copernicus (and of Raphael), which you yourself have allowed to be correct.

3. You state—"The reason why we have been so particular about the dates of his early life will be found in the following passage from Mr. Colenso's letter:—'At the early age of 28 (substitute 23) Copernicus proceeded to Rome, where he was kindly received by the celebrated astronomer Regiomontanus, and appointed to a chair of Mathematics, and there pursued his astronomical studies, being also a Church man.' *Now, Regiomontanus died at Rome, aged 40, July 6th, 1476, when Copernicus was little more than three years of age.* There is little pleasure in tripping up

men of Mr. Colenso's age, but when they make statements such as the above they pass the limits of even charitable tolerance.... Here we may leave Mr. Colenso."

4. I now give you my authority (to do so is my chief reason for writing this), viz., the last complete edition of the "Encyclopaedia Brittanica," vol. VII., art. "Copernicus;" where it is said (*inter alia*):—"At the age of twenty-three Copernicus set out for Italy, and passed some time at Bologna, where he attended the prelections of the astronomer Dominico Maria, and also made some astronomical observations. He then proceeded to Rome, where he was kindly received by Regiomontanus, and honored with his friendship, as he had previously been with that of Professor Maria at Bologna. Here he was appointed to a chair of Mathematics, which he filled with much distinction, &c., &c."

5. But in all fairness to the editors of the "Encyc. Brit.," I should also mention that this error of theirs (*as to date*), which you have corrected, is also set right in their article on Regiomontanus (vol. XV, p. 391, art. "Muller," &c.), where it is said "He was born in 1436—he went to Rome (his second journey) in 1476 (where Pope Sixtus IV. had provided for him the Archbishopric of Ratisbon, and had sent for him to reform the calendar;)—but as he had found faults in the Latin translation of George de Trebizona, his son assassinated him on his journey thither; but others state that he died of the plague."

6. I could write a good deal more, but I forbear, not, however, on the account of "age" (as you courteously put it), for I had supposed—having been so taught— that "age" should bring wisdom.

7. I may, however, briefly say that I should have willingly rejoined to Father Chesnais' letter (and again have shown him where he was wrong), had he not written of me personally therein in the manner that he did, which seemed to me the more strange coming from a son of proverbially polite France! Therefore, I could not lower myself to reply.

§ 1884 WELLINGTON GOSSIP.
Hawke's Bay Herald 29 September.
The Maori Lexicon. The question of the compilation of the Maori Lexicon came before the House yesterday in the shape of the following questions by Mr. Samuel, the member for New Plymouth:—"What was the date and what the nature of the agreement made with Mr. Colenso for the preparation of a Maori Lexicon?" "Is there any probability of the work being published?" "Why has not the Government sooner enforced performance of the agreement?" Mr. Ballance, in reply, gave a history of the agreement. He added that the Government intended to call on Mr. Colenso to finish the work.

❖ 1884 THE MAORI LEXICON.
Hawke's Bay Herald 1 October.

SIR,—In your paper of this morning you have another item respecting the "Maori Lexicon" and myself,—in addition to the telegram you gave us on Saturday last, 27th. And as there appears to be some error or confusion, or both, on the part of the late Actors in it (as reported), I write now to say, that I will at once place copies of the original official Parliamentary Paper respecting the said "Maori Lexicon," in the Reading Room of the Athenæum, and of the Working-Men's Club, Napier; and also in those of the Public Libraries at Hastings, Waipawa, Waipukurau and Wairoa, for public information—I am, &c.,

WILLIAM COLENSO.

Napier, September 29, 1884.

❖ 1884 MR. COLENSO IN REPLY.
Daily Telegraph 20 December.

SIR,—In your article in the DAILY TELEGRAPH of this evening, writing on the "Seventy-mile Bush," you say:—

"The opening of the Seventy-mile Bush may be said to date from the time when Mr. Parke, then Chief Surveyor of the Province of Wellington, cut his way through the forest.... Previously to this the bush had never been penetrated by a European," &c.—

Permit me to correct this error. I, with my party of Maoris, first travelled through that Bush from Wairarapa to Manawatu (Ngaawapurua) in 1846; and subsequently every year, down to 1853, I went over the same ground, in going my annual rounds, and in visiting those Maoris who were then living at two isolated villages (Ihuraoa and Te Hawera) nearly central in that long forest; and this I did either in my going to or returning from Wairarapa.

The track (or rather course, unknown before even to Maoris of that early day,) was soon largely used by the Maoris, even to their driving of tame pigs from Table Cape for sale in Wellington town! there being no demand for them in all the intervening country.

Here I may observe, that you will find these journeys of mine mentioned at page 69 of the little book on "the Ruahine range," lately printed at your press.

After 1853, Dr. Featherston, then Superintendent of the Province of Wellington, applied to me officially for a description, &c., of my track through that forest, (this District being then a part of that Province,) which I made out and sent to him; and subsequently Mr. Parke, then a Government Surveyor of Wellington, came through on my old beaten track, chaining it, &c., &c. He kindly gave me a copy of his rough sketch route, telling me, that it agreed with mine; which I also recognised.

Another observation of yours in the same article, I should like to remark on; namely, where you say,—

"Bishop Colenso shook the theological world and thrust the Zulu assegai through it by pointing out that the simplest arithmetic threw doubt upon the Exodus, since it was impossible for such vast numbers of cattle and sheep to find pasturage in the desert, where scarce a blade of grass grows, and the streams are but feeble tricklings. Forestry arises to confute Bishop Colenso, by replying that the present aspect of the desert is caused by the absence of trees. Of old, when there were extensive forests in those districts, there was doubtless plenty of pasturage and water."

Here, I fear, the warmth of your feelings or the height of your Editorial imagination, in favour of your favourite theme—Forestry, have led you astray. I, on my part, feel the more inclined to write on this error of yours, from the fact of my being a firm believer in the arithmetic and teachings of Bishop Colenso respecting all those legends and tales of the ancient Jews, (which, I may further say, I have also proved to be correct, and which have not and cannot be logically refuted,) as well as from my being his nearest relative living, and therefore doubly ready to take up any charge of that nature against his teaching,—or, rather, the only reasonable deductions from those given premises.—

To return: Did it never occur to you, that if that lonely sterile desert country was so well-filled anciently with "extensive forests and plenty of pasturage and water" (as you say), that in the event of those forests having been all entirely consumed by the wandering Israelites, or by others after them,—the rich soil that bore that fine vegetation would have remained? Geology, or even Physical Geography, answers this.—

Again: What did the ancient Israelites themselves, the inhabitants and traversers of that Country and therefore well acquainted with it, what did they say of it? Let me quote a passage or two from their ancient books; which I allow were in all probability never written by Moses (as is still popularly supposed), nor by any one of his early day,—not till nearly 1000 years after him; but should you be ready to contend that they were,—Well, "all right!" I accept it; but all the worse for you and your argument!—

What of their early and common "murmurings," owing to their great want of food and water?—

What of the Quails and the Manna, this latter, too, daily supplied during their "40 years."

What of their want of water? and the wondrous supplies! and the marvellous legend of the peripatetic and ambulating rock (even adopted by Paul), that followed them all their long and lonely way during those 40 years?

And, what of those fearful and telling statements,—so often and feelingly mentioned and dwelt upon by both early and late prophets,—concerning that "desert land and waste howling wilderness;" and "that great and terrible wilderness wherein the fiery serpents and scorpions and drought, where there was no water," &c (*Deut.* 8, 15.)

I could both quote and say more, much more, on this subject, but this, I think, will suffice.—I am, &c.,

WILLIAM COLENSO.

Napier, December 19, 1884.

❖ 1885 ON EDUCATION.
Daily Telegraph 27 January.

SIR—I have been patiently waiting for the time of your extra excitement and labour to pass away; and now that I hope such is the case I venture to send you this communication. I feel the more encouraged to do so, from your having had lately in your paper several articles and notices on Education—particularly on Technical Education and its importance and great advantages to our rising generation.

A short time ago I was reading, here in the woods, Professor Tyndall's admirable inaugural address of the 62nd Session of the Birkbeck Literary and Scientific Institution; and I could not help thinking how very much there was in it highly suitable for ourselves, here,—both Teachers and Learners, and in these two classes I include *all*. And so I quickly made up my mind to ask you to give your numerous readers a few striking portions from it, which I also have condensed and extracted to form the main portion of this letter.

In the unavoidable absence of the Lord Mayor, Alderman and Sheriff Whitehead presided, who was supported by several gentlemen of note,—the audience being very large.

The Chairman said he was glad to find that among the subjects taught there was that of Technical Education. The City Corporation and the Guilds of the City had done much of late years to promote technical education of various kinds, not only in London but the provinces also, thus bringing about a better state of things in the manufacturing districts—particularly, those of Yorkshire. In Bradford a few years ago it was customary to send the youths of that town to the weaving schools of Germany for the purpose of learning the rudiments of the trade they intended to carry on in the Yorkshire town. Thanks mainly to the Clothworkers' Company there was now a weaving school in Bradford, that company having contributed £5,000 towards the erection of the building, £500 towards the machinery required, and £500 annually towards the maintenance of the school. The result was that, instead of Yorkshire boys being sent to Germany to learn the rudiments of their trade, German lads were sent to Bradford to acquire this knowledge. Facilities for acquiring technical education had also been afforded to the artisans of Bradford, and in both these instances the technical schools were almost entirely maintained by the City Guilds.

Professor Tyndall, in the course of his address, said it was in compliance with an express desire that he should base his address on the experiences of his own life.

—In the days of his youth, he directly derived profit from Dr. Birkbeck's movement. About 1842, he was a member of the Preston Mechanics' Institution, and doubtless the instruction he then and there received entered into the texture of his mind and influenced him in after life. After quitting school in 1839 he joined a division of the Ordnance Survey, intending if possible to make himself master of its operations, as a first step towards becoming a civil engineer. Draughtsmen were best paid, and he became a draughtsman. But he habitually made incursions into the domains of the calculator and computer, and thus learned all their art. In due time he mastered all the mysteries of ordinary field work, and afterwards successfully made trigonometrical observations. On leaving the Ordnance Survey in 1842 his salary was a little under 20s a week; and he had often wondered since at the amount of genuine happiness which a young fellow of regular habits, not caring for either pipe or mug, might extract even from pay like this.

In 1847, he accepted a post as master in Queenwood College, Hampshire.— Here he learned, by practical experience, that two factors went to the formation of a teacher. In regard to knowledge he must, of course, be master of his work. But knowledge was not all. There might be knowledge without power—the ability to inform without the ability to stimulate. Both went together in the true teacher. A power of character must underlie and enforce the work of the intellect. There were men who could so rouse and energise their pupils—so call forth their strength and the pleasure of its exercise—as to make the hardest work agreeable. Without this power it was questionable whether the teacher could ever really enjoy his vocation—with it he did not know a higher, nobler and more blessed calling than that of the man who, scorning the cramming so prevalent in our day, converted the knowledge he imparted into a lever, to lift, exercise, and strengthen the growing minds committed to his care.

We blessed God for our able journalists, our orderly Parliament, and our free Press; but we blessed Him still more for "the hardy English root" from which these good things had sprung. We needed muscle as well as brains, character and resolution as well as expertness of intellect. Lacking the former, though possessing the latter, we had the bright foam of the wave without its rock-shaking momentum.—He did not work for money, nor was he even spurred by "the last infirmity of noble mind." He had been reading Fichte, Emersen and Carlyle, and had been affected by the spirit of those great men. The Alpha and Omega of their teaching was loyalty to duty. Higher knowledge and greater strength were within reach of the man who unflinchingly enacted his best insight. It was a noble doctrine and held him to his work.

In concluding Prof. Tyndall asked his audience to accept his address as a fragment of the life of a brother who had felt the scars of the battle in which many of them were now engaged. Duty had been mentioned as his motive force. In Germany one heard this word much more frequently than the word glory. The philosophers of Germany were of the loftiest moral tone. In fact they were preachers of religion as much as expounders of philosophy.—He asked two Prussian officers whom he met in the summer of 1871, at the Pontresina, how the German troops behaved on going into battle,—did they cheer and encourage each other? The reply he received was, "Never in our experience has the cry, 'Wir müssen siegen'—we must conquer—been heard from German soldiers; but in a hundred instances we have heard them resolutely exclaim, 'Wir müssen unser Pflicht thun'—we must do our duty." It was a sense of duty rather than love of glory that strengthened those men and filled them with an invincible heroism. We in England had always liked the iron ring of the word "duty." It was Nelson's talisman at Trafalgar. It was the guiding star of Wellington. When, in his days of freshness and of freedom, our Laureate wrote his immortal ode on the death of the Duke of Wellington (portions of which both he and others might well take to heart at the present moment,) he poured into the praise of duty the full strength of his English brain:—

"Not once or twice in our rough Island story
The path of duty was the way to glory:
He that walks it, only thirsting
For the right, and learns to deaden
Love of self, before his journey closes
He shall find the stubborn thistle bursting
Into glossy samples which out-redden
All voluptuous garden roses."

—I am, &c.,

WILLIAM COLENSO.

Norsewood, January 25, 1885.

❖ **1885 SCARES.**
Daily Telegraph 11 May.

"1 Witch. Thrice the brinded cat hath mew'd
2 Witch. Thrice; and once the hedge-pig whined.
3 Witch. Harper[12] cries:—'Tis time, 'tis time."
—*MACBETH, ACT IV.*

SIR—I have recently returned to town from a long and peaceful sojourn in the Seventy-mile Bush. While there I was ever and anon being startled by the sudden screams of the distant railway whistle, (often heard resounding through the forest on a dark and dreary windy night,) and by the feverish and symptomatic apprehensive cries issuing from the diurnal Newspaper press of Napier; but I soon got used to both; yet thinking the latter the worse of the two and wholly uncalled for and unreasonable. Owing however to them, the above lines from Shakespeare often came rushingly into my mind,—with not a few others from our old writers equally applicable.

You, too, (permit me to say,) unconsciously added fuel to the fire, in so solemnly informing us, that a Napier parson and his old charwoman or sextonness, had both had in one night, a revelation or nightmare or dream of war bloody war having begun! For this, unhappily I got regularly chaffed, as I could not tell the many,— Why, Whence, or by Whom such a portentous and dreadful revelation had come to them;—whether from above or below,—whether through those naughty *seances* (of which all had heard), or through some better or worse channel: and this, I regret to say, is still unsolved.

You, Mr. Editor (as a long resident in Napier) as well as myself, have seen and passed through several Scares. If habit, as some say, "is second nature," we should by this time have become pretty well used to Scares of almost every political and human

---

12 This original word may be, perhaps, appropriately altered by Napierians to some other more suitable 2-syllabled word, retaining however the initial letter H. W.C.

kind or invention, albeit often accompanied by great screaming and thundering, and by frightful alarms and dire portents—ingeniously or stupidly got up for the nonce, after the fashion of the old story of "the 3 Black Crows."

Let me see; let me count over on the tips of my fingers a few of those more prominent Napier (or Hawke's Bay) Scares. Not to go too far back,—there was the predicted terrific tidal wave, that was to swallow us up quick; what a still greater excess of intense fear that ogre would have caused us, if the late terrible Java earthquake (that gave (?) those fiery sunsets last summer) had preceded it! There was the night invasion of the Hauhaus, and the dreadful state of excitement caused by some one seeing a light at night on the Western Spit beach, where the late Wm. Morris and his two travelling companions to the town, being benighted, were quietly camping and snoring. There was the general Vegetable blight Scare, that destroyed all our Cabbages and Turnips and Brocoli, including even the once universal wild "Maori Cabbage." There was the malignant Swamp and Fever Scare. There was the Small Pox Scare. There was the Harbor Scare,—terrible while it lasted, and of which the ghost is not yet laid. There has also been several Election Scares, which may also be repeated—such being so profitable, you know! And now, to crown them all, is this last,—the big Russian, or Perilous-need-of-Defences Scare! And this last one happening, and enduring, too! under the sweet and powerful public music of M. Remenyi, so highly extolled in the very same Napier Papers. Alas! Orpheus was anciently said to have had better luck with his stringed instrument among the wild beasts of the forest in his day. Verily, ye men of Napier and of Hawke's Bay, it seems to me that you are getting more and more childish and timorous, (at least outwardly so,) and growing unreasonable—like a cow's tail downwards! If you don't take care, of you ere long it may be chronicled—*ante tubam trepidat.*

I should however have told you, what it more particularly was that caused me far up in my quiet mountain solitudes to think so much of this present magnified huge and ugly Russian Scare; seeing that I had plenty there of far more pleasing matters to occupy both my time and attention; it was just this. A few days before I left Napier, I happened to open an old parcel of Botanical plates that I had received from London in 1855, and there I found a copy of the London "Times" Paper, of August 22, 1855, containing a full and particular and highly-graphic account of the attack by the combined fleets of England and France on Sweaborg—that grand old Russian fortress and town in the Baltic. This Paper I took with me to the woods, and there read and considered it; and now (with permission) I will give some literal extracts from it, which I am sure will be read with much interest by many of your readers, and may also be reasonably and profitably considered by them. Indeed, I should have sent the said Paper to you long ago for republication of this portion of it, but I thought,—Better, perhaps, wait, and let the mewings and whinings subside, and the witches' cauldron (now in brewing) boil over, and so (in part) put out the fire of their own kindling.—

"The Bombardment of Sweaborg."

(From our own Correspondent.)

Before entering into the details of the bombardment of Sweaborg it may be advisable to give your readers a brief description of the place itself, in order to render the following explanation fully intelligible.

Sweaborg stands in the Gulf of Finland, three miles south-east of Helsingfors. The fortifications extend over six islands, called Langorn, Lilla Swartoe, West Swartoe, East Swartoe, Vargon, and Gusvavstaard; the last five are connected by bridges and occupy a space of about 1,200 by 650 yards. Vargon is the capital, the strongest fortress, and also the central one. The works are of granite, and as massive as the foundations on which they stand, being, for the most part, constructions out of the solid rock. Sweaborg is said to mount 810 cannon, has casements for from 6,000 to 7,000 small arms, and barracks for a garrison of 12,000 men.

In describing the bombardment of Sweaborg, I shall endeavour, as nearly as possible, to relate the facts in the order in which they actually occurred.

On the 7th of August, at 9.30 a.m., signal was made from the flagship, "Outward and Icewardmost ships weigh." The fleet, consisting of 9 British line-of-battle ships, 13 steam-frigates and sloops, 16 mortar vessels, and an equal number of gunboats, sailed from Nargen, and after a pleasant run of five hours anchored at a distance of about 5,000 yards from the fortress of Sweaborg. In the course of the same evening the French fleet joined, and immediately commenced throwing up a mortar battery on the island of Langorn, situated some 2,000 yards to the north of the cluster of five islands which form the principal part of the fortress of Sweaborg. During the 8th both fleets were busily employed preparing for action; the mortar vessels were towed into position, about 3,700 yards from the fortress, with 400 fathoms each of cable to "haul and veer on," as circumstances might require. This arrangement proved of the greatest advantage, and much credit is due to the originators of this excellent idea. The line-of-battle ships remained in the same order they had at first anchored in. The steamers Magicienne, Vulture, and Euryalus took up a position in rear of the mortar vessels, for the purpose of being ready to give them and the gun-boats any assistance they might require. The Lightning and Locust were ordered to hold themselves in readiness to tow out any gun or mortar vessels that might be injured, or otherwise rendered incapable of remaining longer under fire; in fact, every possible arrangement having been made which prudence and foresight could suggest, the signal was made from the flagship at 7.15 in the morning of the 9th, "Gun and mortar vessels open fire with shell." At 7.30 a.m the first mortar was fired, and taken up along the whole line, the gunboats running in to within 3,000 yards, and getting their range. The enemy returned our fire very briskly with red-hot shot and shell, but, although their range was good, the damage inflicted was comparatively trifling, owing, principally, to the excellent handling of the gunboats and mortar vessels, the former being continually on the move, and the latter hauling or veering on their 400-fathom cable, as soon as they found the Russian shot falling too close to be pleasant. At 10.20 the first Russian magazine exploded, and a fire broke out in the arsenal. About v noon a second magazine exploded; and at 12.15 a most terrific explosion took place, followed by a succession of minor ones. The force of this was so immense that a battery of guns *en barbette* was literally blown to pieces by it. At 12.40 more magazines exploded. At this time the dockyards, arsenal, barracks, all the Government buildings, store-houses, &c., were burning furiously. The sight was most grandly imposing. The yards and poops of the line-of-battle ships were crowded with the excited seamen, who cheered vociferously after every explosion, as only British sailors know how to cheer. To add to this frightful din, the liners Cornwallis, and Hastings, and steam frigate Amphion opened their broadsides at the same moment; and, as if to crown the whole, the Arrogant, Cossack, and Cruiser chimed in by commencing a heavy fire, with good effect, on a large body of troops which they chanced to espy on a small island to the eastward of the fortress. The cannonade continued with little abatement up to 8 o'clock p.m., when the gunboat recall was hoisted. Several of the mortar vessels were also found to be injured from the quick and incessant firing, and had to be brought out to undergo repairs: those, however, which were not damaged, still kept up their fire, in conjunction with the French mortar battery, until 10.30 p.m., at which hour the rocket boats from the fleet went in and kept up their part of the performance until daylight. The scene during the night was grand beyond description: the whole of Sweaborg appeared one mass of flame, the rockets and shells adding not a little to the awful splendour of the fiery landscape.

At 5.30 a.m. on the 10th the fire again opened from our whole line, and continued throughout the day, at the end of which little appeared left to be done; all the mortars, French and English, were more or less injured. Some idea, however, of the services rendered by these vessels may be gathered from the fact that during the two days' bombardment not less than 1,000 tons of iron were thrown into a space of about half a mile in diameter, and upwards of a 100 tons of powder were expended. This, incredible as it may appear, applies to the English mortar vessels alone, and does not include the quantity (which was equally large in proportion) used by our gallant allies on that occasion.

On Friday night, the 10th instant, the rocket boats again went in and played with great effect. On Saturday no fighting took place, and Sunday was a day of rest. On that day everything was quiet and in repose; even the mighty deep bowed in reverence to a holy influence and was still. The tolling of the bells at Helsingfors was distinctly to be heard; the dull and plaintive sounds, mingled with the strains of sacred music from our men-of-war, came floating over the calm waters, and offered a strange but soothing contrast to the noise, turmoil, and excitement of the two preceding days.

On Monday morning, the 13th instant, the two fleets got under way and returned the same day to Nargen, having performed in an incredibly short space of time, with comparatively no loss, one of the most wonderful exploits recorded in modern times."

(Remainder in our next issue.)

—I am, &c.,

WILLIAM COLENSO.

Napier, May 9, 1885.

❖ 1885 "BOMBARDMENT OF SWEABORG" CONTINUED.

Daily Telegraph 12 May.

I proceed to give a few more extracts from the same Paper, "from another correspondent," also an eye-witness, who seems to write more fully, giving several further interesting particulars.

"Aug. 8th. French at work at their battery all night, and will complete it, we hope, by to-morrow. The weather could not be better for us; not a ripple on the water. This morning the Imperial flag was flying at Sweaborg, from which we infer that the Emperor, or the Grand Duke, have come to have a look at us. Thousands of people crowd the rocks and heights along the shore, to watch us all day long, and the harbor is perfectly alive with boats carrying troops to different island batteries. At 9.30 p.m. a general signal was made,—"Have steam up by 3 a.m."

9th. A glorious morning, and all hearts beating quick with anticipation of to-day's work. 7.30 a.m. Signal made, "Mortar vessels open fire with shell." The bombardment will last 18 hours. 8 a.m.—First shell fired; nine gunboats commenced firing, and the action became general along to the eastward as far as the eye could reach, and to the westward as far as a gun could reach; every rock and garden and house seemed full of guns.

At 10 a.m. we set fire to Fort Vargon, and at 11.5 the magazine blew up with an awful explosion, and for a few minutes the Russian fire slackened. The enemy's fire is very good when once they get the range; to prevent their doing this the gunboats kept moving in circles formed by four or five in each, and as each brings the bow gun to bear upon its object it is fired, then, turning as sharply round as possible, the broadside gun is pointed and fired, and they then proceed to complete their circle, while doing which they have time to reload.

12 Noon (exactly).—A monster explosion took place, which lasted without intermission more than two minutes; it was like a volcano in a state of eruption, vomiting forth lighted shells, roofs of houses, and beams of timber. Following this, in the course of half-an-hour, three other explosions took place, which set fire to the barracks and town in four places.—Up to the time I close this (8 p.m.) I am not aware of a single casualty happening to our whole flotilla.

About 9.30 p.m. the rocket boats commenced practice, when, it being quite dark, a most magnificent spectacle presented itself. The Citadel, Admiralty house, storehouses, and other public buildings on Vargon were all on fire; a beautiful breeze from the N.E. fanned it into a fierce blaze, and the red flames, rising at least 150 feet high, seemed to riot among the clouds of black smoke and lick them up. At this moment the rockets commenced their fearful rush through the air, like mighty meteors, leaving long streams of fire behind them; and the mortars, which had ceased firing for a while, to allow them to cool, began to boom again, and their shells, mounting high in the air, twinkled like stars, as the revolving shell showed its lighted fuse occasionally. We could trace it on its mission until it fell and exploded, when a bright flash, followed by smoke and a shower of sparks thrown upwards, told the havoc it spread around. The rockets and mortars continued firing until 2.30 a.m. of the 10th.

At 3.30 a signal was made to the gunboats to go into action again, (they had been withdrawn to take in a fresh supply of ammunition,) and soon after 4 the bombardment was general again. The three-decker which was moored across the entrance to the harbour, with such an imposing look about her, had been removed during the night, and placed behind the town, over which we can just see her masts. We made her old position too hot for her, and it is reported she has been on fire three times. I hear that five of our mortars were disabled yesterday, not by the enemy, but by large holes (some of them big enough to put a hen's egg in) forming in their chambers. Whether this is from the firing, or from defective casting, or the metal, it is difficult to say. They were partially repaired by Mr. Ward, Inspector of Machinery, who poured an alloy of zinc and tin into the holes, and some were afterwards fired 70 rounds before the piece fell out. At 6.15 a.m. another explosion took place on Vargon; our fire continued without intermission, and at 12.30 p.m. we succeeded in setting fire to a part of the dockyard and Swartoe, and at 1.30 to a great number of sheds, reported to contain 100 new gunboats not in use; if so, we are quite certain they are useless now, for not a vestige of them remains. This fire spread itself to the town adjoining, and at one time we could see three long streets in a blaze at once.

At 2.40 p.m. some French gunboats, wishing to take up a better position, sent a couple of gigs to sound a little to the westward, when the town of Helsingfors opened fire upon them from some batteries close under their beautiful Church. It would be an easy task indeed for us to burn Helsingfors to the ground, but we have spared it, and only attacked their fortress, from a wish not to destroy private property; but when our mercy is treated with such base return, we are almost provoked to turn the heads of our little gunboats in that direction. Yet it is evident they expect us to respect certain places, and avoid firing on certain spots, for on one huge building to the westward of Helsingfors is a piece of canvass stretching from chimney to chimney, with the words "Lunatic Asylum" painted in large black letters upon it, yet within 300 yards of it they have three immense batteries—one immediately under it, and the others on either side; and about half a mile to the east of it several hundred men were engaged building a mortar battery and magazine, and covering the latter with sand. This little transaction caused Admiral Penaud [commanding the French fleet] to observe, that "there was much more honour in burning Sweaborg; but there would be more satisfaction in destroying Helsingfors."

Aug. 11.—Our rocket boats went in again last night and fired for about three hours. A boat belonging to the Vulture had two men severely and several others very slightly burnt by one of their own rockets. It seems the stall was not properly screwed into the rocket, so that when it was fired, instead of its going right ahead, it must have fallen from the staff and turning backwards, passed across the boat and burnt the crew; most of the men jumped overboard in time to save themselves.

12th. The bombardment ceased this morning at 1 a.m., at which time the whole place seemed to be on fire. A little after noon Admiral Penaud visited each French ship, to thank the officers and men for their exertions during the late engagement. He was received wherever he went with three cheers. Admiral Dundas [English] issued a general memorandum with the same object, which was read to the men of each ship by their respective captains.

With this almost entire destruction of Sweaborg I expect we must be satisfied, and not look for any other great operation in the Baltic this year. But there still remains a great deal that may be done; indeed, a great deal more might have been done at Sweaborg but for the failure of our mortars. The blow, however, which we have so successfully given, and which, I believe, was more successful than was ever anticipated, will be severely felt by Russia. It shakes her confidence in her stone walls, and makes her tremble for every town along her coasts, when she sees that a few small boats, many of them actually old dockyard lighters, after having a gun or mortar put into them, are able to destroy stores, public buildings, and property worth millions, and defended by between 500 and 000 guns, without the slightest accident or casualty, for I have just learnt that *neither French nor English have lost a single man*, for those wounded in the Cornwallis wore not engaged upon the fortress, and those wounded in the gun and rocket boats were only, with two exceptions, slight burns from our own rockets.

13th. At 6 a.m. all the fleet got under weigh from off what remains of Sweaborg, and anchored in Revel roads again at noon. At the time we left the fires in the were still burning."

Having made those extracts I will just offer a few plain and brief remarks upon, them, premising, that such will naturally occur to almost every one of your readers.

1. The strength of those immense granite fortifications,—including their large number of cannon and troops; and yet how very little service they rendered, both in defending the place and in injuring the enemy at sea.

2. The enormous amount of damage done by the ships and boats, and that in a very short time and from a great distance.

3. The astonishing fact of not a single casualty caused by the enemy occurring on board of the combined fleets.

4. The exceedingly good handling of the attacking gunboats and mortar vessels.

5. The judicious concluding remarks of the second "Correspondent," as to the value of shore defences against maritime attacks.

And now I will conclude with a few observations, which I would earnestly recommend to the consideration of my fellow townsmen.

Before that I went inland, the common talk among us *re* the supposed impending war, was to the effect, that we might lookout for a visit from the enemy for the sole purpose of plunder. But this is a mistaken—or only a one-sided—view of the matter; as we may clearly see in the bombardment of Sweaborg, and also in the more recent conduct of the French in Chinese waters. War has ever a two-fold object: 1. the crippling of the foe by destruction of property and life: 2. by loot—in any shape—

if possible. One can scarcely imagine a Russian fleet, or even a single ship of war, coming to such an insignificant little-known and out-of-the-way place as Napier for the purpose of plunder, nor, indeed, for that of destruction of property (the place being far too small and remote), unless incited thereto by defiance and threats, by brag and colonial "cheekiness." I can, however, well imagine such a thing happening in sheer retaliation for low abuse and insolence, as a kind of severe chastisement; for all natures are not alike noble—as the Lion and the Mastiff—especially when aroused. On my seeing repeatedly what was in our Papers about the enemy and our local "defences,"—the low abuse and disparagement of the one, and the great and wonderful things to be effected by means of the other,—I felt (shall I write it?) lowered, humbled, at a loss for my countrymen! All such vapourings might be very good fun for narrow-minded short-sighted Editors to indulge in, over a cigar in their cosy sanctums and arm-chairs; but serving to remind me of the fable of the Frog and the Ox; and of the following refrain in the very old laughable ballad—which some of my compeers in age may recollect:

> "By their language and air, every officer there,
> Was a sort of a Cromwell-protector;
> And to judge by their swagger, and flourish of dagger,
> Each man—an Achilles or Hector."

And, in conversation on this subject with a few friends from the town, while in the woods, I said,—If I were the commander of a Russian ship of war in these seas, and knew the English language and had happened to look over some Hawke's Bay Papers, or knew their contents, and time and Orders would permit; I would just run in near enough to Napier and give them a few shells, by way of punishment for their gasconading; concluding my work with a note— "There, gentlemen, you have brought this on yourselves; that is for your cheek!" If ever such a visitation should really happen here by Russia or by any other superior hostile power, (which, may God forbid!) then remember, sufficient damage could be done to us in a very short time without landing, and without coming near to the shore!—

Here some one may impatiently exclaim, "What then, Old Man, would you advise us to do? Funk?" And my reply would be, "No, no, not so; be prepared for emergencies; for strong able resistance, even to the death if required, and if such could be advantageously used; but don't invite it." I know very well the trite and hackneyed saying,—"The way to have peace is to be prepared for war;" and this is also true in many cases, but certainly not in ours here; for do what we could, even to the utmost stretch, we could never be prepared for such a war as that,—a maritime visitation, *Destruction inflicted from a distance!* As well talk of being prepared against an eruption from our burning mountain Tongariro,—or a fall of meteoric stones,—or an earthquake! In all such cases it is well to remember the old adage,—"Let sleeping dogs lie": for (to quote again from that old ballad)

> "The fat English Knight said undoubtedly right,—
> That the best part of valor's discretion."

For, seeing we are isolated, and weak as to "Defences," let us rather imitate the staunch and serviceable "Friend,"—who, while he would not fight against the opposing ship, yet waited coolly on the deck at the bulwarks for the boarders, and when the first one attempted to board his ship, collared him and pitched him overboard into the sea, with a, "Friend, thou hast no business here!"

Let our unwelcome foe once land here on our shores, and so give us a tolerably fair chance of meeting him,—then, I trust, our men, especially our crack marksmen and sharpshooters, would give him a proper welcome, which the survivors (if any) should never forget.

For my own part, I confess I cannot see the probability of good ever resulting to the whole Colony from those loudly talked of "Defences," which are now being carried out. And were they not counselled and designed by old and eminent professional men (Military Engineers), I should be inclined to laugh at them. Something, to be sure, may be done to be of small service,—as, for instance, against the visitation of a single small ship of war, a privateer, or filibusterer, in such narrow and naturally defended entrances as Wellington Heads, Port Chalmers, and Auckland, to protect their inner harbours, but even this I doubt—that is, their real utility.

One thing, however, in absolutely certain, and that is, their great *Cost*! Cost to make and Cost to keep them up,—a heavy sum total, and one which this young Colony in her present circumstances can very hardly bear. I trust I do not write this in any thing approaching to a mercenary spirit—very far from that; rather is it, because those heavy outlays are unproductive, and (in my estimation) useless, while more extra money than we can well raise is absolutely needed for Education and Public Works of real utility and pressing need. Indeed, I should not care to touch on this matter of Cost at all, were it not that I have good reasons for believing that we have some among us who rejoice in the prospect of heavy Government expenditure,—utterly careless as to where the money is to come from, or how obtained,—whether by increased taxation or by further borrowing,—or any how, or for any purpose, as long as such is profusely and recklessly squandered! This evil spirit, which has hitherto done so much harm to this young, struggling, and growing Colony, is still (I deeply regret to I say) living and strong and active among us.—I am, &c.,

WILLIAM COLENSO.

Napier, May 12, 1885.

❖ 1885 THE HOTEL QUESTION AT MAKATOKU.
Hawke's Bay Herald 21 May.

"I speak as to wise men; judge ye what I say."

SIR,—The plain striking and truthful remarks in your paper of yesterday (Monday), from "an occasional contributor,"—on the Hotel question at Makatoku,—seem to call on me to say a few words in support of them; that is, of the principal facts which he brings forward. Seeing, that I, too, happen to know a little concerning that matter, and the real want, of the whole large Bush district. For I have been both residing and travelling about within it certainly more than 3 months of the past year (and so in former years), and in my doing so have both used my eyes and ears and thought in connection with this subject.

"Contributor" is quite right when he states—that *more drinking* has taken place in that locality during the past 12 months, since all the four hotels were at once and suddenly closed by the Licensing Committee, than during the 12 months preceding, when they were all open: Mr. Rechab Harding to the contrary, notwithstanding.

In my opinion the Licensing Committee of 1884 did a great wrong to the Public— and particularly to the *travelling* public—by so closing all those hotels; they might have lessened their number, leaving, say, 2,—one on each line of road (Coach & Train) for the benefit of the public.

Not unfrequently during my repeated and rather long sojournings there, and especially when travelling, as I almost daily do for several miles along the great highway and *only* coach road between Napier and Wellington, have I met with travellers, strangers,—of all grades,—some on foot and some riding, who have enquired, where they could get refreshment,—or *suitable* accommodation? and what could I say?

It is all very well for those who are *not* travellers, or who are *interested monetarily* (whether in their little shops, or in church and Sectarian matters,) or who are *rabid teetotallers*, for them to say—"Oh! there is such and such an Accommodation House!" (I only know of 2 within 60, or more, miles.) And, for several good and valid reasons that I could state, and which even reasonable teetotallers would readily allow,—I say, that those 2 Houses are not really good and suitable accommodation, for the present travelling public. Possibly, in years gone by, they were such, but present wants and requirements need something more, something better, or, at all events, more suitable.

For instance: I would take a teetotaller—the most unreasonable and selfish and monomaniac among them, a positive "one-idea" man, whom I will call John,—and I would ask him, if journeying and stopping necessarily through heavy rain at a teetotal accommodation house in the Bush,—"What do you take for supper, John, Tea or Coffee?" "Oh!" he might reply, "Coffee; for I never take Tea, as it always gives me a headache, and prevents me from sleeping." "Ah! yes, very good, John, but there is no Coffee here, and none to be had nearer than Napier." Now, I feel sure, that John, or Bill, teetotaller, would not like to hear that. But there is no help for it; either Tea (the Bush Teetotal-Accommodation house Tea! Ugh!!) or cold water! And so, again, on getting up in the morning, and, it may be, starting afresh in the rain—with his cold comfort! Still, such might only be for a single night, and so could be borne; but what if such continued for a week or more?

Again:—as I lately put it to one of my Scandinavian acquaintances, who had donned the *bit* of Blue, and who is a religiously-disposed man:—"You smoke, I think?" "Yes, I do," was the reply. "Well," I rejoined, "I don't, and I do not like tobacco; and I believe, with many others, that tobacco is much more hurtful to our rising generation than strong drink. Suppose we (my party) were to combine, and not caring for the comfort and requirements of the larger number or our fellow-men, were to get a law passed prohibiting the use of tobacco. How would you like that?" "Oh! not at all," he replied "that would never do; that would be very unfair; we would not submit to it; in fact we could not live without tobacco." "Ah! yes," I said, "that will do; I have it from your own mouth. And you are a Christian! a follower of Him whose principal tenet was,—'Do unto others as you would have them do unto you.'"—

Now, just so, as I take it, is it with a man who needs his glass of Beer, or of Wine, or of Spirits; all, too, made from different material, and of various sorts and kinds to please tastes, and suit the natural requirements of man. Why should a man (any man) not be able to obtain in a free country what he really needs? I, myself, have met with cases up in that big bush, during the last 10–12 years, in which my having a little good Brandy with me (for my own private use, if required,) has proved of great service,— among others to poor half-dying teetotallers in the time of their greatest need, with no Doctor nor medicine near, and all spirituous liquors condemned by them as "an accursed thing." Not, however, that they (many of them) really believed it. No, no; they had been talked over, and in a time of excitement, and led by others, had agreed for the nonce to become teetotallers: and now the sure consequence was, that there were no really good and useful spirituous liquors handy, or to be had!

I do not wish, Mr. Editor, to make this letter too long, and so I cut it short; merely making two remarks which naturally arise from the past and present state of things up in the Bush.

1. That, seeing that there is no hotel on the long and almost dreary line of highway of more than 40 miles, and the only road, between Waipawa and Danevirke, (over which all stock—often "mobs" of sheep each containing many thousands—have to be slowly driven in all kinds of weather,) that the new Licensing Committee will see their way reasonably clear to grant a License to one hotel on that long, line of road; and, also, to one hotel upon the Railway line through the Bush, which is also greatly needed. For, (as I showed in a letter in your columns about a year ago,) really good hotels, kept by suitable people, and furnished with pure and proper drinks of all kinds in use among us, (not adulterated trash which is poison!)—under also the lawful supervision of the police—such would prove to be a great means of bringing more money into those at present poor parts, and therefore a great blessing to that Country, and particularly beneficial to the travelling public,—of whom I am one.

2. That should the new Licensing Committee, in their carrying-out of their legal powers so strain them as to refuse to allow of any hotels in all that extensive and scattered District,—that then, I think, a reasonable and strong public movement should be at once made, to remove the Court-House at Ormondville from its present unsuitable site in the Bush to Takapau on the adjoining plain,—where there is a Hotel, and where professional men and their clients and witnesses, and Magistrates, too, and Jurors, and the Public generally attending the sittings

of the Court, could have their reasonable and needful wants and refreshments supplied, and no longer be bamboozled and hampered and oppressed by an insignificant minority. And so leave all that Bush and its Bush Villages to their inhabitants and to their loved quietude and isolation,—until they should "come to themselves," and see and put away their selfish error.

And this removal of that Court-House to a more suitable place for the public benefit, I think, could be easily brought about, as such would not come under "Local Option," and would be supported by an overwhelming majority.—I am, &c.,

William Colenso.

Napier, May 19, 1885.

❖ 1885 "VERITAS VINCIT"—TRUTH CONQUERS.
Daily Telegraph 26 May.

SIR,—In the Supplement to your Paper of Saturday evening last you have published a sermon by Rev. De Berdt Hovell: will you permit me to offer two very short remarks upon it? (which, also, are not my own but drawn from a higher source.) I am the more induced to do this from Mr. Hovell's opening words:—"Far be it from me to launch out into any new sea of speculation; seeing that the revealed word of God is clear and precise enough on this question to satisfy even the most curious."

My *first* observation is,—that such teaching or belief is *not* that of the Scriptures.

My *second* is,—that such teaching is unorthodox and wholly opposed to the Creeds of the Catholic Church, and to the authoritative official standard of the Church of England; whose IV. Article on this particular subject, "*The Resurrection of Christ*," I quote:—

"Christ did truly rise again from death, and took again his body, with flesh, bones, and all things appertaining to the perfection of Man's nature; wherewith he ascended into Heaven," &c.—

And this doctrine the Rev. De Berdt Hovell, as a Licensed Minister of that Church, has both assented and subscribed to, and been sworn to observe.—

I will conclude with a quotation from a great Doctor of the ancient Church, which I would beg to recommend to Mr. Hovell's particular consideration:—"Resurrexit Christus, absoluta res est. Corpus erat, caro erat, pependit in cruce, positus est in sepulchro, exhibuit illam vivam qui vivebat in illa." *Greg. Serm.* 158. *De Tempore.*

I am, &c.,

William Colenso.

Napier, May 24, 1885.

P.S. I feel constrained, in a postscript, on this occasion, to ask you, Mr. Editor, to reconsider your former expressed determination,—"Not to allow of any religious controversy in your Paper." In my doing so, I know I have with me a large number of your readers in Town and Country, many of whom have at different times, spoken (and written) to me about it, lamenting it. For, it seems to us, your Subscribers and readers, not fair that you should on almost every Saturday in your "Supplement," give a Sermon (for, I suppose, Sunday reading,) which too, frequently (as in this instance) contains extremely strange and far-fetched notions of religion. It seems to us—the many, that your columns should either be open to all decent writers and seekers after Religious truth, or closed against all, and not (as hitherto) open to a select few only. Otherwise, you yourself may unintentionally become the great disseminator of error in matters of religion,—which, I am sure, you cannot desire to do. Of course there is the danger of what is called "religious controversy," but surely all such could be reasonably guarded against or kept within due bounds,—just the same as is now done by all respectable Editors in political and personal matters; even the mere length of a letter, or sermon, might be well fixed; also, the disallowing of all anonymous writers.

Of one thing I feel well assured,—(looking back on the past 50 years, and considering the uphill persevering progress of Truth, in spite of all difficulties, and of all opposition from Churches,)—that the time is not far distant when all truly respectable Newspapers of the day will allot sufficient space to the honest enquirers after Truth,—Truth in all her various forms and opinions,—particularly in Religious matters—the highest and most important of all to man. Free Public Opinion will both demand and obtain this right from a free and enlightened Press. Moreover, be it ever remembered, that from such search and publicity, Truth and True Religion have nothing to fear. For, as the Roman historian Tacitus justly remarks,—"Truth is *established* by scrutiny and deliberation."

W.C.

❖ 1885 LOCAL OPTION.
Hawke's Bay Herald 27 May.

SIR,—Permit me to add a word or two more, by way of explanation, to my letter that appeared in your columns of Thursday last. This I find I am obliged to do from a remark made by your "Argus" in his "Jottings" in yesterday's HERALD. (Although I must confess, that, as I happen to know "Argus" and also his 'cuteness, I cannot but believe that he saw my meaning clearly enough.) I should have said a little more at the time,—and so have fully set forth my meaning,—only I feared to trespass too largely on your space.—

I fully agree with "Argus," as to Local Option being carried out by the inhabitants of any village or locality apart from outsiders, where such villages or localities are isolated or confined to themselves, (say, like Ashley-Clinton, Makareta, Kumeroa, and others in the large Bush Districts)—but where those villages are on the main lines of public roads, such also (as in their case), being *the only great Colonial thoroughfares*, (as I had shown in my letter,) it is a different thing altogether. In all such cases, especially when far apart or distant from other townships, (as I had also shown in my letter,) then the outsiders and particularly the travelling public should also be allowed to have their "say" in the matter; because it was for them as well as for the inhabitants of the said village or locality, that those roads were made and are being kept up at the public expense.

And this argument is still the stronger—cuts the deeper, when further considered in connexion with public Government buildings—as Court-houses. For the Court-house at Ormondville was not erected there mainly for the benefit of that small village (like, for instance, their two little chapels, and the public school-house,) but for the whole large district including outsiders and the travelling public.—I am, &c.,

WILLIAM COLENSO.

Napier, May 26, 1885.

❖ 1885 TO THE EDITOR.
Daily Telegraph 3 August.

SIR,—You have fulfilled your promise to your readers, and have given them in the supplement to your last Saturday's paper the sermon by the Bishop of Waiapu—on the exclusion of the Bible from schools. My object in writing you this note is, to inform you and your readers that I will send you a letter in reply thereto (or, rather, containing remarks thereon) for publication in your next Saturday's supplement; which I hope may be of some service in assisting them to form a right judgement on this important question. I am, &c.,

WILLIAM COLENSO.

Napier, August 2, 1885.

[We publish sermons weekly for the pleasure they give to our country readers. None of the sermons that we have published can be said to be of a controversial character, and we most distinctly decline to accept for publication any contribution that would lead to a religious discussion.—Ed. D.T.]

❖ 1885 MR. COLENSO AND THE REV. W. BAUMBER.
Hawke's Bay Herald 1 October.

(Per favour Editor H.B. HERALD.), To the Rev. Wm. Baumber, Napier.

Dear Sir,—

Permit an entire stranger to thank you thus openly for those very excellent and truthful words uttered by you last evening as Chairman at the Anniversary of your Wesleyan Church Sunday School: as reported in the HAWKE'S BAY HERALD of this morning. May they be generally made known through out the Colony, and may the Divine blessing attend them!—

You, sir, in those few plain and honest words have really struck at the root of the whole matter. (I call it *on* a single root.) As concerning the proper use of the Bible, (the not making a senseless reasonless *fetish* of it, as if it contained spells and charms!) the Home duties of parents,—the Government Day Schools,—the Sunday Schools,—the true cause of growing Larrikanism among us,—and the fearful fruits thereof in the near future, unless timely and reasonably met and suppressed.—

Again do I heartily thank you for this expression of your honest convictions; I do so, as an old Sunday School Teacher, as a Protestant Minister, as a Parent, and as a

Colonist—earnestly desiring the welfare of the Country; and I would that more, nay *all*, of our Working Protestant Ministers could thus think with you, and so act together in cordial concert.

I am, Dear Sir,
Yours truly
WM. COLENSO.

Napier, Sept. 30, 1885.

§ 1886 GENERAL ASSEMBLY.
Grey River Argus 24 July.

Colenso's Maori lexicon would not be finished for some time yet. The letter "A," a very important one, was completed, and it was proposed to complete the work in parts. Government would only pay for the work as it was completed, and would not incur any expenditure beyond what was necessary. No distinct progress was made in the work last year. Stout moved that the House at its rising adjourn till half-past two on Monday. Agreed to. The House rose at 5.30 p.m.

❖ 1886 SCARES.
Daily Telegraph 20 November.

SIR,—In your paper of yesterday (Thursday) you inform us, that Cr. Cotton last night said, in his place in the Borough Council,—"Dr. Menzies was as much entitled to a testimonial as Dr. MacIntyre of Timaru, for he had detected the outbreak of small pox, and thus saved the country from a scourge, and an immense outlay probably, in stamping it out."—

Although I actually gasped over this! and involuntarily cried, "Judge!" and, "What next?" I shall, at present, restrain myself, and make no remark upon it;—only this,— that during my long residence here in Napier, (in which I have seen with pleasure, year after year, the steady and prosperous growth of our thriving town, notwithstanding croakers and detractors,) I have known no less than five ugly scares,—viz., the Maori night attack! the great overwhelming tidal wave!! the dangers of the central swamp!!! the small pox!!!! and the Russian!!!!! and, to me, all very nearly alike—all GROUNDLESS. And now, I am led to suppose, from "the jumping of the cat," that we have to expect, at least, two others: one, (dolefully led by Cr.Graham, like another Cassandra,) as to the certain dreadful effects from the old and mired saltwater lagoon, if left to Nature;—and one, (by some other equally veracious, honest, and inspired prophet— it may be Golder,) as to the certainty and nearness of coming earthquakes! with Walter Scott's Dominie, one can only exclaim, "Prodigious!"

I have said, that at present I shall abstain from making any remarks on Cr. Cotton's sage observation; neither should I care to bring it to your especial notice, were it not, that it so happened, that on the very night before (Wednesday), I was reading the interesting and instructive debate that took place in the British House of Commons, on the 10th September last, on this very subject of small pox; when the heavy and increasing annual vote of £175,970 for *vaccination*, was before them in Committee of Supply. And from that debate I make a short extract, containing a few notable official items, for the especial benefit of Cr. Cotton; and, of course, for those who think with him on such matters,—if any such are to be found.

"Mr. A. O'Connor moved to reduce the vote by the sum of £16,500, the item for public vaccinators. He contended the system was immoral stupid and cruel; and opposed to the parental instincts of tens of thousands of conscientious people. The charge had grown, year by year; and this public vote was supplemented by a further charge of £120,000, which came out of the pockets of the ratepayers. In Birmingham, out of 9000 births, he found 8000 cases of successful vaccination reported; the per-centage of children unaccounted for as regarded vaccination being 1.5. Under these circumstances one might reasonably suppose, if the system was to be maintained, that Birmingham would be singularly free from the small pox. But what was the effect? Epidemics there of small pox had always been of the most severe description. In London, where it was said children were successfully treated, small-pox was not only epidemic, *permanently endemic.*" [Please note that, Cr. Cotton; and no scare!] In London last year the number of persons under treatment for small-pox was 9000, being an increase of 4000 on the previous year. On the other hand, the small-pox hospitals at Leicester, where not more than 40 per cent. of the children were vaccinated, were tenantless. One-third of the population of the country did not believe in vaccination, while a decided majority were opposed to compulsory vaccination. The system of reward to officers for the effective poisoning of healthy children, was a direct incentive to a most cruel form of persecution.... In the reports of medical officers, there was nothing more substantial to be found, than the argument,—that if so and so had been, so and so would not have happened." [This to thy right eye Cr. Graham.] "Let those who believed in vaccination be vaccinated; but let them not trouble their neighbors, seeing that those who were vaccinated considered themselves protected against small-pox."

It will be seen, that in the above extract I have given remarks touching both sides of the question of vaccination; I might have omitted those bearing on its utility, which I consider established—but only when the lymph (or vaccine matter) is obtained from a strictly healthy subject, and not used on infants of very early ages. I am obliged, as it were, to make this remark, to anticipate opponents; who might not know that I myself have vaccinated thousands—including my own children.—I am, &c.,

WILLIAM COLENSO.

Napier, November 19, 1886.

❖ 1886 "ANTIMONY."
Hawke's Bay Herald 8 December.

"Eripit interdum, modo dat medicina salutem."[13]

SIR,—Much has been said of late respecting this drug; the papers have been repeatedly full of it; but, as far as I have seen, it has only been mentioned with disapproval, almost amounting to horror, as a virulent "poison;" not a word said in its defence, or to show its great use and beneficial service in medicine,—in skilful and cautious hands.

For some time I have thought of writing a few words to the Press on this subject; if only to remove from the public mind the general impression—of Antimony being only a "poison," and of very doubtful use in medicine. Of course, this common belief is now strengthened through the modern prohibitory law respecting its sale by Druggists: as well as by the manner it has been of late (for the last two months) spoken of in the papers; including the statements of Medical and other professionals in our Law Courts respecting it:—not one word (as far as I can learn) having been said in its lawful defence and support.

I know very well that in my writing on this subject I shall lay myself open to the charge of being an intruder,—perhaps a quack, or charlatan! but now, as before, *I speak only of what I know.*

And here, I think, a sagacious saying of our celebrated Englishman Locke, may not inaptly be adduced:—"Were it my business to understand physic, would not the safer way be to consult Nature herself in the history of diseases and their cures, than espouse the principles of the dogmatists, methodists, or chymists?"—

Now it so happens, that I myself have had pretty much to do with Antimony as medicine in its various preparations during my life; and that not only in prescribing and administering it to others, but in using it myself, and have found very great benefit from it on many occasions. A few of the more prominent cases I will mention.

When very young (a growing schoolboy) I was long subject to an internal disorder; doctors and their remedies were tried, also the nostrums of old women (never in those days despised in country places), and also some of those other nostrums painfully collected and published by Rev. John Wesley in his book of "Primitive Physic," (which, at that period, 60–70 years ago, was in high repute, especially in Cornwall) —all, however, proved to be of little if any service. About that time a Danish Doctor (said to be the physician to the King of Denmark) came over to the much warmer climate of Mount's Bay to spend the winter, on account of his health, he being consumptive, and I soon became one of his patients; and after taking his medicines, undergoing operation, and suffering much (all to no purpose), I left him. At this time I was advancing towards manhood (in my teens!) and I began to study Medicine a little, having the opportunity of so doing;—for I was early intended for the Medical profession, owing to our esteemed family Doctor being one of my godfathers. Among other strong medicines that I prescribed for myself, for my obstinate internal complaint, I may here briefly notice *Sulphuric Acid*; and this not merely

---

13 Medicine sometimes destroys health, sometimes restores it. Ovid. I.S.G.

the diluted article of the Pharmacopæia, but the stronger raw article of commerce,—which, of course, I diluted in my own way, but was always obliged to suck it up through a glass tube, and this did me some real service. After a while, however, I took Antimony, (the very notorious and much-abused Tartarised Antimony, or Emetic Tartar of the present time!) and of this drug I have taken as much as 2 grains, and on occasion 2½ grains, at a dose; and from this medicine I derived very great benefit.

So much for my early experience.

In coming to Hawke's Bay to reside in 1844, I brought with me a large and varied assortment of useful Medicines obtained from Apothecaries Hall. And, as may be readily supposed, I had plenty of *gratuitous* practice! (I may here mention that for several years from the year 1835 I was in sole charge of the Church Missionary Surgery at Paihia, in the Bay of Islands; there being at that early period no resident Surgeon in the Bay, or indeed, in all New Zealand.)

In 1846, the first visitation of Influenza appeared among us here in Hawke's Bay; and it was a sad time! for the epidemic was very severe and protracted. Now, then, was again seen the great benefits from the judicious use of Antimony (Em. Tartar). I had a large household, including Maori domestics, boys and girls; and my common practice was, during the raging of that Epidemic—first, to weigh out every morning 6 grains of Antimony, and dissolving this in a large bowl of water, to place it on a table in the hall, with a table-spoon and a dessert-spoon by its side; and of this we, all hands (sufferers from influenza) took a spoonful every 3 hours; and this use of it was kept up for several days. I proved this to be exceedingly beneficial in most cases, including my own self and family; in all, I may say, where the seat of the disorder was more especially confined to the chest. And this practice I always carefully followed, in succeeding years in my own house, whenever influenza appeared.

In cases of Croup I have also found Antimony to be a most beneficial medicine; as well as in certain cases of Indigestion, Bilious Complaints, and severe chronic maladies. Used outwardly as an Ointment I have also proved it to be of great service in Hooping Cough, severe swellings, &c.—I believe that the celebrated Dr. Jenner was the first to recommend the use of it in this way. For my own part I consider Tartarised Antimony to be the best and most useful of all the Antimonial preparations, because it is so easily managed.

In all chronic disorders where it is likely to be of service, its use must be continued for a long time. I never heard (until of late) of its administration in minute doses being considered by physicians of eminence as poisonous. When taken in *large* doses, of course, it acts as an active corrosive poison; but even then its symptoms are immediately produced and well-known.

I could say a great deal more on this head, but I forbear. At present I merely give you a little of my own experience.—I am, &c.,[14]

WILLIAM COLENSO.

Napier, December 4, 1880.

---

14 It is quite possible that some of Colenso's symptoms may have resulted from chronic antimonial poisoning, common in printers in those years. I.S.G.

❖ 1887 MR. COLENSO AND THE BOROUGH COUNCIL.
Hawke's Bay Herald 19 February.

SIR—I am just returned from the 70-mile Bush; and my attention has been drawn to your report, of our Borough Council proceedings in the HERALD of yesterday (17th). In which Cr. Cotton, when speaking of the proposed new road from Napier Terrace to Milton Road, said:—

"He (Mr. Colenso) was asked, when the roads committee should go up, and he said, 'Oh, some fine genial day, when the wind doesn't blow, and I can go with you and show you the place. I will let you know.' Well, that was a very long time ago, but Mr. Colenso had not yet made known when the committee should go."

I would lose no time in stating publicly, that I am wholly ignorant of this statement; especially of the concluding words:—"*I will let you know.*" I could never have used them for I have been throughout the whole past year waiting for this long promised visit of the specially-appointed Sub-Committee. And here, I think, I may very properly mention brief conversations I have had from time to time during the past 6–8 months, with several of the Borough Councillors, and also the Town Clerk, the Road Overseer, and Mr. Rochfort, C.E. who surveyed the new road and drew the plan,—as to when, if ever, the long-talked-of visit was to be made by the appointed Sub-Committee. Indeed, I recollect saying on one occasion to Cr. Cornford, (in reply to his remark, that they (3) could never find spare time to come together,)—"Why not come singly? and make notes, and then meet at your leisure down in town and talk it over among yourselves."

Of one other thing I am also certain (from your report), viz.—Had Cr. Cornford condescended to visit the place and *see the ground*, he would never have so far demeaned himself, as to call the highly-approved, useful, simple, and little-expensive road—"a gigantic scheme of (expensive) roads"!!

I write briefly in haste to correct the errors referred to in your issue of tomorrow —I am, &c.,

WILLIAM COLENSO.

Napier, Friday evening,
February 18, 1887.

1887 SHIPWRECKED MARINERS.
Daily Telegraph 17 May.

"And the barbarous people shewed us no little kindness:—and when we departed they laded us with such things as were necessary."
— Acts.

SIR,—In the few plain words above quoted, we are told of the humanity and true charity of the heathen people of Melita to the shipwrecked strangers of Paul's ship. Words which will last as long as the 4 Gospels, and be as largely circulated. In this respect not unlike what the Great Teacher Jesus himself said, of the woman of Bethany respecting her kind care in early and readily anointing him with oil,—"Wheresoever the Gospel shall be preached throughout the whole world, this that she hath done shall be spoken of for a memorial of her."

In your paper of last evening (Saturday), you inform your readers:—"One of the men belonging to the Northumberland is anxious to know who is the agent here for the Shipwrecked Mariners' Society, as he is a member, and when wrecked at a port of Chili last year, he was forwarded Home and received an outfit." And, in your issue of the evening before, you state:—"The seamen of the shipwrecked Northumberland are in need of some clothes. Several of the seamen this morning said, they were willing to go to Port Chalmers, but as they were without a change of clothes they could not go, when all they possessed was what they stood up in. If anything is to be done for these unfortunate men it should be done quickly." &c., —

Now, this, to me, is very sad,—indicating real distress, want, on the part of *shipwrecked strangers* at the Port, which should not be. For the last few days I have been daily on the look-out to learn what you there on the spot at Napier, have done, and have been trying to do, *for the shipwrecked strangers,*—who lost their all in bringing stores to and for Napier. And while I read of a large general and overflowing amount of sympathy shown to our 3 townsmen (and their families), who lost their lives in vainly endeavouring to succour the shipwrecked strangers, I see little or no indications of any really good thing having been done for "poor Jack!" Indeed, I saw it stated, that any overplus remaining from the subscriptions so promptly and properly raised for the decent burial of the one poor, fellow who was drowned by the capsizing of the "Boojum," (who though a resident in Napier had no connections there,)—such remaining money was to be used for a tombstone and fence round his grave:—here again, not a thought for "poor Jack!"—

A public meeting, I see, is to take place on Tuesday night, (17th. inst.,) for the purpose of deciding on some proper plan respecting subscriptions raised in connection with our late disasters.—

Unfortunately for me, I cannot possibly be present. (As I came here to the Bush for a special purpose, which I have not yet accomplished owing to the almost constant rain, and which, as the winter is fast coming on, I must do before I return to Napier.) This proposed scheme of a serviceable and really useful "Jubilee Fund" is a good one, and one that should be largely supported by Napier and Hawke's Bay: provided, that it clearly means what it seems to say; of which, I have some doubts, and hence I now write.

Is it, to raise a fund, or the beginning of a fund, for the real purpose of assisting *shipwrecked mariners?* almost invariably strangers of various nationalities and creeds: or, Is it to raise funds to benefit the families of those who have been, or who may be I drowned in boats, etc., of our Harbour?—our own townspeople, who have their relatives and their friends, and it may be (in some cases) their properties, here. To me the two classes are widely distinct; insomuch that they cannot be made one of—cannot come under the same head or List . The *first* class, the really shipwrecked *strangers in a foreign land* having lost their all, are in *immediate need of everything*, and should and must be helped "right away": the *second* class should also be aided according to their real needs and varying circumstances, to be reasonably enquired into. I have never yet found my fellow-townsmen, backward in any matter of this latter kind and class; friends and neighbours of the bereaved living ones are always sure to abound, and to stir up (if such a thing were required) any amount of sympathy in Hawke's Bay.—

I have read the Bishop of Waiapu's letter in the "Herald" respecting a "Mariners' Relief Fund"; and if it be the Bishop's meaning, that such is to be *for the benefit of the real shipwrecked mariner in distress in a foreign land*, then such may be well-worthy of being called a "Jubilee Relief Fund" (although the Editor of the Herald had no need to make such a blare over it, as if such an idea had only *now* originated!—the same being an old one, and in part already provided for. Of course, this is owing to his ignorance of the past.) But, if the Bishop means, merely or mainly, to meet this recent melancholy occurrence of the sudden deaths of three of our townsmen, then, I say, such is out of place, and not required under the present, or any similar circumstances. All such untoward events and casualties had ever better be met and dealt with as they arise; such things are of common occurrence, and will ever be so:—"the poor ye have with you always, and whensoever ye will ye may do them good."—

I could write a good deal more on this head (for my heart is full), but I forbear. I enclose a cheque for £8 8s 0d, (which has been ready a few days, and which, I fear, I ought to have sent you before,)—for this *one purpose only*, viz., to aid the shipwrecked mariners the officers and crew of the Northumberland; which, please, use at once at your own discretion; and should you have a Subscription List for this purpose, then place the said sum as follows:—

Rev. W. Colenso   ..   ..   £5 5s. 0d.
Mr. W. Colenso, junr. (a sailor)   £3 3s. 0d.

And another cheque shall, if required, be forwarded to you.

I am, &c.,

WILLIAM COLENSO.

Dannevirke, Sunday, May 15, 1887.

❖ 1887 PRESERVATION OF TIMBER.

West Coast Times 13 July; reprinted from Napier News.

"William Colenso" writes as follows to the Napier News:—

SIR,—In your paper of Monday 1st you state, "All who are interested in the preservation of timber will be glad to hear of Professor Poleck's discovery, that timber which had been long immersed in water is thereby rendered free from liability to dry rot."

I do not know who this Profesor Poleck is (not having even heard his name before), neither do I know his residence or country, but this modern "discovery" of the Professor's has been known to the New Zealanders perhaps for ages. Hence they always procured and used such timber for the building of their principal chiefs' houses, although to do so entailed a much larger amount of labor on themselves; destitute too as they formerly were of iron or any other metal.

When the chiefs of Hawke's Bay in 1843–45 united to put up a dwelling house and a church for me at Waitangi, they obtained the timber for posts and pilasters mainly from the bed and banks of the river Tukituki (a great distance up the stream, even to beyond Te Mata, Mr. J. Chambers) where it had long been imbedded and immersed. The difficulty of getting some of those long and thick logs, with their broken branches, out of deep water and from under high banks, was very great, and took a considerable body of Maoris a long time.

When dried and split and worked to a smooth surface (patiently dubbed down with a smooth act set transversely), the timber looked well; it was of various shades of dark color,—from red to a deep chocolate brown or even darker; some also, often had a peculiar partly honeycombed appearance, as if worm eaten or half rotten; but all the kinds were said to be alike indestructible.

There are still some early settlers residing in Hawke's Bay who will recollect the neat appearance of the inside pilasters of my house (detached study) at Waitangi made from such immersed timber—which was so often admired, but by no one more so than the late Bishop of New Zealand (Dr. Selwyn), and by Sir D. M'Lean, who had both travelled much among the Maoris.

No doubt the dark flat and wide slabs of wrought timber, formerly used as pilasters in the constructions of their chief's houses, also as doors, both for them and for their storehouses, have often been noticed by settlers and visitors. Such timber was obtained from similar sources.

Another fact I may mention, further illustrating the same. In 1845 I set out a piece of land adjoining my house, about two acres, to be dug, fenced, and drained. To please the Maoris, and more, to get it done at all, all the neighboring tribes must have a hand in the job, so as to obtain a share of the pay. The natives of Kohinurakau took the north side of the fence, and their posts were apparently weak, being very slender, about 2 and 3 x 4, composed of that kind of submerged and buried wood obtained from the river Tukituki under their pah (village). At first I objected to such slight posts, but I was assured these would stand good longer than the bigger or bulkier ones of new totara, &c., so they went on with their job. When I left that place some twenty years afterwards, that slender pale fence which I had often seen rocking in times of a gale or flood was still standing. Not a single one of those slight posts had ever given way.

❖ 1887 MR. COLENSO AND THE MAORI LEXICON.
Hawke's Bay Herald 2 September.
Under the above heading Mr. Colenso writes as follows to the Wellington Post:—
Sir,—My attention has been drawn to your mention of me and of a work (the Maori Lexicon) on which I was long engaged, in the leading article of your paper of the

24th instant, and as it is wholly erroneous, I trust you will publish this letter. You say—
"Take for example the compilation of the Maori Lexicon, which Mr. Colenso was authorised to prepare. For many years the House voted this gentleman large sums of money, yet when in 1880 he presented the result of his labors up to date to Parliament it was found he had not got beyond the letter A. It is doubtful if he ever completed the work involved in that indefinite article. Shortly after the vote was stopped," &c. Now, the truth is this (which you there at headquarters, with Parliamentary documents, Hansards, &c., &c., at hand, should have known):—I commenced that work in 1866, under agreement for "seven years." But, though continually inspected, and reported on and approved of, the Government of the day arbitrarily stopped it in March, 1870, since which time down to the present I have never received a penny from them, and during those 4¼ years that I was hard at work on it I only received £980 (net) or £230 per annum. At the late Sir D. M'Lean's pressing request: (he being then Native Minister) I, in 1875, sent in proposals for the carrying out of the said work, one being an offer to do so at my own expense; another to give the Government £500 to be allowed to do so. (See Parliamentary Paper of 1887, G.11, herewith.) But to all my proposals no answer was returned. In 1879 Mr. Bryce, being Native Minister, stated in the House "that the work (of the Maori Lexicon) had been definitely abandoned, that the colony did not intend to proceed with it." [Hansard, vol. xxiv., p. 611.) On my seeing this I wrote to him, again asking permission to carry it on and publish it at my own expense. This, however, was refused. Early in 1885 the Hon. Mr. Ballance and the Premier took the matter up, urging me to recommence the work, &c. At first I refused, time with me being past; but believing them, as they both wrote and spoke fairly, I gave way, began afresh, and worked hard at it day and night. In February, 1886, I sent in the first instalment (as stipulated) containing the letter A, in 249 pages, copied ready for press. Subsequently on my asking for payment (including all that I had done in past years from 1870, at the request of Sir D. M'Lean, together with outlay to Maori helpers, &c.)—altogether a bare £300—it was refused. And so the work was again stopped. Can you point out my errors in all this? The time will assuredly come when justice will be done to my memory by my countrymen and the colony, though I shall then be far away; and, also, the blame rightly laid. As an act of common justice, I think you should publish in your paper the Parliamentary Paper above referred to.

In conclusion, I cannot thank you for placing me in the same category with Mr. John White."

§ 1887 TYPO SAYS.
Inangahua Times 11 November.
The paper read by Mr. Colenso before the Philosophical Institute supplies an important chapter in the early history of the Colony, and, incidentally contains much information as to the first books printed in New Zealand, the settling of the orthography of the Maori tongue, &c. We hope to see it in full in the next volume

of the Transactions. In seconding the vote of thanks, Mr. R.C. Harding referred to Mr. W. Colenso as the William Caxton of the Colony. He also inquired as to the whereabouts of the old Stanhope press—the first printing press in the colony, but no one could answer. Can any of 'Typo's' readers supply the information? If it passed safely through the Maori troubles, it is probably in use as a proof-press—or stowed away in some lumber-room. It ought to be in the Colonial Museum. Will our contemporaries pass this query along?

❖ **1888 CHRISTIANITY *VERSUS* MAHOMETANISM.**
Hawke's Bay Herald 17 January.
SIR.—In common I trust with many of your European subscribers and readers I would heartily thank you for the highly interesting mid long paper by the Rev. Canon Taylor on "Christianity v. Mahometanism" so thoughtfully given in your issue of this morning. I have some time known it, (from the London Standard of October 8th.,) and as an old subscriber should have asked you to republish it in the HERALD, but I feared it would prove too long for your columns.

I write now to give your readers (with your permission) what you may have omitted, which, I think, should have been given with Canon Taylor's noble out-spoken and truthful paper: viz., that at the said great Church Congress "held at Wolverhampton in the fine big Drill Hall, capable of seating 2000 people, that number of Members were present. The Bishop of Lichfield presided, and on the platform supporting him were the Archbishop of Canterbury, the Bishops of Carlisle, Durham and Bedford, the Earl of Harrowby, Earl Nelson, Lord Norton, Lord Talbot, and a number of other distinguished laymen, together with many dignified clergy." And this Congress lasted a whole week.

As an old Missionary to Pagans (not to Mahometans), and also as an old Minister of the Protestant Church of England,—I thank GOD for having permitted me to see the day when a canon of the Church of England could so righteously speak and teach before such a high assembly of dignitaries of the English Church "with confidence, no man forbidding him" (as it was once said of Paul).

Permit me to add, that I feel doubly on this matter; and that not merely from being an old belief of mine, (only however arrived at through much study and research,) but because of a memorable long dispute I once had here—in the street at "Manor's corner,"—with the Rev. D'Arcy Irvine (quondam "examining chaplain" of the Bishop of Waiapu) who not only would have it, that Mahomet was an impostor and a limb of Satan, and now (or then) most deservedly roasting and grilling, &c.,—after the true and charitable orthodox fashion!—but that I (poor soul!) was just as bad, or worse, and should be alongside of him! Very possibly the Rev. D'Arcy Irvine, used to such kind and noble thoughts and feelings, may have forgotten all about it,—but I have not, never shall.

While on this subject, and in conclusion, I would also thank you, Mr. Editor, for your able and truthful article on behalf of the disciples of Confucius,—the steady industrious and quiet Chinamen,—which appeared in the HERALD a few days ago. The sublime truths anciently taught by the great Chinese Teacher Confucius to his countrymen, and also by the equally great Indian Teacher Buddha to his people, (though, at present, but little known, and even maligned, here among us in Napier, by narrow-minded orthodox men of small calibre,)—will yet become the prized common property of the thinking world; together with those of the ancient Greek and Roman Philosophers—Socrates, Plato, Marcus Aurelius, Seneca, and others;—and, afterwards, those more plainly taught by the great Jew Teacher and Reformer Jesus,—all will be (at last!) classed, as being Inspiration from the great Father of all—God (*i.e.*, the meat not the bones): for "Great is Truth and will prevail."—I am, &c.,

WILLIAM COLENSO.

Napier,

January 16, 1888.

❖ 1888 BIS DAT QUI CITO DAT.

Hawke's Bay Herald 20 March.

SIR,—Referring to the very sad news given to us in your paper of this morning, of the extensive and highly calamitous fire and great loss of property at Norsewood three days ago—and thanking you for your prompt and stirring appeal to us (our and their fellow-settlers) to come forward early and assist those unfortunates in this their trying hour of suffering and want and loss:—I have great pleasure in sending you enclosed a cheque for £20 towards raising a subscription fund for that purpose.

For I believe in the sterling natural truth of the above quoted ancient motto,—"He gives twice who gives in time." Moreover, I feel greatly for those poor hardworking patient Scandinavians (whom I have long known), now burnt out of house and home:—having, unfortunately, suffered myself in a similar way,—in 1852,—when I not only lost my dwelling-house and all by fire, but had no sympathising neighbors near me! nor even stores in the district, whence I might have procured common necessaries!!

I trust this great and pressing emergency will be at once largely and nobly and cheerfully met. Solitary guineas from gentlemen and well-to-do settlers will scarcely do much good in this extensive and extreme disaster. May it be remembered by Christians of every denomination among us,—as well as by those of the good old Jewish Church,—"He that hath pity upon the poor lendeth unto the Lord:" and, true "Charity ever begins at home."—Far better (may I be permitted to remark, without giving offence) *to give here to real want* than to Melanesan Missions, or to "Dr. Barnardo's (distant) Home."—

One stipulation, however, I would venture to make, *viz.*, that our subscriptions be for the relief of the Scandinavian residents at Norsewood, and *not* to aid or recoup losses which *may* fall on town and Country Mortgagees of property there.—I am &c.,

WILLIAM COLENSO.

Napier, March 19, 1888.

❖ 1888 "FAIR PLAY IS BONNIE PLAY."
Hawke's Bay Herald 22 March.

SIR,—In your issue of this morning you give us the following item of news from "Your own correspondent" at Waipawa;—written yesterday, Tuesday 20th.—

"Last Sunday an alarm was raised in the Maori pa, and in a few minutes males and females were mounted and in chase of some youths who had been stealing watermelons. They were met by the youths' parents, and a war ensued in which the poor Maoris got the worst of it."

—I am very sorry to read such a communication:—Sorry for the "Youths" of that rising township, (were they "larrikins" or school-boys?)—more sorry for their misguided "parents,"—and (must I write?) still more sorry for "Your own" there, who could write you such a serious matter in such an indifferent careless semi-jocular strain! He and they may live long enough to see the *sure fruits* of their own sowing.

Such doings, however, I regret to say, are not new in this country; that is the difference between *meum* and *tuum* (mine and thine): between a European stealing from a Maori and a Maori from a European. I have seen and known too much of it in my time; and I am not now going to write upon it; but to give you (and those Waipawa folks in particular) an instance of how our justly-famed navigator, Capt. Cook, fairly managed a similar trespass and theft,—acting up to the good old English notions of our forefathers.

Cook says:—"One of the towns was very near us, from which many of the Indians (Maoris) advanced, taking great pains to show us they were unarmed, &c. In the meantime some of our people (crew), who, when the Indians were to be punished for a fraud, assumed the inexorable justice of a Lycurgus, thought fit to break into one of their plantations and dig up some sweet potatoes: for this offence I ordered each of them to be punished with 12 lashes, after which two of them were discharged; but the third, insisting that it was no crime in an Englishman to plunder an Indian plantation, though it was a crime in an Indian to defraud an Englishman of a nail, —I ordered him back into his confinement, from which I would not release him till he had received 6 lashes more." (1st Voyage, vol. II., p.366: 4to. ed.) This happened in the Bay of Islands, in November, 1769.—I am, &c.,

WILLIAM COLENSO.

Napier, March 21, 1888.

❖ 1888 THE LATE RENATA KAWEPO.
Hawke's Bay Herald 18 April.

SIR,—In your issue of this morning you inform your readers of the lamented decease on Saturday last of the aged and well-known Maori chief, Renata Kawepo. Of course we had first heard the sad news up here in the Bush District on Saturday night.

In your mention, however, of his return from the North (Bay of Islands) to Hawke's Bay, you have (unknowingly) published a few errors, which I would briefly correct. In my doing so at this particular time (with my old friend lying unburied), I would both apologise, and also observe, that I would not do it were it not for my belief, that what you (the oldest journal in Napier and Hawke's Bay) should say about Renata, will be eagerly copied and republished throughout the colony.

You state, "that Renata was converted to Christianity, and became a missionary with the object of bringing his people to the faith he had adopted. His first visit to this district as a missionary was to Patea, and thence round various settlements which were subject to him as a Chief."

Now this is erroneous. I brought Renata with me from the Bay of Islands to this place, on my coming here to reside in 1844,—being my second visit to Hawke's Bay, along with a few other Maori domestics. And it was some considerable time after our arrival that I made him an assistant teacher in my schools; whence he gradually rose, and at last became an assistant in holding Divine Services in my absence from the Mission Station; in which situation for some time he was very useful and did good service.

At that time there were *no* "various settlements subject to him as a chief;" such a thing was never dreamt of. Indeed, none of his own particular tribe resided here in Hawke's Bay (with the solitary instance of his sister, who was then one of the many wives of the chief Tiakitai)—his tribe (what remained of them) were all living far down the River Manawatu—between which place and Hawke's Bay there was at that period no communication.

After some time Renata visited Manawatu, and it was chiefly owing to his eventually marrying a young woman of that tribe and place, and the Hawke's Bay tribes having mainly become Christians, that several of them migrated hither to Hawke's Bay, and settled down around him at his little and rising village—Te Pokonao—near where Farndon is now.

It was not for several years (until, at least, I had been to Patea over the Ruahine range two or three times) that I sent Renata thither.

I could fill a small volume with much of interest concerning Renata whose eventful biography is a very strange one; particularly that of our first decade of years here together; which, also, is only known to myself.

In conclusion, I would beg of you, (and also of other Editors of newspapers here in the Hawke's Bay District,) not to be too ready to insert hearsay, or supposition or interested details concerning Renata and his life during those early years—or say, from 1844 to 1860.—I am, &c.,

WILLIAM COLENSO.
Dannevirke, April 16, 1888.

❖ 1888 THE INFIDEL AND THE ORTHODOX MAN.
Hawke's Bay Herald 15 May.

If the uncircumcised keep the righteousness of the law, shall not his uncircumcision be counted as a circumcision? .... For he is not a Jew, which is one outwardly, &c—Rom. ii., 26, 27.

SIR,—Your correspondent, the Rev. A.S. Webb, in his letter in your Paper of Saturday last, 12th inst., on "Infidelity aud Reform," seems, to me, to confound the true meanings of two words therein used, or played on, by him, viz. Infidelity and Orthodoxy. It is not likely, however, that he does so in his own mind; but merely from his manner of using them in his letter,—which might possibly deceive the unwary. And as one concrete example is worth a whole lot or bundle of metaphysical or philosophical disquisitions, I will just give a handy one,—taken, also, from the columns of that same Paper. For instance: Some one among you at the Port might be led to suppose that a man dressed up in a tawdry soutane with silver crosses and bullion fringes, and reciting or intoning a Creed of the Church with his face to the East, must therefore necessarily be an orthordox man:—or, in other and plainer words, a true believer and follower of the simple and lowly Jesus!

Be that as it may. I happen to have here with me in my travelling box, a very excellent work by the late Dean of Westminster, entitled "Christian Institutions"; a book that I highly prize from its containing a large amount of valuable historical information and true Christian thoughts;—and from it, with your permission, I will make an opportune extract bearing largely on the matter in question.

"It used to be said in the wars between the Moors and the Spaniards that a perfect character would be the man who had the virtues of the Mussulman and the Creed of the Christian. But this is exactly reversing our Lord's doctrine. If the virtues of the Arabs were greater than the virtues of the Spaniards, then, whether they accepted Christ in word or not, it was they who were the true believers, and it was the Christians who were the infidels.

"When the Norman bishops asked Anselm whether Alfege, who was killed by the Danes at Greenwich, could be called a martyr, having died not on behalf of the faith of Christ, but only to prevent the levying of an unjust tax;—Anselm answered— 'He was a martyr, because he died for justice; justice is the essence of Christ, even although his name is not mentioned.' The Norman prelates, so far as their complaint went, were unbelievers in the true nature of Christ. Anselm was a profound believer, just as Alfege was an illustrious martyr. When Bishop Pearson in his work on the Creed vindicates the Divinity of Christ without the slightest mention of any of those moral qualities by which he has bowed down the world before him, the Bishop's grasp on the doctrine is far feebler than that of Rousseau or Mill, who have seized the very attributes which constitute the marrow and essence of his nature. When Commander Goodenough, on one of the most edifying, the most inspiring, deathbeds which can be imagined, spoke in the most heroic and saintly accents to his sailors and friends, there were pious souls who were deeply perplexed because he had not mentioned the name of Jesus. It was they who for the moment were faithless, as it was he who was the true believer, although he had not spoken expressly, in a language which they could understand, of the Saviour, with whose spirit he was so deeply penetrated.

"They who believe in the singular mercy and compassion exhibited in the Parable of the Prodigal Son, or in the toleration and justice due to those who are of another religion, as shown in the Parable of the Good Samaritan, they, whether they be Christians in name or not, and whether they have or have not partaken of the sacrament, have received Christ, because they have received that which was the essence of Christ,—his spirit of mercy and toleration.

"Such are some of the ways in which the life of Christ is still lived on the earth." (*pp.* 38, 39.)

There are other portions of Mr. Webb's letter I should also like to take up, but I must forbear, having already exceeded in length for your spare space; much rather choosing to give Dean Stanley's judicious, plain and honest words, (containing as they do a sound hearty ring,) than my own. Some of Mr. Webb's remarks I fully agree with and thank him for, while some savour much of disingenuous casuistry, and others contain the very opposite of what I conceive to be the truth;—as when (for instance) he says,—"that 'Carpenter's Son' whom *we many of us worship as being Himself the Mighty Everlasting God.*"!!! Alas! how truly is the saying often verified—"From the sublime to the ridiculous is only a step."—Such is sure always to be the case by both men and ministers who love the faith of their Church or party more than they love the truth.

—*I am, &c.,*

WILLIAM COLENSO.

Dannevirke, May 14, 1888.

§ 1888 A CORRESPONDENT WRITES.
Bush Advocate 29 May.

"Many of your readers will regret to hear that our worthy scientist, the Rev. William Colenso, is about leaving our district for the winter, he having pressing duties to attend to in Napier. He has been residing at Mr. Baddeley's Railway Hotel for some time past, not only as a matter of choice for the unsurpassing salubrity of the locality and its bracing climate, but for its proximity to a splendid fern bush, and other notable novelties in the wild shrubbery line, amongst which in good weather he invariably took his eager walks in the interest of science. At the same time, though thus actively engaged, he did not at all forget local interests, but has taken a special delight in bestowing most liberally and unostentatiously the means at his disposal towards the advancement of the district to a higher and nobler platform. On last Sunday evening, owing to the Revs. Robertshaw and Stewart being both away at Woodville, there would have been no service in Danevirke had it not been for Mr. Colenso, who willingly filled the gap when spoken to on the matter, and preached a very eloquent and edifying sermon on the prodigal son, which was of the most evangelical type, to a very crowded and attentive audience in the new Presbyterian Church. To me, and to many of his auditors, if not to all, it was really refreshing to note the fervid and fluent utterance of an elderly gentleman verging on being an octogenarian, one who had spent many of his late years most successfully in the laudable pursuit of science, which with some scientists, when not directed with the good spirit that rules the universe, tends to lead to scepticism of gospel truths, but not so with him. Like Sir Isaac Newton, he only sees better the puny littleness of the best efforts of men, and that enabled him to raise his voice on the occasion with much power and pathos, humbly reechoing the Great Master's utterance as recorded in St. Luke's Gospel."

❖ 1888 THE "MAORI RELIC."

Bush Advocate 29 May.

SIR,—Having seen your remarks, in your paper of the 26th inst., concerning a notched bone in your possession, as affording "a very valuable proof as a relic belonging to a time before the Maoris arrived here," my curiosity was aroused; and so I called at your office and examined it. I may also say that I had previously seen what had appeared in the columns of the Napier *Herald* respecting it, copied I believe from your paper, and upon that I had rightly concluded what it really was.

I now find it to be a very common instrument indeed, being nothing more than a barbed bone made for killing pigeons, which 40 years (or more) ago I have seen both made and used in the mountain forests in the interior, on the East side of the Ruahine range, and have dined off the pigeons so taken.

This barbed bone was attached as a head to a very long light spear made of tawa wood, generally about 40 feet long; this was partly secured to a suitable tree in the forests, in the proper season, on which pigeons were known (and further invited by baits) to perch, and then, in using, quickly sent upward with a jerk into their bodies, of course entering from the lower part of the abdomen. Through the barbs the bird (though strong on wing and in fluttering) was secured.

The whole method of procedure (including the obtaining and the manufacture of those barbs and spears, etc., etc.) is very interesting, but much too long for your columns, even if I had the required time.

I may add, that from the appearance of the worn bit of bone (3 inches long), and particularly from its blunted barbs, I should suppose it to have been an old one, almost worn out, perhaps on that account thrown away. I have seen some newly made ones of nearly twice the size, with their barbs many, very sharp, tips reversed, and acute. No doubt the bone is human, such being very commonly used by Maoris for all such purposes—barbs for sea-fishing hooks, etc.—not having any known metal.

The old Maoris would call it a *tara*, or a *tara-matia*, or *tara-wero-manu*.

I note you seem to adhere to the *myth* of the Maoris coming to this land!—I had thought I had fully exposed that many years ago.—I am, etc.,

WILLIAM COLENSO.

Dannevirke, May 28, 1888.

§ 1888 NEWS OF THE DAY.

Bush Advocate 29 May.

The Rev. W. Colenso, of Napier, conducted service in the Dannevirke Presbyterian Church on Sunday evening last, when, despite the rain which fell, there was a very large congregation. The Rev. gentleman chose for his text the 20th and 21st verses of the 15th chapter of the gospel of St. Luke, from which he preached a most instructive and interesting sermon. The late cold and boisterous weather we have experienced the last week or two must have brought a few pigeons down from the range again, if we are to judge by the greater number of shots fired in the adjoining forests. We are not, however, likely to have them in any considerable number, if at all, before we see the Ruahine covered with snow. Should we hear that there is good sport to be had, we will not fail to inform our Napier friends, who, we hope, will be able to come to the Bush for a day's sport and return home with bags full and without having had to buy the contents.

❖ 1888 MR. COLENSO EXPLAINS.
Daily Telegraph 13 June.
SIR,—In your issue of this evening you have made two (at least) prominent misstatements respecting what I said last night in my address to the members of the Hawke's Bay Philosophical Institute. As, I believe, you had no reporter present, I would hope you have done so unwittingly.

Nevertheless, I am (as the saying goes,) "in two minds," whether to correct them or not; perhaps I had better do so at once, especially as one of them affects the well-doing of our Society; although your *canards* will have had twenty-four hours' start ahead of veracity, making it a rather desperate stern-chase.

1. You say:—"According to rule 3 of the Hawke's Bay Philosophical Society members are not expected to debate matters which may arise, and the President last night, referred to the danger of the Society's meetings degenerating into a low debating club. This was as much as to say that the statements—misstatements very often—of the members once uttered must be swallowed whole, and that young members must maintain silence although the questions brought forward might require elucidation to bring them down to the level of ordinary minds." Allow me to give you rule 3:—"If any discussion should occur after the reading of a paper, no person shall be at liberty to address the meeting more than once, except when called upon through the chairman, for explanation. The member contributing a paper shall have the right to reply to observations made upon it."

Is not that rule very different to what you have represented it to be? Does it not provide for ample reasonable discussion?—and please note, "observations" from any *"person"present*. Does it not run in almost the same groove as the debates in our Houses of General Assembly? I refrain from making any remark on your straining and high-coloring. I certainly did call on my fellow-members to keep up the status of our Society (as a branch of the Colonial N.Z. Institute, and so to observe her rules), and not to allow themselves to degenerate in the way you have stated.

2. You, also, say:—"In opening the present session of the Hawke's Bay Philosophical Society, the Rev. W. Colenso, F.R.S., the President, took occasion last night to

deplore, the lack of interest in scientific matters shown by the people of this colony. In making this charge the worthy president did the colonists a great injustice," &c., &c.

To this I reply I never said any such thing; rather the very contrary. What I said had reference to our own Hawke's Bay district, and to our own local Society; and that in a very different manner to this statement of yours. I will just copy for you the words I used.

"In this ship, or hive, there should be no drones. Our society is both smaller and poorer than other kindred ones in this N. Island—Auckland and Wellington; happily there is no distinction made on this account; nevertheless we here in Hawke's Bay must feel it, and therefore it is the more imperative upon us, as a determined and devoted though small band, devoid of those large blessings which our older sisters enjoy,—in rich endowments,[15] princely gifts, resident learned scientific men, extensive libraries and museums, —to be active, to be penetrated with that genuine *esprit-de-corps*, which not unfrequently more than makes up for the want of everything else."—I am, &c.,

WILLIAM COLENSO.

P.S.—As I have good reasons for believing that my address will be shortly published. I will take good care that a copy shall early be sent to you.—W.C.

Napier, June 12th, 1888.

❖ 1888 THE TEETOTAL CRUSADE.

Hawke's Bay Herald 25 June.

SIR,—From your Paper of this morning I find that the fanatical hireling Teetotal Lecturer Glover is again on the war-path, again going his rounds among us, spouting away at a furious rate, especially in the back-woods towns and villages—albeit to dwindling audiences. However, as long as the *collections* are sufficient to pay his way, I suppose this kind of thing will be cropping up occasionally, and like Phrenology and Spiritism and Fortune-telling and the "Harmy" must be endured, until our race become wiser through sad and dearly-bought experience.

In your condensed account of his late big-sounding utterances at Waipawa, you tell us,—"As Mr. Glover puts it, publicans should not be paid for the loss of what they never possessed. A license is only a permission under restriction to make the most of selling liquor, and there remains no claim in law or equity for compensation." Now it so happens that I was only this very night reading my London Paper (*Standard*), lately to hand, which coming together proves to be a curious coincidence! or, if you will, a complete upsetting of all such flap-doodle; and as it gives the highest legal authority in England on this very point; I will, with permission, make an extract which I trust may prove of some service even to the superficial Lecturer himself, and to his still more noisy and illiterate local Subs.—

---

15 This original word may be, perhaps, appropriately altered by Napierians to some other more suitable 2-syllabled word, retaining however the initial letter H. W.C.

"Lord Coleridge and the Publicans.—Lord Chief Justice Coleridge presided yesterday afternoon at the twenty-sixth annual meeting of the Church of England Temperance Society, held in the Library of Lambeth Palace. His Lordship, referring to the compensation clauses in the Local Government Bill, after expressing his sympathy with the temperance movement, said he wished to give a clear expression of his views on the question whether the publicans should be compensated. Those views were founded entirely upon what he believed to be the law. In one sense—and no lawyer on either side of the House of Commons would venture to question it—there was no vested interest in the trade. But let them seriously consider what would be said on the other side. Publicans were a set of men whom they might think were engaged in a mischievous traffic, but the trade had been sanctioned by law for a great many years: and it was the custom in all cases where the public-houses were respectably conducted, aud there was no complaint of misconduct on the part of the publican, to renew the licenses from year to year, and in this way a very large interest had grown up, and it would, in his judgment, be wrong to say there was no vested interest in the profession or trade carried on by those to whom licenses had for many years been granted. As he would have to vote on the question in the House of Lords, he considered it his duty to state his views. Unless he did so, when he voted for compensation, he would be open to censure from his temperance friends. Whatever might be the extent of the legal rights of the publicans, they had no right to ruin them because the mind of England had changed on the drink question. Canon Ellison said, the Executive of the Society had adopted the view his Lordship had expressed, and they were glad to have it endorsed by the highest legal profession in England."

It is refreshing to read such clear calm equitable and dignified sentiments expressed by a leading supporter of the Temperance Cause; so very different to the dissonant far-fetched and dishonest talk (I might fairly say—ravings) of the Teetotallers! Would that our Teetotallers could but see the great difference the enormous distinction between their narrow views and those of Temperance,—with which they have nothing to do, "neither part nor lot in this matter."—I am, &c.,

WILLIAM COLENSO.

Napier, June 23, 1888.

❖ 1888 WHAT'S IN A NAME?
Hawke's Bay Herald 27 June.

"And last of all an Admiral came,
A terrible man with a terrible name!—
A name which you all know by sight very well;
But which no one can speak, and no one can spell."
—SOUTHEY.

SIR,—For some time past I have noticed an advertisement in your paper, stating, "that a Special Meeting of the Hawke's Bay County Council will be held on the 6th July, 1888, to consider altering the name of the 'Patea Road Board' and the 'Patea Riding' to the 'Erewhon Road Board' and 'Erewhon Riding.'" And as this seems to me to be a very curious kind of hybrid thing, I trouble you with a few remarks upon it.[16]

1. I think it is wholly new:—that is, to attempt to make such a radical change; and therefore should be well considered before it is done, and becomes a precedent.

2. Hitherto the rule has been with us to maintain in their integrity the ancient and proper Maori names of places.

3. Where such Maori names have been changed (even into fair and reasonable English names), as in Abbotsford for Waipawa, Port Napier for Port Ahuriri, the three rivers Esk, Alma, and Plassy, for Petane, Tukituki, aud Ngaruroro;— the foreign or newly imposed names have dwindled into disuse and are almost forgotten.

4. Where roads or streets have necessarily been named, as here in our town, it has been our good fortune to have really first-class intellectual and respectable English names given to them—names that often evoke a sigh, or proud swelling patriotic feelings when spoken or written, or even only heard! And this thoughtful and pleasurable naming of our streets and roads has been often noticed with approbation by educated tourists and visitors, as well as in works published in England.

5. The proposed new-fangled word as a name for a Riding, &c., seems, to me, to savour of the ridiculous—or even lower still, for (1) it is not an English word, there not being any such in our language: (2) it is also not even a word taken from any civilised tongue: (3) it is merely the English word *Nowhere* spelled backwards like a witch's prayers!: (4) and, lastly, it is the mere trifling name of a common modern ephemeral novel!

6. Such being the case, I trust the members of the Hawke's Bay County Council will please bear all that in mind when duly considering the subject; seeing too, that in their doing so, they will be deciding for the *future* as much (if not more) than for to-day. Let it not be enquired by a generation to come,—"Whence came such a foolish unmeaning nonsensical name? How widely different to all the names of places both *Maori* and *pakeha* around about us! How came it to pass?"

7. If it be said,—A change of name is necessary in order to distinguish between Patea interior and Patea west-coast; such can very easily be done (if really required) by adding North or South, East or West, or some such short and fitting distinguishing word to Patea; as obtains already in towns and Road boards here in our own District, viz., Havelock North, Kaikora North, Hastings South; and in many others scattered throughout the colony, as, Palmerston North, Greytown South, Alexandra South, Waiwera South, Waimate North, South Dunedin, South Malvern, Upper Riccarton, Upper Moutere, &c. Moreover, supposing such a change of name to be advisable, as between the two Pateas, I don't see why we should give up our use of the name, which as the old Maori name, more properly belongs to our Patea: the term on the West Coast is that, of the *River* Patea, and not of the land there.

16 'Erewhon' remains the name of a sheep station on the Hastings–Taupo road. I.S.G.

8. If a man—the owner, say—chooses to give a queer outlandish name to his Homestead,—as Ratshole, or Toadstool, or the Goose and Gridiron, or the Three Jolly Beggars, or Patshall, or Windwhistle House,—I do not see why we should follow suit (more particularly Grave Councillors), and so be the means of supporting his whim and transmitting down his vagaries to posterity.

9. For my part I doubt the absolute correctness of the saying—

> "What's in a name! that which we call a rose
> By any other name would smell as sweet.
> Rather would I choose to say with Campbell,—
> Who hath not owned, with rapture-smitten frame,
> The power of grace, the magic of a name,"

And you, yourself, Mr. Editor, have not unfrequently said as much, when you have occasionally come out in your comic vein, with your "Smith, Jones and Robinson" clan, and "a' o' that ilk."—Just try it: banish Tennyson Street for Smith Street, Shakespeare Road for Erewhon Road! *Bah!!*

10. Twenty-five years ago I wrote thus, (in my prize Essay "on the Maori races,")—"Language adheres to the soil, when the lips which spoke it are resolved into dust. Mountains repeat, and rivers murmur, the voices of nations denationalised or extirpated in their own land."

In conclusion: I sincerely hope, that the members of the Hawke's Bay County Council will keep before them their grave responsibility as elected Councillors when considering this subject, and think deeply and well ere they decide:—(1) Whether any radical change of name is really required: and (2) If so, to give the new named Riding a becoming name,—one, that neither they nor their grandchildren may ever be ashamed of.

—*I am, &c.,*

WILLIAM COLENSO.

Napier, June 23, 1888.

❖ **1888 TEETOTALLISM AND TEMPERANCE.**
Hawke's Bay Herald 29 June.

SIR,—I should like to say a little more upon this Temperance subject, although I have no time to spare for it, and you—at this busy Parliamentary season—no spare room; but I do so from the circumstance of both Mr. Glover and Mr. M'Nicoll being strangers here, and from the fact (as seen in their letters which have appeared in your paper yesterday and to-day) of their confusing Teetotallism with Temperance, and so using it! I will be as brief as possible and being well-known here, together with my views on this subject, among my own people, shall not return to it again.

Mr. M'Nicoll says,—"Mr. Colenso closes his letter by stating that temperance people are intemperate, having 'neither part nor lot' in the matter of temperance." Let me tell Mr. M'Nicoll two things:—

1. That I assisted (largely, I may say, and that without pay,) in forming the *first* Temperance Society in New Zealand, in 1835)—probably before either Mr. M'Nicoll or Mr. Glover was born—attending Public Meeting in open boat over some miles of sea; at a time when we had no Railway Carriages to go about in at ease! nor even horses and roads to use, nor churches in which to hold meetings, nor friends to encourage and receive us free of cost, nor money (*unknown* then!) to gather: that I wrote the Report, &c., of that meeting, and printed it with my own hand (being the *first* book in English printed in N.Z.),[17] and that, in all probability, I am the only surviving originator and supporter of that early Temperance movement in this land.—2. That I have been an upholder of Temperance principles and a temperate man all my days albeit without Fanaticism, or (if they would rather) visionary notions and ideas, farfetched Utopian schemes, mere *ignis fatuus* or Will-with-the-wisp, which can never become universal.

What I mean by Temperance, is this, (the ancient, the classical, the Scriptural and the proper English definition of the word or term),—moderation, self-restraint, decorum, seemliness; to which, as I take it, all Christians as such are bound by their Baptismal pledge:—temperate *in all things,*—not merely in drink, that is to say alcoholic liquors, (many teetotallers gulge tea by the pint or quart! not to mention their own peculiar *Cordials!!*)—but in eating, smoking, play, dress, talking, sleep, &c. To me, the intemperate man is to be found in two distinct classes, or companies, in that one regiment:—1. The drunkard, the glutton, the inveterate smoker, the immoderate in dress and vain body ornaments, in pleasures, and in idleness and frivolity, in gossip and low unprofitable talk:—and 2. the total abstainer from the good things that the Great and Good Father of all hath given to man for his use and comfort, with His blessing on man's progressive improvement in their manufacture, and in his proper use of them. Whether Teetotaller or Vegetarian, anti-tobacconist and antivivisectionist, ascetic or fanatic of any kind,—all alike belong to this class: each with an ill-directed zeal acrimoniously (and too frequently dishonestly) seeking to bring mankind into his own narrowminded way, and looking scornfully on all the rest as being "in the broad way of destruction," if not already "lost"! Further: as an old temperate man, I have often told some of our more conspicuous local teetotallers,—"Come out honourably, don't skulk, or seek to gain advantages (pirate-like) under a flag that does not belong to you. Douse my honest and brave old English flag of Temperance, and run up your own partisan slim or narrow pennant of Teetotallism, and I will then honour you—as a party; aye, and help you too: but, mark! only just as I would (and have done) in administering strong Medicines, as Opium, Arsenic, Croton Oil, Corrosive Sublimate, and Strychnine, desperate cases requiring desperate remedies: never thinking that one treatment is suitable alike for all. Indeed, there have been instances in which I have recommended the unfortunates to become total abstainers."

And, as "one concrete example" is worth more than a whole boat-load of talk, I have one handy: Suppose the "Harmy," or their "Captain," were to say to Mr. M'Nicoll—"We are the two Wesleyans; we adopt John Wesley's early plan, and manner,

17 Note.—This curiosity Mr. M'Nicoll or Mr. Glover may see, if they choose to call on me. W.C.

and doctrines; we are Wesleyan Methodists as well as you; so—." And what reply would the Wesleyan Minister, Mr. M'Nicoll, make? Would he say, with frankness and love,—"All right: come on brother with me"?—Here, methinks, I might ask of Mr. M'Nicoll, (seeing he has posed in his letter as being Mr. Glover's "personal friend," and also supported him,)—"Why not allow Mr. Glover the use of his cosy and respectable Wesleyan Church in Clive-square, to deliver his lecture in tonight; and not allow his "dear personal friend" to drill away to the cold and cheerless Army Barracks, in midwinter too, for that purpose?

Both writers seem to take umbrage at my plain use of the word "hireling" for a paid itinerant Lecturer: I do not see anything wrong in this. For, 1st, it is a proper English (Anglo-Saxon) word: 2nd, Dr. Johnson, in his Dictionary, defines it, "one who serves for wages": 3rd, it is so used in Scripture: and, 4th, also, by several of our superior British poets. And, (again, curiously enough!) in your own paper of yesterday, wherein I read of an imported Parson from England into America, being recently legally objected to as being a labourer for hire—"a contract labourer." Will those writers give the difference between this word and "hireling"?

To Mr. Glover (a stranger and only a passing visitor) I would say one word. I should not have come out on this occasion had it not been for two contrary things happening together;—his statement at Waipawa (as shown in your paper) respecting compensation, which I view as dishonest; and the very opposite one (quoted by me in my letter) lately made by the President of the Church of England Temperance Society, he being also the highest legal authority in England. For, as I have long with sorrow viewed it, commercial and social dishonesty is far too rampant here already, to allow of any thing or matter to be spoken of publicly and taught, that might tend to increase it. As another "concrete example,"—look at the shameful number of bankrupts and insolvents from all ranks, ever increasing among us! And here I may also fully adduce the public testimony of the highest Church authority in England, the Archbishop of Canterbury, lately given by him at his opening the Public Hall for four working-men's Clubs at Bethnal Green, London; his Grace said,—"The two real evils of Bethnal Green were Drunkenness and early reckless marriages. Drunkenness was an offence against all mankind, and early reckless marriages were offences almost as great.... Self-restraint was the road which governed both kinds of intemperance.... There were no royal roads to either leisure or means. There was only one way by which men could obtain a fair share of God's good things, and that was by the road of diligence, industry, and thrift."

Mr. Glover particularly calls my attention to the utterances of "the most learned man living, Mr. Gladstone," and to "100,000 working-men meeting in Hyde Park," &c. Now, as to the first, Mr. Gladstone: for many years I was a consistent supporter of him, but now (with honest John Bright) I have been obliged to leave him—and that for his modern fanatical (visionary Utopian) schemes or speeches, which contain the utter ruin of my Native land! and all done to please his low allies, enemies to British rule. I know of no more melancholy modern instance of the great debasement prostitution and loss of talent and learning than in this one of Mr. Gladstone; when considering it, in conjunction with his early and long and arduous career, I am often reminded of Milton's Satan in his Paradise Lost.

As to the second, the meeting of 100,000 men in Hyde Park (or in Trafalgar Square, or in scores of places in unhappy Ireland,)—what of that? Perhaps Mr. Glover may believe in the old misused saying, *Vox populi, vox Dei*, (the voice of the people is the voice of God,)—that the cry of the many—the idle the discontented the squanderer the loafer,—whether "Hosanna!" or "Crucify him!" must carry the day; forgetting, apparently, that as the wind blows the leaves are directed. I, however, have lived long enough to see the true value of all that; rather with the Duke in Shakespeare I would say—

> —*"I love the people.*
> *But do not like to stage me to their eyes;*
> *Though it do well, I do not relish well*
> *Their loud applause, and aves vehement;*
> *Nor do I think the man of safe discretion,*
> *That does affect it."—*
> —*"Measure for Measure."*

I am, &c.,

WILLIAM COLENSO.

Napier, June 27, 1888.

§ 1888 EDITORIAL.
Evening Post 17 September.
We have to thank the author, Mr. William Colenso, F.R.S., F.L.S., &c., of Napier, for a copy in pamphlet form of a paper recently read by him before the Hawke's Bay Philosophical Society, entitled "Fifty Years Ago in New Zealand:
A commemoration, a jubilee paper, a retrospect, and a plain and true story."
It contains matter of much interest.

§ 1888 NEWS OF THE DAY.
Bush Advocate 27 November.
Mr. William Colenso, who is now on a tour to the Bush district in the interest of science, will address the people on Thursday evening at 7 o'clock in the Presbyterian Church, Dannevirke, on a subject of the most vital importance to the community at large.

❖ 1889 VENEERED INFIDELITY.
Hawke's Bay Herald 30 January.

"O foolish Galatians! Who hath bewitched you, that ye should not obey the truth."
—Paul.

SIR,—I (with, no doubt, many of your subscribers and readers) heartily thank you for your able article of this day on "Veneered Savages." I agree with you in your plain yet forcible observations; and would fain hope such may have some good effect.—

But why have you (or, say, one of your daily contemporaries here) not come out in a similar way but stronger, on the Veneered Infidelity stalking publicly, shamefaced and rampant here in Napier? I have been absent 2 months from Napier residing in the Bush, yet while there seeing your paper (with others); and the question has not unfrequently been put to me, (on reading the blasphemous mouthings of this newly-arrived American lecturer Daniells—though gilded and sweetened for the nonce,) —"Why do the Napier folks endure or support such things?" And my only answer has been,—"Such, unfortunately, has long been their peculiar custom or fashion,— to take up with anything new or strange, no matter of what kind or description, high or low; only (too often) the lower and more abusive of all that is good proved and long established the better!" We have had it, in low theatricals, in politics, in racing and gambling (including the totalisator and all its attendant crimes and horrors), in rinking, and now in what is falsely termed Religion! And for most of these utter abominations—Rinking, Table-turning and "Spiritism," Mormonism, and Adventists—we are indebted to our far ahead cousins in America.

I could better understand why the low the vulgar the careless and the scoffer should unite in supporting (for the time) this man Daniells,—Even to their bearing him on their shoulders in triumph, crowning him with laurels, and putting silver into his purse: but how any members, or frequenters of Christian churches, any readers of the Bible, any thoughtful, any respectable steady moral person, any well-wisher of the community should do so, is the thing that astonishes me!—

Because, Jesus himself—our Great Teacher and the Head of his Church; warned his disciples that such would be, and be carried on even to that extent as "to deceive the very elect;" laying down the safe and simple rule for them to follow,—"Go ye not after them,"—listen not to them. And, also, because, plenty of such opposition arose very early in the infant Christian Church; which called for the serious and plain warnings of the Apostles themselves, as we find them recorded in their several Epistles concerning such innovators;—and all such (it should be borne in mind) was seemingly done for the faith or the Christian Religion!—Paul could even thus write of those plausible designers to the Corinthian Church:—"Such are false apostles, deceitful workers, transforming themselves into the apostles of Christ. And no marvel, for Satan himself is transformed into an angel of light. Therefore it is no great thing if his Ministers also be transformed as the Ministers of righteousness whose end shall be according to their works."—2 *Cor.* xi. 13–15.

We have lately heard of one of the great London publishers, Vitizelly, having been prosecuted and fined £100, with costs and loss of all his books, for his publishing a translation of some filthy French novels,—Vitizelly, too, pleading Guilty; such being injurious to morals. But how much more, I would ask,—aye, stand forward in the public arena of Clive Square, Napier, and ask and demand,—How much more readily should this blatant blasphemer of the Holy Scriptures (albeit his being "silver-tongued") be prosecuted and fined, and his wares (or "Kit of tools") be condemned, for his daring polluting the river of God—the water of life, the Holy Scriptures? And thus unsettling the minds of many and even imperilling the salvation of their souls! Don't let anyone get up and tell me of the poor creature's zeal arising from his ignorance!—hence, too, much of his apparent simplicity and even devotion!! Why the Devil himself, we are told by St. Matthew, daringly quoted Scripture to Jesus, thinking thereby to gain his own ends and carry the day!

And, as I said to some friends in the Bush, so I say now:—Give me the t'other notorious American Lecturer Ingersoll, with all his glaring and coarse faults, and defects,—there was something open and manly about him; before this fellow with his cunningly-contrived, smooth, insidious and destructive tales.

In conclusion; this one word of faithful warning would I utter:—Men of Napier! look to yourselves; give the teachings of this deluded man no place, no quarter! I, your old man, plainly tell you, (and I know what I am writing about,)—that nothing you may ever have done will ever cause you so much uneasiness and bitter distress of mind at the last, (in the day of serious thought, and reflection, should such even be granted you,) as this one error, or sin, or crime, namely, that of your having wilfully received and supported the false and soul-destroying teachings of this American Daniells. Remember the words of Jesus, (thrice repeated by Matthew, by Mark, and by Luke,)—"Whosoever speaketh against the Holy Ghost, it shall not be forgiven him; neither in this world, neither in the world to come." —*Matt.* xv. 32, &c.,

—*I am, &c.,*

WILLIAM COLENSO.

Napier, January 29, 1889.

P.S. By way of postscript I append an advertisement clipped from London Standard, Nov. 30, 1888.

The greatest and most dreadful wars and European revolutions between 1889 and 1891, changing 23 Kingdoms into 10—Britain's Loss of Ireland and India, and subjection to France, previous to the Rise of the Antichrist Napoleon as King of Syria and his Seven Years' Covenant with the Jews on April 21st, 1884—their Sacrifices Restored, November 8th, 1881 (Daniel vii., 24; viii, 14: ix., 27), and his subsequent Massacre of Millions of Christians during 1260 days from August 14th. 1897, to January 26th, 1901—Coming Earthquakes, Famines, Pestilences.—Second Advent of Christ, Resurrection of Saints, and Ascension of 144,000 Living Christians to Heaven without dying on March 5th, 1896, and His Descent on Earth, April 11th

LETTERS 1880-1889

(Nisan 22, 1901), being exactly 2345 years from Nehemiah's command to rebuild Jerusalem on Nisan 22, B.C., 445 (Dan. ix, 25; vii., 14; xii, 11, 12; Nehem. 11).

❖ **1889 PROPERTY TAX VALUATION.**
Hawke's Bay Herald 9 March.
SIR,—I was pleased in seeing in your issue of this morning an article headed "Property Tax Valuation," something of the kind having long been wanted. But you have unwittingly committed a grave error in your so doing; probably through your referring to and copying from, the old Property Tax Act of 1881, which has been repealed; instead of looking-up the Property Assessment Act of 1885;—and, in your so doing, actually confirmed by your editorial sanction the common mistake about it!

For the clause you refer to, (now 95 of the later Act,) which, you say,—"cuts the other way, and provides that if the Commissioner refuses to reduce what an owner may consider *an excessive valuation, the owner can compel the Commissioner to buy at that valuation.*" This clause however, is *not* as you give it, very far from it; though many, I know, have generally believed it to be so.—The said clause runs thus:—

"If any person shall be dissatisfied with the amount at which the whole or any portion of his property is assessed, he shall be entitled to call upon the Commissioner either to reduce the assessment to the sum at which it was valued *in the statement of such person, or else to purchase the property at the sum at which the same was valued in such statement;* and the Commissioner shall, *at his discretion, reduce the assessment accordingly; or shall, upon obtaining the consent of the Governor in Council, and upon having the property duly conveyed,* assured, or assigned to the Crown, purchase the same as hereinbefore provided." (In clause 94.)—*N.B.* At whose expense?

I may briefly add, that "Cash value" means "the market value at which property may be purchased for cash." (Clause 2)

There are also other important alterations in this last Act, which it might be well for you to lay before your readers.—I am, &c.,
WILLIAM COLENSO.
Napier, March 8, 1889.
[Mr. Colenso is quite correct.—ED. *H.B.H.*]

§ **1889 TITLE.**
Hawke's Bay Herald 31 May.
William Colenso objected to the valuation of a property in Hyderabad-road, £200. Mr. Colenso complained that though the last valuation was reduced by the Board to £100, an increase of 100 per cent had been made.—Mr. Williams said he was sick at the time the reduction was made, and could not be present to support his valuation. In reply to the chairman Mr. Williams said the land had not increased in value in the three years.—Reduced to £150.

Mr. Colenso also objected to the assessnent of a section in Milton-road, £350. —Mr. Williams contended that the property had been improved by quarrying. —Mr. Colenso said it was merely the entry to the quarry, and could not be utilised until the quarry was worked out.—Valuation sustained.

Mr. Colenso further objected to the valuation of his residence and seven acres of land, £2860, which was in increase of £700.—Mr. Colenso said his hill property was valued altogether at something like £8000, though he had lodged an objection only to the valuation of one part.—Valuation sustained.

Mr. Colenso further objected to the valuation of four sections in Sale-street and Munro-street, £500. He said that was the previous valuation, but the Reviewers reduced it to £350—Reduced to £450.

Mr. Colenso also objected to the assessment of town section 560, Hastings-street, £600.—Mr. Colenso said Mr. Williams last time valued the property at £400, and he contended that it had not increased in value.—The Chairman: I suppose the improvement of the Marine-parade has added to the value?—Mr. Colenso: I don't believe in the "improvement" and never did. I look upon it as the greatest bug-bear that ever happened to Napier.—Valuation sustained.

❖ 1889 THE CROWN OF THORNS.
Hawke's Bay Herald 1 July.

SIR,—I have been a wee bit amused this dull wet morning in reading in your paper of this day your notice of "The Crown of Thorns." That is to say,—of "the cheek" of that correspondent to an American paper; who goes on to relate an "incident," which (he says) took place when he and his party were lately travelling in the Holy Land. As if such a discovery of that thorny plant, and its probable use, were only then made for the first time! On the contrary, the plant itself has been well known, often described, and commonly received as having furnished that especial wreath, for about 140 years.

It was discovered by Hasselquist, a distinguished Swedish Botanist and pupil of Linnæus, while travelling in Syria and Palestine in 1750 for the purpose of Botany. He died a martyr to science in those burning deserts, in 1752, at the early age of 30.

Indeed, there are two shrubby thorny plants there indigenous to that country, and both common; either might have served for that especial purpose.

1. *Paliurus aculcatus*, Lam., (*Rhamnus paliurus*, Linn.) This is supposed by many to be the plant from which the crown of thorns was composed; and from the pliability of its long slender branches, it seems highly probable. Its fruit has a very singular appearance, resembling a head with a broad-brimmed hat on,—the French call the shrub *Porte-chapeau*. Fifty years ago it grew in my garden in the Bay of Islands, and on my coming hither to reside in 1844, I brought away cuttings which grew well until killed (with many others) by a deep deposit of mud left on the ground from a very severe flood in 1845.

2. *Zizyphus spina-Christi*, Willd., (*Rhamnus spina-Christi*, Linn.) Hasselquist says of this plant,—"In all probability, this is the tree which afforded the crown of thorns put upon the head of Christ. It grows very common in the East. This plant is very fit for the purpose, for it has many small and sharp spines which are well adapted to give pain: the crown might be easily made of these soft, round and pliant branches; and what in my opinion seems the greater proof is that the leaves very much resemble those of ivy, as they are of a very deep glossy green. Perhaps the enemies of Christ would have a plant somewhat resembling that with which emperors and generals were crowned, that there might be a calumny even in the punishment." No doubt, Linnæus agreed with him, and hence gave the plant its trivial name, "*spina-Christi*"—Christ's thorn, which it still bears; but notwithstanding that, the former one, *Paliurus aculcatus*, is now generally believed to have been the plant. Dean Alford in his Greek Testament, in his brief note on the Crown of thorns, (Matt. 27, 29,) seems to confuse several plants, which, as he truly says, were unfit for the purpose. Those remarks, however, of the Dean's, are good,—"It does not appear the purpose of the Crown was to wound, or simply for mockery—and equally uncertain is it, of what kind of thorns it was composed." And,—"some *flexile* shrub or plant must be understood":—unfortunately, adding,—"possibly some variety of the cactus or prickly pear." (!!!) Whereas the Cactus family are inhabitants of tropical S. America and found nowhere else. The Dean was a better theologian, or, rather, Grecian than a Botanist and Scientist. I should, however, mention that other theological writers before him had made the same mistake. Dr. Clarke, for instance, findiug the *Cactus* (Opuntia) *Ficus Indicus* common in Syria and Palestine imagined it was indigenous there, and so has a good deal to say about it. But the Cactus never was known until after the discovery of America, when the Spanish, Dutch, and other traders, having failed in bringing the valuable Cochineal plant into their settlements in the Mediterranean, and the Cape of Good Hope, introduced the thorny Cactus *Ficus Indicus*, in the vain hope that the Cochineal insect would feed upon it. Finding a congenial climate the Cactus took possession of the soil, and passes for indigenous.—I am, &c.,

WILLIAM COLENSO.

Napier, June 27, 1889.

❖ **1889 A QUEEN'S BENCH DECISION.**
Hawke's Bay Herald 16 July.
SIR,—I thank you for your able and truthful leader of Saturday last (13th.)—also, for your sub-leader—same issue.—I cannot understand why any thinking person can take up pen in defence of the "Harmy" *processions*, &c.—I send you, enclosed, a clipping from L. *Standard* of May 2nd—this decision of Judges in Q. Bench Court—one would think should settle the question—as far as to the illegality of all such disagreeable noisy public interruptions.—I am, &c.,

W. COLENSO.

Danmevirke, July 15, 1889.

The following is the clipping enclosed by our correspondent:—
[The clipping is a report of a case in St. Alban's, England, in which a man was found guilty of causing a nuisance by playing an accordion loudly.]

§ 1889 A NEW ZEALAND CAXTON (PRINTERS' REGISTER).
Bush Advocate 24 August.
It was in 1834 that the Church Missionary Society sent out to their station at Paihia a printer, their object being to print the New Testament in the Maori language. It is really not so long ago, for many of us can remember King William IV, and it was only three years prior to our good old Queen's accession. Yet, judged by progression, whole ages have passed in those fifty-odd years. England, of course, has advanced in all knowledge, in manners, and let us hope, in morals; but the difference between the England of 1834 and now cannot be compared with the changes in New Zealand during the same period. In that country the white race was only beginning to make an impression—all was savage; cannibalism, even, was not uncommon; and only on the coast was there any safety, and often not there. But now populous towns cover the land, and the printing press is a dominant power.

Just fifty-five years ago a young man named William Colenso was chosen by the Board of the Missionary Society to go out in the double capacity of printer and missionary. The story of his trials even before leaving England is very remarkable, and reveals the old tale of how red-tape ruled then as now, whether it was a Government department or a board of directors. Just as our officials despatched to Egypt whole consignments of guns and no gun-carriages, so the Missionary Society was above being advised by a practical printer who knew his wants. In vain did young Colenso beg for a proper equipment as printer. They gave him types, of course, and a Stanhope press, but no cases, no leads, nor reglets, nor furniture, nor imposing stone, nor roller composition, no roller stocks, *nor paper!* but to make up he had a big roller-mould. In seventeen weeks Sydney was reached, but nine weeks then elapsed before a craft of any kind could be got to sail to the dangerous shores of New Zealand. At last the mission station was reached, and the press and type taken to shore with great difficulty, as light canoes had to be fastened together like a raft to bear the weight of a demy Stanhope. The Maoris crowded around, and as many old flint muskets had been bartered to them by passing ships, they looked with hungry eyes at the type; for though they had learned in a clumsy way how to use firearms and had powder, they were very short of bullets. The missionary station where the press was erected was called Paihia. There three missionaries lived with their wives and families in three separate houses, which, with schools, and chapel, and stores, made a hamlet. The object was to print the New Testament in the Maori tongue, the alphabet and grammar of which had been perfected by the Rev. W. Williams, one of the three missionaries. Nought could be done without paper. Luckily, however, a small quantity of writing-paper was found by the missionaries' wives, and with that twenty-five copies of St. Paul's Epistles to the Ephesians and Philippians were printed in 8vo. Thus on February 17th, 1835, amidst a crowd of wondering natives, was issued in the Maori tongue the first book ever printed in New Zealand. Only a practical printer can imagine what makeshifts were necessary even for so small a pamphlet, when there was only home-made furniture and reglets, and paper leads, and no roller, nor ball, nor inktable. The next issue was the Gospel of St. Luke, of which, having received some paper from home, 1,000 copies were printed and bound.

On May 19th, 1836, the first book in English was printed, if one can call an unpretentious 8vo pamphlet of eight pages by such a name. It was the First Report of the New Zealand Temperance Society. This was followed by the New Testament, 5,000 copies of which were worked off. Our printer wanted help sadly, and tried hard to get some steady Maori converts to work at the bar; but a little of this was quite enough, and their Christian willingness soon wore off, as work was entirely contrary to their nature, especially work which was the same sort day after day, and always in the same place, the last being an insuperable objection. Their wages certainly were not excessive, being 3s. a week—not in cash, for there was no money, but in goods. This was then a high rate of payment, but it failed to entice the ease-loving natives many of whom never did any work. The New Testament was completed in December 1837, and soon created a demand from many stations in New Zealand where the missionaries were known or Christianity extended. A large number were sent to England to be bound, and brought back, and another edition being soon called for, the Missionary Society had it reprinted by Watts of Union Court, Fleet Street, and sent over.

The narrative of the various shifts and fortunes which befell the young press— its increase, and the spread of printing generally in the islands, must be left for another occasion. We will only add that W. Colenso, the New Zealand Caxton, is still alive and hearty, although in the nineties, and is always pleased to chat over his youthful trials. The particulars narrated above have indeed been gathered from an exceedingly interesting 8vo pamphlet, which has the following title: "Fifty Years Ago in New Zealand. A Commemoration, a Jubilee Paper, a Retrospect; a Plain and True Story. Read before the Hawke's Bay Philosophical Institute, October 17th, 1887. By William Colenso." It is unusually well printed by R.C. Harding, Napier, and bears date 1888.

LETTERS 1890–1899

WILLAM COLENSO 1890–1899

1890 *The authentic and genuine history of the signing of the Treaty of Waitangi* published by Govt. Printing Office; three papers in *Transactions of the New Zealand Institute* 23.

1891 Six papers in *Transactions of the New Zealand Institute* 24.

1892 Six papers in *Transactions of the New Zealand Institute* 25.

1893 Seven papers in *Transactions of the New Zealand Institute* 26.

1894 Re-establishes relationship with Church of England; five papers in *Transactions of the New Zealand Institute* 27.

1895 *May* thumb seriously injured in train door; sends £1000 to Penzance; five papers in *Transactions of the New Zealand Institute* 28.

1896 Offers £1500 and free site for Napier museum; two papers in *Transactions of the New Zealand Institute* 29.

1897 *April* serious accident at Woodville, slow recovery.

1898 Letter 'A' of lexicon printed; *Certain errors* published by Dinwiddie & Co; two papers in *Transactions of the New Zealand Institute* 31.

1899 *February 10* William Colenso dies; his plant specimens sent to Cheeseman for identification; two papers published posthumously in *Transactions of the New Zealand Institute* 32.

1904 Colenso's plant specimens returned to Hawke's Bay; arrangements made for transfer to Wellington.

§ 1890 PRESBYTERIAN CHURCH.

Bush Advocate 30 January.

On last Sunday night the Rev. W. Wallace preached a vigorous sermon in the Presbyterian Church, Danevirke, to a large audience. In finishing his discourse he said that this being jubilee week[1] he would, in a few sentences, review the history of New Zealand—how discovered—and named after the southernmost province of Holland, how it was originally surveyed by Captain Cook, the famous British explorer of the Pacific Ocean, in 1769, and subsequently became the favourable resort of British, French, and American whalers, who established whale fisheries on the coasts, the relics of whose land stations are still to be found along the southern shore, and on both sides of the Straits which divide these islands. The rev. gentleman then described how Australian traders began to visit New Zealand, and the commerce which sprung up, and the occasional appearance at Sydney of a Maori chief on board a trading vessel attracted public attention to the country. In the year 1840, just 50 years ago on the 29th of this month, New Zealand became a British colony, the sovereignty of the British Crown being formally proclaimed by Captain Hobson, the first Governor, and the native rights ceded to the sovereign of Great Britain by the famous treaty of Waitangi in the Bay of Islands, on the north-eastern shore of the province of Auckland. Our most esteemed and now venerable friend, the Rev. William Colenso, who had often worshipped with them in that pulpit and Church, besides, in other ways, materially lending a helping hand to the cause of Christianity in the Bush districts, was the only living European witness to the signing of that treaty, fraught as it is with so much interest to our beautiful and prosperous Island, so bountifully bestowed by benignant providence with boundless resources of industrial pursuits, and whose salubrious and sunny shores afford ample room for many people who are elbowed out in the Old Country, and who could be free, healthy, and happy in this climate of perpetual spring, which, according to the views held by some of the leading newspapers of the Australasian group, is destined to be the ultimate sanatorium of the southern hemisphere.

§ 1890 NAPIER.

Observer 8 February.

Napier was the only place that observed the Jubilee religiously. The only celebration in Squatteropolis took the form of a thanksgiving service at the Cathedral. Among the clergymen present was the Rev. W. Colenso, F.R.S., who saw the ship Herald anchor in the Bay of Islands in 1840, and was present at the signing of the Treaty of Waitangi.

---

1   50 years since the signing of the Treaty. I.S.G.

❖ 1890 THE REVEREND W. COLENSO AND THE JUBILEE.
Auckland Weekly News 8 February.

Mr. W. Wildman having telegraphed to Mr. W. Colenso, of Hawke's Bay, inviting him to come to Auckland at the time of the Jubilee, received in reply the following interesting letter:—

Napier, January 24, 1890

Dear Mr. Wildman,

I can scarcely tell you in a few words how very greatly your kind telegram of yesterday affected me on receipt thereof. It was so unexpected and so very generous on your part. As I don't benefit by the town delivery of letters I did not receive it until late this day, and then by chance; but I replied by wire (briefly) as you wished.

The chief causes of my not accepting your invitation are: my chronic rheumatism (often severe), my age (nearly 80) preventing my undertaking the long and rough overland journey, and my being always such a great sufferer at sea from *mal-de-mer;* at the same time my general health is fair if I keep quietly within my old gearings.

For many reasons I should like to be there with you at Auckland on this occasion: (1) From my having both witnessed and assisted at the creation of the colony in the Bay of Islands (Auckland Province) in 1840; and (2) from my wish to add my testimony (that of a living witness) to that fact against the vainglorious and intolerable assumption of Wellington,—which to me, from my intimate actual knowledge of the past, and of the hundreds of whites located at the North, in and about the Bay of Islands, with our respectable merchants, stores, hotels, bank, churches, shipping and extensive trade, is worse than preposterous. I could say a good deal on this head but I forbear.

The Government undertook to publish my authentic account of "the signing of the treaty of Waitangi" (written entirely at the time, and also corroborated by Mr. Busby, then the late British Resident), and as I read the proofs (revise) a fortnight ago I hope you may have some copies with you by the Jubilee day.

I venture to think that not a few Aucklanders (by this term I mean of the whole province) will find it interesting, as well as historical and correct.

I much regret, however, the Government declining to publish with it my two appendices pertaining to the formation of the colony (on the score of not wishing to enlarge the little book). The first of those two was of public matters prior to 1840; the second of matters closely following the same—viz, in that year, until the seat of Government was removed to Auckland. These, however, may yet be published by me.

Heartily wishing you every possible success—without a flaw! and trusting that much future good (though it may be for the present hidden from view) may follow this Jubilee year and commemoration to Auckland and to her whole province, and to the colony at large.

I am &c.

WM. COLENSO.

P.S. Be very sure to send me an Auckland paper containing a full account of your doings.

❖ 1890 THE INK PLANT.
Bush Advocate 15 May.

SIR,—In your paper of the 13th inst. you inform your readers that "In New Granada a plant grows that is locally known as the ink plant; its scientific name is *Coriaria thymifolia*. Without any previous preparation its juice can be used as ink, etc."

I suppose you are not aware that this same plant is common here in New Zealand, especially in certain localities. I originally detected it, 45 years ago, growing profusely among the common fern on the hills near Pohue (on the old Maori track to the Mohaka river and Taupo), and afterwards, though more sparingly, near Te Pakipaki, and also on the low grounds between the river Ngaruroro and the Middle road, north of Havelock. It is still more common in Otago, and is the "ground tutu" of the settlers in those parts. It is nearly allied to our common, large, and well-known tutu (pronounced "toot" by settlers), *Coriaria ruscifolia*, of which the juice was largely used by Maoris some 45 or 50 years ago as a substitute for ink, in the scarcity of the British article. I doubt, however, its permanency.—Yours, etc.,

W. COLENSO.

Danevirke, May 14, 1890.

❖ 1890 THE REV. W. COLENSO ON FOOTBALL.
Hawke's Bay Herald 12 June.

SIR,—In your paper of this morning you give your readers certain items of information received from your "Own Correspondent" at Woodville; closing with his statement, that "the Rev. W. Colenso, preaching at Trinity Church last evening, was very severe upon the athletic young man, especially the footballer," &c., &c. Now, had your correspondent given the whole of what I said, or even only a little more than he has done, it would save my writing to you.

I did say what he has stated, and more to the same effect; but on these grounds and with these (and other) provisos.

And to show you more clearly how it came about, I should first tell you what my text was, being the ground of my discourse: viz. "My joy shall be in the Lord." Ps. 104, (The second Lesson, appointed, being also the appropriate last chapter of Joshua—in which Joshua, in his last words to his people, told them, that "he and his house would serve the Lord.")

Having shown from this and other similar texts, something of the reality, the *joy*, of true religion in the Jewish Church, from the O.T., as well as in that of the primitive Christian in the N.T., (by many ample proofs of *joy* and rejoicing,)—and contrasting that with the slack, faint-hearted, outward joyless services of the Christian Church of this day;—and, moreover, calling the attention of my congregation to what Moses had said on this very subject, in his parting solemn words to the children of Israel,— viz.: "All these curses shall come upon thee, and shall pursue thee, and overtake thee, till thou be destroyed,.... because thou servedst not the Lord thy God with joyfulness and with gladness of heart, for the abundance of all things." (*Deut.* 28, 47.) I pointed out the various sources of human *joy* among us; from that of A.1,—*viz.*, a man and his wife living happily together and with their children attending regularly at church, (again exemplifying,—that "the voice of joy and health is in the dwelling of the righteous;")—down, by a pretty gradual succession, to the lowest grade of animal human *joy*, that of the athlete and the footballer. Bringing forward the many recent examples I had seen and known, at Woodville and elsewhere, when, on Saturday afternoons in particular, young men would wear themselves out till sundown—even in pouring rain and dressed up in thick coats of frieze! returning faint and weary and worn out, dragging their legs pitiably along the roads!! And then, on their being subsequently asked, "Why they were not at any church on the Sunday?" the reply would be, "Because they were too tired, quite done up, through their severe football exercise on the Saturday afternoons." All such I denounced as wrong, (though no strict Sabbatarian,)—adding that all low animal and brutalising games so followed up and made their chief *joy*, invariably drew away men from all intellectuality, all science, all games of mind and skill (as chess), all real knowledge, and all true religion. And further, (from recent statements made by eminent English physicians,) that no boisterous brutal athletes, (footballers and pugilists in particular,) have been known to live beyond the age of 40; and this, without taking into account the great number of deaths, and many serious casualties, we almost daily read of in the papers as happening, through these rough lowering brutalising games.

Further, that I liked fitting athletic exercises kept within their proper bounds, and not made a "craze" of.—*viz.*, their great aim and chief *joy* of their hearts. And that such games as football were fitted only for school-boys, or for Maori men as they were 50 years ago: that, with Paul, I believed it to be far better on becoming a man, to put away childish things, &c., &c.—Yours, &c.,

WILLIAM COLENSO.

Dannevirke, June 10, 1890.

❖ 1890 CHURCH MATTERS.

Bush Advocate 16 August.

SIR,—I noticed in your paper of Tuesday last a strange anonymous letter headed "Church Matters," and I had hoped some one of your many readers here in Danevirke would have taken it up and replied to it in your paper of yesterday. As, however, no one has considered it worthy of notice, I would say a few words about it,—although it is an old and standing rule with me never to condescend to notice anonymous cowardly letters. I am an Englishman, and like a fair open fight; not secretly lurking behind a flax bush, or hedge to get a shot or a stab at a victim, and then a run! "Fair play is bonnie play," as my Scotch friends say. Of course it may be said, and that with some truth, that as long as the subject written on in newspapers (say an anonymous letter) is truthful, or beneficial, or fair, it matters not who wrote it; and to this I might subscribe (though the devil can quote Scripture). But there is this great difference: (1) An apparently fair matter may be brought forward by an enemy merely to bring about strife, he secretly chuckling over his success! (2) An anonymous writer (in these degenerate mercenary days) may write for pay! indeed, such is commonly and daily done; on one day for, and on another day against, the same thing, by the same writer! and so blowing both hot and cold! (3) What may appear to be fair to one bigoted party, is not so to another: As, for instance, the lamentable local option, and teetotal fads, or Mother Seigel's pills or, the crusade against tobacco, or the vegetarian folly, or the fashionable bankruptcy following, or the football craze, or the gambling and totalisator nuisance. But the writer of a letter in the public papers in honestly giving his name to his letter shows a conviction of his principles, and his not being ashamed to own them; while he leaves his readers who may know him to form their own judgment respecting him, and what he says. But all that by the way. Now then, to the said letter: The writer publicly and flippantly calls on the Rev. Mr. Robertshawe to give up his sermon, publicly announced in his Anglican Church last Sunday, in order that he, and others may hear a travelling "preacher and lecturer, Mr. Knott, in the Presbyterian Church next Sunday evening," just as if Mr. Robertshawe could thoughtlessly or very easily do so. This, alone, serves to show the true position of the writer—as being one of those young men, (he mentions) with itching ears! who, "unstable as water," are even "halting between two opinions, and too often are the troubles of churches and congregations." Still his request would not be so very bad were this present case anything like a former one which happened here, and of which he may have heard (he not then being a resident in Danevirke), and which he and others may suppose to form a precedent; I mean the Sunday of the first opening of the Scotch Church here, when the Rev. Mr. Robertshawe kindly and christianly closed his own Church services that all might have the opportunity of joining on such a festal occasion, and hear the Rev. Mr. Paterson preach. But there is no likeness between the two cases, for Mr. Paterson, a Presbyterian Minister, came hither purposely for that one occasion, while this Mr. Knott was here only last week holding forth in the Presbyterian Church, and is also advertised in your paper to come out again "on Monday evening next in the Town Hall!" thus affording those "young men" several opportunities of hearing him. And I may further mention that last Sunday I preached a special sermon in the Woodville Anglican Church, which had been also advertised in the Woodville Examiner, but it never occurred to me (and I am happy to say it was never done by any of my friends and hearers) to call upon my good friends, the Ministers of the other Churches there—the Rev. R. Saunders and the Rev. J. Saunders—to put off their preaching and Church services on the account of my advertised and special sermon, though it was of much general interest. I omit all reference to the small size of the Presbyterian Church; also the soft sawder and "ground bait" so cunningly referred to in the conclusion of his letter. As a well-wisher to, and a pretty frequent resident in, Danevirke I write this long letter, which I can truly and without misgiving call—*pro bono publico.*—I am, etc.,

WILLIAM COLENSO.

August 15, 1890.

❖ 1890 A REPLY TO OLD RATEPAYER.
Bush Advocate 30 October.[2]

Sir,—I wish to say a word respecting a letter signed "Old Ratepayer," that appeared on Tuesday last. I do not intend to remark upon the whole of its contents, but merely on one of its sentences, which is quite enough for me, for "as the sample is, so is the sack."

The writer says:—"I can find terrible evidence that the results of the existence of five drinking shops are such as no sane man would seek to justify. In our streets on week days and Sundays alike, in the morning, at noon, and at night, we can see poor unfortunates robbed of manhood and respectability tottering along to a drunkard's grave."

Now, the fitting reply to this calumniator—this defamer of your rising and quiet township—would be in an English word of three letters. It is a *lie*, or Thou art a *liar*, aye, and a big one too.

Indeed, were I a little younger than I am, I would go a little further, and challenge him to the proof, and then, on his failing, give it to him without mercy, although, I fear from his style and tone, he is one of those "old," thick-skinned, hardened fellows (most liars are!) spoken of by Hudibras:—

> *"Some have been beaten till they know*
> *What wood a cudgel's of by th' blow!*
> *Some kick'd until they can feel whether*
> *A shoe be Spanish or neat's leather."*

It so happens that I have been residing here nearly a month in the oldest hotel in the township, and with two other hotels within sight and within call from my parlor (there are 4, not 5); and that I have had to traverse continually the streets of Danevirke, more regularly, I may say, on Sundays, morning, noon and night, in my going to and from Church, and never have I once met or seen a drunken man in the street!

Indeed, your active and indefatigable policeman—seen on duty in all weather, and at all times, would take good care of that; and I may further observe that the low and dirty writer of that lying letter (for, as our forefathers said, "It is a dirty bird that defiles its own nest") in so scribbling not only lowers this striving rising township, but its police, and its Magistrates,—including yourself, Mr. Editor, a J.P., and I think you should not have inserted such a bare-faced lie in the columns of your paper, without the defamer of Danevirke signing his own proper name to his letter; or, at least, a short note of your own appended to it.

That some of our hard-working fellow countrymen, living a toiling and solitary life in the bush, while engaged in their heavy work of bush-felling, without comforts (especially in the winter just past, and the present wet and stormy spring season), that some of them may and have drunk a little too much beer (or say "whiskey" to please Old Ratepayer) when they now and then meet in this place, and that "for auld lang syne"—I would not deny; also, that at such seasons they may be and are a little jolly—

---

2 'Old Ratepayer's' letter was published on 28 Oct 1890, and was in reply to a letter by 'Traveller' on 23 Oct. I.S.G.

noisy it may be to the finer nerves of "Old Ratepayer"—but such things at such times are to be expected, and will occur.

It was but a short time ago that I mentioned with much pleasure to a gentleman how pleased I was to see such a large number of good-looking, respectable, decently dressed young men here, and not one of them under the influence of liquor.

—*I am, etc.,*

WILLIAM COLENSO.

Danevirke, Oct. 30, 1890.

❖ **1890 OLD RATEPAYER'S LETTER.**

Bush Advocate 6 November.

SIR,—I am just returned from Woodville and as I find your little town has had another visit from players, I cannot help thinking that Danevirke is very fond of games, plays, charades, and amusements of all kinds.

I am about returning to Napier, and the Prince of Wales' birthday is close at hand, with Father Christmas not far off; and as I shall not be here then I am tempted to offer a mite of amusement (for those who have cut their wisdom teeth!) in two short plays: One a Comedy, and one a Tragedy.

1. COMEDY: "*Every man in his own humour.*"

Act 1.—Concerning mice, or a mouse; that is, what the ancients thought or said of a mouse.

Once on a time the mountains (like Ruahine, near Danevirke) were sending forth awful noises, hollow groans. The people of the township were terrified, appalled, and fell on their knees through fear, invoking the aid of their Gods. When, lo! out crept a mouse from a crack in the side of the cavern in the mountain; and then it was known what caused those dreadful sounds—only a ridiculous mouse!

Again, the great Greek poet Homer, has a famous tale (which has often made me to laugh heartily), called, the Battle of the Frogs and Mice, which dreadful pitched battle lasted till sundown, and prodigies of valour were performed by the combatants on both sides. Now, of one of those Mice, Homer says, "He was more a Mars in armour than a mouse, and *Meridarpax* his resounding name." What a valiant mouse that must have been! Ugh! It makes one shudder to think of it. How the poor frogs must have scuttled away, and dived into their deep dark pools before him! Seeing him stand up to the fight with a long reed spear, which, to their terrified imagination, was like "a weaver's beam," or a *draper's* yardstick.

Act 2.—Concerning charades, puns or plays on words.

Our British poet Cowper, in his laughable poem "The Jack-*daw*" says of him—

"He sees that this great roundabout,
The world with all its motley rout,
Its customs and its businesses;
Is no concern at all of his,
And says—What says he? Caw."

While here in your paper of this day you have told us how our good and able man of the *Law* "eloquently addressed the Court." And here, also, in our living fences, we have that pretty, highly-esteemed English shrub, commonly called "May," now coming into full bloom, which, with its delightful scent and its fresh, bright green leaves, pleasingly serves to remind us all of our Fatherland. This shrub is also called the Whitethorp, and the *Haw*-thorn (and its berries Haws), so that he that runs may read those four words of one syllable—Daw, Caw, Law, and *Haw*—all rhyming so fittingly. Shall I say, one of these short words form half of my blundering charade?

In Woodville this morning I picked up a pin, and in so doing my thoughts went off at a tangent to consider the thousands of *pins* that were daily lost; and this led me to consider the thousand-and-one kerosene *tins*; what can become of them? From tins my rhyming faculty went on to *wins* (I suppose from having seen so much of that word of late in the reports of races), and then the transition to *sins* followed as a matter of course; and in passing by Thomas' fine butcher's shop I noticed a rare lot of sausages in *skins*. Now, these five little words, each of one short syllable, rhyme excellently well, and one, or fourth-fifths of one, of them will have to be joined to the t'other half (above) to make out my charade. And I fancy some clever Danevirkian will be able to do it, and so find "the interpretation thereof."

2.   TRAGEDY: *"A Warning to liars."*

And as I am leaving you, Mr. Editor, for a short season, and have my pen in hand, and an hour to spare, I may as well briefly notice the letter of "Old Ratepayer" in your paper of this day, in reply (he says) to mine. Not, however, that I am thinking of killing two birds with one stone. No! No! I am not going to remark on all his low tarradiddle vulgar, ill-arranged talk. I shall merely quote his own words to put him down. In his first letter of October 28th he said:—"In our streets on weekdays and Sundays alike, in the morning, at noon, and at night, we can see poor unfortunates robbed of manhood and respectability tottering along to a drunkard's grave." (And that was all of it that I took up, and denied, saying,—"the fitting reply to this calumniator, this defamer of your rising and quiet township, would be in an English word of three letters,—it is a *lie*, or thou art a *liar*, aye, and a big one too.") Now, in his present letter, he endeavours to tone that infamous lying sentence down, (as if ashamed of it himself—perhaps through some of his older, wiser, and better-informed friends, but still not manly enough to acknowledge his great error,) saying,—"Mr. Colenso calls me a liar for stating that drunkards may daily be seen in our streets. I do not intend to say anything in proof of my assertion." Nothing in my estimation is worse than the low, mean, base, and cunning attempt to shuffle out of a lie, or to strive to prop it up;—that true old English Divine, G. Herbert, truly says,—

> *"Dare to be true, nothing can need a lie,*
> *A fault which needs it most grows two thereby."*

All of us, I fear, are, at least now and then found tripping, and so uttering a lie,— often done in hasty speaking; some of them are cunningly termed "white lies;" but notwithstanding all that can be said in their behalf such lies are *not* "white."

Moreover, he again, and now deliberately, styles himself *"Old* Ratepayer." Is not this also a *lie?* I will not say he has never paid any rates, but I dare say he is *not* an *"Old* Ratepayer,"* and challenge him to prove it.

Here, in a sheep-breeding, pig-rearing country, we may daily see the effects of crossing between two strains, or classes of a pair of each kind of those animals; and it has often occurred to me (bearing in mind what one daily sees in all our papers)— that the greatest lie, or rather the greatest power or faculty of lying, is to be found in the moral cross between a "Teetotaller" and a "Draper"! they each seem born or reared to it; and so in time become hardened, and get to say strange and false things; yet, possibly, believing them to be true! At all events never once feeling the slightest uneasiness,—never knowing the faintest qualm of conscience about them! Young, our British poet, says (in his "Night thoughts"),

"Men may live fools but fools they cannot die."

But I, in my long and varied experience, have seen the error of that saying; for men too often, alas! die with a lie in their right hand.

Some of those deluded infatuated creatures are almost always having a dig at the poor drunkard, as the lowest of the low, the worst of the worst. But I would again venture to remind them, that it is *not* said of the drunkard, but of *"all liars* their part shall be in the lake that burneth with fire and brimstone": and again repeated,— "Without the holy city are the dogs, and *everyone that loveth and maketh a lie."* (Rev. XXII.)

"Old Ratepayer" says,—"If he writes again, he shall certainly put his name to it." O dear me!, what a boon! what a concession! what a gift to Danevirke! Why, Man, it is well-known already!

Methinks, here, on reading this, some one may say,—"And now, what is the upshot of all this?" "What?" I reply: "Why the carrying out of the ancient Oriental Proverb,—'Answer a fool according to his folly, lest he be wise in his own conceit.'"

In conclusion, I would apologise, Mr. Editor, for the great length of this letter; but it contains two plays (fitted for the times), and I shall not again trouble you as I am leaving the Bush; at the same time I may say that I shall not follow the sainted Westlake (*Draper*, &c.) to San Francisco.—I am, &c.,

WILLIAM COLENSO.

Danevirke, November 4, 1890.[3]

3 Colenso wrote to R.C. Harding (12 Nov 1890), 'I note yr. saying you need an interpr. for my last (?) letter in "Bush Advoc." This surprises me—at all events, it was & is well understood there. Haw-kins is the name of the saucy forward young Australian draper (or cheap John) and it was purposely written in that way (on my return to D. from W.) to raise a laugh as well as to remind him of serious things, for he poses as a religious man of first water!!—to me, it is "unstable water" &c. formerly he was w. the Methodists.' I.S.G.

❖ 1890 TO THE EDITOR.

Evening Press, Wellington, 22 November.[4]

SIR,—A fortnight ago, while residing at Dannevirke in the 40-Mile-Bush, a friend at Wellington kindly sent me a copy of your paper of Octr. 24th, containing "interesting reminiscences" of "an old identity"—Mr. Ebenezer Baker. On reading it I was impressed with the large number of semi-historical errors it contained; and this impression was shortly afterwards increased, on my receiving from Woodville, a copy of another Wellington paper, the "Evening Post" of Octr. 27th, containing that same "notice" somewhat abbreviated, scored with red crosses,—and the question put, "What do you think of this?" No doubt, those copies of two Wellington papers had been sent to me owing to my pamphlet containing the authentic account of "the signing of the Treaty of Waitangi," (written by me at the time,) having lately been published by the Government on the Jubilee Commemoration. Being fully conversant with all that is mentioned, or touched on, in your "interesting remembrances," I should have corrected them and replied at the time, only I considered, that as I was soon to return to Napier, I could better do so from documentary evidence in my possession.

And here I would observe,—that I now write only in the cause of historical truth; and that with a perfect knowledge of all those various events and matters given in your sketch of Mr. E. Baker, and of the public circumstances of those early times. Mr. Baker's father and myself were friends; we lived side-by-side at Paihia Mission Station for many years, and there, on my landing from England in 1834, I first saw the subject of your notice—a little curly-haired boy of 4 years. Yet, while I mention this, I must also add the Ciceronic maxim,—*"Amicus Plato, amicus Socrates, sed magis amica veritas."* And, although it is possible (if Mr. E. Baker really gave your reporter all that is there stated, which I greatly doubt,) that I may not please Mr. Baker in these corrections and remarks, I will nevertheless take good care that "nothing extenuate nor ought of malice" shall be "set down" by me in this letter.

1. I demur to your statement, that Mr. E. Baker "is with very few exceptions the oldest Colonist in the N. Island if not, the whole of New Zealand." Not so: most of the early Missionaries who preceded Mr. Baker's father had large families, many of them the seniors of Mr. E. Baker; of whom Archdn. S. Williams and his lady living here are examples.—

2. "Mr. E. Baker's father was the *third* Missionary to land in N. Zealand, having come out in 1827." Again, not so. Here I give the sequence of the early Missionaries, from official sources—placing the Rev. S. Marsden, the founder of the Mission, *first,* though there were two others, Missionaries, in New Zealand *before* him—Messrs Kendal, and Hall.

---

4   This copy was sent with the same letter to R.C. Harding asking him to vet it or amend it. It was apparently published 22 Nov 1890 in the Supplement to the *Evening Press,* but that issue cannot be found. I.S.G.

1814.	Marsden, Kendal, Hall, King.

—C. Davis (who returned to England, and was lost with his ship at sea, on his voyage back to N. Zealand).

1819.	Kemp, Fairburn, Butler.
1820.	Shepherd.
1821.	Puckey.
1823.	H. Williams, and (present) Archd. S. Williams.
1824.	G. Clarke, R. Davis, S. Davis.
1825.	J. Stack.
1826.	W. Williams (late Bp. of Waiapu), J. Hamlin.
1828.	W. Tate, C. Baker.

(I do not here include Revs. S. Leigh, N. Turner, and others, Wesleyan Missionaries, who were also residing in N.Z. in 1823.)

3. "Lieut. Hobson" (should have been "*Capt.*") "administered the then primitive Government from the Kerekere (?) mission house." Not so, but from Okiato, 3 miles further up the harbour,—formerly Lieut. Clendon's residence

4. "When Lieut. Hobson came to New Zealand he stayed with Rev. Charles Baker, who ultimately gave up his house to him and resided at Paihia." Not so: Mr. C. Baker had been stationed by the Committee meeting in January, at Waikare, nearly 20 miles further S. from Paihia, and in April 1840 (his house having been finished) he removed thither with his family.

5. "The first printing press, an old missionary press, was used at his house at Paihia, where the first Maori Bible was printed by the Rev. W. Colenso, about 1839." Incorrect:—the first printing press in N.Z. was set up in a commodious wing of that "mission house" in January, 1835, which room was built and used for a Boys' School-room (sons of missionaries), and the complete Maori New Testament was printed there in 1837. I do not know what is meant, or intended, by the term here used—"*an old missionary press*";—it was selected in London by the Church Missionary Society, and I had brought it out with me in 1834.

6. "When Sir Benjamin Franklin visited the Bay of Islands, after his explorations in the Antarctic Ocean in the Erebus and Terror, he made his head quarters at the Mission house,"—No such person was ever there! Sir James Ross was Commander of that expedition. (Sir *John* Franklin (not Benjamin) was at that time Governor of van Diemen's Land (now Tasmania). Sir James Ross did not make his head-quarters at that "Mission house", he kept closely on board of his ship. [see below.] The said house (from Mr. C. Baker's finally leaving it in April 1840, sixteen months before the arrival of the Antarctic Expedition in the Bay of Islands,) was let to a person named Tibby, who took in respectable boarders, among whom were several well-known to me, as Mr. Felton Mathew Surveyor-General, Dr. Sinclair, Dr. Dieffenbach, &c.

7. "Mr. Ebenezer Baker and an elder brother (now deceased), as boys piloted him [Sir Benjamin Franklin] about the bays and creeks in a canoe." Astonishing!

I dare disbelieve this. (1) Mr. E. Baker with his brother were then residing at Waikare—at the fresh-water head of that long arm—many miles (20) by sea distant from the anchorage, and those ships. (2) I never knew a single instance of any of the sons of the Missionaries there being allowed (or even being able!) to do such a thing. (3) It was the winter season. (4) Sir J. Ross, and all his officers, were very particular (for several weighty reasons), they had unremitting scientific duties to perform, and were well supplied with boats and with men. I will quote a few words from his published account:—

"The unceasing round of hourly observations" (on shore at the observatory, as well as on board of the two ships,) "was soon brought into operation, and provided full occupation for all of the executive officers of both ships, except only the senior lieutenants, who remained in charge of the vessels. The medical officers, in their turn," (Messrs. McCormick, and J.D. Hooker,) "made short excursions into the interior, for the purpose of increasing our collections of natural history; but the natives at the time of our visit were beginning to feel deeply, and express in terms of severe bitterness, their great disappointment at the effects of the Treaty of Waitangi, so that I did not consider it advisable to permit those officers to extend their researches to any considerable distance from the position we had taken up. And although it was necessary to despatch boats several miles up the river," (on the Kawakawa arm, directly divergent from Waikare) "for the purpose of obtaining the spars we required, yet I thought it proper they should be well-armed and prepared to resist any attack which the natives seemed well disposed to make; indeed so strong was the impression on my mind of the readiness of the natives to seize any favourable opportunity of regaining possession of their lands and driving the Europeans out of the country, that I always felt much anxiety during the absence of our people."— "*Sir James Ross' Voyage to the S. Seas,*" vol.II, p.62. (5) I, myself, was the only one of the Mission who ever accompanied any of those officers, particularly the Botanist of the Expedition, my friend, the present Sir J.D. Hooker; who, on several occasions, went with me in my boat to Waikare forests, and to Waitangi, and to Kerikeri waterfalls: (*vide* his published works).

8. "When Sir Benjamin Franklyn" (*B.F.* again!) was at the Bay of Islands Lady Franklyn was given one of the Mission House horsehair arm chairs, which the Maories attached poles to and carried her about the country."—Lady Franklin, the wife of Sir John Franklin Governor of van Diemen's Land, visited the Bay of Islands in the *early summer* of 1841; but the Discovery ships in the *winter* of that same year. At that time (as I have already stated) Mr. E. Baker was living with his father at Waikare. Lady Franklin, having sprained her ankle, was so carried about (when on land), but not by Maoris while in the Bay of Islands; the boat's crew did all that, and was always kindly attended by the late Capt. Beckham. The term here again used—"the Mission house," is, to say the least of it, misleading: (1) the house in which Mr. Charles Baker, Catechist, had

resided at the N. end of Paihia was never known by such a name: (2) if any one of the three missionaries houses in that station was, or should have been, so called, it was the one at the S. end, occupied by the Rev. H. Williams, (but I never once heard it so called,—who, perhaps, also supplied the "horsehair arm chair," if such an article of luxury was then to be found in the Mission. More likely, however, it was loyally and kindly furnished by Mr. James Busby, late the British Resident, for the Lady of the Governor of V.D.L., as he did possess such furniture, and if so then the article itself is now in my possession, having been purchased by me at the auction of Mr. Busby's goods.—

9. "He" (Mr. E. Baker) "as a boy of 10, and was present at the signing of the Treaty of Waitangi." I doubt this very much; a similar mistake having been made by other Colonists who were also boys at that time. (1) I have no recollection of any of the sons of the Missionaries being present at Waitangi on that occasion; such, indeed, was wholly opposed to the regular dealings of the Missionaries with their children, who were always carefully kept away from all the great meetings of Maoris, fearing the ultimate results, even when such were held on, or near to, the Mission Station. (2) But I dare say he was present at the English township Kororareka (now Russell), two days after the signing of the Treaty,—when the great Demonstration and rejoicings took place, to which all Europeans were specially invited (I know his eldest brother, William, and their father, were there). (3) And, also, it was there, very likely, where he heard the first Proclamation read, on the 30th of January,—as is related in my pamphlet.

10. "In his intercourse with the natives he was a witness of their cannibal customs at that time, having seen human flesh carried about and afterwards eaten." This, also, astonishes me! If Mr. E. Baker really said this,—I should like to know where, and when; for I am obliged to greatly doubt it.—

11. I note, the common Maori names of places are incorrectly given, and this, too, repeated.—

12. And, lastly, as the well-known name of "Benjamin Franklin" has been twice given in your notice, I would observe that this present year, 1890, is the Centenary of the death of the celebrated Dr. Benjamin Franklin, the American *Printer*, philosopher, and politician.

In conclusion, I heartily join in your closing words:—"We offer Mr. Baker hearty congratulations on the celebration of his natal day, and join with his many friends in wishing him 'many happy returns of the day'."

I trust my letter may not prove too long for your columns. It has ever been, and is, my permanent wish, to do all in my power to correct the many errors respecting the early days and doings in this Colony that are still existing, which are frequently freshly brought forward by the Press in New Zealand,—notably that of the day in which Capt. Cook took possession of this N. Island on N. Zealand. Which important event is always wrongly given in all our Colonial Almanacs, &c., &c.,—although so long back as fourteen years ago, I gave its proper authentic history and true date;—

published in the *"Transactions N.Z. Institute,"* vol. X, p.99. Harding's Almanac, printed here in Napier, being the only one that has adopted the correct date.

I am, &c.,

WILLIAM COLENSO.

❖ 1891 KEEP HOLY THE SABBATH DAY.

Bush Advocate 23 April.

SIR,—I read in your paper of yesterday a rather lengthy account of two young men of this place who went a pigeon-shooting on Sunday last, and who were lost for the night in the bush. This you conclude with: "The wanderers ask us to express their thanks to those who were kind enough to come out to look for them. We do, so cheerfully, especially as in this case, 'all's well that ends well.'"

I feel inclined, (impelled, I may truly say,) to offer a few remarks on that matter, and to do this I am the more particularly disposed for five reasons:—

1. It is a sad desecration of the Sunday, (Lord's Day, or Sabbath), to be engaged in *so wilfully breaking it*, and this I notice, is too common here in the Bush. (In my thus writing I would observe—for those who don't know me—that I am no rigid Sabbatarian, very far from it, as my published book on the rational observance of the Sabbath shows.)

2. It was my privilege to read here in St. John's Church last Sunday morning these striking words of Jesus Christ, "he that is faithful in that which is least, is faithful also in much; and he that is unjust in the least, is unjust also in much. If therefore ye have not been faithful in the unrighteous riches, who will commit to your trust the true riches." (Luke 16), and these words I consider very applicable here.

3. If I were an employer of men, and I found that any of them *so wilfully* trampled on God's command, and the good Christian customs and laws of our father, I would "sack" such an one directly, believing that he could not possibly be faithful to me in his work.

4. You have lately had the marvellous Phonograph here exhibiting to the people of Danevirke: they have seen and heard how truly human voices words, and speakings were stored up and recorded as facts, and are we to suppose, that such sad doings as those of the two young men you mention, are not also stored up, and remembered by our ever-present God? May their consciences speak powerfully to them in time. You, Sir, finish with—"All's well that ends well," true, but the *end* of that sin is not yet!

5. I find some of my Presbyterian friends here very zealous in the cause of teetotallism, (a new "fad," a thing unknown even by name to their forefathers), but I hear of nothing being publicly said by them against this common and bigger and crying vice of Sabbath breaking! Against which the noble voice of Scotland was ever boldly lifted up! Why is this? Are the speakers and preachers afraid of coming out too strongly? Fearing the paltry monetary consequences which might follow? I hope not.

I know, full well, the temptation is great, is strong, with pigeons in the woods around, a gun at hand, weather fine, and a ramble almost needful after six days close confinement in office or store, but would it not be far better (to endeavor at least), to get a half-holiday weekly, during the season, even if it cost a few shillings than to act in this way, robbing God of his just due, and so running all risk of consequences? "I speak to wise men, judge ye what I say."

I read also in your paper of "a boy named Christian Harden, sixteen years old, having been accidentally shot at Mauriceville, on Sunday, while pigeon-shooting." Was it any consolation to him in his dying moments, or to his poor sorrowing parents, that he had met his fate while breaking God's command?—I am etc.

WILLIAM COLENSO.

Danevirke, April 22, 1891.

§ 1891 KEEP HOLY THE SABBATH.
Bush Advocate 25 April.

SIR,—I notice by a letter which appeared in your paper of last Thursday headed "Keep the Sabbath Day holy," and signed, William Colenso, that that worthy gentleman is again amongst us, in full possession of his usual health and vigor. Indeed it is a matter of much pleasure to us all here in the Bush district, that a gentleman of ample means, of such suavity and learning, both in the regions of science and theology, should condescend to isolate himself from the comforts of home and town life to live with us periodically, and take such a great interest in the affairs and conditions of our little town. But it is really the fact, and we all should feel grateful to him for it; and considering his advanced age, I take it that he as it were stands on the brink twixt time and eternity, and beholds wickedness leading in the van, whilst righteousness is seen shrunken in the shade. He then at this juncture wields his mighty and facile pen and denounces the evil of Sabbath desecration which is so rampant in our midst, mentioning that he had referred to the matter on last Sunday in St. John's Church. So far I am quite in accord with the rev. gentleman, but, I really think as an independent free thinker, he was ill-advised in singling out the Presbyterian sinners, who appear to be in his estimation too zealous in the cause of total abstinence from spirituous liquors, but apparently remiss in publicly denouncing against Sabbath breaking. I am not going to discuss this matter now, but merely tell our rev. friend, that I was told for a fact, the Presbyterian Minister, Mr. Wallace, was actually in the field before him, as he preached a vigorous sermon a fortnight ago, against the evil consequences of Sabbath desecration showing the consequence of its evils for time as well as for eternity, and making at the time special mention of pigeon-shooting. I regret to think that Mr. Colenso, by showing an animus against teetotallers lost his usually clear head for the nonce and so struck hard against his Presbyterian friends, who appeared for the moment to be in his mind's eye. For really I do not believe the Presbyterians are worse than the Anglicans or any other denomination for Sabbath desecration. In fact it is proverbial that a true Presbyterian and Wesleyan will never work on Sunday, they would suffer martyrdom first. I certainly can argue the point, but won't now, that the William Colenso who wrote the book referred to in his letter cannot, on the ground of logic and consistency, be the evangelical William Colenso who has written the letter against Sabbath desecration.—I am etc.,

FREE THINKER.

❖ 1891 THE SEA SERPENT.
Daily Telegraph 8 August

SIR,—I have read the accounts lately given in our papers, of a fresh appearance of the great Sea Serpent! Having often read very many similar accounts of this nondescript from my early boyhood, I pay little attention to them now. It has, however, occurred to me, that such as described (omitting all the garnish and dressing, so common on all such occasions!) may have been caused by the sudden projection upwards of the huge and very long deep sea weed Macrocystis pyrifera, which abounds in deep water off all our N.Z. coasts, and girds the S. temperate zone. Specimens measuring between 100 and 200 feet are common in the open ocean. Admiral D'Urville, a good authority, states it to grow in 8, 10, and even 15 brasses of water, from which depth it ascends obliquely and floats along the surface nearly as far,—this gives a length of 200 feet. Sir J. D. Hooker (who often met with it and other like gigantic ocean weeds when in the discovery ships 60 years ago, and who has written largely on them), says of it. "that it grows to a very large size, always in deep water. At Cape Horn, and at Kerguelen's Land, it generally rises from 8 to 12 fathom water, and the fronds (long slender branches) extend upwards of 100 feet on the surface. But the largest specimens they saw were between the Crozet Islands, where very far from either shore, in what is believed to be 40 fathom water, stems of Macrocystis rose at an angle of 45° from the bottom, and streamed along the surface for a distance certainly equal to several times the length of the "Erebus" (discovery ship); data, which, if correct, give the total length of the stems of about 700 feet."

Another peculiarity of this gigantic seaweed is this, that its "long branches from the root are simple and pinnate (not branched), bearing long broad leaves; these branches are each shaped like an immense isosceles triangle, or a long narrow inverted V, or the top of a lance, or somewhat like a big feather of a large fowl—is broadest at the bottom or top of the stem where it reaches the surface of the sea, and gradually tapers to the top, and that on each side of this long and thick stem, the long bladdery close-growing or broad leaves pitted and undulated and reflecting light fall-off and hang down like the web of a feather, or like some of our ferns. I have collected and sent to Sir J. D. Hooker specimens of this plant, which I obtained from Castle Point, and he described them in his Flora of N.Z.

The only difficulty with me is, the sudden projection upwards of the plant; but this I think might be reasonably accounted for *on that occasion* by an earthquake; and the shock of a rumbling one we had here (and elsewhere) on that morning, and at about that hour, and (if I mistake not) it was more strongly felt at Poverty Bay. A sudden submarine explosion, especially if vertical and confined, would as surely effect it, as our strong westerly winds carry out horizontally the long lithe branches of our Weeping Willows, which we so often see. Besides we have plenty of such sudden vertical explosions, and geysers, in and among our volcanic hot springs in the interior.

I could say more on this subject, but time with me is too precious just now.

—*I am, &c.,*

WILLIAM COLENSO.

Napier, August 6, 1891.

❖ **1892 A QUERY.**
Hawke's Bay Herald 11 March.
SIR,—I notice in your paper of Wednesday the following statement:—"Two cases of *delirium tremens*, both from Danevirke—the most drunken place for its size in the colony—have ended fatally in the Waipukurau hospital."

I write to ask you to give us the name of your informant; and please don't hesitate. I believe the story to be utterly untrue. I have been residing eight weeks at the Railway Hotel in Danevirke, with two of the other three hotels always in sight, and during that time I have not seen nor heard of one drunken man!

I would fain hope, that you, as editor of your old and hitherto respectable paper, are not become infected with the lying virus of the "Drink Question" which has so disgraced your columns of late! How strange it is, that otherwise sane and tolerably educated and well-disposed men, the moment they take up their "fad" against all drinking are carried off their legs by its current and "lie by the hour!"—I am, &c.,

W. COLENSO.

Waipawa, March 10, 1892.

[We suggest that Mr. Colenso should apply to the hospital authorities.—Ed. *H.B.H.*]

❖ **1892 THE DRINK QUESTION.**
Hawke's Bay Herald 15 March.
SIR,—Permit a few lines with reference to two scurrilous letters in your paper of this morning, in which my name is prominently and (I would hope) mistakenly mentioned.

1. From "A Bushman,"—but only to tell him, through you, that had he the manliness to put his name to his letter, I would reply fully thereto. I am an Englishman, and I can take no notice of "Bushrangers"—that is, of sneaking anonymous scribblers. At the same time, I think I know the writer; no true "Bushman," but a low well-known "character" of Dannevirke town, and one of the "G.T.S." clique.—

2. From "D.N. Adams," who evidently had been reading and dreaming over that astounding cablegram which appeared in your columns last week, viz., that the Emperor of Germany could pulverise the Czar of Russia,—and the Czar could

throw half a million of troops on the boundaries of Prussia: and so, like the frog in the fable, endeavors to imitate!

(1) I never charged temperance reformers with "lying by the hour." But I did, and do, charge such shallow creatures and faddists as D.N. Adams and others like him—who have of late come out so conspicuously in your columns, to suit their own vagaries which they foist on the unwary as being connected with "temperance"! All such are not *true temperance men*, (to which class I have ever belonged,)—but Rechabites, Good Templars, Blue Ribbonists, Reformed Drunkards, Prohibitionists, Local Optionists, Ascetics, &c., &c. Here I would say to D.N. Adams and all others of his kidney,—Fly your own proper flag,—Endeavor to act openly, manly;—Let alone *my* "Temperance" Flag;—Cease being pirates.

(2) Those whom I specially mentioned in my short letter of the 10th inst., were those who *were recent writers in your paper*, who "the moment they take up their fad against all drinking, are carried off their legs by its current, and 'lie by the hour.'"—And this, I repeat, your papers bear me out in.

(3) D.N. Adams says—"Let me mention a few of these liars. The Bishop of Waiapu, Sir W. Fox, Sir H. Atkinson, the Hon. Thomas Dick, Mr. Justice Ward, Mr. Thomas Tanner, and nine-tenths of the clergymen of all denominations." This is the *first* time that I have heard of any one of those respected gentlemen having written in your paper on this subject. But, alas! here is another indication of 'lying by the hour'!

(4) I pass by his "challenge" (so *apparently* fair), because he does not understand the simple and first grounds of his subject; and I have little doubt of his champion being one like him.

Another word; What a pity! that the poor fellow F. Gutt, who committed suicide here in the "Temperance Hotel" on Saturday last, (as fully reported by you in your paper of this day)—that he did not commit this sad act at one of our hotels and under the influence of drink! What a dreadful loss to D.N. Adams and Co.!! And then (another reference) a telegram in your paper of this morning from Oamaru thus:— "Drunkenness is very prevalent in this town, six or eight cases coming before the magistrates almost daily." Compare that with your own in your paper of Wednesday last, (which was one of the two subjects in my former short letter)—*viz.*, "Dannevirke the most drunken place for its size in the colony."—I am, &c.,

W. COLENSO.

Napier, March 14, 1892.

§ 1892 TO THE EDITOR.
Hawke's Bay Herald 19 March.

SIR,—The Rev. W. Colenso has replied, and in a style far different from that ordinarily adopted by clergymen, but if the reverend gentleman is satisfied with his production it is not for me to cavil. If he is pleased to indulge in railing abuse, well and good. Calling an opponent ill names is to say the least bad form. Mr. Colenso says he never charged temperance reformers with "lying by the hour." Well, I leave the public to judge from his own letter whether or not I was justified in drawing the inference that he included all in his denunciation. There is certainly nothing in his letter to lead one to suppose that he only referred to the persons engaged in the present correspondence, and I do not think his quibbling will help him any. What your reverend correspondent is pleased to call my "vagary" is one common to men who see so many of their fellow men ruined through their indulgence in strong drink—a desire to aid the weak, to raise the fallen, and to assist in removing from amongst us a traffic which is admitted by all right thinking men to be a snare and a curse.

I can well understand why Mr. Colenso concluded to "pass by my challenge," but permit me to say that it is pure assumption to assert that "I do not understand the simple and first grounds" of my subject. Mr. Colenso should show this, not merely assert it.

The weak distinction between temperance and total abstinence, which Mr. Colenso evidently seeks to draw, would be amusing were it not so painful. Has he yet to learn that custom gives authority in the use of words and phrases? Mr. Colenso asks to have his "temperance" let alone. By all means, Mr. Colenso, we will let your temperance alone if you will have the goodness to acquaint us with its quality. Does the reverend gentleman allude to temperance of language? If so, might I ask him— without any intention of interfering—to add to his temperance brotherly kindness, and to brotherly kindness charity?

In my challenge I undertook to find a man the equal of Mr. Colenso in scholarship and experience, and only consented to meet him myself upon the platform should he fear to meet a "foeman worthy of his steel." Mr. Colenso's reference to Oamaru is unfortunate—for him. Oamaru is a town of five or six thousand inhabitants.—I am, &c.,

D.N. ADAMS. March 15, 1892.

❖ **1892 SEVENTH DAY ADVENTISTS.**
Hawke's Bay Herald 7 April.
SIR,—I was really sorry (and something more) in reading in your issue of yesterday such a long and (to me) sickening notice of those wretched men the Adventists! one of the lowest and worst sects of falsely-called "Christians" known to me—who through that kind of pulling aided by you unsettle and lead astray the simple, the quiet, and the unwary.

I enclose an advertisement of theirs—often repeated in the columns of the London *Standard* (once a fortnight, or so)—perhaps such may have escaped your notice, and I would thank you to make a fit and proper use of it early in your paper. I have long ago (and again recently) told some of their leaders my opinion of their blasphemous doings—even to the saying that I shall rejoice to see them served as a false prophet was served in the reign of one of the Tudors (?) who had prophesied the King's death at that day 12 months:—"Keep him well. Do him no harm: until that day arrives. If the King dies, honour that prophet; if not, hang him." And hung he was, and serve him right—and so (as I have said) I would treat Daniells—after their predicted day of March, 1896.

You may make what use you please of this letter—publish it, if you will, and I shall further thank you.—I am, &c.,

W. COLENSO.

Dannevirke, April 6, 1892.

❖ 1892 BARON ROTHSCHILD ON LABOR.
Hawke's Bay Herald 12 November.

SIR,—I send you, subjoined, an extract from the London *Standard* of September 16th, containing a portion of a recent dialogue between two eminent public men in France on the great Labor Question, which seems to me to contain some just and admirable common sense remarks and opinions, given in a few plain and pregnant words on that important subject: Trusting you may find room for them in your columns. I may also say that I am the more inclined to ask of you this favor, for these reasons:—They are eminently suited to our present circumstances here in this colony, and they are almost epitomes of similar wholesome views and teachings contained in Holy Writ.—I am, &c.,

W. COLENSO.

Danevirke, November 11, 1892.

PARIS, Wednesday night.

M. Jules Huret, who is publishing in the *Figaro* the results of an inquiry into the labor question, after having taken the evidence of working men and women, conceived the idea of obtaining Baron Rothschild's views on the question. Accordingly, he travelled to Dinard, where the head of the Paris branch of the Rothschild family is spending the summer, and found no difficulty in gaining an interview with the great banker. In answer to inquiries as to what he thought about the present labor crisis and the Socialist movement, the Baron said:—

I do not believe that any crisis exists just now. There have been temporary crises caused by unfortunate failures, such as that of the Barings' Bank in London, but the general situation in Europe has undergone no change, and I do not regard it as unsatisfactory. As to an uneasy feeling among the working classes leading to a menacing Socialist current, for my part I do not believe in the existence of any such movement. I feel sure that the working classes, generally, are very well satisfied with their lot, and that they do not trouble their heads with what is called Socialism. It is absolutely untrue that good workmen demand an eight hours day; it is only the lazy and incapable ones that do so. The men with wives and children, steady, orderly men, have no idea of being prevented working the time they consider necessary for their requirements and those of their children.

The conversation turning upon capital, M. Huret remarked that the Socialists said that capital meant other people's labor. The Baron replied:—

How so? Barring unfortunate exceptions, the result of unavoidable accident, every man, as a rule, possesses that share of capital which is commensurate with his intelligence, his energy, his own individual labor. Of course luck and chance occasionally interfere with the lot of individuals. No doubt worthless people are favored by chance, and deserving persons meet with unfair usage; but the same law is applicable to all alike, on every rung of the social ladder; and the only general law, the only just law, is that which lays down that all men alike must work. You ask whether there will always be rich and poor? You might as well ask whether there will always be the sick and the healthy. War against capital is mischievous and foolish; Anti-Semitism is foolish and hideous. This double war is waged by one and the same class of minds. If, unfortunately, such insanity obtained a footing in any country, the result would be its definitive ruin.

The interview came to a close with the following dialogue:—

M. Huret,—People regard you, M. L. Baron, as the happiest man on earth, with all your milliards.

The Baron.—My milliards? I saw in a paper the other day that I possess three milliards of francs (one hundred and twenty millions sterling). This is sheer insanity. Well, no matter the figure. Does wealth secure happiness? Ah, no! happiness is quite another thing. Of course, if there were not some compensaton attached to wealth it would not be worth while to work so hard for it, but real happiness at bottom means work.

M. Huret.—How about the unearned increment ? Do you not think there is some justification in the attacks on the law of inheritance by which a man is put in possession of wealth he has not earned?

Baron de Rothschild.—Are you married?

M. Huret.—Not yet.

Baron de Rothschild.—When you are a husband and a father you will never allow the law of inheritance to be attacked.

❖ 1893 "JACKATYE."

Hawke's Bay Herald 6 March.

Sir,—In your paper of this day, (that is, in its "supplement,") you have a strange outrageous story headed "Jackatye," and said to be taken from the *Pastoralists' Review* (of this—whether book or paper—I know nothing, never having heard of it before).

This story purports giving freely an account of "Jackatye," and of an encounter that once took place between him and the first Bishop of New Zealand, Dr. Selwyn, and as the whole of it is a most audacious falsehood, without one single atom of reality or truth, and as I am the only European who has it in his power to disprove and to deny it,—I think it a duty incumbent on me to do so.

Bishop Selwyn, in making his periodical visits, as a matter of course always came to and remained at the Mission Station, and during his stay we were always together, and when he should leave on his way north I always accompanied him to Waikari—my northern boundary.

The Bishop never once visited Waimarama on the outer coast where Tiakitai (not "Jackatye") resided; and no such meeting of theirs ever took place.

The Chief Tiakitai was never baptised, (as the framer of the story states he was—even to the giving his new and European name!), neither was he drowned *in that way* mentioned by him.—I am, &c.,

W. COLENSO.

Napier, March 4, 1893.

❖ **1893 "NOXIOUS WEEDS."**
Daily Telegraph 15 March.

SIR,—In your issue of this evening you have an article with this heading; and you commence by saying, "some interesting information comes from Wellington respecting the manner in which noxious weeds arrive in New Zealand, and spread over the country. The settlers are sometimes astonished at discovering now forms of hurtful vegetation, and wonder how an unwelcome visitor got into their pastures." Further on giving a list of noxious weeds containing nineteen names, which, you say, were "found growing on ship's ballast of fine sand that was spread over a part of the reclamation land in Wellington," and that "Mr. Kirk had examined the miscellaneous crop and so defined the foregoing list;" and that now "the mystery" of their arrival here in New Zealand "has been partially if not wholly solved."

Well, your information has astonished me! Shall I say, "Quite taken away my breath?" No; caused me to burst out in a loud guffaw! And why? (1) Because all those so-called "noxious weeds" (with many others) have long been common here in Napier, and also inland in the country villages and townships, and in the Bush; and (2) that sixteen of those nineteen enumerated by you were absolutely published by Sir J.D. Hooker in his "Handbook of the New Zealand Flora," in 1864 (thirty years ago!), as then being common naturalized weeds in New Zealand; and with them he also gave more than one hundred others!

More likely, more reasonably, the "mystery of those weeds being found there, growing on that discharged ship's ballast, spread over the land, is mainly owing to their seeds having been blown thither from the neighboring hills, &c.,—seeing, too, that Wellington is not wanting in suitable zephyrs!—I am, &c.,

W. COLENSO.

March 14, 1893.

❖ 1893 THE MORETON GALLERY.
Daily Telegraph 10 April.

The following letter has been addressed by the Rev. W. Colenso, F.R.S., to Mr. S.H. Moreton, in reference to that artist's gallery of pictures

Napier, April 7ᵗʰ, 1893.

MR. S.H. MORETON, A.S.A.

Napier.

Dear Sir,—I was very greatly pleased on Wednesday last in reviewing your admirable works, and I hope to revisit your gallery at an early date, for having had some *small* experience in the '30's and early '40's in your special lines (as shown by your *drawings* and by your *roughing it* in the wild and uninhabited spots of this land), I can, perhaps, the more fully appreciate your labours.

But it has occurred to me since leaving your exhibition and looking into your catalogue of pictures, that you may have some difficulty in making up the total number required, at the low charge of only one shilling each, to enable you to dispose of them according to terms of art union, and therefore I write to you now.

To aid therein I will take, say, fifty tickets, but only conditional, viz.: If you can obtain the number required without my fifty, then I would withdraw my offer, as I do not wish to appear greedy in the matter.

If a word from me would have any weight with the professed lovers of Nature's grand and sublime Alpine scenery, so faithfully depicted by your ready and masterly pencil, and with the encouragers of high art, so little known and less estimated among us, I would say to all such—especially those resident in the country towns and districts—*do not fail to see this show*: it will repay you, and give to many of you wonderful and magnificent, new and truthful ideas.

Heartily wishing you all success, and thanking you for visiting Napier,

> I am, Dear Sir,
> Yours sincerely,
> W. COLENSO, F.R.S.

P.S. You can make any use you please of this note,—*W.C.*

❖ 1893 TRANSLATIONS INTO MAORI.
Hawke's Bay Herald 14 June.

SIR,—In your issue of this morning you have a statement concerning a translation into Maori of the two old popular English works—the "Pilgrim's Progress," and "Robinson Crusoe"—which is erroneous (as is frequently the case respecting old Maori matters). You say, those translations by Mr. Kemp were made under the Governor Sir G. Grey "so far back as 1847 and 1848"; and, also, that they went "through three editions."

I have copies of them: "Robinson Crusoe" was published in 1852, and "Pilgrim's Progress" in 1854; both, also, bearing the Governor's notification of those respective dates. I never heard of three editions.

You, also, state,—that "last Session the Maori Members applied to the Government for a fresh edition of the Pilgrim's Progress and Robinson Crusoe;" and, "It is believed the request will be granted";—and this is my chief reason for writing to you.

An excellent translation of the *whole* "Pilgrim's Progress" in its two parts, was early made (in the '30s) by one of our Church-of-England Missionaries, Mr. W.G. Puckey, at the Kaitaia Mission Station; these MSS. I possess. Mr. Puckey was one of our very best Maori linguists (if not the best *par excellence*), especially in all pure colloquial Maori; and his MSS. contain the *entire* work without omissions, whereas that by Mr. Kemp was only of the *first* part. If there is to be a fresh publication of the "Pilgrim's Progress," I hope that this translation by the late Mr. Puckey may be used, and that for several reasons (having read and studied them both I may be allowed to say this much). Unfortunately my MSS. are bulky, written closely, yet clearly, on foolscap folio on both sides, and without margin, paper being both dear and scarce in those days! and therefore are not in the usual state of MS. "Copy for Press." But in the hands of careful compositors used to book work (such as I have known in London), these MSS. could be used.

Moreover, I should be *now* willing for my MSS. to be published:—Provided, I had the final supervision of the sheets as issued,—and, that the said MSS. should be carefully handled and returned to me.

I have said "*now*" (at this present time), "willing" for this translation to be published— this I will briefly explain. I was not so inclined when the translation was finished; and that, mainly, from the reason of it being a "*Dream*"; believing, (1.) that such would serve to strengthen largely the Maori people in their many injurious superstitions respecting Dreams; and (2.) that on being asked by them,—"Is it true—is it real?" obliged to answer "No"; when the fixed rejoinder would be sure to follow,—"Why, then, print what is not true? We Maoris have lots of similar stories, fables, legends, and dreams"—and that response would then the more naturally be made, because they had seen nothing printed in the Maori tongue but the sacred Scriptures and of these they could not get a full supply. I could say more under this head.—I am, &c.,

W. COLENSO.

Napier, June 13, 1893.

❖ 1893 TO THE EDITOR.

Napier Daily Telegraph 15 September.

A correspondent sends us the following:—"You and your contemporaries have often to complain of the errors and blunders received per 'wires,' and published by you; and not unfrequently the fault has been placed on the unlucky comp, proof-reader or printer's devil. Here in your issue of this evening is a notable instance. In your telegram from New Plymouth, it is stated:—'The position of the moon and *Saturn* in conjunction last evening at 6 o'clock attracted general attention. The young moon was on his back, and *Saturn* appeared touching at the northern horn.' Now it was not the new moon and *Saturn* but the new moon and Venus (the bright 'evening star'), and it was not a *conjunction*, but an *occultation*. Alas for the astronomical love of New Plymouth! if such is to be taken as a fair sample; seeing, too, that such a phenomenon must have been witneseed by the many, and made matter of common talk there. A friend and myself, having been aware of this occultation, and deeming it of importance as well as interesting from the size of the planet occulted, we had made the necessary calculations and preparations for observing it, but the state of the atmosphere utterly precluded our doing so! This was felt by us the more keenly from the fact of the sky on the previous evening being so delightfully clear, and the narrow illuminated rim-like crescent of the new moon showing so plainly."

[Editor, *Napier Daily Telegraph*, 16 September 1893: "The letter inserted by us yesterday as from a "correspondent," on the occultation of the new moon and Saturn, was from the pen of the Rev. W. Colenso, F.R.S.]

❖ 1893 THE LATE MR. PULLEN.
Hawke's Bay Herald 23 November.

SIR,—I was pleased to see in your paper a few days back, a prompt call for assistance on behalf of the distressed wife and family of the late J.B. Pullen, who for some years had been the zealous caretaker of the Theatre Royal, and who died on the 9th inst., and I have been waiting to see how it would be responded to. For you informed us— that the deceased man was very assiduous and very useful in his various occupations; a fact acknowledged (you say) by all, and especially by those who had been performers in the theatre. And it occurred to me, that, knowing that fact, you should have come out more openly, more equitably, and called on (at least) the three classes I now proceed to name,—to come forward *quickly* in this good cause.

1. The theatre-supporters, who flock in crowds to every performance! which is carried on almost every night in the week, and who, also, must have been largely benefited by the poor man's active and strenuous endeavours.

2. The bands of local amateur players and concert singers who have often (especially of late in their repeated "*Les Cloches de Corneville*," &c., &c.,) performed therein to "overflowing houses," and reaped largely.

3. This present or late large batch of performers, who were carrying-on in the Theatre on Thursday night while a poor man lay dying in an adjoining room,— and also on the Friday night while lying dead; and who again did so on the Saturday night (the day of his hastened burial), and also on the following Sunday evening! Surely, *here*, at all events—seeing the Theatre was crowded (as you say), and that too early during Church hours,—a share at least of the amount collected might be disgorged!

In these three classes coming out quickly and fairly lovingly, they will be (I hope) doing a little in the *only way* of "making to themselves friends of the Mammon of unrighteousness" as advised by the Great teacher.

I could say more but I refrain; only this:—Seeing the Theatres here are so extensively patronised, I think a rule or by-law something like this should be established, namely,—that all performers therein (especially non-resident strolling players) should be made to contribute a fixed per-centage of their gains for charitable purposes—especially such as this.

I dare to think of myself, that I would not willingly be the *last* to help in all such cases (particularly as in this one, being my neighbour,) but *I am late* on this occasion. I gladly now enclose my mite, £2 2s.—I am, &c.,

WILLIAM COLENSO.

Napier, November 14, 1893.

[We have had to hold over Mr. Colenso's letter with many others to give room for the addresses of candidates, &c. Mr. Colenso will have seen, since he wrote, that the amateurs of Napier are giving material assistance,—ED *H.B.H.*]

§ 1893 ADVERTISEMENT.

Napier Daily Telegraph 19 December.

FOR COUGHS AND COLDS.—Gowing's Linctus is still in steady demand as it has been for the past 30 years. The Rev. W. Colenso, F.R.S., thus writes of this remedy:—"I consider it to be a vauable and safe medicine, of great service in Coughs, Colds, Bronchial Affections, and Irritation and Dryness of the Throat. I always carry a bottle with me when I visit the bush district."—H. Owens, Chemist, Napier.

❖ 1894 FLOODS.

Hawke's Bay Herald 16 January.

SIR,—In common with many others I have been much interested (or I may truly enough say concerned) in reading the public accounts of the late disastrous flood at Clive and its adjacent low-lying lands; and also, in considering Mr. Knorpp's (old) "river conservation scheme," recently republished by you; and the official "report" of Messrs Carr and Kennedy, C.E.'s., on the same subject to the River Board at Clive, also published by you in your issue of the 8th inst. And, no doubt a very great cause of my thinking so much over this late calamity, arises from my having often suffered from floods myself during my long residence of nearly 20 years in that neighborhood; when, too, I experienced a bigger flood than this one of December last, and was wholly *alone*—as to European neighbours and aid! And happening to mention this circumstance in conversation with a few friends, I have been solicited to give the public some account of it; this I now propose to do in your columns,—premising, that all I shall now write about that one big flood is strictly copied from my journal written at the time; which also was duly forwarded to the C. M. S., London,—it being a part of the duty of their missionaries to keep a daily journal for the society. And as the very site of my old residence has been long ago washed away by the floods and ever encroaching sea, I may first point out its position, so as to enable your readers and the residents in general of Napier and Hawke's Bay to know something more about it.

I first visited the Hawke's Bay district and travelled largely through it more than 50 years ago (in 1843), and returned hither in 1844 to reside permanently. In 1843 Archdeacon W. Williams (afterwards Bishop of Waiapu) and myself—in travelling north from Castlepoint—halted at Te Awapuni (a pretty large pa or fenced village of the Maoris) on the Waitangi creek, where, after long discussion by the chiefs it was finally arranged that a small rectangular block of land containing 10 acres, on the opposite side of the creek, should be granted as a Mission Station; and this plot the late chief Te Hapuku and myself stepped out, with no small difficulty from the dense and entangled herbage growing on it. A long row of blackberry bushes running nearly east and west (to the north of Farndon, and near the east bend of the said Waitangi creek) still marks the ditch and dyke fence and Boundary to the south of my old outer grass paddock. At that time, and for several years after, the Waitangi creek—where it ran parallel with the seabeach and joined the Ngaruroro river—was only a very small and narrow water-course. I have often crossed it at low water without taking off my boots; and there was also a large piece of high and dry stony land, containing several acres, and covered with low herbage, lying between the said Waitangi creek and the outer north boundary of the Mission station.

In returning overland, on foot, to the Bay of Islands from Hawke's Bay, in 1843, I took with me four strong young Maoris (men), one from each sub-tribe; and during my absence in 1844 (a much longer one than I had expected), the resident Maori chiefs—being aided by some skilful Maori housebuilders, friends from Poverty Bay, erected a very large and substantial house for me, on a rising knoll—the highest thereabouts—within the said marked-off plot;—this, of course, I had to finish and to render habitable—with floors, partitions, doors, windows, chimneys, &c.,—a work extending over several years, partly owing to the building being a very large one, the main portion 50 x 36, one storey, but very lofty, with its floors and extra deep joists of kauri timber, and the joists crossed over large whole pine, tree trunks newly felled in the Big Bush and brought down the river Ngaruroro for that especial purpose: so that the floors of the house were raised several feet above the ground around it: and all this extra labour and trouble and expense I underwent through (fortunately) detecting on my arrival in 1841, many small water-loving and marsh plants growing there about the house, though the ground was then perfectly dry, being the middle of summer; and here and there, also, small washed and rounded pebbles of pumice, scattered among the tufts of herbage and fern,—which eloquently, though silently, told their tale! I now relate this, by way of letting folks know something of my then situation and position.

And here, no doubt, someone will naturally say,—"Why, on earth did you two select such a low spot for a Mission Station; when you had all Hawke's Bay open before you?" But the fact was—there was no selection in it, no choice whatever; either that, or none! And this arose from a curious cause, or reasons, viz.—1. That a missionary in coming hither to reside for all the Maoris must not belong to one sub-tribe more than to another, for if he were to reside near to a pa (or large village) he would then be considered as belonging to that sub-tribe there dwelling, and so the others would not (and could not, according to Maori custom and to their extreme jealousy) visit him freely. 2. That therefore, as this tongue of lowland, surrounded on three sides by the Waitangi and Ngaruroro rivers was *tapu*, (a strictly tabooed preserve for pigs and for marsh and water birds and for eels,) this small plot, a kind of "No Man's Land," was by all agreed to as being equally free to all of them; but even this was only determined on after two or three days' deep consultation by the Maori chiefs then and there assembled.—I now give the extracts from my old Journal.

"1847. June 23rd.—Returned late this evening to the Mission Station, having been absent from the 12th inst., viewing the Maoris in the villages to the north— Tangoio, Aropaoanui, Petane, and Wharerangi, a most disagreeable journey owing to the cold and wet winter weather, short days, and no roads,—walking through mud and marshes, slippery, clayey hills, and wet fern! Wind very high to-day with every appearance of a heavy gale coming on.

"24th.—A very stormy day indeed of wind and rain; the most so of any gale from the N.E. since I came hither to reside; great fears expressed by the Maoris living near me of a heavy flood.

"25th.—Pouring rain all night without intermission; the wind, too, terrifically strong, and the sea awfully roaring and lashing over the high bank in front of the house; the bank itself being 2 or 3 feet higher than the ground on which the house stands, and only 150 yards from it. Rain continuing all day, and the waters rising rapidly all round; the low plains disappearing fast. We hoped, however, that our dwelling house would escape, it being situated on a rising spot, with its floors raised more than 2 feet above the ground. Towards evening our raised pathways through the garden and paddock began to disappear, and our Maori domestic lads were obliged to evacuate their house, and we to abandon the kitchen (detached) which was now under water. The incessant dashing of the waters against the fences, &c., being fearfully agitated by the stormy wind, added not a little to the appalling nature of the scene. At 8 pm. the verandah floor, although about a foot above the raised pathway, was under water, and at the same time the floor of our newly erected store was also covered. The wind now subsided, and the rain ceased, but the furious sea effectually damming up the only open and narrow mouth of the 3 rivers (which here disembogue into the ocean) caused the waters rushing from the hill country to be returned again over the low lands with frightful velocity. The water had still, however, 6 inches to rise to reach the level of the dwelling-house floors, and 15 inches to reach the floor of the study in the garden; so we still dared to hope we might yet escape. Our goats and pigs, which crowded about us, we took away in canoes to a little rising bank or ridge only a few feet in diameter, a short distance off, there to await the result; our dogs and cats came into the house; while the remnant of our poultry (which had escaped the flood in March last) took refuge on the fence, and on the roof of the house. Narrowly, indeed, did we watch the rise of the water,—as breathlessly as any Egyptian sage ever watched the Nilometer. Seeing it was still rising rapidly we proceeded to make platforms within the house by joining tables together, &c., and to raise up boxes and cases on each other, and to pull out the lower drawers of chests of drawers, &c., &c. At 9 p.m. my Maori teacher Renata came across the plains from his little village in a canoe, stating that his place, which is a much higher spot than this of ours, was totally under water, and the river Ngaruroro coming over its banks in that direction at a fearfal rate. The few Maoris who happened to be there, women and children, fled to their *patakas* (raised food platforms on posts) for refuge, while the men, with a large number of others from all the villages around, had proceeded to the sea beach to try to cut the dam through. I got my whaleboat and oars and big canoe fastened to the fence of my entrance gate, to be in readiness if we should be obliged to leave; which done, we sought for bricks in the back yard wherewith to raise the fireplace on the hearth in the sitting-room, so as to be able to keep a little of that necessary article at hand; those bricks (left from building our two chimneys) could only be obtained by one of my young Maori lads diving for them, and bringing them to Renata, who was staying with us. At 10 p.m. the waters began to enter the house, and soon rushed through, making a clean sweep. I then threw open all the doors and windows (French casements) to give the flood free egress. Now we were obliged to carry the dogs out and place them in the big canoe, and to begin to take refuge ourselves upon tables and chairs, and piled boxes. There we sat in the cold night, looking at each other and the still rising flood, and fearing that the worst was yet to come, as it wanted 4 hours of high water. We also feared that the flood would raise the floors *en masse*—as they were only now kept down by the slight rush and reed partitions, which were merely nailed to the rafters of the roof,—and so force off the heavy roof above us! We still cherished a hope that the study might escape, as its floor was 9 inches higher than that of the dwelling-house; and so we kept anxiously looking at the legs of the tables and chairs as their knobs were successively reached by the water, and when it had risen 6 inches over the floor of our sitting-room, I lost no time in paddling to the study in a canoe (which was brought into the sitting-room through the verandah and open doorway) over the flowers and shrubs and gooseberry bushes! We got there just in time to do what we could (which was little enough!) to secure the books, papers, specimens, boxes, &c., &c., from present wet, for before we had finished the water began to pour in over the floor! This was the only blow that I acutely felt. I had considered the stores and goods which would unavoidably be lost and spoiled as scarcely worth a thought, but when I left my books and papers to their approaching fate it cost me a pang. It was now a still serene night—or rather morning, the declining moon shone brightly,—not a cloud in the sky,—not a sound to be heard save the swiftly rushing ripple of the current as it shot past—the faint snorting of a drowning pig, which ever and anon broke upon the ear,—the plaintive wail of the sandpiper as it flitted about, seeking rest for the sole of its foot, and the quick succeeding waves of the sea which vehemently dashed over the high bank in front of the house in mad confusion. However, we returned in our canoe to the dwelling-house, and took our seats as before upon our temporary platforms of tables, stools, and boxes. During our absence at the study, Renata, who had remained behind in charge of the fire, had again to raise the fire-place, making the fourth tier of bricks built up on the iron dogs; and now we could only just see the little fire by looking horizontally, as it was only a few inches (less than the thickness of another brick,) below the flat open arch of the chimney fire-place. Renata had kept the young Maori diving for bricks in the cold muddy water, a job he did not like, owing to the strength of the current, the night season, and the increasing difficulty of finding the scattered bricks which had to be groped for; and, worst of all to a Maori! no fire to warm himself by."

[And here I should also mention a curious device of Renata; he, naked save his big shaggy black body mat, had a chair early allotted to him for a seat, but, the water rising rapidly, he put 4 bricks under the 4 legs of the chair to raise it, and this he had to repeat twice over, so as to be quite above the flood, and there he sat still, and slept (at last!) for some honrs, squatting quietly—without even the solace of a pipe, such not being in common use in those happier days. I confess, I felt uneasy on Renata's account, fearing he might fall off his perch in his sleep, and so get a cold bath, and wet his thick warm mat.]

To continue:—"Just at this time a very large and raised log (a whole white pine trunk with its bark on), on which the turkeys had taken refuge, was carried off over the close lower fences (6 feet high). With great difficulty we saved 5 of them out of 10. At 3 o'clock a.m. two or three Maoris in a small canoe came up to the house, bringing the pleasing news that the great dam, or high beach bank, had been cut through, for which we all truly and devoutly thanked God and took courage. Shortly after we found the water to be at a stand, and in about an hour to decrease—slowly indeed, but surely. We now hoped the worst was over, and being much fatigued and cold (for it was very cold from it being midwinter as well as from having so much water about us), we endeavored to wrap ourselves up, and to get a little sleep, squatting on our platforms, ere day should break upon us.

"26th.—We, each and all hands, dozed 2 or 3 hours upon our confined seats—like fowls upon their perches—which refreshed us a little for future action. For by daylight the fast retiring waters plainly showed what a benefit they had brought us, in a stratum of fine mud, which not only covered the floors, but had found its way into every box or case however tightly nailed into which the waters entered. In some places the deposit of mud was from 10 to 16 inches thick; the general layer being from 3 to 8 inches. We worked hard all day in getting two or three rooms put a little to rights. About 3 p.m. my horse came up—where or how he escaped we could not tell. The few natives who remained in their village, Te Awapuni pa, on the opposite shore of the river where the land is considerably higher, were obliged to retreat by degrees before the rising flood—which completely covered the whole village (overthrowing its strong fences), together with the church yard and floor of the large church beyond it; a portion, too, of the newly erected and strong close (paled) totara fence of the church-yard was thrown down. A whole stack of wheat floated down from its staddle on the high ground at Te Ngaaue (a village 4 miles off beyond Pakowhai), and curiously enough was carried by the current into the village here (Te Awapuni), and there set down whole between the houses, as if it had been originally stacked there, bringing with it a whole colony of rats, and, on the outside, a large number of *Pukeko*—(*Porphyrio melanonotus*). About noon it again recommenced raining heavily, and blowing strongly from the N.E.

"Sunday, 27th.—Morning fine, but the whole country for miles in every direction under water or mud, or both!

"23th–30th.—Still raining hard and blowing strong. Scarcely any getting outside of the doors, goods and stores all ruining from so long exposure to the wet; some large cases having been nearly 2 feet submerged in water, and others completely beneath. The weather during the whole of this month had been little else than rain.

"July 1.—Weather clearing; all hands turned to work, to scrape mud out of houses and rooms—to open boxes, and cases. Iron and tinware, books, clothing, drapery, salt, oil, sugar, and other groceries, carpenters' tools, &c., &c., in a most pitiable condition. Such was the subtle state of the mud or slime that it found its way into close and new cases which had never been opened since their first nailing down in England! In the afternoon it again came on to blow with rain.

"2nd.—Heavy rain all night, but morning fine. Continuing our onerous work of yesterday. This afternoon Tareha, one of the principal chiefs of this district, and his relative Isaac, brought back my horse; the animal had actually swum across the harbor at Ahuriri, spite of the enormous current, and got in safety to the opposite shore to the great astonishment of the Maoris residing there. It seemed as if the horse had had quite enongh of the marshes of Heretaunga, and was going back to its old quarters at Wairoa or Poverty Bay. The Maoris, however, followed it, and after some difficulty (for they had never handled a horse before) succeeded in capturiug it. Tareha's object in coming was, mainly, to condole with me. Among other things he said—'No one ever dwelt here on this spot before you; it has always been only the dwelling-place of eels.' We scarcely knew what to do with the horse, as nearly the whole neighbourhood is under mud, which is in some places very deep; and if returned to the ridge of the dry stony beach leading to the Port, where there is scarcely a single bite of grass, it would again try the sea at Ahuriri;—as to our few cows we know nothing of them."

In a few days we heard the cows were safe; they had been early noticed by Maoris of Pakowhai going towards the distant hills through the waters of the rising floods, and they kindly drove them on in that direction. The horse was again taken across the creek to the dry shingle beach, and there tethered by a long rope and left in charge of a Maori: but though its life was preserved on this occasion it perished during the following year from another severe flood—(during my absence on my long annual journey) to the great grief of the Maoris, who composed and sang songs and dirges over it, after sharing among them the black hair of its mane and tail! It was a fine young animal, reared and broken in at Poverty Bay, a bright bay with black points, very docile, quite a pet with the Maoris, who would often bring it a bundle of leafy shrubs from Tukituki, as there were none around me, neither grass for some years; name Cæsar. It was never ridden by me, and being the first horse introduced to Hawke's Bay deserves a brief notice. And here I may also mention that my best cow—a pretty well-formed red poley, picked from Rev. S. Marsden's herd at Parramatta, N.S.W.—was also (unfortunately for me) killed by the large pig dogs of my Maori neighbors. Having mentioned the Maori Renata as heartily rendering good assistance at the time of the flood (and so did all the others, domestics: we were about 10 there gathered together on that eventful night, the larger number being women and children), I should also add that this Maori is the same Renata Te Kawepo who years afterwards became so well known here among the settlers as a prominent and wealthy chieftain, and who died a few years ago. I had brought him hither with me from the North in 1844, and for several years Renata did good and trusty service both to me and to the Church.

I have incidentally mentioned having a large stock of groceries, &c., in hand; this, also, may require explanation. On my coming hither in 1844, knowing my complete isolation, I brought with me a ton of flour, half ton of rice and sugar, two half chests of tea, &c., &c., because then there were no shops nor stores nearer than Auckland and Wellington, and no vessels visiting here; and so it continued to be for some time after my arrival. I was early obliged to purchase largely at Wellington, hence my loss became heavy; and, as a matter of course, it all fell on me—in spite of repeated appeal, the C. M. Society then not being wealthy.

During my long residence there I witnessed many other severe floods, some very heavy (which always depended on the mouths of the rivers being closed), but none before or since so big as the one in June 1847. I may, however, mention that I suffered more loss from a big flood in 1845 than I did from this one, owing to my being totally unprepared for that earlier one, and knowing nothing of its severity; on that occasion I lost nearly all my large stock of flour, sugar, rice, &c., (and all hands suffered according for some time)—and, alas, my first crop of rye-grass and white clover growing on cleaned and enclosed ground, an acre and half, dug with worry, great labour, and expense; this was totally buried in silt, and smothered and killed when young, and had to be resown the following season.

I have also known a much deeper deposit of silt (fine mud) than was left by the big flood of June 1847. On one particular occasion there was an enormous deposit, measuring in some spots on my own paddocks 2 feet 4 inches deep after the waters had drained off. Of this early flood, during which the dammed up waters remained for a long time high, I had to write an official account for the Superintendent of Wellington (Dr. Featherston), at his request; Hawke's Bay being then deemed part of the Province of Wellington.

I got, at last, to welcome a gently rising tranquil flood that merely covered the paddocks and gardens a few inches in depth, and soon drained off, especially if followed by rain; as such natueal irrigation always wonderfully enriched the grasses and soil. On one occasion I noticed a peculiar natural phenomenon; the advance waters from the two rivers, Ngaruroro and Tutaekuri, quietly meeting and mingling in my flat paddock; that of the Tutaekuri being almost clear and of a bluish cast, while that of Ngaruroro was yellowish and very muddy, by which they were well defined. Of course, whenever the Tutaekuri overflowed and ran east towards Cape Kidnappers, joining the other two rivers, the flood was very high. I have said that during the flood the Maoris of the large pa, Te Awapuni, had to desert it, and to retreat to the higher ridge of the shingle hank (a raised beach) leading to the port; on this occasion leaving in the night they had to make two or three bivouacs as the rising waters gained on the ground. This, however, they had done during a former flood, and also again afterwards. It was a curious natural sight—one that often raised the question among our early and observing settlers and visitors—to see the pumice stones and boulders forming an almost regular border-line high up on this long shingle bank, as if placed there in a row end to end by children in play. This line, however, showed the height of the inundation; those worn lumps and boulders of pumice having been carried thither by the flood and quietly deposited, presenting a kind of high-water mark.

On my arrival here in 1844, the Maoris were scattered in many very small villages all over the plains, from Clifton (the cliffs of Cape Kidnappers range of hills) to Taipo and Puketapu, and inland as far as Pakipaki, causing me an immense amount of heavy and laborious travelling, always on foot, to visit them and their sick. What made it the more difficult was there being no roads, not even pathways, leading to their hamlets; and the jungle on all those marshy flats was of the coarsest and most luxuriant character, intersected in all directions with deep ditches and pools of mud and water, making it difficult to find one's way through it. Indeed, the Maoris themselves rarely or never travelled anywhere overland, choosing always to go by water in their small canoes, particularly on all those tidal rivers and their branches, coming and returning with the tide and river current; time then with them being of no importance.

Four things I had early noticed in my travelling across those flats respecting the rivers of this great low delta or watershed: 1. That they had often changed their channels (owing to the loose nature of the ground, and probably earth disturbance). 2. That they were much higher on their immediate banks (though running through lands pretty nearly level on both sides) than the land itself was a little way in from the river. 3 The margins of those banks also carried a much more dense vegetation than the land immediately beyond them, owing to the vegetation itself on the margins of the streams always catching and retaining floating plants and debris at times of overflowing. 4. That this was a great natural means of causing the overflowing waters to move slowly and to spread more equably with less force of ourrent. Moreover, everywhere concealed among the reeds and coarse cutting grasses of those marshy flats were innumerable prostrate trees and big branches and rotten logs, which also served to retard the current of the rising floods. But on the arrival of settlers in this district those natural features began to disappear; by their clearing and firing the said dense jungle, their using and destroying the logs and prostrate trees, and through their cattle breaking down the high margins and banks of the several streams, and the consequent rolling of their debris into their channels; hence it is that the rivers and streamlets have become shallowed, and not merely from shingle or silt brought down by the current from a distance above. Farther, the enormous quantity of surface water now flowing from the numerous artesian wells must also be considered as largely tending to augment a flood and to give an impetus to its current.

The wise old Maoris well knew of those floods, and in a measure were generally well prepared for them. Their losses at such times were chiefly confined to their canoes and eel and fish pots and traps (all, however, being their valuable and substantial property), and whenever any one of their low-lying villages was inundated (which, I believe, was never occasioned except when the mouth, or mouths, of the rivers were dammed) their general mode of acting was to unite and cut through the thrown-up sea-bank as quickly as possible This was done several times by them during my early years at Waitangi; and my belief has ever been, that such a work only is required to keep all those lowlying lands on those rivers and at their mouths free from floods,—*to see that their mouths are kept open*; and that, particularly such should be the case with the mouth of the Ngaruroro river, separate from that of the Tukituki. This is the old proved plan; and is the natural and reasonable and cheaper and most effectual mode of dealing with the floods, in my estimation.

There is yet another patent factor which should certainly not be lost sight of, viz., *volcanic action*; and that for these reasons: That the whole of this district has been not only subject to it, but that the tendency has ever been in one direction—upheaval, of this we have plenty of proof all around us; and (geologically speaking) as to time, much of that action has taken place in recent ages. Indeed, I myself have known and marked such earth surface alterations, as to altitude, during my early years here; and while earthquakes were pretty frequent, and severe too, 40 years ago (say from 1843 to 1855), there have not been any strong ones in this district for the last 30 years; but we well know that those ancient powerful forces are all here handy, stored in reserve in Nature's magazine, though for the time being latent; and when by her need—called into action—no warning notice is ever given.

My letter is unpardonably long for your columns (although I have striven to condense it), yet, as it is on a grave and important subject, affecting many among us, much of it unknown, and not, I think, wholly uninteresting to Hawke's Bay settlers, I trust its length will be forgiven by the public and yourself.—I am, &c.,

WILLIAM COLENSO.

Napier, January 15, 1894.

❖ 1894 MOUNTAIN GRASS.
Hawke's Bay Herald 2 February.

SIR,—Permit me to correct an error in your paper of this morning concerning your mountain grass, which I the more readily desire to do as you say it is a correction by some "well-informed correspondent,"—who also gives a wrong botanical name to the grass in question, calling it *Holcus indicus*. There is no such species of *Holcus* known as *H. indicus*. Your grass is *Holcus lanatus*, a very common European grass, and now become a Cosmopolite; its universal old English name is *"meadow soft grass."* It has long been naturalised in New Zealand (here, on the sides of this hill, for instance).

Hooker in his "Flora of New Zealand," written nearly 50 years ago, mentions it. Moreover there are but two species of this genus *Holcus*; this one, and *H. mollis*, much like it in general appearance. Wherever your "well-informed correspondent" picked up the foreign and far-fetched term of *"indicus,"* is a mystery to me. And so I may say of the low provincialism—"Yorkshire fog"!! Why take up and continue to use such a term? For two or three years, I myself, who had never before heard of this name, —never met with it in print,—could not understand what was meant by it.

And just so of another introduced weed, here in the Colony called "the Californian Thistle,"—as if, forsooth, it were new and a plant of that American State! whereas it is also a common British weed—*creeping*, or *plume, thistle*, its proper botanical name being *Crucus arvensis* (*NOT Cardtuus arvensis*).

But it would fill a column or two of your paper to point out those common glaring modern botanical names and errors respecting many old well-known British weeds that have been introduced and now are naturalised here among us. Too much fuss made about them.—I am, &c.,

W. COLENSO.

Napier, February 1, 1894.

❖ 1894 THE "WILD IRISHMAN".
Hawke's Bay Herald 6 February.

SIR,—In the vivacious and amusing narration, entitled,—"Up the Kaweka with a mustering Party," lately given to your readers in three numbers of the HAWKE'S BAY HERALD, mention is made of some of the peculiar and striking plants of that elevated region, especially of one termed the "Wild Irishman." And as with this plant you have prominently coupled my name, I may be permitted to add to your remarks about it; seeing, also, that the said strange mountain plant is so very little known among us.

My first practical and experimental experience of this plant took place nearly 60 years ago (in the autumn of 1845), on the high summits of the Ruahine mountains, when I attempted to cross the range on my way to visit the Maoris living isolated at Patea; and in my writing a semi-scientific account of that journey (with special regard to the botany of that region then unknown), I have thus recorded my introduction to and acquaintance with this plant—a species of *Aciphylla*—styled by you the "Wild Irishman";—but of its names more anon.

Of all the peculiar and novel plants which grew on the mountain tops, the large new species of *Aciphylla* was the one which we were all the more likely to remember,—not only for a few weeks but for all time! It gave us an immense deal of unpleasantness, trouble, and pain,—often wounding us to the drawing of blood. I suppose, that each one of the party (six Maoris besides myself), speaking quite within probability, received at least 50 stabs from these plants, which my Maori companions, (in shoulder mats without boots or trousers) justly termed *infernal!* I will attempt to describe it. Imagine a living circle of 5 feet diameter (the size of the full-grown plant), with all its many harsh spiny ray-like leaves radiating alike outwardly from the crown of its carrot-shaped root, forming almost a plane of living elastic spears, composed of sharp and stiff points or flat spikes, each several inches long; these make up the leaf, and many of them are set on each long leaf stalk of nearly 2 feet in length: from the centre rises the strong flowering stem, an erect orange-coloured spike or stalk 5 or 6 feet high, containing many hundreds of small flowers, gummy (or having a varnished appearance) and strong-scented, each a little cluster securely guarded with similar miniature sharp spiny bracts or leaflets. The general appearance of these plants, at times, reminded me of a lot of shallow umbrellas opened and fixed upside down on the ground. Of course there were hundreds of smaller plants, also forming circles, of all sizes—from 3 inches diameter upwards; while some still younger (seedlings) were just pushing up their needle-like points (not in a circle, but drawn together) through the mossy soil. These larger plants rarely ever intermixed their spear-shaped leaves to any great extent); they seemed as if they had just touched each other, with their living circle of points, and when we should put down our feet as warily as possible on some tolerably clear spot between them, we were often caught on all sides as if in a man-trap, and not infrequently roared pretty loudly from the pain—while our vain attempts to extricate ourselves often increased it. More than once each one of us was so seriously caught as not to be able to move without assistance.

On one occasion in particular we all (save one—the sufferer) had a hearty laugh over one of these plants:—One of our party, a strong robust Maori, had been pricked or stabbed rather severely by a large *Aciphylla*, insomuch that the blood spurted out: at the sight of this he got enraged (a very natural thing for a Maori in those early days,) and throwing off his back-load, and obtaining the long handled axe, which another was carrying, he hastened towards the plant, vowing he would cut it up by the roots! The spear-like leaves, however, spreading out all round it like a circle of fixed bayonets—being longer (including their big leaf stalk) than the helve of the axe and very tough and elastic, quite kept him from doing any harm to the plant, which seemed to mock his impotent rage; so, after gaining a few more pricks from it for his labour, he was obliged, doubly vexed though he was at our looking on and laughing, to give up the unequal combat. This story was too good to be lost, especially to a fighting race like the Maori, and the joke was long kept up after our return, and repeated with additions at the expense of the poor fellow.

I may here mention, that when I next travelled over the range from Hawke's Bay, I took two extra Maoris with me specially armed with long-handled axes to clear the way a little, otherwise baggage bearers could never have got over those spots which abounded with *Aciphylla*. My bearers, too, having been warned, some by experience on that former occasion and some by hearsay, took with them sundry old cast off clothing and pieces of matting to use as a defensive armour.

One of those little open summits bore the name of Maunga Taramea (Mount Taramea) from the plant growing so profusely there. Taramea ~ *the rough spiny thing*, being the Maori name of this plant, not unlike in meaning the botanical name of *Aciphylla* ~ *needle-pointed leaf*, given to the genus by Forster, the German botanist who accompanied Cook on his second Voyage to New Zealand. But Forster's plant, on which he founded the genus, is another species (*Aciphylla squarrosa*); it is very much smaller than this one in all its parts, and has fine narrow pale-green lax leaves—though sharp enough! He got it at Dusky Bay in the South Island; I, also, early found it in Palliser Bay and Wairarapa. Wild pigs grubbed up and ate its thick succulent carrot-like root, which is aromatic, and I think edible for man.

Our Ruahine plant is thus described by Sir J.D. Hooker:—

"Aciphylla Colensoi, Stem 6 to 9 feet high. Leaves forming a circle 5 to 6 feet diameter of bayonet-like spikes, two feet long, pinnate; leaflets 8 to 10 inches long, half-inch broad, very thick and coriaceous, narrow linear acuminate, &c.

"N. ISLAND, top of Ruahine mountains, *Colenso*. MIDDLE (S) ISLAND, Nelson mountains, above 2000 feet, *Bidwill, Monro*, &c. Canterbury, ascending to 5500 feet, *Raoul, Haast*, &c. Otago, *Lindsay*. There are apparently two varieties; both are called "Spear-grass," and "Wild Spaniard." Monro states that it forms a thicket impenetrable to men and horses."—"*Handbook Flora, N.Z.*", p. 92.

A description of this plant with a coloured plate is also given by the late Dr. Lauder Lindsay, F.L.S., in his "Contributions to the Botany of New Zealand,"—a copy of this scarce work is in the Library of the Hawke's Bay Philosophical Institute.

As stated in the "Narration," I brought plants of this species from the mountain (with many others), and they did well and flowered in my old garden at Waitangi, until a heavy flood which submerged them and leaving a deep deposit of fine mud killed them all.

Hooker describes five species of *Aciphylla*; and says of the plant,—"a very remarkable genus, confined to N.Z., and the Australian Alps." The Australian 2 to 3 species, however, are small.

I may also add another curious and interesting item concerning this Ruahine plant *Taramea*, as it is little known. I copy from a paper read before our H.B. Philosophical Institute in 1891, (and published in "Transactions N.Z. Institute," vol. XXIV,)— "Reminiscences of the ancient Maoris" § VI. "of their fine smelling sense and taste for perfumes," and, after mentioning several, I go on to say:—

"The choicest and the rarest was obtained from the peculiar plant *Taramea* (*Aciphylla Colensoi*, Hook,) which inhabits the Alpine zone, and which I have only met with near the summit of the Ruahine range, where it is very common and very troublesome to the traveller that way. The gum-resin of this plant was only collected through much labour toil and difficulty, accompanied, too, with certain ceremonial (taboo) observances. An old *tohunga*, (skilled man and priest) once informed me, that the *Taramea* gum could only be got by very young women—virgins; and by them after certain prayers, charms, &c., duly said by the *tohunga*. This prized perfume is quaintly and lovingly extolled in a sweet little nursery song by the Maoris." (See more concerning it in the place quoted.)

Although my letter is already long, I must fain say a few words about the names used in the original narration. And, first, of the " Wild Irishman." This low uncouth vulgarism has been (unthinkingly) given "down South" to a species of thorn, a close-growing spiny shrub with very small and few leaves and long spines—appropriately named by the old Maoris—*Tumatakuru*—Face-smiter, and by the French Botanist, Raoul *Discaria toumatou.* I early discovered this plant at Poverty Bay in 1838, and also grew it in my garden at Paihia, Bay of Islands, (as is stated in Hooker's "London Journal of Botany," vol. IV, p.17, 1844,) but Raoul first fully described it with a place in his *"Choix de Plantes,"* in 1846, he having found it at Akaroa. In those Southern parts, according to the late Sir Julius von Haast it grows tall—"15 feet high." In 1838–1842 it was common at Poverty Bay on the flats near the sea, and I have seen it growing scantily in the Hawke's Bay District. (2.) It appears from Hooker, (who, no doubt, received the information from his Southern scientific correspondents,) that our big *Aciphylla* was termed "Spear-Grass," and "Wild Spaniard" by the settlers in the S. Island; while "Spear-Grass" is a fair enough common English name for the plant (although it is not a grass, and there are several large and sharp true grasses), the latter name of "Wild Spaniard" is another equally objectionable term; surely the Maori name of *Taramea*, if not the botanical generic one of *Aciphylla*, is far better than either—neater, fitting, and more euphonious. And here I would observe that I am not certain of the "Wild Irishman" of the "Kawekas" being identically the same species as the large *Aciphylla* of Ruahine; as, from the description given of it in the narration, it seems to be a smaller plant, and I have seen no specimens; but the difference in size may arise from the ground having been long used as a sheep run, and so the larger plants have perished, or been cleared off, and those seen only young ones. (3.) Of the name of the country visited: that high hill land to the west of Napier is called in the narration "the Kawekas;" and here, as I take it, is another error in etymology which should be abandoned. Kaweka is the old proper name of that mountain district; and if the Maori name is to be retained (as I hope it may be, not only there but in most places), the terminal letter s, not being Maori, and not agreeing (as a kind of English termination) with Maori idiom and rule, should be dropped.—I am, &c.,

W. COLENSO.

Napier, February 3, 1894.

❖ 1894 THE BISHOPRIC.

Hawke's Bay Herald 18 April.

SIR,—In your paper of this morning you have a strange letter on the vacant Bishopric, signed "Parishioner"; abounding in errors, and, of course, with erroneous conclusions. If "Parishioner" will have the common manliness to give his name (either publicly, or privately to me through you,) I will—with your permission, answer it. *"Inimicus homo hoc fecit."*[5]—I am, &c.,

WILLIAM COLENSO.

Napier, April 7, 1894.

---

5   'An enemy hath done this' (Matthew 13: 28). I.S.G.

❖ 1894 THE LATE PRESIDENT CARNOT.
Hawke's Bay Herald 29 June.

SIR,—As one of your old original subscribers, please allow me to say, that I was not a little surprised this morning in reading in your paper an atrocious letter written on the late shocking murder of the President of France. Such an abominable scribble I think I have never before known to be published by you in your old established and respectable paper. But I am not going to tackle it; it is too low, too anarchical, for me; besides, it is well known that I never notice anonymous letters; and this one, too, without even a disguised name!

My object, however, in writing is, (1.) to say, that I think you should not insert [6] having immoral tendencies; (you do, **** exercise your undoubted right in ****;) and(2.) that, having published it, you **** also give to your readers and to the public generally, the name in full of the wretched writer. Let me know who the creature is, (I would hope:—a visitor, a mere bird of passage, and not a Napier resident,) even to run the risk of his being "tarred and feathered." Sure I am, Mr. Editor, that the steady thinking industrious settlers of New Zealand will—to a man—lament the sad untimely end of President Carnot, and with the civilised world truly feel for the French nation in their very severe and unexpected calamity and national loss.—I am, &c.,

WILLIAM COLENSO.

Napier, June 26, 1894.

❖ 1894 A CORRECTION.
Hawke's Bay Herald 12 July.

SIR,—For the sake of the rising generation I would ask permission to correct an error in the letter from your correspondent "Hopeful," in your paper of this morning. —I do so, because it is a very common one. He concludes his letter by saying,— "Burns wrote, 'An honest man is the noblest work of God.'"

Of course, I am well aware, that Burns has that line in his delightful heart-felt poem the "Cotter's Saturday Night"; but the idea was *not* original with Burns.The line occurs in Pope's "Essay on Man," (Epistle IV, line 248) whence Burns got it. And, indeed, in the large and superior editions of Burns' works, the line itself is always placed between quotation marks, and Pope, I may observe, died before Burns was born.

But I would go a step further: and state (again) my belief—that Pope did not originally use the superlative, "noblest," but either the comparative, "nobler," or the positive, "noble"; more likely this latter, as the word is undoubtedly the more correct one there, and more in keeping with Pope's well-known careful grammatical writing. Though, very likely, Burns, to make it more suitable for his subject, altered "noble" to "noblest."

In my so saying, let no one suppose for a single moment, that I would ever write or utter a word of detraction against Scotland's first and greatest poet—Burns; for I

---

6   The paper is torn, and some words obscured. I.S.G.

have ever had the highest opinion of him as a true and great poet, of whom Scotland may ever and increasingly be truly proud.—I am, &c.,

WILLIAM COLENSO.

Napier, July 10, 1894.

§ 1894 EDITORIAL.
Manawatu Herald 28 August.
In the course of an exceedingly interesting paper read in Napier by the Rev. W. Colenso contrasting the present with the past, he mentions that in the forties it was thought to be lucky if an answer to a letter could be received from Home under twelve months; as an instance of the time taken for a letter to reach here from England, he handed round a couple of envelopes he had received, and the post marks showed that one had been posted at Farnham, England on December 27th, 1850, reaching Wellington on June 24th, 1851, and Napier September 5th. The other, posted at Farnham on October 16th, 1852, reached Auckland on April 18th, 1853, and Wellington on May 6th.

❖ **1894 TO THE EDITOR.**
Hawke's Bay Herald.
7 letters written 20, 23, 26, 29 November; 6, 13, 21 December (publication dates unknown).[7]

❖ **1894 A NEW PEST.**
Daily Telegraph 10 December.
SIR,—I take the liberty of enclosing some leaves of a chrysanthemum. Under the cuticles of the back part of these are the chrysalides of a pest that is new to me, and probably to others. Can you get some kind entomologist to identify these for the benefit of myself and the curious who may not be acquainted with them?—I am, &c., W.W. Yates.

We forwarded the leaves to the Rev. W. Colenso, F.R.S., who writes to us as follows:—

Sir,—I am now able to reply to your note of enquiry of the 3rd inst, containing some chrysanthemum leaves, having on them the larvæ of some insect. On examining them I found them to be unknown to me and probably not indigenous; so I sent them to Wellington to Mr. Maskell, (who is facile princeps in all such matters,) and from him I have just received an interesting report concerning them. Mr. Maskell says:—"The insect is the larvæ of a fly, Phytomyza affinis, Fallen: it came to Wellington a couple

---

7   These seven letters, along with a further three written in 1897, were republished as a booklet, *Certain errors of the Church of Rome* and will be republished in *Colenso's published papers*, 2, forthcoming. I.S.G.

of years or so ago; but yours are the first specimens which I have seen from elsewhere. As the fullgrown insect is very active on the wing, I have no doubt that it will rapidly spread. This fly attacks apparently almost all the *Compositæ* in New Zealand; and as this grub bores under the surface of the leaves and mines them in numerous channels it is not only most destructive but very difficult to get at. (You will find an account of it by me in vol. xxvi. of our *"Transactions"* p. 663.)"

On referring to the vol. of "Transactions N.Z. Institute" for 1893, (mentioned by Mr. Maskell,) I find, that he had sent Home specimens to Mr. C. Whitehead, Adviser to the Department of Agriculture in England, to ascertain the true affinities; and Mr. Whitehead, in replying, says, "This insect is very troublesome in England to many plants, mainly of the compositæ. It is found in enormous quantities on chrysanthemums and on allied plants—I do not think arsenical washes would be effectual in preventing egg-laying. Spraying with paraffin or carbolic acid would be far more likely to keep the fly from depositing eggs."

I may add, that I had gathered a few leaves from sonchus (sow-thistle) last autumn, both at Woodville end here on Scinde Island, which had been so curiously "mined" and discoloured by this same insect, but such did not possess any larvæ, and I had supposed at first sight the leaves were visited by a fungus:" I am, &o.,

WILLIAM COLENSO.

Napier, December 8, 1894.

❖ 1894 THE DISCOVERY OF MOA REMAINS.
New Zealand Herald. 15 December.

SIR—This morning I received from a friend a copy of the Poverty Bay Herald of the 6th instant which contains a long and interesting article extracted from your paper, entitled "The Maori and the Moa"; and as there is one statement therein that is erroneous (not, however, begun by you), I wish to correct it—partly because I may be the only living person who has it in his power to do so and partly because it refers to an old resident at the North in the *Auckland* Province. I fear, however, that you may not have any now residing with you who once knew him. The sentence I allude to is the following:—

"The first announcement respecting the moa was made in Mr. Polack's book about New Zealand published in 1838, and there he states that he had found bones near the East Cape."

I shall copy verbatim what Polack has said; he had been writing on the kiwi:—

"That a species of the emu, or a bird of the genus struthio, formerly existed in the northern island, I feel well assured, as several large fossil ossifications were shown to me when I was residing in the vicinity of the East Cape, said to have been found at the base of the island mountain of Ikorangi. The natives added that, in times long past, they received the tradition that very large birds had existed, but the scarcity of animal food, as well as the easy method of entrapping them, had caused their extermination." (*l.c.* Vol. I, p. 303) and again, "I feel assured, from the many reports I received from the natives, that a species of struthio still exists in that interesting

419

island, in parts, which, perhaps, have never yet been trodden by man. Traditions are current among the elder natives, of atuas, covered with hair, in the form of birds, having waylaid former native travellers among the forest wilds, vanquishing them with an overpowering strength, killing and devouring, etc. These traditions are repeated with an air of belief that carries conviction to the younger natives, who take great delight in the marvellous and improbable" (*l.c.*, p. 307).

Before, however, that I remark on what I have here quoted, I would state —(1) That I knew Polack well, and was not unfrequently in his store at Kororareka (he was a general dealer in "marine stores," particularly spirits); (2) that he was a great collector of all manner of "curios," both natural and artificial (as indeed his published volumes show), which he also sold; (3) that he did not wholly write his book (indeed he could not possibly do so), the London booksellers helped him, but his peculiar stiltified and strained phraseology everywhere appears; (4) Polack's coasting craft (a cutter used in collecting flax) was wrecked in Tolago Bay, and through that misfortune he (being in her) was obliged to remain there some time, until another vessel arrived and took him and his companions away—I saw the hull there, high and dry and broken, in January, 1838; (5) from Polack's published account we find that during his long sojourn at Tolago Bay he never visited the country or coast north and south of Tolago—not even Poverty Bay, so near by! (I knew well it would not have been an easy matter for him to do so).

Now for his statement: his (so-called) "*vicinity* of the East Cape" was Tolago Bay, some 60 miles further S. The "fossil ossifications" (strange term!) came from "the base of the inland mountain (Hikurangi)," near the East Cape: very likely these were only *portions* of bones from the shanks of *tibiæ*, the processes thrown away, as the natives there (East Cape) cut up such into slips as lures for their large sea-fishing hooks,—some of them I still possess. Had there been a perfect bone Polack would have secured it, and brought it away. Polack, having come to New Zealand from Sydney, knew all about the emu, etc., then so common there. Polack, who commonly deals largely in Maori names of things (birds, fishes, trees, etc.) never once used the term moa.

I did not see Polack's book until about 12 to 14 years ago, when I obtained a copy from London; and even this I did not go through (nor cut), and I only *first* heard of Polack's statement (*supra*) from my friend Mr. Hamilton at Dunedin, about three years ago, Mr. Hamilton, in his long paper on the "Bibliography of the Moa" (*Trans. N.Z. Inst. vol. xxiv, p. 95*), brings forward Polack for the first time, but, just as in your article, the Professor says:—"The first announcement of the former existence of large struthious birds in New Zealand was by Mr. J.S. Polack, who in his book 'New Zealand,' published in 1838, stated that he had found their bones near the East Cape of the North Island."—I am etc.,

WILLIAM COLENSO.

Napier, December 12, 1894.

§ 1895 BUSH WANDERINGS.
Hawke's Bay Herald 16 April.

I saw that well-known scientist, the Rev. Mr. Colenso, in Danevirke a few days ago. He carries his age well, and those who have the honor of his acquaintance must revel in a past history of this country. I am told the old man has seen most of the great events take place in the growth of our nation's life, and that he is almost the only remaining link between the past and present. How greatly ought such a man to be valued and what a pity it will be should his vast stores of historical information pass away when his time comes to go. I for one should be glad to learn that he has put on record the great events through which he has passed. Even now his old spirit seems to glow with fervor, and his stirring words in Church the other Sunday would have done credit to much younger men. He is a ripe scholar, full of years, and a man it seems to me worthy of the highest respect and admiration. He appears to be highly respected hereabout.

❖ 1895 PALMISTRY.
?Bush Advocate c. 20 April.

SIR,—When at Danevirke a short time ago I saw in your paper an advertisement announcing a Bazaar about to be held for the benefit of the Danevirke Brass Band, and among other wonders a cunning woman was to be brought there from Palmerston to tell fortunes by palmistry! However, it so happened, that the promoters of the Bazaar, on learning that such cheating as Palmistry was illegal, wisely caused it to be published in the following number of your Paper that Palmistry would not be allowed at the Bazaar; this was right. I have lately again, met with a recent case in the London papers, in which the brazen-faced prophetess or cheating-woman was severely punished for her palmistry. I extract this and send to you for insertion in your paper, that my good friends in the Bush district generally, (including the police), may know a little more about it, and how severely it is punished in England. At the same time I cannot shut my eyes to the fact, that you have there in Danevirke and its neighbourhood, far worse cheats, false prophets, and "fads" than this of palmistry.[8]—I am, etc.,

WILLIAM COLENSO.

Napier, April 19, 1895.

London Standard

February 18th, 1895

Sophia Robson *alias* 'Madame Minerva,' was charged at the Mansion House Police Court yesterday with having pretended to tell fortunes by means of palmistry. Mrs. Whatley, a cook at the Cloak-lane Police Station, spoke to an interview with the

---

8   This is taken from a clipping of the letter (ATL MS-Copy-Micro-0485-1) on which Colenso wrote 'the "fads": Salvation Army! Mormonism!' I.S.G.

prisoner at the instance of the police, and Mr. Alderman Green, considering the case proved, inflicted a fine of £25, or a month's imprisonment in default.

❖ 1895 WAS IT A JUST JUDGEMENT?

Hawke's Bay Herald 26 April.

SIR,—I thank you for publishing in your paper of this day the able and fitting letter from "Humanity,"—and him, too, for writing it: I hope, also, it may be productive of good. I had very nearly written a letter myself on the same thoughtless and harsh decisions: of such we have seen too many of late throughout Hawke's Bay; and the marvel with me has ever been—Why the public put up with it?—When inland a month ago, and speaking on a public matter, I said,—"No man with a pronounced moral or political 'fad,' should be entrusted with the office of a parish schoolmaster, or Minister"—and to that I would add—or J.P. Such creatures are always narrow-minded, perhaps born so! I could say a great deal more on this subject, but I forbear,—I am, &c.,

W. COLENSO.

Napier, April 25, 1895.

❖ 1895 THE RE-UNION OF CHURCHES.

Hawke's Bay Herald ?4 June.

SIR,—Can you kindly find room for this short communication of mine, containing a recent important public letter from the Archbishop of Canterbury re Re-union with Rome. It is a fitting and full reply to Prior Vaughan's vainglorious statement contained in your late Sydney telegram in the HERALD of this morning, in which utterance of the Prior, no doubt, "the wish was father to the thought."

Moreover, the Archbishop's brief letter is also, a full confirmation of what I had publicly said in your columns a few months ago, in my letters on this subject; and, I trust, your republication of his Grace's plain and truthful statement, may prove of service here among us, and be a means of saving some (of our pleasure-loving and thoughtless folks) from being carried away by the sophistries and blandishments, the music and fair speeches of erring and meretricious Rome (*semper eadem*).
—I am, &c.,

W. COLENSO.

Napier, June 3, 1895.

"The Rev. Prebendary Webb-Peploe, as Chairman of the National Protestant Union, lately sent to the Archbishop of Canterbury a copy of Lord Halifax's speech on Reunion with Rome, and asked his Grace to make some public pronouncement upon it. In reply the Archbishop has written the following letter, and has authorised its publication:—

"Lambeth Palace,

"March 28th, 1895.

"Dear Mr. Webb-Peploe,—I have given full consideration to your letter and its important enclosure. I feel, however, I should be setting a precedent fraught with much difficulty hereafter were I to put forth official utterances with respect to the speeches of clergy or laity to members of the private societies to which they may belong. I did not gather that the speech in question was to be regarded in any other light than as the expression of the individual opinions of the speaker; and, indeed, if I am not misinformed, it has already been made clear in the newspapers that he did not express the sentiments of the society generally.

"But while I must abstain from the task of commenting upon the speeches then delivered (a task which might indeed be endless), I have no hesitation in saying that, in my opinion—to quote your own words—'any corporate union with Rome, so long as she maintains her distinctive and erroneous doctrines, and advances her present unproductive and unscriptural claims, is absolutely visionary and impossible.'—Believe me, sincerely yours,

(Signed) "ED. CANTUAR."

——(London Standard, April 5, 1895.)

❖ 1895 THE TODAS.

?Hawke's Bay Herald c. 12 June.

SIR,—I was much interested in reading, in your issue of this evening, a paper on "the Thodawar tribe (India) and their habits," written by Mr. A. Lascelles, now in India, which was read at the meeting of the Hawke's Bay Institute on Monday evening last, as it reminded me of my having read a similar but fuller account of that peculiar race nearly 20 years ago, in a scientific volume on that hill (or mountain) tribe, written by Col. Marshall of H.M. Bengall Staff Corps, and well illustrated throughout by the autotype process, to which is added a grammar of their language, by the Rev. O.U. Pope, D.D., Headmaster of the "Bishop-Cotton" School, at Bangalore. Col. Marshall writes from actual observation (aided by Tamil scholars), having spent his furlough among that tribe. Mr. Lascelles does not say he had witnessed what he relates.

I may notice what I believe to be an error of your compositor—the naming the tribe in question the "Zodas"; whereas it should have been the Todas, (also written *Tuda* by Dr. Pope in his Grammar). I am the more inclined to deem this an error of the press, from the fact of the well-known Indian word *Tamil* being also printed *Zamil* in your paper. Moreover Col. Marshall says, that the *Tadawar* tribe are a distinct people, but living in close proximity to the Todas.

I may further add, that I was led to purchase a copy of Col. Marshall's book, (on its publication by Longman & Co., in 1873, at a guinea) from having seen notices of it which led me to hope I might find some ancient latent connection between the Todas language, habits, and customs and our own Maoris, (I, then, working on the N.Z. Lexicon) but in this I was disappointed.—I am, &c.,

W. COLENSO.

Napier, June 11, 1895.

❖ 1895 THE APPOINTMENT OF TEACHERS.
Hawke's Bay Herald 20 June.

SIR,—Thank you heartily for your article this morning on "The Appointment of Teachers." Indeed I may truly say doubly so; because I had first read your report of the school committee's doings last night, and had arrived at similar conclusions; and then, on reading your able remarks, agreeably found myself quite in thinking with you.

As an old teacher of youth, and also as Inspector of Schools, I lament—I feel disgusted—at the hasty untoward action of the School Committee. In so saying, I have nothing whatever against Mr. Hislop, (very far from it,) a gentleman whom I do not know, not even by sight, (and so I may also say of the other applicants). It may be, that Mr. Hislop is the most fit and proper person among all the applicants for the office in question, but that is not shown in what took place. (1.) By the Committee refusing to look at the high-class testimonials sent in for their inspection. (2.) By the Committee ignoring the superior academical qualifications of all the other applicants; together with the number of years they severally had been engaged in teaching, and also the high positions they now hold in their various schools and colleges. (3.) By the Committee setting aside the plain official instruction from the Education Board, namely,—"All other things being equal."

At the same time I am quite ready to allow, (what, indeed, I have always held and published,)—that mere academical distinctions, however high, are not sufficient of themselves to make a good useful serviceable teacher. Indeed, I should place *"aptness to teach,"*—that rare ability to lead, to get to love learning and to learn, to educe, in our boys,—as of far greater or paramount importance, truly "A1," in this matter: and this with strict reference to all teachers—Clerical as well as lay.

But, as I view it, a double injury has been done by the School Committee; unwittingly, it may be, nevertheless it is there, fixed. Again showing the truth of the poetical axiom, (too often forgotten) that

Evil is done by want of THOUGHT,
As well as want of heart,

—"A double injury," did I say? Yes, a double injury—if not a still larger one.

(1.) Injury to those respectable applicants.

(2.) Injury to our big rising and toiling generously-minded aspiring youths; who have been long aiming rightly at scholastic distinctions; some of them (I know) looking forward to their attainment, in order the better to become teachers themselves. And now they find our sapient school committee—that such is all bosh! worthless!!—

(3.) Injury, moreover, to our schools in the near future; for when a vacancy occurs in a school, and the usual advertisement is published, who will respond? Who apply? Not, I suppose, any superior class teacher of ability and distinction, to be again trodden under foot by——.

The chairman could truly say, that the large majority of the committee "had made up their minds beforehand"!—no doubt. But, if so, why go to the expense and trouble of advertising at all? And why, needlessly, cause trouble, expense, and dissatisfaction amongst the distant applicants? Moreover (it may be, that) those very applicants themselves may become losers of positions, &c., in their several schools, through their having been so unceremoniously treated.

Now, after all, the main question is not answered. Why has Mr. Hislop been so chosen over the heads of others—far higher in academical rank, and long known as "A1" teachers in our public schools; and therefore, possibly, better men? Is it owing to friendship? or to private influence? or to a determination at all risks to elect a townsman? or, even to a lower unworthy cause,—to his supporters having a *fad* of their own, and privately knowing that Mr. Hislop will carry out their *fad*? I am obliged to mention this last mean hypothesis, seeing that there are *faddists* in the committee, who only last week carried the reading of their *fad*—the teetotal book of their Great Mogul, Dr. Richardson, in the public school! Here, again, displaying "want of thought," for if one such book (the pet of the noisy minority) be taken in to be read in the school, then, in common justice, such will shortly be followed by others, from the majority of our more reasonable townsmen.—I am, &c.,

W. COLENSO.

Napier, June 18, 1895.

❖ **1895 INTRODUCTION OF BEES.**
Hawke's Bay Herald 10 December.

SIR,—I was not a little surprised (I may say, and amused!) in reading in your paper of the 7th instant a letter written from England to you, purposely and fully stating that "Bees were introduced into New Zealand in 1845!" and that there is a silver medal extant attesting it, of which a photograph was also sent to you. I am sorry (in a certain sense) to have to upset the pretty picture you, and your English correspondent have given us, but now for the plain dry facts, without! alas! the embellishments of a silver medal, or of a photograph, or of "a deserved recognition." Our Scotch friends truly say: "Facts are chiels that winna ding, an' canna be disputed."

(1.) When I came to Hawke's Bay, on my second visit, to reside in 1844, I brought my hive of bees with me.

(2.) That special hive was made in the Bay of Islands for me, containing a swarm from the bees of my esteemed friend Mr. James Busby, of Waitangi, (for many years British Resident there down to the time of the signing of the Treaty of Waitangi), Mr. Busby having introduced bees into New Zealand a few years before.

(3.) I may add that Mr. Busby had reared several hives of bees, and with many others, I had gone from the Paihia mission station (near by) to Waitangi, to see the bees at work; as Mr. Busby had also the new addition to the old-fashioned box hives, of a glass vase, or room, fixed on the top. And I had also partaken of the new honey in its comb made there, and kindly distributed by Mr. Busby to his friends as a novelty.

(4.) The Rev. W.C. Cotton, (mentioned in the English letter to you, and who arrived in the Bay of Islands with Bishop Selwyn, in 1842,) was a great bee-lover, and had written a nicely illustrated book on bee-keeping. He had a hive of bees at Waimate, from Mr. Busby's, in 1842–3.

(5.) There being no flowering plants producing honey around me at Waitangi in those early days, and I getting tired of artificially feeding my bees, and fearing to lose them all if I let them go, there being no shelter, and the fierce westerly winds very strong, I sent them by special messengers to the "Big Bush," (then standing between the modern towns of Hastings and Clive,) and they were liberated there; they did well; and from them I believe all the bees of this provincial district, and farther, are descended.

(6.) Moreover, I think there were bees at the old Church Mission Station at Poverty Bay prior to 1844, and a swarm from Mr. Busby's hives. The present Bishop of Waiapu, or his brother, Mr. J.N. Williams, of Frimley, could no doubt satisfy you on this head.

(7.) Such a medal with its pseudo inscription would be sure to evoke much controversy in "days to come," if not now so clearly explained and shown to be untrue. But, in my saying this, I mean only in the one primary sense, of the first introduction of bees into New Zealand, and without any reference to the sending them hither direct from England.

Thinking over the whole subject brings to mind several somewhat similar matters of hoary antiquity, aye, and of modern times, too; in which men and manners, acts and dates, sculptures, inscriptions, writings and medals, have been handed down to posterity, causing no little research and controversy. And then, as to the "honour"— well (without quoting Shakespeare), at such times a quaint distich from Goethe's *Faust*, where, in the inimitable scene on the Brocken (blasted mountain-top), in the Walpurgis-night, Mephistopheles accosts one of the old witches riding on a sow, saying—

"Honour to whom honour is due:
Here, Mother Baubo, is honour to you."

I am, &c.,

W. COLENSO.

Napier, December 9, 1895.

❖ **1895 DANEVIRKE OR DANNEVIRKE?**
Hawke's Bay Herald 11 December.
SIR,—Permit me (for the information of the public generally) to correct a glaring error in the letter of your "Own Correspondent" at Waipawa, which appeared in your paper on Saturday last. Had it been merely one of his ordinary usual ones I should not care to notice it. He says: "An official notice has been sent to the local post-office from headquarters to the effect that in future the official spelling of the name of the town shall be Dannevirke! I wonder who is responsible for this new barbarism?" Now Dannevirke (with two n's) is both the original name

of the said town, and the properly spelled orthographical one in accordance with the old Scandinavian language, and so "the new barbarism" (or brass ignorance) pertains to your "Own Correspondent." I may add that I have often had to call the attention of visitors there (as well as to reply to questions from abroad) as to the proper spelling of the word, which, however, has always been painted correctly on the Government signboard at the railway station, as well as printed so in the Government railway time-tables.—I am, &c.,

W. Colenso.

Napier, December 10, 1895.

§ 1896 NO THOROUGHFARE.

THE Public are hereby informed that thoroughfare through my enclosed grounds on the hills, Napier, can no longer be allowed. Persons trespassing after the last day of this month (February), will be prosecuted. That none may plead ignorance, and that this notice may be fully known, it will be advertised for one whole week in each of our three daily town papers.

W. Colenso.

** See my letter in another column. February 20, 1895.

❖ 1896 SHORT CUT TO NAPIER TERRACE.

Hawke's Bay Herald 21 February.

SIR,—From an advertisement in another column the public will know, that all thoroughfare through and over my ground is permanently closed, and this applies to *all alike*, including a few friends and neighbors to whom I had given permission, as I cannot possibly make any distinction.

I have now leased my premises to the Napier Golf Club, who will join with me in keeping off trespassers. But I had previously determined to put a stop to this incessant trespass, which had increased so rapidly at the end of last year, and should have done so, but for the very dry and hot weather which had burnt up the grass in my paddocks, and I really pitied the small school children living on the hills, some of whom, unfortunately, had to go home to dinner in the extreme heat of the day.

All losses and injuries (hitherto quietly borne) have been many and great, all my ducks, and a number of my fowls killed by dogs of trespassers; fences, and side cuttings well grassed and firm, shamefully broken down; trees and shrubs continually wantonly plucked, wrecked, and thrown on the path; gates left open, so the horses got out and became impounded; the fields trampled in all directions—not caring even to keep their one track or pathway, and, not least, no privacy, and the fear and danger from fire (smokers' matches).

That there is great need of a shorter road (than the long round-about one by Milton-road from its saddle) to connect Napier Terrace and Barrack Hill, the cemetery and botanic gardens, and indeed all the southern part of Scinde island with the town, is well known to all who have to travel over that ground; and this, I may say, was an additional reason with me for hitherto allowing so much of daily trespass. And this shorter road may yet be had; the first three chains of it, from Napier Terrace to suburban section 32 (church land), having been already by the Government reserved for a road, and much (nearly two thirds) of the land required to make a good carriage road would come through my grounds, and *I am still willing to give it*—as, indeed, I offered it to the Borough Council sixteen years ago, furnishing them at the same time with Mr. Rochfort's carefully prepared plan of the proposed road showing its gradients, and that it was twelve chains shorter than the present road. And this new road would not only be so much shorter but be a far better road for travellers than the present disagreeable, close, hot, and tedious upper Milton-road.

The other owners of the land required are the Church Trustees (who I believe will again readily consent to grant their portion), and Mr. R.D.D. M'Lean—for a short distance only, but should Mr. M'Lean not consent, that would make no difference, as I can easily meet that, by giving a little more land, and while the new road according to Mr. Rochfort's plan would join on to Milton-road at my upper gate there, the cutting and gradient would be very different from the present steep horse track up my hill.

And so—in closing my private grounds against the public, as I view it, they will become the gainers; for they have the alternative of a good carriage road ½ chain or more wide in their own hands and this thought goes a great way toward supporting me—although the cost of fencing would come heavy upon me. Let the matter be taken up heartily by the people of the borough, especially by those who reside on the hills, and the Council seeing now the absolute necessity of the thing, must grant their request.—I am, &c.,

WILLIAM COLENSO.

Napier, February 15, 1896.

❖ 1896 A STRANGE INSECT.
Daily Telegraph 9 March.

A few days ego one of the runner boys of the Daily Telegraph found upon his coat a strange looking insect between four and five inches long. It was forwarded to the Rev. W. Colenso, F.R.S., and the following letter, in which he has kindly given a description of the insect, will therefore explain itself:—

SIR,—On my return from the Bush District last evening, I found here in my house the specimen of a large Orthopterous insect you had kindly sent me for examination, &c.

It is a species of Bacillus (Acanthoderus) and near B. horridus (or B. coloreus, Col.) Without close and microscopical examination I cannot say if it is really distinct from those species of that genus already known and described, seeing, too, that the males of each species differ from the females. In "Transactions N.Z. Institute," vol. XVII., pp. 151-155, I have described four new species (besides others in other volumes), and all of course in papers originally read here at our branch-Institute meetings; and I have still remaining other specimens undescribed—through want of time.

These insects, commonly known as the "Stick Insect" are common in the Bush woods, on trees and shrubs. Some of the species attain to a large size, 6 and 7 inches long, and are very prickly. This one you sent me, a female, measures 4½ inches (body and head) in length; but has nothing striking about it. I have kept them alive sometime feeding them with green leaves; and the female insect has laid 54 eggs, small and curiously shaped and marked, and even engraved! and the young fry have also been hatched here under glass, (see the vol. "Transactions" referred to p. 162, for a minute description.) This specimen of yours has also laid 3 eggs in the box in which it was confined.—I am, &c.,

W. COLENSO.

Napier, March 7, 1896

❖ 1896 OF A DESTRUCTIVE NEW ZEALAND ROOT FUNGUS.
Hawke's Bay Herald 23 March.

SIR,—Yesterday I received from the Director of the Royal Gardens, Kew, London, a copy of the official *Kew Bulletin* for January, 1896; containing, among other things, a full and particular account of this terrible native pest—which may, I fear, prove far more destructive than the codlin moth, or the acacia, or the American apple blights. It is now some time since I first discovered this fungus, and sent specimens of it to Kew—but those were incomplete. Nine months ago I was again at Woodville, and visited Mr. G. Lindauer's[9] garden and orchard, where I had full proof of the sad havoc caused by this small plant! Several of his large and hitherto flourishing apple trees (10–12 feet high) were killed by it. These had been lately dug up by Mr. Lindauer, and showed how greatly their roots and bases of trunks had been infected by it —a most disagreeable sight. I recommended him to burn up every portion, even to the making strong fires in the big holes or pits whence he had dug the trees. Other apple trees near by had not at that time shown signs of infection. Afterwards at Dannevirke, I heard of this root fungus infecting certain flower and shrub roots, also potatoes. It will further appear, from statements in the said Kew paper, how very mischievous this fungus has been in the Waikato and Auckland districts:—

"Amongst the numerous root diseases of various plants caused by parasitic fungi, none are better known, or extending over a greater area than the *pourridié* of the French, which occurs in France, Italy, Switzerland, Austria, and South-west Germany, and has recently been recorded from three widely separated localities in Britain. The fungus causing this disease is called *Dematophora necatrix*, (Hartig), which frequently devastates vineyards and orchards; its attacks, however, are unfortunately not confined to vines and fruit-trees; potatoes, beans, beet, &c., are also destroyed, and Hartig states that the mycelium soon kills young maples, oaks, beeches, pines and spruces. During the spring of the present year (1895), a sample of soil was received by the Royal Horticultural Society, from Mr. Hooper, Cambridge, Waikato, New Zealand,

---

9   Gottfried Lindauer of Woodville had painted Colenso's portrait, which was presented to him on 12 November 1894. I.S.G.

containing roots of apple trees attacked by a fungus; with a communication stating that the roots of fruit trees which penetrated the places where the fungus appeared to reside became infected, the fungus penetrating the tree and ultimately killing it. This material was forwarded to Kew for investigation. Sterile mycelium alone was present, which appeared to agree in every detail with that of *Dematophora necatrix*, and the fungus was provisionally referred to that species in a brief report published in the Journal of the Royal Horticultural Society (xix., part 1, 28). The following account will give an idea of the injury caused by this fungus, as observed by Mr. R. Allan Wight, of Auckland, N.Z.:—

'This fungus, in the mycelial stage, attacks a great variety of tree roots, amongst the most conspicuous of which are the apple, pear, peach, and all other common orchard trees. The white thorn is also subject to its attacks, and several of the native trees and plants. It also attacks the cabbage, potato, docks, sorrel, fern, and in fact is almost omnivorous, which is a marked peculiarity. In hedges of white thorn, where roses have been planted at intervals, the thorns are killed, and the roses remain intact and quite uninjured. In an orchard it will appear in patches, killing the fern and sorrel. It then attacks the bark round the stem, just under the ground, which speedily rots, presenting the appearance of having been cooked, and has an offensive smell; it then proceeds along the roots, and the tree soon shows withered leaves, which drop off, leaving it bare; and by and by it falls over and lies on the ground. Its movements are uncertain; sometimes a tree here and there dies; sometimes a whole row, and very often acres are swept off. Many entire orchards of fine trees are killed in a few years. This fungus is never found in clay or other damp soils, but always in very friable lands. Professor Kirk, of Wellington, says it is *Lycoperdon gemmatum* (Batsch), and that "tar water" is a certain cure. The last statement is assuredly an error, and I think the first is also. For a great many years I have endeavored in vain to procure the fruit of this fungus, using all the means that suggested themselves to me, without any success. I have seen large quantities of the *L. gemmatum* growing in orchards where there is root fungus, and I have seen a very great many orchards, and watched several closely where hundreds of trees were attacked, and could never find the mycelium connected with the *Lycoperdon*. …. The pest is most plentiful on the skirts of the primeval forests, and on fern lands adjoining where no cultivation has ever been resorted to. Whole crops of potatoes are destroyed on such lands, and on dry land, where native tree stumps remain it is very prevalent. My own opinion is, that it is a fungus native to, and probably peculiar to New Zealand (in the North Island only). All my experiments with sulphur and lime have failed. Kerosene oil used in winter has alone been of any use, and that has been used pure in winter without killing the trees. The fungi of New Zealand are legion, and very destructive, but this is the worst, and particularly as it is confined to dry soils. Where I am now writing 500 trees have been killed within the last two years, and all remedies tried have failed. The apple scab, the shot hole fungus, the oidium of the vine are terrible pests in New Zealand, and the settlers have more to fear from fungus growths than insect pests.'

"As previously stated, the material received from New Zealand was, in the first instance, referred to *Dematophora necatrix*. Further development of the fungus, and the receipt of additional fruiting specimens from the same country showed that this was a mistake, neither does the fungus belong to any known species. It will, therefore, be described as new, under the name *Rosellinia radiciperda* .... During the period of this investigation a parcel of New Zealand fungi, collected and communicated by the Rev. W. Colenso, F.R.S. was received at Kew, and amongst the number was a species of *Rosellinia*, marked 'at the base of a fallen and decayed apple tree.' Careful examination of this specimen revealed the presence of sclerotia bearing conidia identical with those of the fungus under consideration, mixed with the perithecia or ascigerous condition of Colenso's specimen (figs. 1–6) and, further, it appears that the perithecia originate from the sclerotia, which previously bear the conidial form of reproduction.

PREVENTIVE MEASURES.

"Notwithstanding the fact that the New Zealand fungus proves to be distinct from the European root fungus, yet the general habit, mode of attack, and structure of the two are so similar that the same methods of combatting the disease will apply to both. The most frequent and rapid mode of spreading is by means of the mycelium travelling in the soil, and a good method of isolating diseased patches is to cut a narrow trench, from nine inches to a foot deep round, such care being taken to throw the excavated soil into the diseased portion and not outside of it. This method, which was first suggested by Hartig, for the purpose of preventing the spread of subterranean fungi in the German forests, cannot be too strongly commended. The amount of success depends entirely on the thoroughness, combined with an intelligent mode of carrying out the work; half attempts invariably result in a loss of capital without benefit. It may be enough to suggest that the disease may be spread by the spores of the fungus, or infected soil being carried by the shoes of laborers, by dirty tools, wheels of carts, animals, &c., from diseased centres. Diseased and fallen trees, and especially stumps and roots, should be at once destroyed by burning. The soil surrounding diseased stumps should be burned after the stumps have been removed, so as to destroy the smaller diseased portions of the root that remained behind. A second preventive method, which has proved of service in France, is to lay bare the trunk as far below the surface of the soil as can be done without injury to the tree, and to densely coat the exposed trunk and adjoining soil with powdered sulphur. This should be repeated when the channel round the trunk becomes filled up with earth. Stagnant water should not be allowed to remain in the soil, as this favors the spread of the fungus."

Believing that the importance of this communication will make amends for its length,—I am, &c.,

W. COLENSO.

P.S. The plate containing drawings and dissections of this plant will be exhibited in Mr. J.W. Craig's window for a week.—W.C.

Napier, March 21, 1896.

❖ 1896 A NEW INSECT.
Daily Telegraph 27 April.

Last week a somewhat remarkable insect, having fourteen pairs of legs and long antennae, was found in a house in Emerson street. It was the smaller of two seen, the larger escaping. The specimen captured was sent to the Rev. W. Colenso, for his verdict upon it, and in return that gentleman writes as follows:—

SIR,—The insect you have submitted to me for examination, belongs to the class Myriapoda, order Chilopoda, and to the genus Scutigera. It is very much like the species Scutigira arancoides, (Scolopendra coleoptra, Linn., and Fab.,) an European species but, I think, quite distinct: that species is said to be venomous, and is much dreaded in Hungary. This insect is new to me, never having seen one before, and I almost doubt it being indigenous;—perhaps introduced in the egg state (with many others) through shipping.

We have here in N.Z. 2 species of the genera Julus and Scolopendra, allied insects belonging to the same order; this last contains the well-known Centipede so common (and large too) at the North. And I may mention a remarkably fine and (illegible) specimen of Julus, measuring 6 inches in length, (which was found living at Dannevirke in a bunch of bananas from Fiji.) I exhibited and described this insect two years ago at our Institute meeting, and published also in "Transactions N.Z. Institute." vol. xxvi p.106,—Julus (Spirostreptus) Fijiensis.

Fresh forms of insects are being continually introduced into the Colony from abroad, among fruit and other Island produce. You say, in your accompanying note, that another but larger one was also seen in the house where this one was captured. If this one should also be obtained, I should like to see it.—I believe they mostly roam at night, seeking food. I am, &c.,

W. COLENSO.

Napier, April 25, 1896.

❖ 1896 ROOT FUNGUS.
Hawke's Bay Herald 5 May.

SIR,—In your issue of March 23rd, you kindly published my letter containing some particulars respecting a root-fungus (*Rosellinia radiciperda*), which is such a pest in some of our apple orchards;—destroying the otherwise healthy trees by hundreds, while hitherto no effective means had been known to subdue it. I have since received several communications respecting it; and one, in particular, contains an interesting account of the way in which this new and trying plague was fought and killed. I should, therefore, also like to make this public through the columns of your paper, for the benefit of apple-growers, seeing, too, the remedy is both simple and at hand. Mr. A. Olsen,[10] painter, of Norsewood, in a recent letter to me, says:—"I have seen your letter in the HERALD respecting the root-fungus. I have had pretty much experience with it. About six or seven years ago I had many apple-trees killed by it, and tried several

---

10 See *Colenso's collections*. Andreas Olsen collected Ruahine plants for Colenso. I.S.G.

remedies in vain. At last, however, I succeeded in this way: I dug away the earth round about the stem and main root of the tree affected by the fungus, and then scraped away all the rotten bark and stuff adhering, until the stem and root were quite dead: then I sprinkled the root with lime, or if I had no lime at hand, wood ashes, and laid the roots bare for some time, until I saw the tree was recovering; by this means I have now several trees that I have saved, and they are doing well. One can easily see when the tree is affected by the fungus; the leaves turn red and yellow, and if the tree so attacked is attended to early it can be saved. The tree soon shows its return to healthy life, and freedom from its destroying enemy."—I am, &c.,

W. COLENSO.

Napier, May 4, 1896.

§ 1896 A MUNIFICENT GIFT.
Poverty Bay Herald 13 May.

REV. W. COLENSO'S PRESENTATION TO HAWKE'S BAY.

A TOUCHING SCENE.

WORDS OF WISDOM FROM A GRAND OLD MAN.

[SPECIAL TO HERALD.]

NAPIER, to-day.

There was something very touching in a scene at the Philosophical Institute, in which the Rev. W. Colenso played the principal part. The old man's heart is thoroughly in his scientific pursuits, and a visitor to his residence on Colenso Hill will ever find him wrapt up in his studies of the glories of nature.

The want of a proper museum has perhaps not been more keenly felt by any Hawke's Bay settler than by the aged Maori missionary. Mr. Colenso's sympathies with all objects having for their purpose the intellectual advancement of the community in which he has passed so many years of his life, are well known, but no one was prepared for the munificent offer which he made at the Philosophical Institute's meeting.

In unfolding his scheme, he said his first donation would be £1000, and he would give a freehold site. (Great applause). This site would be town section 109, near the public school. He wanted to make up £4000. How was it to be done? Mr. John Harding had made an offer last year to give £200 towards a museum. This year, as wool had risen in price and things were well with him, perhaps Mr. Harding would be inclined to double that and give £400, or perhaps £500. At any rate, when another £500 was paid up he would give a second donation of £500. (Applause). That would be £2000. Mr. Douglas McLean had written to him, stating that he was prepared to give £500, and if that were done he (Mr. Colenso) would give a third amount of £500. Then another £1000 would be wanted. For that they must all put their shoulders to the wheel. He believed it could be got in this way. A museum here would also be for the East Coast, not only for Hawke's Bay proper or for the old provincial district, but for Poverty Bay and Gisborne and the country stretching up to the East Cape.

He declared that the building was to be used solely for the purposes of a museum and library. There were to be no concerts, no Liedertafels, no Bohemians, no "spouting," no mutual admiration societies (laughter), no globe trotters, no tourists, and no parsons. (Laughter.) He would not give a penny for persons of that sort. (Great laughter.)

In concluding Mr. Colenso said his offer would be open until December 31st, and he would like to see the matter started ere he departed, assuring his hearers that unless they showed themselves worthy of it they would not get the £2000.

Mr. Colenso's inaugural address was one of the finest ever heard in the institute, and it was delivered with wonderful clearness for a man eighty-seven years old. In the course of his address, he said: "Fairly considering an institution such as this, especially in a newly settled country, and with special reference to the great number of educated youths yearly leaving school, one was tempted to ask 'Why is it that so few of them are found here with us?'—if not as enrolled members and co-workers, yet as visitors to the museum and library and hearers at their meetings, which were now thrown open to the public." Was it so, he asked, that out of these many youths and young men, several of whom were gainers of high prizes at various school examinations, and of whose future career high hopes were entertained, there were none to be found in love with nature and natural science in all its varied forms so as to continue and carry on these studies begun at school? Our youths were the hope, the strong hope, the backbone of this young and rising colony, destined in due time, under God's destiny, to become a great and mighty nation or a fair and flourishing portion of a still mightier Empire, and therefore they should be seeking to grow, to improve in knowledge and wisdom. Nothing was more sure than this, that school knowledge and attainments, allowed insensibly to wither and rust, soon became forgotten, and once forgotten were seldom if ever found again; and here he asked, not only as their elected president *pro tem*, but as a very old man of some understanding in these matters, and therefore speaking from experience, to proffer a little sound advice. The powerful and active enemies of science and of general learning, especially here in the colony, were too great love of holidays and idleness, of frivolity and of fleeting pleasures, which yielded no enduring satisfaction, which generally, if not invariably, looked for more, never being satisfied and mostly leaving "an aching void," and should there be, before the final close, a few hours or days free from pain and extreme weakness for reflection, then the sad heartrending vista presented itself of time lost, of noble, almost God-like faculties abused, of a waste of life.

In conclusion he said: "I, as an aged minister of religion and a fervent disciple of nature, and with increasing convictions of the truth, soon by me to be realised, would say one word more to my audience *re* our talents and our time here: that as you sow you will reap hereafter. Young friends: don't waste time; don't abuse talents. Seek to make the best use of both."

❖ 1896 THE PROPOSED MUSEUM.
Hawke's Bay Herald 19 May.

SIR,—I was very much surprised on Saturday last (16th instant), in seeing in your paper the following sentence contained in a letter from Mr. John Harding:—"Will Mr. Colenso please tell me, who informed him that I had promised £200 to the (Museum) fund?" And my first thoughts were to write to you immediately, and to refer you to Mr. Harding's own letter in one of the Napier papers of last year, in which he had plainly made the said offer. But as Mr. Hill, Inspector of Schools, had arranged to meet me here on Saturday night,—and as we two had talked, about that offer at the time of its publication,—I resolved to wait his arrival. Well, he came, and we soon entered on the subject, and Mr. Hill assures me of the *great* mistake I had made; for Mr. Harding's offer at that time was "£25," or "£50," and not £200. Depending on Mr. Hill's accuracy, *I am very sorry* I made such a great mistake; and now make this public apology to Mr. Harding, (having also already written to him). I cannot account for it. It was not done in a hurry—off-hand, as it were, at our meeting on Monday night, (11th)—for it had been in my memorandums and calculations and mind for two or three months past. Possibly the wish may have been father to the thought (expressed), and then there is (for certain) the "old man's" defective memory—Alas!—I am, &c.,

> W. COLENSO.

Dannevirke, May 18, 1896.

❖ 1896 PROHIBITION AND THE CLERGY.
Hawke's Bay Herald 17 July.

SIR,—Your paper of this morning—and of a few late days, in which so much has been said *ad captandum* on the subject of Prohibition—brought strongly to my mind two old lessons: one, a subject, and one, an object, lesson. The former being the short, neat saying of the German philosopher Göethe,—"In this world there are so few voices and so many echoes." And, the latter being a copperplate engraving I have in an old folio volume of Voyages and Travels, showing, "The manner in which the Apes fight the Lyons in Barbary";—in this plate the apes are depicted drawn up together behind a sand-heap, flinging sand into the advancing lions' eyes! Many of those and similar thoughts have arisen in my mind from perusing the letter in your paper of this morning, signed "John Hosking."

If time with me permitted, and your columns were also open, I should like to take up "John Hosking's" letter line by line, to show the gross erroneousness of it, the wine question (as set forth in the Bible) having been closely and fully studied by me (and that aided from first class and original sources), 40–50 years ago, when I had both time and opportunity for the work,—and *no bias.* Moreover, I may be permitted to briefly mention that I am the only one of us remaining, who 60 years ago (1836) formed the *first* public *Temperance* Society in New Zealand, and wrote and printed with my own hands the report of that meeting—(the same being the first book in English printed in New Zealand). That meeting was a *true* temperance one—not a

Teetotaller nor a Prohibition meeting—so often, now-a-days, impudently vamped up and obtruded on our notice under the Temperance flag!

John Hosking has (strongly and designedly) brought forward a huge display of learning; all which, however (as mentioned by him), has been repeatedly published by teetotallers, and particularly by one of their leaders, Dr. Lees, some 25 years ago in an early edition of *"Kitto's Cyclopedia of Biblical Literature,"* under the heads of "The Lord's Supper," "The Passover," "Fruits," and "Wine"; but in the newer edition of that work Dr. Lees' erroneous articles were excluded, those subjects being furnished by more truthful and competent hands.

John Hosking says (of wine):—"The Hebrew word *Yayin* denotes intoxicating wine. This class of drink is invariably condemned; it is *prohibited."* (The italics are J.H.'s) "I find (*sic*) the word *Yayin* so used 120 times in the Old Testament."

I agree with John Hosking, in *Yayin* "denoting intoxicating (or fermented) wine;" but my position will be to show that the use of *Yayin* is neither condemned nor prohibited.

Now for a few facts from Holy writ. I have lately had to read publicly in our Church on Sundays, lessons from the first book of Samuel. In the first chapter we find the high priest Eli charging Hannah with drunkenness; he told her to put away her *Yayin* from her; in denial she replied she had drunk neither *Yayin* nor *shechar* (strong drink). Again, in the very same chapter we are told, that Hannah brought up her son Samuel to Eli, and with him "three bullocks, one ephah of flour, and a bottle (goat skin)" of *Yayin* into the house of the Lord at Shiloh. In the tenth chapter of the same book we have *Yayin* again mentioned in a similar manner. Samuel told Saul he should meet three men going to God at Bethel, one carrying three kids, one three loaves of bread, and another a bottle (goat-skin) of *Yayin.* And again in chapter twenty-five we have the remarkable and natural account of a present of two goat-skins (the cask or keg of those times) of *Yayin* made by the lady Abigail to David—(taken from the store of wine they were using at their sheep shearing)—which present David gladly accepted. Now, had David been a Teetotaller or Prohibitionist, would he not have refused it as a thing accursed?

Farther: *Yayin*, the fermented juice of the grape, was by Divine command used in the most sacred services of God's worship. The lambs offered continually every day at morning and evening sacrifice were offered with the fourth part of a *hin* of *Yayin* for a "drink offering" which is also expressly named as "a sweet savour unto the Lord." Thus, also it was—throughout the bigger monthly sacrifices of the year (with a ram and a bullock), a drink offering of *Yayin* continually to the Lord. (Exodus xxix. 38–46, Numbers xv., xxviii.)

In Psalm civ. 156, *Yayin* is said "to make glad the heart of man," being also Divinely linked with "oil," and with "bread which strengthens man's heart;"—the three essential elements of an Eastern banquet; the object being to set forth the bounty of God's provision for man.

Throughout the history of the Bible we find that wine (*Yayin*) was used on festive and joyous occasions, because of its agreeable and exhilarating properties and, also, that man did use it to excess. It is this excess alone that is condemned and not use.

It was even provided, for those of the Israelites who resided at distance from Jerusalem, that on the yearly going thither to worship, they should carry their tithes in money: —"And thou shalt bestow that money (there) for what thy soul lusteth after, for oxen, or for sheep, or for wine (*Yayin*) or for strong drink, or for whatever thy soul desireth; and thou shalt eat there before the Lord thy God and thou shalt rejoice, thou, and thine household (Deut. xiv. 25, 26). Here was Divine sanction for the use of wine and strong drink, dangerous and tempting as they are. As a good divine formerly wrote on this passage, "What was to protect the drinkers against excess in the use? Their faith in the presence of God, and their accountability to him; they were to eat *before the Lord*. This is the sole and effectual protection against every temptation arising out of the use of any good creature of God." Even as St. Paul counsels—"Whether ye eat or drink, or whatsoever ye do, do all to the glory of God." (1 Cor. x. 31.)

John Hosking cites from Leviticus X, (as if it were a positive command like —"Thou shalt not steal,")—"Do not drink wine (*Yayin*)." But he omits to give the reason of that sentence. Thus, after the sin and awful public death of the two priests, Nadab and Abihu, it is written, "The Lord spake unto Aaron saying, do not drink wine nor strong drink (*Yayin* nor *shechar*), thou nor thy sons with thee, when ye go into the tabernacle of the congregation, lest ye die." From this it is clear, that *Yayin*, and other drinks, were commonly used by the Jews.

I have heard some shallow short-sighted persons confidently affirming that wine and alcohol were not creatures of God! and, therefore, not included in St. Paul's assertion, —that "Every creature of God is good, and nothing to be refused, if it be received with thanksgiving." (1 Tim., iv., 4) Nothing, with them, extracted by man from any natural product is a creature of God! Of course, not sugar, nor any of the many good things we have for food, and clothing, and for medicine, separated from their natural compounds.

In one of the letters in your paper, some one, writing on this subject, has chosen John the Baptist for his exemplar and lawgiver. I, however, with the Christian Church, regard Jesus as such; and would remind that writer of John's own solemn words,—"He must increase, but I must decrease." Our Lord, too, placed himself in contradistinction to John, saying, "John the Baptist came neither eating bread nor drinking wine, and ye say, He hath a devil: the Son of Man is come, eating and drinking, and ye say, Behold a gluttonous man; a wine-bibber; a friend of publicans and sinners; but wisdom is justified of all her children" (Luke vii., 33).

I once told one of those paid, noisy, strolling, itinerant teetotal (or, now, Prohibitionist) lecturers that I consider *alcohol* as one of the choicest gifts of God to man; that I placed it together with the printing press in the very van of all his blessings: but, unhappily, man, in *both* matters, too often perverted the blessing into a curse. And so I say now, after many years' *experience*; and if I too am called "a gluttonous man and a wine-bibber," and farther identified with "publicans and sinners"—by the "unco guid" and teetotal party—I shall not complain. "If they have called the Master of the house Beelzebub, how much more shall they call them of his household".—I am, &c.,

WILLIAM COLENSO.

Napier, July 15, 1896.

§ 1896 PROHIBITION AND THE CLERGY.

Hawke's Bay Herald 20 July.

SIR,—"William Colenso" has spoken! Prohibitionists wipe your pens! The Hebraist of Hawke's Bay, the Philosopher of Napier (the Athens of New Zealand) has broken the silence. Surely the controversy must end now. When "William Colenso" condescends to use such adjectives as "paid, noisy, strolling, itinerant" teetotallers; when he, with very questionable modesty, reminds us of "apes depicted drawn up together behind a sand heap and flinging sand into the advancing lions' eyes" a very simple question arises. Who are the apes? Who are the lions? Who are the sand-flingers? Where does the greatest quantity of mud generate?

"William Colenso" dares not dispute my position, unless he is anxious to be made a laughing-stock to the Hebraists of New Zealand. So he admits that I am right in saying that there are different words in Hebrew translated by the one English word wine in our English Bible.

I said that intoxicating liquor is condemned in the Bible, and that God never sanctions an object that is a curse to His family. If "William Colenso" will dare say the opposite, let him do it. "Great men are not always wise, neither do the aged understand judgment."—always. If "W.C." will read the Encyclopedia Brittanica, on wines, he will find that my statements as to the different kinds of wine are borne out. It says "One of the greatest faults of our otherwise admirable version of the Bible is, that the translation of the same original word is often improperly varied at the expense of perspicuity: while, on the other hand, ambiguity is sometimes occasioned by the rendering of two original words in the same sentence by one English word, which, however, is used in different meanings. Not only two, but *thirteen different* and *distinct* terms are translated by the word *wine*, either with or without the adjectives, 'new,' 'sweet,' 'mixed,' and 'strong.' Some of the kinds of wine were good, some bad; some to be used frequently and freely, some seldom and sparingly; some to be utterly and at all times avoided. Let the passages in which the word wine occurs be compared, and it will be seen that this principle must be kept in view if we are to make the Bible consistent with itself; and if we do so, we shall find that Scripture, thus properly interpreted, will be found to give no sanction whatever to the common notion of drinkers. It will be *difficult*, if not *impossible*, to find a *single passage* in which drinking of intoxicating drinks is spoken of as adding in any way to the excellence of moral character, while total abstinence from such drinks has received the broadest marks of the Divine approval." With such an authority as this at my back, "William Colenso" must excuse me if I tell him straight that I am not prepared to accept his dictum on the question, although he has studied it for 60 years. To go to the Bible for a sanction of a drink that was first made in the Middle Ages, long after the canon of Scripture had closed, shows the weakness, the invincible bias, the blind superstition, of those who will not see. Let me give a few instances of the voice of the Bible upon this question. Perhaps "W.C." will give me his attention. "It is good neither to eat flesh, nor to drink wine (*oinon*), nor anything whereby thy brother stumbleth, or is offended, or is made weak."—Romans xiv., 21. "Wine (*yayin*) is a mocker, strong drink (*shakar*) is raging; and whosoever is deceived thereby is not wise."—Proverbs xx., 1. "Be not among winebibbers (Heb. *al tehi be-sovai-yayin*), among riotous eaters of flesh; for the drunkard and the glutton shall come to poverty; and drowsiness shall clothe a man with rags."—Prov. xxiii., 20,21. "Who hath woe? Who hath sorrow? Who hath contentions? Who hath babbling? Who hath wounds without cause? Who hath redness of eyes? They that tarry long at the wine (*yayin*); they that go to seek mixed wine." The last clause has it in Hebrew *labahim lakhqor mimsak*,—they that go after yayin made stronger by drugs. "Look not thou upon the wine when it is red, when it giveth his color in the cup, when it moveth itself aright. At the last it biteth like a serpent, and stingeth like an adder."—Prov. xxiii., 29–32. "Woe unto them that rise up early in the morning, that they may follow strong drink (*shakar yirdophu*) that continue until night, till wine (*yayin*) inflame them"—Isaiah v., 11. "Woe to the crown of pride, to the drunkards of Ephraim, whose glorious beauty is a fading flower, which are on the head of the fat valleys, of them that are overcome with wine (Hebrew *halumai yayin*, smitten of wine drunk). "But they also have erred through wine (*yayin*) and through strong drink (*shakar*) are out of the way: the priest and the prophet have erred through strong drink." (Read carefully, Mr. W.C.), "They are swallowed up of wine, they are out of the way through strong drink; they err in vision, they stumble in judgment." Isai., xxviii, 1, 7. "Whoredom and wine and new wine take away thy heart." Hosea iv. 11. "Awake ye drunkards and weep; and howl, all ye drinkers of wine, because of the new wine; for it is cut off from your mouth." Joel I, 5. (This is a prophecy of the result of the next licensing election, I hope). "For while they be folded together as thorns, and while they are drunken as drunkards they shall be devoured as stubble fully dry." Nahum. I, 10. (And they would make a wonderful blaze.) "Woe unto him that giveth his neighbor drink, that puttest the bottle to him, and makest him drink also." Habbakuk II, 15. "And take heed to yourselves lest at any time your hearts be overcharged with surfeiting, and drunkenness, and cares of this life, and so that day come upon you unawares." Luke xxi, 34. "Let us walk honestly as in the day; not in rioting and drunkenness, not in chambering and wantonness, not in strife and envying." Romans xiii., 13. "And be not drunk with wine, wherein is excess; but be filled with the spirit," Ephesians v., 18. "Abstain from all appearance of evil." I. Thess. v. 22. "A Bishop then must be blameless, the husband of one wife, vigilant, sober. Not given to wine." I. Timothy iii, 2, 3. Also Titus I. 7, 8; II. 2, 3, 12. Time would fail me to give all the passages condemning intoxicating liquor in the Bible. It requires more than the bare assertion of "William Colenso" to relegate the testimony of the word of God against the curse of liquor to the limbo of exploded delusions.

"William Colenso" says that he has "heard some shallow shortsighted persons confidently affirming that wine and alcohol were not creatures of God, and therefore not included in St. Paul's assertion, that every creature of God is good, and nothing to be refused, if it be received with thanksgiving." I. Tim. iv. 4. To call one's opponents "shortsighted and shallow" is very unbecoming on the part of the Sage of Napier, but we'll let it pass. Blocks of granite, poisoned berries, rats, mice, toads, alligators, snakes, monkeys, and even apes, are "good creatures of God," but we don't want to make meals of them just yet.—I am, &c.,

JOHN HOSKING, *Wesleyan Parsonage. Hastings, July 17, 1866.*

§ 1896 PROHIBITION AND THE CLERGY.
Hawke's Bay Herald 23 July.

SIR,—My friend the Rev. W. Colenso has sent me a copy of the HERALD of the 17th instant, containing his reply to the Rev. J. Hosking, and in our public library I see papers containing that gentleman's rejoinder, and other letters on the subject. The main question is one on which Mr. Colenso and I have long since agreed to differ; but he had a light task in demolishing an opponent who maintained two such untenable propositions as that *yayin* [always] denotes intoxicating wine, and that its use is always condemned or prohibited. And I was pained to see that in replying he could find no better answer than an elaborate sneer: "The Sage has spoken," &c. I would that the reverend gentleman, and other temperance speakers and writers whom I need not name, could realise how petty, how unworthy their sacred calling, and how damaging to the cause they maintain, such advocacy is. In this case, Mr. Colenso's four score years, his long and distinguished services to the Church and the scientific world, his wide and unostentatious benevolence, should have been a protection against vulgar abuse. To a sneer there is no answer—no refutation; but it has no weight either as argument or evidence. Fortunately for the unlearned, it is not so much profound scholarship, as patient study and impartial examination that is needed to arrive at a conclusion in cases of verbal disputation. When a word occurs 140 times in a book, in every possible variety of context, an ordinary intelligence should have no serious difficulty in settling its meaning or meanings. And as in most cases where fierce strife has arisen over definitions, the reason has been that the debaters, giving a fundamental principle of language, have insisted on limiting a word to one of its varied meanings. Whole sects have been founded on no better basis than the rigid interpretation of a word which has been freely used in a variety of senses. The Greek words *oinos, baptizo, ainos*, are prominent examples. We can imagine "cranks" a thousand years hence maintaining that "tea" in English in the nineteenth century signified "beef tea" and nothing else; this would be as reasonable as the contention that the word "wine"—the same in form and meaning in Hebrew, Latin, Greek, and English—means fermented wine and that alone. Numerous instances can be given where it bears that meaning, others can be adduced where the meaning is impossible; the context must decide. Mr. Colenso makes light of Dr. Lees' qualifications, and even appears to cast doubt on his integrity. Here Mr. Colenso is wrong. It might be quite fair to assume a bias—few are free from that, but Dr. Lees' honesty is beyond suspicion, and his scholarship unquestioned. He was the first to scientifically and systematically investigate the subject of ancient wines. The article in the Encyclopedia Britannica, quoted by Dr. Hosking, if not actually written by Dr. Lees, embodies all his conclusions. Here, as in the important subject of vaccination, this great book of reference rises above popular prejudices, and is in advance of the time. Had Dr. Hosking studied Dr. Lees' works with more care he would not have fallen so easily a victim of Mr. Colenso's bow and spear.

In his researches Dr. Lees has not only collated and studied every passage in the sacred text bearing on the subject, in the original, the LXX., and the Vulgate, but he has gone exhaustively through the Greek and Latin classics and the dense forests of patristic literature. He is the one specialist in this field. He has proved that what are commonly known as "temperance drinks"—sherbet, &c.—were among the ancient wines; that *salt* entered largely into some of them; and that fresh grape-juice, boiled down into a thick preserve or jam, was "wine." To make it potable water had to be added—hence the custom of the "mixed chalice," to which a mythical meaning in after times attached. And his labors have borne practical fruit. It was an old argument that fermentation was inevitable—that no art, especially among the unscientific ancients, could preserve the wine unfermented. But these same ancients were something like the clever Maoris of old, who could teach our scientific folk wrinkles not a few. It is true that they did not talk about "microbes" and "sterilisation," but they had practical knowledge which the Pasteur institute has not attained. It is a fact that Frank Wright's unfermented wine (used in most of the churches in this city for sacramental purposes) is protected from fermentation by a recipe placed on record by Pliny, and brought to light by Dr. Lees. The parable of the "New wine in old bottles" is unintelligible on the supposition that the new wine had begun to ferment. Your correspondent "Anglicanus" is a good example of the kind of folk who plunge into a controversy without any equipment at all. I had those same "flagons of wine" flung at me in your columns in years gone by. The learned Adam Clarke, 70 years ago, showed that there were neither flagons nor wine in the original. "Anglicanus" apparently wants his pastor or bishop to do what he ought to be able and willing to do himself. Let him "search the Scriptures"; look up the passage in the Revised Version. I was sorry to see in your paper the old and ribald story of the man who "searched the Scriptures through and found only one man who wanted to drink water. He was in hell." If intended for a jest, it is very poor and very profane. If for argument—well, the man lied. Of many instances two stand out prominently: David, who longed for the water of the well of Bethlehem; and our Lord, who at Jacob's well, asked water of the woman of Samaria. Water, the emblem of Divine faith, is throughout Scripture mentioned with honor, as one of God's chief blessings. Wine is mentioned also with honor, and again condemned as a curse and type of Divine wrath. The wine so minutely described in the Book of Proverbs as a "mocker" is certainly intoxicating—all the familiar phenomena of fermentation are set out in detail. But we read also of wine "in the cluster," and the joyous vintage song—the motto of the temperance societies of to-day: "Destroy it not (O brewer and distiller!), for a blessing is in it." But I find no warrant for Dr. Hosking's statement that the Scriptures forbid wine, or are "prohibitionist." Such assertions irritate me like the kindred talk about "Christ the Social Reformer," or the "Great Democrat." The Holy Scriptures are on a higher plane. They ignore "our little systems," they are above faction and party. They supply general principles, the application of which each must discover for himself.—

I am, &c.,

R. COUPLAND HARDING.

Wellington, July 21, 1896.

❖ 1896 PROHIBITION AND THE CLERGY.
Hawke's Bay Herald 23 July.

"A Daniel, still say I; a second Daniel!—
I thank thee Jew, for teaching me that word."
—SHAKSP Mercht of Venice, Act IV scene i.

SIR,—Max Müller has very naturally and truly observed in his Gifford Lectures: —"Every kind of evidence is made to tell by writers who have a theory to defend." Now I had quite intended that I, in my letter of last week in reply to "John Hosking," having said my say, should not write again. And I should not now do so, were it not for his own closing and (as he no doubt supposed) clinching sentence from the New Testament, in his reply letter in yesterday's HERALD, viz., "A Bishop must be—sober, *not given to wine*" (the italics, as usual are "J.H.'s,") and it is just this one little well-known and plain English word "given" that has prompted me to write again; for, verily, "John Hosking" shows, he does not understand its meaning! and has also led me to choose my Shakespearian motto, at the same time not intending to say that "John Hosking" is a "Jew."

"Not given to wine." Of course, the meaning of this word is,—addicted to, a lover of, &c. Now, had John Hosking deigned to look into the Revised Version of the New Testament, he would have found the true meaning of the Greek better rendered, thus:—"A bishop must be—no brawler," or as in the margin, "not quarrelsome over wine," and so it is in Titus, i, 8—the only other place in the New Testament containing that word.

"Paroinon"—the Greek word in question, there used by St. Paul—is also farther rendered by Dean Alford in his Greek Testament thus—"*not a brawler* (properly, 'one in his cups,' a man rendered petulant by much wine), and perhaps," Alford says, "the literal meaning should not be lost sight of." To which I would add a further testimony from Parkhurst (Gk. Lex.)—"A tippler, one who sits long at the wine;" with his apt quotation from Lucian—"*methyson kai paroinos*, &c.,—a person drinking and tippling not only till he sings and dances, but till he becomes abusive and enraged." Schrevelius (Gk. Lex.) renders the word—"a tippler, drunken, intoxicated." Conybeare and Howson also render the term—"not given to wine or brawl."

Those verses alone, *rightly considered*, respecting the use of wine in the Christian Church, have ever been with me sufficient to decide all controversy concerning fermented drinks. How "John Hosking" could reasonably adduce that word and sentence in support of Teetotallism or Prohibition is beyond my comprehension! It is mine in support of Temperance.

I do not know "John Hosking," neither have I spoken with any person who knows him, and therefore I am ignorant as to his age, &c., but suppose him to be an inexperienced young man—this from his hasty, irrelevant writing; so stiltified, too! (If I may use that term) concerning himself.

If "John Hosking" would condescend to accept advice from an aged veteran in the Army (not an enemy to the great cause of Temperance), I would suggest to him to be more thoughtful, considerate, and modest in his statements, particularly in his public writings. (2 Tim. ii, 24).

And as I shall not write again to your paper on this subject; and as I have again seen in your columns the aged Paul's advice to his son Timothy respecting the use of wine, once more twisted and travestied in quotation, I am inclined to give the new and plainer rendering of that sentence from the Revised Version, viz,, "Be no longer a drinker of water, but use a little wine for thy stomach's sake, and thine often infirmities."—I am, &c.,

WILLIAM COLENSO.

Napier, July 21, 1896.

❖ 1896 A PLEA FOR THE STARVING.
Hawke's Bay Herald 10 August.

SIR,—Permit me through your paper to ask you to set forth speedily some useful plan by which to relieve the poor—the very poor—the starving, the outcast, the wanderer, the stranger, the homeless,—who are daily visiting Napier seeking work; and who do not know where to go, or what to do, to obtain a meal or a bed at night. Do, please, come out strongly and quickly in their behalf; for it is a great necessity, a serious trying matter which cannot be put off. Human beings are starving in our midst, and the winter not yet over.

For some months I have had many poor fellows visiting me; sometimes even four and five of a day! and though willing to help, I cannot do all they need—cannot even approach it; and therefore it is that I write to you, that through your generous and ready public call, something serviceable and fitting may be done and that speedily.

In other towns, though much smaller and poorer, an almoner is to be found ready at hand to help all such necessitous cases; and an almoner should be found here, one always handy and at his post,—his room or office being central and publicly known.

Three weeks ago, the cases being numerous and pressing, I called on the Town Clerk and laid the matter before him, for him to tell the Mayor. Captain Bower (seemingly) agreed with me that something should be done, and that, too, quickly; and also promised to let me know of some fit person being appointed as almoner to meet such cases. But I have not heard from him, and hence I write to you.

If money is wanting, let the Mayor call an urgent public meeting "right away," and let such be subscribed and collected, or (better still) if the Borough possesses the necessary power to levy a special rate for this purpose, let such be done. I am sure many in Napier would gladly pay their share to help, to save their fellow countrymen; for my own part I would willingly do so—aye, I would rather pay double (if needed) what I have now to pay for harbor rates, and have done with that.

Not a few of those who have called on me are fine able young fellows—not so much seeking pecuniary help as work; and some (I have observed) though starving were above asking alms; still possessing that fine old English feeling! God help them.

Only a short time ago a poor old man was committed to gaol here for a fortnight for asking alms! As a "vagrant"; such may have been right in his case if a resident townsman; but I equally pity the Justices who could inflict such a sentence, together with the householder who laid the complaint, and the policeman who had (in the performance of his duty) to "run him in."

Do, please, use your able pen. Remember who said,—"Ye have the poor always with you, and whensoever ye will ye may do them good: I was a stranger and ye took Me in, naked and ye clothed Me," &c.—I am, &c.,

WILLIAM COLENSO.

Napier, August 8, 1896.

❖ 1896 MR. COLENSO EXPLAINS.

Daily Telegraph 28 September.

SIR,—Recently, while in the Bush district, I saw a notice in your paper (August 28th) of the death of Mrs. Mary Ann Henderson, of Napier, aged 82; "said to have been the first white woman who came to Hawke's Bay." At first sight I knew this to be an error—and a great one; and I determined to write to you about it; but a very serious cold, and, also, wishing to make enquiries concerning her arrival, have hitherto prevented me.

And now I write, merely (1) to *deny* her being the *first* white woman who came to Hawke's Bay; and (2) to state, that there were several here before her, some of whom still remain among us.

One intelligent old settler of 43 years residence in Hawke's Bay, to whom I had also written for information respecting her arrival among us, in his reply, laughs at the outrageous statement made by you and says,—"there were dozens here before her!"

If this error were not corrected by *one who knows*; no doubt, in days to come, your statement concerning her arrival here would be strenuously brought forward as a true one.—I am, &c.,

WILLIAM COLENSO.

Napier, September 25, 1896.

❖ 1896 THE MOA.

The Press 14 November.

SIR,—I have received a copy of your paper of 2nd inst., containing a long and very interesting paper by Captain Hutton on the "Moa."

There is much, very much, in the paper that is really "food for thought," gleams of sunshine (as it were) now and then occurring amid the dark mazes of an entangled wood—all on a subject or subjects of high interest to this rising colony and to science in general, which are sure to be taken up and carried on in days to come. There are, however, two prominent errors (as I view them):—1. (The minor one.) In which Captain Hutton mentions Polack as being "the first to publish anything about the moa." 2. (The other.) The adhering so pertinaciously to the old threadbare legendary story of "Hawaiki," and of the Maoris' emigration therefrom to New Zealand—as if such were physical facts.

I have frequently said, written and published, that the sooner that myth be abandoned (as forming any foundation for truth re the Maoris being here) the better, for it will ever prove a terrible stumbling-block, and sure to become the prolific cause of many more erroneous deductions.

I shall post with this a copy of the *New Zealand Herald*, containing a letter of mine written nearly two years ago, on Captain Hutton's quotation from Polack's book.[11] I could say a good deal more on the subject, but I forebear; merely adding that Polack also published 2 vols. additional (not a second edition) in 1840 on New Zealand, in which he brought forward everything he could think of respecting the Maoris, illustrating his second work with many good wood cuts of articles of Maori manufacture (taken of course from what he took Home with him, and these can be depended on, but not his so-called portraits of Maoris and views of scenery). Yet he never once mentions or alludes to the "large fossil ossifications" on which Captain Hutton dwells. Now, Professor Owen had published his first paper on the Moa (Dinornis) in 1839, which caused so much talk at Home at the time, and Polack was then residing in London, as we find from the date he gives in his introduction, and no doubt must have heard all about it. There is much in Polack's four volumes re New Zealand of his day that is valuable, but such is like gold in quartz, &c., and must be well worked and sifted to obtain it. Unfortunately Polack is so egotistical, and so addicted to drawing the long bow, and uses high flown stiltified language in every paragraph—even concerning the smallest unimportant matter—that it requires extra patience to bear with him, especially for me who knew him so well.—Yours, &c.,

W. COLENSO.

Napier, November 9, 1896.

---

11 The Discovery of Moa Remains. *New Zealand Herald* 15 Dec 1894. I.S.G.

§ 1897 EDITORIAL.
Mataura Ensign 23 February.

Judging by the course of recent events the people of Napier do not appear to be much overburdened with a spirit of patriotism or a desire to contribute toward their town's prosperity. About a year ago the Rev. W. Colenso made a most handsome offer to the public of the place generally that he would contribute £1500 and a free site for a museum on condition that they subscribed the remaining necessary amount to place the institution on a proper footing. At a meeting of the Hawke's Bay Philosophical Society (the body through which the offer was made), held the other night, it was stated that the rev. gentleman's generous offer had been supplemented from outside by only £163, whereupon Mr. Colenso gave vent to most righteous indignation, and, besides resigning the Society, said that his books and money would go to his native town of Penzance. Eventually oil was poured upon the troubled waters, and Mr. Colenso so far relented as to promise that he would reconsider his determination to resign.

❖ 1897 MR. COLENSO EXPLAINS.
Hawke's Bay Herald 1 March.

"Speak of me as you find—nothing extenuate."—SHAKESPEARE.

SIR,—I have recently heard of some amount of misunderstanding existing respecting one phrase, or rather, one misplaced word in your condensed report of the proceedings of the Hawke's Bay Philosophical Institute, at its annual meeting held last week. And, as I have been appealed to about it (and have good reasons for knowing that it is made a handle of for perversion by a small clique among us, who ought, however, to know better), I write this by way of explanation, although my friends who were present at the meeting to whom I have spoken, assure me there is no occasion for it.

The one word found fault with, is the word "respectable;" that is, as it now stands in your report, which runs thus:—"Of the 20 names handed in to the secretary as willing to contribute towards this project there was not one wealthy man, not one respectable, not one old settler amongst them."

Now, I believe I may boldly and truly say—I did *not* use those words as there reported in that one condensed sentence; indeed, I could not do so. For (1.) I had in my hand the list of the kind donors to the said scheme for museum and library (which I had received a fortnight before, and was therefore well acquainted with), and in that list are the names of old and dear friends and of townsmen of high respectability, among whom are Bishop Williams, Dr. de Lisle, Dr. Moore, Messrs Hill, Banner, Craig, and Ringland; and from the country, Father Binsfield, Dr. Todd, Messrs R.N. Blakiston, J. Powdrell, A. Harding, and J. Holder, and others, (2nd.) What I did say, and I think dwelt on, and that with full and painful reference to the large number of non-subscribers to this great public good (accepting your published words as a basis), was—"There was not one wealthy man, not one of the old-established respectable settlers, owners of large estates, fathers of families, amongst them"—*viz.*, the few names in the list. And I may observe that I was the more led to make this remark—(1) Because I had certainly expected *large* assistance from those men as early settlers—with their princely domains, thousands of acres, and many tens of thousands of sheep, &c.—to say nothing of the present good season's clip of wool, &c., &c.; and (2) because I had at the large May meeting, when I launched my offer, inadvertently (yet trustingly) mentioned Mr. John Harding's name as a joint contributor to the scheme (who had formerly freely proffered his subscription, but who now, I found, did *not* come forward!) and had also the great pleasure of publicly announcing, in contrast, the name of our respected and lately-elected member to the House of Representatives, Mr. R.D.D. M'Lean, as being the only large subscriber to the museum; both of those gentlemen being alike very old residents and large sheepfarmers.

I would also remind your readers, that at the May meeting in 1896 (already referred to) it was clearly and distinctly laid down that this projected museum and library was not for Napier (solely), but for the East Coast of New Zealand. I quote from your paper of the time: "A museum here would be a museum for the East Coast, not only for Hawke's Bay proper or for the old provincial districts, but for Poverty Bay and Gisborne, and the country stretching up to the East Cape. The people of those districts could not possibly have a museum of their own. Auckland, as they knew, had a museum for the whole of Auckland province, &c." I fear the forgetting of this—a main object in the success of the proposed plan—has also been the means of it having been overlooked.

And—as I do not intend to write again on this subject, I may be allowed to briefly mention two or three errors, or omissions, in your report of the 16th inst., (I would it could be given *in extenso*, even if I have to pay for it). (1.) I did *not* say—"His books and money" (meaning, the whole) "would now go to his native town of Penzance in Cornwall":—but, part only. (2.) You omitted, (a) what I said about Mr. M'Lean's generous offer; that that in part mainly depended on the standing committee of the late Sir Donald M'Lean's Memorial Fund agreeing thereto; and (3.) my promised subscription of £500 to back up and support Mr. M'Lean's plan. Both, however, of these omissions you kindly allowed and supplied in your next morning's issue; and I only mention them now, in conclusion, to show to the distorters and carpers, that even in your report there were admitted omissions. To all such invidious folk I would quietly and individually say *nosce te ipsum.*[12]—I am, &c.,

     W. COLENSO.

Napier, February 26, 1897.

[Mr. Colenso spoke under great excitement and in a low tone, making it difficult for our reporter to follow him, and it is quite possible that he misunderstood Mr. Colenso in this matter, though the report is a faithful transcript from his shorthand notes. —Ed. *H.B.H.*]

---

12 Know thyself. I.S.G.

§ 1897 WOODVILLE CORRESPONDENT.
Hawke's Bay Herald 3 April.

A painful accident happened to the Rev. W. Colenso, F.R.S., on Thursday (writes our Woodville correspondent). He had been on a visit to the Whariti ranges, and while being driven along Woodlands road on his return, the horse in the vehicle fell, both the driver and Mr. Colenso being thrown out. The former was unhurt, but the latter was found to have broken one of his arms at the elbow-joint. A conveyance was obtained, and the sufferer taken to Jull's Hotel, where Dr. Milne subsequently set the injured limb. The patient is doing fairly well, but owing to his advanced years it will be some time before he recovers from the shock.

❖ 1897 THE RECORD REIGN.
Hawke's Bay Herald 8 June.

SIR,—During my prolonged and enforced sojourn in the bush district I have on several occasions observed, in the various papers that I have seen respecting the approaching Jubilee of Her Majesty our Queen, that her accession to the throne took place on the 22nd of June, whereas it really took place on the 20th of that month, as is clearly shown in the order for the form of prayer for thanksgiving, issued by Her Majesty on the 21st June, 1837, as printed in the Book of Common Prayer of the Church of England:—"The twentieth day of June; being the day on which Her Majesty began her happy reign." This latter and correct date I have seen nowhere noticed.—I am, &c.,

> *W. COLENSO.*

Danevirke, June 7, 1897.

❖ 1897 THE RECORD REIGN.
Hawke's Bay Herald 24 June.

SIR,—I have been greatly interested in reading your full and ornate account of the church service in Napier on Sunday last, 20th instant, the record day of the Queen's accession, as given in your paper of yesterday. The more particularly, may I say, through my inability to be present and to join them. But, at the same time, pleasure has again been alloyed with pain (as is frequently the case) on reading your able and well-meant editorial in the same paper, on the same and closely allied subject, where your strange ultra-statement and also your omissions are so conspicuous. Conspicuous, I may be allowed to say, from my having been a witness of the long past, of these very matters so stigmatised, and also omitted by you; hence, too, it is, in the cause of truth only that I now write.

1. Your error: you say (writing of Dean Hovell's arrival in Napier some 20 years ago, and of our English Church there)—"He came to find a congregation divided against itself, an unsightly wooden church, and a tumble-down parsonage." This "unsightly" sentence I deny *in toto*; having been one of the principal subscribers

towards the erection of that "unsightly wooden church," long our pride, and a constant worshipper therein—holding a whole pew for self, family and household.

But even if our *early first* little wooden church of nearly 40 years ago (built when Napier was a very small place and a part of the province and diocese of Wellington,) were all that you are pleased to term it:—Is it fair, is it creditable, now to run it down? "The boy is father of the man"; and I have yet to learn that the stately oak, Britain's pride! looks back with contumely and scorn on the puny sapling or insignificant acorn from whence it sprang. I have read in our British histories of the introduction of Christianity into Britain, and of the first humble erections of chapels for Christian worship there being formed of wicker work, or of "wattle and dab," (just as our early Maori Mission Churches were 60–50 years ago,) but I have never yet read of the writer who could traduce them. Those humble origins were the forerunners or precursors of those stately Cathedrals of an Old Country about which you have also been writing lately in your paper. Probably you are not aware of the fact, that a large portion of your "unsightly wooden church" was removed bodily to, and still forms the chancel end of St. Augustine's Church in Napier, where its neat suitable outlines are a conspicuous ornament—often admired by visitors for their appropriate simplicity, and not less so by myself and others of the congregation worshipping in that church. (I omit, for the present at least, saying anything respecting your equally erroneous statement,— "a congregation divided against itself," &c., which I could as easily refute.)

2. Your omissions (as I view them): First, you forget or overlook, in rightly mentioning "The stately Cathedral of brick and stone—as being a monument to Dean Hovell's persevering work"; that before that period a cathedral could *not* have been built in Napier. For, first (as mentioned above) Napier was part of the ecclesiastical diocese of Wellington; second, the first Bishop of Waiapu resided at Poverty Bay, and had it not been for those serious troubles and dangers arising from the Maori war at that time, which caused him to remove to Napier, he (the Bishop) might have continued to reside there, the more central position, and if so, then no Cathedral here in Napier, nor Dean) nor Deanery. Moreover (and as I take it), our worthy Dean's chief "monument," irrespective of favorable circumstances over which he had nothing to do, arises from his indefatigable loving care and industry in visiting the sick and poor of his parish, coupled with his able and faithful preaching of the truth—the word of GOD.

Secondly: In your enumeration of wild, savage, and heathen countries subsisting as such at the accession of our most worthy Queen, you omit New Zealand; and, also, two, at least, of the greatest factors in the matter of Her Majesty and Britain obtaining this colony, viz., the translating, printing, and distributing among the Maori tribes of the New Testament in the Maori tongue (A.D. 1837), the same year as that of Her Majesty's accession; through which the hitherto wild and ferocious New Zealander became largely tamed; and the Treaty of Waitangi (1840), by which this country became annexed to Britain.

Having been myself an actor in those—all but forgotten—matters, I deem it but right to myself, to those dear co-workers who have "crossed the stream," to posterity, and to the sacred cause of truth, to write you this long letter on an important matter, the first prints, I may truly add, of my injured right hand and arm, now partially restored.[13] *Vivat Regina.*—I am, &c.,

WILLIAM COLENSO.

Dannevirke, June 22, 1897.

[We did not profess, in the brief space at our disposal, to give a complete sketch even of the history of Church matters in Napier in the last 20 years, nor would we decry what the early settlers did. But Mr. Colenso seems to have forgotten that the part of the old parish church which now forms the chancel end of St. Augustine's was erected *after* Dean Hovell came to Napier. It was the exception to the unsightly church. —ED. *H.B.H.*]

❖ 1897 MAJOR ROPATA.
Hawke's Bay Herald 6 July.

SIR,—I have read with interest in your paper of the 3rd instant your brief memoir of the late Major Ropata Wahawaha, M.L.C, who died on the 1st instant. Having known the old chief, and also been deeply interested in the clever and long letters he wrote to his tribe from Sydney (on his visit thither with Sir Donald M'Lean), in which he so well and ably described in pure Maori the many new sights, &c., &c., he then saw for the first time there (several of his letters having been published by the Government of the day in the *Waka Maori*, the Maori newspaper of that period), and believing you are in error as to his age ("90") from your informant not being acquainted with the past and so calculating from insufficient data, I should like to correct the same and so set you right.

You say, "Major Ropata said he was a full-grown boy at the date of the introduction of the Gospel into New Zealand. Taking that date as 1814, and allowing him to be seven years of age at the time, it would appear that at the date of his death he was 90 years old."

On the contrary I take it thus: (1) "The date of the introduction of the Gospel into New Zealand, in 1814," far away in the North (Bay of Islands) and not made much of at the time by the Maoris, and long confined to the Ngapuhi tribes, their deadly enemies, could scarcely ever have been heard of by these East Coast tribes. But what the Major meant, was the introduction of the Gospel by the missionaries there among his own tribe at East Cape and on to Poverty Bay, which was in 1837. The first Bishop of Waiapu (then the Rev. W. Williams) and myself having been selected by the committee of missionaries to do so; we landed at Wharekahika (Hick's Bay), and travelled leisurely by the coast to Poverty Bay—an adventurous journey; and saw the Maoris (Ngatiporou tribe of Waiapu especially) dwelling in hundreds in their large and substantial war pas—Rangitukia and Whakawhitira being the largest—in all their pristine glory! Well do I remember the grand open reception we met with from the principal old chief, Te Houkamau, on our landing. Soon after our visit trained

---

13 He refers to the crash, from a gig overturning, when his right arm was broken (see above). I.S.G.

Christian Maori teachers were sent among them, who were also well received and Christianity was established; and in their first schools, I have no doubt, Major Ropata was taught to read and write, and in those same schools I myself also taught hundreds of Maoris in subsequent years, before I came to Hawke's Bay in 1843. And not long after the Rev. W. Williams and family removed from Te Waimate (Bay of Islands) to Poverty Bay, and so founded the Christian mission there.

(2) "Major Ropata said he was a full-grown boy at that date;" such a Maori term would *not* be used (as you have it) for a boy of "*seven* years of age;" rather say, 14–16, or more. This would bring his age to about 75, which I take to be pretty nearly correct. I have also other data which serve to strengthen me in my belief, which I could give if needed.—I am, &c.,

WILLIAM COLENSO.

Dannevirke, July 5, 1897.

❖ **1897 TO THE EDITOR.**
Hawke's Bay Herald 24 August.

❖ **1897 MR. COLENSO IN REPLY.**
Hawke's Bay Herald 8, 22 September.[14]

❖ **1897 THE RELIEF OF "SWAGGERS."**
Hawke's Bay Herald 14 September.
A LETTER FROM MR COLENSO.

At the meeting of the Charitable Aid Board yesterday the following letter was read from the Rev. W. Colenso:—

"I have the honor to call your attention to the contents of this letter. It is written in the hope of something real and useful being done by your Board to meet the many cases of the poor straggling wanderers—strangers, who almost daily visit this town and me, seeking work, food, necessary clothing, and a night's lodging. I have had as many as six applications in one day,—commonly from two to four, and that at all hours, generally before 9 a.m., and after sunset, on their reaching town, and sometimes on Sundays. I do what I can for them all, in a small way, to relieve their present needs—in a meal, and a night's shelter at the City Buffet, in Emerson-street; but some of them, both aged and young, decent-looking men, often want more than those small helps, as boots, clothing, a blanket, &c. I suppose that this is more or less known to and experienced by you all individually. And what I wish to have done by the Board is, to appoint some person residing handy in the town to act as almoner —some humane person, and to assist those poor unfortunate strangers in their pressing hour of need. No doubt some of those stragglers are men of indifferent character, yet

14 These three letters are included in 'Certain errors of the Church of Rome' 1898, republished in *Colenso's published papers 2*. Father Grogan's reply (*Hawke's Bay Herald* 15 Sep) was proudly reprinted in the *New Zealand Tablet* of 1 Oct 1897. I.S.G.

they are human beings in want, in distress, needing present help; equally with such a one having fallen overboard into the sea, whom all hands rush to save. Besides, you have an almoner in the country, at Waipawa, who has also sub-almoners under him in all the townships, and poor men and strangers in distress in those places obtain their wants supplied by them without difficulty. Why, then, should not such an officer have been long ago appointed in Napier? Possibly you may say that your secretary in his office in town, from 10 to 4 on some days of the week, fulfils that duty; but I fear such is not the case—cannot be done by him, simply because he is not in his office when these poor men mostly turn up here in Napier, before 9 a.m. and after 4 p.m., and also on Sundays. Besides, I am (at present) ignorant as to whether his instructions allow of his helping such persons—strangers. I could say more under this particular head, but I refrain. It is not from any desire to be relieved from helping these strangers that I now apply to the Board—that is, as to expense or cost—for I am willing to contribute my full quota in an early cheque; but it is to be relieved from the continued worry of their calling on me in all weather, and so wasting my time and often increasing rheumatic pains, and, in truth, frequently upsetting me for the day with their sad experience and tales, which I now, in my old age, cannot so well meet as formerly."

The Chairman said no doubt Mr. Colenso was very humane and generous in giving charity to those who called on him for it, but he pointed out that there were ample facilities for people getting assistance from the Board. The secretary was in his office three days a week. So far as giving aid was concerned he (the chairman) was placed in a somewhat similar position to Mr. Colenso, as people called on him at all hours for assistance.

Mr. Cohen deprecated the idea of declaring that there was an "open house" for swaggers in Napier, which would draw men to the town.

Mr. Ormond said if it were understood that men on going to the Refuge could get relief for a night it would meet the difficulty. The place would be open for the night to people destitute, and gentlemen in the position of Mr. Colenso could refer callers to the Refuge, provided it were understood that that institution was available for the purpose. He understood from a conversation with Mr. Colenso that he did not give swaggers money but gave them orders for meals at the Buffet.

The Chairman said practically the secretary was in his town office five days a week.

Mr. H. Williams suggested that a reply be sent to Mr. Colenso asking him to refer applicants that came to him on to the Refuge.

The Board resolved to instruct its secretary (with the aid of the Chairman) to attend to such cases on application being made, and Mr. Colenso is to be asked to send applicants who come to him on to the Board, temporary accommodation being afforded at the Refuge.

❖ 1897 DAFFODILS.
Hawke's Bay Herald 15 October.

SIR,—I was much interested this morning in reading your article on "The Modest Daffodil." One sentence, however, I must take great exception to. You say (from Mr. Clayton's lecture)—"The history of the plant from the earliest records to the present time was a quaint and curious one; *one or two varieties in* 1879," &c. This startled me; as I well recollect seeing several, during successive spring seasons, in gardens in the West of England before I left the Old Country, more than 60 years ago. This is, also, well supported by botanical works that I happen to have; for instance, in the early volumes of "Curtis's Botanical Magazine" (A.D. 1795–1809) there are well-executed colored plates of 24 varieties: indeed of these 24, no less than nine are given in the volume for 1795, more than a 100 years ago! I have no later volumes of the said work than for 1809, although it has been continued down to the present time: yet, as in six of those 15 volumes new varieties are brought forward, I have no doubt of many more having been described and figured before 1879. I bring this to the notice of your readers towards rescuing the memory of our old British florists, who worked so largely under difficulties unknown to the present generation, and without the encouragement given in modern times by Mammon and Fashion.—I am, &c.,

W. COLENSO.

Napier, October 11, 1897.

❖ 1897 IMPRECATORY PSALMS.
Hawke's Bay Herald 20 November.

SIR,—In your issue of Thursday (18th), in the report of the Diocesan Synod proceedings, you give two motions made by me, with a very condensed *resumé* of what was said about them; and, as I take it, placing me in rather an unfair light, more, however, to be found in the remarks of other speakers; which, if left unnoticed, may be the means of still further objectionable observations or thoughts respecting me, where your paper is extensively read. Therefore, with your permission, I would say a few words concerning them in two short letters.

"The Rev. Mr. Colenso moved,—'That on those days in which an imprecatory psalm follow as appointed for use, the minister be allowed to use another Psalm instead thereof.'" This subject has been for many years on my mind; increasing in strength from the frequent remarks I had from time to time heard. The present I thought a good opportunity, as our Bishop had lovingly told us of the kindness and humanity of the large number of the American Protestant Bishops at the late Lambeth Conference and I had long known that in their book of Common Prayer (precisely in the main as ours), there were no less than ten varying selections from the more beautiful, simple, natural, and godly Psalms, any one of which may be used instead of the Psalm appointed for the day at the discretion of the minister. Of course this early amendment of the American Episcopal Church was to obviate the reading of those few Psalms containing those horrid Jewish curses and wishes and prayers,—

so utterly repugnant to the teaching and acting of our Lord, and to the character of our God, and Father, and consequently anti-Christian. Even the very contrary of our own very poor deal logs here. Such as: "Let the children be fatherless and vagabonds and beg their bread, and seek it in desolate places; let the extortioner consume all that he hath," &c. "The Lord hath said—that thy feet may be dipped in the blood of thy enemies, and the tongues of thy dogs red through the same." "Consume them in thy wrath, consume them that they may perish," &c. "Blessed shall he be that taketh thy children and throweth them against the stones," &c. (Pss. 109, 59, 68, 137.)

The celebrated Dean Farrar, of Canterbury (England), in a recent work of his on the Bible truly calls them "sweeping curses," and inveighs strongly against them. The Dean asks,—"In the blessing pronounced on those who should take the little children of the Babylonians and dash them against the stones, are we to see a supernaturally dictated sentiment of divine morality, or are we to detect a fierce utterance of Jewish hatred, which directly contradicts the exhortation of Jeremiah?"

Now in our own English Book of Common Prayer an instruction is given as to the proper reading of the Psalms, in these words:—"Note, also, that on occasions to be appointed by the Ordinary, other Psalms may, with his consent, be substituted for those appointed in the Psalter." And I had supposed that I was acting quite within it in bringing forward this motion. Bearing in mind, that by the term "Ordinary" in England, the Bishop of the Diocese for the time being is not meant but an inferior ecclesiastical officer; yet, no doubt here, as things are, the Bishop could rightly act. Our Bishop, however, decided as given by you, that the permission sought for by me was only for special services, which (while I confess I cannot see) it is my duty to observe; though to that I might reply "Just so, for it is only on those special occasions."

Mr. Tanner, in his reply to Mr. Eccles, observed "That even the Church of Ireland had not thought fit to expunge those Psalms from its Prayer Book." (As if I had ever once thought of such a thing!) Archdeacon Williams argued on "The closeness of the tie between the Mother Church and us":—which very thing I had sought to keep close to in my motion. The Rev. Mr. Hobbs said, "We should wait for reforms in this direction from the Mother Church."—And this with the needful reform made in the American Church more than a 100 years before—in 1789!—in their Prayer Book before him.

I could say much more—but you have no spare room, and I am weak—in body. Of one thing I feel assured, that this same matter will crop up again—and (it may be) again, until the proper object sought is attained.—I am &c.,

W. COLENSO.

Napier, November 19, 1897.

§ 1897 BUSH NOTES.
Hawke's Bay Herald 11 August.

The Rev. W. Colenso, of Napier, appears to be held in gratifyingly high esteem in this district. He is deservedly respected on account of his vast knowledge, but what has principally contributed to endear him to the people of Norsewood is the warm affection which he has ever manifested towards the place and the lively interest he has ever taken in its welfare. This, I may say, is a trait which, generally speaking, never fails to have great weight with the Scandinavian people, who as a rule are a most affectionate race. Once gain their confidence and merit by your actions and a continuance of their confidence and a kindly interest in their concerns will awaken in their hearts a corresponding feeling of affection towards you. The meeting held in connection with the silver jubilee commemoration on Friday evening received Mr. H.P. Mortensen's motion to include the reverend gentleman in their list of guests very warmly, and the references of Mr. A. Olsen to the services rendered the district by their guest elect served to give a spice of enthusiasm to this part of the proceedings.[15]

❖ 1897 THE MORE SUITABLE CHURCH LESSONS.
Hawke's Bay Herald 22 November.

SIR,—I thank you for publishing my letter on the Imprecatory Psalms in your issue of this morning; and now, with your permission I would also say a few words concerning my second motion on the benefit resulting from reading the more suitable lessons from Holy Scripture in the churches. (I copy from your paper of the 18th instant.) "The Rev. W. Colenso moved,—'That on those few occasions when the lessons as appointed in the calendar to be read may be the better omitted for the chapter or portion immediately preceding or following the same, that the minister be allowed to read such portion instead of the appointed one, for the greater edification of the congregation.'—seconded by Mr. Tanner—the Dean strongly protested that even the General Synod had no power in face of constitution and canons to proceed in the direction indicated.—The Rev. John Hobbs argued that the motion was not necessary, the matter being in the hands of the Bishop—the motion was lost."

I briefly said: (1) The reading of the Scriptures in the Church of England at daily morning and evening services was done regularly, especially the second lessons from the New Testament, which followed in orderly succession; it being also the pride, the glory of our English Church that the Scriptures were read to the congregation in the common tongue; and, that where such were so read daily there needed no alteration. The case, however, was different where the Scriptures were only publicly read two (or, at most, three) times a week; and, at such times, the detached lessons which followed in course for those two or three services might not (and in some days could not) be the most profitable for the congregation. This was a point that could not be denied, as

---

15 Colenso stayed at the Mortensens' guest house 'Fernhills' when in Norsewood. Andreas Olsen farmed nearby, at Makotuku, and collected specimens from the Ruahines for Colenso. I.S.G.

I (and I had no doubt all ministers) had not infrequently proved. That then, on such occasions, the chapter immediately preceding or following the fixed lesson might be the better one to be read, from it being more suitable, and should be read instead. And further, this simple substitution was the more to be desired, seeing that the daily reading of the Scriptures in families at home was not now so well observed here in this new colony as formerly in England. And (2) that the principle of occasional selection of a lesson was quite in accordance with the rules of the Prayer Book of the Church at the discretion of the minister; as shown (a) In the first lesson for Sunday's evening service, throughout the year, where for every Sunday *two* chapters are mentioned, one of them only to be chosen, and read by the Minister; (b) also, in the case of a moveable holy day, the same happening to fall on a Sunday, then "the lesson appointed either for that Sunday or the holy day may be read at the discretion of the Minister." (c) "If Evening Prayer is said at two different times in the same place of worship on any Sunday, the second lesson at the second time may at the discretion of the minister be any chapter from the four Gospels, or any lesson appointed in the table of lessons from the four Gospels." (d) "Upon occasions to be appointed by the Ordinary, other lessons may with his consent be substituted for those which are appointed in the calendar." Therefore, from all those rules and allowances of occasional selection, it seemed to me quite clear that what I sought was in accordance with them; especially as it was merely a simple change for the better edification of the congregation. But, as on the former motion, it was decided against me. However, and notwithstanding, I thought on Galileo of old, and told the Synod,—"I joy a coming age will think with me!"

I felt sorry for this decision (may I say, hastily arrived at?). It seemed so opposed to the principles and plain rules of the Church, and to common sense; moreover, because in this case, as also in the former one of those objectionable Psalms, I have heard it said that we did not always read in our Church services those portions of Holy Scripture which were the most beneficial for the people, and I could not deny it. The Word of God is in the Bible (though not confined to that holy book), and should be diligently sought out and extracted, just as our miners do gold, all parts of the Bible not being alike from God, neither of essential service to man; yet, as our Church truly says,—"Holy Scripture containeth all things necessary to salvation." I could say a good deal on this subject; living "thoughts that breathe in words that burn," but I forbear; choosing rather to close my letter with a few sentences from Dean Farrar (whom I also quoted in my former letter), fresh utterances of true knowledge and wisdom, which, thank God! have long been part of my own belief.

The Dean says:—"There are many Christians who hold that every word of the Bible is supernaturally dictated and infallibly true. That position is untenable. It has not been held always, nor everywhere, nor by all; there is not the least merit involved in its acceptance: it is not helpful to the religious life of the individual or of nations. It has, on the contrary, been prolific of terrible disasters. The acceptance of it may be due, not to faith but to faithless materialism and a petrified tradition; the notion of it is not a sign of unbelief, but a duty to truth, and to the God of Truth ...."

Men constantly fight on behalf of their own mistakes, limitations, prejudices, and traditions, because they forget that the ever broadening light of human knowledge, which saves mankind from torpor, is light from heaven, and is a part of the Divine economy of revelation …. God has given man a lamp which is sufficient to enable him to discern truth from falsehood in all essential things. Having bestowed on man his Reason and his Conscience, He does not speak to him by voices in the air. God never reveals to man what He has enabled man to discern for himself." *Vale, valeat quantum*—I am, &c.,

WILLIAM COLENSO.

Napier, November 20, 1897.

❖ 1897 AUSTRALIA OF THE PAST.
Hawke's Bay Herald 4 December.
SIR,—In your paper of this morning—in your interesting article on "Australia of the past," you have two items, quotations, that, I think, are scarcely accurate,—at least, not without some correction or explanation: viz., (1.) "On 7th February, 1788, the colony of New South Wales was taken possession of in due form," &c., &c., (quoting from Marcus Clarke). And, again, (2.) "It is scarcely known to the majority of the Australian people that Phillip was the man who founded their country, and that Cook was never inside the Heads of Port Jackson," writer Louis Becke.

Now in Cook's voyages, (Admiralty edition published in 1873), we find, that on his leaving New Zealand (Cape Farewell), in March 1770, his ship anchored on April 28th in Botany Bay, so named by him, and there he remained until the 6th May. During his stay he made an accurate chart of that bay, which is given in his voyage. He also, he says, "caused the English colors to be displayed on shore every day, and the ship's name, and the date of the year to be incised on one of the trees near the watering place." And, on leaving, he further says, "at this time we were between two and three miles distant from the land, and abreast of a bay or harbor in which there appeared to be good anchorage, which I called Port Jackson. This harbor lies three miles to the northward of Botany Bay," and, four months after, on August 23rd, he says:—"As I was now about to quit the eastern coast of New Holland, which I had coasted from lat. 39 deg. S., to this place, lat. 10½ deg. S., I took possession of the whole, in right of His Majesty King George the III by the name of New South Wales." (With several other interesting notices—one I may mention, *viz.*, their joyous feasting on two large sharks and two large sting-rays they had caught, "one of these rays weighing 240 pounds and the other 336 pounds after its entrails were taken out." (Mention of this timely capture is also made in Sir Joseph Banks's journal of that voyage, lately published, with this additional remark, that "the tripes of the rays made a very excellent dish, much relished.")

All that taking *possession* and naming in due form, was done 18 years before the arrival of Governor Phillip; and, as I take it, it was entirely owing to Cook's discovery, his taking possession, and because of his full report of the country, that

Governor Phillip was sent out thither. To me, the fulsome adulatory recital of the taking possession of New South Wales by Governor Phillip; and also the invidious depreciating remark, that "Cook was never inside the Heads of Port Jackson," had been both better omitted, especially when what he and his able party of scientific men did at Botany Bay, so very near to Port Jackson, under all their trying circumstances, is duly considered. One might just as soon attempt to detract from Cook's fame in this our colony of New Zealand, by saying (though he first passed through the strait bearing his name), "Cook never entered Wellington Heads."

To us the name of Cook is far too high for all time—"above all Greek, above all Roman fame"—to be so easily tarnished. But so it is! Who is Louis Becke? Such carping writers—"who hint a fault and hesitate dislike"—serve to remind one of the poetical aphorism:—

"The aspiring youth that fired the Ephesian dome
Outlives in fame the pious fool that raised it."

I trust that in the days to come the New Zealand colonists in general, and those of Hawke's Bay in particular, will ever keep a sharp look-out ahead, and never allow the name of our immortal navigator Cook to be depreciated.—I am, &c.,

W. COLENSO.

Napier, December 2, 1897.

§ 1898 FROM OUR ORMONDVILLE CORRESPONDENT.
Hawke's Bay Herald 16 May.

A chat with the Rev. W. Colenso is a privilege to be remembered for years, so entertaining is this veteran in the search for knowledge. He is, one might say, literally consumed by an insatiable craving for more of this precious possession, and the performance of his task of adding to his large store seems almost as essential to him as the air he breathes, and the warm bright weather which is so cheering to the convalescent. No man in the province is (as) enthusiastic over matters pertaining to the diffusion of knowledge, and we venture to say that, notwithstanding his advanced age, and the effects of his recent accident, no man does more or works harder for his fellows in this way.

The results of his delving into the mines of knowledge are at once so numerous, and comprise a range so extensive that we of the younger generation have to regard him with mingled feelings of wonder, admiration—and (we hope, justifiable) envy. As an example in matters educational to our youth we can quote no better, and trust that they will show their appreciation, of his achievements by endeavoring to follow in his footsteps. Such action would at once carry with it the hall mark of sincerity, and would more than anything else, tend to brighten the declining days of this worthy pioneer, with the sense of succeeding in leaving the world better than he found it. Science —his beloved science—he is passionately devoted to, and it is this fact which has caused his wonderfully active mind to chafe so over the comparative inaction to which the Woodville accident doomed him.

Mr. Colenso has now recovered so far that he is able to write without fatigue; and though, for a long time, he was not able to walk about much, the present up-country trip has so benefited him that he has recovered the use of his limbs to quite a considerable extent, and has been performing wonders in the walking line. That he is not easily daunted is proved by the fact of his having, assisted by Rev. J.C. Eccles, of Woodville, again ascended the hill which cost him so dear last year. "Some people," humorously remarked the old gentleman, "call it foolhardiness, and others call it something worse. However, I prefer to have an independent mind of my own and to follow my own ideas." His memory is vigorous as of yore, and he was very solicitous in his enquiries concerning friends of years gone by from whom he had not heard for some time. Sympathising with them in their misfortune, and "rejoicing with those who had cause to rejoice" over their prosperity. It afforded him great pleasure to hear of their well being. Increasing progress in his recovery gives him considerable satisfaction. His hopes for future progress are bright, "although," he adds, "while I am getting better I am getting no younger." Your readers, I am sure, will be pleased to learn that he is enjoying good health, and will heartily endorse his hopes for the future. The crowning joy of his life would be the knowledge that his life work had been marked by success, and that this may be so is our heartiest wish for Napier's "grand old man."

§ 1898 A PIONEER.
Ashburton Guardian 18 May.

It is stated by the Woodville Examiner that the Rev. W. Colenso, F.R.S., is the only white man now alive who witnessed the signing and took part in the Treaty of Waitangi. The treaty was signed in the year 1840, and although Mr. Colenso is now in his eighty-seventh year, he is hale and hearty, and nothing pleases him better than recounting his early experiences in the colony. Mr. Colenso was the first printer to arrive in New Zealand. He arrived in the year 1834. Before leaving London the London Missionary Society would not allow Mr. Colenso to select his own plant, and the result was that when Mr. Colenso unpacked the boxes on reaching Paihia, in the Bay of Islands, he discovered to his annoyance that no cases to hold the type and no printing paper had been sent. Before he could get cases made Mr. Colenso had to set the type from small heaps on the floor, and had to wait about twelve months for a supply of printing paper from Sydney.

❖ 1898 AN IMPORTANT MATTER.
Hawke's Bay Herald 24 June.

SIR,—I notice in your paper of this morning, that a report from the Select Committee to the Education Board recommends (1) the sale and removal of the care-taker's house adjoining the infant's school in Carlyle-street, and (2) the purchase of the large corner section on the opposite side of the same street as a playground for the infants—several hundreds in number; and that such has been "adopted" by the Education Board. I regret very much to hear this, and therefore I once more write a few words on this important subject.

No doubt the doing so would give the little ones more room (which they badly need), but at what a *cost*! and at what a great and ever increasing *risk*, Carlyle-street (like Emerson-street, its northern end) being far too narrow, and the principal line of traffic in Napier, and the said proposed play-ground away from the school on the opposite side of the street—I shudder when I think on it. I omit remarking on the high figure asked for the said piece of land, situate as it is in the very heart of the town. And it is just the same with the principal Boys' and Girls' School adjoining in Clive Square, which has also long been "cabin'd, cribb'd, confin'd, bound in," on every side and crammed with scholars; and, as a matter of course, the already large number of scholars are also continually increasing.

Why not boldly "take the bull by the horns," (as the saying is,) and remove both schools to a better and more suitable locality? Of course, to do so would cost a considerable sum, but it would prove to be beneficial to all, and by far the cheaper in the end; and once done well—it is done for ever.

During the last year of my holding the office of Inspector of Schools for Napier and the Hawke's Bay province, the Board of Education wrote to me officially, to point out to them the most suitable site in the town for its Public Schools. I did so: and in my letter to the Board recommended the 7-acre piece of ground in Carlyle-street, then vacant, and since called the *Recreation Ground*; that plot is still the fittest site for our town schools, where all the children would have ample room for play grounds. The place being at present set apart and used as a Recreation Ground (mostly for idlers), is as a feather in the balance when compared with the public good—in the far nobler use and proper purpose to which it should have been long ago set apart and dedicated. "It is never too late to mend."—I am, &c.,

W. COLENSO.

Napier, June 22, 1898.

❖ 1898 PHOSPHORESCENT WOOD.
Hawke's Bay Herald 24 August.

SIR,—In your two papers of yesterday and to-day (22nd and 23rd inst.) your country correspondents have told us of a piece of decaying wood which is singularly phosphorescent, and much seems to be made of it—as if such was a very remarkable or rare production. Whereas such luminous substances are by no means uncommon, and to be met with all over the globe, both on land, in the ocean, and in the several kingdoms of Nature—zoological, vegetable, and mineral; also, in both living and dead states in the animal kingdom, and very common: Witness, the glow worms living, and mackerel and the sea jellies (*Medusa* sps.) dead in our own native land in the summer season. Indeed, "fish abiding in the dark," in a certain incipient state of decomposition is well known.

And, as I have not infrequently met with such luminous vegetable substances (decaying woods) in my former travelling days and sojournings in our New Zealand forests, it seems strange that old settlers living in the Bush (or interior) should not have often noticed them, especially in certain seasons when the low forests are damp after rains. At such times and in such places I have seen some curious, strange, and weird-like appearances; one in particular, though seen 50 years ago, I shall never forget.

We were travelling from Ngaawapurua, a village on the Manawatu River, towards Wairarapa; the weather had been wet and hindered us, and we started late in the day for the village of Te Hawera, situate in the dense and long forest; I wishing to get there, if possible, that night, as the next day was Sunday, and I knew the isolated and scattered Maoris would be assembled, awaiting me. We were soon benighted in the deep gloom of the forest. I had travelled through those forests before, but there was no proper or continuous track. We had taken with us chunks of a dry large woody creeper which burnt steadily and slowly when ignited, to serve as a kind of lantern; as the night advanced the darkness of the ancient and close virgin forest became almost palpable and "Egyptian," when we got into a broken mass of phosphorescence, arising from decaying wood and large *fungi*, which spread out on all sides and extended many chains! The luminosity was grand, clearly showing the trunks and stems and leaves of trees and ferns, and the dead unshapely prostrate rotting logs. But the peculiar pale colors of various hues of that strange light, together with the coldness of those gleams, and the deep silence, and the Stygian blackness surrounding—altogether caused an unpleasant unearthly kind of thought and feeling—almost causing one's flesh to creep! We (or I) could fancy all manner of strange outrageous and mocking spectral or demon faces, more suited for the revelry of Faust's Walpurgis night, with Mephistopheles and the witches on the Brocken, than for a small and quiet party plodding our way through a low-lying New Zealand forest. My travelling party of Maoris had never before witnessed any such a scene, and often in after years related it. Our travelling slow match, with its red light and sparks, was paled and lost before that grand phosphorescent show. Sometimes streaks and small patches of luminous slime would adhere for a while to my clothing in passing through the forest. Only on one other occasion did I ever witness a similar large display of natural cold and pale light, or sheets of lambent flames, issuing from the earth, and that too, was by night, at the time of the great earthquake in the 60s, through which I could see the trunks of trees, &c. This, however, was of a very different nature. I am, &c.,

W. COLENSO.

Napier, August 23, 1898.

[We are heartily glad to see that Mr. Colenso's handwriting is as clear as ever, showing that he has quite recovered from his severe accident in the Bush.—Ed.]

❖ 1898 THE KUMI.

Hawke's Bay Herald 16 September.

SIR,—In your paper of this morning you have a short local on the strange animal lately seen near Gisborne, in which you bring me forward as saying (to your informant) that "In the absence of fuller particulars I believed it to be one of the large lizards mentioned in Cook's voyages." That, however, is but a small portion of what I said to him, and not (perhaps) the most likely hypothesis of the several mentioned by me. However, I should not care to write about it now, only for another error in the same notice, namely, that by Captain Hutton. I told your informant (seeing that the moa—of celebrity—was also prominently brought forward in your account of the said animal from Gisborne) that it was likely the mythical *saurian*, or monstrous lizard, formerly stated by the old Maoris to be the moa's guard, at its cave, on the top of the mountain Whakapunake. I now quote briefly from my first early paper on the moa, containing mention of the said fabulous lizard; and also of other real living Maori ones, as obtained by me from the old tohunga Maoris more than 60 years ago.

"During the summer of 1838, while at Waiapu, East Cape, I heard from the Maoris of a certain monstrous animal, called a *moa*:—that it dwelt in a cavern on the precipitous side of a mountain,—that it lived on air,—and that it was guarded by two immense *tuataras*, who, argus-like, kept incessant watch, while the moa slept; also, that if anyone ventured to approach the dwelling of this wonderful creature, he would be invariably trampled on and killed by it. A mountain named Whakapunake, at least 80 miles distant in a southerly direction, was spoken of as the residence of this creature; there, however, only one existed, which, it was generally contended, was the lair of its race." (I here omit a great deal more said of the moa; and give a portion of a note from the same paper on the *tuatara*—then, also, unknown to science.)

"The tuatara, a saurian,—is common in some parts of New Zealand, particularly on rocky headlands, and islets lying off the coast. I have one at present in spirits, which I had alive for nearly three of the winter months; during which time, although I repeatedly tried to get it to take some kind of food, I could not succeed. From its habits I supposed it to be a hybernating animal. It measured 19 inches in length, &c., &c., and appeared a perfectly harmless creature. It was taken, with two others, (also possessed by me,) on Karewa Island, off Tauranga harbour, Bay of Plenty."

"The natives speak of another species, possessing a forked tail; and assert that a larger species, which inhabits swampy places, has been seen 6 feet in length, and as thick as a man's thigh. The largest, however, that I have ever known did not measure above 2 feet in length." (*Tasmanian Journal of Natural Science*, vol. II, p.81. Published under the kind auspices of the lamented Sir John Franklin, then Governor of Tasmania.)

Then, as to Captain Hutton's remark, as given by you—that the large animal lately seen near Gisborne was a *tuatara*, a specimen having been obtained near Auckland, &c., this could not be; from the fact of this strange animal having been called by them a "*kumi*"—the name of the mythical big lizard—the companion or guard of the moa. No Maori would, or could, have confounded that scarce monstrous creature with the small and well-known tuatara. Possibly, with your permission, I may have a little more to say on this subject. I await, however, further news re the kumi from Gisborne, hoping it may not prove to be a hoax!

It is, perhaps, worth mentioning that the name *kumi*, given to this big lizard, is the proper name for their measure of *ten fathoms. This* serves to join it on to those cleverly constructed legends of those immense saurians as related by the ancient Maoris; translations of the same are given by me in vol. XII., "Transactions N.Z. Institute.—I am, &c.,

W. COLENSO.

Napier, September 15, 1898.

❖ 1898 THE MAORI BIBLE.
Hawke's Bay Herald 17 September.

SIR,—You have greatly surprised me in your paper of this morning with a short notice concerning myself taken from "a London paper," which is partly wrong. And as it contains a grave error (and I do not wish to wear peacocks' feathers) I feel called on to set it right. It is stated (*inter alia*) that, "I translated the Bible into Maori," which is not correct. The translation of the whole Protestant Bible into Maori was not completed by any one of the Church of England missionaries. The first entire edition of the New Testament was mainly translated from the original Greek by the Rev. W. Williams (afterwards the first Bishop of Waiapu), who also prepared it wholly for press: it was printed and bound by me. Portions also of the Old Testament—as many chapters of Genesis, Exodus, Deuteronomy, Isaiah, and Daniel, with Jonah and the Psalms entire—were translated by others of the early missionaries; Mr. Puckey and the Rev. Dr. Maunsell taking prominent parts—in these translations I assisted; all those were also printed by me. And, of course, all that was done long before the first Bishop (Dr. Selwyn) came to New Zealand. Subsequently the whole translation of the Bible went through a complete critical revision by a Board elected by Bishop Selwyn, in which the late Bishop Williams and Rev. Dr. Maunsell largely worked. I have purposely abstained from giving particulars concerning the whole work of translation of the Bible into Maori from first to last, which, however, are well known to the Church Missionary Society (London) as well as to me.—I am, &c.,

W. COLENSO.

Napier, September 16, 1898.

❖ 1898 "THIS TO THY RIGHT EYE, PHILIP."
Hawke's Bay Herald 1 October.

SIR,—In your paper of this morning you tell us that the R.C. Archbishop Redwood, preaching on Sunday at St. Patrick's Church, South Dunedin, said:—"We live in an age of adulteration. If ever there was a century remarkable for its adulteration it is this nineteenth century with all its boasting. It is a dishonest century, and you can hardly get anything that is genuine." Plain and strong words these, containing a large amount of truth, but a little extra thought on the part of the preacher might have led him to trace back and consider the origin of the *greatest adulteration*, namely, the Church of Rome, which so heinously adulterated Christian teaching and the Holy Scriptures, so that the pregnant words of Our Lord to the leaders and teachers of the ancient Jewish Church are equally as applicable to the Romish Church and her adulterated teachings of this day:—"Well did Isaiah prophesy of you hypocrites ... in vain do they worship me teaching doctrines and precepts of men .... Making void the word of God by your own tradition, which you have given forth. And many other such like things you do." (*Mark* vii.) Through which grievous departure of the Church of Rome from the teaching of the early Christian Church may be fairly ascribed all the numerous adulterations of true Christian teaching down to the present day—and "the cry is, still they come," which wretched spawn is already so prominent broadcast among us here in Hawke's Bay! for "the people," so easily galled and cheated in matters of religion, "love to have it so!"—I am, &c.,

W. COLENSO.

Napier, September 30, 1898.

§ 1898 LOOKING BACKWARD—AND FORWARD.
Hawke's Bay Herald 24 September.

TODAY the HAWKE'S BAY HERALD celebrates its forty-first birthday, the first issue having seen the light on September 24th, 1857.... In a communication to the *Herald* not long since the Rev. W. Colenso referred casually to an event occurring fifty years since in this district—a personal reminiscence. How many are there among us who can throw their minds back the space of half a century, and see this country as it then was in the dawn of its development as a British colony? The trials and vicissitudes of such a space of time would blot out the recollection of those early days from the average mind, though indeed it is generally recognised that in old age the memories of early life are often more vivid than the occurrence of recent events. Doubtless the veteran stands alone as one who knew the physical conformation of this island in that early day of its history as a colony. The Maori race was a power then, an item to be reckoned with, the coast only fringed with white inhabitants, whose principal occupation was the pursuance of the whaling industry, or barter with the natives. The pakeha inhabited these shores on sufferance, and the intelligent, warlike Maori was a very different individual to his degenerate representatives of the present. The interior was all but an unknown country, and our first knowledge obtained of it was through the medium of such indefatigable explorers as the veteran who still remains with us, like Ulysses, "a part of all that he has met." How short the space permitted man to work his end; an infinitesimal section of time in which to develop, to take from nature and to impart for the guidance of the future's truthseeker. When a man's passions and aspirations have ceased to distract his mind from the contemplation of the truths and beauties of natural phenomena his day is waning, and the short span in the eve of life alone is left to him, whereas:

"Life piled on life
Were all too little, and of one to me
Little remains—but every hour is saved
From that eternal silence. Something more,
A bringer of new things.

* * * * *

"Death closes all, but something ere the end,
Some work of noble note, may yet be done,
Not unbecoming men that strove with gods."

It is history now that Mr. Colenso walked from end to end of the island, and gained at that period a knowledge of its characteristics and natural capabilities which few possess at this day, and those who have since acquired such enlightenment owe it principally to the laborious efforts of such pioneers as the Rev. W. Colenso, pursued through great trials and difficulties. What a change to the conditions of the country—a change which we who have been bred to the circumstances of these latter days cannot comprehend. How many of the numerous population which, compared to that of half a century since, now inhabits this district will in the course of another fifty years time be able to turn their minds back to this date and quote reminiscences of the happenings of today? They will be few, and fewer still those who can bring to bear upon them the intelligence and erudition possessed by this great solitary figure, standing out in relief as a memento of that long past.

We do not value to their full extent the efforts of these men. ....

They are many and vast, and how many and how vast we cannot quite comprehend, but veterans who have attentively watched these changes, and taken a delight in their inspection, can impart something of their import to us. That valuable collection of material on such subjects, the "Transactions" of the New Zealand Institute, will in future form the basis of our scientific and natural history, and among them the labors of the Rev. William Colenso will be treasured as a precious gift from an able and searching mind.

❖ 1898 GOVERNOR EYRE.
Hawke's Bay Herald 6 October.

SIR,—In your paper of this morning you have a letter from Mr. Hindmarsh, in which he says, that "Your article in last Saturday's HERALD on Governor Eyre was so full of errors that he ventures to point them out." However, in his doing so, he has committed not a few errors himself, being (as it appears in his opening remarks) much inclined to depreciate or "run down" Governor Eyre, Police Court fashion! Saying—"He had emigrated to New South Wales when 16 or 17; he was in Adelaide, having brought a mob of cattle overland," &c., &c.

Now, I knew Governor Eyre personally pretty well, and for some time corresponded with him both privately and officially; and have a copy of his work—*Discoveries in Central*

Australia, 2 vols, presented to me by him. And having, from my earliest days, been deeply interested in Australian explorations and discoveries, and read with avidity those of Oxley, Sturt, Mitchell, and Grey; and, also, intimately known Cunningham and other scientific men, who labored so long and efficiently in that country, whose names are high on the historic roll, I think it right to say a few words concerning Governor Eyre.

Before that Mr. Eyre went on his long and perilous journey in 1840, from Adelaide to King George's Sound, throughout more than 24 degrees of longitude, he had performed several journeys in the unknown interior of Australia: Colonel Gawler being then the Governor of South Australia. For eight years previous Mr. Eyre had been resident in Australia, during which he had visited many of the located parts of New South Wales, Port Phillip, South Australia, Western Australia, and Van Diemen's Land. In the years 1836–1840 he had conducted expeditions across from Liverpool Plains, in New South Wales, to the county of Murray, from Sydney to Port Phillip, from Port Phillip to Adelaide, and from King George's Sound to Swan river, besides undertaking several explorations towards the interior north from Port Lincoln and from Adelaide.

I have myself pretty often, 50–60 years ago, had to bear up against many hardships in my travelling throughout the length and breadth of the North Island of New Zealand; but mine shrink into insignificance when compared with those endured and overcome by Mr. Eyre on that terrible journey, during which his overseer and other companions were murdered by the blacks, his stores stolen, and abandoned, and he with only one black lad reached Albany on foot in the uttermost state of destitution, after a journey of one year and 26 days. I have ever considered that overland journey of Mr. Eyre as being one of the wondrous ones of modern times.

It was after that journey Mr. Eyre was invited by the Governor of the colony to undertake the task of re-establishing peace and amicable relations with the numerous native tribes of the Murray River and its neighborhood, whose daring and successful outrages in 1841 had caused great losses to, and created great apprehensions among the colonists, hoping that his personal knowledge of, and practical experience among the aborigines might prove serviceable, and from September 1841 until December 1844, he was closely occupied with the duties of his office, so that Mr. Eyre had a very good initiation for the higher office of Lieutenant Governor of New Zealand; however greatly he may have subsequently erred while Governor of Jamaica.—I am, &c.,

W. *COLENSO.*

Napier, October 5, 1898.

❖ 1898 EVOLUTION AND HUXLEY, NO. 1.
Hawke's Bay Herald 7 October.

SIR,—As you have kindly inserted my letter containing a few sentences in defence of Governor Eyre in your paper of this morning, I will, with permission, trouble you again on a similar theme,—only vilely carried to a far greater excess of language.

Your paper of the 3rd last, contains a low abusive letter written by some creature at Hastings, who, rightly enough (though unwittingly!) signs himself *"Tadpole"*—for this bit of brash I thank him. Because a tadpole just emerged from the spawn of a frog and living in its proper home, the mud of a marsh or stream, cannot possibly have any elevated ideas, or know much of the world beyond its ken, though it may improve in knowledge on becoming a full grown croaker. Now this dweller in mud,— this "Tadpole" comes out in this way:—"Sir, kindly grant me a line or two on this Evolution question. Haeckel, John Stuart Mill, Huxley, Tyndall, Darwin, and Spencer, leading Evolutionists, were (and are) all *infidels.*

At present I will confine my remarks to the late Professor Huxley. I select him for two reasons: (1.) My having brought him so prominently forward in my last Presidential address to the H.B. Phil. Institute, (1896) particularly showing what he had done for both technical and higher education at Home, in the Empire at large, and throughout our colonies: and (2.) to tell your readers what this *"Infidel"* has written and published regarding our Bible and its superior teaching, which, it is hoped, may have the greater weight just now. Huxley says:—"I have always been greatly in favour of secular education, in the sense of education without theology, but I must confess I have been no less seriously perplexed to know by what practical measures the religious feeling, which is the essential basis of conduct, was to be kept up in the present utterly chaotic state of opinion on these matters without the use of the Bible. Take the Bible as a whole; make the severest deductions which our criticism can dictate for shortcomings and positive errors; eliminate, as a sensible lay teacher would do if left to himself, all that is not desirable for children to occupy themselves with, and there still remains in this old literature a vast residuum of moral beauty and grandeur. And then consider the great historical fact that for three centuries this book has been woven into the life of all that is best and noblest in English history; that it has become the national epic of Britain, and is familiar to noble and simple from John o' Groat's house to Land End; that it is written in the noblest and purest English, and abounds in exquisite beauties of a merely literary form; and, finally, that it forbids the veriest kind who never left his village to be ignorant at the existence of other countries and other civilisations, and of a great past, stretching back to the furthest limits of the greatest nations in the world. By the study of what other book could children be so much humanised, and made to feel that each figure in that vast historical procession fills, like themselves, but a momentary space in the interval between two eternities, and earns the blessings or the curses of all time, according to its efforts to do good and hate evil, even as they also are earning their payment for their work? (*"On Science and Education,"* Contemporary Review 1870, *p.* 397.)

Nor is this Professor Huxley's only testimony to the unique glory of the Scriptures. In another able essay he says:—"It appears to me that if there is anybody more objectionable than the orthodox bibliolater it is the heterodox Philistine who can discover in a literature which in some respects has no superior, nothing but a subject for scoffing and an occasion for the display of conceited ignorance of the debt he owes to former generations. The Bible has been the Magna Charta of the poor and of the oppressed; down to modern times no State has had a constitution in which the interests of the people are so largely taken into account; in which the duties, so much more than the privileges, of rulers are insisted on, as that drawn up for Israel .... Nowhere is the fundamental truth that the welfare of the State in the long run depends on the welfare of the citizen, so strongly laid down .... I don't say that even the highest Biblical ideal is exclusive of others or needs no supplement. But I do believe that the human race is not yet, possibly never may be, in a position to dispense with it." (*Essays on Controverted Questions*, pp. 55–58.)

Had I, myself, been bemired by this tadpole, I should not have written, for my old rule is not to answer anonymous letters; but it is far different when one sees the *dead*— the *illustrious* dead, the pride and glory of our race, abused in this coarse offensive way. I am, &c.,

W. COLENSO.

Napier, October 6, 1898.

❖ 1898 EVOLUTION AND HUXLEY, NO. 2.
Hawke's Bay Herald 8 October.

"True Faith and Reason are the soul's two eyes."—*QUARLES.*

SIR,—"Tadpole" says, in your paper (quoted fully by me yesterday), that "Huxley, Darwin, and Spencer, leading evolutionists, were (and are) infidels." Of Huxley I wrote yesterday in my letter No. 1. I would now say a little in defence of Darwin (not, however, that such is really needed). And here I may be permitted to briefly remark, *in limine*, that having yesterday in Synod to say a few words respecting my personal knowledge of the late Rev. S.M. Spencer, when we were students together under Bishop Selwyn 55 years ago,—I am now led still farther back to a brief personal acquaintance with Darwin 63 years ago when residing in the Bay of Islands. For it may be that I am the only person living in the colony who had the pleasure and benefit of conversation with Darwin in this land; and possessing his able published works, and holding and supporting the great truths set forth in them, I consider it both a duty and a privilege to have to write for your columns a few imperfect yet well-intended lines in vindication of this great man. Moreover, this particular crisis (when so much had been of late said in your columns respecting evolution, and the Church of England clergy being assembled here in Synod,) seems a most fitting opportunity for my using my pen. And having thus mentioned my brethren of the clergy, and wishing to gain their ear, I think I cannot do better than to quote for their especial benefit from two of our great devout Church-of-England authorities—writers whose works have ever been highly esteemed by us—viz. Hooker, and Bishop Ken. Hooker says:—"That authority of men should prevail with men either against or above Reason is no part of our belief. Companies of learned men, be they never so great and reverend, are to yield unto Reason." (*Eccl. Polity*, Book II. ch. VII, 6.) And dear

Bishop Ken, (whose Morning and Evening Hymns are so prized and frequently used in our Church,) quaintly says:—

"Three volumes he assiduously perused,
Which heavenly wisdom and delight infused,

God's works, his conscience, and the Book inspired."
—Bishop Ken, *Hymenotheo.*

In these pregnant words is food for thought. And, following out my line of thought, I think I cannot do better than quote from a well-known living high authority—the present Dean of Canterbury (England) Dr. Farrar, what he too has again recently published respecting Darwin, in his new work on the Bible; as his words will (rightly) have more weight than anything I could write—

"Which of us does not remember the burst of scorn and hatred with which the theory of *Evolution* was first received? Mr. Darwin endured the fury of pulpits and Church Congresses with quiet dignity. Not one angry or contemptuous word escaped him. The high example of patient magnanimity and Christian forbearance was set by *him*; the savage denunciations and fierce insolence came from those who should have set a better example. What has happened since then? The hypothesis of Evolution, taken in its whole extent, is still an hypothesis only. Proofs final and decisive are confessedly wanting. On the admission of its supporters links are still missing from the evidence in its favour. Yet before Mr. Darwin's life was over two things had happened. On the one hand his hypothesis had been accepted as a luminous guide to inquiry by the large minority of the leading scientists of Europe and America; and even those who reject its extreme inferences fully admit that it rests on a wide induction and furnishes an explanation for many phenomena. That there is such a law as that of natural selection in the struggle for existence all are now agreed. Further, the theory of Evolution has now been admitted as a possible explanation of the phenomena of life by leading theologians, and we have been told on all sides, that, if it should prove to be true, there is nothing in it which is contrary to the creeds of the Catholic faith. Not a voice was raised in opposition when Mr. Darwin was laid with a nation's approval in his honored grave at Westminster Abbey; and—seeing how noble was his example, how gentle and pure his character, how simple his devotion to truth, how deep his studies, how memorable his discoveries, even apart from the view which is mainly associated with his name—I regarded it as an honour that I was asked to be one of the bearers of his pall; and to preach his funeral sermon in the nave of 'the great temple of silence and reconciliation.'"

Further, Dean Farrar says:—"The din and furious battle between science and that which was mistaken for religion has been chiefly waged over the first chapter of Genesis. That chapter is of transcendent value, and in a few lines corrected the Idolatry, the Polytheism, the Atheism, the Pantheism, the Ditheism, the Agnosticism, the Pessimism of millions of mankind. No science has ever collided with, or can ever modify, its true and deep object, which was to set right an erring world in the supremely important knowledge that there was one God and Father of us all, the Creator of heaven and earth, a God who saw all things which He has made, and pronounced them to be very good. It was written to substitute simplicity for monstrous complications, and peace for wild terrors, and hope for blank despair."

In all such conflicts a self-styled theology, intruding into regions of which it is profoundly nescient, exhibits nothing but its own impotence and rage. No sight is more disturbing than that of religious teachers who, knowing little of anything, and nothing of science, and not exhibiting the smallest sign of moral elevation over others, but often very much the reverse, assume oracular airs of superiority over the patient students of God's works. Nothing but rout has ever followed such attempted usurpation. Whatever inferences may have been drawn from the misapplication of the narrative of creation, there is no sane person who now believes that the world was made in six solar days; or that the trees and plants were created before there was any sunlight; or that all the stars were created after the earth was covered with vegetation; or that all the fishes and birds were created previously to all quadrupeds and reptiles; or a multitude of other details which have been inferred from regarding the first chapter of Genesis as a scientific document instead of regarding it as a religious revelation.

It is now understood by competent inquirers, that geology is God's revelation to us of one set of truths, and Genesis of quite another. May your numerous readers, Mr. Editor, readily and thankfully support Dean Farrar in his noble and truthful eulogism on Darwin; and his fitting remarks on the Mosaic cosmogeny,—I am, &c.,

W. COLENSO.

Napier, October 7, 1898.

❖ 1898 A RARE PLANT.
Hawke's Bay Herald 28 November.
SIR,—I read with pleasure in the HERALD of Thursday last your notice of a curious and fine plant from Queensland (*Doryanthes*), now flowering for the first time in Mr. Robjohns' garden, after 16 years of cultivation.

Here, too, in my garden is another fine plant—*Fourcroya gigantea*—now in full flower, for the first time, and of a similar age; its tall, stout, erect spike of flowers, some 15 feet high, like the mast of a small boat, bearing thousands of scented blossoms, hanging in long graceful festoons around it, reminding one of those Venetian masts decorated with narrow streamers used at public rejoicings. This, however, is not an Australian, but a South American plant, and worthy a notice in your paper.—I am, &c.,

W. COLENSO.

Napier, November 25, 1898.

❖ 1898 SOME IMPORTANT MATTERS.
Hawke's Bay Herald 3 December.
SIR,—I thank you for giving us in your paper of this morning two important cablegrams: (1) that "the Kolle-Turner process for the treatment of rinderpest had saved 700,000 head of cattle to Cape Colony." (2) That "Mr. Balfour" (that thoughtful

and clear-headed British statesman) "in his Bristol speech, referring to the agitation and friction in the Church of England at present, urged that it would be wise if the Church used its episcopal power to tide over the Ritualistic difficulty." I mention these two items together; the thoughtful mind will discover my reason for so doing, my meaning.

It is pleasing and hopeful to find, from late English papers to hand, that the Bishops of the Church of England are prompt and moving in this matter. The Bishop of Winchester, at his Diocesan Conference on 22nd September, in his able address, said:—"Bishops and clergy alike have been of late years too lax, or, to use an expressive local phrase, too "casual" in the matter. That episcopal authority will now be exercised decisively and if need be sternly, wherever in England any difficulty of the sort occurs I do not doubt .... Would that I could see no danger of another sort! I think it real and growing .... It lies deeper and extends more widely; it is far more difficult to specify or to define. It may be described as a growing tendency among certain men to blur, or ignore, or explain the distinctive character of the Church of England; the Church, not Catholic only, but Reformed; to forget, or at all events not to adhere to, the principles for which the Reformers cared and fought and suffered; a tendency to belittle (by implication if not in words) the changes wrought out for good by English Churchmen, in the century and half of effective fruitful controversy which we lightly call the Reformation. I think the matter is vital to our Church's healthy life .... May I just say that in accentuating what the Prayer-book enjoins or allows with regard to private confession, some teachers seem quietly to forget the history of the words, and to ignore the significant changes that our Church deliberately made. Hence a danger neither fanciful nor small. Another, and that surely the gravest danger of all, is to be seen in the teaching and usages of an increasing number of parish priests with regard to the Holy Communion—devoted enthusiastic men and women are swinging back, half unconsciously, into something perilously like the materialistic doctrines of the fifteenth century. Is there no danger that some of our people in some of our churches are, in this particular matter, insensibly drifting away from the true 'proportion of the faith' of the Church of England, and that with the drift there comes a corresponding peril of something sadly like the materialistic superstitions of pre-Reformation days? Conditions change, and the pitfalls that we now dread are not all the actual pitfalls of those days. Then the worshippers' Communions had become rare; now they are numerous, and often the roll is largest in the very churches wherein the risk I speak of is most real .... I am not alluding now to overt acts in direct contravention of the book of Common Prayer; .... I am speaking of what is more nebulous, more difficult to grasp,—a tendency, a tone, an atmosphere of teaching and of worship which for some minds has a perilous attraction. I speak as to wise men, judge ye what I say."

The Church Congress, also, commenced its business at Bradford on 27th September. The Bishop of Ripon, the president, made an able speech, from which I cull a few striking and pleasing quotations. With him on the platform were the two Archbishops of Canterbury and of York (who both spoke and also preached) and several other English and Irish Bishops. The president said:—"It would be affectation to deny that there were elements in our Church which may, if we are not careful, go far to cripple her usefulness and to hinder the readiness of her obedience. Our internal divisions are, perhaps, our greatest foe. There were men whose tendency was more Catholic than Protestant; there were others whose tendency was more Protestant than Catholic; but the most Protestant claimed to be Catholic, and there was a sense in which the most Catholic was not ashamed to call himself Protestant. There is a noble Catholicity, and there is a noble Protestantism, and it would be sad indeed if these terms should be prostituted or narrowed in meaning. If Protestantism means the claim of the human spirit to direct access to the Father of Spirits, the protest against the idea of vicarious responsibility, and against every attempt to check the freeness and fulness of the message of Divine forgiveness,—then, it is a term which no Church need fear to use, for it means the preservation of primitive and essential Christianity.... If Catholicity is confounded with the practice of customs which have only a mediæval sanction; if it claims to be identified with notions of ecclesiastical officialism which were unknown in the Church of Christ during the first century and a half of her purest life; if it insists on transforming permissible opportunities of help into necessities of Christian life and practice; if it takes the ideals of Catholicity from the un-Catholic corruptions of the Latin Communion, then we feel that Catholicity is robbed of its majestic voice, and has become the snarl of intolerant sectarianism. Every new epoch has added new dogma to faith, and with every new dogma has gone further from the simplicity of Christ. The future of the world does not belong to Latinism, and so the vision of Protestantism will be fulfilled. The religion of the future will neither be Protestant nor Catholic, but simply Christian. The dogmas of the Churches which have separated communion from communion will fall off as autumn leaves before the fresh winds of God. Many views which in the very Providence of God have played their part in cleaning the thoughts of men will pass into forgetfulness. Men will not grieve to see the old things go, for a larger faith will be theirs; they will not think God's world will fall apart because we tear up parchments more or less. The Church of God will renew its youth, it will be content with a simpler symbol because it will have learned Christ. It will not need any longer Trent, or Westminster, or Lambeth, or the Vatican to lead it. It will be satisfied with simpler thoughts and a purer faith. It will be satisfied to realise that there is one Lord, one faith, one baptism, one God and Father of all."

I fear I may have occupied too much of your paper, but my excuse is, that here in these living words we have "thoughts that breathe and words that burn." Much good, I hope, will be effected by them through their being read and thought over by your numerous readers (Bush and elsewhere) on this coming Sunday.—I am, &c.,

W. COLENSO.

Napier, December 2, 1898.

§ 1898 THANKS.

Hawke's Bay Herald 6 December.

Sɪʀ,—Kindly allow me a little space to thank the Rev. Mr. Colenso for his letter in Saturday's issue, and not only this one, but many others of his which appeared in the HERALD before now. May he have health and strength for many years to come is the fervent wish of ....

AN ADMIRER.

❖ 1898 THE SLAVE-TRADE.

Hawke's Bay Herald 10 December.

Sɪʀ,—In the supplement to your paper of Saturday last you have given your readers an interesting (though sad) account from the "Times of India," of the Slave-trade, as it is carried on by the Arabs on the Oman Coast, together with some fitting remarks on the iniquity of that traffic in human flesh. Recently, too, in several of our colonial papers the "massacres" by the Arabs and by the Turks—showing their extreme carelessness and low value of human life, whether of their own particular nation or of those other peoples subject to them (as, for instance, the Armenians,) have largely been made use of: forgetful (as it seems to me) of the far worse doings of our own British forefathers with their slaves! So that the rising colonial generation, with the Maoris around them none being slaves, are likely to remain ignorant of such mal-treatment by our nation of their unfortunate slaves, unless they are informed of it. And as one truthful concrete example is worth a bushel of abstract sentences, however finely and logically spun-out and coloured, I wish, with your permission, to tell them a bit of our true colonial history—not, however, New Zealand. I will take the small island of Barbadoes in the British West Indies (lately brought prominently forward in our papers as having been again visited by a dreadful hurricane, causing great loss). Of this island I fortunately possess an excellent, ample, and truthful history, in a curious and quaint old folio volume, written by a Church of England minister, long resident there, the Rev. I. Hughes, M.A., F.R.S., Rector of St. Lucy, illustrated with many full-size copper-plate drawings in natural history (each plate bearing also the coat-of-arms of one of his noble subscribers to the book, which was largely patronised by the Royal Family, the bishops, and several of the highest nobility both at Home and abroad; the subscribers thereto whose names are given numbering more than 600!) Mr. Hughes, from his long residence in the island, from his being an accomplished scholar, and from his faculty for seeking and describing everything, however small or mean, and to publish the same in plain and simple language, was evidently well fitted for his work; which, no doubt, bore high repute as a standard work in its day.

He says: "The greatest length of the island is 20 miles and its greatest breadth 14 miles, containing, in the whole, 54 square miles; in acres, 106,470." (A piece of land, I may observe, much smaller than a portion of our Hawke's Bay plains, as seen from Napier hills.) Though small in extent and generally level, its highest hill, a cliff, only rising 915 feet above the sea, Mr. Griffiths writes of its gullies and forests being but little known. "Of black slaves," he says, "we have between 65,000 and 70,000, though formerly we had a greater number, yet we were obliged, in order to keep up a necessary number, to have a yearly supply from Africa. The hard labor and often the want of necessaries, which these unhappy creatures are obliged to undergo, destroy a greater number than are bred up here. The capacities of their minds in the common affairs of life are but little inferior, if at all, to those of the Europeans .... As to the slavery of these African negroes this hardship is not so insupportable to them; for they are very little better than slaves in their own country .... The only happiness, even in temporals that these poor creatures meet with, is when they fall into the hands of masters influenced by the principles of humanity and fear of God. On the other hand when they are so unfortunate as to have owners unpolished in their manners and insatiable of riches (who, like the Egyptian tyrants, require bricks without straw, or, more literally, expect severe labor from an hungry belly, or a naked back), they have scarce a gleam of rest from hard toils and heavy stripes, but whilst sleep, with its short interval eludes the painful scene, which must again be renewed with the returning dawn. Such taskmasters consider not that compassion to the miserable is a just debt. Here there are many complicated scenes of misery, in the condition of so many thousands of our fellow creatures who are continually liable to the insults of the imperious lusts of the debauched, and whose own and their children's children's incessant labor will never be at an end but with their lives .... However, is it not of some weight to consider, that if the negroes are bought and transported into Christian settlements, at least a few among many thousands imported, may probably come to a better knowledge of their duty to God and man .... Though to bring them in general to the knowledge of the Christian religion,— the difficulties attending it are, and I am afraid ever will be, insurmountable."

Thus far Mr. Griffiths. And when we consider that the several other West India islands forming the group were in similar circumstances, we shall be deeply impressed with the hundreds of thousands of unfortunate human beings formerly enslaved in our British colonies, compared with whom the "1500 to 2000 slaves annually landed at Sur" seem few indeed! and the touching romance of "Uncle Tom's Cabin" sinks into insignificance. "'Tis strange, but true; for truth is always strange; stranger than fiction."—BYRON. I have no hesitation in stating my belief that the slaves at present made and sold by the Arabs of the Oman Coast, are far better off in every respect than those others formerly were in Barbadoes (and other also of our West Indian islands) under their "Christian" masters.

Mistake me not! I am no advocate for slavery even in its least distressing form. And, as an Englishman, I rejoice at our Imperial Government having entirely and for ever done away with slavery in all the British dominions proper (which event I well remember); our brothers in the United States having also done the same.

Moreover, it is well known the Mahometans treat their slaves fairly well, especially if they become Mahometans, which is very likely. And it does not always follow that the children of those slaves must also ever remain as such; sometimes they even rise to posts of distinction among them. Further, bearing in mind that slavery as an institution has ever existed from the earliest time in our world's history, and that the highest civilised and most enlightened nations have only by very slow degrees and within the memory of man abandoned it, we, in so rabidly declaiming against the same being still carried on in a smaller way by the less civilised nations, after the manner of their forefathers, only show our ignorance and folly. Such conduct reminds me strongly of some of those over zealous doings of certain police, who, in their ardour for carrying out the law of kindness to animals, bring up men for shortening the tail of a puppy, for tying the legs of a fowl taken in a basket to market for sale, and for selling a glass of hore-hound beer! Instances of all these I find in the latest English and Scotch newspapers to hand; and I also find that the worthy English and Scotch Magistrates dismissed the several charges, notwithstanding the strenuous opposition of the prosecuting sergeant.

Let us seek, Mr. Editor, to have a right and fairly-balanced judgment in all things. —I am, &c.,

W. COLENSO.

Napier, December 8, 1898.

❖ **1898 THE LA PEROUSE EXPEDITION.**
Hawke's Bay Herald 26 December.
SIR,—In your paper of yesterday you have given your readers the news from Sydney, of "a vessel having recently visited La Perouse islands and recovered from the natives a number of relics of the ill-fated La Perouse expedition, including pieces of old flintlock guns and Spanish coins bearing the date 1727 and 1728." And to this you add, in your article, some interesting information respecting La Perouse, closing with these words:—"In February 1788 he sailed from Botany Bay on a further voyage of discovery, but he and his two ships were never more heard of till 1821, when the captain of an English sailing ship discovered that the La Perouse expedition had been wrecked upon a coral reef near the New Hebrides."

There is some error in those two statements, which I should like to correct believing that I can well do so; from the fact of my having been a fellow-passenger with Captain Dillon, the discoverer of those relics, during our long voyage of more than four months from London to Sydney, 1834 (with only very few passengers), and probably the only man now living who had so long closely companied with him and conversed on the subject: I, also, saw him again in after years in the Bay of Islands. Besides that, I have the long and full and particular account of his two voyages to those islands (in 2 vols.), with lists of everything he recovered, (preserved in Paris,) for which he was amply rewarded by the King and Government of France.

The errors I wish to correct are these: 1. That it was not in 1821, but in 1826, when Capt. Dillon first heard at the little isle of Tucopea of some foreign European articles among the natives of that isle, and obtained a few of them; but it was on his return to Tucopea from Calonita in 1827, (in a ship specially fitted-out for that purpose,) that he collected at the neighbouring and larger island of Mallicolo, where La Perouse's two ships were wrecked, such a quantity of relics of all kinds belonging to that unfortunate expedition. 2. That I cannot suppose those "*Spanish* coins of 1727 and 1728" to be relics from La Perouse's *French* ships, lost there in 1788, sixty years afterward; besides, why should *French* ships have *Spanish* coins? Moreover we know, that the Spaniards were often in that part of the Pacific, many of the isles having been also discovered and named by them; on one of those islets near Mallicollo a small Spanish colony remained for some time so early as 1595 under Admiral Mendanz. Several other ships (not French) have also been wrecked and plundered by the natives of those groups of islands during this century. One, in particular, is mentioned by Captain Dillon. "In 1828, an American brig from River Plate was lost on one of those islands with 40,000 Spanish dollars on board .... The crew were saved, and part of them escaped to reside among the natives with as many of the dollars as they could conveniently carry off." From those ships Spanish coins were more likely to have been obtained than from La Perouse's French ships in 1788. Even in my early days here in New Zealand, before it became a colony, Spanish dollars were very common in circulation in the Bay of Islands and among the Polynesian Islands; in fact they were almost the only coin, and were in high request as an article of barter as well as for their monetary value.—I am, &c.,

W. COLENSO.

Napier, 'Xmas Eve, 1898.

§ 1898 EDITORIAL.
Hawke's Bay Herald 29 December.
In yesterday's issue, and on the authority of a London correspondent, we stated that the Rev. W. Colenso had been elected an honorary member of the "Royal Geographical Society." The honor conferred on Mr. Colenso, it seems, comes from the "Royal Geological Society of Cornwall," the late English mail having brought Mr. Colenso intimation to that effect from the president and honorary secretary of the Cornish society. This society, we may add, stands very high, having the Queen for patron and the Prince of Wales (as Duke of Cornwall) as vice-patron. We congratulate our veteran citizen upon this further recognition of his untiring efforts in the cause of his beloved science.

§ 1899 FROM OUR ORMONDVILLE CORRESPONDENT.
Hawke's Bay Herald 18 January.
Napier's grand old man, the Rev. W. Colenso, occupied the pulpit at the Ormondville Anglican Church on Sunday morning last, and preached a very interesting sermon of a very orthodox nature. There was a good attendance to listen to his remarks, and the hearing accorded him was most appreciative. During the course of his remarks he

took occasion to bestow a well-deserved compliment on the playing of the organist, Mr. J. Scholes.

§ 1899 EDITORIAL.
Poverty Bay Herald 9 February.
The Rev. W. Colenso, of Napier, has made another gift of £1000 to his native town of Penzance, Cornwall. The sum is to be added to previous gifts, and the interest of the whole is to be shared annually, under the title of "The Colenso Dole." It is stipulated that the dole shall be open to the poor of all creeds, but Cornishmen are to be preferred, and especially *bona fide* townsmen of the borough of Penzance, moreover always preferring the unfortunate, struggling, prudent working man, to the unthrifty and lazy and men of drinking habits. The Penzance Borough Council, as evidence of their recognition of Mr. Colenso's liberality towards his native place, unanimously decided to present him with the honorary freedom of that ancient borough.

THE FINAL CHAPTER

§ 1899 DEATHS.
Hawke's Bay Herald 11 February.
COLENSO.—At Napier, on 10th February, 1899, Rev. William Colenso, F.R.S., F.L.S., in the 88th year of his age. The funeral will leave his late residence tomorrow (Sunday), 12th instant, at 3 o'clock.—W.M. Newman, Undertaker.

§ 1899 THE CLOSE OF AN EVENTFUL LIFE.
Hawke's Bay Herald 11 February.
DEATH OF THE REV. W. COLENSO.
The Rev. W. Colenso, F.R.S., F.L.S., died early yesterday morning at his residence, Milton-road, his end coming peacefully. At 4 a.m. he called his housekeeper to procure him some refreshment, and when Mrs. Anderson returned he seemed to be sleeping. Not wishing to disturb the sleeper, she did not wake him, but subsequently finding that he did not move, she went to his bedside and found him dead. The deceased, who came from an old Cornish family, was born in 1811, and was a first cousin to the late Bishop of Natal.

In October, 1887, Mr. Colenso read a "Jubilee Paper" before the Hawke's Bay Philosophical Society. This was intended "to commemorate more particularly the completion of the printing of the New Testament in the Maori tongue at Paihia, in the Bay of Islands, in the year 1837—60 years ago—an event that caused a great sensation at the time, both in New Zealand and at Home (although now in part forgotten), and one that was productive of incalculable good to the Maori race; together with the introduction of the printing press into this country; and also the gradual formation of the present written Maori language, with many peculiar and little-known circumstances pertaining to these pre-historic times, and incidental thereto."

In the year 1833, the Church Missionary Society having determined to send out a printing press and type, and all necessary material to the mission in New Zealand, were seeking a missionary printer to be in charge. In the end of that year Mr. Colenso, then residing in London, was introduced to the secretaries of that society at their mission house, and engaged to come out to New Zealand with the press as a missionary. In 1834 he left London for Sydney en route to New Zealand, and after a long passage of 17 weeks the vessel arrived at Sydney. At that time there were only three clergymen of the Church of England residing in all Australia—two of them (the Revs. Messrs Cowper and Hill) in Sydney, and the Rev. S. Marsden at Parramatta. As no vessel could be found willing to leave for New Zealand, owing to fear of the Maoris, Mr. Colenso was obliged to remain eight or nine weeks at Sydney. At last, after much entreaty, a small schooner of 67 tons was got ready, and he sailed on the 10th December for the Bay of Islands. After a long and eventful voyage of 20 days (suffering much from want of water, as well as from a complication of peculiar miseries), he landed at Paihia mission station in the Bay of Islands on December 30th, and in the following few days got the press, type, &c., safely on shore.

At this time there were three missionaries with their wives and families living at Paihia—the Rev. H. Williams, the Rev. W. Williams, and Mr. C. Baker. On the 17th February, 1835, Mr. Colenso pulled proofs of the first book printed in New Zealand, the printing office being filled with spectators to witness the performance. The printing of the New Testament, consisting of 356 pages, was accomplished by the middle of December, 1837—naturally a cause of great rejoicing with Mr. Colenso, who relates that many remarkable incidents happened at this time, showing the extreme value placed by the Christian and well-disposed Maori chiefs on the sacred volume. The powerful chiefs of Kaitaia (near Ahipara and the North Cape), Panakareao, wrote to Mr. Colenso for a single copy; and in order that it should arrive the more dignified, he sent it all the way by a special messenger (a long journey of several days through a wild and little known dense untravelled forest), and with it he sent Mr. Colenso one pound in gold for payment, strictly limiting his request to one copy only. It was the first sovereign Mr. Colenso ever saw with a Maori or in this country, and the letter and the gold were well secured, being wrapped up in folds of cloth, and bound and worn turban fashion night and day on his head. As not many of the principal Maori chiefs or their sons could then write, many of them travelled on foot and barefooted to Paihia, from very great distances, to obtain a copy, at the same time running no small risks in their doing so, owing to the unsettled unavenged old feuds which still existed. Several distinguished early foreign visitors also got single copies by asking— as the Bishop of Australia, Admiral du Petit Thouars, of the French navy, Captains P.P. King and Harding, of the British navy, Commodore Wilkes, of the American exploring expedition, and others.

In 1842 the Bishop of New Zealand, Dr. Selwyn, arrived, accompanied by his chaplain, Rev. W.C. Cotton and others, and in the following year a printer having arrived at Paihia from the Society in England to take charge of the mission press, Mr. Colenso went to reside with them at St. John's College, Te Waimate. On Mr. Colenso's coming to reside in Hawke's Bay in 1844 he brought with him a small Albion press and types which he again found to be of great service, though having a people scattered over a very large district to attend to, with its consequent heavy travelling on foot, there being then no roads, he could not use his little press so much as he wished. The deceased was at one time Inspector of Schools in Napier; and was also Treasurer for Hawke's Bay in the Provincial Government days. He was the first member for Napier in the General Assembly, which sat in Auckland in 1861.

Mr. Colenso was on several occasions president of the Hawke's Bay Philosophical Society, before which institute he read many valuable papers on scientific matters. His portrait graces the museum of that institute, to remind the visitor of a life which bound together the past and the present generations. In Mr. Colenso's death a lone and solitary figure has passed away. He had dipped deep into the volume of Nature, had plucked secrets from her bosom which the future inhabitants of this country will value far above the passing profit of the moment, and which but for his keen perception, his acumen, would have been buried. The future historian, when examining into the earlier records of this country, will find in the traces left by this veteran, the most ample information as to all that was remarkable and characteristic in the peculiar period when Europeans first set their feet on Maori soil. On the verge of a new century he has gone, the labors of nearly a century to mark his passage. To the last moment he was busily engaged in preserving that which would keep the period in which he lived and moved in prominence in future years.

To quote his farewell words to the Hawke's Bay Philosophical Institute: —"I, as an aged minister of religion, and a fervent disciple of Nature, and with increasing convictions of the truth (soon by me to be realised), would say one word more to my audience re our talents and our time here; that as you sow now, you will reap hereafter. Young friends, don't waste time; don't abuse talents; seek to make the best use of both. Our bodies will remain, but our minds will go with us. And in a few beautiful and expressive lines of our classical English poet, Thomson—already quoted from by me—I close—

> *"Father of light and life! thou good supreme*
> *O, teach me what is good! teach me Thyself!*
> *Save me from folly, vanity, and vice,*
> *From every low pursuit! and feed my soul*
> *With knowledge, conscious peace, and virtue pure.*
> *Sacred, substantial, never fading bliss."*

§1899 ODE ON THE DEATH OF WILLIAM COLENSO.
Daily Telegraph 11 February.

"Proud Ocean, circling round New Zealand's Isle,
Mourn in loud murmurs on thy sea-girt strand!
Ye stars of Heaven, that o'er her gently smile
'Mid the dark hours of midnight, guard thy land!
For lo! our teacher and our friend lies sleeping,
While round his bier a myriad eyes are weeping.
Ye distant mountains, cloud-wrapt, cold and bleak,
Whose rugged heights by man have ne'er been scaled,
Echo a mourning nation's loss from peak to peak,
As in full years a prophet dies bewailed.
And Death! who spares nor age, nor power, nor worth,
Claims him her own, and calls him from the earth.

"Wake! long neglected lyre, in measured tones
Breathe music to the wind, all soft and sweet,
As in its onward march it wildly moans,
Or softly whispers hope and peace complete.

Then shall our hearts be soothed, and 'mid the gloom,
Shall dream of rest, and life beyond the tomb."

PENLYRIA
Repo Kite,
Napier, February 11, 1899.

§ 1899 THE LATE MR COLENSO.
Hawke's Bay Herald 13 February.

The funeral of the late Rev. William Colenso took place yesterday afternoon, and was attended by a very large number of settlers from all parts of the district. Amongst the wreaths sent was one from the congregation of the parish in Woodville, where Mr. Colenso often preached, in token of loving remembrance. The service at the graveside was impressively conducted by Dean Hovell, assisted by the Bishop of Waiapu.

The Rev. T.A. Cato, preaching at the Cathedral last night from the text "It is finished," made feeling reference to the death of the late Rev. William Colenso, and said that he felt sure the people of Napier, especially the poor, would greatly miss the many benevolent actions of the deceased gentleman. He referred to Mr. Colenso as an early pioneer of the colony, and one who had gone through many trials and vicissitudes, with exemplary patience and forbearance. The choir, after the sermon, sang the hymn "Days and moments swiftly flying," and at the conclusion of the service Mr. Sharp played the "Dead March" from "Saul," the choir and congregation remaining standing.

Messrs C.H. Edwards, E.W. Knowles, and J.B. Fielder are the executors of the will of the late Mr. Colenso. The deceased leaves £1000, to be invested by the Mayor and Councillors, and divided annually amongst 20 of the poorest families of Napier. The sum of £500 is bequeathed to the annual purchase of prizes for children attending the State schools in Napier; £500 for poor and distressed seamen or other strangers desiring assistance; and £500 to be invested for the object of assisting discharged prisoners from Napier gaol; £200 to the Hawke's Bay Philosophical Society, which body also receives all his dried plants, specimens, natural history specimens, framed portrait of Sir J. Hooker and Allan Cunningham, an enlarged photograph of the donor, and a photo of an ancient bronze bell with Tamil inscription, found in New Zealand, all these gifts to be held in trust by Mr. S. Hill and Dr. Spencer and Mr. J.W. Carlile (the two latter deceased since the signing of the will). The bell referred to goes to the Colonial Museum, Wellington, which also receives a copy of the New Testament in Maori, printed by Mr. Colenso at Paihia, Bay of Islands, in 1837; £100 is bequeathed to the Anglican Church, Woodville, to be devoted to the completion of the chancel in memory of Bishop Stuart; his theological works to the Waiapu Diocesan Library, as well as a complete subscriber's set of the "Transactions of the New Zealand Institute," and the MSS. of the "Census of the Maori Population of Hawke's Bay and Neighborhood," as taken at the request of the Bishop of New

Zealand in 1845. The Maori Dictionary manuscripts go to the Government, on certain terms, and the deceased's scientific books are included in his general estate.

§ A TRIBUTE TO THE VETERAN.
Hawke's Bay Herald 13 February.[1]
[By H. Hill.]

Yesterday the grave closed over the mortal remains of one who has for many years held a foremost place amongst (us) as a citizen, and as a man of science. The spectacle was an imposing one, as befitted the occasion. All classes of the people were represented at the funeral, for all were able to show in this way the esteem and respect in which the late Rev. Mr. Colenso was held. The scene at the grave side was sad, and withal beautiful. An old man full of years and honors, was borne to his last resting place. Yet no wife, no child, no relative was there to mourn his passing away. But friends and associates and admirers—all classes, all creeds, as well as those of no creed—were there to do honor at his burial to the man who, whilst living loved the poor, the homeless, and the unfortunate and though dead had not forgotten to make "mention of them in his will."

> *His house was known to all the vagrant town,*
> *He chid their wanderings, but relieved their pain,*
> *Careless of their merits or their faults to scan.*
> *His pity gone ere charity began.*

Such was the man of 88 years who, of us all, had resided longest in this district and had witnessed the birth of Napier and seen the marvellous changes through which it has passed since the year 1843, when as the first European he came here to do missionary work. He had then resided in New Zealand nine years. Coming to the country as a printer, and imbued with scientific tastes and strong religious convictions, he was not the man to remain idle during the intervals of rest from the printing press. Already his name was known to the motley crowd in the Bay of Islands as an enthusiastic collector of plants, and we find the celebrated Darwin making his acquaintance in 1835 during the voyage of the Beagle; Allan Cunningham, the botanist, in 1837; and Sir Joseph Hooker in 1843. Cunningham died in 1839 at Sydney, but he appears to have made a deep impression upon Mr. Colenso, for only in December last a long conversation took place between the writer and Mr. Colenso concerning Allan Cunningham, whom Mr. Colenso mentioned in loving terms as a noble character and an ardent student of botany. But he was proud of the acquaintance of Allan Cunningham for another reason. Cunningham knew Sir Joseph Banks, the botanist who accompanied Cook in his first voyage to New Zealand, and thus, as he used playfully to remark, he was the link that joined the century gone with the century going.

The acquaintance made with Sir Joseph Hooker remained unbroken to the last. It was in July 1886 that a letter arrived from Sir Joseph informing Mr. Colenso that

---

1   Nearly all of the national and provincial papers carried Colenso's obituary. I.S.G.

he had been unanimously chosen for honors by the Royal Society, it being the only occasion on which such an honor had been conferred without a single objection being raised. The Royal Society is supposed to contain none but princes in the world of science, and as is natural, Mr. Colenso was proud of the honor conferred upon him. Even so long ago as 1864, when Sir Joseph Hooker was occupied in the preparation of the "Handbook of the New Zealand Flora," he had written in the preface:—"In every respect Mr. Colenso is the foremost New Zealand botanical explorer, and the one to whom I am most indebted for opinions and information." And he maintained his position to the last. No other man has written so many papers in the "Transactions of the New Zealand Institute" on botany, Maori customs, natural history, and legendary lore, and I believe that one of his botanical papers is now being printed in the Transactions to be issued shortly. Here is an example of steadfastness and diligence, seldom to be found among men, and it is worthy of being held up to the pupils of our local schools, who have also been remembered by this veteran of science in his will.

Less than a year ago the first portion of his Maori–English Lexicon was issued from the Government printing office. It bears a dedication to his old friend Sir George Grey, who, I believe, was dead before a special presentation copy reached London. For 32 years the Government of this country has been meddling and muddling with the issue of this work, the only result being the printing of the letter A. The manuscript is left in the pigeonholes of the room in which Mr. Colenso spent so many years of his active life, to the everlasting disgrace, be it said, of officialdom and mediocrity of mind among those who ought to lead the destiny of our country to better things. But the history of this transaction dealing with the Maori-English lexicon has yet to be told. The last word has certainly not been said on the subject, for the full and complete facts are known and Mr. Colenso's name will yet be vindicated before the world.

Of his private life it is difficult to write. He hated shams of all kinds, and the new ways of the world, in whatever direction, were to him an abomination. The "boys of yesterday" who came to him were too often repulsed by his pungent remarks on the forwardness and lack of knowledge of the younger generation. He had outlived his own generation, and the new generations, with new thoughts and new ways, were not to his liking. Yet he had a tender and loving heart, and no man was ever more ready to help those in distress, and likewise young children, with many of whom he corresponded until within a few days of his death. As a citizen he has left behind him a good name, worthy of all praise. As a scientific student and collector and as a philologist he has done excellent work for his country such as was needed in the early days of settlement, and his mark has been left on the "sands of time," for the benefit of other men and other students. When the history of Early New Zealand comes to be written the name of William Colenso, F.R.S., F.L.S., printer, missionary, scientist, philologist, and, best of all, humanitarian, will be found among the list of the honorable roll of men who spent their talents in laying a strong foundation for the future of this land, and who when dying remembered the poor, the outcast, the unfortunate, and the young children in his will, without regard to age, creed, or nationality.

"Lay me low, my work is done;
I am weary, lay me low,
Where the wild flowers woo the sun,
Where the forest breezes blow,
Where the butterfly takes wing,
Where the creepers drooping grow,
Where the wild birds chirp and sing
I am weary, let me go.
I have striven hard and long
In the world's unequal light.
Always to resist the wrong,
Always to maintain the right,
Always with a fearless heart;
Taking, giving blow for blow,
Willie, I have played my part,
And am weary—let me go.
Stern the world and bitter cold.
Irksome, painful to endure,
Everywhere a love of gold.
Nowhere pity for the poor,
Everywhere mistrust, disguise,
Pride, hypocrisy, and show,
Draw the curtain, close mine eyes,
I am weary—let me go."

Such were the sentiments and wishes addressed 19 years ago to his son by the man with whom we have parted for a time. He has now been laid low in full anticipation of a glorious rising. The good fight of faith has been fought—he has entered into his rest and his works will follow him.

§ 1899 LATE REV. MR. COLENSO.
Hawke's Bay Herald 14 February.

SIR,—Referring to the lamented decease of the late Mr. Colenso, who is acknowledged by all that knew him to have been kindly disposed to his fellow-creatures, and who would have resented, during his life time being charged with vanity or any selfish motive for his philanthropic action, I am impelled to write these few lines to point out what I consider an outrage on the memory of the deceased gentleman. I refer to the fact that portions of the will were made public on Saturday last prior to the funeral. This sacreligious outrage and breach of confidence someone is responsible for, seeing that the contents of the will should remain sacred at least till the remains of the testator were buried. It seems to me, sir, and I think that all decent-minded people will agree with me, that an explanatian for the unseemly publication of portions of the will of the late Mr. Colenso demand some explanation from the executors, who must meantime be held responsible for the premature and indecent public announcement.—I am, &c.,

One Who Knew the Good Old Man.

February 13, 1899.

§ 1899 EDITORIAL.
The Northern Advocate 18 February.

The Rev. W. Colenso, F.R.S., F.L.S., one of New Zealand's earliest settlers, died this week at Napier, aged 88. He introduced to New Zealand the first printing press, which was landed at the Bay of Islands on January 3, 1835. He was a devoted student of science and probably the best Maori scholar and antiquarian in New Zealand. He left several charitable bequests.

§ 1899 EDITORIAL.
Hawke's Bay Herald 23 February.

A correspondent writing to the Auckland Herald on the late Rev. William Colenso, says:—"An ably-written 'Life of William Colenso' would be a most valuable addition to New Zealand literature. Mr. Henry Hill, the inspector of schools for Hawke's Bay, was to the last a trusted friend of the great man, and to him I imagine the task would be most congenial. Our Government might at least acknowledge a great wrong done to a man now dead by arranging for the publication of such an interesting work."

§ 1899 EDITORIAL.
The Colonist 28 February.

The Rev. William Colenso, whose death at Napier was recorded last week, was a printer of the old school, and as conservative in this respect as he could well be. Any attempt to coach him in the up-to-datedness of the printing art was to offer him grievious insult, and was met with profound contempt. In the days of Provincialism he was for many years Superintendent of the Province of Hawke's Bay, and while in office he made it his hobby to revise the proofs of every scrap of Council printing before it was finally machined. And beautiful exhibits these revises were when returned to the printer. What with the substitution of small capitals for large capitals, and *vice versa*, and the italicisation, and the ultra free use of commas, semi-colons, dashes, parentheses, and all the other points in the category, the time taken by the compositors in correcting the stuff was even more than that taken in setting it. But it was all good for the trade, and 'Billy's' venerable smile was never more serene than when initialling as correct the prodigious lists of extras, and the Council smilingly paid for it all. Of the deceased scholar it may also be said that during his political career no man was more revered in the Council than he, and that no matter how intense the excitement of an electioneering contest, the courtesy extended to his fellow candidates was uniform and gentlemanly.

§ 1899 THE LATE MR. COLENSO:
SIR JOSEPH HOOKER'S EULOGIUM.
Hawke's Bay Herald 13 June.

At the meeting of the Hawke's Bay Philosophical Institute last night the following motion was passed on the motion of Mr. H. Hill, seconded by Mr. J.W. Craig:— "That this branch of the New Zealand Institute places upon record the great loss it has sustained by the death of the Rev. William Colenso, F.R.S., F.L.S., who from its foundation was closely connected with the society as secretary, president, and member of the Council, and as a contributor of papers on botany, anthropology, and kindred subjects, has done much for the advancement of science throughout the world." In speaking to the motion Mr. Hill read the following letter from Sir Joseph Hooker:— "The Camp, Sunningdale.—April 15th, 1899.—My Dear Sir,—Your very kind letter of February 21st reached me in Devonshire, whither it was forwarded four days ago. The touching tribute of affection for my dear old friend Colenso quite overpowered me. A small testimony of his long, warm affection for me would not, I need hardly say, have been unexpected, especially from one who had on several occasions sent gifts to my children and to myself in aid of the publication of unremunerative works—always spontaneous as they were—and not seldom from the gratification that the liberal action afforded him. It was in 1841 (not 1843, as in your charming tribute to his memory) that I first made the acquaintance that at once ripened into friendship with Colenso, and ever since (except during my travels in India) we have unremittingly corresponded, most closely indeed during the critical period of his clerical career, when he unburdened his sorrowing heart to me—sure of my deep sympathy, though powerless to aid.[2] All you say of him is most true, and finds a repeating echo in my brain. He stands quite alone in the history of the colonisation of New Zealand, as a Christian, philanthropist, and naturalist combined in one. His portrait hangs before me in my study, and his initials carved in stone appear over a bow window of my house, or rather between the two bows. I shall get it photographed and send you a copy. I am glad indeed that he has left his plants in trust for the Philosophical Society .... I do hope that the municipality yielded to his wish that it should accept and endow it. Our last communication from him was a souvenir to my wife of a charming little book of views in New Zealand about a month ago. I cannot tell you how much I shall miss him, for he was the very last of my old correspondents of the 40's. To have had him as one for 58 years of my life may well be a source of deep thankfulness during the remaining days that may be spared to me. If not troubling you too much, I should exceedingly like to have some account of his last illness. His last letters to me were in as vigorous a hand as his first; and he described himself in good health for his age.—

Truly and gratefully yours,

J.D. HOOKER."

---

2 There is a gap between 3 Feb 1852 and 28 Aug 1854 in the Kew collection of correspondence from Colenso to Hooker, suggesting Hooker did not file the most personal letters during Colenso's bleakest period. I.S.G.

§ 1899 AUCTIONEERS.
Hawke's Bay Herald 31 August.
C. B. Hoadley & Co.'s sales. Preliminary notice. Important sale of Napier Hill building sites. C.B. Hoadley & Co. have received instructions from R.L. Colenso, Esq., to offer for sale by Public Auction, early in October, ALL THAT MAGNIFICENT HILL PROPERTY, Formerly the Residential Estate of the late Rev. W. Colenso. This Property is something over 30 acres in extent, and will be subdivided into suitable-sized Building Allotments, commanding most beautiful land and seascape views.

§ 1899 COLENSO'S LIBRARY, NAPIER.
Nelson Colonist 8 September.
Efforts to secure the late Mr. Colenso's unique library for the town have failed, his son having sold it to Messrs Angus and Robertson, of Melbourne.

§ 1899
Hawke's Bay Herald 9 September.
Mr. Ridley L. Colenso writes as follows:—
"SIR,—A paragraph in your Friday's issue re the late Rev. W. Colenso's library, is correct but misleading. A Hawke's Bay Philosophical Institute deputation viewed the library, and came to the conclusion that there were far more books than they would know what to do with, especially as of some of the more valuable works duplicates were already in their possession. They consequently decided to approach Messrs Angus and Robertson's representative in order, if possible, to secure those books they required. The town of Napier could have had the whole collection at Angus and Robertson's prices."

§ 1899 DIOCESAN SYNOD.
Hawke's Bay Herald 27 September.
On the opening of the Synod ... The Rev. E. Robertshawe moved,—"That this Synod desires to place on record its deep sense of loss in the death of the Rev. W. Colenso, F.R.S., whose kindliness and liberality endeared him to all classes of the community."—The motion was seconded by the Very Rev. the Dean, and supported by his Lordship the President, the Revs. F.E.T. Simcox and J.C. Eccles, and by Messrs H. Burdett and H. Hill, each of whom added some tribute to the memory of the late Mr. Colenso, and testified to the far-reaching and unostentatious nature of his generosity.—Mr. Simcox suggested it would be fitting that a memorial to his name should be placed in the Cathedral, a proposal which met with approval from subsequent speakers.—Mr. Hill read an extract of a letter from Sir J. Hooker, showing the highest esteem and personal friendship for Mr. Colenso as a scientist, philanthropist, and Christian.—The members of the Synod stood while the motion was put and carried.

§ 1903 LEGISLATIVE COUNCIL.

Evening Post 30 July.

The Hon. Mr. Bowen asked the Attorney-General what steps had been taken towards the publication of the late William Colenso's Maori lexicon, and to whose custody the manuscript has been confided? The Minister stated that no steps had yet been taken to publish, and that the document was in the custody of the Native Minister. He would bring the matter before his colleagues, and subsequently give further information.

INDEX OF LETTERS

1840–1859

1847   1   April 28: To the Editor. *New Zealand Spectator and Cook's Strait Guardian 27*
1848   2   May 6: To the Editor. *New Zealand Spectator and Cook's Strait Guardian 29*
1857   3   November 10: To the Editor. *Hawke's Bay Herald 34*
1858   4   February 20: Open Column. *Hawke's Bay Herald 35*
      5   May 8: Open Column. *Hawke's Bay Herald 36*
      6   May 22: Open Column. *Hawke's Bay Herald 41*
      7   June 5: To the Editor. *Hawke's Bay Herald 43*
      8   June 22: To Messrs Gollan & Fitzgerald. *Hawke's Bay Herald 46*
      9   July 3: Open Column. *Hawke's Bay Herald 48*
    10   July 24: Open Column. *Hawke's Bay Herald 50*
    11   August 14: Open Column. *Hawke's Bay Herald 57*
    12   August 28: Open Column. *Hawke's Bay Herald 60*
    13   October 16: Open Column. *Hawke's Bay Herald 65*
    14   October 23: Tracts for the Times No. 1. *Hawke's Bay Herald 66*
    15   October 30: Tracts for the Times No. 2. *Hawke's Bay Herald 68*
    16   November 13: Tracts for the Times No. 3. *Hawke's Bay Herald 69*
    17   November 20: Tracts for the Times No. 4. *Hawke's Bay Herald 71*
    18   November 27: Tracts for the Times No. 5. *Hawke's Bay Herald 73*
    19   December 4: Tracts for the Times No. 6. *Hawke's Bay Herald 75*
    20   December 11: Tracts for the Times No. 7. *Hawke's Bay Herald 77*
    21   December 18: Tracts for the Times No. 8. *Hawke's Bay Herald 79*
1859 22   January 8: Tracts for the Times No. 9. *Hawke's Bay Herald 82*
    23   January 22: Tracts for the Times No. 10. *Hawke's Bay Herald 85*
    24   February 5: Tracts for the Times No. 11. *Hawke's Bay Herald 87*
    25   March 5: Open Column. *Hawke's Bay Herald 91*
    26   March 26: To the Editor. *Hawke's Bay Herald 92*
    27   April 30: Tracts for the Times No. 12. *Hawke's Bay Herald 93*
    28   May 7: Tracts for the Times no. 13. *Hawke's Bay Herald 97*
    29   August 6: Open Column. *Hawke's Bay Herald 100*
    30   August 6: To the independent electors of the town of Napier. *Hawke's Bay Herald 101*
    31   October 22: Open Column. *Hawke's Bay Herald 105*

1860–1869

1860 32   February 4: Open Column. *Hawke's Bay Herald 111*
    33   February 11: To the Editor. *Hawke's Bay Herald 112*
    34   April 14: Open Column. *Hawke's Bay Herald 114*
    35   May 12: Open Column. *Hawke's Bay Herald 118*
    36   August 25: Open Column. *Hawke's Bay Herald 120*
    37   September 8: To the Editor. *Hawke's Bay Herald 127*
    38   October 27: Open Column. *Hawke's Bay Herald 128*
    39   November 3: Open Column. *Hawke's Bay Herald 129*
    40   November 17: Open Column. *Hawke's Bay Herald 132*
    41   November 24: Open Column. *Hawke's Bay Herald 132*
1861 42   January 5. To the electors of the district of Napier. *Hawke's Bay Herald 136*
    43   January 19: Open Column. *Hawke's Bay Herald* (1) *138*
    44   January 19: Open Column. *Hawke's Bay Herald* (2) *138*
    45   February 23: Open Column. *Hawke's Bay Herald 139*
    46   July 20: To Mr. H.B. Sealey, of Napier. *Hawke's Bay Herald 140*
1862 47   March 20: Open Column. *Hawke's Bay Times 143*

48 June 28: Open Column. *Hawke's Bay Herald 144*

1863 49 January 26: To the electors of the town of Napier. *Hawke's Bay Times.* Republished 28 January as a leaflet and in *Hawke's Bay Herald. 156*

50 February 6: Correspondence. *Hawke's Bay Times 160*

51 February 14: To the Editor. *Wellington Independent 164*

52 August 29: Open Column. *Hawke's Bay Herald 167*

53 September 4: M. Fitzgerald v. Colenso. *Hawke's Bay Times 168*

54 September 30: Open Column. *Hawke's Bay Herald 172*

55 October 2: Correspondence. *Hawke's Bay Times 173*

56 October 9: Correspondence. *Hawke's Bay Times 174*

1864 57 April 15: Correspondence. *Hawke's Bay Times 174*

58 April 21: To the Secretary, Wellington Chamber of Commerce. *Wellington Independent 175*

59 May 13: Macaulay's New Zealander on London Bridge. *Hawke's Bay Times 175*

1865 60 May 15: Correspondence. *Hawke's Bay Times 179*

61 July 29: To the Editor. *Hawke's Bay Herald 182*

62 October 26: To the Editor. *Wellington Independent 184*

63 December 4: Correspondence. *Hawke's Bay Times 186*

64 December 4: The Colenso Bell. *Hawke's Bay Times 187*

65 December 9: Mr. Colenso and separation. *Hawke's Bay Herald 188*

66 December 11: Correspondence. *Hawke's Bay Times 190*

67 December 19: To the Editor. *Hawke's Bay Herald 192*

1866 68 February 26: Correspondence. To His Honor Donald McLean .... *Hawke's Bay Times 193*

1867 69 August 13. The Blight Bird. *Hawke's Bay Herald 196*

1868 70 August 8: The Guernsey Lily. *Hawke's Bay Herald 199*

71 September 8: The Educational Rate. *Hawke's Bay Herald 200*

72 November 17: To the Editor. *Hawke's Bay Herald 202*

1869 73 February 23: The Education Rate. *Hawke's Bay Herald 203*

74 March 26: To the Editor. *Hawke's Bay Herald 204*

75 March 30: To the Editor. *Hawke's Bay Herald 206*

76 April 9: To the Editor. *Hawke's Bay Herald 207*

77 August 3: Native Affairs. *Wellington Independent 210*

78 September 24: Lieut. Saxby's Prediction. *Hawke's Bay Herald 212*

79 October 1: Cook's Centenary. *Hawke's Bay Herald 215*

1870–79

1870 80 December 16: To the Editor. *Hawke's Bay Herald 219*

1871 81 Fiat Justitia; being a few thoughts respecting the Maori prisoner Kereopa now in Napier gaol, awaiting his trial for murder. Respectfully Addressed to the considerate and justice-loving Christian Settlers of Hawke's Bay, and also to our Rulers, in a Letter to the Editor of the "Hawke's Bay Herald." *223*

1872 82 January 3. Should Kereopa be Hung? *Nelson Examiner & New Zealand Chronicle 223*

1874 83 December 26: Early Days of the New Zealand Press. *Otago Witness 230*

1877 84 February 14: Mr. Colenso and Temperance. *Hawke's Bay Herald 237*

1878 85 January 19: The Education Act. *Hawke's Bay Herald 238*

86 March 9: The Late Bishop Williams. *New Zealand Herald 240*

87 April 9: The Inspectorship of Schools. *Hawke's Bay Herald 242*

88 May 4: To the Chairman Board of Education, Napier. *Hawke's Bay Herald. 247*

89 July 17: Philosophical Society. *Hawke's Bay Herald 248*

90 September 6: Sunday-School Picnics. *Hawke's Bay Herald 249*

91 September 24, 27, 28; October 1, 5, 22, 31; November 14, 15, 21, 29;

92 December 4, 12: A few thoughts and facts concerning the "Sabbath" and its due observance. *Hawke's Bay Herald 250*

1879   93   March 5: The Communion. *Hawke's Bay Herald 251*
        94   April 4: Fair Play. *Hawke's Bay Herald 251*
        95   May 19: The Innocent Punished. *Hawke's Bay Herald 253*
        96   July 11: Mr. Colenso and St. John's Church. *Hawke's Bay Herald 254*
        97   October 4: Mr. Colenso on the Drainage Poll. *Hawke's Bay Herald 256*

1880–1889
1880   98   March 30: The New Building Regulation. *Hawke's Bay Herald 261*
        99   April 9: Mr. Colenso and the Municipal Council. *Hawke's Bay Herald 263*
        100   May 28: A Mountain of a Molehill—*alias* Roasting a Maori. *Hawke's Bay Herald 264*
        101   June 7: The Bible in Schools. *Hawke's Bay Herald 265*
        102   June 8: The Bible in Schools II. *Hawke's Bay Herald 267*
        103   June 28: Mr Colenso on a Small Inland Tax. *Hawke's Bay Herald 271*
        104   July 24: Early Printed Books. *Hawke's Bay Herald 272*
        105   December 6. The Athenæum's last meeting. *Hawke's Bay Herald 273*
1881   106   January 1. More Serious Errors! *Waipawa Mail 274*
        107   January 5. Correspondence. *Waipawa Mail 275*
        108   January 8: Mr. Colenso on an incident of old New Zealand .... *Wanganui Herald 275*
        109   January 15. A few thoughts on the late sad murder at Opunake. *Waipawa Mail 278*
        110   January 22, 26, 29, February 2, 5, 9, 12, 16, 19, 23, 26, March 2, 5. The first European fighting and killing at Taranaki: A striking incident .... *Waipawa Mail 281*
        111   July 13: Turning to the East. *Napier Daily Telegraph 282*
        112   September 23: Mr. Colenso in Denial. *Hawke's Bay Herald 282*
        113   September 27: Newspaper Errors. *Daily Telegraph 283*
1882   114   April 11: The Fever Scare. *Hawke's Bay Herald 283*
        115   April 13: The Fever Scare. *Hawke's Bay Herald 284*
        116   April 21: The Treatment of Native Prisoners of War. *Timaru Herald 286*
        117   May 11: The New Zealand olive. *Daily Telegraph 286*
        118   May 12: The New Zealand olive. *Daily Telegraph 286*
        119   June 26: Stilling the Waves. *Daily Telegraph 290*
        120   September 18: Proposed New Bye-laws. *Daily Telegraph 291*
        121   November 23: To the Benevolent: a case for charity. *Daily Telegraph 293*
        122   November 28: The Case for Charity: the poor widow and her 6 little ones. *Daily Telegraph 294*
1883   123   January 2: Shortsightedness. *Daily Telegraph 295*
        124   February 28: A Word about Te Kooti. *Hawke's Bay Herald 297*
        125   March 14: "Much Ado about Nothing!" *Hawke's Bay Herald 303*
        126   June 23: Dr Colenso, the late Bishop of Natal. *Hawke's Bay Herald 304*
        127   July 13: Mr. Colenso and the Auckland Weekly News. *Daily Telegraph 305*
1884   128   January 25. Scinde Island. *Hawke's Bay Herald 308*
        129   February 23: Stamford-Street files. *Hawke's Bay Herald 310*
        130   March 10: A last word on Stamford-Street. *Hawke's Bay Herald 311*
        131   April 11: Stamford-Street. *Hawke's Bay Herald 313*
        132   May 8: Mr. Colenso and Nebuchadnezzar. *Daily Telegraph 313*
        133   June 10: Mr. Colenso on bush licenses. *Hawke's Bay Herald 314*
        134   June 16: Mr. Colenso on "Strongbow". *Hawke's Bay Herald 316*
        135   June 18: Correspondence. *Daily Telegraph 319*
        136   July 1: Father Des Chesnais' Lecture. *Hawke's Bay Herald 322*
        137   August 18: Mr. Colenso and the Auckland Freeman's Journal. *Hawke's Bay Herald 325*
        138   October 1: The Maori Lexicon. *Hawke's Bay Herald 327*
        139   December 20. Mr Colenso in Reply. *Daily Telegraph 327*
1885   140   January 27: On Education. *Daily Telegraph 329*
        141   May 11: Scares. *Daily Telegraph 331*

142 May 12: "Bombardment of Sweaborg" continued. *Daily Telegraph 335*

143 May 21: The Hotel Question at Makatoku. *Hawke's Bay Herald 339*

144 May 26: "Veritas Vincit"—Truth Conquers. *Daily Telegraph. 342*

145 May 27: Local Option. *Hawke's Bay Herald 343*

146 August 3: To the Editor. *Daily Telegraph 344*

147 October 1: Mr. Colenso and the Rev. W. Baumber. *Hawke's Bay Herald 344*

1886 148 November 20: Scares. *Daily Telegraph 345*

149 December 8: "Antimony". *Hawke's Bay Herald 347*

1887 150 February 19: Mr. Colenso and the Borough Council. *Hawke's Bay Herald 349*

151 May 17: Shipwrecked Mariners. *Daily Telegraph 349*

152 July 13: Preservation of Timber. *West Coast Times;* reprinted from ... *Napier News 351*

153 September 2. Mr. Colenso and the Maori Lexicon. *Hawke's Bay Herald. 352*

1888 154 January 17. Christianity *versus* Mahometanism. *Hawke's Bay Herald 354*

155 March 20: Bis dat qui cito dat. *Hawke's Bay Herald 355*

156 March 22: "Fair play is bonnie play." *Hawke's Bay Herald 356*

157 April 18: The Late Renata Kawepo. *Hawke's Bay Herald 356*

158 May 15 The Infidel and the Orthodox Man. *Hawke's Bay Herald 357*

159 May 29: The "Maori relic." *Bush Advocate 360*

160 June 13: Mr. Colenso explains. *Daily Telegraph 361*

161 June 25. The Teetotal Crusade. *Hawke's Bay Herald 362*

162 June 27: What's in a name? *Hawke's Bay Herald 363*

163 June 29: Teetotallism and temperance. *Hawke's Bay Herald 365*

1889 164 January 30: Veneered Infidelity. *Hawke's Bay Herald 369*

165 March 9: Property Tax Valuation. *Hawke's Bay Herald 371*

166 July 1: The Crown of Thorns. *Hawke's Bay Herald 373*

167 July 16. A Queen's Bench decision. *Hawke's Bay Herald 373*

1890–1898

1890 168 February 8. The Reverend W. Colenso and the Jubilee. *Auckland Weekly News. 380*

169 May 15: The Ink Plant. *Bush Advocate 381*

170 June 12: The Rev. W. Colenso on Football. *Hawke's Bay Herald 381*

171 August 16: Church Matters. *Bush Advocate 382*

172 October 30: A reply to Old Ratepayer. *Bush Advocate 384*

173 November 6: Old Ratepayer's letter. *Bush Advocate 385*

174 November 22: To the Editor. *Evening Press, Wellington 388*

1891 175 April 23: Keep Holy the Sabbath Day. *Bush Advocate 392*

176 August 8: The Sea Serpent. *Daily Telegraph 394*

1892 177 March 11. A Query. *Hawke's Bay Herald 395*

178 March 15: The Drink Question. *Hawke's Bay Herald 395*

179 April 7: Seventh Day Adventists. *Hawke's Bay Herald 397*

180 November 12: Baron Rothschild on Labor. *Hawke's Bay Herald 398*

1893 181 March 6: "Jackatye". *Hawke's Bay Herald 399*

182 March 15: "Noxious Weeds." *Daily Telegraph 400*

183 April 10: The Moreton Gallery. *Daily Telegraph 401*

184 June 14: Translations into Maori. *Hawke's Bay Herald 401*

185 September 15: To the Editor. *Hawke's Bay Herald 402*

186 November 23. The Late Mr. Pullen. *Hawke's Bay Herald 403*

1894 187 January 16: Floods. *Hawke's Bay Herald 404*

188 February 2: Mountain Grass. *Hawke's Bay Herald 412*

189 February 6: The "Wild Irishman". *Hawke's Bay Herald 413*

190 April 18: The Bishopric. *Hawke's Bay Herald 416*

191 June 29: The Late President Carnot. *Hawke's Bay Herald 417*

192 July 12: A Correction. *Hawke's Bay Herald 417*
193 Publication dates unknown: To the Editor. *Hawke's Bay Herald*
These letters republished as a booklet, *Certain errors of the Church of Rome,* and further
republished in *Colenso's published papers 2: 1884–1899,* forthcoming in this series; written
24 August; 8, 22: 20 September, 23, 26, 29 November; 6, 13, 21 December 1894. *418*
194 December 10: A New Pest. *Daily Telegraph 418*
195 December 15. The Discovery of Moa Remains. *New Zealand Herald 419*
1895 196 April *c.* 20: Palmistry. *?Bush Advocate 421*
197 April 26: Was it a just judgement? *Hawke's Bay Herald 422*
198 June ?4: The Re-union of Churches. *Hawke's Bay Herald 422*
199 June 11: The Todas. *Hawkes Bay Herald 423*
200 June 20: The Appointment of Teachers. *Hawke's Bay Herald 424*
201 December 10: Introduction of bees. *Hawke's Bay Herald 425*
202 December 11: Danevirke or Dannevirke? *Hawke's Bay Herald 426*
1896 203 February 21: Short Cut to Napier Terrace. *Hawke's Bay Herald 427*
204 March 9: A Strange Insect. *Daily Telegraph 428*
205 March 23: Of a Destructive New Zealand Root Fungus. *Hawke's Bay Herald 429*
206 April 27: A New Insect. *Daily Telegraph 432*
207 May 5: Root Fungus. *Hawke's Bay Herald 432*
208 May 19: The Proposed Museum. *Hawke's Bay Herald 435*
209 July 17: Prohibition and the Clergy. *Hawke's Bay Herald 435*
210 July 23: Prohibition and the Clergy. *Hawke's Bay Herald 442*
211 August 10: A Plea for the Starving. *Hawke's Bay Herald 443*
212 September 28: Mr Colenso Explains. *Daily Telegraph. 444*
213 November 14: The Moa. *The Press 445*
1897 214 March 1: Mr. Colenso Explains. *Hawke's Bay Herald 446*
215 June 8: The Record Reign. *Hawke's Bay Herald 448*
216 June 24: The Record Reign. *Hawke's Bay Herald 448*
217 July 6: Major Ropata. *Hawke's Bay Herald 450*
218 August 24: To the Editor. *Hawke's Bay Herald.* Sept. 8, 22: Mr. Colenso in Reply. *451*
219 September 14: The Relief of "swaggers". *Hawke's Bay Herald 451*
220 October 15: Daffodils. *Hawke's Bay Herald 453*
221 November 20: Imprecatory Psalms. *Hawke's Bay Herald 453*
222 November 22: The More Suitable Church Lessons. *Hawke's Bay Herald 455*
223 December 4: Australia of the Past. *Hawke's Bay Herald 457*
1898 224 June 24: An Important Matter. *Hawke's Bay Herald 459*
225 August 24: Phosphorescent Wood. *Hawke's Bay Herald 460*
226 September 16: The Kumi. *Hawke's Bay Herald 462*
227 September 17: The Maori Bible. *Hawke's Bay Herald 463*
228 October 1: "This to thy right eye, Philip". *Hawke's Bay Herald 463*
229 October 6: Governor Eyre. *Hawke's Bay Herald 465*
230 October 7: Evolution and Huxley, No.1. *Hawke's Bay Herald 466*
231 October 8: Evolution and Huxley, No.2. *Hawke's Bay Herald 468*
232 November 28: A Rare Plant. *Hawke's Bay Herald 470*
233 December 3: Some Important Matters. *Hawke's Bay Herald 470*
234 December 10: The Slave-Trade. *Hawke's Bay Herald 473*
235 December ?26: The La Perouse Expedition. *Hawke's Bay Herald 475*

LETTERS BY SUBJECT

Numbers in these lists refer to the number given to each letter in the Index by Date.

Charity   121, 122, 151,155, 180, 186, 211, 219

Christianity   3, 90, 91, 92, 93, 96, 101, 102, 111, 119, 132, 136, 137, 139, 144, 146, 147,
                            154, 158, 164, 166, 170, 171, 175, 179, 190, 193, 198, 215, 218, 219, 221,
                            228, 230, 231, 233

Education   35, 71, 73, 85, 87, 88, 101, 102, 123, 140, 146, 147, 200, 224

Land   48, 53, 103, 129, 130, 131, 150, 203

Maori   1, 2, 26, 31, 37, 38, 39, 40, 52, 54, 56, 60, 72, 76, 77, 81, 83, 100, 106, 107,
                            108, 109, 110, 116, 124, 138, 153, 156, 157, 159, 162, 184, 217, 227

Miscellaneous   59, 63, 64, 75, 78, 80, 89, 94, 95, 98, 105, 113, 114, 115, 126, 127, 135, 141,
                            142, 148, 149, 160, 167, 183, 185, 191, 192, 196, 197, 199, 208, 214, 215,
                            234

Missions   86, 174

Natural History   69, 194, 195, 201, 204, 206, 213, 226

NZ History   79, 108, 110, 128, 139, 168, 174, 181, 187, 201, 202, 212, 216, 217, 222,
                            223, 227, 229, 235

Plants   7, 11, 58, 70, 117, 118, 125, 152, 166, 169, 176, 182, 188, 189, 201, 205,
                            207, 220, 225, 232

Politics, National   4, 10, 12, 13, 32, 41, 42, 43, 51, 57, 62, 66, 67, 68, 72, 74, 103, 106, 107,
                            165, 180

Politics, Provincial & Local 5, 6, 8, 9, 14, 15, 16, 17, 18, 19, 20, 21, 22, 23, 24, 25, 27, 28, 29, 30,
                            33, 34, 36, 44, 45, 46, 47, 49, 50, 55, 61, 65, 74, 97, 99, 112, 120, 145, 162

Printing   83, 227

Temperance/Prohibition 84, 133, 134, 143, 161, 163, 172, 173, 177, 178, 209, 210